THE PROPHET-KING

The Johannine Monograph Series
Edited by Paul N. Anderson and
R. Alan Culpepper

THE VISION OF THE Johannine Monograph Series is to make available in printed, accessible form a selection of the most influential books on the Johannine writings in the modern era for the benefit of scholars and students alike. The volumes in this series include reprints of classic English-language texts, revised editions of significant books, and translations of important international works for English-speaking audiences. A succinct foreword by one of the editors situates each book in terms of its role within the history of Johannine scholarship, suggesting also its continuing value in the field.

This series is founded upon the conviction that scholarship is diminished when it forgets it own history and loses touch with the scintillating analyses and proposals that have shaped the course of Johannine studies. It is our hope, therefore, that the continuing availability of these important works will help to keep the cutting-edge scholarship of this and coming generations of scholars engaged with the classic works of Johannine scholarship while they also chart new directions for the future of the discipline.

Volume 1: *The Gospel of John: A Commentary*, by Rudolf Bultmann
Volume 2: *The Composition and Order of the Fourth Gospel*, by D. Moody Smith
Volume 3: *John's Gospel in New Perspective*, by Richard J. Cassidy
Volume 4: *Bread From Heaven*, by Peder Borgen
Volume 5: *The Prophet-King*, by Wayne A. Meeks
Volume 6: *The Testament of Jesus*, by Ernst Käsemann

THE PROPHET-KING

MOSES TRADITIONS
AND THE JOHANNINE CHRISTOLOGY

BY

WAYNE A. MEEKS

WIPF & STOCK · Eugene, Oregon

Wipf and Stock Publishers
199 W 8th Ave, Suite 3
Eugene, OR 97401

The Prophet-King
Moses Traditions and the Johannine Christology
By Meeks, Wayne and Anderson, Paul N.
Copyright©1967 E. J. Brill
ISBN 13: 978-1-4982-8884-2
Publication date 7/15/2017
Previously published by E. J. Brill, 1967

To

Bernhard Citron

ὃς ἀνώμβρησεν σοφίαν ἀπὸ καρδίας αὐτοῦ

—Jesus ben Sirach 50.27

TABLE OF CONTENTS

FOREWORD

The Itinerary of The Prophet-King by Wayne Meeks

By Paul N. Anderson

Among modern analyses of the origin and development of John's Christology, the socio-religious analysis of Wayne A. Meeks advances one of the most compelling and suggestive theses in recent years, addressing the riddles pertaining to the puzzling presentation of Jesus as a prophet-king like Moses in John 6:14-15. Whereas the *Logos* motif of the Johannine Prologue and the Father-Son relationship in the Johannine narrative convey high-christological thrusts, his receptions as a rabbi, teacher, and prophet elsewhere in John's story of Jesus are far more mundane and earth bound. While he is rejected in Judea for failing to live up to Davidic royal expectations (7:40-52), Jesus is declared to be "the King of Israel" by Nathanael of Cana (1:49) and the crowd in Jerusalem (12:13), and he is labeled "King of the Jews" by Pilate at his trial and crucifixion (18:39; 19:19-22). In his appearance before Pilate, however, Jesus also affirms his being a king, but rather than asserting political prowess, his kingship is one of truth (18:36-37). Rather than a king, though, he is acclaimed as a prophet by the Samaritan woman, the Jerusalem crowd, and the blind man (4:19; 7:40; 9:17), and when the Galilean crowd seeks to rush him off for a coronation as a prophet-king like Moses in John 6:14-15, Jesus responds by fleeing into the hills. The question is *why?* Was the origin and development of John's presentation of Jesus here political, historical, theological, sociological, or some combination of the like? These are the issues Wayne Meeks addresses in his first of several important monographs, and his work continues to impact New Testament studies to this day.[1]

---

1. Wayne A. Meeks, *The Prophet-King: Moses Traditions and the Johannine Christology*, NovTSup 14 (Leiden: E.J. Brill, 1967); see also his early essay on the subject, "Moses as God and King," *Religions in Antiquity: Essays in Memory of Erwin Ramsdell Goodenough*, Studies in the History of Religions 14, Jacob Neusner, ed. (Leiden: Brill, 1968) 354-71.

In charting the course for his study, Meeks poses a corrective to insightful commentaries by Edwin Hoskyns and others, wherein the grounded realism of the Fourth Gospel is appreciated, but its contemporary religious milieu is ignored.[2] Of course, Hoskyns was interested in the Johannine tension between history and theology, but in Meeks' judgment, making use primarily of the Old Testament and a cluster of citations from Philo, rabbinic sources, and later Christian literature offered too small a repository for understanding John's socio-religious background. Conversely, despite Rudolf Bultmann's identifying of twenty-eight similarities between John's presentation of the mission of Jesus and the Gnostic Redeemer-Myth,[3] the Mandaean literature is itself later. It most likely was influenced by John rather than contributing to the Johannine tradition. Further, identifying John the Baptist as a proto-Gnostic figure is less than compelling historically, and Johannine parallels with the Qumran writings account for some of its features just as readily. Here the works of Ferdinand Hahn, Francis T. Glasson, and others point the way forward, focusing on the themes of the eschatological prophet, kingship in the Levant, and Moses in contemporary literature and in the Gospel of John.[4]

In approaching his subject, Meeks first of all reviews the Mosaic, prophetic, and kingly themes in the Gospel of John, seeking to identify ways they cohere with reference to John's Christology (Chapter 2). He then explores these themes within non-Rabbinic Jewish sources (Chapter 3), the Rabbinic haggadah (Chapter 4), early Samaritan sources (Chapter 5), and finally the Mandaean texts (Chapter 6). From these analyses, Meeks contributes not only a fresh understanding of John's Christology, but he also accounts for its history-of-religions development within its Palestinian Jewish milieu (Chapter 7). It would be a mistake, however, to simply regard the value of Meeks' analysis as casting light upon the Palestinian context within which John's memory of Jesus sprouted and grew. As the scope of Meeks' lifetime contributions to New Testament studies would

2. Edwin C. Hoskyns, *The Gospel of John*, F. N. Davey, ed. (2nd edn., London: Faber & Faber, 1947).

3. Rudolf Bultmann, *The Gospel of John: A Commentary*, R.W.N. Hoare, J.K. Riches, and G.R. Beasley-Murray, trans. (1971, repr. Johannine Monograph Series 1, Eugene: Wipf & Stock, 2014).

4. Ferdinand Hahn, *The Titles of Jesus in Christology: Their History in Early Christianity*, Harold Knight and George Ogg, trans. (1963, Cleveland: World Publishing Company, 1969); T. Francis Glasson, *Moses in the Fourth Gospel* (London: SCM, 1963).

suggest, within this monograph lie the seeds of understanding more fully the Jewish character of John's memory of Jesus, Samaritan and Galilean tensions with Judean leaders regarding what sort of messianic deliverance was envisioned, ongoing dialogues within the evolving Johannine situation, and the emerging character of early Christianity itself with extensive implications for understanding John's contested Christology and its continuing meanings. While these enduring contributions took a lifetime to develop, their impetus is here seen in Meeks' first monograph: *The Prophet-King*.

The Presentation of Jesus as Prophet, King, and Prophet-King in the Fourth Gospel

While other approaches to John's Christology have focused on titles with exalted or theological meanings, Meeks' selection of "prophet" and "king" focuses on understandings of Jesus rife with political and mundane associations. In fact, this is the first major treatment of the *prophet-king typology* in Jewish life and culture to be performed, period. Part of the interest is to establish a historical sense of rootedness in contemporary contextual settings so as to illumine a fuller understanding of John's presentation of Jesus as the Christ. While the Johannine Jesus indeed fulfills a host of scriptural allusions, both typologically and predictively,[5] one must inquire as to what those texts and associations would have meant to originative audiences—both in oral and written stages of the Johannine tradition. If the evangelist was indeed a dialectical thinker, as Barrett and others have pointed out,[6] the dialectical and grounded associations within southern, central, and northern Palestine (Judea, Samaria, and Galilee) must be taken into account if John's story of Jesus is to be appreciated in its fullest. Therefore, the range of contemporary religious literature provides a helpful backdrop for understanding the origins of John's memory of Jesus as well as its later developments.

As a history-of-religions approach, however, the work of Meeks pushes back hard against the Bultmannian School, which identified the agency of Jesus as rooted in early Gnostic Baptistic traditions, flowering later in the Mandean literature (pp. 1-31). Even after the discovery of the Dead Sea

5. Paul N. Anderson, *The Riddles of the Fourth Gospel: An Introduction to John* (Minneapolis: Fortress, 2011) 83-85.

6. C.K. Barrett, "The Dialectical Theology of St John," *New Testament Essays* (London: SCM, 1972) 49-69.

Scrolls, Bultmann's inference that John the Baptist, if he were connected with the Essene movement or the Qumran community, exposes thereby the Gnostic character of Qumranic Judaism.[7] After all, the Dead Sea is to the east of Jerusalem, so Gnostic influence might have had some impact even on the Essene sectarians on its way toward Palestinian Judaism, which then evolved into Mandean Gnosticism—wherein John the Baptist was a heroic figure. And, if followers of the Baptist became the first followers of Jesus (John 1:19-51), this would explain the originative character of the Johannine I-am sayings, the sending motif, and the *Logos*-hymn, which introduces the Fourth Gospel. Therefore, the Gnostic Redeemer-Myth, in Bultmann's view, formed the theological basis for the Johannine Father-Son relationship, inviting the hypothesizing of a Revelation-Sayings Source supposedly underlying the discourses of Jesus in John. A major problem with Bultmann's approach, however, is that the Odes of Solomon and other Mandean literature were likely written over two centuries after the Gospel of John,[8] so these connections are better explained on the basis that the Johannine Gospel influenced their development rather than being influenced by the Gnosticism they came to represent in the 3rd and 4th centuries CE.

This is why the approach of Ferdinand Hahn seems compelling, and why Meeks was well advised by N.A. Dahl in following his lead. If it can be shown how Palestinian Judaism understood the motifs of "prophet" and "king" within the time and context of the Johannine tradition's development in the first century CE, important groundwork will have been laid in understanding the content of the Johannine Gospel in historical and theological perspective. In Hahn's approach, advances rooted in Second Temple and intertestamental Jewish literature provide several ways forward. First, the title *Christos* ("Christ," "Messiah," "Anointed One") is associated with a variety of authoritative leaders within Judaism, including prophetic, royal, priestly, and political figures.[9] Therefore, messianic associations were more fluid than fixed in contemporary Judaism. Second, the anticipation of the

7. Paul N. Anderson, "John and Qumran: Discovery and Interpretation over Sixty Years," *John, Qumran, and the Dead Sea Scrolls: Sixty Years of Discovery and Debate*, Early Judaism and its Literature 32, Mary Coloe, PVBM and Tom Thatcher, eds. (Atlanta: SBL Press 2011) 15-50.

8. Although James Charlesworth dates the Odes of Solomon around 100 CE, which seems early to most scholars, *The Old Testament Pseudepigrapha*, Vol. 2, James H. Charlesworth, ed., Anchor Bible Reference Library (New York: Doubleday, 1985) 726-34.

9. Hahn, "Christos," *The Titles of Jesus in Christology*, 136-222.

eschatological prophet in later Judaism incorporated both the typologies of Elijah (Mal 3:1, 23-24) and Moses (Deut 18:15, 18), while also assimilating the royal-prophetic associations of the Suffering Servant of Second Isaiah.[10] Rather than assert a Davidic understanding of royalty, however, Hahn builds upon royal understandings of Moses in Maccabees, Philo, and Qumran, and the Samaritan anticipation of the *Taheb* (the prophet like Moses). Third, the Elijah-Moses typology is certainly connected with the ministry of John the Baptist in the Synoptics, and Josephus describes several messianic leaders in first-century Judaism that draw upon prophetic associations in seeking deliverance from Roman occupation in political terms. As a result, Meeks teases out the details of this trajectory with great success in ways that illumine understandings not only of the primitive Johannine Jesus tradition, but which also provide valuable clues to the evolving Johannine situation and the contextual thrust of John's story of Jesus.

In analyzing the thematic functions of Jesus as prophet and king in John's narrative, Meeks notes several important features (pp. 32-99). First, Jesus is regarded as a prophet by some in John 7:37-52, although his identity as such is debated by the religious leaders in Jerusalem. In favor of Jesus' being regarded as "the Prophet" is the fact that he has performed signs, and yet this identity is denied by the Judean leaders because he does not hail from Bethlehem, the city of King David. Second, given that prophetic and royal messianic associations are here intertwined, it is ironic that the understandings of the Jewish leaders are tied facilely to geography. Thus, we see in the Johannine critique of the Jerusalem-centered rejection of the northern prophet the Judean leaders' failure to conceive of the spiritual character and heavenly origin of the Messiah, which the Galilean prophet-king embodies. Third, the ironic miscomprehension of the Judean leaders is accentuated by their allegations that Jesus, in speaking of himself, is the presumptuous and false prophet described in Deuteronomy 18:19-22, when his words indeed come true, attesting his authenticity. Fourth, in John's trial of Jesus, his "kingship" being one of truth is presented in sharp relief against political prowess. Encompassing all the elements of Israel's authentic prophet, the "good shepherd" is willing to lay down his life for his sheep, and they recognize his voice. Fifth, acclamations of Jesus as the true "king of Israel" in John's calling and Jerusalem-entry narratives (John 1:49; 12:12-19) reflect an independent tradition designed to lead later audiences

---

10. Hahn, "The Eschatological Prophet," *The Titles of Jesus in Christology*, 352-406.

from initial miscomprehension to fuller comprehension of Jesus as a humble leader, whereby in affirming their faith, they become linked with the "true Israelites" of John 1:45-51. Sixth, it is in John 6 where the motifs of prophet and king are linked together following the feeding of the multitude, as the crowd hails Jesus as "the prophet who is to come into the world" and seeks to make him a king by force (John 6:14-15). Ironically, Jesus flees their political designs on his future, reflecting a historically grounded set of messianic expectations in Galilee, which Jesus partially embraces but also qualifies in the rest of his ministry.

Meeks then sets the history-of-religions backdrop against which John's story of Jesus deserves to be most closely read (pp. 100-75). Among *non-rabbinic Jewish sources*, Moses is portrayed as a divine and royal figure—superior to all others—a prophet, lawgiver, priest, and king. In Philo's *Life of Moses*, three types of Mosaic prophetic oracles include oracles spoken by God, oracles answering human questions, and divine words delivered while in ecstasy by the prophet. Therefore, as a hierophant, a mystic, and a "divine man," Moses is also portrayed as ascending into heaven and thus conveying heavenly knowledge of the world below (pp. 100-31). By contrast, Josephus portrays Moses not as a king, but as a legislator, commander, and sovereign leader. While silent on royal and priestly associations, Josephus does portray Moses as the archetypal Hellenistic commanding leader, also describing his work as a paraclete—an advocate—pleading for grace on behalf of the Jewish nation. Josephus also embellishes the theme of an authentic succession of Moses, whereby recent prophetic figures are compared, contrasted, and thereby judged (pp. 131-46). The presentations of Moses in apocryphal and pseudepigraphal writings do feature some links between Moses as a prophet and a king,[11] wherein Moses comprehends and explains the state of the world as a vice-regent with God. And, as Moses was adopted into Pharaoh's household, he would indeed have had a royal upbringing. In addition to ascending into heaven and being Israel's intercessor (paraclete), Moses is attested as God's authentic ambassador because of his signs and wonders, as made clear in *Wisdom of Solomon* (pp. 146-64). In Qumranic literature, the connection with Deuteronomy 18 is especially

---

11. The clearest association is found in a fragment cited by both Eusebius and Clement of Alexandria, "The Exodus," a poem attributed to an otherwise unknown person named Ezekiel, which offers an apocalyptic perspective on things past, present, and future emerging from Moses' dream (Meeks, *The Prophet-King*, 147-53).

pronounced with reference to the anticipation of an eschatological prophet like Moses, and while the Teacher of Righteousness is associated with such, explicit identifications are lacking (pp. 164-75). Therefore, anticipations of the eschatological prophet-king like Moses in the non-Rabbinic literature are many, though not entirely parallel to John 6:14-15.

Within *the rabbinic haggadah*, Moses is presented as a king, and within this literature the divine character of that kingship is sometimes conflated with priestly status (pp. 176-215). Royal associations also accompany the shepherding role of Israel's leader, and Moses as the supreme prophet is remembered as originator of prophecy and the source of the prophets' succession. Moses also plays the role of Israel's defense attorney before God, and his ascent of Sinai becomes spiritualized and extended as ascending to heaven in approaching the *Shekinah*-presence of the divine throne. Thus the eschatological role of Moses envisions his appearing, along with Elijah, returning at the appointed time to lead Israel again through the wilderness into the Promised Land. In these and other ways, Moses is portrayed in the rabbinic literature as sometimes a greater king than David, and his messianic roles included caring for, instructing, and redeeming Israel at the appointed time.

Within *Samaritan sources,* the royal role of Moses is even more pronounced (pp. 216-57). In what proves to be the most significant of his chapters in terms of the religious background of John's presentation of Jesus as the Messiah/Christ, Meeks shows how the figure of Moses dominates Samaritan religious literature of the times, whereas messianic associations with David are largely absent. As Samaritans also had their own Pentateuch, their traditions reflect individuated developments involving some interfluential exchanges with contemporary Judaism, though the particulars of intertraditional exchange are elusive. Samaritan sources portray Moses as "the faithful prophet," "the great prophet," "the righteous prophet," and "the true prophet," by whom the secrets of Yahweh are revealed in the Torah. He is also called "the apostle of God," and while kingly references to Moses are more rare, he nonetheless founded the kingdom of Israel as the pivotal figure between Joseph and Joshua. Thus, Meeks concludes (p. 256):

> This inquiry into Samaritan sources has shown that Moses was for the Samaritans the supreme prophet, indeed virtually the only prophet. His prophecy was understood as the mediation to Israel of heavenly secrets, imparted by God when Moses ascended Mount

Sinai into "the unseen world." These secrets, including the Torah, brought "life" to the world, and both the Torah and Moses himself are symbolized by such terms as "water" and "light." Closely related to Moses' prophetic office is the notion that he was God's "apostle," belief in whom was equivalent to belief in Yahweh, himself.

Within the *Mandean literature*, however, royal references are more common, and prophetic references are less common (pp. 258-85). While Mandean salvation and redemption myths are difficult to systematize, they do bear a semblance with such Johannine revelational themes as "light" and "life," and "the King of Light" is associated with the hidden Creator, who both creates and redeems the world. Conversely, kings of darkness and rebellion distort the truth and oppose the redemptive work of God. In the heavenly spheres, Mandean demiurges serve as divine envoys, bringing the water of life and the gift of light from the πλήρωμα to the world of humans, availing deliverance from the powers of darkness. Despite these similarities, however, direct connections between Mandean sources and Jesus' being a king of truth in John 18:37 are lacking. Connections with Moses, however, are primarily associated with enthronement motifs, and references to prophets are also set in two oppositional categories. On one hand, false prophets characterize those in opposition to the Mandeans, whereas John the Baptist is hailed as their true prophet. Finally, though, king and prophet are not associated together in Mandean literature, so the Johannine linking of these two images cannot be attributed to Mandean influence.

Mosaic traditions in *the Fourth Gospel*, therefore, cohere more closely with Jewish and Samaritan sources than any others, confirming the view of E. R. Goodenough, that Mosaic mystical piety played an important role within Jewish traditions contemporary with the emergence of the Johannine tradition.[12] Thus, such an ethos avails the clearest backdrop for understanding the prophet-king like Moses motif within the Gospel of John, elucidating the religious backdrop of some of the most puzzling elements of Johannine Christology. Direct mentions of Moses in the Fourth Gospel affirm that the Torah was given through Moses (1:17), Moses lifted up the bronze serpent in the wilderness (3:14), manna was given by Moses (*and* God, 6:31-58); and yet, the gifts availed through Moses are surpassed by the gifts availed through Jesus Christ (1:16-17).

12. Pp. 286-319. E.R. Goodenough, "John a Primitive Gospel," *Journal of Biblical Literature* 64 (1945): 145-82.

As the center of Jewish piety, Judean leaders put their hope in Moses while not seeing that Moses wrote of Jesus (5:39-47). They claim to be disciples of Moses (9:28-29), and yet they fail to glimpse the truth of Jesus, as witnessed to by the walking lame man in John 5 and the seeing blind man of John 9. Parallel to the ascension of Moses on Mount Sinai and followed by his heavenly enthronement in contemporary Jewish literature, the Johannine Jesus not only descends from heaven in order to carry out the will of the Father, but he also returns whence he came, fulfilling his apostolic commission and thereby being glorified (3:13; 6:62). While no one has ever seen God (1:18; 5:37; 6:46; 1 John 4:12), Jesus has (like the Mosaic theophany), thus forming the heart of Johannine-Jewish polemic. As such, Jesus as the prophet of whom Moses wrote in Deuteronomy 18:15-22, serves as the apostolic agent sent from God, speaking (only) God's words and performing signs, demonstrating his divine agency. Confirming his authenticity, his words come true, and he even speaks them ahead of time to show that he indeed is the true prophet like Moses—despite being accused of being the presumptuous prophet (Deut 18:19-22)—challenging competing claims of Mosaic authority by the Judean leaders.

As a result of these clear presentations of Jesus in John as the prophet-king like Moses in the light contemporary literature, the following inferences can be made. First, the forensic character of Jesus' revelation betrays ironically the judgment of the world in the trial of Jesus before Pilate (John 18-19). In rejecting the apostolic agent of God, the unbelieving world is self-condemned. Jesus thus becomes the world's accuser in its rejecting the Revealer. Second, the Good Shepherd motif in John 10 bears clear associations with the leadership of the virtuous king in contemporary Jewish literature, as the authentic shepherd lays down his life for the sheep, in contrast to thieves and robbers; and he knows his sheep, and they recognize his voice. Third, given the geographical symbolism in the Fourth Gospel, Jesus goes back and forth between Galilee and Judea—through Samaria—and while he is rejected in Judea, he is embraced in Samaria and Galilee. Given Kundsin's work on topographical and contextual Galilean and Samaritan features in John, we clearly have a tradition originating in Palestine, though finalized in the diaspora. Within that later setting, the depiction of Jesus as greater than the law-giver Moses (1:17), the well-provider Jacob (4:12), and nation-father Abraham (8:53) served a set of pointed rhetorical thrusts. Thus, if John's audience did not adhere to the prophet-king like Moses, they

would cease to be true followers of Moses, as Moses wrote of Jesus. And,
Jesus is not simply presented as a "new Moses" in John;[13] rather, Jesus is
"greater than" Moses, who simply witnesses to Jesus as does John the Baptist. From these features, the common inferences can be made regarding
the developments and provenance of the Johannine tradition (pp. 318-19):

> First, the Johannine traditions were shaped, at least in part, by inter-
> action between a Christian community and a hostile Jewish com-
> munity whose piety accorded very great importance to Moses and
> the Sinai theophany, probably understood as Moses' ascent to heav-
> en and his enthronement there. Second, it is clear that the Johannine
> church had drawn members from that Jewish group as well as from
> the Samaritan circles which held very similar beliefs, and it has been
> demonstrated to a high degree of probability that the depiction of
> Jesus as prophet and king in the Fourth Gospel owes much to tradi-
> tions which the church inherited from the Moses piety.

While reviews of Meeks' book were few in number, they nonetheless picked
up on these two points. The Johannine tradition and its developments show
evidence of Mosaic rhetoric marshaled in addressing religious challenges in
Jerusalem-centered Judea as well as in Torah-centered Judaism in the diaspora.[14] As a result, Meeks' work launched a series of developments regarding the background and foreground of the Johannine tradition over the
next several decades, eventually impacting history-and-theology analyses
of John's presentation of Jesus as the Messiah-Christ.

The Johannine Backdrop:
Hellenistic, Jewish, or Both?

As a result of Meeks' analysis, the religious background of the Johannine
tradition cannot be said to be simply biblical, as though the evangelist were
merely citing Jewish scripture (Hoskyns and others), nor can it be said to
represent the Gnostic Redeemer-Myth, as though its primary backdrop

13. Versus Glasson and others; see also Marie-Emile Boismard, *Moses or Jesus: An Essay in Johannine Christology*, B.T. Viviano, trans. (1988, Leuven: Peeters, 1993); Severino
Pancaro, *The Law in the Fourth Gospel: The Torah and the Gospel, Moses and Jesus, Judaism and Christianity According to the Fourth Gospel* (Leiden: E.J. Brill, 1975).

14. See, for instance, the review in *Biblische Zeitschrift* 13:1 (1969): 136-38 as well as
that by Ľudovit Fazekaš, *Theologische Zeitschrift* 27:1 (1971): 53-54.

were third- and fourth-century Mandeanism (Bultmann and others). Rather, in the light of contemporary Jewish literature, John's presentation of Jesus as the Messiah-Christ shows a distinctively northern Palestinian perspective, somewhat at odds with Judean Davidic typologies that antici- pated a messianic figure who would elevate the Jerusalem-based center of Judaism and restore the priesthood and Judean aristocracy to their right- ful place of honor. In presenting Jesus as a prophet-king like Moses, John's northern messianic perspective poses a challenge to centralizing tenden- cies within the Judean populace, and in that sense, the Samaritan embrace of a Mosaic prophet as the anticipated Messiah-Christ would have borne extensive similarities in Galilee, as well.

In his investigation of Samaritan messianic expectations, Meeks built upon the works of Karl Kundsin, Hugo Odeberg, John Bowman, John Mac- donald and others,[15] and yet his monograph then established the connec- tions between Samaritan and Johannine studies more than any other single work.[16] Given the fact that Samaritan studies had long been overlooked in history-of-religions analyses of New Testament studies, elucidating the Sa- maritan ethos and its messianic expectation of a Mosaic *Taheb* contributes significantly toward understanding both the mixed reception of Jesus in Jerusalem and its ambivalent presentation of Judean leaders in the Gos- pel of John.[17] Then again, while links between Samaritan and Johannine messianic understandings are impressive, the character and particulars of

15. In addition to Nils Alstrup Dahl's guidance, Meeks builds upon the works of Karl Kundsin, *Topologische Überlieferungsstoffe im Johannes-Evangelium*, FRLANT 22 (Göt- tingen: Vandenhoeck & Ruprecht, 1925); Hugo Odeberg, *The Fourth Gospel: Interpreted in its Relation to Contemporaneous Religious Currents in Palestine and the Hellenistic- Oriental World* (Uppsala: Almqvist & Wiksell, 1929); John Bowman, *Samaritan Stud- ies, Bulletin of the John Rylands Library* 40:2 (1958): 298-327; and John Macdonald, *The Theology of the Samaritans* (London SCM, 1964). Note Meeks' appreciation for Dahl's work in his later essay, "The Restless Curiosity of Nils Alstrup Dahl," *Religious Studies Review* 29:3 (2003): 247-50.

16. Thus, just as studies of Jesus as prophet in the Fourth Gospel can be divided as works preceding and following Meeks' monograph, the same can be said of Samaritan and Johannine studies: Sumkin Cho, *Jesus as Prophet in the Fourth Gospel*, New Testa- ment Monographs 15 (Sheffield: Sheffield Academic Press, 2006) 33-53.

17. Following directly on Meeks' monograph are C.H.H. Scobie, "The Origins and Development of Samaritan Christianity," *NTS* 19 (1973): 390-414; E.D. Freed, "Samari- tan Influence in the Gospel of John," *CBQ* 30 (1968): 580-87; and George Wesley Bu- chanan, "The Samaritan Origin of the Gospel of John," *Religions in Antiquity*, J. Neusner, ed. (Leiden: E.J. Brill, 1968) 149-75.

the relationship remain uncertain.[18] Nor is it clear what the implications of Samaritan-Johannine links might be. Along these lines, some scholars have argued that John's story of Jesus was crafted to convert Samaritan and/or Jewish audiences to believe in Jesus as the Messiah-Christ;[19] still another view is that the Fourth Gospel was crafted in order to provide a means of reconciling otherwise estranged Jews and Samaritans.[20] Most significant, however, is the fact that Samaritan messianic expectations inform a grounded understanding of how a Galilean prophetic figure would have perceived and been perceived by religious leaders in Jerusalem, Judea, Samaria, and elsewhere.[21]

This set of north-south tensions can be seen in the symbolic geographical references in the Johannine narrative, as the Judean leaders declare that no prophet arises from Galilee but rather should come from David's city, Bethlehem (John 7:40-52). Jesus is thus referred to pejoratively as "a Samaritan" and a demoniac by the Judean leaders (John 7:20; 8:48, 52; 10:20), and virtually all of the negative references to the *Ioudaioi* in John target religious leaders in Jerusalem and Judea.[22] That being the case, John's geographical symbolism presents the prophet-king from Nazareth

18. As Margaret Pamment has argued, it is also possible that parallels between Samaritan writings and the Fourth Gospel reflect either the use of similar biblical texts or the possibility that Samaritan theologies were influenced by Christian presentations of Jesus as the Christ: "Is there Convincing Evidence of Samaritan Influence on the Fourth Gospel?" *ZNW* 73 (1982): 221-30.

19. E.D. Freed argues that John was written to convert Jewish and Samaritan audiences, "Did John Write his Gospel Partly to Win Samaritan Converts?" *NovT* 12:3 (1970): 241-56; James D. Purvis sees John's story of Jesus as a polemic against Samaritan Mosaism, perhaps represented by Simon Magus or Dositheus (cf. Origen, *Contra Celsum* I.57), "The Fourth Gospel and the Samaritans," *NovT* 17:3 (1975) 161-98.

20. Craig S. Keener, "Some New Testament Invitations to Ethnic Reconciliation," *EQ* 75:3 (2003): 195-213.

21. B.P. Robinson, "Christ as a Northern Prophet in St John," *Scripture* 17 (1965): 104-08. See also Abram Spiro, "Stephen's Samaritan Background," Appendix V in Johannes Munck, *Acts*, Anchor Bible 31 (New York: Doubleday, 1967) 285-300, for another example of tensions with temple-centered Judaism in Jerusalem.

22. On this point, inferred anti-Semitism within the Fourth Gospel is anachronistic and controverted by the textual facts, as none of the general references to "the Jews" in John are negative: Paul N. Anderson, "Anti-Semitism and Religious Violence as Flawed Interpretations of the Gospel of John," *John and Judaism*, R. Alan Culpepper and Paul N. Anderson, eds, Resources for Biblical Study 87 (Atlanta: SBL Press, 2017) 265-311.

as juxtaposed over and against the anticipated Davidic Messiah of Judea.[23] From the Johannine perspective, Pilate's rhetorical question: "Am I a Judean?" bears with it something of an adversarial sting (John 18:35).[24] Despite the prominence of the Judean mission of Jesus in John, this does not imply, however, that the evangelist was from Jerusalem. More plausible is the view that John's presentation of multiple visits to Jerusalem by Jesus posed a realistic alternative to Mark's single visit culminating at the end of his ministry.[25] Further, at odds with Mark's presentation of the rejection of Jesus in his hometown (Mark 6:1-6), in John the Samaritans and Galileans in the midlands and the north receive him openly (John 4:45). Thus, John's rendering of Jesus' ministry poses a dialectical engagement of alternative gospel traditions, if the evangelist were familiar with Mark's narrative or its synoptic incorporations, even in part.[26]

It is at this point that John's presentation of Jesus and his mission clashes with Matthew's rendering, where Jesus instructs his followers not to travel among the Samaritans (Matt 10:5), whereas the itinerary of Jesus in John "must" involve the passing through of Samaria on the way to Jerusalem (John 4:4). Whether this is a matter of divine necessity, it certainly represents a geographical reality, and Luke also includes travel among the Samaritans in his story of Jesus (Luke 9:51-56). Note, though, that in the Fourth Gospel, the Samaritan woman becomes the apostle to the Samaritans, and they not only receive him as the Messiah, but they also welcome

---

23. As argued by Meeks in "Galilee and Judea in the Fourth Gospel," and developed more fully in the contributions of Sean Freyne, *Jesus, A Jewish Galilean: A New Reading of the Jesus-Story* (London: T. & T. Clark, 2004); "The Galilean Jesus and a Contemporary Christology," *Theological Studies* 70 (2009): 281-97.

24. See Meeks' essay, which takes this theme further, "'Am I a Jew?'—Johannine Christianity and Judaism," *Christianity, Judaism, and other Greco-Roman Cults: Studies for Morton Smith at Sixty*, Vol. 1, Jacob Neusner, ed, Studies in Judaism in Late Antiquity 12 (Leiden: Brill, 1975) 163-86.

25. So argued by Paula Fredriksen, "The Historical Jesus, the Scene in the Temple, and the Gospel of John," *John, Jesus, History; Vol. 1, Critical Appraisals of Critical Views*, Paul N. Anderson, Felix Just, SJ, and Tom Thatcher, eds., Symposium Series 44 (Atlanta: SBL Press, 2007) 249-76.

26. With Richard Bauckham, "John for Hearers of Mark," in his *The Gospels for All Christians: Rethinking Gospel Audiences* (Grand Rapids: Eerdmans, 1998) 147-72, a primary interest of John's story of Jesus is to provide an alternative rendering to Mark: Paul N. Anderson, "Mark and John—the *Bi-Optic* Gospels," *Jesus in Johannine Tradition*, Robert T. Fortna and Tom Thatcher, eds. (Louisville: Westminster John Knox, 2001) 175-88.

Jesus and his disciples to stay with them for two days, extending them a hospitable welcome (John 4:1-43). If the Johannine evangelist were aware of Matthew's narrative, his presentation of the Samaritan mission of Jesus and his followers might reflect a corrective to Matthean ethnocentrism or at least the sentiment it represents. Whatever the case, John's presentation of Jacob's Well and a worship site on Mount Gerizim cohere with archaeological findings,[27] and yet the words of the Johannine Jesus defining worship as being in spirit and in truth (John 4:21-24) reflect a more universal view of authentic worship over and against more provincial ones.[28]

In these and other ways, John's presentation of Jesus as the Mosaic prophet, received favorably in Galilee and Samaria and with some unevenness in Judea and Jerusalem, coheres with Samaritan and Galilean perspectives of the day. Therefore, while John's story of Jesus was developed further within a Hellenistic diaspora setting, its traditional memory was deeply rooted in Palestinian Judaism and its variegated expressions.

The Dialectical Johannine Situation:
History and Theology Continued

As a result of Meeks' analysis, not only is the religious backdrop of the Johannine tradition illumined, but so is the foreground of the Johannine situation and its dialectical character. Rather than seeing only a single set of engagements with Jewish leaders in a diaspora setting—Ephesus, Alexandria, the Negev, or elsewhere—the Johannine situation likely involved engagements with Samaritan, Jewish, Gentile, and Christian audiences either in Palestine, or the larger Mediterranean world, or both. Along these lines, John's rhetorical presentation of Jesus as a prophet greater than Moses would have challenged would-be disciples of Moses to believe in Jesus, lest they deny their professed religious values. Here Meeks' argument goes

27. Robert J. Bull, "An Archaeological Footnote to 'Our Fathers Worshipped on this Mountain,'" *New Testament Studies* 23 (1977): 460-62.

28. E.D. Freed, "The Manner of Worship in John 4:23f," *Search the Scriptures: New Testament Studies in Honor of Raymond T. Stamm,* J.M. Myers, O. Reimherr, and H.N. Bream, eds. (Leiden: E.J. Brill, 1969) 33-48; Paul N. Anderson, *The Christology of the Fourth Gospel: Its Unity and Disunity in the Light of John 6,* WUNT 2:78 (1996; 3rd printing with a new introduction and epilogue, Eugene: Cascade Books, 2010) 234-49. See also Marie E. Isaacs, "The Prophetic Spirit in the Fourth Gospel," *Heythrop Journal* 24 (1983): 391-407.

beyond simply asserting that Jesus is presented as the new Moses in the Fourth Gospel; Jesus surpasses Moses, fulfilling the ultimate Jewish typologies of divine agency.[29] According to Meeks, John's presentation of Jesus as the Mosaic prophet thus reflects something of the evolving Johannine situation and its experience, including rejection from local Jewish audiences and a growingly sectarian existence.[30] Along these lines, further developments in Johannine studies can be seen.

First, with the pivotal work of J. Louis Martyn,[31] it is no surprise that the work of Meeks contributed significantly to the view that what we have in the Fourth Gospel is a two-level reading of history and theology. In Martyn's sketching of the Johannine situation, a curse against the followers of Jesus of Nazareth (the *Nazoreans*) was added to the twelfth of eighteen benedictions, introduced by Gamaliel II during the Yavneh Council period (estimated between 85-115 CE). Martyn argued that this development was directly linked to the *aposynagōgos* references in John (9:22; 12:42; 16:2). While Meeks disagreed with Martyn over the role of the *birkat ha-minim* as a precipitator of synagogue expulsion, they did concur that conveyed in John's story of Jesus is the breaking away of Johannine believers from local Jewish communities of faith, reflected in the narrative itself.[32] In Meeks' view, John's binary presentation of Jesus as the eschatological Mosaic prophet forced audiences to take a stand for or against Christ and his community, which was now meeting in house churches; to stay behind in

29. In addition to the works by Glasson, Boismard, and others, Sumkin Cho's *Jesus as Prophet in the Fourth Gospel* shows the development of scholarly understandings of the Johannine Jesus not simply as a prophetic figure, but as *the* prophet predicted by Moses in Deuteronomy 18:15-22.

30. Wayne A. Meeks, "The Man from Heaven in Johannine Sectarianism," *Journal of Biblical Literature* 91 (1972) 44-72 (published also in *The Interpretation of John*, John Ashton, ed., 2nd edn., Edinburgh: T&T Clark, 1997, 169-206. Note, however, the challenge to the view of Johannine sectarianism by Kåre Sigvald Fugsleth, *Johannine Sectarianism in Perspective: A Sociological, Historical and Comparative Analysis of Temple and Social Relationships in the Gospel of John, Philo, and Qumran*. NovTSup 119 (Leiden: Brill, 2005), seeing the Johannine situation as more cultic and cosmopolitan than sectarian.

31. First published in 1968, J. Louis Martyn's *History and Theology in the Fourth Gospel* (3rd edn., Louisville: Westminster John Knox, 2003).

32. Wayne A. Meeks, "Breaking Away: Three New Testament Pictures of Christianity's Separation from the Jewish Communities," *"To See Ourselves as Others See Us": Christians, Jews, "Others" in Late Antiquity*, Jacob Neusner and Ernest S. Frerichs, eds. (Chico, CA: Scholars Press, 1985) 93-115.

the synagogue is to "love the world" rather than embrace life-producing truth.[33] In addition to John's scandal of particularity, however, the Fourth Gospel also includes the most universal and open soteriology in the New Testament, as all have access to the light—a fact too easily missed by readers of John.[34]

A second set of developments in Johannine research came to see John as either written for a Samaritan community or designed to convince Samaritan audiences to believe in Jesus as the Messiah/Christ. While the above works of Bowman, Freed, Macdonald and others argue for a close link between the Johannine Jesus movement and Samaritan communities either in Palestine or in the diaspora, the Samaritan approach to the Johannine situation has not endured within Johannine scholarship overall. Nonetheless, Raymond Brown's reconstruction of the Johannine community included the presence of Samaritans, in one way or another, functioning to elevate the Johannine Christology as a factor of embracing Mosaic pietism. In Brown's sketching of the history of the Johannine community, the second phase saw the addition of Samaritan converts to Christianity among Johannine believers, following their expulsion from the local synagogue.[35] These believers in Jesus as the Mosaic Prophet and Messiah (ca. 90 CE) entered the Johannine community, discernible in a two-level reading of John 4, and it was during this phase that the Johannine narrative was written. This led to John's embellished presentation of Jesus' signs and discourses, posing an either-or depiction of the Son's representation of the Father. The inclusion of Samaritan actants in the narrative, however, does not necessarily imply the presence of Samaritan members of John's community or audience at the time of its composition. Thus, Brown's two-level

---

33. While Adele Reinhartz agrees with much of Meeks' analysis, she disagrees that all who might have been impressed with the Johannine Jesus would have also been willing to accept its binary opposition of believers and nonbelievers. *Befriending the Beloved Disciple: A Jewish Reading of the Gospel of John* (New York: Continuum, 2001) 156-59.

34. See R. Alan Culpepper, "Inclusivism and Exclusivism in the Fourth Gospel," *Word, Theology and Community in John*, John Painter, R. Alan Culpepper, and Fernando F. Segovia, eds. (St. Louis: Chalice Press, 2002) 85-108; and Paul N. Anderson, "The Way to Salvation in John: Particular or Universal," *The Riddles of the Fourth Gospel*, 34-35, 183-86.

35. Raymond E. Brown, *The Community of the Beloved Disciple: The Life, Loves, and Hates of an Individual Church in New Testament Times* (New York: Paulist, 1979) 22, 36-40.

reading of the Fourth Gospel on this score must be considered suggestive rather than conclusive.[36]

A third development alongside the contributions of Meeks and others involves an important advance on the history-of-religions character of the mission of Jesus as the Christ in the Fourth Gospel. While Marinus de Jonge faults Meeks for not connecting John's presentation of Jesus as the Mosaic Prophet more explicitly with the Father-Son relationship,[37] others have developed that link more extensively.[38] Central within these studies is the role of Deuteronomy 18:15-22 as a means of confirming the authenticity of the Mosaic Prophet, and Peder Borgen has shown convincingly that within the Jewish agency schema of Merkabah mysticism, the one who is sent is in all ways like the sender.[39] This feature would thus account for one of John's key theological riddles: the egalitarian and subordinate relation between the Father and the Son, bolstered by a contemporary religious convention. Therefore, central within the Johannine Father-Son relationship is the Jewish sending (*shaliach*) motif,[40] wherein the Son is to be equated with the Father precisely because he does nothing except what the Father has

36. I see it as one of the weaker elements of Brown's overall theory; Paul N. Anderson, "The Community that Raymond Brown Left Behind—Reflections on the Dialectical Johannine Situation," *Communities in Dispute: Current Scholarship on the Johannine Epistles*, Early Christianity and its Literature 13, R. Alan Culpepper and Paul N. Anderson, eds. (Atlanta: SBL Press, 2014) 47-93.

37. Marinus de Jonge, "Jesus as Prophet and King in the Fourth Gospel," in his *Jesus: Stranger from Heaven and Son of God: Jesus Christ and the Christians in Johannine Perspective*, SBLSBS 11 (Missoula: Scholars Press, 1977) 49-76.

38. Ernst Haenchen, "Der Vater, der Mich Gesandt Hat," *NTS* 9 (1963): 208-16; Rudolf Schnackenburg, "'Der Vater, der Mich Gesandt Hat' Zur Johanneische Christologie," *Anfänge der Christologie: Festschrift für Ferdinand Hahn zum 65. Geburtstag*, Ferdinand Hahn, Cilliers Breytenbach, and Henning Paulsen, eds. (Göttingen: Vandenhoeck & Ruprecht, 1991) 275-92.

39. Peder Borgen, "God's Agent in the Fourth Gospel," *The Interpretation of John*, 2nd edn, John Ashton, ed. (Edinburgh: T. & T. Clark, 1997) 83-96, first published in Jacob Neusner, ed., *Religions in Antiquity* (Leiden: E. J. Brill, 1968) 137-48. Note also contemporary cases of rejecting a prophetic figure as the presumptuous prophet of Deut 18:19-22 (as in John 7): Wayne A. Meeks, "The Divine Agent and His Counterfeit in Philo and the Fourth Gospel," *Aspects of Religious Propaganda in Judaism and Early Christianity*, Elisabeth Schüssler Fiorenza, ed. (Notre Dame: University of Notre Dame Press, 1976) 43-67.

40. See especially Craig Evans' work on the *shaliach* motif in the Fourth Gospel: Craig A. Evans, *Word and Glory: On the Exegetical and Theological Background of John's Prologue*, JSNTSupS 158 (Sheffield: Sheffield Academic Series, 1993).

instructed.[41] Given that there are no fewer than twenty-four parallels between Deuteronomy 18:15-22 and the Father-Son relationship in John, the prophet-like-Moses agency schema not only accounts for many of John's elevated christological features; it also accounts for subordinated ones and the Son's representative relation to the Father.[42] A full-length treatment of the Johannine agency schema was contributed by Jan-A. Bühner, and even so, his indebtedness to the work of Meeks and the trajectory he forged is evident within that monograph.[43]

Interestingly, while this was not the primary interest of Meeks in his work, the elucidation of Jesus' mission within the schema of the prophet-king like Moses casts valuable light on John's first level of history in addition to its later developments. In particular, the presentation of Jesus as the Mosaic prophet bears a closer resemblance to what might be imagined as the self-understanding of Jesus and his mission, commanding a greater historical likelihood than Davidic messianic associations.[44] Thus, one would not be surprised to learn that the provocative deeds and words of Jesus

41. Thus, rather than seeing subordinate and egalitarian presentations of the Father-Son relationship in John as representing opposing christological views, they should be seen as flip-sides of the same coin, reflecting a Jewish agency typology: Anderson, *The Christology of the Fourth Gospel*, 184-85, 229; *The Riddles of the Fourth Gospel*, 27-29, 85-87, 131-34, 216-18. See also Wayne A. Meeks, "Equal to God," *The Conversation Continues: Studies in Paul and John in Honor of J. Louis Martyn*, Robert T. Fortna and Beverly R. Gaventa, eds. (Nashville: Abingdon, 1990) 309-22.

42. Paul N. Anderson, "The Having-Sent-Me Father—Aspects of Agency, Encounter, and Irony in the Johannine Father-Son Relationship," *Semeia* 85, Adele Reinhartz, ed. (1999): 33-57. See also A.E. Harvey, "Christ as Agent," *The Glory of Christ in the New Testament: Studies in Christology*, L.D. Hurst and N.T. Wright, eds. (Oxford: Clarendon, 1987) 239-50; Paul W. Meyer, "'The Father': The Presentation of God in the Fourth Gospel," *Exploring the Gospel of John; In Honor of D. Moody Smith*, R. Alan Culpepper and C. Clifton Black, eds. (Louisville: Westminster John Knox, 1996) 255-73.

43. Jan-A. Bühner, *Der Gesandte und sein Weg im vierten Evangelium: Die kultur- und religionsgeschichtlichen Grundlagen der johanneischen Sendungschristologie sowie ihre traditionsgeschichtliche Entwicklung* (Tübingen: Mohr Siebeck, 1977).

44. The presentation of Jesus as a charismatic prophetic figure is supported by the corroborative impression of all four canonical Gospels, and even though the Gospel of John was likely finalized last, it still conveys early impressions of Jesus of Nazareth in addition to the Christ of faith. Cf. Paul E. Davies, "Jesus and the Role of the Prophet," *Journal of Biblical Literature* 64:2 (1945): 241-54; Henry J. Cadbury, "Jesus and the Prophets," *Journal of Religion* 5 (1935): 607-22; see also the work of the John, Jesus, and History Project (2002-2016), which benefited from the wise counsel of Wayne Meeks at the outset of its organization.

were legitimated by appeals to a Mosaic-Prophet commission early on, and that in response to later challenges to the Jesus movement within the Johannine situation, appeals to the representative authority of Jesus as the prophet-king like Moses would have been especially potent.[45] Palpable also is the political thrust of messianic associations among the Gospels, and the messianic secrecy of Mark is corroborated by Jesus' fleeing of the crowd's designs on Jesus' future in John 6:15, as they seek to rush him off for a nationalistic coronation.[46] While John's Jewish agency motif was developed more fully within the *Logos*-hymn of the Johannine Prologue, its pervasive presence within the rest of the mundane Johannine narrative informs modern understandings of the Jesus of history as well as the Christ of faith.[47]

While it is unlikely that specific Samaritan audiences are targeted within a two-level reading of John's story of Jesus, nor is it likely that the Johannine situation reflects much of a Samaritan presence within its later community developments, John's characterization of Moses and his supersession by Jesus is clear within the rhetorical construction of the Johannine narrative.[48] On a multi-level reading of the text, however, the authority of Moses can be seen to be leveraged by the opponents and advocates of Jesus alike. Within Jerusalem and its environs, religious defenders of the Mosaic Law and the cultic establishment plausibly appealed to Sabbath prescriptions and temple practices. In answering those objections, Jesus reciprocally appealed to the Mosaic promise of a Prophet, who would speak and act directly on God's behalf.[49] In later stages of the Johannine situation, as

45. Anderson, "The Having-Sent-Me Father."

46. Anderson, *The Christology of the Fourth Gospel*, 170-93.

47. Paul N. Anderson, "The Johannine *Logos*-Hymn: A Cross-Cultural Celebration of God's Creative-Redemptive Work," *Creation Stories in Dialogue: The Bible, Science, and Folk Traditions, Radboud Prestige Lecture Series by R. Alan Culpepper*, BibInt 139, R. Alan Culpepper and Jan van der Watt, eds. (Leiden: E.J. Brill, 2016) 219-42.

48. Stan Harstine, *Moses as a Character in the Fourth Gospel: A Study of Ancient Reading Techniques*, Journal for the Study of the New Testament Supplement Series 229 (London: Sheffield Academic Press, 2002).

49. On the Mosaic agency schema and the historical Jesus in John, see Paul N. Anderson *The Fourth Gospel and the Quest for Jesus: Modern Foundations Reconsidered*, Library of New Testament Studies Series 321 (London: T&T Clark, 2006) 33-39, 59-60, 90-96, 107-10, 119-20, 138-42, 156-57, 161-62. On the self-understanding of Jesus and his mission, see also Wayne A. Meeks, "Asking Back to Jesus' Identity," *From Jesus to John: Essays on Jesus and New Testament Christology in Honour of Marinus de Jonge*, Martinus C. De Boer, ed. (Sheffield: JSOT Press, 1993) 38-50.

Deuteronomy 6:4-9 would likely have been cited in combatting the perceived ditheism of John's elevated Christology, followers of Jesus likely cited Deuteronomy 18:15-22 as a means of connecting the authority of the Son to his ambassadorial representation of the Father. As Meeks would put it, if one would truly aspire to be a follower of Moses, one must consider embracing the kingly Prophet of whom Moses wrote.

Conclusion:
The Itinerary of the Prophet-King Continuing

It is a rare thing that the doctoral dissertation of Wayne Meeks addressed one of the most puzzling of the Johannine riddles in such a way as to set the trajectory for his own career and also to influence generations of New Testament scholarship continuing to address a multitude of puzzling Johannine idiosyncrasies. Puzzling indeed is John's presentation of Jesus, being rejected in Jerusalem because he does not fit the royal expectations of Davidic messianism, while at the same time claiming to be a king before Pilate and hailed as a kingly prophet like Moses by the Galilean crowd. As a result of Meeks' exhaustive research, such a riddle cannot be explained away as simply a theological concoction or a rhetorical ploy. Nor is John's elevated Christology explicable on the assumption that it betrays later assimilation of Hellenistic redeemer myths. Rather, John's story of Jesus reflects Samaritan and Galilean anticipations of an eschatological prophet like Moses, who would speak on God's behalf, bringing liberation by the power of grace and truth—at times at odds with religious and political claims of authority and the leveraging of power. After all, Jesus fled the Galilean crowd's designs on a hasty coronation in John 6, and before Pilate in John 18, he declared that he is a king, but that his kingdom is one of truth, which is why his followers cannot resort to force to further it. As the Johannine Prologue reminds future hearers and readers of the narrative (John 1:17), "The law indeed was given through Moses; grace and truth came through Jesus Christ."

PREFACE

The following monograph was a doctoral dissertation accepted by the Faculty of the Graduate School of Yale University in 1965. It is published here without substantial alteration.

My thanks are due above all to Professor Nils Alstrup Dahl, who first suggested to me an investigation of the notion of Jesus' kingship in John 18.36f., and to Professor Paul W. Meyer, my dissertation adviser, for his friendship, his unfailing precision, and his keen exegetical sense. Professor Paul Minear provided valuable criticism, and Professor Paul Schubert has constantly given me warm encouragement as well as sound training in philological and style-critical method.

For many insights into the rabbinic literature I am indebted to Professor Brevard S. Childs and Professor Judah Goldin and to my good friend and former colleague Jacob Neusner. They of course share no responsibility for my errors. I owe a great deal also to conversations with my friends and erstwhile fellow students W. Sibley Towner and Fred O. Francis.

My graduate study and research were made possible by a Campus Ministry Grant from the Danforth Foundation and by a Kent Fellowship. To the Trustees of the Foundation and to the officers and fellow members of the Society for Religion in Higher Education I am deeply grateful.

Publication of this monograph would have been impossible without the assistance of a generous but anonymous donor, whom I wish to thank on this occasion. The indexes were prepared with the help of Mrs. Brenda Partin, under a grant from funds made available by the Board of Directors of the former Indiana School of Religion. I am much indebted for this assistance.

I will not attempt here to thank the one person to whom I owe most of all. I only mention that, besides her other excellences, my wife is an astute editor with a merciless eye for jargon.

Finally, my thanks to Dr. F. C. Wieder, Jr., the competent and helpful director of E. J. Brill, and to the editors of *Novum Testamentum* for including my work in the *Supplements* series.

The essay is dedicated to the man who started me on the way of biblical scholarship.

Indiana University   WAYNE A. MEEKS
Bloomington, Indiana
Advent 1966

LIST OF ABBREVIATIONS

Adv. Haer.	Irenaeus, *Adversus Haereses.*
ALUOS	*The Annual of Leeds University Oriental Society* (Leiden: E. J. Brill).
Antt.	Josephus, *Antiquitates judaicae.*
ARN	*Abot de Rabbi Nathan,* ed. Schechter.
Assump. Mos.	*The Assumption of Moses.*
ATD	*Das Alte Testament Deutsch* (Göttingen: Vandenhoeck & Ruprecht).
Bamidbar R.	*Bamidbar rabbah*: "Midrash Rabbah" on Numbers.
Bereshit R.	*Bereshit rabbah*: "Midrash Rabbah" on Genesis.
Bib. Antt.	Pseudo-Philo, *Liber Antiquitatum Biblicarum.*
BJ	Josephus, *Bellum Judaicum.*
BJRL	*Bulletin of the John Rylands Library*
BZAW	Beihefte zur Zeitschrift für die alttestamentliche Wissenschaft. (Berlin: Alfred Töpelmann.)
BZNW	Beihefte zur Zeitschrift für die neutestamentliche Wissenschaft. (Berlin: Alfred Töpelmann.)
C.Ap.	Josephus, *Contra Apionem.*
CD	The Damascus Document
CP	*The Canonical Prayerbook of the Mandaeans. (Qulasta.)*
Debarim R.	*Debarim rabbah*: "Midrash Rabbah" on Deuteronomy.
Did.	The Didache.
Ep. Barn.	The Epistle of Barnabas.
ET	English translation.
FRLANT	Forschungen zur Religion and Literatur des Alten und Neuen Testaments. (Göttingen: Vandenhoeck & Ruprecht.)
GCS	*Die griechischen-christlichen Schriftsteller der ersten drei Jahrhunderte.* (Leipzig: J. C. Hinrichs.)
GL	*Left Ginza,* ed. Lidzbarski.
Gosp. Peter	The Gospel of Peter, ed. Harnack.
GR	*Right Ginza,* ed. Lidzbarski.
HE	Eusebius, *Historia ecclesiastica.*
HNT	*Handbuch zum Neuen Testament.* (Tübingen: J. C. B. Mohr [Paul Siebeck].)
ICC	The International Critical Commentary on the Holy Scriptures of the Old and New Testaments. (Edinburgh: T. & T. Clark.)
IDB	*The Interpreter's Dictionary of the Bible.* (New York: Abingdon Press, 1962.)
JBL	*Journal of Biblical Literature.*
JE	*The Jewish Encyclopedia.* (New York: Funk & Wagnalls Company, 1907.)
JJS	*The Journal of Jewish Studies.*
JThSt	*The Journal of Theological Studies.*
Jub.	The Book of Jubilees.
KEK	Kritisch-exegetischer Kommentar über das Neue Testament. (Göttingen: Vandenhoeck & Ruprecht.)

Kohelet R.	*Kohelet rabbah*: "Midrash Rabbah" on Ecclesiastes.
LXX	The Septuagint.
Mart. Polyc.	The Martyrdom of Polycarp.
Mekilta	Unless otherwise specified, *Mekilta de R. Ishmael*, ed. Lauterbach.
MT	Masoretic Text.
n.s.	new series.
NTS	*New Testament Studies.*
Or. Sib.	*Oracula Sibyllina.*
Praep. Ev.	Eusebius, *Evangelicae Praeparationis.*
Ps. Sol.	The Psalms of Solomon.
RB	*Revue Biblique.*
RGG	*Die Religion in Geschichte und Gegenwart.* (3d ed.; Tübingen: J. C. B. Mohr [Paul Siebeck].)
RQ	*Revue de Qumran.*
RThP	*Revue de Theologie et de Philosophie.*
Sam. Josh.	Samaritan Joshua: *The Samaritan Chronicle or the Book of Joshua the Son of Nun,* trans. Crane.
SBT	Studies in Biblical Theology. (London: SCM Press Ltd.)
Shemot R.	*Sheᵐot rabbah*: "Midrash Rabbah" on Exodus.
Shir. R.	*Šir ha-širim rabbah*: "Midrash Rabbah" on Canticles.
Sifre Dt.	*Sifre de Be Rab* on Deuteronomy.
Sifre Num.	*Sifre de Be Rab* on Numbers.
Strom.	Clement of Alexandria, *Stromateis.*
Syr. Bar.	The Syriac Apocalypse of Baruch.
Talm. B.	*Talmud babli*: The Babylonian Talmud.
Talm. Y.	*Talmud yerušalmi*: The Palestinian Talmud.
Targ.	Targum, targumim.
Test. Lev.	The Testament of Levi.
Test. XII	The Testaments of the Twelve Patriarchs.
ThLZ	*Theologische Literaturzeitung.*
ThWbNT	*Theologisches Wörterbuch zum Neuen Testament.* (Stuttgart: W. Kohlhammer.)
Wayikra R.	*Wayikra rabbah*: "Midrash Rabbah" on Leviticus.
ZNW	*Zeitschrift für die neutestamentliche Wissenschaft.*
ZThK	*Zeitschrift für Theologie und Kirche.*

The following abbreviations refer to the Qumran texts:

1QS	*serek ha-yaḥad* ("Manual of Discipline").
1QSa	"Règle de la Congregation."
1QSb	"Recueil des Bénédictions."
1QH	*hodayōt* ("Hymn Scroll").
1QM	*serek ha-milḥamā* ("Rule of the War").
1QpHab	*pešer habakkuk* ("Commentary on Habakkuk").
1Q 16	"Commentaire de Psaumes."
1Q 27	"Livre des Mystères."
4QFlor	"Florilegium," ed. Allegro (*JBL* 75 [1956], 174-187).
4QTest	"Testimonia," ed. Allegro (*ibid.*).
4Q PB	"Patriarchal Blessings," ed. Allegro (*ibid.*).
4QpIsᵃ	Commentary on Isaiah, ed. Allegro (*ibid.*).
4QpNah	Commentary on Nahum, ed. Allegro (*ibid.*, pp. 89-95).
4QMa	Fragment of an older recension of the Rule of the War, ed. Hunzinger (*ZAW* 69 [1957], 131-151).
4Q Sl 39	"The Angelic Liturgy," ed. Strugnell.

4Q Dib Ham   "Words of the Heavenly Lights," ed. Baillet (*RB* 68
                  [1961], 195-250).
Tractates of the Mishnah and Talmuds are abbreviated as in Herbert
Danby, *The Mishnah*, p. 806.
Works of Philo Judaeus are abbreviated as in the Loeb edition, Vol. X,
pp. xxv-xxxvi.

CHAPTER ONE

INTRODUCTION

PURPOSE OF THE INVESTIGATION

In John 6.14f. we read, "So when the men saw the sign [the feeding miracle] which he had done, they said, 'This is truly the prophet who is coming into the world.' So Jesus, recognizing that they were about to come and seize him to make him king, fled[1] to the mountain alone." Who is "the prophet who is coming into the world?" Why does the "sign" of the multiplication of loaves indicate his identity? Why is it so self-evident that "the prophet" is to be made "king"?

In 18.37 Jesus, having tacitly admitted to Pilate that he is a king, explains his "kingship": "You say that I am a king. For this purpose I have been born and for this purpose I have come into the world: to testify to the truth." Again there is mention of "coming into the world." More important, it is clear that the purpose of Jesus' kingship as defined here is essentially that of a prophet. What "king" is this whose "kingship" is "not of this world" (18.36), whose royal function consists of prophetic "testimony"?

The following investigation undertakes to clarify the way in which the motifs represented by the two terms "prophet" and "king" in the Fourth Gospel not only are interrelated, but interpret each other. A study of similar combinations of the prophetic and royal motifs in representative sources from the Mediterranean religious world of the first Christian centuries will help to define the range of connotations of these two motifs and especially of the composite figure wherever it appears. At the same time these comparisons may contribute new information to the widely discussed but far from resolved question of the Johannine "background" by focusing attention upon one limited constellation of ideas and imagery which perhaps characterized the groups toward which the evident polemic and apologetic elements of John were directed. Finally the investigation will permit some deductions

---

[1] Or "withdrew." φευγει ‭א‬* lat syr^cur is to be preferred as *lectio difficilior* (below, p. 88).

about the Johannine christology and about the Christian community that described Jesus as "the Prophet" and "the King of
Israel."

THE RELATION OF THE PRESENT INVESTIGATION
TO THEORIES ABOUT THE JOHANNINE BACKGROUND

Since this investigation will involve not only detailed analysis of
passages within the Fourth Gospel but also a wide-ranging survey
of extra-biblical sources, it is necessary at the beginning to recognize
that not all scholars agree as to the necessity, or even the relevance, of
such comparative studies for the task of New Testament exegesis.
This is not the place, of course, for an abstract discussion of this
question, nor even for a survey of all the divergent positions toward
it which have been assumed by commentators on the Fourth Gospel
in this century. Instead, two figures are chosen whose positions
with respect to the question of "background" are opposite, yet
who have each achieved a deserved pre-eminence in Johannine
studies of the last half century.

The commentary of Hoskyns

Among English commentators the late Sir Edwyn Clement
Hoskyns[1] perceived most clearly and wrestled most profoundly
with the theological problem implicit in all historico-critical studies
of John: What is the relation between the theology of the Fourth
Gospel and history? Hoskyns insists upon the "fleshliness" of Jesus
in the Fourth Gospel and upon the "realism" with which the
evangelist views the world.[2] Yet, paradoxically it seems, he pays
virtually no attention to the environment within which the Fourth
Gospel came to be written. Two questions must be asked: (1) Why
does Hoskyns avoid discussing the Johannine milieu? (2) Is this
avoidance justified on his own grounds?

Hoskyns has a fundamental theological reason for passing over
the discipline of the history of religions in his approach to the
Fourth Gospel. He wishes to ward off the notion that historical
research of itself can "explain" the gospel as it stands. There is a
"tension" within the Fourth Gospel, he recognizes, but it is at root

---

[1] *The Fourth Gospel*, ed. Francis Noel Davey (2d ed. rev.; London: Faber
and Faber Limited, 1947), 604pp.

[2] *Ibid.*, pp. 17f. *et passim*.

a *theological* tension inseparable from "the meaning of the history of Jesus" as the evangelist himself was led to see it. This tension cannot be dissolved, then, without giving up the evangelist's own solution to the most basic theological problem of Christianity;[1] no additional historical knowledge will enable the Fourth Gospel "to come to rest."[2] Behind this considered judgment lies Hoskyns' assumption that the fourth evangelist is to be regarded primarily as a theologian. His gospel, therefore, is not to be "explained" by means of the elements which fed into it, but must be regarded as a *novum*, the result of creative reflection upon the Christian tradition. The Fourth Gospel is to be tested by the degree to which it makes more intelligible, that is, sets within a coherent theological pattern, the traditions and statements to be found in the other New Testament books.[3] To some extent this position corresponds, as Hoskyns notes,[4] with the view of such church fathers as Clement of Alexandria, for whom John was "the spiritual gospel."[5] At the same time Hoskyns, when he takes over the epithet "the theologian" for John, wants carefully to avoid the separation of interpretation from history that is implicit in Clement's language and still, Hoskyns felt, in the whole generation of modern Johannine studies prior to his own work.[6] "The theologian" for Hoskyns is not to be distinguished from "the historian," but is precisely the man who presents clearly the "theological tension" which he has seen in the "flesh and blood" history.[7]

From this cursory review of Hoskyns' standpoint it can be seen that he did not intend by any means to deny the relevance of

---

[1] *Ibid.*, pp. 130f. and chap. VII *passim*.

[2] *Ibid.*, p. 20, cf. pp. 129ff.

[3] *Ibid.*, pp. 133f.

[4] *Ibid.*, p. 17.

[5] τὸν μέντοι Ἰωάννην ἔσχατον, συνιδόντα ὅτι τὰ σωματικὰ ἐν τοῖς εὐαγγελίοις δεδήλωται, προτραπέντα ὑπὸ τῶν γνωρίμων, πνεύματι θεοφορηθέντα πνευματικὸν ποιῆσαι εὐαγγέλιον. (from the *Hypotyposeis, apud* Eusebius, *HE*, VI, xiv, 7).

[6] Hoskyns, pp. 17f., cf. chap. II *passim*.

[7] *Ibid.*, p. 131. This is also the theme of the important essay, written by Davey from Hoskyns' fragmentary notes, "The Fourth Gospel and the Problem of the Meaning of History" (now chap. VII). Davey is not always able to carry through this theme with the same consistency, as for example when he seems on p. 112 to see before the evangelist only the alternatives of "handling the material as a chronological historian" or "as a theologian." Such a statement of alternatives hopelessly modernizes the evangelist's situation; it also denies Hoskyns' fundamental concern, which Davey has elsewhere in this chapter expressed quite ably.

historical inquiry for his exegetical task, but only to limit *the theological function* of such inquiry. The supposition to be avoided was that the historian might obtain a standpoint outside the Fourth Gospel from which he could criticize the theological statements of the gospel by means of a "bare history" supposedly purged of "interpretation."[1] But so far as *understanding* the gospel's statements is concerned, Hoskyns is perfectly ready to make use of historical method. This is evident above all in his use of the First Epistle of John as a means of obtaining a picture of the intra-church situation against which that letter —and by implication the gospel —was written.[2] Moreover, "the Fourth Gospel depends for its understanding upon the recognition that its author is moving within the orbit of historical tradition, a tradition with which he presumes his readers to be at least generally familiar."[3] Consequently, any knowledge of those traditions one can obtain contributes to one's ability to understand the gospel, although Hoskyns is more skeptical than some scholars about the possibility of obtaining knowledge of the traditions in the form in which they existed prior to the synoptic gospels.[4]

When Hoskyns sets to work, however, it becomes evident that there is another limit to the extent of historical inquiry, a limit which controls his selection of sources, but which has not been established overtly in his theological introduction. Two examples will illustrate this limit. In discussing "living water" (John 4.10), Hoskyns says:

> The recognition of the parabolic character of water is characteristically biblical ... [There follow citations from Revelation and references to other New Testament and Old Testament passages, to Ben Sirach, to the Targums, to a summary by Billerbeck, and to Philo]. These Old Testament and Jewish references are quite sufficient to explain the background of the discourse; it does not seem necessary to add (as Bauer does in

---

[1] It is noteworthy that Hoskyns' polemic against the "historicizing" and "mythicizing" directions thus brings him in this particular to a stance remarkably similar to that of the scholar I have chosen to represent the opposite approach, Rudolf Bultmann. It is no wonder that Bultmann could speak so highly of Hoskyns ("The Interpretation of the Fourth Gospel," *NTS* 1 [1954/55], 91).

[2] Hoskyns, chap. III *passim*.

[3] *Ibid.*, p. 59.

[4] *Ibid.*

a detached note to v. 14 inserted in the second edition of his commentary) references to Mandaean and Hermetic texts. Such parallels belong to the study of comparative religion rather than to the exegesis of the Fourth Gospel.[1]

Again, commenting on the "shepherd" of John 10, Hoskyns cites a number of parallels in various religions, but adds:

> To place the parable in the Fourth Gospel upon the background of such general mysticism is to obscure the delicate allusions to the Old Testament, and to destroy that vigorous sense for history which it is the main purpose of the Evangelist to expose as the ground of Christian truth.[2]

Thus it is evident that Hoskyns does not reject the study of the historical background of John as a part of the task of exegesis; he only operates with a narrow definition of what that background may be. His exegesis takes account above all of the "self-contained allusiveness" that characterizes John,[3] then of the allusions to the Old Testament[4] and of allusions to the "orbit of historical tradition" common to the early Christian communities.[5] In addition he inserts occasional references to Philo, rabbinic sources, and the church fathers. By what criterion does Hoskyns decide that these sources exhaust the traditions that may have contributed important ideas and images to the evangelist's "workshop"?[6] Is the criterion dogmatic, as the statement quoted above seems to imply ("Such parallels belong to . . . comparative religion rather than to . . . exegesis . . .")? Or is it a historical criterion, which concludes that the circles represented by other extant sources could not have impinged upon that represented by John? The question is not discussed. Instead Hoskyns appears to regard it as axiomatic that only the Old Testament and (orthodox) Christian literature are of primary importance in illuminating the Fourth Gospel. But by assuming this position unargued, he ignores the complexity of the religious syncretism which, as has become increasingly apparent in

---

[1] *Ibid.*, p. 241.
[2] *Ibid.*, p. 368.
[3] *Ibid.*, p. 67.
[4] *Ibid.*, pp. 64f.
[5] *Ibid.*, pp. 59, 68ff.
[6] "There was a workshop in which the Fourth Gospel was fashioned, a workshop filled with particular ideas and particular experiences and containing, it seems, other *Christian* literature" (p. 20, emphasis mine).

the last generation, pervaded the Mediterranean world of the first century. Consequently he has himself implicitly denied that "vigorous sense of history" in the Fourth Gospel for which he so brilliantly argued.

Bultmann and the gnostic redeemer-myth

In sharpest possible contrast to Hoskyns' position, Rudolf Bultmann[1] argues that it is impossible to understand the Fourth Gospel properly without first becoming acquainted with a peculiar pattern of ideas and images that was extremely influential in the evangelist's environment. In his view the Fourth Gospel presents a puzzle to the reader: not only has it resisted attempts by scholars to fix its place in their reconstructions of the development of early Christian thought, but the fundamental conception of the gospel itself remains unclear, its imagery fragmentary and disjointed.[2] Yet Bultmann is fully aware of the unity of the gospel, which emerges from what Hoskyns calls the "self-contained allusiveness." The resultant riddle expresses itself for Bultmann finally in these terms: although the central conception of the gospel is that Jesus is the messenger from God who brings revelation, *what* he reveals is nothing more than *that* he is sent as revealer.[3] Such a self-contained but far from self-evident conception cannot stand by itself, Bultmann reasons, but must presuppose a well-known account of such a super-terrestrial messenger and of the message he brings. "In fact there stands behind [this central conception] a powerful *myth*, and

---

[1] Bultmann has set forth his argument in a large number of articles and larger works. Most important for our purposes: "Der religionsgeschichtliche Hintergrund des Prologs zum Johannes-Evangelium," ΕΥΧΑΡΙΣΤΗΡΙΟΝ, ed. Hans Schmidt ("Hermann Gunkel zum 60. Geburtstage . . ."; FRLANT, n.s. XIX, Part 2, 1923), pp. 1-26; "Die Bedeutung der neuerschlossenen mandäischen und manichäischen Quellen für das Verständnis des Johannes-evangeliums," *ZNW* 24 (1925), 100-146; and *Das Evangelium des Johannes* (6th ed., KEK; 1959), 563 pp. and Ergänzungsheft, 58 pp. The clearest systematic statement remains the *ZNW* article, which I mainly follow here. Summary statements are found also in the article "Johannesevangelium," *RGG*, 3d ed., Vol. III (1959), cols. 840-850 and *Theology of the New Testament* trans. Kendrick Grobel, Vol. II (New York: Charles Scribner's Sons, 1955), pp. 6, 10-14.

[2] Here it is not a question of the unevennesses in the narratives and discourses which Bultmann, like many other commentators, seeks to remove by theories of redaction and displacement of the text. Rather it is the perplexing character of the "Grundkonzeption" to which Bultmann points in his 1925 article.

[3] *ZNW* 24, p. 102.

recognizing it is the first step towards a correct understanding of the Gospel of John."[1]

Already in 1922 Bultmann had posited such a mythology behind the Prologue, which he had illustrated by reference to Jewish notions of a hypostasized "Wisdom." But the immediate *Vorlage* of the Prologue, he thought, had probably been a baptist hymn glorifying John the Baptist as the incarnate *Logos-Sophia*. The prose insertions containing an anti-John polemic were the work of the evangelist, who thus reduced the Baptist to the status of a mere "witness" and transferred his exalted attributes to Jesus.[2]

By 1925 Bultmann had before him Lidsbarski's translations of Mandaean texts (the Book of John, the Liturgies, and the *Ginza*) as well as descriptions of the Manichaean texts from Turfan. In them he saw the full-fledged myth he had previously deduced, on the basis of Reitzenstein's and Bousset's research, from the scattered "Wisdom" speculations. He was now certain that the myth basic to the Mandaean ideology was the same as that presupposed by John. He undertook to demonstrate this identity by collecting terminological and/or conceptual parallels between John and Mandaean texts (with some additions from the Turfan fragments, the Odes of Solomon, the Acts of Thomas, and a few other apocryphal books), illustrating twenty-eight characteristics of the redeemer-figure.[3] The fact that the sources for the "gnostic" myth

---

[1] "In der Tat steckt hinter ihm ein gewaltiger Mythos, den zu erkennen der erste Schritt zum rechten Verständnis des Joh-Ev ist" (*ibid.*, p. 103).

[2] ΕΥΧΑΡΙΣΤΗΡΙΟΝ, pp. 23-26; cf. *Ev. Joh.*, pp. 4f.

[3] *ZNW*, 24, pp. 104-139. The twenty-eight characteristics form a good outline of the "gnostic redeemer-myth" as Bultmann understood it then and later: (1) The revealer is the eternal divine being, who was in the beginning. (2) He was sent from the Father into the world. (3) He came into the world. (4) At the same time he is one with the Father. (5) The Father equipped him with authority. (6) He has and imparts life. (7) He leads out of the Darkness into the Light. (8) The word-pairs Life and Death, Light and Darkness, in John as in the literature being compared, correspond to the word-pair Truth and Falsehood. (9) The Messenger is without fault or falsity. (10) He does the works which his Father appointed for him. (11) In revelation discourses he speaks of his person (*ego eimi*). (12) He knows his own, and they know him. (13) He gathers or selects them; they are or become his possession. (14) To the powers of this world the Messenger appears as a stranger; they do not know his origin, for it is different from theirs. (15) Those who hear the preaching of the Messenger are hardened. (16) The messenger is renounced and hated in the world. (17) He will depart as he came; as he descended, so he will ascend. (18) Then one will seek him without finding him. (19) By his ascent he is "justified" (20) As the Redeemed [*sic*: evidently however "Erlöster" is a misprint for "Erlöser," since the

were all much later than John he regarded as irrelevant, since the myth itself was indubitably older.[1]

The last point is fundamental to Bultmann's whole method. His judgment as to the antiquity of the basic "redeemer myth" was derived, first of all, from the hypotheses of Reitzenstein and Bousset, who had sought a genealogical explanation of the idea of a "redeemer" and were increasingly inclined to find its origin in ancient Iranian speculations about the "primaeval man." Bultmann, therefore, never appears to doubt that the "redeemer myth" in all its essential parts existed long before the Hellenistic Age. For his judgment on the relative age of the Johannine and the Mandaean patterns, however, he argues from specific comparisons between the respective texts. Assuming, on the basis of the innumerable parallels he cites, that both John and the Mandaean texts belong to the same circle of ideas, he then argues that the fragmentary, relatively simpler pattern of John could not be a stage on the way to the elaborate myth, but must have been excerpted from it, with some deliberate alterations.

At the same time Bultmann found in the apparent prominence accorded John the Baptist in the Mandaean sources a striking confirmation of his hypothesis of a Baptist origin for the Johannine prologue.[2] Now he expanded this thesis by noting that (1) the polemic against an elevated status for John was not confined to the Prologue, but occurred at several points in the early chapters of the Fourth Gospel, and (2) the "revelation discourses," which so largely create the distinctive character of the Gospel, have certain stylistic similarities to the Prologue.[3] Bultmann was now ready to develop his source hypothesis in the form that controls the structure and argument of his commentary: the Prologue and the revelation discourses belonged to a document of the Baptist community, which exalted John and gave him the central role of a redeemer sent from the Light-world to the demon-ruled earth, where, taking human

---

passages Bultmann quotes (pp. 131f.) do not contain the notion of "the redeemed redeemer."] the Messenger leads the redeemed with him. (22) He prepares a dwelling place for his own. (23) He has shown or prepared for his own the way. (24) He is the Door. (25) He frees the captives. (26) His ascension is the catastrophe of the cosmos. (27) He is the Judge. (28) He is the Son of Man.

[1] *Ibid.*, p. 139.
[2] *Ibid.*, pp. 142f.
[3] *Ev. Joh.*, index, s.v. "Quellen: Offenbarungsreden"; cf. *RGG* III, cols. 842f.

form, he revealed himself, thus effecting a separation between the world and "his own," who heeded his preaching, recalled their origin in the Light-world, and thus learned the way back home, whence John preceded them after accomplishing his mission. The evangelist, Bultmann asserts, took over this source, but excised certain distinctively gnostic elements —the cosmological basis of man's fateful situation and the pre-existence of the essential self — using the broken myth to depict Jesus' activity as redeemer.[1]

Bultmann welcomed the thesis of Lidzbarski and Reitzenstein that the Mandaeans originated in Palestine among the baptizing sects of Transjordan, but he went one step beyond their arguments by confidently asserting that "the origin of the Mandaeans —regardless of what elements may have determined the further development of the sect —lies among the adherents of John the Baptist."[2] This meant that a direct line ran from John's disciples, whose writings the fourth evangelist had appropriated and against whom he had contended, to the Mandaeans of present-day Iran and Iraq. Furthermore the literature of this group, although in its present form it was not assembled before the Islamic invasions of Babylonia in the seventh and eighth centuries,[3] has preserved, despite accretions of fantasy and folklore, one of the purest extant forms of the "early oriental" "gnostic redeemer myth."[4] Since,

---

[1] *RGG* III, cols. 846f.

[2] *ZNW* 24, p. 143. Lidzbarski is much more reserved: "Wahrscheinlich haben die Mandäer die Tätigkeit Johannes des Täufers, die ja aus derselben Bewegung hervorgegangen ist, im Westen miterlebt, vielleicht an ihr teilgenommen. Dass sie lediglich auf Johannes zurückgehen, wie vielfach angenommen wird, glaube ich nicht" (*Ginza; Der Schatz oder das grosse Buch der Mandäer* ["Quellen der Religionsgeschichte"; Göttingen: Vandenhoeck & Ruprecht, 1925], p. X). Reitzenstein takes a similar position (*Die hellenistische Mysterienreligionen, nach ihren Grundgedanken und Wirkungen* [3d ed. rev.; Leipzig: B. G. Teubner, 1927], p. 418; more clearly, *Die Vorgeschichte der christlichen Taufe* [Leipzig: B. G. Teubner, 1929], pp. 265f. Both these works were written after Bultmann's article).

[3] Kurt Rudolph, *Die Mandäer*, Vol. I: *Prolegomena: Das Mandäerproblem* (FRLANT, n.s. LVI, 1960), p. 23. There are evidently pre-Islamic elements incorporated into the collection, however. Rudolph judges particularly the hymns to be quite early, in part going back at least to the second century A.D. Moreover, potsherds and a lead tablet containing Mandaean magical inscriptions have been found, datable in the 5th/6th and 4th centuries respectively. In the opinion of specialists, these texts demonstrate "dass bereits im 3. und 4. Jh. 'wesentliche Elemente der mandäischen Literatur' vorhanden gewesen sein müssen" (*ibid.*, p. 28, citing Schlier).

[4] The clearest statement of this opinion, which is presupposed by Bultmann's commentary, is by Hans Jonas: "Er ist so der am meisten 'orienta-

therefore, Bultmann argues that the main features of the Johannine christology are drawn from a gnostic redeemer myth which had previously been historicized in the person of John the Baptist, he can move directly to the Mandaean texts for elucidation of that christology. These texts, along with the writings of Ignatius (who in Bultmann's view was himself influenced by Syrian gnosticism) and the Odes of Solomon, become the most important source of parallels in the commentary.[1]

The results of Bultmann's daring synthesis are impressive. Indeed it is no exaggeration to say that he has carried the field in Johannine studies, at least in the sense that the question of the extra-biblical background for the christology of John has become unavoidable. Even C. H. Dodd, who stands nearest to Hoskyns in his approach to John, nevertheless devotes more than one-fourth of his commentary on the Fourth Gospel to "The Background."[2] On the other side, Bultmann has largely supplanted older approaches by the "religionsgeschichtliche Schule" and others to the gospel's background. For example, B.W. Bacon's "Hellenists" are representatives of "the syncretistic Jewish Gnosticism of northern Syria, and especially of Samaria."[3] Gillis P. Wetter's attempt[4] to locate the essential christology of John in the type of the Hellenistic *theios anthropos*, principal figure in the "popular religion" of Hellenism, ascribes to this figure many features which for Bultmann are characteristics of the "gnostic redeemer myth."[5] Hugo Odeberg's suggestion of a background in "Jewish salvation mysticism" con-

---

lische,' volksmässige –und d.h. zugleich: der unmittelbarste Ausdruck gnostischen Seelenlebens geworden. In ihm bietet sich daher das Eigenwesen der Gnosis am reinsten so dar, wie es nach grösstmöglichem Abzug aller 'Pseudomorphose' nur erscheinen kann –also eine optimale Erscheinung derselben" (*Gnosis und spätantiker Geist*, Part 1: *Die mythologische Gnosis* [FRLANT, n.s. XXXIII; 1934], p. 95). This statement is cited with approval by Rudolph, pp. 141f.

[1] Cf. *RGG*, III, col. 847.

[2] *The Interpretation of the Fourth Gospel* (Cambridge: The University Press, 1953), pp. 3-130.

[3] *The Gospel of the Hellenists*, ed. Carl H. Kraeling (New York: Henry Holt and Company, 1933), p. 121.

[4] *Der Sohn Gottes; Eine Untersuchung über den Charakter und die Tendenz des Johannes-Evangeliums* (FRLANT, n.s., IX; 1916), 201 pp.

[5] Note especially the pattern of descent/ascent, p. 101ff. Here is one of the weakest links in Wetter's chain of arguments. In the first place he is able in this chapter (V) to offer only the most meager evidence that the *theioi anthropoi* were characteristically thought to be of divine origin. The citations he gives are all from literature which might be suspected to have

nected with an exalted view of the Old Testament patriarchs[1] deserves new attention on the bases of the illuminating studies by Gershom G. Scholem.[2] But while his collections of parallels (to the discourses in the first twelve chapters of John alone) are suggestive, his general category of "salvation mysticism," which he himself sometimes calls "gnosticism,"[3] is too vague to be helpful, and his exegesis of the Johannine text is controlled by ideas found in the parallels to the point of ignoring the connections within the text itself. Bultmann's work can justifiably be given pre-eminence above all these, for the facts which each of these theories seeks to explain find their places to a remarkable extent within the enormously detailed and strikingly self-consistent exegesis contained in Bultmann's commentary. The same judgment must be rendered towards the more recent advocates of an Essene background of John, on the basis of the Qumran texts.[4] So far nothing more convincing than

been influenced directly or indirectly by Christianity. Especially is this clear in his discussion of the question πόθεν εἶ σύ; He cites only Apollonius of Tyana (*Vita* IV, 44; cf. I, 21) and the Fourth Gospel (19.9). Yet he only asserts, without proof, that the two are independent. (For the opposite view, cf. Pierre Labriolle, *La Réaction païenne; Étude sur la polémique antichrétienne du Ier au VIe siècle* [Paris: l'Artisan du Livre, 1942], pp. 175-189.) Moreover, in his discussion of the Fourth Gospel itself Wetter shows no insight into the function of the phrase πόθεν ἐστίν in the development of the gospel, so that he finds embarrassment in the evangelist's failure to answer the question, where in fact the evangelist is driving toward a significant theological statement. In general Wetter's book suffers from his superficial exegesis of John.

[1] *The Fourth Gospel, Interpreted in its Relation to Contemporaneous Religious Currents in Palestine and the Hellenistic-Oriental World* (Uppsala: Almqvist & Wiksells Boktryckeri, 1929), p. 215 *et passim*.

[2] *Major Trends in Jewish Mysticism* (3d ed.; New York: Schocken Books, 1954), 460 pp.; *Jewish Gnosticism, Merkabah Mysticism and Talmudic Tradition* (New York: The Jewish Theological Seminary of America, 1960), 126 pp.

[3] Odeberg, p. 215.

[4] For example, A. Feuillet, "La litterature de Qûmrân et les écrits johanniques," *Études* 3 (1959), 440-456; Ethelbert Stauffer, "Qumran und die Evangelienforschung," *Universitas* 14 (1959), 487-495 [I have not personally seen these two works]; Lucetta Mowry, "The Dead Sea Scrolls and the Background for the Gospel of John," *The Biblical Archaeologist* 17 (1954), 78-97; W. F. Albright, "Recent Discoveries in Palestine and the Gospel of St. John," *The Background of the New Testament and Its Eschatology*, ed. W. D. Davies and David Daube (Cambridge: The University Press, 1956), pp. 153-171; F. M. Braun, "L'arrièrefond judaïque du quatrième évangile et la communauté de l'alliance," *RB* 62 (1925), 5-44. The influence of the Qumran sect on John is contested vigorously by Howard M. Teeple, "Qumran and the Origin of the Fourth Gospel," *Novum Testamentum* 4 (1960), 6-25.

the citation of a few isolated parallels, or the general similarity of "limited dualism," has been produced by these advocates. Perhaps it is not too much to say that, if they could prove their case, they would thereby only succeed in bringing the Qumran ideology under the umbrella of Bultmann's "gnostic myth."[1]

Dissolution of the synthesis

For the reasons outlined above, Bultmann's commentary stands as the landmark with which everyone undertaking anew to explore the Johannine christology must first reckon. Nevertheless, the presuppositions behind its tightly woven argument are now called into question at three significant points.

First, the connection of traditions or actual sources behind the Fourth Gospel with the sect of John the Baptist is undermined by the recent analyses by two of Bultmann's own pupils of the Johannine Prologue. Both Ernst Käsemann[2] and Ernst Haenchen[3] present convincing arguments that not a baptist but a Christian hymn was used by the evangelist.[4] But, as was shown above, Bultmann's source-critical analysis of the Prologue was his starting point for the hypothesis that the "revelation discourse" was derived from a baptist sect. Therefore Haenchen categorically rejects the hypothesis of a "discourse source."[5]

Second, the historical connection between John the Baptist and

---

[1] Bultmann himself, with dubious justification, has hailed the Qumran texts as proof of the early penetration of gnostic influence into Jewish Palestine (*Theology*, II, 13, n.; cf. *Ev. Joh.*, Ergänzungsheft, p. 11).

[2] "Aufbau und Anliegen des johanneischen Prologs," *Libertas Christiana*: *Friedrich Delekat zum 65. Geburtstag*, ed. W. Matthias and E. Wolf (München: Chr. Kaiser Verlag, 1957), pp. 75-99.

[3] "Probleme des johanneischen 'Prologs,'" *ZThK* 60 (1963), 305-334.

[4] Beyond this point they diverge on the questions of the extent of the hymn (Käsemann: only verses 1 (2), 3-5, (9), 10-12; Haenchen, rejecting the strict criteria of meter and strophic structure applied by Bultmann and Käsemann, thinks all of vv. 1-5, 9-11, 14, 16f. belonged to the original) and of its interpretation (Käsemann: v. 5 already speaks of incarnation; Haenchen: vv. 5, 9-11 speak of a futile revelation of the *logos asarkos* after the model of the old Wisdom myth, as a motivation for the incarnation first described in v. 14). Haenchen takes the further step of showing that the status given to John the Baptist here (ἄνθρωπος ἀπεσταλμένος παρὰ θεοῦ: elsewhere in the gospel almost exclusively the designation for Jesus!) does not harmonize with the over-all view of the evangelist. Hence the prose insertions are not his work, but the rather clumsy redaction of an editor, perhaps the same who added chap. 21.

[5] P. 309.

the Mandaeans is likewise rejected in the most thorough study of
the Mandaeans since Lidzbarski's own labors, the large monograph
of Kurt Rudolph.[1] Beginning with the remarkable fact that John
does not appear in the baptismal ritual of the Mandaeans,[2] Rudolph
proceeds to show that all the traditions regarding John in Mandaean
sources are secondary, with no historical verisimilitude. Moreover,
John is no redeemer figure for the Mandaeans: "The notion that
John is regarded as an incarnation of Anoš is completely without
foundation. . . . There is nothing of this notion in the texts, and
there is no 'incarnation idea' in Mandaean."[3] While the Mandaeans
must have taken over traditions in which John and Jesus were
viewed as opponents,[4] these traditions play no decisive role in the
over-all structure of Mandaean thought. "For the Mandaean religion
as a whole, John is not constitutive."[5] Consequently, in Rudolph's
well-substantiated opinion, the Mandaean texts afford no basis
whatever for reconstructing the character and history of the baptist
movement whose existence is surmised from New Testament allusions and polemical notes.[6]

As a result of these researches, Bultmann's reconstruction of a
specific historical bridge by which he sought to explain the fourth
evangelist's acquaintance with the gnostic redeemer myth must
now be regarded with extreme skepticism, if not rejected altogether.
However, even its rejection is not fatal to Bultmann's over-all
approach, since in his view the gnostic myth itself was an ancient,
very widely diffused entity, which maintained its essential contours
regardless of the particular community or body of literature in
which it found expression. Therefore the Mandaean texts, even if

---

[1] See above, p. 9, n. 3.

[2] "Der Kult ist an der 'Jordan' gebunden, aber nicht an den Täufer
Johannes" (Rudolph, p. 65).

[3] *Ibid.*, p. 69.

[4] *Ibid.*, p. 75.

[5] *Ibid.*, p. 73.

[6] "Kann man nun nach dem obigen Bild von einer Beziehung zwischen
Täufergemeinde und Mandäern sprechen? Etwa in dem Sinn: 'Die mandäischen Texte haben Bedeutung für die Rekonstrucktion einer im NT nur aus
der Polemik und Apologie des 4. Evangeliums unsicher zu erkennenden,
aber in ihrer Geschichtlichkeit nicht zu bestreitenden Täuferbewegung als
Parallel-oder Kontrasterscheinung zum Urchristentum'? Mit Bezug auf die
Bewegung Johannes des Täufers halte ich dieses Unterfangen für völlig
haltlos. . . . *Johannes der Täufer und seine Jüngerschaft haben nach dem Befund
der uns zugänglichen Quellen keine Beziehung zu den Mandäern gehabt"* (ibid.,
pp. 79f., italics original).

there is no historical connection between Mandaeans and any sects
known by the evangelist, can still stand as a most important witness
to the form of the myth which, *ex hypothesi*, was also known to
John. Rudolph himself is careful to reserve this possibility.[1] But
now even this fundamental point in Bultmann's theory is called into
question by the renewed inquiry into the "gnostic redeemer myth"
itself by Carsten Colpe.[2]

Colpe singles out as the decisive accomplishment of Bultmann,
for the history-of-religions approach to New Testament research,
the fact that "he distilled out of the literature a veritable *model* of
the gnostic redeemer myth."[3]

This "model" brought into a coherent pattern the discoveries and
hypotheses of men like Reitzenstein and Bousset. On the basis of
this forceful synthesis, Bultmann and his school proceeded on the
assumption of a pre-Christian Gnosis in the sense of "a myth of the
redeemed redeemer, the 'Urmensch' as 'cosmogonic potency and
anthropological principle.'"[4]

Yet the very power of Bultmann's synthesis, which gave it such
extensive influence in New Testament studies, had at the same
time the important negative effect that, for the Bultmann school,
further detailed investigation of the individual elements that composed the gnostic synthesis was no longer pursued as a special task –
especially after the epoch-making exposition by Hans Jonas, under
Bultmann's aegis, of the gnostic "understanding of existence."[5] A
particularly important consequence was that the New Testament
scholars were virtually cut off from thirty years of Iranian studies.[6]
Yet Bultmann's original synthesis was derived from the general
"thesis of the old-Iranian origin of Gnosis and of the late-Jewish
apocalyptic," according to which "the Son of Man and the gnostic

---

[1] "Unbeschadet davon erkenne ich die Bedeutung der mandäischen Texte
für die Interpretation der urchristlichen Literatur (als 'orientalischer Kommentar,' Windisch) an, besonders für den johanneischen Schriftenkreis"
(*ibid.*, p. 80, n. 2; cf. pp. 141f.).

[2] *Die religionsgeschichtliche Schule: Darstellung und Kritik ihres Bildes vom
gnostischen Erlösermythus* (FRLANT, n.s. 60, 1961), 265 pp.

[3] *Ibid.*, p. 57. At the same time, Colpe justly notes, "wurde Bultmann
aber auch der Eigenart des Neuen Testaments methodisch viel besser gerecht
als seine Vorgänger . . ." (p. 58).

[4] *Ibid.*, p. 60; the quoted phrase is Vielhauer's.

[5] *Ibid.*

[6] *Ibid.*, p. 140.

Anthropos had their forerunners in an Iranian *Urmensch* figure, most likely in Gayomart."[1]

The central section of Colpe's monograph reports his own investigation of the old Persian texts, building upon the vastly improved knowledge of Iranian sources obtained since Reitzenstein's time. He concludes that no direct or indirect connection can be posited between the gnostic *Urmensch* and the Gayōmart of the Avestas.[2] Indeed the Iranian primaeval man did not have any echo in late Judaism or in Gnosis.[3]

Carrying his criticism of the conventional model of the "gnostic redeemer myth" a decisive step further, Colpe then calls into question the whole concept of a "redeemed redeemer." This term never in fact occurs in gnostic sources, although it can be deduced logically from the various versions of gnostic myth. The term expresses the fact that the redeemer is often identified, implicitly or explicitly, with the primaeval man and thus also with the individual men or souls to be saved. But the expression actually covers several different possible relationships, so that Colpe, after analyzing nine representative gnostic systems, concludes that one can speak of the "urmensch-redeemer" or of the "redeemed redeemer" only at the cost of disregarding the diverse hypostatizations by which historical gnostic systems in fact *separate* "the redeemer from the primaeval man, the various redeemer figures from each other and from the primaeval man, the upper, saving light-substance from the lower light-substance that is to be saved, and both these substances from the primaeval man and the various redeemer-figures."[4]

In short the whole "model" of the "redeemer myth" in the form that Bultmann and his pupils have employed it has to be thoroughly revised, using more appropriate categories than those that heretofore have dominated the discussion and avoiding the temptation to press upon the gnostic systems the modern scholar's logical reduction of them to their "basic ontological structure."[5] But before a more adequate model can be constructed, a thoroughgoing analysis of the fundamental concepts of gnosis must be carried out. This task Colpe assigns himself for his second volume, still to be publish-

---

[1] *Ibid.*, p. 65.
[2] *Ibid.*, p. 153.
[3] *Ibid.*, p. 169.
[4] *Ibid.*, p. 185; cf. the summary on pp. 186-189.
[5] *Ibid.*, p. 186.

ed. The following paragraph, in which he summarizes one aspect of the problem to be investigated, is worth quoting in its entirety because of its direct applicability to Johannine research:

> Therefore one has to investigate whether certain concepts and ideas of relatively early times can only be interpreted as traces of the whole myth—in this case they would be foreign bodies in the context of the traditions in which we now find them— or whether they are fully understandable as integral components or expressions of their own contexts within their traditions—in this case, in so far as one can maintain their relationship with a myth at all, they are components that have entered the myth at a later time, perhaps with altered structure.[1]

The former alternative is precisely the position which Bultmann takes for granted[2] and upon which he rests his whole case for the "Mandaean" gnostic background of John's revelation discourses. The requirement that this alternative be investigated afresh, without positive or negative prejudgment, by means of a careful analysis of specific individual phenomena, is a direct result of the new fluid situation in gnostic research.[3]

All of this carries immediate and far-reaching implications for New Testament studies. Particularly it supports the validity of the present investigation of a narrow aspect of the Johannine christology in the face of Bultmann's elaborate theory that had seemed to account so cogently for the *total* christological picture in John. Just as Colpe calls for a precise, philologically based exploration of the redeemer myth wherever it occurs within gnostic sources, so it is appropriate in a study of the Fourth Gospel to focus attention upon a single phenomenon or group of closely related phenomena. This is the only means by which scholarship can move from Bultmann's great synthesis, now made problematical, toward the possibility of a new synthesis which may account more adequately for the additional facts and insights that have come to light.

For several reasons the figure described by the merging of the functions and titles of "prophet" and "king" is an appropriate phenomenon with which to begin further efforts toward understanding the Fourth Gospel's christology. This figure is one which is demonstrably important in the thematic development of the

---

[1] *Ibid.*, p. 202.
[2] See above, pp. 11f.
[3] Colpe, p. 201.

gospel itself.[1] Furthermore, the figure is identifiable: exegesis can begin with the actual occurrences of the two titles and with the functions specifically associated with them in their contexts in the gospel. Finally the "prophet-king" figure may have a direct relationship to the problem of the gnostic redeemer,[2] while at the same time this terminology does not carry the burden of implying a preconceived "myth".

PROPHET AND KING IN PREVIOUS JOHANNINE RESEARCH

The king

"King" as a christological appellative in the Fourth Gospel has never been the object of a special investigation. The reason for this neglect, of course, is that it is commonly assumed that the term "king" refers to the Messiah, the Son of David.[3] Since it is generally held that the Johannine interpretation explicitly denies the political element of the Davidic ideology, the title "king" is ordinarily thought to have no special significance. Willy Staerk in fact argues that the concept "King of Israel" particularly recedes among the christological titles in John, replaced by the ascendant idea of "the

---

[1] The exegetical support for this statement must await systematic treatment in the next chapter.

[2] The resemblances of the redeemer in several gnostic systems to a "prophet" are self-evident. Whether all the prophets who figure in gnostic literature can forthwith be regarded as "redeemers" is an open question, however. (Cf. Colpe, p. 198. Orally Prof. Colpe has further suggested, as a working hypothesis, that the existence of a gnostic redeemer myth properly so-called may always presuppose the prior existence of some historical prophet who has been docetically interpreted.) The occurrences of "prophet" and "king" as actual designations for the redeemer in Mandaean sources will be the object of investigation in a later chapter.

[3] An exception is Oscar Cullmann, who regards the title βασιλεύς as only "a variant of the *Kyrios* title" (*The Christology of the New Testament*, trans. Shirlie C. Guthrie and Charles A. M. Hall [Philadelphia: The Westminster Press, 1959], p. 220). Cullmann's support for this assertion is not at all clear. He begins with the assumption that the conflict with emperor worship is one of the main elements involved in fixing the κύριος title. Then, since βασιλεύς occasionally figures in situations of conflict between Empire and Christians, he concludes that the two are "interchangeable" (*ibid.*, p. 221). Beyond this bare assertion, his further argument seems to consist only in first positing a theological difference between the connotations of the two titles in Christian usage, then citing several passages (one, 1 Tim. 6.15, erroneously referred to Christ instead of God, as the context requires) that refute this hypothetical difference.

Son of God."[1]

Against a view like Staerk's stands first of all the constitutive position of the kingship of Jesus in the Johannine passion narrative. Not only is the repetition of the title impressive,[2] it is so coordinated with the alternation of scenes, punctuated by Pilate's "going out" and "going in," that it governs the whole direction of thought, from Pilate's first question to Jesus, "Are you the King of the Jews?" to the final solemn proclamation to "the Jews", "Behold your King!" and their shout of rejection, "We have no king but Caesar!"[3] While Jesus' kingship is also an important motif in the synoptic trial scenes, John has not merely taken over the traditional imagery,[4] but has vastly expanded and emphasized this particular motif.[5] Balancing this dramatic climax of the gospel there stands in the beginning, at the focal point of transition from the testimony of John (1.19-34) and the resultant joining of the first disciples to Jesus (1.35-44) to Jesus' first sign (2.1-11, cf. 1.50), the solemn confession by the one who is "truly an Israelite": "Rabbi, you are the Son of God, you are the King of Israel." The

---

[1] "Hinter dieser rein religiösen, im pneumatischen Wesen des Christus begründeten Gottessohnschaft tritt die Vorstellung von dem jüdischen Messias, im besonderen die vom König Israels, völlig zurück. . . ." (Soter; Die biblische Erlösererwartung als religionsgeschichtliches Problem. Part I: Der biblische Christus [Gütersloh: Verlag C. Bertelsmann, 1933], p. 106).

[2] βασιλεύς occurs 12 times in the Johannine passion narrative (6 times β. τῶν Ἰουδαίων, 2 times β. ὑμῶν [i.e., τῶν Ἰουδαίων], 4 times without modifiers), compared with 6 times in Mk. (β. τ. Ἰουδαίων 5 times, β. Ἰσραήλ once), 4 times each for Mt. (3 times β. τ. Ἰουδαίων, once β. Ἰσραήλ) and for Lk. (3 times β. τ. Ἰουδαίων, once without modifier).

[3] An extended analysis of these scenes is included in the next chapter.

[4] It is assumed throughout this inquiry that Jn is dependent upon a source, probably written, but not identical with any of the Synoptics, for the passion narrative. For the evidence, which need not be discussed here, see Martin Dibelius, "Johannesevangelium," RGG, Vol. III (2d ed.; 1929), col. 353; cf. Bultmann, Ev. Joh., pp. 491, 493, 497f., 502f., 515 and, most recently, C. H. Dodd, Historical Tradition in the Fourth Gospel (Cambridge: The University Press, 1963), pp. 65-173. For a contrary view, see John Bailey, Traditions Common to the Gospels of Luke and John ("Supplements to Novum Testamentum," VII; Leiden: E. J. Brill, 1963), 121 pp., who argues for the dependence of Jn. on Lk.

[5] Thus Bultmann correctly says, "Er hat das traditionelle Motiv, dass Jesus als angeblicher βασιλεύς angeklagt wird, durch die Dialoge Jesu mit Pilatus in den Mittelpunkt gestellt, und er hat also die Paradoxie des königlichen Anspruchs Jesus deutlich gemacht . . ." (Ev. Joh., p. 503). Cf. Vincent Taylor, The Names of Jesus (London: Macmillan and Co., Limited, 1953), pp. 76f.

idea of Jesus' kingship, far from receding in John's gospel, has gained new significance.[1]

It is also incorrect to argue that the titles in the Fourth Gospel are "leveled" or simply equated. Wetter, for example, asserts that "Messiah," "Christ," "the Prophet," "the Son of Man," and "the Son of God" are all interchangeable for the fourth evangelist.[2] Since for Wetter the christology of John stems mainly from the "divine man" figure of popular Hellenistic piety, the variety of titles is merely comparable to the numerous epithets applied to various Syrian "prophets."[3] To a degree Bultmann's exposition of John implies an analogous position. Although in the exegesis of particular passages he is careful to mention the background of specific titles of Jesus, yet since the fundamental shape of Johannine christology comes from the gnostic redeemer myth, the various traditional names add nothing of consequence. There is some truth in these points of view, since one must not make the mistake of supposing that the titles, as fixed semantic counters, "carry" the christology of the gospel. Instead the christology is expressed through the interrelationship of the titles and above all by the total structure of the gospel. Furthermore, an argument like Wetter's might seem to be supported by the frequent association of different titles in the same narrow context, like the confession of Nathanael just mentioned, where "Son of God" stands alongside "King of Israel."[4] Nevertheless, John's use of the titles betrays an awareness of their discrete connotations. For example, the questions to the Baptist in 1.20-28 distinguish clearly among several eschatological personages expected by the Jews, while 7.40-41 demonstrates the evangelist's knowledge of the distinction between "the Christ" and "the Prophet," a distinction often ignored by modern scholars.

If the importance of the king motif in John is granted, then it remains to determine the range of connotations which "king" may have here and, if possible, the identity of any figures who may have

---

[1] Other allusions to Jesus' kingship in John will be discussed in Chap. II (below, pp. 81-98).

[2] Wetter, p. 12.

[3] *Ibid.*, p. 10.

[4] In fact there are three titles employed in the conversation between Nathanael and Jesus: υἱὸς τοῦ θεοῦ, βασιλεὺς τοῦ Ἰσραήλ, and υἱὸς τοῦ ἀνθρώπου. Perhaps it is significant that the same three, or their equivalents, play a role in the interrogation by Pilate: υἱὸς τοῦ θεοῦ 19.7; βασιλεὺς τῶν Ἰουδαίων 18.33,39; 19.3 (14, 15), 19, 21; ὁ ἄνθρωπος 19.5.

been associated with the title "King of Israel" or "King of the Jews" in the environment in which the gospel took shape. At this point New Testament scholarship has been almost unanimous: the King of Israel is assumed to be equivalent to *Messiah ben David*. There are of course ample reasons in the early Christian traditions for presuming this identification. That Jesus was crucified as "King of the Jews" is one of the most firmly fixed elements in the passion narratives, and analysis of the stories shows that from the very beginning Christians saw in the placard announcing this charge an ironic testimony to Jesus' messiahship. Furthermore, it is apparent that for most of the circles represented by the New Testament writings the eschatological king, the Messiah, was also the descendant of David.[1] In this respect these Christian traditions agree with the dominant portrait of the Messiah in the documents of later "normative" Judaism.[2] However, the discovery of the Qumran documents has forcibly called attention to the diversity of Jewish eschatological expectation in the period before the First Revolt.[3]

---

[1] This is the view of all the Synoptics, despite the problematical passage Mk 12.35ff. (on which see Ferdinand Hahn, *Christologische Hoheitstitel; Ihre Geschichte im frühen Christentum* (FRLANT, 83; 1963), pp. 259-262, cf. pp. 113-115, and 191). But the Davidic origin of Christ is also firmly rooted in the early formula Rom. 1.3; cf. 2 Tim. 2.8, and in the probably liturgically derived passages Rev. 5.5; 22.16; cf. 3.7. It is taken for granted in Heb. 7.14. Moreover a heightening of interest in Jesus' connection with David, connected with the development of Christian apologetic and polemic based on scripture proofs, is evident both in Mt. and in Lk.-Acts, although *Barn.* 12.10f. shows that some circles were impelled in polemical contexts to reject the notion.

[2] Cf. Emil Schürer, *Geschichte des jüdischen Volkes im Zeitalter Jesus Christi* (4th ed.; Leipzig: J. C. Hinrich'ssche Buchhandlung, 1907), II, 29, especially pp. 612-621; George F. Moore, *Judaism in the First Centuries of the Christian Era; The Age of the Tannaim* (Cambridge: Harvard University Press, 1927), II, 323-376; Paul Volz, *Die Eschatologie der jüdischen Gemeinde im neutestamentlichen Zeitalter* (Tübingen: J. C. B. Mohr [Paul Siebeck], 1934), pp. 173-186; Sigmund Mowinckel, *He That Cometh*, trans. G. W. Anderson (New York: Abingdon Press, 1954), chap. IX; Staerk, pp. 48-55. All these distinguish between the "national" and the "universal" or "apocalyptic" expectations, represented respectively by the Davidic Messiah and the heavenly Son of Man. Mowinckel in particular develops this schematization to an extreme. Staerk sees the two forms as stages in one line of development, beginning with a mythical "Paradise-king" who is then "historicized" in the Davidic figure, while the mythical figure reappears in the Son of Man of Dan 7.

[3] Cf. A. S. van der Woude, *Die messianischen Vorstellungen der Gemeinde von Qumrân* ("Studia Semitica Neerlandica" III; Assen: Van Gorcum & Comp., 1957), especially his criticism of Mowinckel, p. 168 *et passim*.

By no means may the "normative" picture of Judaism be projected back into the period before 70 A.D.,[1] and the situation in many circles of Judaism undoubtedly remained quite fluid for several centuries after the destruction of Jerusalem.[2] In particular the Qumran texts reveal a sect that expected not one but two Messiahs, as well as a third eschatological figure designated "the Prophet,"[3] while avoiding altogether the term "king" as a designation for the royal "Messiah of Israel."[4]

All these facts should warn against the assumption that the equation "King" = "Messiah" = "Son of David" would have been equally valid for all circles of biblically and Jewishly oriented Christians of the first century. If such groups as the Samaritans, on the one hand, and the Hellenistic Jewish writers, on the other, are taken into consideration, then the range of possibilities for interpreting "King of Israel" on the basis of Old Testament is even more broadly extended, as will be shown in subsequent chapters. With these expanded possibilities in mind, new significance accrues to the fact that the only occurrence of the Son of David notion in John is in a polemic which denies Jesus' Davidic legitimation.

The Prophet

Like the "king", "the Prophet" has seldom been accorded independent significance by students of the Fourth Gospel. C. K. Barrett, for example, in his comments on 1.21 refers only vaguely to "a belief, or hope, that a new prophet, or one of the prophets of old, would be sent to the assistance of Israel."[5] For reasons which

---

[1] On the dangers of this anachronism in New Testament research, see the excellent review article by Morton Smith, "A Comparison of Early Christian and Early Rabbinic Tradition," *JBL* 82 (1963), 169-176.

[2] Even archaeological evidence points to this conclusion. Synagogues that deviated notably from "normative" standards often suffered iconoclastic defacement as late as the 5th and 6th centuries A.D.: see Erwin R. Goodenough, *Jewish Symbols in the Greco-Roman Period* ("Bollingen Series" XXXVII; New York: Pantheon Books), Vol. I (1952), 7-17, 184-187, 189, 193f., 197, 199, 201, 206-208, 211f., 214, 245f.; Vol. IV (1954), 44. But above all, cf. the studies of Jewish mysticism and/or gnosticism by Gershom Scholem (above, p. 17, n. 40).

[3] Cf. van der Woude, pp. 185-189, 245-249. The most important texts are 1QS IX, 11; 4QTest 1-19; CD XII, 23f.; XIV, 19; XX, 1; XIX, 10f.

[4] See below, p. 166.

[5] *The Gospel According to St. John; An Introduction with Commentary and Notes on the Greek Text* (London: S.P.C.K., 1955), p. 144.

are not apparent, he thinks 6.14 represents "a different use of ὁ προφήτης," probably referring to the Prophet like Moses (Deuteronomy 18, 15ff.), but merely as a title for the Messiah.[1] Barrett was unacquainted with the Qumran texts at the time of writing;[2] it would hardly be possible today for a commentator to avoid the question of the Prophet's identity as a distinct eschatological figure.[3] Even some older exegetes were aware of the question from the evidence of the Johannine text alone. For example, H. A. W. Meyer could say already in 1869, "ὁ προφήτης is designated by the article as the *known, promised* Prophet, . . . the one intended by Dt. 18.15, a text whose application to the Messiah himself (Acts 3.22; 7.37; Jn 1.46; 6.14) was at least not universal (cf. 7.40) and not shared by the questioners [in 1.21]."[4]

Even among those who have recognized that "the Prophet" has a specific significance in the Fourth Gospel, opinion has diverged as to what precisely that significance is. A number of scholars have sought to explain the figure, at least in so far as he is identified with Jesus, solely from Hellenistic comparisons. A larger number have regarded the Prophet as explicable on the basis of Old Testament and Jewish ideas alone.

In his monograph on "the Son of God," Wetter argues for a purely Hellenistic background for the term "prophet" in John. For comparison, he discusses the wandering prophets of Syria-Palestine described by Celsus, as well as the more philosophically conceived divine messengers such as the Stoic σοφός, Appollonius

---

[1] *Ibid.*, p. 231.

[2] *Ibid.*, p. viii, n. 1.

[3] See the excellent discussion by Van der Woude, pp. 76-89 (*a propos* of the passage IQS IX, 9b-11). Cf. also J. Giblet, "Prophétisme et attente d'un Messie prophète dans l'ancien Judaïsme," *L'Attente du Messie*, ed. L. Cerfaux *et al.* ("Recherches Bibliques"; Paris: Desclee de Brouwer, 1954), pp. 85-130, and R. Schnackenburg, "Die Erwartung des 'Propheten' nach dem Neuen Testament und den Qumran-Texten," *Studia Evangelica*, ed. Kurt Aland *et al.* ("Texte und Untersuchungen zur Geschichte der altchristlichen Literatur," Series V, Vol. 18; Berlin: Akademie-Verlag, 1959), pp. 622-639. Still Harald Riesenfeld could treat "the eschatological prophet" as a figure virtually interchangeable with "the Messiah," even though he knew some of the Dead Sea documents, apparently because he regarded both as belonging ultimately to the same mythological "pattern" ("Jesus als Prophet," *Spiritus et Veritas*, ed. Auseklis, Societas Theologorum Universitatis Latviensis ["Festschrift for Karl Kundsin"; San Francisco: Rev. A. Ernstons, 1953], pp. 135-148, especially p. 141.

[4] *Kritisch exegetisches Handbuch über das Evangelium des Johannes* (5th rev. ed.; KEK; 1869), p. 101.

in Philostratus' portrait, Philo's Moses, and the Hermetic prophet. The Fourth Gospel, he thinks, is much closer to the former, more popular kind of piety, and "the Prophet" which appears in John "as a synonym for 'Son of God' "[1] is equivalent to the *theios anthropos* of popular Hellenistic piety. The interpretation of Walter Bauer, in his commentary on John, moves in a similar direction.[2] Bauer thinks it unlikely that the term "the Prophet" derives either from the Old Testament or from early Christian traditions. Instead he seeks parallels in the mystery religions, among the gnostics and Mandaeans, and in the Hermetic Corpus. Erich Fascher, in his pioneering philological study of προφήτης,[3] follows Bauer in placing the Johannine Prophet within a Hellenistic perspective, since his basic functions in John are as an "all-knower," a wonder-worker, and a bringer of *gnosis*.[4] But Fascher perceives that the absolute usage, *the* Prophet, is non-Hellenistic and in fact best understood as anti-Hellenistic.[5] Howard M. Teeple, despite his own investigation of "the Mosaic eschatological prophet," thinks it impossible that Jesus could be identified with the prophet of Mosaic type, since the evangelist makes him superior to Moses.[6] Instead

---

[1] Wetter, p. 25. This statement cannot be supported. προφήτης occurs 8 times in Jn. (1.21, 25; 4.19, 44; 6.14; 7.40, 52; 9.17, apart from the plural 8.52); in none of these passages is there any reference to the title "Son of God." Wetter himself cites only 1.19-27 –but "Son of God" is not among the titles named in the questions to John! Actually Wetter is assuming what he wishes to prove, that "Son of God" is the fundamental title given Jesus in the Fourth Gospel, and that all other titles point to the same notion.

[2] *Das Johannesevangelium* (2d ed., rev.; HNT, VI; 1925), pp. 3of.

[3] ΠΡΟΦΗΤΗΣ, *eine sprach- und religionsgeschichtliche Untersuchung* (Giessen: A. Töpelmann, 1927), 288 pp.

[4] *Ibid.*, p. 208; cf. Bauer, p. 31.

[5] *Ibid.*, pp. 51f. and p. 209: "Als der λόγος ist er Gottes Wort an die Menschheit und damit der Prophet schlechthin. Hat das A.T. in seinen Propheten mit Energie gegenüber der Vielgötterei den einen Gott gepredigt, so verkündigt das Christentum einer Welt, in der es von Orakel und Wander-propheten wimmelt, dass dieser Gott nur einen Propheten hat, der auf diesen Namen allein Ausspruch machen darf."

[6] *The Mosaic Eschatological Prophet* ("JBL Monograph Series," Vol. X; Philadelphia: Society of Biblical Literature, 1957), pp. 95f. Similarly Schnackenburg, p. 639. Hardly convincing, as T. F. Glasson justly remarks (*Moses in the Fourth Gospel* [SBT, 40; 1963], pp. 24f., n. 2). All Christian typology contained the notion, implicit or expressed, that Christ and his gifts were superior to their prototypes discovered in the OT. One has only to think of Hebrews, the most "typological" of all NT writings, to see that the superiority of the new covenant and new cult founded in Christ's sacrifice to the Levitic cult in no way excludes the author's use of the latter for his basic symbols. Teeple's argument could equally be turned against his own

he accepts Fascher's judgment that, in Teeple's words, "the Fourth Gospel presents Jesus as *the* Prophet of the Hellenistic miracle-worker type. . . ."[1]

On the other hand many commentators see in "the Prophet" of John 1.21; 6.14, and 7.40 a definite eschatological figure of Jewish expectation, to be identified with the "prophet like Moses" promised in Deuteronomy 18.15, 18.[2] Among recent works, three are especially important. Against Bultmann and Barrett, Van der Woude argues convincingly, on the basis of the Qumran sect's eschatology, that John 1.21 and 7.40 cannot be separated from 6.14f. and that Deuteronomy 18.15, 18 lies behind all three passages.[3] Glasson agrees in his chapter on "The Prophet,"[4] and adds to the Johannine attestations of "the Prophet" 7.52 on the strength of Bodmer Papyrus P66.[5] Most important is the substantial treatment of "The Eschatological Prophet" which Ferdinand Hahn adds as an appendix to his recent Christology.[6] Hahn finds numerous allusions to the eschatological prophet of the Moses type in John and attributes

---

conclusion, since Christ is undoubtedly regarded by the fourth evangelist as superior to the Hellenistic prophets after whom, according to Fascher and Teeple, he is portrayed.

[1] *Ibid.*, p. 120.

[2] For example: H. A. W. Meyer, p. 101; Theodor Zahn, *Das Evangelium des Johannes* (4th ed., rev.; "Kommentar zum Neuen Testament," IV; Leipzig: A. Deichert'sche Verlag, 1912), p. 112; recently Alfred Wikenhauser, *Das Evangelium nach Johannes* (2d ed. rev.; "Regensburger Neues Testament," IV; Regensburg: Verlag Friedrich Pustet, 1957), pp. 59f. Joachim Jeremias finds a Moses typology in these passages but distinguishes Jn 1.21 and 7.40, in which "the Prophet" and "the Messiah" are separate figures, from 6.14f., in which the two are merged ("Μωυσῆς," *ThWbNT*, IV, 862f., 876f., but cf. *Golgotha* ["ΑΓΓΕΛΟΣ Beiheft," I; Leipzig: Verlag von Eduard Pfeiffer, 1926], 83f., where he connects 6.14 and 7.40f. closely together). Volz, pp. 193f., avoids a definite identification of "the Prophet" with Moses. Renée Bloch, "Quelques aspects de la figure de Moïse dans la tradition rabbinique," *Moïse, l'homme de l'alliance*, ed. H. Cazelles *et al.* (special issue of "Cahiers Sioniens"; Paris: Desclée & Cie., 1955), p. 162, thinks of Moses only as the type of the Messiah rather than of "the Prophet." Schnackenburg is even more cautious than Volz, emphasizing the variety of Jewish views of eschatological prophetic figures (p. 627).

[3] Pp. 82f.

[4] Chap. III, pp. 27-32. Glasson's monograph has many imaginative suggestions, to which I am indebted. On the whole, however, his interest is more homiletical than historical, and he exercises little exegetical control over the allusions that occur to him.

[5] *Ibid.*, pp. 29f.

[6] Pp. 351-404; cf. also his excursus on the Transfiguration, pp. 334-340. For a critique of Hahn's position, see below, pp. 26-29.

them to the community traditions taken over by the evangelist.[1]

It should be noted that the two positions which have just been outlined are not mutually exclusive, despite the tendency of Johannine studies to separate into self-contained schools. For example, it is well known that Hellenistic Jews sometimes described Moses in terms very similar to the Hellenistic prophet-hero, the *theios aner*.[2] Hence it is not impossible that the "prophet like Moses" could at the same time carry traits of the Hellenistic prophet of the type described by Wetter and Fascher. In fact both Wetter and Fascher implicitly recognize this possibility when they suggest that the portrait of Jesus in the Fourth Gospel is drawn in a situation of polemic against those, among others, who regard Moses as the prophet *par excellence*.[3] A critical evaluation of the various possibilities summarized above, as well as the possibility of either combining or supplanting them, requires first of all a more precise description of the prophetic figure in the Fourth Gospel itself.

The prophet-king

One of the principal contentions of this dissertation is that the prophetic and royal elements in the Johannine christology are not to be understood separately, but exactly in their combination and mutual interpretation. Yet the relation between the two has never been explored. Several examples will expose the question which has been left not only unanswered but, for the most part, unasked. Commenting on John 6.14f., where "the prophet who comes into the world" and "king" are brought into direct juxtaposition, H. A. W. Meyer simply assumes a tautology: "the prophet" is "the Messiah."[4] The difficulty of uniting this identification with his own recognition that Messiah and Prophet are *separate* figures in John 1.21 and 7.40[5] remains unresolved in Meyer's commentary, and in this respect his work is typical not only of his generation but even of the most recent commentaries. Bauer saw no connection between

---

[1] *Ibid.*, p. 397.

[2] Especially true of Josephus: cf. Ludwig Bieler, ΘΕΙΟΣ ΑΝΗΡ; *Das Bild des "göttlichen Menschen" in Spätantike und Frühchristentum*, Vol. I (Wien: Buchhandlung Oskar Hofels, 1935), pp. 18f., and Jeremias, *ThWbNT*, IV, 854-856.

[3] Wetter, pp. 167ff.; Fascher, p. 209.

[4] Meyer, p. 254.

[5] *Ibid.*, pp. 101, 316.

the two verses 6.14 and 15.[1] Bultmann[2] and Barrett,[3] as already
mentioned, separate "the Prophet" in 1.21 and 7.40 from the same
term in 6.14, associating the former with the prophet like Moses,
but leaving the latter undefined. Among specialized studies, the
same simplification prevails. Staerk sees in John 6.14f. evidence
that "in popular christology" the exercise of prophetic functions is
"sufficient basis for the Messianic claim."[4] For Volz "in John 6.14f.
Prophet and messianic King flow together."[5] Riesenfeld[6] and
Schnackenburg[7] adopt essentially the same position. It is to the
credit of Van der Woude, in his excursus already mentioned, that
he recognizes the anomaly existing in John 6.14f. He refuses to take
the easy but unsupported escape of separating this passage from
1.21 and 7.40. But then he is faced with the perplexing problem
that the evangelist clearly distinguishes between "the Christ" and
"the Prophet" in the latter two passages, while "the Prophet" and
"king" are united in the former. Van der Woude does not solve this
perplexity; he can only speak of a "wavering line of separation
between the Prophet and the 'Messiah.'"[8]

By far the most comprehensive discussion of "the Prophet" as a
christological designation in the New Testament is the essay by
Ferdinand Hahn which has already been cited. To a large extent
Hahn both incorporates the results of the previous investigations
already mentioned and supplants them in his own synthesis. For
this reason, and because he does give some attention to the specific
problem of the merging of the prophetic and the royal eschatological
figures, a brief consideration of his conclusions is appropriate here.

Hahn develops the thesis that the conception of the eschatological
prophet was an important strand in the eschatology of early
Judaism, in two distinct forms. The first is the expectation of a
return of Elijah, based on Micah 3.1 and its secondary interpretation
in 3.23f. The second is the view, derived from Deuteronomy 18.15,
18, that a prophet like Moses will come at the end of time. In post-
biblical Judaism—within which he includes Samaritan eschatology

[1] Bauer, p. 89.
[2] *Ev. Joh.*, pp. 61f.; cf. 148, n. 2.
[3] Barrett, pp. 144, 231.
[4] Staerk, p. 66.
[5] Volz, p. 194.
[6] Riesenfeld, p. 143.
[7] Schnackenburg, p. 630.
[8] Van der Woude, p. 83.

—Hahn finds two essential features belonging to the Moses-type prophet: (1) certification by miracle and (2) emphasis on teaching, including the idea of restoration or modification of the Torah. In addition "the wilderness" plays a part in the prophet's expected activity.

Hahn is undoubtedly correct that the Moses and Elijah traditions are the two major strands in the expectation of an eschatological prophet,[1] even though the evidence he cites is admittedly sparse, forcing him to rely very much on indirect clues and hypothetical reconstructions. It must be questioned, however, whether he has not imposed too rigid and exclusive a scheme upon the materials. It seems much more likely, as Schnackenburg argues,[2] that there may have been a variety of differing views in ancient Judaism about the eschatological prophet, and that these views may not have been kept so rigorously separate from one another as Hahn supposes.[3] Still, these two main categories form a useful heuristic scheme.

In the New Testament Hahn finds the Elijah typology applied very early to John the Baptist, probably already by the baptist sects themselves.[4] Partly because of this association of the Elijah typology with John, the Christians make little use of it in describing Jesus. The Moses typology, on the other hand, was applied to Jesus—in Hahn's opinion, by the earliest Palestinian community—and had some independent development within the Hellenistic branch of the early church, before it was finally submerged by the dominant royal messianology.[5]

Hahn's direct evidence for the early application of the Mosaic prophet notion to Jesus comes exclusively from Luke-Acts.[6] He labors to show that this is not a Lucan peculiarity, but stems from traditional material which Luke has incorporated. However, in order to support this view, he is forced to disagree with most recent

---

[1] Cf. the similar view of Teeple, *Mosaic Prophet, passim.*

[2] Schnackenburg, p. 627.

[3] One of the great weaknesses of Hahn's very remarkable book as a whole is his propensity to force the New Testament's christological statements and allusions into categories which often seem quite artificial. These in turn are associated with "Traditionsschichten" so narrowly defined that it stretches the reader's imagination to conceive of living communities in which such traditions could have maintained their antiseptically isolated existence.

[4] Hahn, pp. 371-380.

[5] *Ibid.*, 380-404.

[6] *Ibid.*, pp. 382-390.

scholars who have analyzed the Lucan literature, and his own
counter arguments are none too convincing. In view of the prominent place which Jesus' prophetic office plays in Luke's total theological development,[1] he would be on safer ground to assume that
the third evangelist himself has constructed this "prophetic christology" in its present form. Of course this assumption would not
exclude the possibility that the evangelist was acquainted with
traditions which already identified Jesus as the prophet like Moses.

Of more direct relevance to the present investigation, however,
is Hahn's discussion of the occasional merging of the prophetic and
the royal eschatological figures. With precision he recognizes in
John 6.14f. "das Nebeneinander und Ineinander beider Vorstellungen."[2] Since he quite correctly insists on the distinction between
"Messiah" and "Prophet," thereby avoiding the common but misleading expressions "messianic Prophet" or "prophetic Messiah,"
he regards this as a typical instance of the rather frequent *secondary
combination* of the two separate figures. In some of the other
instances which Hahn cites, this explanation seems adequate. In
the passages from Acts the association of the Messiah with the
prophecy in Deuteronomy 18 might very well be a purely Christian
construction. The tendency in Rabbinic texts to apply the formula,

---

[1] It will be sufficient here to mention a few significant passages. First of
all, the programmatic introduction of Jesus' whole mission, Lk. 4.18-30,
portrays his task as prophetic. I can see no justification for Hahn's insistence
that this ,,cannot be regarded as a Lucan re-working of Mk. 6.1-5" (p. 394,
against Bultmann, Conzelmann). The two key passages in Hahn's argument,
Acts 7 and 3.12-26, are striking in their parallelism, which is most readily
accounted for by Luke's construction. Lk. 24.21, Ἰησοῦ τοῦ Ναζαρηνοῦ, ὃς
ἐγένετο ἀνὴρ προφήτης δυνατὸς ἐν ἔργῳ καὶ λόγῳ is best understood as a Lucan
theologoumenon which expresses in compressed form Luke's view of Jesus'
total ministry as depicted in the gospel. This view includes the necessity for
a prophet to die in Jerusalem (13.33: unique to Lk.), a statement integrally
related to the most prominent structural element in the gospel, the journey
to Jerusalem (9.51-19.46). Furthermore, the προφήτης δυνατὸς ἐν ἔργῳ καὶ
λόγῳ has a clear echo (or, vice versa) in the description of Moses, Acts 7.22:
δυνατὸς ἐν λόγοις καὶ ἔργοις αὐτοῦ. To be sure, this "prophetic christology"
represents for the evangelist an incomplete view of Jesus, which has to be
corrected by the resurrection faith which is instructed in the proofs-from-
prophecy (cf. Paul Schubert, "The Structure and Significance of Luke 24,"
Neutestamentliche Studien für Rudolf Bultmann, ed. W. Eltester [2d ed.,
BZNW, XXI; 1957], pp. 173-177). In short it seems to me that Hahn's
"two-stage christology" is an apt description of Luke's second-generation
construction, not of the pattern of development of the primitive community's
faith.

[2] Hahn, p. 370.

"As was the first Redeemer [Moses], so will be the last Redeemer," to the Davidic Messiah can also be explained as a secondary merging of these two traditions. On the other hand, such an explanation is impossible for the Samaritan *Taheb*, since it is unthinkable that the Samaritans would have constructed their redeemer figure from a combination of the *Davidic* Messiah with a purely prophetic personage. It is far more likely that they would have found both royal *and* prophetic features already present in the Moses tradition, stemming perhaps from very early times. As a matter of fact, Hahn himself accepts the thesis of Bentzen and others that the "servant" of Second Isaiah, a figure combining both prophetic and royal functions, belongs to the type of Moses.[1] There are certainly some instances, then, of the combination of royal and prophetic eschatological functions where the Davidic messianology can hardly have played any part.

Hahn left unnoticed the main dilemma that John 6.14f. presents. If eschatological king and Davidic Messiah are identical, how can this text unite the king with "the Prophet," while elsewhere in the gospel "Christ" and "the Prophet" are kept distinct? The hypothesis of an *ad hoc* combination of Mosaic Prophet and Davidic King cannot remove this perplexity.

Now if the well-known description of Moses by Philo, as at the same time the ideal king, the most perfect of prophets, and the prototypal high priest, is recalled, then the working hypothesis for the following inquiry may be expressed more precisely: Certain traditions about Moses provided for the Fourth Gospel not only the figure of the eschatological prophet, but the figure who combines in one person both royal and prophetic honor and functions.[2]

THE PROCEDURE

The investigation of the "prophet-king" will proceed in three stages. First of all, the Johannine passages which speak of Jesus as

---

[1] *Ibid.*

[2] Such a suggestion was put forward by Jeremias, *Golgotha*, pp. 83f., in conjunction with a rather far-fetched typological identification of Jesus with the "rock" that followed the Israelites in the wilderness (as in 1 Cor. 10.4), equated in legend with Mt. Zion. Bultmann (*Ev. Joh.*, p. 158, n. 2) rejects the idea, since he supposes that Moses was never expected as a *king*. In Chapters III-V below it will be shown that several circles regarded Moses as the first –and prototypal –King of Israel.

προφήτης or βασιλεύς or of his βασιλεία and other passages which have an evident thematic relation to these will be analyzed in the next chapter. This analysis, which will concentrate upon the internal connections of the Johannine text, without extensive reference at this point to extra-biblical literature, will serve three purposes. (1) It will demonstrate the significance of the combination "prophet-king" in the literary and theological structure of the gospel. (2) It will delineate the functions and characteristics proper to the prophet-king figure in John. (3) It will indicate whether this figure is connected with other prominent motifs in the gospel.

The second stage of investigation will use the results of the first, in effect a tentative description of the "prophet-king," in a search for analogous figures in the religious environment within which the Fourth Gospel may be reasonably supposed to have emerged. Since attempts to define the Johannine milieu have not come to rest, the limits within which relevant sources may be found must be left broad. Geographically, the whole Mediterranean world comes into question. Chronologically, the scope of the survey will be the Roman-Hellenistic period, with narrower limits to be determined case by case, since the date of the source is often not the same as the date of origin of the traditions it contains. The character of the sources also must not be prejudged. After a century of study of the Johannine background, there is still no agreement whether "Jewish" or "Hellenistic", "Palestinian" or "Diaspora" traditions may have been the dominant influences on the fourth evangelist. Because the working hypothesis associates the "prophet-king" with traditions about Moses, these traditions will be studied with special care. The question of possible gnostic influence on Johannine christology may for present purposes best be put in this form: Is there a gnostic redeemer characterized as a "prophet-king" in the way Jesus is in the Fourth Gospel? Because of the great significance attached to the Mandaean gnostic traditions by Bultmann and his pupils, the published Mandaean texts are chosen as representative gnostic sources for the investigation of this question.

The sources therefore fall into several natural groups: (1) Jewish sources outside the Rabbinic circle of tradition and editing (Chapter Three), (2) Rabbinic haggadah about Moses (Chapter Four), (3) the earliest extant Samaritan sources, so far as they are published (Chapter Five), and (4) the Mandaean texts (Chapter Six).

The investigation of each group of sources will proceed within narrow limits, since it is necessary to concentrate only on a single phenomenon, the interrelationship of the motifs represented by "prophet" and "king". On the other hand, each appearance of this phenomenon will have to be understood in relation to its function within its immediate literary context and within the larger ideology of the group represented by the source in question.

The third stage of investigation will make use of the findings of the second stage for a more extensive analysis of the Fourth Gospel. At this point it will be appropriate to inquire to what extent, if at all, patterns which were discovered in the non-Johannine traditions and documents may be found echoed in the Fourth Gospel. Then it should be possible to determine whether there are other elements, less obvious than those which appeared in the first stage of analysis, that may be connected with the prophet-king motif, so that exegesis may discover a connected development of this motif throughout the gospel.

On the basis of the full investigation it is reasonable to expect new light on the content of Johannine christology and on the nature of the Johannine circle and its opponents.

CHAPTER TWO

THEMATIC FUNCTIONS OF PROPHET
AND KING IN JOHN

This attempt to follow two motifs through the Fourth Gospel begins with the direct uses of the representative words and subsequently proceeds by exegetical analysis to discover whether there are indirect allusions elsewhere to the same themes.

Of the two passages in the Fourth Gospel which apply the title "the Prophet" directly to Jesus, the best starting point is 7.40 and its immediate context, because this passage raises immediately the question how "the Prophet" is related to "the Christ" and to the Son of David ideology. To inquire how the passage (7.37-52) fits into its larger context —if at all —leads to the delineation of several expanding themes.

The evangelist's attribution of the title "king" to Jesus, on the other hand, is best understood by first examining its function in the place where it appears most clearly at the center of attention, in the trial before Pilate. To this will be added an exegesis of the two passages in which "King of Israel" occurs, the confession of Nathanael and the acclamation by the Entry crowds.

From the exegesis of the two large blocks of material mentioned above, there emerge both a certain parallel development and an interrelationship between the theme of Jesus' role as prophet and that of his role as king. From that point it will be possible to analyze the passage in which "the Prophet" and "king" are expressly connected, 6.14f.

THE CONTROVERSY AT TABERNACLES

John 7.37-52

Prophet and Christ

The beginning of a new section of narrative is clearly marked in John 7.37 with the temporal note, "on the last, the great day of the festival." Jesus makes a solemn proclamation identifying himself as the source of "living water" for all who thirst. There follows a division among his hearers, which introduces a controversy about Jesus' identity. This is the real subject of the remaining verses of the chapter. Among "the crowd" some say, "This is truly the Prophet," but others say, "This is the Christ." Yet a third group then raises an objection based on scripture proofs, asserting that Jesus cannot be the Christ, since the Christ does not come from Galilee but from Bethlehem and from the seed of David (verses 40-42).

The σχίσμα which Jesus' words produce among the crowd is a familiar motif in John. In 9.16 the Pharisees interrogating the blind man healed by Jesus divide over the question whether Jesus is from God. Again in 10.19 "the Jews" are separated in response to Jesus' words; some say he is a demoniac, others that "these words are not those of a demoniac." The γογγυσμός of 7.12 is in effect a synonym, for some say that Jesus is a good man, others that he "leads the crowd astray." This motif corresponds of course to the total pattern of response which Jesus' words and deeds evoke in the Fourth Gospel. In particular the σημεῖα invariably produce a division between those who "believe" and those who become hostile toward Jesus and seek to kill him.

But the σχίσμα depicted in 7.40-43 differs from the others mentioned in one important respect. Here not only is there a division between those who favor and those who oppose Jesus, but also a further division of those who favor him into two groups, one ready to see in him the eschatological prophet, another asserting that he is the Messiah. This division shows, in the first place, that the evangelist recognizes a clear distinction between the two eschatological figures, just as in the questions to John the Baptist, 1.21, 25. Moreover, the juxtaposition of the two titles in this manner raises the questions of their relationship to one another and of Jesus' relationship to the hopes they represent, in the view of the Johannine Christian community.

For John, Jesus is definitely the Christ (1.41; 11.27; 20.31). Furthermore, while the evangelist can use the term in the fashion of general Hellenistic Christianity as a proper name (1.17; 17.3), he is quite aware also of its "official" signification and, alone of all New Testament writers, equates it explicitly with the transliterated Hebrew Μεσσίας (1.41; 4.25). Is the identification of Jesus as "the Prophet" also a proper Christian affirmation? The use of the adverb ἀληθῶς already suggests that it is; compare its use in 1.47; 4.42; 6.14; 7.26; 8.31; 17.8.[1] Jesus is called "a prophet" in 4.19 and 9.17, in each case by one who is in some sense a paradigm of incipient faith. Both instances mark only a first stage of understanding and confession. In chapter 4, the Samaritan woman advances to the recognition that Jesus is also Μεσσίας = Χριστός (verse 25), and her countrymen to the final confession that he is ἀληθῶς ὁ σωτὴρ τοῦ κόσμου (verse 42). In chapter 9 the former blind man is led to the recognition of "the Son of Man" (verse 35). While it cannot be assumed with Fascher that προφήτης has the same meaning as ὁ προφήτης "since John knows no other prophet than Jesus,"[2] still the two forms are doubtless related. At least 4.19 and 9.17 assert that Jesus is a true prophet, not a false prophet or γόης.

The decisive evidence, however, that "the Prophet" as well as "the Christ" is understood positively in 7.40f. is to be found in the handling of the question in the remaining verses of the chapter. In a broad sense the structure of the argument is chiasmic. In verse 41a a group asserts that Jesus is "the Christ." This is immediately rejected by those who insist that "the Christ" cannot come from Galilee, for "does the Scripture not say that the Christ comes from the seed of David and from Bethlehem, the village whence David came?" (verses 41b-42). In verse 40 the first group had said, "He is truly the Prophet." But this is denied in verse 52, on precisely the same grounds: "Search [the Scriptures; compare 5.39] and see that [the][3] Prophet does not arise from Galilee." Thus the two titles

---

[1] This accords with the significance of words on the root ἀληθ- throughout the gospel. Fascher's failure to recognize this significance, together with his failure to distinguish between οἱ Ἰουδαῖοι and Ἰσραήλ in John, leads him into the error of interpreting ἀληθῶς Ἰσραηλίτης in 1.47 as a pejorative expression, so that Nathanael, like the scripture-proof enthusiasts of 7.42, 52 and the Samaritan woman of 4.19, represents an older, improper view of the redeemer, to be overcome in each case by Jesus' γνῶσις (p. 179). Dodd (pp. 239f) also thinks that "the Prophet" in the evangelist's view is "an inadequate, or even misleading, description of the real status of Jesus."

[2] *Ibid.* Jn. 11.51 excludes this generalization, which is rightly rejected by Bultmann, *Ev. Joh.*, p. 61.

[3] Fascher is correct in relating v. 52 to v. 40 (p. 179). Owen (*apud* E. Nestle, *Novum Testamentum Graece* [24th ed.; Stuttgart: Privilegierte Württembergische Bibelanstalt, 1960], *ad loc.*) long ago conjectured that the definite article stood in the original text; MS support is now provided by P66*. Even if the article is rejected, however, my argument about the structure of the passage is not fundamentally affected. (On the problems of this reading see Gordon D. Fee, "Corrections of Papyrus Bodmer II and the Nestle Greek Testament," *JBL*, 84 [1965], 68, and the references given there [n. 8].)

are treated in an exactly parallel manner, and the controversy over their attribution to Jesus provides the framework of the whole section, verses 40-52. It follows then that the first two groups in verses 40b-41 express the truth, Christianly understood, about Jesus.

Is the Christ of Davidic origin?

That Jesus belonged to "the seed of David" was a commonplace of broad circles of the early Christian communities.[1] But that he was "from Nazareth" is at least equally as ancient and firmly established a tradition.[2] The origin of the tradition that the Messiah's birth must be in Bethlehem is not quite clear, although there is evidence that Micah 5.1-5 was interpreted messianically in relatively old rabbinic traditions.[3] The suggestion by Dodd that the tradition may have been Christian from the start and based on the historical fact that Jesus was born in Bethlehem[4] cannot be maintained. On the contrary, it is much more probable that the motif of birth in Bethlehem, at whatever point it came to the attention of Christians, raised formidable difficulties in the light of the firm recollection of Jesus' origin in Nazareth of Galilee. Each of the infancy narratives of Matthew and Luke offers a different solution to these difficulties.[5] According to the former, the home of Jesus' family is assumed to have been in Bethlehem. Only later, as a result of the danger from the Herodian house and because of explicit warning "in a dream," did Joseph move to Nazareth, for which Matthew adds the still further support of a proof-text (Matthew 2.22f.). In Luke, on the other hand, Mary's home (for in Luke's account she rather than Joseph is the central character) is in Nazareth (Luke 1.26f.); the change of scene to Bethlehem is motivated by the census decree of Caesar (2.1-5).

---

[1] Above, pp. 19f.

[2] Mk. 1.9; Mt. 4.13; 21.11; Lk. 4.16; Jn. 1.45f.; cf. Mk. 1.24 par.; 10.47; 14.67; 16.6; Lk. 24.19. Also the etymology (cf. Mt. 2.23) that derives the designation Ναζωραῖος from the place name, whatever the problems about its accuracy, at least presupposes the common knowledge that Jesus was from Nazareth.

[3] Cf. Louis Ginzberg, *The Legends of the Jews*, Vol. V (Philadelphia: The Jewish Publication Society of America, 1955), p. 130 and the references given there.

[4] Dodd, *Interp. of the F. G.* p. 91.

[5] Cf. Bultmann, *Die Geschichte der synoptischen Tradition* (5th ed.; FRLANT, n.s. XII; 1961), pp. 319, 323.

The same problem is reflected in John 7.41-42.[1] Here the opponents appeal directly to "the Scripture" in asserting that "the Christ comes from the seed of David and from Bethlehem . . ." The simplest explanation for the evangelist's inclusion of this objection is that it played a role in the polemic between the Jews and the Christian community he represents.[2] But John offers no explanation in the manner of Matthew and Luke; neither David nor Bethlehem is mentioned elsewhere in the Fourth Gospel. How is this silence to be accounted for? Several explanations are offered by commentators.

Some scholars have seen in John's silence the genuine embarrassment of a circle of Christianity in which the legends of birth at Bethlehem were as yet unknown. No answer is supplied to the question of the Jews because the evangelist knows none.[3] But if he knew no reply to the taunt, why should he give it wider currency by repeating it? Much more common is the supposition that the question of John 7.42 is one of those "misunderstandings" in this gospel by which Jesus' opponents are made unwitting spokesmen for the evangelist's own viewpoint. Barrett thinks that "we may feel confident that John was aware of the tradition that Jesus was born at Bethlehem . . .; he writes here in his customary ironical style."[4] A. Descamps, disputing particularly the viewpoint of such "rationalist authors" as Loisy, also speaks of irony. The words of the Jews, like the "banal or hypothetical words" of the Samaritan woman in 4.12, 15, 25, express the truth well known to any Christian reader.[5] Even Dodd suggests this as one explanation,[6] although it accords poorly with his hypothesis that John is a missionary tract addressed to educated pagans. Glasson also is of two minds on the question, for while he confidently says that "the writer was quite conversant with the fact that Jesus was of David's line," he adds a few lines later that "the implication is that it is not a Davidic

---

[1] Compare also the objection of Nathanael, 1.46.

[2] Cf. Alfred Loisy, *Le quatrième Évangile* (2d ed.; Paris: Émile Nourry, 1921), pp. 274f.: ". . . si donc l'objection n'ést pas dissimulée, c'ést qu'elle avait cours dans le milieu où fut écrit l'évangile johannique . . ." Cf. also Fascher, p. 179, who sees behind this argument the missionary experience of the church.

[3] Wetter, p. 98; Loisy, pp. 274f.

[4] Barrett, p. 273.

[5] "Le messianisme royal dans le Nouveau Testament," *L'attente du Messie*, ed. Lucien Cerfaux, *et al.* (Paris: Desclée de Brouwer & Cie., 1954). p. 66.

[6] Dodd, p. 91.

kingship [which is attributed to Jesus in John]." He even goes on to suggest a connection, unfortunately not pursued, between Moses' kingship, as attested in Philo, and that of Jesus.[1]

This explanation pays more attention to the method of the Fourth Gospel than does the former, but it presupposes that the readers could not understand John without thorough acquaintance with the synoptic tradition. Yet other ambiguous or ironic "misunderstandings" by Jesus' opponents in John are eventually exposed in the development of the gospel. The information necessary for the perceptive reader to recognize them as *mis*understandings is available within the gospel itself. But "David" and "Bethlehem" are never mentioned again. There is nothing whatever in the Fourth Gospel that would lead the reader to suppose that Jesus was born in Bethlehem. Furthermore, the parallelism between verses 42 and 52 is ignored by an interpretation that places the weight upon what is said positively about "the Christ" in verse 42, since nothing is said positively about "the Prophet" in verse 52. What is parallel in the objections is that neither figure, according to Scripture, is "from Galilee." If the Christian is to understand the objections as ironically expressing the truth, then what is relevant is only the fact that Jesus *is* from Galilee—a fact which the Fourth Gospel has made sufficiently plain from the beginning.

A more satisfactory version of the "misunderstanding" explanation is that which spiritualizes the question of Jesus' origin. Several of the authors quoted hold this view as well as the second, regarding them as differing "levels" of interpretation. Thus Barrett says, "John's irony goes far deeper. . . . The birthplace of Jesus is a trivial matter in comparison with the question whether he is ἐκ τῶν ἄνω or ἐκ τῶν κάτω (8.23), whether he is or is not from God. . . ."[2] A similar position is taken by Dodd.[3] Wetter,[4] and Loisy.[5] Bultmann, who thinks that "the evangelist knows nothing, or wants to know nothing, of Jesus' birth in Bethlehem," sees in this scene a polemic against all human dogmatics that tries to control the criteria by which God's mystery is judged.[6] This is certainly a more

---

[1] Glasson, p. 31.

[2] Barrett, p. 273.

[3] Dodd, p. 91.

[4] Wetter, p. 98.

[5] "L'origine divine du Christ paraissait être la vraie réponse à toutes les difficultés" (p. 275).

[6] *Ev. Joh.*, p. 231 and n. 2; cf. p. 233 on Jn 7.27.

adequate explanation, and it can be supported even further by careful examination of the question πόθεν ἐστὶν ὁ Ἰησοῦς, one of the most important of the ironically ambiguous themes of the gospel. Apart from the present passage and Nathanael's skeptical question in 1.46, the most important passage is 7.25-29. "Some of the Jerusalemites" wonder whether the rulers in fact know that Jesus is the Christ. But, they object, "As for him, we know where he is from (πόθεν ἐστίν); when the Christ comes, no one will know where he is from (πόθεν ἐστίν)." The reply by Jesus (verses 28f.) shows that they do *not* know where he is from, since they do not know the one who sent him. Similarly in 6.42 it is objected, "Is this not Jesus the son of Joseph, whose father and mother we know? How now can he say that he has come down from heaven?" The objection of 7.27 is precisely reversed in the objection of 9.29: "We know that God has spoken to Moses, but as for him, we do not know where he is from (πόθεν ἐστίν)." The answer of the former blind man is significant: "Why this is an astonishing thing, that you do not know where he is from, though he opened my eyes! . . . If he were not *from God*, he could do nothing" (9.30,33). Finally Pilate, after hearing the accusation that Jesus "makes himself Son of God," asks Jesus, πόθεν εἶ σύ; "But Jesus gave him no answer" (19.9). Pilate, like "the Jews," cannot know where Jesus is from. The correlative theme is that where Jesus is going is not known: by "the Jews" (7.33-36); by Thomas (14.4f.). Both aspects are summarized in Jesus' self-testimony: "My testimony is true, because I know where I am from and where I am going. But *you* do not know where I am from or where I am going (8.14).[1] In keeping with this general theme, perhaps the best explanation of the controversy in 7.41-42 is that the reader is being led by this means to see that the significant question is not whether Jesus is from Galilee or Judaea, but that he is from *God*.

Nevertheless this line of interpretation fails to explicate the emphasis in the Fourth Gospel on Jesus' origin in Galilee. It is not

---

[1] Just as Jesus' origin and destination are a mystery known only by faith, so also his gifts are mysterious in origin: the wine at Cana (2.9); the πνεῦμα (3.8), exactly correlated with Jesus himself; the "living water" (4.11); the bread to feed the five thousand (6.5: Jesus' own words: contrast the synoptic account Mk 6.36-38 par.). Are the statements of perplexity about Jesus' body in the resurrection narrative also connected in some way with this pattern? 20.2: οὐκ οἴδαμεν ποῦ ἔθηκαν αὐτόν; 20.13: οὐκ οἶδα ποῦ ἔθηκαν αὐτόν; 20.15: εἰπέ μοι ποῦ ἔθηκας αὐτόν.

the case merely that his earthly place of origin is insignificant, for in 7.40-52 itself his Galilean origin is emphasized over against the presumed Judaean origin of the Messiah and the unspecified but non-Galilean origin of the Prophet.

A careful analysis of John 4.43-54 sheds light on the significance of Galilee in the Fourth Gospel. In this short narrative the statement is five times repeated that Jesus left Judaea and went to Galilee (verses 43, 45, 46, 47, 54). The proverb quoted in verse 44, known also from the synoptic tradition, raises problems in this context: αὐτὸς γὰρ ᾽Ιησοῦς ἐμαρτύρησεν ὅτι προφήτης ἐν τῇ ἰδίᾳ πατρίδι τιμὴν οὐκ ἔχει. In the synoptic version Jesus' πατρίς is Nazareth. In the Johannine context, however, the following words require that Judaea be understood as the πατρίς.[1] Yet this contradicts the general view in John that Jesus is from Nazareth of Galilee. Some commentators explain the contradiction by conjecturing different sources[2] or a redactional gloss.[3] James Moffatt suggests instead the transposition of verse 44 after verse 45 or, better, after verse 46.[4] Bultmann, while leaving the text intact, regards verse 44 as a parenthesis. The οὖν of verse 45, he thinks, connects with verse 43.[5] Syntactically this seems an arbitrary means of removing difficulties; even greater problems arise when the context is considered. Bultmann correctly interprets αὐτὸς γὰρ ᾽Ιησοῦς ἐμαρτύρησεν as a fulfillment formula, to be translated, "For Jesus himself had testified."[6] That is, at some previous time Jesus had spoken of his rejection in his own πατρίς, which is now to be fulfilled. But how is it fulfilled in this narrative? Verse 45 immediately records that "when therefore (οὖν) he came to Galilee, the Galileans *received him*," and verse 50 relates that "the man [the

---

[1] Thus Dodd says, "Jerusalem is the πατρίς of Jesus in the Fourth Gospel" (p. 352; cf. Barrett, p. 205 and R. H. Lightfoot, *Locality and Doctrine in the Gospels* [New York: Harper & Brothers, 1938], p. 145. Strictly speaking he should have said, "Judaea," since the present context mentions only the two countries, not cities (Bauer, p. 73). But Dodd ignores the conflict between his statement and Jesus' Galilean origins.

[2] Julius Wellhausen, *Das Evangelium Johannis* (Berlin: Georg Reimer, 1908), p. 23.

[3] Emanuel Hirsch, *Studien zum vierten Evangelium* ("Beiträge zur historischen Theologie," XI; Tübingen: J. C. B. Mohr [Paul Siebeck], 1936), pp. pp. 9, 55.

[4] *An Introduction to the Literature of the New Testament* (New York: Charles Scribner's Sons, 1911), p. 553.

[5] *Ev. Joh.*, p. 150; cf. Bauer, p. 73.

[6] *Ibid.*, n. 4.

βασιλικός of Capernaum] *believed* the word which Jesus said to him."
Only by a very strange logic can such language be supposed to
describe a *rejection* of Jesus, yet that is what Bultmann's interpretation requires.[1] His only support for the assertion that the Galileans' acceptance of Jesus was "not genuine" is the statement,
"unless you see signs and wonders, you will not believe" (verse 48).
In a synoptic context this statement would be derogatory, but the
σημεῖα in John have a very different meaning from that in the
Synoptics. The condition of those who must see signs in order to
believe is exactly that of the *disciples of Jesus* (2.11 and often).
Their belief is genuine, though without understanding before Jesus'
"glorification." Here the man of Capernaum *does* see a sign (verse
54) and *does* believe (verse 50). The reception of Jesus by the
Galileans does not fulfill Jesus' saying about the prophet's lack of
honor in his fatherland. The fulfillment must be sought rather in
the failure of "the Jews" to receive him on his first visit to Jerusalem (2.13-3.21), and Jesus' πατσίς is not Galilee, but Judaea. Yet
the perplexity remains that in this gospel Jesus comes from Galilee.

The perplexity can be illuminated by another observation. Only
the Johannine version of the proverb contains the adjective ἴδιος.[2]
With this observation it becomes apparent that the proverb is
made to say the same thing as John 1.11: εἰς τὰ ἴδια ἦλθεν, καὶ οἱ
ἴδιοι αὐτὸν οὐ παρέλαβον.[3] Jesus' πατρίς, his ἴδια, is Judaea. Jerusalem in John is the center of "the world," the place of decision.
But the πατρίς is not Jesus' *native* land, but his *own* land. In his
πατρίς he is not received, but when he goes to Galilee (his native
land), there he is received (4.45). Verse 45 therefore becomes a
paradigm of 1.12, ὅσοι δὲ ἔλαβον αὐτόν, ἔδωκεν αὐτοῖς ἐξουσίαν τέκνα
θεοῦ γενέσθαι.[4] The Galileans are those who "receive" Jesus.

---

[1] "Indessen ist der Beifall, den Jesus nach v. 45 in Galiläa findet, noch
nicht echte Anerkennung, so wenig wie der Glaube der Jerusalemer 2₂₃
echter Glaube war" (*ibid.*).

[2] Its appearance in a few MSS of Mt. and Mk. is the result of scribal
harmonization.

[3] Cf. Lightfoot, p. 146.

[4] For this reason I cannot accept Ernst Haenchen's ingenious proposal
that 1.11 in the original hymn and in the evangelist's own understanding
spoke of the wandering Wisdom that found no acceptance in the world, thus
motivating the incarnation, while v. 12 is only the clumsy addition of a
redactor who misunderstood the passage (*ZThK*, 60, p. 329f.). The coming
of Jesus to "his own" and his rejection are too integral to the whole structure
of the gospel to support this view. Cf. I. de la Potterie, "Jésus roi et juge

In this way Nathanael, who is a Galilean and not a "Jew," is nevertheless the "real Israelite" who recognizes Israel's king (1.49), and Nicodemus, when he takes Jesus' side among the "rulers of the Jews," is behaving like a "Galilean" (7.52). The journeys to Jerusalem in John symbolize the coming of the redeemer to "his own" and his rejection by them,[1] while the emphasized movement from Judaea to Galilee (especially 4.43-54) symbolizes the redeemer's acceptance by others, who thereby become truly "children of God," the real Israel. Thus, while "the Jews" symbolize the natural people of God, who however reject God's messenger, "the Galileans" symbolize those who are estranged from the natural people of God, but become truly God's people because they receive God's messenger.[2]

Galilee therefore takes on a very important symbolic reference in the Fourth Gospel. Hence, while it is legitimate to speak of a spiritualization—or, better, of a second, hidden meaning—of the question of Jesus' origin, one must reckon with the likelihood that this is the spiritualization of an already existing tradition of the *Galilean* origin of a savior figure. Alternatively, the tradition, perhaps connected with the northern, ultimately Ephraimitic circles, may have mentioned no place of origin, but still may have accorded better with Jesus' historical origin in Galilee than did the Davidic ideology of the Judaean King-Messiah. Thus John 7.37-52 contains both (1) a polemic against the Davidic, Judaean ideology of the eschatological redeemer and (2) a further re-interpretation that makes neither the northern nor the southern origin of the redeemer of ultimate significance in comparison with Jesus' *heavenly* origin.

---

d'après Jn 19, 13," *Biblica* 41 (1960), 246: "Le prologue avait indiqué le thème dominant du recit: 'il vint chez lui et les siens ne l'ont pas reçu' (1,11)." The seeming contradiction between 1.11, οὐ παρέλαβον and 1.12, ὅσοι δὲ ἔλαβον, does not require the hypothesis of a redactor, but only an observation of the Johannine style. Cf. especially, 3.32, τὴν μαρτυρίαν αὐτοῦ οὐδεὶς λαμβάνει and 3.33, ὁ λαβὼν αὐτοῦ τὴν μαρτυρίαν.

[1] Cf. Dodd's illuminating comments on chap. 7 (pp. 351f.).

[2] The case of the Samaritans in chap. 4 is similar. In this light 4.22b, "Salvation is from the Jews," is understandable and need not be removed as a gloss. Salvation is *from* the Jews; they are God's "own" people. But it is the non-Jews, the Samaritans, who recognize and accept it (4.42: ὁ σωτὴρ τοῦ κόσμου).

John 7: its internal and external order

Aporiae in John 7

The sequence of event and discourse in chapter 7 has seemed so disconnected to most commentators that proposals for rearranging the text abound. A number of scholars[1] agree in transposing 7.15-24 to a position before verses 1-14, where, since the same scholars all remove chapter 6 from its present setting, these verses are brought into direct connection with chapter 5. The reasons offered for this transposition by Archbishop Bernard and Rudolf Bultmann are identical and representative. Fundamental, of course, is the fact that the "themes of 7.15-24 are throughout the same as in c.5."[2] There are specific connections between 7.16f. and 5.19, 30; between 7.18 and 5.41-44; between 7.23b and 5.9; between 7.24 and 5.30. Second, the question about Jesus' knowledge of the γράμματα in 7.15 connects well with his statement about the γράμματα of Moses in 5.47, which then provides the needed motivation for the question. Third, 7.25, with its references to Jesus' speaking "openly," forms a natural sequence to 7.14. Fourth, Jesus' question in 7.19, "Why are you seeking to kill me?" is extremely abrupt, since 7.12ff. tells of a "favorable reception."[3]

These arguments should be considered in turn. First, while the allusions to chapter 5 in 7.15-25 are clear and emphatic, such references to themes and episodes previously mentioned are a dominant characteristic of the Fourth Gospel as it now stands. It is this self-allusiveness that gives to the gospel its involuted, rather intricate structure. Unless one is prepared to assume that the whole gospel was originally quite different, with a tightly logical topic outline—like that which results from the ingenious rearrangements found in Bultmann's commentary—, then the occurrence of the same themes in two places is not in itself sufficient reason for demanding that these two places be given adjacent positions.[4] The

---

[1] F. Warburton Lewis, James Moffatt, G. H. C. Macgregor, J. H. Bernard, Rudolf Bultmann: see W. F. Howard, *The Fourth Gospel in Recent Criticism and Interpretation* (4th ed. rev. C. K. Barrett; London: The Epworth Press, 1955), p. 303.

[2] J. H. Bernard, *A Critical and Exegetical Commentary on the Gospel according to St. John* (ICC; 1929), I, xix; cf. Bultmann, *Ev. Joh.*, p. 177.

[3] *Ibid.*

[4] On the whole question of the displacement and redaction theories contained in Bultmann's commentary, see D. Moody Smith Jr., *The Compo-*

second argument, based on the occurrence of γράμματα in both 5.47 and 7.15 is invalid. In the first place, the use of γράμματα in both places might be fortuitous. More important, the proposed rearrangement severs the discussion of Jesus' διδαχή in verses 16 and 17—the real subject of the controversy—from its very natural introduction by ἐδίδασκεν in verse 14. The third argument, that 7.25 would follow naturally upon 7.14, is correct, but the present sequence is not unnatural. The important question, which must be discussed below, is whether the content of verses 15-24 is in any way related to that in 25-36.

The fourth argument is crucial. Is the question of 7.19c so abrupt that some motivation for it, not present in the present context, must be sought elsewhere? Bernard's statement that 7.12ff. describes a favorable reception is inaccurate. Instead a γογγυσμός over Jesus among the crowds is described, corresponding, as was said above, to the σχίσματα described elsewhere. Some of the crowd are favorable, some opposed to Jesus. Nevertheless, the question is abrupt — and the reply in verse 20 shows that the audience hears it as unmotivated! "You have a demon," they say; "who is seeking to kill you?" If the question were not so abrupt, then this reply would be. At this critical point, then, the proposed rearrangement solves too much. It smoothes an abrupt transition that is manifestly intentional. Just why this abrupt transition should have been built into the dialogue is a question which will be pursued further below.

The tendency of the proposed rearrangement to multiply problems is reflected also in the subsequent recasting of the remainder of chapter 7 in Bultmann's commentary. Bultmann recognizes an introduction in 7.1-13, followed by four scenes: (a) verses 14, 25-30; (b) verses 31-36; (c) verses 37-44; (d) verses 45-52. But since the sending of the servants to arrest Jesus and their return ought to take place the same day, (b) and (c) are then transposed. The first scene now seems too brief, however, so Bultmann takes the final step of inserting 8.48-50, 54, 55, one of the "fragments" out of chapter 8, which fits well into this context.[1] The brilliance of this construction is unquestionable, and it can scarcely be doubted that the resulting chapter develops with a much more orderly sequence of thought than does the transmitted text. Nevertheless, the very

_____

sition and Order of the Fourth Gospel (New Haven and London: Yale University Press, 1965), particularly pp. 116-179.

[1] *Ev. Joh.*, p. 216.

complexity of the construction throws doubt on the hypothesis that requires it. Furthermore, if the original text was so concise and systematic as Bultmann's construction, then its disintegration into the present disarray demands an explanation, which Bultmann does not provide.

Now if it can be shown that the received order of the chapter has a sound logical sequence of its own, then elaborate rearrangement becomes unnecessary. Alternatively, even if Bultmann's reconstruction is accepted as the "original" order, an attempt to understand the text as transmitted would at least explain how the "inferior" order might have arisen.

Reading the chapter as it stands, one discovers that the major points of division are well marked. The first thirteen verses form an introduction to the whole. The discussion between Jesus and his brothers sets the stage for his appearance ἐν παρρησίᾳ while at the same time demonstrating the ambivalence of his self-manifestation, which can never be really "open" to "the world", but only to faith.[1] In addition, as was already pointed out, the description in verse 12 of a "great murmuring" about Jesus among the crowds introduces the major subject of the chapter, which comes to most explicit expression in the "division" in the crowd in verse 43.

After this introduction there are two main divisions, each marked by a notation of time: verses 14-36 (ἤδη δὲ τῆς ἑορτῆς μεσούσης) and 37-52 (ἐν δὲ τῇ ἐσχάτῃ ἡμέρᾳ τῇ μεγάλῃ τῆς ἑορτῆς). Analysis of the second of these has already shown that its framework is provided by the controversy whether Jesus is legitimately called either "the Prophet" or "the Christ."[2] The unity of the first division is generally called into question because the theme of the Jews' intention to kill Jesus (verses 19-26) seems unrelated to its context. Yet attempts to create a unity of thought by connecting verse 19—and of chapter 5 produce new problems. The troublesome verse 19 is therefore a good place to begin an analysis of this section.

The abruptness of the question. "Why are you seeking to kill me?" does not stem from the psychological lack of preparation in the scene which the reader must imagine. The real perplexity is not that of "the crowd" but of the reader, and it does not derive from

---

[1] The function of the introduction is well described by Dodd, pp. 351f., who finds chapters 7-8 a unified whole, framed by ἐν κρυπτῷ (7.4) and ἐκρύβη (8.59) (p. 348).

[2] See above, pp. 34ff.

lack of preparation in the verses prior to verse 15, but in the harsh transition within verse 19 itself. What is the connection between the statements of verse 18, "He who speaks from himself seeks his own glory, but he who seeks the glory of him who sent him is true, and there is no unrighteousness in him," and the mention in 19 of Moses as the law giver and of the Jews' disobedience, with the question about the intent to kill Jesus? This is the crux of the problem.

The theme of verses 14-18 is the origin of Jesus' teaching. Repeatedly he insists, in slightly varying language, that his teaching is from God, *not from himself* (ἀφ' ἑαυτοῦ). T. F. Glasson suggests that such language alludes to Deuteronomy 18.18-22, a passage in which God speaks to Moses of the prophet in the future.[1] The passage follows:

> ". . . I will raise up a prophet for them from among their own people, like yourself: I will put My words in his mouth and he will speak to them all that I command him; and if anybody fails to heed the words he speaks in My name, I myself will call him to account. But any prophet who presumes to speak in My name an oracle which I did not command him to utter, or who speaks in the name of other gods—that prophet shall die." And should you ask yourselves, "How can we know that the oracle was not spoken by the Lord?"—if the prophet speaks in the name of the Lord and the word does not come true, that word was not spoken by the Lord; the prophet has uttered it presumptuously: do not stand in dread of him.[2]

Here the essential characteristic of the true prophet like Moses is that he speaks Yahweh's words, not his own. There are several other passages in John in which the language is still closer to this Deuteronomic passage. In 3.34 a summary statement about the messenger "from above" says: ὅν γὰρ ἀπέστειλεν ὁ θεὸς τὰ ῥήματα τοῦ θεοῦ λαλεῖ. Verses 35f. show that judgment of life or death hangs on the question whether one receives and believes the testimony of this messenger: compare Deuteronomy 18.18f. The same allusion may be present also in John 8.47, ὁ ὢν ἐκ τοῦ θεοῦ τὰ ῥήματα τοῦ θεοῦ ἀκούει (compare the similar motif in 10.3 and 18.37). In 12.47-50 allusion to Deuteronomy 18.18b is fairly plain. One who does

---

[1] Glasson, p. 30.

[2] The translation is from *The Torah: The Five Books of Moses; A New Translation of the Holy Scriptures According to the Masoretic Text* (Philadelphia: The Jewish Publication Society of America, 1962).

not receive Jesus' ῥήματα is judged by the λόγος which Jesus spoke, because ἐγὼ ἐξ ἐμαυτοῦ οὐκ ἐλάλησα, ἀλλ' ὁ πέμψας με πατὴρ αὐτός μοι ἐντολὴν δέδωκεν τί εἴπω καί τί λαλήσω. Deuteronomy 18.18b reads in part: καὶ λαλήσει αὐτοῖς καθότι ἂν ἐντείλωμαι αὐτῷ. In John 14.10 Jesus says to Philip, τὰ ῥήματα ἃ ἐγὼ λέγω ὑμῖν ἀπ' ἐμαυτοῦ οὐ λαλῶ. ὁ δὲ πατὴρ ἐν ἐμοὶ μένων ποιεῖ τὰ ἔργα αὐτοῦ.[1] Finally, John 17.8, τὰ ῥήματα ἃ ἔδωκάς μοι δέδωκα αὐτοῖς, may be a direct allusion to Deuteronomy 18.18, δώσω τὸ ῥῆμά μου ἐν τῷ στόματι αὐτοῦ καὶ λαλήσει αὐτοῖς καθότι ἂν ἐντείλομαι αὐτῷ.

The ultimate test of the prophet's authenticity, according to Deuteronomy 18.22, was whether what he announced came to pass. Three times in the farewell discourses Jesus tells his disciples things which are to take place—that is, from the evangelist's viewpoint, things which have taken place, thus demonstrating the truth of the prophecies. Clearest is 13.19: "I am telling you right now, before it takes place, that when it takes place you may believe that 'I am.'"[2]

All these probable allusions to Deuteronomy 18, while none is certain, cumulatively give plausibility to the hypothesis that John 7.14-18 intends to depict Jesus as the prophet like Moses. The hypothesis is strengthened by the fact that the characteristic of Jesus' teaching emphasized here, that he does not speak ἀφ' ἑαυτοῦ, is directly identified by the evangelist with the act of prophecy in 11.51: τοῦτο δὲ ἀφ' ἑαυτοῦ οὐκ εἶπεν, ἀλλὰ ἀρχιερεὺς ὢν ... ἐπροφήτευ-σεν.[3]

Now the puzzle of verse 19 must be considered more closely. It reads: "Did not Moses give you the Law? Yet none of you does the Law—why are you seeking to kill me?" The implication is, "If you *did* keep the Torah, then you would *not* be seeking to kill me." Understood in this way, the verse is exactly parallel to a statement in the following chapter, which is equally puzzling in its context:[4]

---

[1] The notion that both "words "and "acts" or "signs" are given by God to his prophet belongs also to the tradition of Moses: cf. Dt. 34. 10-12.

[2] Cf. 14.29; 16.4. (The connection of these passages with Dt. 18.22 was suggested to me by Prof. Paul W. Meyer.) As prophet, Jesus knew πάντα τὰ ἐρχόμενα ἐπ' αὐτόν (18.4). N.b. that the "Messiah" awaited by the Samaritans "will announce all things to us" (4.25).

[3] This characteristic of prophecy is not in itself limited to the *Mosaic* prophet, nor even to specifically biblical concepts of prophecy. For a similar idea in the older Greek sources, see Fascher, pp. 11-54, especially pp. 51f. Parallels are cited in Bauer, pp. 151f., and Bultmann, *Ev. Joh.*, p. 314, n. 4.

[4] For an extremely suggestive discussion of the whole passage 8.37-59, see Nils A. Dahl, "Manndraperen og hans far (Joh 8.44)," *Norsk Teologisk*

"If you are children of Abraham, do the works of Abraham; but now you are seeking to kill me, a man who has spoken the truth to you, which I heard from God. This Abraham did not do" (8.39b-40). In one case appeal is made to Moses, the lawgiver of Israel, in the other case to Abraham, the "Father" of Israel, to show that the intention of "the Jews" to kill Jesus is neither according to the Law nor proper to children of Abraham. In 7.21-24 there follows a kind of paradigm of the principle, "If you kept the Torah, you would not be seeking to kill me." By a *Kal wehomer* argument from the law for circumcision on a Sabbath, Jesus shows that the ἔργον for which he is being condemned is not in truth a violation of the Torah, if only his opponents would judge τὴν δικαίαν κρίσιν, not κατ' ὄψιν (verse 24).

But what is there in the context of verse 19 that calls forth this apparently abrupt mention of Moses, the Torah, and the intention to kill Jesus? If the hypothesis is correct that verses 14-18 allude to Deuteronomy 18.18-22, then the answer lies near at hand. For the Deuteronomic passage speaks not only of the true prophet like Moses, but also of *false* prophets who may arise to lead the nation astray from the worship of Yahweh, and who must be put to death. If verses 14-18 suggest that Jesus is the prophet like Moses, then the official plot to kill Jesus implies the accusation that he is the false prophet.

The false prophet

There is evidence from a variety of sources that the figure of the false prophet, based in large part upon Deuteronomy 18.18-22 and on the other important Deuteronomic passage on this subject, 13.1-6, was a subject of concern, speculation, and legislation in divers circles of Judaism around the time the Fourth Gospel was written.

The Mishnah tractate *Sanhedrin* provides for the trial of a false prophet:

"The false prophet"—he that prophesies what he has not heard and what has not been told him, his death is at the hands of men; but he that suppresses his prophecy or disregards the

Tidskrift 64 (1963), 129-162, and "Der erstgeborene Satans und der Vater des Teufels (Polyk. 7.1 und Joh 8.44)," *Apophoreta, Festschrift für Ernst Haenchen*, ed. Walther Eltester (Berlin: Alfred Töpelmann, 1964), pp. 70-84.

words of another prophet or the prophet that transgresses his own words, his death is at the hands of Heaven, for it is written, *I will require it of him.*[1]

Even apart from the direct quotation of Deuteronomy 18.19b in the last clause, it is evident that the whole *halakah* is an interpretation of Deuteronomy 18.18-22. The Gemara of the Babylonian Talmud makes this dependence explicit and gives historical examples of prophets who prophesied what they had not heard and who prophesied what had not been told them.[2] The Tosefta declares that "he who prophesies in order to abrogate anything of what is written in the Law, is guilty . . ."[3]

The New Testament provides several clues to traditions about the false prophet which evidently had developed in apocalyptic circles of Judaism. In Matthew 24.11 the woes of the last day include the appearance of "many false prophets (ψευδοπροφῆται)" who will "lead many astray (πλανᾶν)." Verses 10-12 have been inserted by Matthew into a Marcan context; whether Matthew composed these himself or drew on an older Jewish or Christian tradition cannot be determined.[4] In Mark 13.22 the mention of false prophets (and false Messiahs, unless this element is a Christian addition) probably belonged to the Jewish *Vorlage.*[5] Again the mission of the false prophets is to "lead astray (ἀποπλανᾶν)"; in this case the further information is given that they will do this by "signs and wonders (σημεῖα καὶ τέρατα)." Revelation 19.20 describes the capture and judgment of "the false prophet who performed the signs (σημεῖα) before him [*scil.* the first beast], by which he led astray (ἐπλάνησεν) those who received the stamp of the beast and those who did obeisance to his image" (cf. 20.10). This "false prophet" is the same as the second beast who arose "from the earth" (Revelation 13.11-18), of whom it is said: "He performs great signs (σημεῖα) so that he even makes fire descend from heaven upon the earth before men. And he leads astray (πλανᾷ) those who dwell upon the earth, by means of the signs (διὰ τὰ σημεῖα) which

---

[1] *Sanh.* 11.5. Translation from Herbert Danby, trans., *The Mishnah* (Oxford: At the Clarendon Press, 1933), p. 400.

[2] Talmud Bab., *Sanh.* 89a.

[3] Danby, trans., *Tractate Sanhedrin: Mishnah and Tosefta* ("Translations of Early Documents, Series III, Rabbinic Texts"; London: Society for Promoting Christian Knowledge, 1919), p. 140; cf. Talmud Bab., *Sanh.* 89b.

[4] Cf. Bultmann, *Geschichte*, p. 129.

[5] *Ibid.*

were given to him to perform before the beast . . ." (verses 13f., cf. 16.12-16). Here the "false prophet" is "mythologized" or at least clothed with mythical symbolism. By this means the false prophet is placed within a dualistic setting not so evident in the synoptic apocalypse. A very similar tradition lies behind the "lawless one" of 2 Thessalonians 2.8-12. The "lawless one" (ἄνομος) is regarded, at least in the present context, as the "anti-Christ" properly so-called. He is the enemy "whom the Lord will destroy by the breath of his mouth and annihilate by the appearance of his coming" (verse 8). Like the false prophet of Revelation, he has his power from Satan (verse 9), though here the dualistic element remains sharply circumscribed by the Old Testament notion that *God* sends the "power of error (ἐνέργειαν πλάνης)"[1] (verse 11). Like the false prophets of both the synoptic and Johannine apocalypses, the "lawless one" performs false δυνάμεις and σημεῖα and τέρατα. The ultimate result, as in Revelation, is judgment. God sends the "power of error" so that those who lack the "love of truth" will "'believe the false one (ψευδός), that all who do not believe the truth but approve the false[2] may be judged" (verses 11b-12).

Common to all the apocalyptic traditions of the false prophet attested in the New Testament are (1) that he will "lead astray" the nation(s) and (2) that he will perform "signs." How is this apparently well established tradition to be explained? Wilhelm Bousset, in his pioneering and wide-ranging monograph on the Antichrist,[3] explained the enigmatic figure behind these texts as a Jewish development from the ancient myth of the chaos-dragon who combatted the Creator. The specific form of the legend attested in the New Testament arose from the reinterpretation of the myth in political and historical terms at a time prior to the New Testament itself. This is not the place to enter into a criticism of Bousset's theory, which has had very extensive influence on subsequent interpretation of New Testament apocalyptic traditions,[4] but it is

---

[1] Cf. 1 Kings 22.19-23: God sends a רוח שקר, LXX πνεῦμα ψευδές, into the mouths of the prophets.

[2] ἀδικία: equivalent to the Hebrew שקר, as often in LXX.

[3] *Der Antichrist in der Überlieferung des Judentums, des neuen Testaments, und der alten Kirche. Ein Beitrag zur Auslegung der Apocalypse* (Göttingen: Vandenhoeck und Ruprecht, 1895), 186 pp. English ed.: *The Antichrist Legend: A Chapter in Christian and Jewish Folklore*, trans. A. H. Keane (London: Hutchinson and Co., 1896), 307 pp.

[4] For example, cf. Dibelius' comments on 2 Thess 2.1-12 in *An die Thessa-*

apparent that the mythical and supposed historical-political elements alone fail to explain precisely those elements of the tradition which are most pertinent for the present inquiry. There is nothing in the mythical background described by Bousset that accounts for the identification of the "Antichrist" as a false *prophet* nor for the stereotyped expectation that he will "lead astray" the elect community. Furthermore, even the "signs and wonders" of the "Antichrist" remain unexplained in Bousset's treatment, even though he devotes several pages to documentation that shows how nearly universal this motif is in the legend. Yet all three of these elements are readily explained by reference to a single Old Testament text, Deuteronomy 13.2-6:

> If there appears among you a prophet or a dream-diviner and he gives you a sign or a portent [אות או מופת, LXX: σημεῖον ἢ τέρας], saying, "Let us follow and worship another god"— whom you have not experienced—and the sign or portent that he named to you comes true: do not heed the words of that prophet [לוא תשמע אל־דברי הנביא ההוא LXX: οὐκ ἀκούσεσθε τῶν λόγων τοῦ προφήτου ἐκείνου] or that dream-diviner. For the Lord your God is testing you to see whether you really love the Lord your God with all your heart and soul. Follow none but the Lord your God, and revere none but Him; observe His commandments alone, and heed only His orders: worship none but Him, and hold fast to Him. As for that prophet or dream-diviner, he shall be put to death [יומת; ἀποθανεῖται]; for he uttered falsehood about [or, apostasy against: סרה על־] the Lord your God—who freed you from the land of Egypt and who redeemed you from the house of bondage—to make you stray [להדיחך; LXX: πλανῆσαί σε] from the path that the Lord your God commanded you to follow. Thus you will sweep out evil from your midst.[1]

This text and Deuteronomy 18.18-22 provide the two *loci classici* in Jewish traditions about the false prophet. The assumption that Jewish forms of the Antichrist legend—even though other, mythical forms may have existed long before—would have been connected with a biblical text, accords with everything that is known about the most varied circles of Judaism in the Greco-Roman period.[2]

---

lonicher I, II; *An die Philipper* (HNT; 1925) and Lohmeyer's exposition of Rev 13 in *Die Offenbarung des Johannes* (HNT; 1926).

[1] *The Torah*, p. 350.

[2] Above all the elaborate interaction of scriptural exegesis, mythical notions, and historical events in the *pešarim* discovered at Qumran graphically illustrate this point. But such diverse documents as Philo's allegories, the *midrashim* of rabbinic Judaism, and numerous apocalyptic writings betray equal, if different preoccupation with scripture.

Outside the New Testament the same or very similar traditions manifest themselves in several places. In the Qumran texts there appears a "man of lies" (איש הכזב)[1] or "preacher of lies" (מטיף הכזב)[2] or "man of scoffing" (איש הלצון).[3] Gert Jeremias finds in this figure a rival teacher who arose within the Qumran sect, alongside the Teacher of Righteousness. His controversy with the latter is described in the Habakkuk Commentary 5.9-12. His defection led to the establishment of a schismatic group, whose continuing polemical relationship with the original community is depicted in the Damascus Document.[4] Of special significance are two passages which speak of this unknown person and his followers. The first, in the "Testimonia" from Cave IV, interpreting a text from Joshua 6.26, says: "But behold, a man accursed, the one of Belial, shall arise, to be a fowl[er's sn]are to his people, and destruction to all his neighbors. And there shall arise [. . . so] that the two of them may be instruments of violence. . . ."[5] Since the beginning of line 25, now lost, must have mentioned a second figure, Van der Woude thinks the reference was to the "Wicked Priest" and the "Man of Lies," interpreted here as a double manifestation of the Antichrist, an earlier form of the same tradition that is adapted in Revelation 16.13; 19.20; 20.10.[6] His hypothesis is supported by the mention of Belial, which is found frequently associated with the Antichrist.[7] At the same time, the Qumran community related the rise of these false preachers to scripture proofs. This is clearly shown by the Damascus Document:

> For in ancient times Moses and Aaron arose by the hand of the Prince of Lights, and Belial raised Jannes and his brother by his evil device, when Israel was delivered for the first time. And in the epoch of the desolation of the land there arose the

---

[1] 1 QpHab 2.2; 5.11; CD 20.15.

[2] 1 QpHab 10.9; Commentaire de Michée 10.2; CD 8.13; 19.26; cf. CD 1.15.

[3] CD 1.14.

[4] Gert Jeremias, *Der Lehrer der Gerechtigkeit* ("Studien zur Umwelt des Neuen Testaments," ed. Karl G. Kuhn, Vol. II; Göttingen: Vandenhoeck & Ruprecht, 1963), pp. 79-126; summary, p. 126.

[5] Lines 23-25, trans. J. M. Allegro, "Further Messianic References in Qumran Literature," *JBL* 75 (1956), 185.

[6] Van der Woude, pp. 121f. The "Wicked Priest" in Van der Woude's view corresponds to the "Beast from the Sea" of Rev., the "Prophet of Lies" to the "false prophet" or "beast from the earth."

[7] Cf. Bousset's excursus on Belial, *Der Antichrist*, pp. 99-100; English ed., pp. 153-156.

'removers of the boundary' [מסיגי הגבול Hosea 5.10] 'and they lead Israel astray' [ויתעו את ישראל: Jeremiah 23.13], 'And the land became desolate' [Ezekiel 19.7], for they 'spoke rebellion' [דברו סרה: Deuteronomy 13.6] against the commandments of God given by the hand of Moses and also by the hand of those anointed with the holy spirit and prophesied falsehood so as to cause Israel to turn away from God [וינבאו שקר להשיב את ישראל מאחר אל: compare Deuteronomy 13.2-6, especially verse 6].[1]

Significantly the time of the community's origin, viewed as part of the eschatological epoch, is compared with the time of the first deliverance of Israel. As in the former time two false leaders opposed Moses and Aaron, so in the community's own age there are false leaders—by the logic of the text, two in number, as in the Testimonia passage. One of these is doubtless the "Man of Lies" or "Prophet of Lies," the satanic counterpart of Aaron, who was Moses' prophet.[2] Again, among the biblical passages used to explain the appearance of the false prophet(s) is found Deuteronomy 13.1-6. There is good reason to believe, then, that the Qumran community's teaching about a false prophet, while it probably took its starting point from a specific historical incident within the community's experience, also made use of a tradition which already combined mythical elements with the Deuteronomic law of the false-prophet—in short, the same tradition that is attested in the New Testament.

Moreover, there are indications that the same tradition emerges occasionally in sources seemingly remote from the New Testament and the Qumran documents. In the Sibylline Oracles, the following passage occurs:

> From the stock of Sebaste Beliar shall come in later time and shall raise the mountain heights and raise the sea, the great fiery sun, and the bright moon, and he shall raise up the dead and shall perform many signs (σήματα πολλὰ ποιήσει) for men: but they shall not be effective in him. Nay, but he deceives (πλανᾷ) mortals, and many shall he deceive (πολλοὺς δὲ πλανήσει), Hebrews faithful and elect and lawless, too, and other men who have never yet listened to the word of God.[3]

---

[1] CD V, 17b - VI, 2a, trans. Chaim Rabin, *The Zadokite Documents* (2d rev. ed.; Oxford: At the Clarendon Press, 1958), p. 20.

[2] Cf. Ex 4.16 and the midrashim on that passage.

[3] *Or. Sibyl.* III, 63-70. Translation by H. C. D. Lancaster, *The Apocrypha and Pseudepigrapha of the Old Testament*, ed. R. H. Charles (Oxford: At the Clarendon Press, 1913), II, 380. Critical text by Joh. Geffcken, *Die Oracula*

Although not explicitly designated a "false prophet," Beliar "leads astray" by means of "signs."

In the published Mandaean texts, several rather isolated passages apply the epithet "false prophet" and the related term "false judge" to various figures. None of these passages has any connection with the tradition here under investigation, with one important exception. The *Right Ginza* contains an extended admonition from "the first messenger" to the Naṣoraeans (Mandaeans), warning against threats of "false prophets" and against various groups which will endanger the sect by the enticement of false teaching as well as by actual persecution. The admonition deals first with the Jews, then with the Christians, and finally, very briefly, with Islam. Traditions of several ages and origins have here been rather loosely woven together. The *Right Ginza*[1] recounts a periodized scheme of world history that without doubt belonged once to Jewish apocalyptic.[2] It begins with the age of Adam, who lives one thousand years to be killed by the sword. Then comes the age of Rām and his wife Rūd, which ends with destruction of the world by fire. Next is the age of Surbai and his wife Sarhabēl,[3] followed after fifteen generations by the age of Noah. After twenty-five generations, the world is destroyed by water, with Noah and his family saved to begin the race anew, now for the third (fourth?) time. "From the ark of Noah until Abraham, the Prophet of Rūhā, arises, until Moses arises, until the city of Jerusalem is built, are six generations [each]."[4] The kings David and Solomon and the building of Jerusalem by Solomon are mentioned. Then comes a paragraph that describes the appearance of "prophets of lies" at the "end of the worlds (*'alma*)," who simulate the form of "the three messengers" (Hibil, Šitil, and Enoš-Uthra). Their appearance

---

Sibyllina (GCS, 8; 1902), 203 pp. For an illuminating discussion of the apocalyptic material imbedded in the Sibylline books, cf. Bousset, *The Antichrist*, pp. 95-100.

[1] Lidzbarski, *Ginza*, II, 1; pp. 45:22-46:28.

[2] This much remains of the thesis of Richard Reitzenstein, who analyzed the apocalypse in detail (*Das mandäische Buch des Herrn der Grösse und die Evangelienüberlieferung* [Sitzungsberichte der Heidelberger Akademie der Wissenschaften: Philosophisch-historische Klasse, Jahrgang 1919; Heidelberg: Carl Winter, 1919], p. 11 *et passim*). His theory of the relation of gospel traditions to the Mandaean apocalypse has been refuted by Lidzbarski, *Ginza*, xii, and others. Cf. Rudolph, I, 24.

[3] Are these "pairs" fragments of a systematization like that found in the Pseudo-Clementines?

[4] GR II, 1, Lidzbarski, p. 46, ll.10-12.

signals the beginning of the scattering of the Jews and of other nations, followed by international turmoil and war.[1] This apocalyptic fragment is followed by a short fragment from a mythological or cosmological tradition, naming the seven planets that lead astray—among which now stand the Holy Spirit, identified with Venus, and Christ. This forms the transition to the anti-Christian polemic, which contains allusions to the gospels.[2] Finally "after all prophets, a prophet will arise from the earth,"[3] who is identified as Mohammed, "the Arab prophet."

In its present context the apocalyptic fragment, which is obviously not entirely coherent, has been adapted in part to specifically Mandaean ideology and made to serve an anti-Jewish polemic. However, at several points it does not really fit the polemic usage. Elsewhere in Mandaean texts the Jewish God becomes an evil spirit; the law is given by the evil Rūhā and the seven planets.[4] Hence it is remarkable that this passage regards the God of the Jews and their Law positively and reproaches the Jews for not having obeyed. This shows that the traditional passage has been only superficially adapted and remains surprisingly close to the form it must once have had in some Jewish apocalypse.[5] That the

---

[1] The text, in Lidzbarski's translation (GR II, 1, p. 46, ll.19-35) reads: "Vom Moses, dem Sohne des Amra, bis zum Ende der Welten werden Gläubige der Kûṣṭä sein; sie werden in diesem Glauben treu befunden werden. Dann werden Lügenpropheten auftreten, die Gestalt von *xxxx* [the lacuna is to be filled with a reference to the "three messengers," as in GR II, p. 44, l.23] annehmen, in jeder Stadt auftreten. Die Völker werden sich verteilen, die Zungen sich verteilen uber jede Stadt, über jeden Ort. Die Juden werden über jede Stadt zerstreut werden. Die Welt wird sich spalten und Tyrannen werden sich eines jeden Ortes bemächtigen. Ein Ort wird über den anderen herfallen, eine Stadt über die andere mit Krieg herfallen, und sie vergiessen Blutströme in der Welt. Ein jeder sucht für sich selber einen Vorteil und kämpft um das, was nicht ihm gehört." Cf. GR 24; Lidzbarski, p. 26, ll.10-12, where the false prophets are described in more mythical terms: they come from the "angels of lack," enter the wombs of human women, "put on bodies and take on the form of men."

[2] For example, the description of Enoš-Uthra in GR II, 1; Lidzbarski, p. 47, l.41 - p. 48, l.14. It is generally recognized that this polemic presupposes an encounter between the Mandaeans and Byzantine Christianity; cf. Rudolph, I, 47-51: "Nur setzen die mandäischen Schriften augenscheinlich in der Hauptsache eine mächtige Kirche nachkonstantinischer Prägung voraus" (p. 51).

[3] GR II, 1; Lidzbarski, p. 54, l.11. Cf. Rev 13.11!

[4] Rudolph, I, 51f.

[5] This ambivalence is typical of Mandaean relationship to Judaism. As Rudolph says, the anti-Jewish polemic is "der eigenartigste Zug der Mandäer, die selbst aus jüdischer Wurzel stammen" (I, 51).

Mandaeans originated in "a 'half-Judaism' on the periphery of official Judaism"[1] has been convincingly argued by Rudolph,[2] who shows in addition that the separation from Judaism was very likely prior to the rise of Christianity.[3] The conclusion may therefore be drawn with reasonable probability, that before the Christian era the Mandaeans took over the Jewish apocalyptic notion of false prophets who would arise at the end of days. Eventually they merged this idea with gnostic or quasi-gnostic teaching about the planets that lead men astray—perhaps attracted to this connection because "leading astray" was an integral part of the false-prophet tradition—and applied the combined imagery to their various opponents, Jewish, Christian, and Islamic. If this line of reasoning is valid, then another witness is found for the pre-Christian existence of the tradition of the false prophet(s).

Jesus as the false prophet

The above excursus on "the false prophet" led to the conclusion that a fairly firm tradition existed in first-century Judaism about "false prophets" who would arise to "lead the people astray" by performing "signs and wonders"—as Moses had done (Deuteronomy 34.10-12)—and by "speaking words which God had not commanded them." Very likely this tradition was connected with midrashic interpretation of Deuteronomy 13.1-6 and 18.18-22. The tradition is elaborated in various ways, of which the eschatological development clearly evident not only in the New Testament, but also in the Sibylline Oracles, the Qumran texts, and even the Mandaean *Ginza*, is particularly important.

Before pursuing the specific relevance of these results for the Fourth Gospel, it is first necessary to observe that according to Jewish tradition, Jesus was executed as a magician and seducer of the people, that is, as a false prophet. Thus a *Baraita* of the Babylonian Talmud says:

> On the eve of the Passover Yeshu was hanged. For forty days before the execution took place, a herald went forth and cried, "He is going forth to be stoned because he has practiced sorcery and enticed Israel to apostasy. Anyone who can say anything in his favour, let him come forward and plead on his

---

[1] *Ibid.*, pp. 93f.
[2] *Ibid.*, pp. 80-101.
[3] *Ibid.*, p. 100.

behalf." But since nothing was brought forward in his favor he was hanged on the eve of the Passover! Ulla retorted: Do you suppose that he was one for whom a defence could be made? Was he not a *Mesith* (*enticer*), concerning whom Scripture says, *Neither shalt thou spare, neither shalt thou conceal him* [Deuteronomy 13.9]?. . .[1]

The kernel of the Baraita, "Jesus practiced magic, seduced, and made Israel apostate," [ישי כישף והסית והדית את ישראל] is repeated in *Sanhedrin* 107b and in *Sota* 47a.[2] This tradition, moreover, can be dated accurately to the middle of the second century because of a quotation by Justin Martyr in his *Dialogue with Trypho*: καὶ γὰρ μάγον εἶναι αὐτὸν ἐτόλμων [οἱ Ἰουδαῖοι] λέγειν καὶ λαοπλάνον.[3] In both cases the characteristics are that Jesus is said to be a "magus" and that he "leads the people astray." Both elements are present in Deuteronomy 13.1-6 and 18.1-22.

Against this background, the logic of John 7.19 becomes clearer. The whole argument of 7.15-24 turns on the question whether Jesus is the true prophet like Moses or whether he is the false prophet. As the true prophet, Jesus insists that his teaching is not his own. He speaks the words God has commanded him, not "from himself." He does not "seek his own glory," that is, he does not speak "presumptuously" like the prophet described in Deuteronomy 18.20. Therefore all who genuinely obey the Torah will obey the commandment of the Torah to "heed" the prophet (Deuteronomy 18.15b). But Jesus' hearers are placed before a dramatic decision, for while they are commanded to heed the true prophet upon pain of divine judgment (Deuteronomy 18.19), they are also commanded to put the false prophet to death (Deuteronomy 18.20; 13.6). The crowd therefore divides. While some say that Jesus is "good," others say, "on the contrary, he leads the crowd astray" (πλανᾷ;

---

[1] *Sanh* 43a, trans. Jacob Shachter in *The Babylonian Talmud*, ed. Isidore Epstein [henceforth: "Soncino Talmud"], Vol. XXIII: *Seder Nezikin, Sanhedrin* (London: Soncino Press, 1935), I, 281f. The statement by Ulla focuses on one element of the charge, הסית, from which he argues that Jesus was a מסית, 'seducer' (Dt 13.6-11), and therefore, according to Mishnah, *Sanh.* vii. 4, not a false prophet (Dt 13.1-5) but a "layman" (הדיוט = ἰδιώτης). But in the original charge on which Ulla comments, כישף . . . והדית את ישראל clearly points to the false prophet.

[2] Cited by Herman L. Strack and Paul Billerbeck, *Kommentar zum Neuen Testament aus Talmud und Midrasch*, Vol. I (München: C. H. Beck, 1922), p. 1023 (henceforth cited as "Billerbeck").

[3] *Dial.*, 69; cited by Billerbeck, I, 1023.

John 7.12)[1]—characteristic of the false prophet. They could have pointed out that the way Jesus led the crowd astray was also characteristic of the false prophet: by "signs" and by words purporting to be from God.

"Prophet" and "Christ" as ordering themes in John 7

If the dialogue in John 7.14-25 turns on the question whether Jesus is the true prophet or the false, then the first major division of chapter 7 (verses 14-36) may be shown to contain a coherent progression of ideas, which is, moreover, exactly parallel to that of the second division (verses 37-52). For if verses 14-25 deal with the question whether Jesus is "the Prophet," it is even clearer that the subsequent verses raise the question whether he is "the Christ." Verse 25 brings to a conclusion the discussion about the Jews' seeking to kill Jesus, which was introduced by a question on Jesus' lips in verse 19. Verse 26 is transitional, stating again the theme of Jesus' teaching παρρησίᾳ, which runs throughout the chapter, and introducing the new question "whether really the rulers do not know that he is the Christ." Denial of this question, on the grounds of a dogma that "when the Christ comes, no one will know his origin [πόθεν ἐστίν]," provides the occasion for a very brief statement by Jesus about his own mysterious origin (verses 28f.), which points to the fact that he comes really from God. That he has not *come* "from himself" (verse 28) corresponds exactly to the theme of verses 14ff., that he does not *speak* "from himself." On the other hand, it is significant that both in verses 26-29 and in verses 41-42 (in the second main division), the dispute whether Jesus is "the Christ" centers on the question "whence he comes."[2] The discussion concludes with verse 31, "Of the crowd, many believed in him, and they said, 'When the Christ comes, will he perform more signs than this man has performed?'"

Unless one assumes in advance that the evangelist would have been more interested in historical verisimilitude than in the pro-

---

[1] Thus I am led to a conclusion near that of Staerk, who says, "Er wird sogar ausdrücklich mit Mose gleichgesetzt, 7, 12, wenn er ἀγαθός genannt wird im Gegensatz zu dem Urteil, er sei ein falscher Prophet [,der] πλανᾷ τὸν ὄχλον 7, 13 [sic]" (p. 67). However, I am unable to discover how Staerk arrived at this conclusion, or how this verse "expressly" equates Jesus with Moses. The commentary by Joh. Jeremias referred to by Staerk at this point is so far unavailable to me.

[2] See above, pp. 35f.

gression of motifs from the reader's point of view, there is no reason to displace verses 32-36 from their present setting. Separation of the sending of the "officers" to arrest Jesus from the account of their return (verses 45-48), far from impeding the train of thought, in fact serves to connect the two main divisions of the narrative. Verse 32, by its mention of the "murmuring of the crowd" (τοῦ ὄχλου γογγύζοντος περὶ αὐτοῦ) returns to the theme announced by the introductory verse 12 (γογγυσμὸς περὶ αὐτοῦ ἦν πολὺς...ἐν τοῖς ὄχλοις), which in turn reappears in the σχίσμα of the second part.[1] The sending of the officers sets the stage for the quasijuridical discussion of Jesus' claims by the "rulers" upon their return (7.45-52).[2] The statement by Jesus and its misunderstanding by "the Jews" in verses 33-36 provides the counterpart to the discussion of his origin in verses 40-52. This new theme, where Jesus is going, is developed further in 8.21-29 and elsewhere.[3]

Chapter 7 is therefore not "disjointed," whether deliberately (Dodd) or accidentally (Bultmann and others). It is introduced by Jesus' paradoxical decision to appear ἐν παρρησίᾳ and by the suggestion that "the crowds" are already divided over his mission and person (verses 1-13). His "open" appearance and its effects are recounted in two major sections, verses 14-36 and verses 37-52. In each section Jesus' appearance and proclamation bring to expression the incipient division of the crowds; that is, just as Jesus moves from "hiddenness" (verse 4) to "openness," so the response of his hearers moves from hiddenness (verse 13: οὐδεὶς μέντοι παρρησίᾳ ἐλάλει περὶ αὐτοῦ) to open decision. His appearance ἐν παρρησίᾳ is thus itself κρίσις—a point underlined by the discourse immediately following this chapter, 8.12-20. Moreover, it has been shown that in each major division of chapter 7 order is provided by the two questions which are raised: Is Jesus the Prophet? Is he the Christ? These questions come to expression only allusively and implicitly in the first division, explicitly in the second. The reiteration of these two questions in so solemn a context suggests that they may play a role in the development of the whole gospel. For

---

[1] Cf. p. 33 above.

[2] Note also the ironic connection between the question of v. 26, μήποτε ἀληθῶς ἔγνωσαν οἱ ἄρχοντες ὅτι οὗτός ἐστιν ὁ χριστός, with v. 48, μή τις ἐκ τῶν ἀρχόντων ἐπίστευσεν εἰς αὐτὸν ἢ ἐκ τῶν φαρισαίων;

[3] See above, p. 38.

this reason the connections between chapter 7 and its broader context must next be explored.

Jesus' teaching παρρησία and the first trial

C. H. Dodd has pointed out that chapters 7 and 8 of John form one cycle whose central theme is Jesus' open manifestation.[1] The whole is framed by the words ἐν κρυπτῷ (7.4) and ἐκρύβη (8.59). Dodd's insight is further supported by the detailed analysis of chapter 7 in the preceding sections. In addition it should be noted that the cycle is framed by the two very similarly constructed miracle stories and accompanying discourses of chapters 5 and 9.[2] These two chapters depict the alternatives which lie before those who respond to Jesus' healing ἔργα and his ῥήματα: the one who falls away because "in fear of the Jews" he does not acknowledge who Jesus is, and the other, the true disciple, who is led "into all truth," so that he even teaches the scribes. Both are thus paradigms of Jesus' statement on discipleship in 8.30-36, and at the same time, as Bultmann suggests, probably vignettes out of the life of the Johannine church in its relationship to a hostile Jewish community.[3]

Chapter 11 again takes up the theme of Jesus' public manifestation. Like chapter 7 it begins with the question whether Jesus ought to go to Judaea. A comparison between Jesus' conversation with his disciples (11.1-16) and his conversation with his disbelieving brothers (7.1-10) is illuminating, both in their similarities and in their differences. This time Jesus determines to go, while his disciples object; the reversal results from the fact that Jesus' "hour" has drawn near (compare 7.6). The account of the raising of Lazarus,

---

[1] Dodd, pp. 345-354.

[2] Cf. especially Bultmann, *Ev. Joh.*, pp. 178f. The close connection between these two chapters and the themes of chapters 7-8 provides strong support for the common view, rejected by Dodd, that chap. 6 is out of place. However, there might be a significant reason for having placed the bread miracle and the discourse on "bread from heaven" alongside Jesus' proclamation about "living water," since both miraculous feeding and miraculous water belong to the wilderness traditions of Israel. Moreover, as will be seen below, the response of those who see the bread miracle is the assertion that Jesus is "the Prophet" and the attempt to make him "king" while the response to his proclamation about living water includes assertions that he is "the Prophet" and that he is "the Christ." Thus, while the cycles of tradition that make up the material of the Fourth Gospel may at some stage have had an order into which chap. 6 fits poorly, there is good ground for supposing that the present order is the work of the evangelist himself.

[3] *Ev. Joh.*, p. 178.

of Jesus' discourses with the two sisters, and of the final plot to kill Jesus ends with this note: "So Jesus no longer went about openly (παρρησίᾳ) among the Jews, but he departed from there to the country near the wilderness, to a town called Ephraim, and there he remained with his disciples" (11.54). Thus Jesus' public teaching and activity are formally concluded.

Jesus' teaching παρρησίᾳ is mentioned in one other significant place: in the trial before the High Priest (18.19-24). The abbreviated Johannine version of this trial has always been puzzling. Missing is the question that is central to each of the synoptic accounts, σὺ εἶ ὁ χριστός;[1] instead there is only the statement that the High Priest interrogated Jesus περὶ τῶν μαθητῶν αὐτοῦ καὶ περὶ τῆς διδαχῆς αὐτοῦ. Since John's passion narrative elsewhere shows essential similarity to the synoptic tradition, it is likely that his source had a reference at this point to ὁ χριστός. Why has John removed this and replaced it by such a seemingly innocuous question? Bultmann argues that the trial before the High Priest has no real significance for the fourth evangelist, who wants to put full emphasis on the trial by the Roman state.[2] Perhaps, however, the question of the High Priest is more significant than it appears at first. Jesus' reply reads, ἐγὼ παρρησίᾳ λελάληκα τῷ κόσμῳ. This "open" speaking by Jesus, now completed (notice the perfect tense!), was exactly the theme found in chapters 7, 8, and 11, above all in 7.14-25. Furthermore, when a question about Jesus' teaching was raised (7.15), he then replied, "If anyone wills to do his [God's] will, he will know concerning the teaching, whether it is from God or whether I speak from myself" (7.17). This is precisely the thrust of Jesus' retort to the High Priest. The teaching, which was "open," not "in secret" (18.20), can be known by the High Priest, but he will receive no further revelation from Jesus. What he lacks is not more information, but the desire to do God's will.

But why is it only about Jesus' disciples and his teaching that the High Priest inquires? If the trial is understood as a case of the "false prophet," then the question is entirely appropriate. Of the false prophet it is required to determine whether he teaches words which have not come from God (Deuteronomy 18.20) and whether

---

[1] Mk 14.61, σὺ εἶ ὁ χριστὸς ὁ υἱὸς τοῦ εὐλογητοῦ; Mt 26.23, εἴπῃς σὺ εἶ ὁ χριστὸς ὁ υἱὸς τοῦ θεοῦ; Lk 22.67, εἰ σὺ εἶ ὁ χριστός, εἰπὸν ἡμῖν.

[2] Ev. Joh., p. 498.

he has "led astray" others (Deuteronomy 13.1-6).[1] If the trial before the High Priest is a trial of Jesus on the charge of being the false prophet, then the two trials deal with exactly the same two questions raised about Jesus in chapter 7: Is he the Prophet? Is he the Christ? The second question is concentrated by the fourth evangelist entirely into the trial before Pilate; only in the place of the title ὁ χριστός stands the one handed down by the earliest tradition of the crucifixion, "the King of the Jews."

TRIAL AND CRUCIFIXION OF THE KING OF THE JEWS
(JOHN 18.28-19.22)

The division of scenes

The movement of Pilate back and forth between the Praetorium and the Jews, an element added to the tradition by the fourth evangelist, serves to divide the second trial into successive scenes.[2] Including the account of the crucifixion and the cross placard (19. 17-22) the narrative has eight clearly marked stages. It will suffice for purposes of this investigation merely to outline these eight stages before going on to examine the elements in each which are directly related to Jesus' kingship. A fuller analysis of the whole sequence may be found in the standard commentaries and the numerous special studies of the Johannine passion.[3]

---

[1] See above, p. 47f. C. H. Dodd (*Historical Tradition*, p. 95) arrives at a similar conclusion by a slightly different argument.

[2] ἐξῆλθεν: 18.29, 38; 19.4; ἤγαγεν ἔξω τὸν Ἰησοῦν 19.13; ἐξῆλθεν [scil. ὁ Ἰησοῦς] εἰς τὸν λεγόμενον κρανίου τόπον 19.17; εἰσῆλθεν 18.33; 19.9, to which must be added Pilate's implied entry at 19.1: ἔλαβεν ὁ Πιλᾶτος τὸν Ἰησοῦν.

[3] I have found the commentaries of Bultmann and Hoskyns most useful. The monograph by Joseph Blinzler, *The Trial of Jesus; The Jewish and Roman Proceedings against Jesus Christ Described and Assessed from the Oldest Accounts* (trans. Isabel and Florence McHugh; Cork: Mercier Press, 1959), 312 pp., is of no value for the present study. Historical in aim, Blinzler's approach is harmonistic and apologetic. Far more reliable is the monograph on the same subject by Paul Winter, *On the Trial of Jesus* ("Studia Judaica," I; Berlin: W. de Gruyter, 1961), 216 pp., although Winter's interest also is mainly historical and thus of little direct relevance here. The articles by Ernst Haenchen, "Jesus vor Pilatus," *ThLZ* 85 (1960), cols. 93-102, and Heinrich Schlier, "Jesus und Pilatus nach dem Johannesevangelium," *Die Zeit der Kirche; Exegetische Aufsätze und Vorträge* (Freiburg i B.: Herder Verlag, 1956), pp. 56-74, are fundamental. But above all the excellent arti-

The eight scenes are as follows:[1]

(1) 18.28-32: Pilate inquires of the Jews about their indictment against Jesus. He receives no clear answer.

(2) 18.33-38a: The dialogue between Pilate and Jesus turns on the fact and nature of Jesus' kingship.

(3) 18.38a-40: Decision is required between Jesus and Barabbas.

(4) 19.1-3: In mockery the Roman soldiers invest Jesus with the insignia of royalty.

(5) 19.4-7: Jesus, still wearing the "royal" paraphernalia, is presented to the Jews with the cry, "Behold the Man!" The Jews demand his crucifixion, on the grounds that "He made himself Son of God."

(6) 19.8-12: Pilate asks Jesus where he is from, but receives no answer. Jesus' cryptic statement about Pilate's authority leads to a new attempt to release him, but the Jews interject the insinuation of treason.

(7) 19.13-16: Pilate presents Jesus to the Jews a second time, installs him on a judge's bench,[2] and proclaims: "Behold your King!" Again the Jews demand his crucifixion, this time asserting, "We have no king but Caesar."

(8) 19.17-22: Jesus is crucified (by "the Jews"?), and Pilate affixes a *titulus* to the cross proclaiming in three languages that he is "King of the Jews." The "high priests of the Jews" object, but Pilate refuses to alter the inscription.

Even this cursory outline reveals the remarkable extent to which Jesus' kingship stands at the center of the whole progression. It is this element which must now be more carefully examined.

---

cles by Josef Blank, "Die Verhandlung vor Pilatus Jo 18, 28-19, 16 im Lichte johanneischer Theologie," *Biblische Zeitschrift*, n.s., 3 (1959), 60-81, and I. de la Potterie, "Jésus Roi et Juge d'après Jn 19, 13; Ἐκάθισεν ἐπὶ βήματος," *Biblica* 41 (1960), 117-147 (English translation, slightly abbreviated, "Jesus King and Judge according to John 19.13," *Scripture* 13 [1961], 97-111), have confirmed and enriched my own analysis of the distinctive Johannine motifs in the trial and crucifixion.

[1] The first seven correspond closely to the six delineated by Bultmann, *Ev. Joh.*, p. 501. He combines my fourth (19.1-3) and fifth (19.4-7) into one. They are closely connected, but the change of place, (ἐξῆλθεν, v.4) shows that two stages are intended. Cf. Blank, p. 61, and Karl Kundsin, *Topologische Überlieferungsstoffe im Johannes-Evangelium* (FRLANT, n.s. XXII; 1925), pp. 41f.

[2] For justification of this statement, see below, pp. 73-76.

The King of the Jews

The dialogue with Pilate (18.33-38a)

Pilate's question, "Are you the King of the Jews?" (verse 33) belongs to the traditional account of the Passion,[1] but the following dialogue (verses 34-38) is the evangelist's formulation. Jesus' counter question to Pilate, "Do you say this of yourself (ἀφ' ἑαυτοῦ) or did others tell you about me?" is striking because of the appearance of the formula ἀφ' ἑαυτοῦ. Elsewhere in the Fourth Gospel this phrase points to the divine origin of revelation through one who, consciously or unconsciously, is a prophet.[2] It is not impossible that a *double-entendre* is present here comparable to that of 11.50f. As the High Priest unwittingly prophesied Jesus' vicarious death, so in the irony of the Johannine Passion Pilate repeatedly proclaims Jesus' kingship. If this is so, then Pilate's retort is doubly ironic. His information is not "from himself," but also not—so far as he knows—from God: it is from "the Jews." The form of his retort is significant: "Am I a Jew?" This is just the question posed by the trial situation, for "the Jews" represent in John the disbelieving world, the world seeking to be rid of the Redeemer.[3] Does Pilate belong to the world that rejects Jesus? Grammatically his question expects a negative answer; the development of the trial, however, places him step by step at the disposal of "the Jews."

The following verses (36f.) contain the only direct statements in the Fourth Gospel on the nature of Jesus' kingship. The first statement defines Jesus' kingship negatively: "My kingship is not of this world"; the second, positively: "You say that I am a king: for this purpose I have been born and for this purpose I have come into the world, to testify to the truth."

The phrase οὐκ . . . ἐκ τοῦ κόσμου τούτου must be understood first of all as a genitive of origin. Jesus' kingship does not derive from the world, but from God. The opposite of ἐκ τοῦ κόσμου τούτου is ἐκ τῶν ἄνω (8.23), which means ἐκ τοῦ θεοῦ.[4] The origin of Jesus' kingship corresponds to his own origin. Since it does not originate in the world, it is not established by worldly power (18.36b), but

---

[1] Mk. 15.2; Mt. 27.11; Lk. 23.3.
[2] See above, pp. 45-47.
[3] Bultmann, *Ev. Joh.*, pp. 59f.
[4] Cf. 16.28; also 3.31; 8.42, 47. In the latter two passages the genitive of relationship is also to be understood.

only by the power of God. From those who seek to make Jesus king by force (ἁρπάζειν) he flees (6.15).

Nevertheless, Jesus' kingship is not "unworldly." Instead one of the characteristics of the Johannine treatment of the trial and the events that lead up to it is that the *political* implications are emphasized. In 11.48 a specifically political motivation is injected into the plotting of the Jewish authorities.[1] John alone mentions the presence of Roman soldiers (ἡ . . . σπεῖρα καὶ ὁ χιλίαρχος) at the arrest of Jesus.[2] In the trial itself, the political-realistic element is introduced by the Jews at 19.12: "If you release this man you are not Caesar's friend; anyone who makes himself a king opposes Caesar." The climactic rejection of Jesus by the Jews is the statement "We have no king but Caesar," in which the "religious" and "political" questions are shown to be inextricably merged. Hence, while the Christian community's precarious relation to the Empire at the end of the first century has doubtless influenced the Johannine form of the trial, it is not quite accurate to call the narrative apologetic. It is certainly not true that the trial scene provides a model by which the Christians can readily show "that they are not seditious."[3] On the contrary, what the trial suggests is that the disciple will always have to decide *vis à vis* the Empire whether Jesus is his king or whether Caesar is.[4]

---

[1] There is no reason to agree with Winter, p. 38, that only the theological interpretation of 11.51 fits the evangelist's purpose, while "the words of the high-priest as recorded in vv. 48, 50 [ascribed by Winter to a source] were felt to be too harsh, too realistic, to be reconciled by the author with his own understanding of the events." Winter's view apparently stems from the prevalent but outdated notion that Jn. is a "spiritual" or "mystical" gospel. He ignores Jn's use of the double meaning as a literary device.

[2] Cf. Bultmann, *Ev. Joh.*, p. 493.

[3] Hoskyns, p. 521; cf. Barrett, p. 447.

[4] An excellent example is provided by *Mart. Polyc.* 9.3, which perhaps alludes to Jn. 19.12-15. Pressed by the Proconsul to "swear by the τύχη of Caesar," Polycarp declares, "For eighty-six years I have served [Jesus], and he has not wronged me. How can I blaspheme my King who saved me (τὸν βασιλέα μου τὸν σώσαντά με)?" Quite different is the understanding of Jesus kingship in the report by Hegesippus of the trial of Jesus' relatives by Domitian: "Questioned about the Christ and his Kingdom— what kind it was and from where and at what time it appeared— they explained that it was neither worldly (κοσμική) nor earthly (ἐπίγειος) but heavenly and angelic, and that it would be at the completion of the ages, when he would come in glory and judge living and dead and repay each according to his practices." That such an *unworldly* (οὐ κοσμική) interpretation could be useful is shown by the result: "At that, Domitian did not condemn them at all, . . . but set them free and stopped the persecution of the church by decree" (*apud*

Moreover, the decision is pressed not only upon "the Jews" but even upon the Procurator, as 18.37-38a indicate. The positive statement of Jesus' kingship defines it in terms of his mission: he has come to testify to the truth. But, as always in the Fourth Gospel, the manifestation of the truth is itself a κρίσις which exposes the position of men with respect to the truth. Thus Jesus adds, "Every one who is of the truth hears my voice."

Here again the trial brings to a climax motifs which have been developed throughout the gospel. In 3.31-36 the μαρτυρία of the one who comes "from above" is identified with God's own words. This μαρτυρία is generally rejected, but anyone who receives it confirms that God is true (verses 32f.). Upon this decision depends the judgment: either ζωὴ αἰώνιος or ἡ ὀργὴ τοῦ θεοῦ (verse 36). The same connection between Jesus' testimony and judgment is found in 5.24-30. Even more clearly μαρτυρία and κρίσις are interrelated in 8.12-20, a passage which picks up the theme of 5.31-41, that Jesus does not testify to himself. Here the two parallel concessive sentences 8.14 and 16 are significant:

$$\text{κἂν ἐγὼ μαρτυρῶ περὶ ἐμαυτοῦ,}$$
$$\text{ἀληθής ἐστιν ἡ μαρτυρία μου . . .}$$

$$\text{καὶ ἐὰν κρίνω δὲ ἐγώ,}$$
$$\text{ἡ κρίσις ἡ ἐμὴ ἀληθινή ἐστιν . . .}$$

The parallelism indicates that μαρτυρία and μαρτυρεῖν are forensic terms in the Fourth Gospel. On good grounds several scholars have proposed that the literary structure of the whole gospel suggests an extended court process between God and the world.[1] The "case"

Eusebius, *HE*, III, xx, 4-5). Somewhat differently Justin (*Apol.* I, 11) also interprets the kingdom which Christians await (προσδοκᾶν) as one that is "with God" (μετὰ θεοῦ), not a "human kingdom" (ἀνθρώπινον βασιλείαν). Both the conversation reported by Hegesippus and the argument of Justin illustrate the apologetic use of a notion of Jesus' "unworldly" kingship in the framework of a futurist eschatology. In this view conflict between Jesus' kingship and that of Caesar could arise only out of misunderstanding or deliberate malice. But this view is very far from that of the Fourth Gospel. Cf. Günther Bornkamm, *Jesus of Nazareth* (tr. Irene and Fraser McLuskey with James M. Robinson; New York: Harper & Brothers, 1960), p. 123, n. 33.

[1] Bultmann, *Ev. Joh.*, pp. 58f., to a certain extent corrected by Schlier, *passim*; cf. Blank, p. 64; N. A. Dahl, "The Johannine Church and History," *Current Issues in New Testament Interpretation*, ed. William Klassen and Graydon F. Snyder (New York: Harper & Brothers, 1962), pp. 139-141; Ch. Masson, "Le témoignage de Jean," *RThP* 38 (1950), 121, quoted by Pottérie, *Biblica* 41, p. 246. The notion is developed independently and with

unfolds in the controversies between Jesus and "the Jews" and climaxes in the trial before Pilate.

The controversy of 8.30-59 between Jesus and the disbelievers who claim first to be sons of Abraham (verse 33), then sons of God (verse 41), shows that their true "paternity" is exposed by their inability to hear Jesus' words. Only one who becomes truly Jesus' disciple by "abiding" in his word is able to know the truth (verse 32). The opponents do not know what Jesus says because they cannot hear his word (verse 43). They cannot hear the word of him who speaks the truth (verse 46) because they are the sons of the Devil (or, of Cain, whose father is the Devil: verse 44),[1] who is a ψεύστης. "For this reason you cannot hear: because you are not of God" (verse 47).

Of all the parallels to the words "He who is of the truth hears my voice" (18.37), perhaps the most significant is the call of the "Good Shepherd" and the response of the "sheep" (chapter 10). Unlike the "thieves and robbers," the shepherd enters by the proper "door," and "the sheep hear his voice" (10.3). He goes before them, "and the sheep follow him, because they know his voice" (verse 4). The voice of the "thieves and robbers" the sheep did not hear (verse 8). The sheep of the "other fold" will also hear Jesus' voice (verse 16). As before, this "hearing" of Jesus' voice is the means of entering life:

> My sheep hear my voice, and I know them, and they follow me, and I give to them eternal life, and they will never be lost, and no one will snatch them out of my hand. [verses 27-28]

On the other hand, the inability to hear Jesus' voice is characteristic of those who reject him and thus are excluded from eternal life. In 10.20, where one of the characteristic σχίσματα is described, those who, like the opponents in 8.30-59, regard Jesus as a demoniac ask, τί αὐτοῦ ἀκούετε;—a question very similar to that put in the mouth of the disciples who "take offense" at Jesus (6.60): τίς δύναται αὐτοῦ ἀκούειν;

---

particular insight by Théo Preiss, "Justification in Johannine Thought," in *Life in Christ*, trans. Harold Knight ("Studies in Biblical Theology," No. 13; Chicago: Alec R. Allenson, Inc., 1954), pp. 9-31 (original in *Homage et Reconnaissance*, 1946).

[1] Cf. Dahl, *Norsk Teologisk Tidskrift* 64, pp. 129ff. Also John Bowman, "Samaritan Studies," *BJRL*, 40 (1958), 304f., n. 4, and José Ramón Díaz, "Palestinian Targum and New Testament," *Novum Testamentum* (1963), 79f.

Against this background Pilate's reply. "What is truth?" takes on new significance. It is no philosophical rejoinder nor the quip of a cynical pragmatist, but only serves the evangelist's purpose to show that Pilate is not "of the truth." Therefore he does not "hear" Jesus' voice. Pilate does not belong to the "flock" of the Good Shepherd, but to the sons of the Devil (or Cain) who seek to kill the messenger of God. Pilate's own question (verse 35) has thus been answered affirmatively: he has joined "the Jews," the disbelieving world that rejects its saviour.

The weight which the Fourth Gospel places on "hearing Jesus' voice" recalls again the figure of the prophet like Moses, for in Deuteronomy 18.15 Moses says: "The Lord your God will raise up for you a prophet like me . . .; him you shall heed (αὐτοῦ ἀκούσεσθε)." Furthermore, the prophet's words are identified with God's own words, just as Jesus' words are throughout the Fourth Gospel.[1] Finally, divine judgment hangs upon whether one hears the prophet's words in Deuteronomy 18.19, just as it depends on hearing Jesus' words in John. Yet Jesus' testimony and the "hearing of his voice" are explicitly connected with his *kingship* in John 18.37 and with the image of the Good Shepherd in chapter 10. In both cases kingship and prophecy are intimately joined. More precisely, the function of the king is absorbed almost completely into the mission of the prophet. This is true no less in the discourse on the Good Shepherd than in the statement about Jesus' βασιλεία, for the Shepherd is surely a royal figure —as so frequently in ancient Near Eastern, classical Greek, Hellenistic, and Old Testament sources.[2] Bultmann's objection that "every feature of a royal figure is lacking" in John 10[3] could just as well be applied to Jesus' βασιλεία according to 18.37. In both passages —and in the whole Fourth Gospel —kingship is being radically redefined. The remarkable thing is that it is being redefined in terms of the mission of the prophet.

Choice between the King and the ληστής *(18.38b-40)*

The content of the third scene of the trial is traditional; both Pilate's question, "Do you want me to release to you the King of

---

[1] Cf., besides the passages just cited, the discussion above, pp. 45f.

[2] In Chapter VII below the figure of the Good Shepherd will be examined more carefully in the light of the numerous parallels to be found in the literature which will be surveyed in the second stage of this investigation.

[3] *Ev. Joh.*, p. 279.

the Jews?" and the response of the crowd, "They cried out again, 'Not him, but Barabbas,'" were taken over by the evangelist, probably from a written source.[1] John, however, has added one comment which introduces an important nuance: ἦν δὲ ὁ Βαραββᾶς λῃστής. Nowhere else in the passion tradition is Barabbas called a λῃστής. But in John 10 the λῃστής is a figure contrasted with the Good Shepherd:

10.1: ὁ μὴ εἰσερχόμενος διὰ τῆς θύρας . . . , ἐκεῖνος κλέπτης ἐστὶν καὶ λῃστής· ὁ δὲ εἰσερχόμενος διὰ τῆς θύρας ποιμήν ἐστιν τῶν προβάτων.
10.8: πάντες ὅσοι ἦλθον πρὸ ἐμοῦ κλέπται εἰσὶν καὶ λῃσταί· ἀλλ' οὐκ ἤκουσαν αὐτῶν τὰ πρόβατα.

The meaning of John 18.40 is clear: the Jews reject their king and choose instead a λῃστής; unable to hear the voice of the Good Shepherd, they follow one of the "robbers" who comes before him.

This scene and the preceding one are thus parallel, and both related to the discourse on the Good Shepherd. In the previous scene Pilate, in this scene the Jews, show that they are not of the flock of the Good Shepherd, not the subjects of the king whose kingship consists in his testimony to the truth. At this point it is well to recall that in chapter 10 what distinguishes the Good Shepherd from other shepherds, that is, what characterizes him as the *Good* Shepherd, is not only his call, but also the fact that he "lays down his life for the sheep" (10.11, 15, 17).[2] But that is also a distinguishing characteristic of Jesus' kingship, as the whole development of the passion narrative shows: he reigns from the cross.

Mock investiture of the King (19.1-3)

The content of this scene is also traditional, although the Johannine version is abbreviated in comparison with that in Mark and Matthew. In the synoptic version, it is explicitly stated that the

---

[1] Mk. 15.9, θέλετε ἀπολύσω ὑμῖν τὸν βασιλέα τῶν Ἰουδαίων; Jn. 18.39, βούλεσθε οὖν ἀπολύσω ὑμῖν τὸν βασιλέα τῶν Ἰουδαίων; Mk. 15.13, οἱ δὲ πάλιν ἔκραξαν; Jn. 18.40, ἐκραύγασαν οὖν πάλιν λέγοντος; cf. Bultmann, *Ev. Joh.*, p. 502.

[2] Paul W. Meyer has shown that the θύρα in Jn. 10.1-18 also symbolizes Jesus' death. My exegesis extends and corroborates his insight that in Jn. 10 (I would add now: also in Jn. 18) "a legitimate claim to be a shepherd rather than thief must rest on legitimate entry– via death" ("A Note on John 10. 1-18," *JBL*, 75 [1956], 234).

clothing of Jesus in the vestments of royalty was part of the "mocking" of the soldiers (Mark 15.20; Matthew 27.31). Luke separates the two in order to construct the new scene with Herod (23.6-12; cf. 22.63f.); in his version all the specifically royal elements of the scene are lost. Potterie points out that "John leaves out several details given in the synoptic accounts, but retains precisely those which serve to emphasize the royal dignity of Jesus: the crown of thorns, the purple garment and the words of the soldiers: 'Hail king of the Jews.'"[1] That the soldiers were *mocking* Jesus is not explicitly stated in John.

In addition, the fourth evangelist has shifted the position of the scene. In the Marcan account Jesus is mocked as "king of the Jews" after he has been condemned as pretender to that title. If the scene is historical, then this is the only point in the sequence of events where it could reasonably have occurred.[2] But in the Fourth Gospel the investiture of Jesus comes near the beginning of the procedure, immediately after the Barabbas episode and immediately before Jesus is first presented to the Jews by Pilate. The rearrangement is hardly accidental. In the Johannine version Jesus, while still inside the Praetorium, is clad in the garb and crown of a king, which he wears throughout the rest of the proceedings as he is twice presented to the Jews with solemn proclamation (19.5, 13f.). In contrast to the synoptic accounts (Mark 15.20; Matthew 27.31) there is no indication in John that the purple robe was removed before the actual crucifixion. In John the scene is not the satirical aftermath of Jesus' condemnation, but the prelude to his paradoxical exaltation.

The first throne name (19.4-7)

The ensuing scene is a close parallel to 19.13-16. In each case Pilate leads Jesus out, wearing the acanthus garland and the purple robe, and presents him to the waiting Jews. In each case the presentation is accompanied by a solemn proclamation, and the two proclamations are precisely parallel: ἰδοὺ ὁ ἄνθρωπος (verse 5); ἴδε ὁ βασιλεὺς ὑμῶν (verse 14). In each case the Jews respond in similar fashion: σταύρωσον σταύρωσον (verse 6); ἆρον ἆρον, σταύρωσον αὐτόν (verse 15).[3] In terms of the theological content of the trial

---

[1] *Scripture*, 13, p. 106 (*Biblica*, 41, p. 239).
[2] Cf. Winter, pp. 102-105.
[3] Cf. Bultmann, *Ev. Joh.*, pp. 501f.; Potterie, *Biblica* 41, p. 239f.; Corssen, "'Εκάθισεν ἐπὶ βήματος," *ZNW* 15 (1914), 340.

narrative it may be true, as Bultmann argues, that the emphasis lies on the two scenes in which Jesus and Pilate are alone in conversation.[1] But in terms of the literary structure itself the presentations of Jesus and the proclamations are the twin climaxes of the whole trial. It is not at all far-fetched to speak, as Blank does, of a "king's epiphany," preceded by "inthronement and investitute" and greeted by the deeply ironic "king's acclamation" by the people.[2]

Once the parallelism between the two presentation scenes is recognized, it is remarkable that the majority of commentators see in ὁ ἄνθρωπος only a sarcastic or ironic reference to Jesus' humanity, intended to awaken sympathy[3] or to demonstrate the ridiculousness of the kingship claim and Jesus' harmlessness[4] or, in addition to the latter, to express the ultimate extent of the paradox that "the word became flesh."[5] The dramatic structure of the two scenes only makes sense if "the Man" is understood as a title, a throne-name given to the "King of the Jews." Hence Dodd and Blank are probably on the right track when they suggest that the title alludes to the "Son of Man."[6] In addition Blank observes that in 5.27 it is precisely the Son of Man to whom *judgment* is given.[7] Barrett is more precise: "ὁ ἄνθρωπος calls to mind those Jewish and Hellenistic myths of the heavenly or primal Man which lie behind John's use of the phrase υἱὸς τοῦ ἀνθρώπου . . ."[8]

There is evidence that "Man" was an eschatological title at least in Hellenistic Judaism. Chiefly certain alterations in the Septuagint in comparison with the Masoretic text point in this direction. A

---

[1] *Ev. Joh.*, p. 502.

[2] Blank, p. 62.

[3] H. A. W. Meyer, p. 617.

[4] Zahn, p. 638; Wikenhauser, p. 327; Blinzler, p. 229; cf. Hoskyns, p. 523.

[5] Bultmann, *Ev. Joh.*, p. 510.

[6] Dodd, p. 437; Blank, p. 75 and n. 38. Blank overlooks the prior suggestions by Dodd and Barrett. Moreover his main reason for finding in ὁ ἄνθρωπος a "reminiscence of the Son of Man title" is faulty. He argues that there is a progression of titles in the trial, from "King of the Jews" (18.33, 39; 19.3) to "Man" (19.5) to "Son of God" (19.7), and that "ein höherer Titel als der Messias-Titel könnte zunächst nur der Menschensohn-Titel sein" (*ibid.*). But the progression is incorrect, since the narrative does not end with 19.7, but goes on to emphasize the "King of the Jews" title. If anything, it is "King of the Jews" that supersedes "Anthropos," not *vice versa!* Cf. Potterie, *Biblica* 41, p. 239.

[7] N.b. ὅτι, Blank, p. 75.

[8] Barrett, p. 450.

striking, if perhaps accidental, parallel to John 19.5 is found in Zechariah 6.12.[1] The context is the command of God to Zechariah to crown Joshua the High Priest as king. Originally the passage described the symbolic coronation of Zerubbabel as future king,[2] but his name was effaced, presumably before the passage was translated into Greek. The divine proclamation which Zechariah is directed to speak to Joshua (Zerubbabel) reads: ἰδοὺ ἀνήρ, Ἀνατολὴ ὄνομα αὐτῷ, καὶ ὑποκάτωθεν αὐτοῦ ἀνατελεῖ, καὶ οἰκοδομήσει τὸν οἶκον κυρίου κτλ. Originally this passage may have carried no eschatological meaning,[3] but it lent itself to eschatological interpretation. The Hebrew already contained an allusion to the fundamental text of Davidic messianology, 2 Samuel 7.12-16 ("He will build a house for my name," verse 13). The Greek version is more suggestive. In place of the original throne-name "Shoot" (צמח)—which itself became in some circles a messianic title[4]—the Septuagint has Ἀνατολή, and the original play on the name in the following verb (Hebrew: יצמח) is preserved in the Greek (ἀνατελεῖ). But this must be connected in some way with the peculiar alteration of Numbers 24.17, which reads:

ἀνατελεῖ [for Heb. דרך] ἄστρον ἐξ Ἰακὼβ
καὶ ἀναστήσεται ἄνθρωπος [Heb. שבט!] ἐξ Ἰσραήλ.

The insertion of ἄνθρωπος without any basis in the Hebrew is also the most conspicuous feature of the Greek version of Numbers 24.7, which differs in other respects as well from the Masoretic text. The latter passage is quoted by Philo in a description of the eschatological warfare between Israel and recalcitrant members of the rest of mankind—the only clearly eschatological passage in all Philo's writings.[5] Numbers 24.17 is interpreted eschatologically in the

---

[1] The passage is cited but not discussed by Bauer, p. 212.

[2] Cf. Karl Marti, *Das Dodekapropheton* ("Kurzer Hand-Kommentar zum A.T.," ed. Karl Marti, *et al.*, XIII; Tübingen: J. C. B. Mohr [Paul Siebeck], 1904), pp. 420f.; (Theodore H. Robinson and) Friedrich Horst, *Die Zwölf Kleinen Propheten* ("Handbuch zum Alten Testament," ed. O. Eissfeldt, XIV; Tübingen: J. C. B. Mohr [Paul Siebeck], 1954), pp. 237-239; Karl Elliger, *Das Buch der zwölf kleinen Propheten* (ATD, XXV; 1950), pp. 119-123.

[3] Yet see Elliger, pp. 121f.

[4] In the Qumran texts: 4Q PB 3; 4Q Fl 1.11.

[5] ἐξελεύσεται γὰρ ἄνθρωπος, φησὶν ὁ χρησμός, καὶ στραταρχῶν καὶ πολεμῶν ἔθνη μεγάλα καὶ πολυάνθρωπα χειρώσεται (*Praem.* 95).

Testament of Judah 24.1,[1] and several times in the Qumran texts,[2] but in the latter in the form known in the Masoretic text. "Scepter" (שבט) not "Man," is the title derived from the passage at Qumran.[3]

An investigation into all the evidence for the expectation of an eschatological Ἄνθρωπος lies far beyond the scope of this inquiry.[4] However the instances which have been cited from Jewish documents alone are sufficient to support the contention that Pilate's announcement, "Behold the Man!" is to be understood as the proclamation of a title. John 19.4-5 depicts a significant stage in the installation of the eschatological king.[5]

Final dialogue with Pilate (19.8-12)

The next scene does not concern Jesus' kingship primarily, but the assertion that "he makes himself Son of God" (verse 7b). This title, whatever its background, for the fourth evangelist is clearly an established part of Christian terminology. As it is introduced into this context by an accusation of "the Jews," so also a "Jewish" accusation provides the transition back to the title "king" (verse 12). Both titles are found together in the confession of Nathanael (1.49); elsewhere in the gospel they do not appear to be connected.

The mention of the title "Son of God" is made to motivate Pilate's fear and his question, πόθεν εἶ σύ; a question that has formed a major theme of the gospel.[6] The reader knows that the

---

[1] καὶ μετὰ ταῦτα ἀνατελεῖ ὑμῖν ἐξ Ἰακὼβ ἐν εἰρήνῃ, καὶ ἀναστήσεται ἄνθρωπος ἐκ τοῦ σπέρματός μου ὡς ἥλιος δικαιοσύνης. Test. Naph. 4.5. speaks of an eschatological ἄνθρωπος ποιῶν δικαιοσύνην καὶ ποιῶν ἔλεος, who is also called τὸ σπλάγχνον Κυρίου, but probably ἄνθρωπος carries no extraordinary meaning here. Cf. Van der Woude, p. 93.

[2] 4Q Test 12; CD VII, 18-20; 1Q M XI, 6; cf. 1Q Sb V, 27f.

[3] On the interpretation of these passages see Van der Woude, pp. 44, 53f., 207-209.

[4] In this connection the essay by Geza Vermes in Scripture and Tradition in Judaism ("Studia Post-Biblica," ed. P. A. H. DeBoer, et al., IV; Leiden: E. J. Brill, 1961), pp. 56-66, is suggestive, but only preliminary. The application of the title "man" in one form or another to Moses is noted in several kinds of tradition in the following chapters, but a very extensive investigation would be required to discover the significance of this fact.

[5] Perhaps it is significant that in the parable of judgment Mt. 25.31-46 both the titles "Son of Man" and "King" are applied to the judge, whose action is compared with that of a shepherd. "King" and "shepherd" certainly belonged to pre-Matthean tradition, perhaps in the beginning a Jewish parable applied not to the messianic king, but to God. The title "Son of Man" was probably added at a later stage. Cf. Bultmann, Geschichte, pp. 130f.

[6] See above, p. 38.

correct answer is ἐκ τοῦ θεοῦ. Pilate, however, receives no answer (verse 9); the time when he could hear Jesus' testimony to the truth is past (18.38). Nevertheless, the answer is implicit in the ἄνωθεν of the subsequent statement about Pilate's authority.

It is not quite clear how the transition to the next scene is to be visualized, since Pilate's exchange with the Jews bridges both the scene inside and that outside the Praetorium. However, it is typical of the Fourth Gospel that the progression of the argument often violates rules of verisimilitude, and the sequence of thought here is relatively clear. Jesus' pregnant and somewhat cryptic statement of the limits of Pilate's power motivates (ἐκ τούτου) Pilate's third attempt to release him. The attempt is countered by "the Jews," who assert for the first time that Jesus' kingship stands in opposition to that of Caesar. Behind this statement must lie much more than just the recollection that Jesus was crucified as an alleged king-pretender. Implicit is not only the conflict between church and empire, reflected in the similar significant but isolated note in Acts 17.7,[1] but also evidently the fruit of Christian reflection on the universality of Jesus' kingship. In the structure of the passage mention of βασιλεύς provides the occasion for the next scene, in which Jesus is presented for the second time as the king of the Jews.

The enthronement and second throne name (19.13-16)

The final stage of the trial depicts the second public presentation of Jesus as king and his rejection. The symbolic description of this action has long been the subject of debate, since ἐκάθισεν can be understood either transitively or intransitively. Parallel accounts increase the perplexity. Of the synoptics only Matthew mentions the tribunal (βῆμα) in the context of the legend of Pilate's wife (27. 19). There καθίζειν is used in the middle voice; it is Pilate who seats himself on the tribunal.[2] In both the Apology of Justin and the Gospel of Peter, however, it is stated that "they [the soldiers] seated Jesus upon a tribunal [Gospel of Peter: 'judgment seat'], and said, 'Judge us!' [Gospel of Peter: 'Judge justly, King of Israel!']."[3]

---

[1] οὗτοι πάντες ἀπέναντι τῶν δογμάτων Καίσαρος πράσσουσιν, βασιλέα ἕτερον λέγοντες εἶναι τὸν Ἰησοῦν. Cf. above, pp. 63f.

[2] καθημένου δὲ αὐτοῦ ἐπὶ βήματος ἀπέστειλεν πρὸς αὐτὸν ἡ γυνὴ αὐτοῦ κτλ.

[3] Justin, *Apol.* I, 35: καὶ γὰρ, ὡς εἶπεν ὁ προφήτης, διασύροντες αὐτόν, ἐκάθισαν ἐπὶ βήματος, καὶ εἶπον· κρίνον ἡμᾶς. *Gosp. Peter* (ed. Harnack), v. 7: καὶ πορφύραν αὐτὸν περιέβαλον καὶ ἐκάθισαν αὐτὸν ἐπὶ καθέδραν κρίσεως λέγοντες· δικαίως κρῖνε, βασιλεῦ τοῦ Ἰσραήλ.

Justin and the author of the apocryphal gospel did not make use of
John 19.13 in its present form, since in their version the seating of
Jesus on the tribunal is part of the mocking by soldiers. Since the
tendency of the fourth evangelist is to expand the tradition and to
separate and rearrange the various elements into distinct stages,
the version of Justin and the Gospel of Peter probably preserves in
this detail the more nearly original form of the tradition. On the
basis of this observation Harnack, following a suggestion by
Westcott, proposed that ἐκάθισεν in John 19.13 ought also to be
read transitively.[1] In a very brief article in 1914 Paul Corssen
developed Harnack's proposal further by showing (1) that from
known examples of Roman criminal proceedings there was no *more*
verisimilitude in the view that Pilate seated himself on the tribunal
only at the very end of the trial than in the admittedly improbable
view that he seated Jesus there and (2) that the literary structure
of the trial scene accorded better with the latter view.[2]

The view of Harnack and Corssen received little acceptance.
Bultmann objects on philological grounds, urging that the direct
object would have to be expressed.[3] To Hoskyns the proposed
symbolism seemed "an unnecessary subtlety."[4] Barrett, seeking to
make the most of both sides, thinks that the meaning is deliberately ambiguous: "in fact," Pilate sat on the tribunal, but "for
those with eyes to see," the Son of Man was enthroned.[5]

Now, however, the brilliant essay of Potterie lends strong support
to the transitive interpretation. The great merit of Potterie's work
is that he combines thorough philological investigation with a sure
grasp of the theological motifs in the trial scene. He correctly rejects
the proposal by Barrett and others of deliberate ambiguity, since
the statements with double meaning elsewhere in John never depend
upon *grammatical* ambiguity.[6] Then Potterie advances three philological arguments, of which the second is by far the strongest. First,
he urges that εἰς τόπον requires a verb of motion, since John, unlike
some New Testament and other Hellenistic authors, does not con-
fuse εἰς and ἐν. The required verb of motion must be ἤγαγεν, but

---

[1] Adolf von Harnack, *Bruchstücke des Evangeliums und der Apokalypse des
Petrus* (2d ed.; Leipzig: J. C. Hinrichs'sche Buchhandlung, 1893), pp. 63f.

[2] *ZNW* 15 (1914), 338-340.

[3] *Ev. Joh.*, p. 514, n. 2.

[4] Hoskyns, p. 524.

[5] Barrett, p. 452.

[6] *Biblica* 41, p. 218 and n. 2.

THEMATIC FUNCTIONS OF PROPHET AND KING IN JOHN

unless ἐκάθισεν is understood as transitive, so that the two verbs
are taken together, an awkward interruption results in the flow of
thought.[1] This is the weakest of Potterie's arguments, since καθίζειν
is very frequently used pregnantly with εἰς and the accusative not
only in Hellenistic Greek but already in classical poetry.[2] Nevertheless, the pregnant sense of καθίζειν would be very much reinforced if it had the same object as ἤγαγεν. The second argument is
decisive. Potterie shows that according to Johannine usage the
position of the complement τὸν Ἰησοῦν *between* the two verbs
indicates that it is the object of both. This is also the case in the
Codex Bezae reading of Acts 2.30 and in Ephesians 1.20, the only
places where καθίζειν is clearly transitive in the New Testament.[3]
Finally, Potterie finds significance in the fact that βήματος is anarthrous. In Hellenistic texts καθίζειν ἐπὶ βήματος expresses the nuance
either (a) that the βῆμα is not the usual one or (b) that the nature
of the action is stressed: to act as judge (intransitive) or to install
as judge (transitive). Neither would fit Pilate if the verb were
intransitive.[4]

The objections to the transitive interpretation on the basis of
psychological and historical probability[5] are quickly disposed of by
Potterie.[6] Actually, once it is recognized that there is no evidence
at all in the Johannine account for a concern to relate the factual
or probable occurrences as such, these objections become irrelevant.
The fourth evangelist is manifestly recounting not what Pilate
would probably have done in the given circumstances, but what the
Christian understands God to have done. Potterie is aware of the
theologically oriented structure of the narrative, and his analysis
of it offers the final support for the transitive understanding of
ἐκάθισεν. The central theological content of the trial narrative in
John is not Jesus' condemnation, as would be expected if it were
Pilate who, at the climatic moment, were seated on the tribunal,

---

[1] *Ibid.*, pp. 221f.
[2] This is the case in 2 Thess. 2.4, ὥστε αὐτὸν εἰς τὸν ναὸν τοῦ θεοῦ καθίσαι,
where καθίσαι is intransitive. Cf. Raphael Kühner and Bernhard Gerth, *Ausführliche Grammatik des griechischen Sprache* (2d part: *Satzlehre*; München:
Max Hueber Verlag, 1904, rp. 1963), I, 543 (§447B) and pp. 313f (§410),
n. 13.
[3] *Biblica* 41, pp. 223-225.
[4] *Ibid.*, pp. 226-233.
[5] Cf. Blinzler, p. 237, n. 3.
[6] Potterie, *Biblica* 41, pp. 233-236.

but Jesus' kingship and his role as judge of the Jews.[1] Nothing needs to be added to this conclusion except the observation that not just the Jews are judged by Jesus, but also Pilate himself and indeed the world.[2]

The enthronement of a king is followed normally by an acclamation by his subjects. In John 19.15 the acclamation is replaced by the words ἆρον ἆρον, σταύρωσον αὐτόν. The evangelist underlines the irony of the rejection in the words of Pilate, "Shall I crucify your *king?*" and the reiterated and now absolute statement of rejection, "We have no king but Caesar." This last statement brings to its fullest expression the political theme which has been observed at several points in the Johannine trial and the preceding narratives, but at the same time it shows that the political element in Jesus' kingship cannot be separated from its religious significance. The high priests' denial expresses *in nuce* the tragic irony of the entire trial: in rejecting Jesus as "King of the Jews" for political expediency, "the Jews" reject the eschatological king toward whom their highest hopes were directed. Rejecting the "King of the Jews," "the Jews" cease to be "Israel," the special people of God, and become only one of the ἔθνη subject to Caesar.

This ironic import of the response is commonly recognized by commentators. But something more is here. It is not by accident that the evangelist carefully fixes the precise moment of Jesus' enthronement as king at the sixth hour on the Eve of Passover (verse 14), that is, at the hour at which the actual observation of the Passover regulations must begin.[3] Passover allusions abound in

---

[1] *Ibid.*, pp. 238-242. "En effet, les circonstances solennelles dont nous venons de parler [the day, the pascal setting, the time, the place] introduisent non pas la sentence judiciaire de Pilate, mais sa déclaration: 'voila votre roi'" (p. 237).

[2] Cf. above, pp. 65-67. N.b. 12.31, νῦν κρίσις ἐστὶν τοῦ κόσμου τούτου, and 16.11, ὁ ἄρχων τοῦ κόσμου τούτου κέκριται. Does Pilate represent the "ruler of this world"? In certain traditions of Judaism Sammael, the "head of all the Satans" (*Debarim R.* 11.9) is the "Prince of Rome" (*Seder Ruhot*, in Jellinek, *Bet ha-Midrasch*, V, 179). Cited by Ginzberg, V, 164, cf. 311f. Cf. Odeberg, p. 45.

[3] According to Mishnah *Pes.*, 1.5-6, all ḥameṣ (leavened grain products) must be burned at the beginning of the sixth hour of the 14th Nisan. The assumption that the purpose of the note of time in Jn. 19.14 is to indicate that Jesus' death was simultaneous with the sacrifice of the passover lambs (Barrett, p. 454; Bultmann, p. 514, n. 5; Hoskyns, p. 525) is not satisfactory; it is not the time of Jesus' death, but of his enthronement as king and judge that is specifically stated (cf. Potterie, *Biblica* 41, pp. 244f.).

the Fourth Gospel,[1] and 19.36 in its present form indicates that Jesus is identified with the passover lamb, whose bones are not to be broken.[2] But anyone familiar with the Passover Haggadah cannot fail to be reminded by the cry of the high priests, "We have no king but Caesar," of the *Nišmat*, the hymn sung at the conclusion of the Greater Hallel:

> From everlasting to everlasting thou art God;
> Beside thee we have no king, redeemer, or savior,
> No liberator, deliverer, provider
> None who takes pity in every time of distress and trouble.
> We have no king but thee.[3]

Therefore one should look for a tradition concerning enthronement and/or judgment at Passover. As a matter of fact, eschatological references in the Passover Haggadah are frequent, and the kingly reign of God is especially emphasized (see below, pp. 77f. and n. 3). Moreover Mishnah *R. Sh.*, 1.2 states: "At four times in the year is the world judged: at Passover, through grain; at Pentecost, through the fruits of the tree; on New Year's Day all that come into the world pass before him like legions of soldiers [or 'like flocks of sheep'] . . .; and at the Feast (of Tabernacles) they are judged through water" (the translation is Danby's).

[1] As a single indication, πάσχα occurs nine times in Jn.– more than in any other NT book. Furthermore, the three passovers mentioned in Jn. play a major part in the chronological structure of the gospel.

[2] Ex. 12.10. ὀστοῦν οὐ συντρίψετε ἀπ' αὐτοῦ; cf. Num. 9.12. The spear-thrust and the statement that Jesus' bones were not broken are closely connected. In each case more than one motif is present: (1) apologetic: against Jewish objections that Jesus never really died, the two statements demonstrate his actual death (cf. Mk. 15.44f.); (2) scripturefulfillment: each incident is supported by a text introduced by the fulfillment formula. The text for "breaking bones" is not quite clear, since the passive συντριβήσεται occurs only in Ps. 33.21, where it is said that God will guard the δίκαιος lest his bones be broken. It is quite possible, as Bultmann urges (*Ev. Joh.*, p. 524, n. 8), that the original tradition was based on the Psalm text alone, while the evangelist himself introduced the Passover allusion by adjusting the quotation in part to Ex. 12.10. (3) In the case of the spear-thrust perhaps there is also a sacramental interest: the sacraments are connected as closely as possible to Jesus' death.

[3]
מן העולם ועד העולם אתה אל
ומבלעדיך אין לנו מלך גואל ומושיע/ סודה ומציל ומפרנס
ומרחם בכל עת צרה וצוקה
אין לנו מלך אלא אתה·

It is unfortunately not possible to ascertain the date at which the *Nišmat* became part of the Seder. It is first mentioned in Talmud Bab., *Pes.* 118a: "What is the 'grace of song' [ברכת השיר, Mishnah *Pes.* 10.7]? Rab Judah [b. Ezekiel, Babylonian Amora, 3d century] said, 'They shall praise thee, O Lord our God' [the יהללוך]; while R. Johanan [b. Nappaha, Palestinian Amora, 2d-3d centuries] said, 'The breath of all living' [the נשמת]." It is likely that the Gemara reflects a difference between Palestinian and Babylonian practice, and that the use of the *Nišmat* in Palestine was quite early.

God's eternal reign as king is the principal theme of the *Nišmat*, and there are some elements that suggest his eschatological enthronement. For example, "For every mouth shall praise thee, every tongue shall swear to thee, and every knee shall bow to thee"[1] is derived from Isaiah 45.23, which is quoted in Romans 14.11 in the context of the final judgment and in Philippians 2.11 is applied to Christ's exaltation. Against this background it is clear that, if the cry of the high priests does allude to the *Nišmat*, it represents not just the rejection of the Messiah, but also of "the one who sent him" (12.44f.; 13.20). God himself, universally praised by every circle of Judaism as the king and judge of all men,[2] is here rejected. And because God the king and judge, who appears in the person of his son and ἀπόστολος enthroned on the tribunal, is rejected, then the judges who reject him become themselves the condemned.[3]

Final "exaltation" of the king (19.16-22)

For purposes of the present investigation, there are good reasons for singling out the first section of the crucifixion narrative to be treated in connection with the trial. The closely parallel designations of place in verses 13 and 17 themselves suggest that the scene on Gabbatha and that on Golgotha have a close connection. Furthermore, as Potterie says, the two scenes "develop exactly the same themes and ultimately have the same theological meaning: the proclamation of the kingship of Jesus . . . and the refusal of the Jews, which constitutes their condemnation . . ."[4]

John 19.17-22 can hardly be called an account of the crucifixion itself, which receives only the scant notice of verse 18. The center of attention is instead the placard which Pilate attaches to the

---

[1]   כי כל פה לך יודה וכל לשון לך תשבע וכל ברך לך תכרע׃

[2] By far the most frequent use of the title "king" in the Judaism around the turn of the eras is to refer to God, especially in the context of his eschatological judgment of the whole world. E.g., 1 Enoch 12.3; 25.3, 5, 7; 91.13f., and especially 9.4; 84.2, 3, 5; 81.3; 63; 3 Macc. 5.35; Mishnah *Abot* 4.29; cf. 3.1, *Or. Sibyl.* III, 56 and the fragment 3.42; Ps. Sol. 2.36; *Assum. Mos.* 10. 1-3; *Test. Levi* 5.1f; 1Q H 10.8; 4Q Ma 12f. Perhaps God's enthronement as king and judge is already eschatological in Ps. 96.13; 98.9; cf. 5.3; 7.7ff.; 9.8f.; 10.12, 16; 50. 1-6; 58; 82; 99.1-4. Cf. H. J. Kraus, *Psalmen* ("Biblischer Kommentar zum A.T.," XV; Neukirchen: Verlag des Erziehungsvereins, 1961), II, 665, 674f.

[3] On the stylistic device of "reversed roles" in the trial narrative, cf. Blank, 64f.

[4] *Scripture* 13, pp. 109f (*Biblica* 41, p. 245).

cross, "Jesus the Nazoraean, the King of the Jews." The fact of the placard itself is of course traditional and one of the most firmly fixed of all elements in the passion traditions,[1] although the wording

---

[1] Against Staerk (p. 88) and Bultmann (*Geschichte*, p. 293) the cross placard with the title "King of the Jews" must be regarded as historical, not the work of *Gemeindedogmatik*. The title "King of the Jews" cannot have been derived from the messianic ideology of Judaism. It never occurs in the Old Testament, and in the literature of inter-testamental Judaism it appears, so far as I can discover, only twice, both times in Josephus. The first occurrence (*Antt.* xiv, 34-36) is in the inscription of the famous "golden vine" which Aristobulus sent to Pompey in the spring of 63 B.C., "From Alexander, the King of the Jews." The second (*Antt.* xvi, 311) refers to Herod. The Hasmonaeans, beginning with Aristobulus I, gave themselves the title "king," but there is no evidence that the title carried eschatological implications. R. H. Charles' thesis that the "Messiah ben Levi" of the supposed original form of the Testaments of the Twelve Patriarchs was an element of the Hasmonaean court-theology has been exploded on the one hand by the form-critical investigations of Marinus de Jonge (*The Testaments of the Twelve Patriarchs* [Assen: Van Gorcum and Company, 1953], 171 pp.) and by the discovery of the double messianic ideology of the Qumran sect. The influence of the Hasmonaean kings was rather to increase the longing for the legitimate king or for God's own kingly rule (*Ps. Sol.* 17) or to produce an avoidance of the term "king" altogether for the royal Messiah (Qumran). In any case "King of *the Jews*" remains an improbable and unattested title for an eschatological figure: even "King of Israel," which would presumably be a more satisfactory formulation, is not directly attested to my knowledge. (Philo, *Som.* II, 44, allegorizes this title as applied to Judah the Patriarch; he may have known a tradition in which the Davidic Messiah, i.e., the Messiah from the tribe of Judah, was so called.)

On the other hand, "King of the Jews" was not an early Christian title for Jesus (cf. Winter, pp. 108f.). It occurs in the New Testament only in the passion narratives and in Mt. 2.2. In the passion accounts, two of the occurrences in Mk. (15.9, 12) are altered by Mt. (27.17, 22) to ὁ λεγόμενος χριστός and omitted by Luke. In Mk. 15.32, a portion of the crucifixion narrative in which references to Ps. 22 and 69 are evidence of *Gemeindebildung*, the title is not "King of the Jews" but "the Christ, the King of Israel." In the Gospel of Peter the change to "King of Israel" has been made even in the juridical question of Pilate (v. 7, cf. Mk. 15.2 par.) and in the cross inscription (v. 11, cf. Mk. 15.26 par.). The occurrence in the Mt. infancy story is probably to be explained on the basis of (1) assimilation of the legend of Herod's attempted murder of Jesus to the passion itself and (2) analogy to Herod's own title.

With a very high degree of probability, then, it may be concluded that the title was forced on the church, not created by it. The most reasonable explanation of its occurrence in the passion narratives is that the cross placard was historical. (Cf. N. A. Dahl, "Der gekreuzigte Messias," *Der historische Jesus und der kerygmatische Christus*, ed. H. Ristow and K. Matthiae [Berlin: Evangelische Verlagsanstalt, 1960], pp. 149-149. The evidence was presented more fully by Prof. Dahl in his 1962 Shaffer Lectures at Yale University Divinity School, "Historical Beginnings of Christological Doctrine," to be published in the near future.)

varies slightly from one gospel to another. After the development in the preceding scenes of the theme of Jesus' kingship, however, the τίτλος[1] takes on greater significance, which is emphasized in the present scene by the specifically Johannine additions to the tradition. These are (1) the indication of the universality of the king's reign, implied by the three languages of the inscription (verse 20); (2) rejection of the proclamation by "the high priests of the Jews"; and (3) the ironic insistence upon its irrevocability by Pilate's reply, ὃ γέγραφα, γέγραφα. The divine king reigns from the cross[2] despite his rejection by his own subjects. That is the final affirmation about Jesus in the crucifixion narrative. Perhaps it also explains the very puzzling fact that in the passion account John makes no alteration in the problematical title "King of *the Jews*,"[3] even though "the Jews" in the Fourth Gospel stand for the disbelieving world. Apart from the evident strength of the tradition itself, the title serves the evangelist's intent, apparent from the structure of the passage, to show that Jesus remains king of the disbelieving world as well as of the believers.[4]

Summary

Several points have emerged in the foregoing analysis of the trial and crucifixion narrative which must particularly be kept in mind in the further stages of this inquiry. First, Jesus' kingship was found to stand at the center of attention in the whole narrative. A signifi-

---

[1] Not an αἰτία, as in Mk. 15.26 – Mt. 27.37.

[2] The paradox has been announced throughout the gospel by the ambiguous ὑψωθῆναι. The recognition of the ironic enthronement in the early church is demonstrated by the Christian alteration of Ps. 95 (96).10 to read: ὁ κύριος ἐβασίλευσεν ἀπὸ ξύλου. Cf. Justin, *Apol.* I, 41 (with the introductory remark, . . . μηνῦον τὸ προφητικὸν πνεῦμα . . . ὅτι μετὰ τὸ σταυρωθῆναι βασιλεύσει ὁ χριστὸς . . .), and *Dial.* 73.1; cf. *Ep. Barn.* 8.5, ἡ βασιλεία Ἰησοῦ ἐπὶ ξύλου.

[3] Contrast *Gosp. Peter* 7, 11, where the title is twice altered to "King of Israel" as in Mk. 15.32 and Jn. 1.49; 12.13.

[4] Contrast the point of view expressed in the Lucan version of the "parable of the pounds," Lk. 19.27. The universality of Jesus' kingship in the Fourth Gospel is one of the reasons why Cullmann's scheme, in which βασιλεύς represents Jesus' relation to the believers and κύριος his relation to the world, cannot be maintained (*Christology*, p. 221; *Königsherrschaft Christi und Kirche im Neuen Testament* (2d ed., "Theologische Studien," ed. Karl Barth, XI; Zollikon-Zürich: Evangelischer Verlag, 1946), p. 9 *et passim.*)

cant element already in the tradition, this motif has been vastly heightened and expanded by the evangelist. Second, Jesus' kingship is inextricably connected with his function as judge, a function which is depicted by the deeply ironic "exchange of roles" apparent in the dramatic structure of the narrative. Furthermore, Jesus' kingship was found to express *God's* kingship, so that the rejection of Jesus by "the Jews" was equivalent to rejection of God, and the judgment effected through Jesus was God's own final judgment. In these motifs themes which have dominated the entire gospel are brought to a climax. Third, significant connections were found between the trial scene and the "parable" of the Good Shepherd. The "King of the Jews" and the "Good Shepherd" are equivalent figures, having the same functions. Finally, the mission of Jesus which defines his kingship was seen to be twofold. (a) His kingship consists in bearing witness to the truth, which is equivalent to the Good Shepherd's "call" to which "his own" respond. Functionally, then, Jesus' *kingship* is identical to the office of a *prophet*. (b) His kingship is inaugurated through his willing death. As the *Good* Shepherd is the one who "lays down his life for the sheep," so the "exaltation" of the king consists in his being "lifted up" on the cross.

THE KING OF ISRAEL: CONFESSION AND ACCLAMATION

In all the Johannine passion narrative Jesus is nowhere called χριστός. The place of that title is entirely filled by βασιλεύς (τῶν Ἰουδαίων). Nevertheless the entire gospel was written ἵνα πιστεύσητε ὅτι Ἰησοῦς ἐστιν ὁ χριστὸς ὁ υἱὸς τοῦ θεοῦ (20.31), and the central section describing Jesus' manifestation ἐν παρρησίᾳ (chapters 7-8) was found to turn on the question whether Jesus was ὁ προφήτης or ὁ χριστός.[1] The centrality of the kingship in the passion narrative thus has two implications. (1) Allusions to Jesus' kingship in the earlier parts of the gospel, which alone might seem unimportant, demand serious attention in the light of the trial and crucifixion narratives. (2) The meaning of the term χριστός in John is to be found in analysis of Jesus' kingship, not the other way around.

The βασιλεύς title in the trial and crucifixion story is the rock of offense in Jesus' rejection by "the Jews." There are two passages

---

[1] See above, pp. 57f.

in the gospel, however, in which "king" is not the point of rejection but the center of confession and acclamation. Both of these passages, and they alone in the Fourth Gospel, contain the solemn title "King of Israel," while "King of the Jews" occurs nowhere outside the passion. Exposition of the two passages can be brief, since their significance depends less upon their isolated content than upon their place within the thematic development of the whole gospel.

Confession by the true Israelite (John 1.49)

The first mention of βασιλεύς is also the most direct: Nathanael, confronted with Jesus' mysterious knowledge of him, responds: "Rabbi, you are the Son of God; you are the King of Israel." The form is that of a confession, like Peter's "You are the Holy One of God" (6.69) and Martha's "You are the Christ, the Son of God, who comes into the world" (11.27). As the first direct confession addressed to Jesus in the gospel—for it has a different character from the μαρτυρία of the Baptist—Nathanael's statement must carry great weight in the gospels' evolving structure. Its significance is heightened by the identity of the person who makes the confession: Nathanael,[1] who is ἀληθῶς Ἰσραηλίτης (1.47). He is the "true Israelite"[2] who recognizes the "King of Israel."

Perhaps there is a clue here to the relation between "King of Israel" and "King of the Jews" in John. To be sure "King of Israel" would be the preferred form of a messianic title, as the tendency to replace or interpret "King of the Jews" by "King of Israel" as well as by "Christ" demonstrates,[3] and this fact alone could explain the Johannine usage. However, it is also true that "Israel" and "the Jews" are given distinct connotations in the Fourth Gospel. Thus Nathanael, who confesses the King of Israel, is the "true Israelite," the countertype to "the Jews" who deny the King of the Jews. In his very act of confession Nathanael manifests that he is the true Israelite and the prototype of the Christian

---

[1] נתנאל of course means "God gives." Barrett's suggestion (p. 153) that the name is symbolic, referring to the disciples whom God gave to Jesus (6.37-39; 10.29; 17.6-12, 24; 18.9) is very plausible, although the name is not emphasized in John's characteristic way by the addition of a Greek equivalent.

[2] On the significance of ἀληθῶς in Jn., see above p. 34; cf. Bultmann, Ev. Joh., p. 73, n. 6: "'Αληθῶς attributiv, etwa gleichwertig mit ἀληθινός; also: 'einer, des Names Isr. wurdig ist.'"

[3] See above p. 79, n. 1.

believer; in their very act of denial the crowds become "the Jews," representative of the disbelieving world. Moreover, verse 51, which is a clear allusion to Genesis 28.12 as interpreted in the midrashim,[1] may intend an identification of Jesus with Jacob/Israel. If so, then the correspondence between the "Israelite" and the "King of Israel" is analogous to the relationship between Jesus and "his own" throughout the gospel. Quite possibly there lies behind this usage a polemic situation in which Christians, over against Jewish opponents, call themselves "the true Israel."[2]

The motif of Jesus' supernatural knowledge of Nathanael points in the same direction. Such supernatural knowledge is of course characteristic of the θεῖος ἀνήρ,[3] but it may serve another purpose in the Fourth Gospel besides showing that Jesus is divine. Above all, the Good Shepherd knows "his sheep" (10.28). Since reason has already been found for identifying the Good Shepherd with the prophetic king of the passion narrative, the indication that the King of Israel knows his true subject is a parallel to the Good Shepherd's knowledge.

Acclamation by the festival pilgrims (John 12.12-19)

The only other occurrence of the full title "King of Israel" is in the account of Jesus' entry into Jerusalem (12.13). Again the position of the passage is significant. As Nathanael's confession stands at the beginning of Jesus' manifestation to the world, the acclamation by the festival crowds outside Jerusalem stands at the end.[4] The entry divides the gospel in half, for "the hour has come for the Son of Man to be glorified" (12.23); "now is the judgment of this world" (12.31). "The Jews" make their decision at this point (12.37-43); in the subsequent trials it is only exposed.

A comparison with the synoptic versions of the entry will help clarify the manner in which the fourth evangelist has adapted the tradition. In all four accounts reference to Jesus' kingship is un-

---

[1] See especially Odeberg, pp. 33-42 and the extensive parallels he quotes; also Bultmann, *Ev. Joh.*, p. 74, n. 4; Barrett, p. 156; Nils A. Dahl, *Das Volk Gottes; Eine Untersuchung zum Kirchenbewusstsein des Urchristentums* (2d ed.; Darmstadt: Wissenschaftliche Buchgesellschaft, 1962), p. 170.

[2] Cf. Gal. 6.16, Ἰσραὴλ τοῦ θεοῦ; Rom. 9.6, οὐ γὰρ πάντες οἱ ἐξ Ἰσραήλ, οὗτοι Ἰσραήλ; 1 Cor. 10.18, Ἰσραὴλ κατὰ σάρκα; Rev. 7.4-8; 21.12; Dahl, *Volk Gottes*, pp. 167-174.

[3] Wetter, pp. 69-72; Bultmann, *Ev. Joh.*, p. 73.

[4] Note especially 11.54.

mistakable, although it is only implicit in Mark, who speaks of "the coming kingdom of our father David" (11.10). Even the Marcan form shows the formative influence of Zechariah 9.9, although only Matthew and John quote the prophetic passage.[1] Billerbeck has collected extensive evidence that the Zechariah passage was interpreted eschatologically in Judaism, probably before the Christian era.[2] The implicit reference to the eschatological king is made explicit and emphatic by both Luke and Matthew, in different ways.

Luke's alterations of the Marcan pericope are minor and principally stylistic. For example, in Luke 19.33 οἱ κύριοι αὐτοῦ introduces a play on ὁ κύριος αὐτοῦ χρείαν ἔχει of Mark 11.3 (Luke 19.34), and 19.38b is an editorial emendation of Mark 11.9b to make it conform with Luke 2.14. Stylistic considerations may also have dictated Luke's insertion of ὁ βασιλεύς into the Marcan citation of Psalm 118.26. F. C. Grant's suggestion of a gloss assimilating Luke to John at this point[3] is attractive but unnecessary. The somewhat awkward construction (its awkwardness explains the variant readings) arises from the simple combination of Mark's two parallel clauses 9b/10a to avoid repetitiousness—just as Matthew has done by the even simpler expedient of omitting the second clause altogether. Luke effects the combination by substituting ὁ βασιλεύς for the problematic phrase[4] ἡ . . . βασιλεία τοῦ πατρὸς ἡμῶν Δαυίδ. However, the change from βασιλεία to βασιλεύς may also have a

---

[1] Bultmann, *Geschichte*, p. 281; Erich Klostermann, *Das Markus Evangelium* (4th ed.; HNT; 1950), p. 112; Hahn, p. 266, n. 2.

[2] Billerbeck, I, 842-844.

[3] "Was the Author of John Dependent upon the Gospel of Luke?" *JBL* 56 (1937), 294.

[4] Ernst Lohmeyer, *Das Evangelium Markus* (4th ed.; KEK; 1954), pp. 231f., and Hahn, pp. 264f. Lohmeyer thinks the whole phrase is a purely Christian formulation since (1) Judaism did not speak of the "coming" of David's kingdom and (2) Judaism did not refer to David as "father." Hahn adds the supposition that "vom 'Vater' David ist offensichtlich nur auf Grund der geläufigen Bezeichnung Jesu als Davids 'Sohn' die Rede." To the latter it may be remarked that it is not altogether "obvious" how the transition between calling Jesus David's son and Christians calling David "our Father" is to be made. Moreover, while אבינו is most often used of Abraham, Isaac, and Jacob, and according to Talmud Bab. *Ber.* 16b *only* of these (probably the source of Lohmeyer's assertion), yet Billerbeck shows that in fact a great variety of notable persons were called "Father," including David (Billerbeck, II, 26; cf. I, 918f.). The origin of the formula βασιλεία τοῦ πατρὸς ἡμῶν Δαυίδ therefore remains in doubt.

theological purpose, connected with Luke's altered eschatology.[1] In any event the title "king," absent from the Marcan version, is expressed in Luke and applied to Jesus.

Matthew omits all reference to the kingdom of David, but inserts into the Psalm quotation the messianic title "Son of David" (Matthew 21.9). In addition, he introduces, with the characteristic fulfillment formula, a composite scripture quotation (blending Isaiah 62.11 with Zechariah 9.9): "Say to the daughter of Zion, Behold your king is coming to you, lowly and seated upon a donkey and upon a foal the offspring of a beast of burden." Matthew also conforms the narrative to the quotation by adding a second animal (21.2, 7), having misunderstood the parallelism of the original verse in Zechariah. Gunther Bornkamm rightly sees in the passage the work of "Matthew as theologian and interpreter," portraying Jesus as the "lowly king."[2]

Despite the obvious similarities between the Johannine account of the entry and the synoptic versions, John is probably independent of the Synoptics.[3] The whole legend of the disciples' procurement of the donkey, the *Märchenmotif* as Bultmann calls it,[4] is missing from John, and there is no reason to regard verse 14 as a substitute for the legend by an author acquainted with it,[5] since εὑρών implies nothing supernatural. From the standpoint of the history of tradition, the Johannine form thus appears earlier than the Marcan. The scripture quotation in John 12.15 differs from Matthew as well as from all known text traditions of both Hebrew and Greek Old Testaments. The coincidence that both Matthew and John quote

---

[1] Cf. 9.27 in comparison with Mk. 9.1, and Hans Conzelmann, *The Theology of St. Luke* (New York: Harper E Brothers, 1960), pp. 104f., 110, especially 198, However, Conzelmann's conclusion that Lk. rejects the concept of Davidic rule because "the simple title king" has for him a "non-political sense" connected solely with the temple (p. 139) has little to commend it.

[2] "End-Expectation and Church in Matthew," *Tradition and Interpretation in Matthew*, by Günther Bornkamm, Gerhard Barth, and Heinz Joachim Held (trans. Percy Scott: Philadelphia: The Westminster Press, 1963), pp. 33f.

[3] Bultmann, *Ev. Joh.*, p. 319. Cf. D. Moody Smith Jr., "John 12.12ff. and the Question of John's use of the Synoptics," *JBL* 82 (1963), 58-64.

[4] *Geschichte*, p. 281.

[5] Bultmann, *Ev. Joh.*, p. 319, n. 4. He thinks vv. 14f. are an addition to the story, but is uncertain whether the addition was already present in the evangelist's source, was added by the evangelist, or is the product of the "ecclesiastical redactor" in the interest of harmonizing with the Synoptics.

the Zechariah passage is therefore best explained by positing a common tradition at some point behind both, which in turn reinforces the conclusion that the Zechariah passage shaped the tradition of the entry at its earliest stages. Like Luke, John adds the title βασιλεύς to the quotation from Psalm 118.26, but there is no more reason on that account to argue John's dependence on Luke[1] than Luke's on John. John adds the full title "the King of Israel," not inserted awkwardly into the participial phrase, as in Luke, but in parallel with it and connected by the epexegetic καί. The title is motivated by the confluence of the fourth evangelist's theological concerns with the royal implications of the whole scene, especially the quotation from Zechariah itself.

The independence of the Johannine version makes it more difficult than in the case of Matthew and Luke to single out the evangelist's alterations. Still the main Johannine elements are quite evident. Above all the kingship of Jesus is underlined, even more than in any of the Synoptics. Both the direct application of the title "King" to Jesus (which resembles Luke's version) and the citation of the Zechariah passage with its "your king" (which resembles Matthew) are found in John. The former is undoubtedly the evangelist's formulation, and it may be that the Zechariah quotation was added also by him, since the very loose quotation of Old Testament texts is a Johannine characteristic.[2] The mention of palm branches—which symbolize victory, including victory over death, throughout the ancient world, but have no necessary connection with royalty[3]—may have been present in John's source. Mark speaks only of "twigs (στιβάδες) . . . cut from the fields."

The other distinctively Johannine elements are (1) the disciples' lack of understanding, in this instance specifically the understanding of the scripture that pointed to the event, before Jesus' glorification;[4] (2) the connection of the entry with the resurrection of

---

[1] Bauer, p. 155.

[2] Cf. Bent Noack, *Zur johanneischen Tradition* (Kobenhavn: Rosenkilde og Bagger, 1954), pp. 71-89, particularly 74f.; Barrett, p. 348.

[3] Against Hoskyns, p. 421; cf. "Palme," *Real-Encyklopädie der christlichen Altertumer*, ed. F. X. Kraus (Freiburg i. B.: Herder Verlag, 1886), II, 578-580; Steier, "Phoinix," *Paulys Realencyclopädie der classischen Altertumswissenschaft*, ed. Georg Wissowa (Wilhelm Kroll and Karl Mittelhaus) [cited henceforth as "Pauly-Wissowa"], Vol. XX, Part 1 (Stuttgart: J. B. Metzler Verlag, 1941), cols. 401f.; Goodenough, *Jewish Symbols*, IV, 144-166.

[4] Cf. 2.17, 22 and 14.26; Barrett, p. 347; Hoskyns, p. 422. Compare the less subtle expression of a similar notion in Lk. 24.27, 45.

Lazarus (17f.); (3) insertion of the remark by the Pharisees, "Behold, the world has gone after him" (verse 19).

Also significant may be the shift in order, in comparison with the synoptic accounts, so that the procuring of the donkey is not mentioned until after the royal acclamation. Hoskyns thinks this represents a deliberate reversal of the meaning of the acclamation, "a protest against it, explained in the discourse that follows . . ."[1] In this view Jesus mounts the donkey to demonstrate that he is not the kind of ruler understood by the crowds, but the "lowly king," who reigns only through his death. The text, however, will not support Hoskyns' interpretation. If Jesus' lowliness had been the point of the reference to Zechariah, then at least the עני πραΰς could have been quoted, as in Matthew. As the text stands there is no emphasis on lowliness, as there was not in the original context of Zechariah nor, for that matter, in Mark.

The disciples' misunderstanding of Jesus' kingship (verse 16) stands within the context of faith. It is not expressly stated that the "crowd" misunderstood Jesus. If that is intended, then their misunderstanding, too, stands within the context of an affirmative response to Jesus, and there is no rejection of or protest against their acclamation in verse 15. The crowd consists of those who have seen the σημεῖον of Lazarus' resurrection or who have heard the μαρτυρία of this sign (verses 17f.).[2] In their response to that sign they represent "the world" that has "gone after Jesus" (verse 19), as "the Jews" in the trial scene represent "the world" which is judged (12.31) and overcome (16.33). Therefore the "crowd" of John 12.12-19 which acclaims Jesus as "the King of Israel" and welcomes him with the emblems of victory joins the "true Israelite" of John 1.45-51.

THE PROPHET-KING

John 6.14-15

At the conclusion of the account of the feeding miracle the fourth evangelist inserts a note which is unparalleled elsewhere in the gospel tradition:

---

[1] Hoskyns, p. 422.

[2] Bultmann is probably right in seeing a forensic connotation in the ἐμαρτύρει of v. 17, as elsewhere in Jn. (*Ev. Joh.*, p. 320).

οἱ οὖν ἄνθρωποι
ἰδόντες ὃ ἐποίησεν σημεῖον
ἔλεγον ὅτι οὗτός ἐστιν ἀληθῶς ὁ προφήτης
ὁ ἐρχόμενος εἰς τὸν κόσμον.
'Ιησοῦς οὖν
γνοὺς ὅτι μέλλουσιν ἔρχεσθαι καὶ ἁρπάζειν αὐτὸν
ἵνα ποιήσωσιν βασιλέα,

There are a few significant variants in the text tradition, but the case is strong for those selected here. The singular σημεῖον, supported by the overwhelming majority of manuscripts and versions, is definitely to be preferred to the plural, supported only by B,a, and the Bohairic.[1] The plural is most likely a copyist's assimilation to verse 2 (cf. verse 26). In verse 15 ποιήσωσιν is to be preferred to καὶ ἀναδεικνύναι attested by the original Sinaiticus. The latter is probably a theological correction by a copyist who correctly understood that Jesus was a king in John and who was therefore affronted by the suggestion that men could make him a king. More difficult is the decision between φεύγει (א* lat syᶜ) and ἀνεχώρησεν (the remaining witnesses). Nevertheless the preference must go to φεύγει as the more difficult reading; piety would tend to avoid the notion of Jesus' "fleeing."[2] The use of the present tense for narrative is also characteristic of John.

The real puzzle posed by the passage has nothing to do with textual uncertainties, however. The notion which this passage takes for granted, but which from the standpoint of common views of first-century Jewish and Christian eschatology is difficult to explain, is that "the Prophet" is naturally to be "a king." Yet the majority of commentators have also taken the identity to be self-evident, and have assumed without further discussion that βασιλεύς here refers to the Davidic Messiah.[3] Even those who have recognized "a certain inappropriateness"[4] here, in light of the fact that

---

[1] Bultmann, Ev. Joh., p. 158, n. 1, "zweifellos," though Barrett, p. 231, finds it hard to decide.

[2] Cf. Barrett, p. 231.

[3] Meyer, p. 254; Staerk, I, 66; Riesenfeld, Kundsin Festschrift, p. 143; Barrett, p. 231. Others speak of a "flowing together" of the separate figures "the Prophet" and "the Messiah"; Volz, p. 194; Bultmann, p. 158, n. 2; Hahn, pp. 370, 392. Somewhat different Zahn, p. 325, who recognizes the distinction and sees in 6.15 an (historical) attempt by the enthusiastic Galileans to make "the Prophet" into a Zealot leader.

[4] Schnackenburg, p. 630: "Eine gewisse Inkonvenienz bleibt, insofern 'der Prophet' in 6, 14f. fast mit der Gestalt des (nationalen) Messias zusammenfliesst, während er an den anderen Stellen von ihr unterschieden ist."

elsewhere the Fourth Gospel clearly distinguishes the Messiah from "the Prophet," find no resolution of the problem.[1]

Jesus' flight cannot imply a rejection of the term "king" as such; it need hardly be emphasized again that for the evangelist Jesus *is* a king. What is rejected is worldly force (ἁρπάζειν, cf. 18.37) and the world's "hour," which is not yet his own (cf. 7.6).[2] Whether the verse implies a "protest against the old eschatology"[3] is a question best answered later.

The relation between the two terms χριστός and βασιλεύς in the Fourth Gospel is not entirely clear. There are many indications that χριστός and βασιλεύς τοῦ Ἰσραήλ are equivalent expressions. In 1.35-51 the testimony of Andrew to Simon, "We have found the Messiah (which is translated 'Christ')" (verse 41), is followed by Nathanael's confession, "You are the Son of God, you are the King of Israel" (verse 49). The identity is further reinforced by Martha's confession (11.27), which is parallel to Nathanael's except that ὁ χριστός replaces βασιλεύς τοῦ Ἰσραήλ. Finally, it was suggested above[4] that the trial of Jesus as "King of the Jews" is a counterpart to the second question of "the crowd" in 7.40f., whether Jesus was "the Christ." Nevertheless, the two titles are never expressly identified nor juxtaposed in one passage, as are, for example, "Son of God" and "King of Israel" in 1.49, "Son of God" and "Christ" in 11.27, and "Prophet" and "king" in 6.14f. Remembering that ὁ χριστός and ὁ προφήτης are carefully distinguished (1.21, 24; 7.38-52), while βασιλεύς and ὁ προφήτης are identified in the passage now under consideration, one may perhaps perceive a deliberate ambiguity, a certain reserve in the Johannine use of χριστός. In any case it cannot be assumed that the use of βασιλεύς automatically implies the background of the Davidic messianology.

In the present passage the intent of "the men who saw the sign" to make Jesus a king, which is revealed to the reader only by the indirect device of Jesus' supernatural knowledge, is based solely on

---

[1] Cf., besides Schnackenburg, Van der Woude, pp. 8of. For a critique of the positions referred to here see Chapter I, pp. 25-29, above.

[2] David Daube's suggestion (*The New Testament and Rabbinic Judaism* [London: The Athlone Press, 1956], p. 19) that a Saul-typology, based on 1 Sam. 10.21ff., may lie behind the "flight" has no real evidence for it, as he himself admits. The rabbinic maxim he cites (from *Tanḥuma* on Lev. 1.1), "he who flies from rulership, rulership will pursue him," is interesting but hardly relevant.

[3] Bultmann, *Ev. Joh.*, p. 158.

[4] P. 61.

their recognition that he is "truly the prophet who is coming into the world." The phrase ὁ ἐρχόμενος occurs eight time in John,[1] always with reference to Jesus except for the debated passage 1.9.[2] Since it is not only "the Prophet" who "comes into the world" in John, but also "the Christ, the Son of God" (11.27) and "every man" (1.9), and since one of the most fundamental themes of John is that Jesus, with whatever title, has come into the world "from above,"[3] 6.14 will certainly not support the conjecture "that this expression . . . was a *terminus technicus* to designate the eschatological Prophet."[4] It is often supposed that ὁ ἐρχόμενος was a messianic title,[5] but this cannot be demonstrated. What the participial phrase, in conjunction with the definite article, does indicate in 6.14 is that "the Prophet" with whom Jesus is identified is one who is a well-known eschatological figure.[6]

Mention of "the prophet coming into the world" naturally calls to mind the prophet like Moses of Deuteronomy 18.15-22,[7] although this is by no means the only possible identification. The cumulative evidence already discovered in John for a pattern of allusions to the Mosaic prophet and to his opposite, the false prophet of Deuteronomy 13 and 18,[8] adds weight to this interpretation. The decisive

---

[1] 1.9, 15, 27; 3.31 (twice); 6.14; 11.27; 12.13.

[2] Whether ἐρχόμενον ought to be understood as accus. masc. modifying ἄνθρωπον or as neut. nom. in a loose periphrastic construction joined with ἦν, with τὸ φῶς as subject, has long been debated. Bultmann, *Ev. Joh.*, pp. 31f., n. 6, offers an argument for the former which is not likely to be overturned. Not only would the separation of the auxiliary verb from the participle by a relative clause be unprecedented in periphrasis, but also the parallelism of v. 9 with vv. 4, 10 shows that τὸ φῶς must be the predicate, not the subject, of ἦν Moreover, in rabbinic writings ((כל) באי העולם) "(all) those who enter the world," is a frequent circumlocution for "human beings" (cf. Billerbeck, II, 358), leading to Bultmann's suggestion that ἄνθρωπος is an explanatory gloss.

[3] Cf. 3.31, ὁ ἄνωθεν ἐρχόμενος = ὁ ἐκ τοῦ οὐρανοῦ ἐρχόμενος, and above, pp. 37-39.

[4] Cullmann, *Christology*, p. 36; cf. p. 26.

[5] Taylor, *Names*, pp. 78f.; Bultmann, *Geschichte*, p. 168, n. 2 (on Mt. 11.3//Lk. 7.19), *Ev. Joh.*, p. 309, n. 1, although Bultmann thinks the real "analogy and manifold root" of the expression is in gnostic usage (*ibid.*, p. 30, n. 3, cf. p. 97, n. 3). For parallels in Mandaean usage, see Bauer, p. 89, and Bultmann, *ZNW* 25, pp. 106f.

[6] Hahn, p. 393: "'Kommend' ist alles, was mit der Heilzeit in Verbindung steht . . ."; cf. the passages cited by Billerbeck, II, 358.

[7] Supporters of this view are listed above, pp. 21–25 The objection by Teeple and Schnackenburg is criticized p. 23, n. 6.

[8] See above, pp. 45-58.

element, however, lies in the nature of Jesus' "sign," for it was "seeing the sign which he had done" which led "the men" to recognize Jesus as the true prophet.

Bread on the mountain and bread from heaven

The narrative of John 6.1-13 is traditional, probably derived from a written source very similar to but not identical with the Marcan account of the feeding of the five thousand.[1] The evident alterations by the evangelist are few: verse 4 sets the context of the miracle by a reference to the approaching Passover; verse 6 introduces the familiar theme of Jesus' omniscience; finally the verses which have been under consideration here, 14f., provide a new climax to the whole account.[2] In addition it will be shown below that the evangelist probably altered verses 12f. as well. For the most part he places his interpretation of the event in the long discourse which follows, verses 26-59. It ist his to which one must turn for an understanding of the σημεῖον from the Johannine point of view.

The most striking feature of the discourse is its chain-like structure which progresses by alternative statements or questions, now by Jesus, now by his opponents, containing repeated key words. Second, this structure is very closely tied to scripture quotations, particularly that in verse 31, "Bread from heaven he gave them to eat." Peder Borgen points in the right direction when he calls the discourse "an exegesis, a midrash, of this reference to the manna miracle with its quotation from Scripture. . . ."[3] At the center of the discourse is the comparison and contrast between the manna which the wilderness generation of Israel received and the bread which Jesus gives, identified finally as himself, his flesh. The question by Jesus' audience, "What sign do *you* do?" followed by their reference to the manna, together with Jesus' reply, "It is not

---

[1] Cf. E. R. Goodenough, "John a Primitive Gospel," *JBL* 64 (1945), 156-158; Bultmann, *Ev. Joh.*, p. 155; Haenchen, "Johanneische Probleme," *ZThK*, 56 (1959), 31-34.

[2] Cf. Bultmann, *Ev. Joh.*, p. 155.

[3] "The Unity of the Discourse in John 6," *ZNW* 50 (1959), p. 277. His recent article, "Observations on the Midrashic Character of John 6," *ZNW* 54 (1963), 232-240, shows that this insight is productive, even though some details of his exposition are questionable. Mr. Borgen's monograph developing this point of view, with detailed discussion of relevant material from first century and later Judaism, appeared after my manuscript went to the printer (*Bread from Heaven* [Supplements to Novum Testamentum, X; Leiden: E. J. Brill, 1965]).

Moses who gave you the bread from heaven, but my father is giving you the real bread from heaven" (verses 31f.), underlines the point of comparison. Here as in 9.28, the decision has to be made whether to be disciples of Moses or disciples of Jesus. Only the latter receive the "real bread," the "food that remains for eternal life." Finally, it is likely that the discourse incorporates themes which belonged to the traditions surrounding Passover. In Jewish tradition the manna is midrashically connected with the Passover bread, and both are interpreted eschatologically.[1] The evangelist's note of the season in verse 4 justifies attempts to discover allusions in the Johannine discourse to Passover traditions, although recent attempts to explain the form and content of the whole discourse as the result of homilies on the Jewish lectionary texts for the season must be regarded as failures.[2] In any case it is

---

[1] Cf. Bertil Gärtner, *John 6 and the Jewish Passover* ("Coniectanea Neo-testamentica," XVII; Lund: G. W. K. Gleerup, 1959), pp. 18ff.

[2] The work of Aileen Guilding, *The Fourth Gospel and Jewish Worship; A Study of the Relation of St. John's Gospel to the Ancient Jewish Lectionary System* (Oxford: At the Clarendon Press, 1960), 247 pp., begins with a hypothesis that is not implausible, but her procedure can only be called fantastic. Following Büchler's reconstruction of a triennial cycle, with its starting point in the chronological statements in the Pentateuch and the midrashim and in the older paragraph divisions of the Masoretes, she uses this cycle as a key to open all doors. The structure of the Pentateuch itself, she finds, is based on the three-year lectionary cycle, which explains un-evenness, doublets, and numerous other perplexities at a stroke, while this discovery on the other hand proves that the cycle was current at least 400 B.C. The same structure is discovered in the Psalms, by means of ingenious exegesis that turns verses into chains of catchwords which allegedly indicated to the lectors the corresponding *seder* from the Pentateuch for each of the three years. Her exegesis of the Fourth Gospel is marked by a curious blend of a radical application of the "myth and ritual pattern" to the text, a naive historicism which finds in the discourses collections of Jesus' actual sermons, delivered in synagogues on the assigned texts in various years, and the most superficial concordance-scholarship. A single example of the last will indicate the level of reliability of the whole: Chap. 18 is said to treat the same themes as chap. 10- in both cases the lections for Hannukah- because the words αὐλή and θυρωρός are found only in these chapters (p. 49), although in Chapter 10 the αὐλή is the "sheepfold" and the θυρωρός its guard, while in chapter 18 both terms occur in the traditional account, drawn from a source, of Peter's denial in the "court" of the high priest's residence.

In a similar direction but more sober is the essay by Gärtner already referred to. He also thinks the gospel tradition was shaped by liturgical practice of the church, which in turn was dependent upon synagogue liturgy. Like Guilding he has a historicizing purpose, for he assumes (with Jeremias) that the more "Jewish" a passage is the more likely it contains authentic words of Jesus or at least earliest Christian tradition (implied on p. 5, openly expressed on p. 38). He offers some suggestive parallels between the Passover

sufficiently evident that the discourse sets Jesus' σημεῖον parallel with God's miraculous care of Israel under Moses' leadership. This adds very strong support to the supposition that "the Prophet" of verse 14 is the Mosaic eschatological prophet. That the gift of "the Prophet" is far superior to the gift given at the hands of the Prophet's prototype is no argument to the contrary.

The discourse serves a further purpose: it deliberately draws attention away from the feeding miracle itself, interpreting it as only a "sign," a symbol for the "real bread." This is made clear in verse 26, where the crowd is reproached for having eaten of the loaves and been filled without seeing "signs." They are then admonished not to work for "the food that perishes (τὴν βρῶσιν τὴν ἀπολλυμένην), but for the food that remains for eternal life" (verse 27). As the subsequent dialogue makes plain, the "food that remains for eternal life" is Jesus himself, "the one who comes down from heaven and gives life to the world" (verse 33). Jesus' "giving" of himself is to be understood as his death. Gärtner calls attention to the future tenses of verbs in verses 27 and 51, which point forward to the passion.[1] In the disputed verses 51-58 the main point, as Barrett emphasizes,[2] is not to describe the Eucharist itself as a "medicine of immortality," but to identify the life-giving bread with Jesus' death, taking the allusion to the Eucharist for granted.

On the other hand verse 27 points back to the narrative of the feeding as well as forward to the discourse on bread of life, for τὴν βρῶσιν τὴν ἀπολλυμένην recalls verse 12, "Gather the fragments that abounded (or, remained), ἵνα μή τι ἀπόληται." While the gathering of the superfluous fragments is part of the traditional form of the story, as a proof of the magnitude of the miracle, only in John is it introduced by a separate command by Jesus. The purpose clause is

---

traditions and John 6, but none is altogether convincing. His supposition that there is a formal analogy between John 6 and the Passover Haggadah (based mostly on Daube's principle of the "four questions," Daube, pp. 158-159, itself far from demonstrable) lacks any persuasiveness. His classification of the four questions in John 6 is highly arbitrary. Finally, his attempt to support his thesis by proposing that the Sitz-im-Leben of John 6 was within a Christian Passover celebration like that attributed to the Quartodecimanians by Lohse and others is equally unconvincing, and cannot in any case strengthen the already weak case on internal evidence.

[1] Gärtner, p. 24.

[2] Barrett, pp. 235ff.; cf. Bultmann, Ev. Joh., p. 175, who, emphasizing the sacramental interest of the section and interpreting it in the light of Ignatius, attributes the verses to the "ecclesiastical redactor."

very probably the evangelist's insertion. With keen perception Daube points out that these two changes shift the emphasis from the miracle of feeding itself—which is described now only in a subordinate clause (ὡς δὲ ἐνεπλήσθησαν, verse 12)—to the gathering of the abundant fragments.[1]

Resemblances between the language of the miracle story in John, and perhaps already in the Synoptics, and the liturgical language of the Eucharist are commonly recognized. But what interpretation of the Eucharist explains the command, "Gather the fragments, so that nothing may be lost?" The eucharistic prayer found in the Didache provides a clue.

Didache 9.4: ὥσπερ ἦν τοῦτο[2] κλάσμα διεσκορπισμένον ἐπάνω τῶν ὀρέων καὶ συναχθὲν ἐγένετο ἕν, οὕτω συναχθήτω σου ἡ ἐκκλησία ἀπὸ τῶν περάτων τῆς γῆς εἰς τὴν σὴν βασιλείαν.

John 11.52 ἔμελλεν Ἰησοῦς ἀποθνῄσκειν . . . ἵνα καὶ τὰ τέκνα τοῦ θεοῦ τὰ διεσκορπισμένα συναγάγῃ εἰς ἕν.
John 6.12b-13a: συναγάγατε τὰ περισσεύσαντα κλάσματα ἵνα μή τι ἀπόληται. συνήγαγον οὖν, καὶ ἐγέμισαν δώδεκα κοφίνους κλασμάτων κτλ.

The similarities were noticed by J. Armitage Robinson, who used them to support his elaborate and untenable hypothesis of the Didache's extensive dependence on the New Testament.[3] There is no proof that the Didache used John as a source,[4] but several

---

[1] Daube, p. 38. Daube's derivation of the Johannine "parable" from rabbinic traditions about Ruth is much less convincing. His citation from Talmud Bab. *Shab.* 113b, "She did eat? in this world, and was filled? for the days of the Messiah, and left thereof? for the Age to Come," is indeed suggestive, but isolated. The mention of "barley" probably belongs to Jn's source and is more readily explained from 2 Kings 4.42 than from Ruth. The connection of συνάγειν (Jn. 6.12, 13) with Ruth 2.15, "She rose to *glean*," is farfetched, as is the suggestion that ἐργάζεσθαι in vv. 27f. comes from Ruth 2.12 and the rabbinic interpretation that Ruth's "work" was seeking refuge under the wings of the *Shekina*.

[2] The editions of the text all insert < τὸ > which is not in the MS. But Lucien Cerfaux, "La multiplication des pains dans la liturgie de la Didachè (IX, 4)," *Biblica* 40 (1959), 944, points out that the unemended text makes good sense if τοῦτο is understood as pronominal rather than attributive: "ceci (c'est-à-dire le pain que le célébrant a devant lui) a été auparavant (ou autrefois) du pain brisé dispersé sur les montagnes."

[3] "The Problem of the Didache," *JThSt* 13 (1911/12), 339-346, especially pp. 346-348.

[4] Cf. Jean-Paul Audet, *La Didachè; Instructions des Apôtres* (Paris: Librairie Lecoffe, 1958), pp. 174f.

scholars have suggested that a common tradition, ultimately derived from Jewish liturgy,[1] lies behind both, so that John and the Didache can interpret each other.[2] The 1959 essay by Cerfaux is sober and convincing. He agrees with Goodenough and Moule that the Didache represents an early eucharistic interpretation of the bread miracle in which the eucharistic bread is thought to come mysteriously from the twelve baskets of the Apostles.[3] He discovers traces of this interpretation in several early liturgical texts, but observes that at a certain point this interpretation is replaced by a view in which the "scattering" is understood in the sense of the sowing of grain.[4]

Cerfaux, like the other scholars mentioned, interprets the Didache prayer as well as John 6 in an exclusively sacramental sense, so that the gathering of the fragments is assumed to mean that the magic bread has to be preserved for sacramental use.[5] He passes all too quickly over the main point of the prayer, which is that the "gathering" of the "scattered" fragments symbolizes the "gathering" of the church. There is good reason for supposing that this is the symbolism intended already in the Johannine narrative, for the clause ἵνα μή τι ἀπόληται is interpreted in verse 39 of the discourse. The context is an elaboration of the phrase "the bread (or, the person) that comes down from heaven" (verse 33), in which Jesus states that he has "come down from heaven" to do the will of God. Verse 39 reads: "This is the will of the one who sent me, ἵνα πᾶν ὃ δέδωκέν μοι μὴ ἀπολέσω ἐξ αὐτοῦ ..." The generalizing neuter for persons[6] corresponds exactly to the τι of verse 12. The theme appears

---

[1] For parallels to Jn. 6.12f. in Jewish prayers, cf. Rudolf Knopf, *Die Lehre der zwölf Apostel; Die zwei Clemensbriefe* (HNT, Ergänzungsband, I; 1920), p. 27, and W. O. E. Oesterley, *The Jewish Background of the Christian Liturgy* (Oxford: At the Clarendon Press, 1925), pp. 131f. In particular the "Additional Prayer," (תפלת מוסף) for Yom Kippur and the tenth *Berakah* of the *Shemoneh Esre* are very close to *Did.* 9.4.

[2] Goodenough, *JBL* 64, 145-182; C. F. D. Moule, "A Note on Didache IX, 4," *JThSt*, n.s. 6 (1955), 240-243 (Moule still inclines toward literary dependence; he ignores the Jewish background); the interpretation by Goodenough and Moule is disputed by Harald Riesenfeld, "Das Brot von den Bergen; Zu Did. 9, 4," *Eranos* 54 (1956), 142-150, defended at length by Cerfaux in the article cited above.

[3] Cerfaux, p. 957.

[4] *Ibid.*, pp. 950-953, 958.

[5] *Ibid.*, pp. 948 *et passim*; similarly Daube, p. 40.

[6] F. Blass and A. Debrunner, *A Greek Grammar of the New Testament and Other Early Christian Literature*, trans. and rev.; Robert W. Funk (Chicago: The University of Chicago Press, 1961), §138.

elsewhere in John: 3.16 states that God gave (ἔδωκεν) the only son, ἵνα πᾶς ὁ πιστεύων εἰς αὐτὸν μὴ ἀπόληται ἀλλ'ἔχη ζωὴν αἰώνιον (cf. 6. 27, "the food that remains εἰς ζωὴν αἰώνιον"); in 10.28 the "Good Shepherd" says of his "sheep," κἀγὼ δίδωμι αὐτοῖς ζωὴν αἰώνιον, καὶ οὐ μὴ ἀπόλωνται εἰς τὸν αἰῶνα. Most important of all, in 17.12 (cf. 18.9) Jesus prays: ἐγὼ ἐτήρουν αὐτοὺς [scil. τοὺς ἀνθρώπους οὓς ἔδωκάς μοι, verse 6] . . . καὶ ἐφύλαξα, καὶ οὐδεὶς ἐξ αὐτῶν ἀπώλετο εἰ μὴ ὁ υἱὸς τῆς ἀπωλείας . . . Perhaps it is neither accidental nor the result of obtuse redaction[1] that chapter 6 concludes with a dialogue between Jesus and the Twelve (verses 66-71) in which Simon confesses that Jesus has the ῥήματα ζωῆς αἰωνίου, but Jesus warns that one of the Twelve is a διάβολος—the equivalent to υἱὸς τῆς ἀπωλείας.[2] There can be little doubt that the "twelve baskets" of 6.13 represent the twelve apostles, of whom "none may be lost," except the "son of lostness," who is so destined. But the passages just cited indicate that it is not only the apostles as such whose loss is to be avoided, much less the physical bread they gather, but "everyone who believes" in Jesus, whom "the Twelve" represent.[3] Perhaps then there is an additional allusion to the twelve tribes of Israel, as in the Jewish prayers whose language so closely resembles that of both John 6.12 and Didache 9.4.

In this context John 11.50-52 must also be carefully considered. If the interpretation of 6.12f. proposed here is correct, then Jesus is not only the one who gives miraculous food, but the one who thereby "gathers" those who are "scattered upon the mountain," that is, the straying children of Israel who come to believe in him. The "prophecy" of the high priest in 11.50 urges Jesus' death ἵνα . . . μὴ ὅλον τὸ ἔθνος ἀπόληται, and the evangelist's note adds that Jesus died not only for "the nation," but ἵνα καὶ τὰ τέκνα τοῦ θεοῦ τὰ διεσκορπισμένα συναγάγῃ εἰς ἕν (11.52). The resemblance

---

[1] Bultmann, Ev. Joh., p. 176. Bultmann evidently had difficulty in deciding what to do with 6.60-71 once he determined to remove it from the transmitted context. For the various attempts to find a place for the passage, compare his analysis on p. 77, p. 154, n. 8, pp. 214f., and the corrections in the Ergänzungsheft to each. In my judgment the passage fits as well at the close of chap. 6 as any of the places Bultmann tried.

[2] Cf. 2 Thess. 2.3 and CD VI, 15 (בני השחת).

[3] Hoskyns recognizes this symbolism: "They [the regenerate believers] are the true and living bread which must not and indeed cannot be lost" (p. 305), but he offers no exegetical foundation for the statement, although he notes that 6.12b "is explained in v. 39" (p. 289) and suggests that the twelve baskets represent the twelve Apostles (p. 290). Cf. also Barrett, pp. 230-231.

between this verse and Didache 9.4 has already been noted; now its similarity with the Johannine interpretation of the bread miracle is equally apparent. As John 6 shows that Jesus provides the miraculous bread, the "true bread" that "remains for eternal life," by his act of giving "his flesh," that is, by his death, so in 11.50-52 it is by dying that he "gathers into one" the "scattered children of God."

The imagery of "scattering" and "gathering," which belongs more to the description of sheep and shepherd than to sowing and reaping or bread-making, is very widespread in the Old Testament, where it describes the dispersion of Israel, usually understood as an act of God's judgment, and his merciful gathering of them, which is anticipated and prayed for.[1] Of all the passages which have been adduced as parallels to both John 6.12 and Didache 9.4, the closest of all seems to have been overlooked. In 1 Kings 22.17 Micaiah the prophet says, "I have seen all Israel scattered into the mountains, like a flock that has no shepherd."[2] Here the puzzling phrase "upon the mountains" of Didache 9.4—which is also implied by the ἀνῆλθεν δὲ εἰς τὸ ὄρος of John 6.3—finds its explanation, especially if the version found in the Targums, the Syriac, and 2 Chronicles 18.16 is adopted, "scattered *upon* the mountains" (על–ההרים instead of אל–ההרים). It is worth noting that the phrase "like sheep with no shepherd" is found already connected with the feeding narrative in Mark 6.34.[3] Apparently the oral tradition of some segments of the early church identified the feeding of the multitude as the act of the shepherd who was to gather Israel.[4] At least it is significant that in the Johannine discourse on

---

[1] "Scattered" as judgment: Dt. 30.1-10; quoted in the prayer of Neh. 1.8f.; Jer. 9.15 (16); 10.21; 13.14 (LXX); Ezek. 20.34; 22.15 (all διασκορπί-ζειν); Lev. 26.33 (a formula found also in Jer. 9.16; Ezek. 12.14); Dt. 4.27; 28.64; Jer. 13.24; 15.7; 18.17; Ezek. 11.17 (all διασπείρειν). God to "gather" (συνάγειν) the scattered Israelites: Isa. 11.12; 56.7f; Hos. 1.11 (LXX 2.2); Isa. 27.12; Jer. 23. 1-6; cf. 32.37 (LXX 39.37); Ezek. 11.17; 20.33ff (note the Exodus and Passover allusions: cf. Dt. 26.8 and the Passover Haggadah).

[2] Thus the MT. LXX reads ἑώρακα πάντα τὸν Ἰσραὴλ διεσπαρμένον [B, Syr, 2 Chron. 18.16: διεσπαρμένους] ἐν τοῖς ὄρεσιν ὡς ποίμνιον ᾧ οὐκ ἔστιν ποιμήν.

[3] Perhaps derived from Num. 27.17. Neither Lk. nor Mt. follows Mk., but Mt. uses the verse in 9.36 where he adds ἦσαν ἐσκυλμένοι καὶ ἐριμμένοι. The latter may have been suggested by the נפצים of 1 Kings 22.17; the rest of the quotation follows Mk. 6.34.

[4] The apparently irrelevant reference to the "plentiful grass" (Jn. 6.10; cf. Mk. 6.39) may also be a subtle allusion to the Good Shepherd's care for the sheep. Cf. Philo, *Mos.* I, 65; Josephus, *Antt.* ii, 264f., on luxuriant grass

the "Good Shepherd" Jesus says, in close conjunction with the statement that he will lay down his life for the sheep, "I also have other sheep which are not of this fold, and I must gather (ἀγαγεῖν) them . . . and there will be one flock, one shepherd" (10.16).

Who is the figure who is to "gather Israel?" In the Old Testament it is primarily God himself, but also the prophets, kings, David, Joshua, and Moses are shepherds of Israel. Elijah was expected to come to "restore the tribes of Jacob" (Sirach 48.10), and in the midrashim Moses is the "faithful shepherd." Either the Davidic Messiah or a figure like Moses could be regarded as one who was to gather the dispersed tribes. However, two things must be noticed: (1) David would never be called "the Prophet,"[1] and (2) there is no basis or evidence for an expectation that the Davidic Messiah would die for the people.[2] Moses, on the other hand, was regarded as the "prince of the prophets" in Judaism, and, as will be shown in the next chapter, his death was regarded as vicarious in some sense.[3] Once again, therefore, support is found for the view that "the prophet coming into the world" who is to be made "king" is a figure related to the traditions about Moses.

Conclusions

From the foregoing analysis it can be seen that the fourth evangelist has set the traditional feeding miracle into the context of the manna from heaven enjoyed by the wilderness generation under Moses' leadership and connected with the eschatological interpretation of the Passover bread. Moreover, good reason was found, though no certainty is possible, for regarding the gathering of the fragments, emphasized by the evangelist as a distinct act, as a symbolic action pointing to Jesus' mission to "gather into one the children of God who are scattered." As the giving of the true bread is explained in the following discourse as a symbol of Jesus' giving of himself in death, so also his death is the means by which

---

on Sinai, where Moses pastured Raguel's flock. This tradition is also known in haggadah; see Salomo Rappaport, *Agada und Exegese bei Flavius Josephus* (Frankfort a/M: J. Kauffmann Verlag, 1930), pp. 29, 117f., n. 144.

[1] The fact that David was thought to have had the gift of prophecy (Ginzberg, VI, 249 f., n. 24) does not contradict this statement.

[2] Cf. Volz, pp. 288f.; Moore I, 551f., III, 166, n. 255; Schürer, II, 648-651.

[3] Cf. Bloch, pp. 127-138.

the scattered children are gathered. The themes of chapter 6, like those of the trial before Pilate, are found to be very close to those of chapter 10, where it is by "laying down his life" that the Good Shepherd establishes the "one fold."

The mission described in this manner is the mission of "the prophet coming into the world" who, it is taken for granted, is to be "king." The identification of Jesus as this prophet-king is by no means denied by Jesus' "flight" to the mountain; only the time and the manner in which the men seek to make him king are rejected.

At every point evidence has accumulated for connecting the "prophet-king" of 6.14f. with the tradition of a prophet like Moses. Whether the Mosaic traditions offer sufficient foundation for this view will be a problem for the following chapters.

CHAPTER THREE

MOSES IN NON-RABBINIC JEWISH SOURCES

In this and the following chapter the conventional separation of
Jewish sources originating in Palestine from those of the Diaspora
has been abandoned.[1] The new discoveries and research of recent
years have shown that the boundary between "Palestinian" and
"Hellenistic" forms of both Judaism and early Christianity are
quite fluid.[2]

There are very good reasons, however, for separating those
sources which have been shaped and preserved by "normative"
Judaism from those which were rejected, neglected, or unknown by
the rabbis. The non-rabbinic sources are witnesses to the diversity
of Judaism in the first century—even in Judaea, as the Qumran
texts show so vividly—which would scarcely be guessed from
reading the Talmuds and the rabbinic midrashim, at least as they
are customarily interpreted. In addition, the sources which have
been used for this chapter have the advantage that their dates can
be fixed, with few exceptions, within fairly narrow limits, while the
dating of traditions reported in rabbinic literature is notoriously
difficult.

MOSES IN PHILO

Introduction

Philo as Greek and Jew

Philo was the "Hellenistic Jew" *par excellence* and, in the prevailing opinion of scholarship, far more Hellenistic than Jewish.

---

[1] Such a classification of the sources used here, apart from the Qumran
documents, is found in Schürer, III, chaps. 32 ("Die palästinensisch-jüdische
Literatur") and 33 ("Die hellenistisch-jüdische Literatur").

[2] E.g., Victor Tcherikover, *Hellenistic Civilization and the Jews*, trans. S.
Applebaum (Philadelphia: The Jewish Publication Society of America,
1961), especially Part I, chaps. 2 and 7, and pp. 344f. and n. 2; Elias Bickermann, *From Ezra to the Last of the Maccabees; Foundations of Post-Biblical
Judaism* (New York: Schocken Books, 1962), *passim*; Saul Liebermann,
Hellenism in Jewish Palestine (New York: The Jewish Theological Seminary,
1950), *passim*; Morton Smith, "Palestinian Judaism in the First Century,"

Isaac Heinemann's meticulous research[1] demonstrated that the oral Torah so central to Pharisaic Judaism was foreign to Philo. The "law" for Philo was the written Pentateuch, in the Septuagint version, and his understanding of the law was thoroughly Greek.[2] Yet it is also true, as E. R. Goodenough points out, that the fundamental importance which Philo gives to the Torah, as the comprehensive guide of all life and source of all wisdom, marks him as a *gesetztreuer* Jew.[3] Moreover there are indications that, while Philo knew no oral *halakah*, he knew some of the haggadic traditions which have found their way into later midrashim.[4] Of course this fact in itself does not indicate whether the traditions were originally "Palestinian," "Hellenistic," or both.

The Use of Philo as a Source

The use of Philo as a source for the Judaism of his milieu is fraught with difficulties. Apart from the complexity of his thought and the formlessness and repetitiousness of the allegorical tracts, the main problem is to discern when Philo is original, when representative. E. R. Goodenough, upon whose pioneering research in Philo much of what follows is based, argues that Philo, in the basic structure of his allegory, is representative. To support this position, Goodenough shows, in the first place, that when the fragmentary elements of Philo's allegorical description of the Patriarchs are gathered from the many different contexts in which they appear in his works, the fragments are remarkably self-consistent. "Philo himself," Goodenough concludes, "could hardly have developed

---

Israel: Its Role in Civilization, ed. Moshe Davis (New York: The Seminary Israel Institute of Jewish Theological Seminary, 1956), pp. 67-81; Goodenough, *Jewish Symbols*, vols. I-III; Jacob Neusner, "Jewish Use of Pagan Symbols after 70 C.E.," *The Journal of Religion*, 43 (1963), 285-294.

[1] *Philons griechische und jüdische Bildung; Kulturvergleichende Untersuchungen zu Philons Darstellung der jüdischen Gesetze* (Breslau: M. & H. Marcus, 1929-1932; rp. Darmstadt: Wissenschaftliche Buchgesellschaft, 1963), 606 pp.

[2] *Ibid.*, pp. 524-527, *et passim*; cf. E. R. Goodenough, *By Light, Light; The Mystic Gospel of Hellenistic Judaism* (New Haven: Yale University Press, 1935), chap. II.

[3] Goodenough, *By Light, Light*, pp. 73f.

[4] An impressive, if small, beginning of the comparison of such parallels was made by Edmund Stein, *Philo und der Midrasch; Philos Schilderung der Gestalten des Pentateuch verglichen mit der des Midrasch* (BZAW, No. 57, 1931), 52 pp. Recently Peder Borgen has taken up the task (reported in his paper "Philo and a Haggadic Tradition," read before the 99th meeting of the Society of Biblical Literature, New York, January 2, 1964).

this great allegory of the Mystery *de novo*, and then broken it up
into the myriad incidental allusions and fragments that he offers."[1]
Second, Goodenough backs up his argument that Philo represents
a substantial movement by collecting an impressive array of literary
and iconographic parallels.[2] Both arguments have to be evaluated
with some caution. Against the first it can be argued that Philo is
not always consistent, and sometimes quite self-contradictory,
while demonstrating that his mind is capable of such ingenuity that
it is perilous to assert that he could not invent a given allegory. In
the case of the second, the pitfalls in the use of "parallels" are well-
known; applied to Philo the most dangerous is the temptation to
read into less explicit parallels Philo's developed allegory as "implicit."

A tentative working method may now be formulated, both for
Philo and the other sources employed in this chapter. Each element
of the portrait of Moses which bears on the problem of this dissertation must be questioned, asking: Which elements can be satis-
factorily explained from known antecedents, Greek or Jewish?
Which elements can be "midrashically" connected with the biblical
text? Which elements grow naturally out of Philo's own over-all
argument and tendency? Which elements does Philo find it necessary to explain; which does he take for granted? In this way the
most salient characteristics of Moses as seen by Philo's circle emerge
with tolerable clarity.

The Significance of Moses for Philo

Moses superior to all others

The most casual reading not only of Philo's *Vita Mosis* but of his
other tracts as well will show that Moses is his primary hero. Moses
is far superior to the Patriarchs; they had to be initiated into the
holy secrets as novices, while Moses officiates from the beginning
as the mystagogue.[3] Noah represents only a "copy" of the "supreme
wisdom" shown in Moses; hence God grants grace to Noah only
through his "powers" but he himself rewards Moses directly.[4]

---

[1] *By Lgiht, Light*, pp. 180f.
[2] *Ibid.*, pp. 265-369; *Jewish Symbols, passim*, esp. vols. IX-XI, which deal
with the Dura synagogue frescoes.
[3] *Post.* 173, below, pp. 120–122.
[4] *Quod deus* 109f.

Moses is the ideal Jew, whose life presents to the Gentile inquirer the highest values of Judaism.[1] The true Jews in turn, that is, those who are capable of "clearly understanding" the symbolic meaning of the Torah, are "Moses' disciples."[2] Moreover, Moses is evidently Philo's own ideal, the true "philosopher,"[3] "sage,"[4] and "theologian,[5] the model to be imitated. Moses himself was God's disciple; he learned from God as they were alone together.[6] He is called the "friend of God," who shares all God's treasures, so far as possible, even his title.[7]

Moses as divine

It is obvious that Philo portrays Moses as something more than an ordinary human being. He is "the divine and holy Moses."[8] Already in his youth his control of his passions caused such astonishment that people wondered τίς ἄρα ὁ ἐνοικῶν αὐτοῦ τῷ σώματι καί

---

[1] The *Vita Mosis* is written "to make his life known to those who are worthy not to remain ignorant of it" (*Mos.* i.1). On the place of the *Vita* in Philo's writings, see Schürer, III, 675. Goodenough argues convincingly that it was intended as an introduction to the whole exposition of the Law (embracing *Abr.*, the lost *de Isaaco* and *de Iacobo*, *Jos.*, *Opif.*, *Dec.*, *Spec. leg.*, and *Praem.*: *By Light, Light*, p. 181).

[2] γνώριμοι Μωυσέως, *QG* iii.8; *Spec. leg.* i. 59, 319ff., 345; *Det.* 86; *Post.* 12; *Conf.* 39; *Quis Her.* 81; *Vit. Cont.* 63; *Hyp.* ii.1; θιασῶται: *Quod deus* 120; *Plant.* 39; ἑταῖροι, *Conf.* 62; φοιτηταί: *Spec. leg.* i.319, 345; ii.256; Cf. *Som.* ii.1.

[3] *Quis Her.* 301; *Conf.* 1.

[4] σοφός: *Leg. all.* ii.87, 93; iii.45, 131, 140, 141, 144, 147 (ὁ τέλειος σοφός); *Det.* 162; *Post.* 18; *Gig.* 47, 50, cf. 27; *Quod deus* 23-26, cf. 110; *Ebr.* 1, 100; *Sob.* 20; *Conf.* 30, 192; *Mig.* 113, 201; *Quis Her.* 19, cf. 21; *Fug.* 157, 165; *Mut.* 19, 104, 128; *Som.* ii.229, 237, 278; *Mos.* ii.67; cf. i.4; *Spec. leg.* iv.143; *Quod omn. prob.* 29, 68; πάνσοφος: *Det.* 126; *Post.* 28, 169, cf. 173; *Gig.* 56; *Agr.* 20, 43; *Plant.* 27; *Mig.* 45, 76; *Abr.* 13; *Spec. leg.* ii.194; iv. 69, 157, 175; *QE* ii.74.

[5] θεολόγος: *QG* ii.33, 59, 64, 81; iii.5, 20, 38; iv. 137; *QE* ii.37, 74, 87, 88, 108, 117.

[6] *Mos.* i.80; ii. 163. Cf. the rabbinic emphasis on Num. 12.8, where it is said that God spoke to Moses alone פה אל־פה; e.g., *ARN* (ed. Schechter), pp. 10f.

[7] *Mos.* i.156, 158; cf. Ex. 33.11; 7.1. Moses is called φίλος θεοῦ also *Sac.* 130; *Ebr.* 94; *Mig.* 45; *Quis Her.* 21; *Som.* i.193f., 231f.; θεόφιλος and θεοφιλής, *Op.* 5; *Leg. all.* i.76; ii.79, 88, 90; iii.130; *Cher.* 49; *Sac.* 77; *Det.* 13; *Plant.* 62; *Conf.* 95; *Mig.* 67; *Mos.* ii.67, 163; *Spec. leg.* i.41; iv. 175; *Virt.* 77; *Quod omn. prob.* 44.

[8] *QE* ii.54, trans. Ralph Marcus in *Philo, with an English Translation by F. H. Colson and G. H. Whitaker* ("The Loeb Classical Library," ed. by E. Capps *et al.*; London: Wm. Heinemann, Ltd., 1929-64) [cited henceforth as "Loeb"], Supplement, II, 102.

ἀγαλματοφορούμενος νοῦς ἐστι, πότερον ἀνθρώπειος ἢ θεῖος ἢ μικτὸς ἐξ ἀμφοῖν.[1] Bieler remarks that the three possibilities all belong to "the Aristotelian definition of the θεῖος ἀνήρ."[2] The features common to Philo's *Vita Mosis* and the *Vita* of a typical Hellenistic θεῖος ανήρ are numerous; they are conveniently summarized by Bieler.[3] Nevertheless, Bieler concludes that Philo's Moses is "not the usual θεῖος of Hellenism, the typical hero of miracle-mongering aretalogies." Rather, "he is the πνευματικός in whom, centuries later, pagan and Christian Gnosis alike saw the perfect man, that Gnosis which announces itself so impressively already in Philo."[4]

Bieler's statement is very judicious, but it raises an important question: to what extent is one justified in speaking of "gnosticism" in Philo? If by gnosticism one means a pattern of myth in which a heavenly redeemer is essential, then only one passage in Philo can be called "gnostic":

> When God lent Moses to earthly things and permitted him to associate with them. He endowed him not at all with the ordinary virtue of a ruler or king with which forcibly to rule the soul's passions; rather He appointed him to be god, and decreed that the whole bodily realm and its leader, the mind, should be his subjects and slaves.[5]

Philo arrives at this remarkable statement by his exegesis of Exodus 7.1: Ἰδοὺ δέδωκά σε θεὸν Φαραω. In Philo's allegorical scheme, "Egypt" consistently represents the body or the whole material universe, while "Pharaoh" represents the "lower mind," that is, the mind turned toward the senses. Thus in this passage, Moses does seem to represent the messenger sent from the world of light into the bodily realm to instruct and thus redeem "his own," the higher minds capable of receiving the divine mysteries. In this light his mission to Egypt parallels that of the Parthian Prince in the *Hymn of the Pearl*. Furthermore the analogy between Moses and God implied by his title θεός is taken so seriously in this passage

---

[1] *Mos.* i.27.

[2] Bieler, II, 35.

[3] *Ibid.*, pp. 33-36.

[4] *Ibid.*, p. 36.

[5] *Sac.* 9. I adopt here the translation by Goodenough, *By Light, Light,* p. 199. The text reads: οὐ μὴν οὐδέ, ὅτε τοῖς περιγείοις χρήσας αὐτὸν εἴασεν ἐνομιλεῖν, ἄρχοντος ἢ βασιλέως κοινήν τινα ἀρετὴν ἀνῆπτεν αὐτῷ, καθ' ἣν ἀνὰ κράτος ἡγεμονεύσει τῶν τῆς ψυχῆς παθῶν, ἀλλ' εἰς θεὸν αὐτὸν ἐχειροτόνει πᾶσαν τὴν περὶ τὸ σῶμα χώραν καὶ τὸν ἡγεμόνα αὐτῆς νοῦν ὑπήκοα καὶ δοῦλα ἀποφήνας. . .

that it approaches consubstantiality. The translation of Moses to "him that is," Philo argues, was not the same as the "adding" of the Patriarchs (in the common biblical phrase, "N. died and was added to his people"), "Since God (θεός), being complete and perfectly equal to himself, does not admit diminution or addition."[1] Moses thus shares God's nature, as in a few other passages,[2] and is accorded the title "God" in the proper sense.

Yet the passage is unique, for elsewhere Philo uses the same scriptural text and a similar argument from analogy in exactly the opposite direction: to show that Moses was called "god" only in a figurative sense. In the tract "That the Worse is Wont to Attack the Better" (161-162), he shows that since Exodus 7.1 says that Moses as θεός is *given* to Pharaoh, the word is only a metaphor for "God is giver (δίδων), not given (διδόμενος), ... active (δραστήριον), not passive (πάσχον)." Hence the text means only that "the wise man is 'god' of the foolish, but in truth he is not God" (ὁ σοφὸς λέγεται μὲν θεὸς τοῦ ἄφροντος, πρὸς ἀλήθειαν δὲ οὐκ ἔστι θεός). Furthermore, while the biblical text is used in "The Sacrifices of Abel and Cain" to show that Moses' translation was the return of the perfect soul to the One who Is, Philo's other descriptions of Moses' assumption[3] clearly depict the apotheosis of a divine *man*, not the return of an incarnate deity, as Goodenough suggests.[4] The distinction is important;[5] while Philo does vacillate in his portrait of Moses, now elevating him virtually to a "second god," again restricting him to the sphere of the human,[6] the vacillation remains within the compass of the θεῖος ἀνήρ. If Bieler finds Philo's Moses something more than the typical θεῖος, that is partly because Bieler has restricted his investigation primarily to the "godlike wise man and prophet," omitting for practical reasons the other major type of θεῖος, "the

---

[1] *Sac.* 10.

[2] *Post.* 28, τῆς ἐαυτοῦ φύσεως, ἡρεμίας, τῷ σπουδαίῳ μεταδίδωσιν; cf. *Gig.* 47ff.; *Quod deus* 23; *Conf.* 30f.; Goodenough, *By Light, Light,* p. 228.

[3] *Mos.* ii. 288-292; *Virt.* 73-75. Actually the same view appears in *Sac.* 8, immediately before the passage just discussed: Moses is translated as a reward, because he is "the perfect man."

[4] *By Light, Light,* pp. 223, 225. Moreover, since Philo accepts the Platonic concept of metempsychosis, the death of any man could be described as the "return" of the soul.

[5] Cf. Bieler, I, 150.

[6] Goodenough, *By Light, Light,* p. 224. Goodenough's discussion of the divinity of Moses, pp. 223-234, is very helpful.

divine king of Hellenism."[1] It is precisely in the second type that Goodenough, with very persuasive evidence, finds the closest analogy to Philo's Moses and, to a lesser degree, Philo's Patriarchs. Bieler's monograph and Goodenough's own essay on Hellenistic kingship[2] thus provide needed complements to each other. To speak of "gnosticism" or "gnostic influence" in Philo is therefore unjustified. Instead, Philo provides a graphic illustration of the kind of syncretistic building material that could lend itself directly to the construction of gnostic systems.

Moses of many names

In a passage in his treatise "On the Change of Names," Philo says, "The Chief Prophet turns out to be many-named."[3] As Goodenough points out,[4] the adjective πολυώνυμος was a frequent epithet for deities in classical and Hellenistic literature,[5] a fact which was probably not lost on Philo, though the names he mentions in this passage remain within the limits of the "divine man." More important is the way in which the various titles are related to one another in the passage. The functions of legislator and of prophet are merged and connected with the name "Moses," which, by some mysterious etymology, is explained "receiving" or "handling." The functions of priesthood are connected with the title "Man of God," and the title "God" of Exodus 7.1 is explained figuratively, as in the passage already discussed.[6] Moreover, all these diverse functions and titles are subsumed under the supreme title ἀρχιπροφήτης.

This passage illustrates the fluidity of titles and descriptive epithets applied to Moses by Philo. The combinations and explanations are almost endless in variety, suggesting that perhaps the titles were given him by scripture and tradition, while their interpretation and interrelationship is to a greater extent his own. Only in the *Vita Mosis*, and in a brief summary again in the treatise "On

---

[1] Bieler, I, 6.

[2] "The Political Philosophy of Hellenistic Kingship," *Yale Classical Studies*, Vol. I, ed. Austin M. Harmon (New Haven: Yale University Press, 1928), pp. 55-102.

[3] *Mut.* 125.

[4] *By Light, Light*, p. 228, n. 193.

[5] Besides Diogenes Laertius, VII. 135, which Goodenough cites, cf. Cleanthes' *Hymn to Zeus*, which begins: κύδιστ' ἀθανάτων, πολυώνυμε, παγκρατὲς αἰοί.

[6] Above, p. 104f.; *Det.* 161f.

Rewards and Punishments,"[1] is there a consistent systematization of Moses' offices, and in these places the supreme title is not prophet but king. This complex must now be explored.

Moses as King in Philo

The Vita Mosis as portrait of the ideal king

The fundamental theme of Philo's Life of Moses" is that Moses was the "most excellent king," the "most perfect ruler." This fact is not at once apparent, for Philo's prooemium introduces Moses as "according to some, the legislator (νομοθέτης) of the Jews, according to others the interpreter of the sacred laws (ἑρμηνεὺς νόμων ἱερῶν)."[2] At the end of the first book, however, Philo tells the reader that "the preceding account has related Moses' royal activity," and then goes on to show that "legislation"—like priesthood and prophecy— is only an adjunct of kingship.[3] These remarks are certainly not just an after-thought, a "coup de pouce" to round out the pane- gyric.[4] Rather, they reveal the deliberate plan by which Philo has arranged his biography. Book I is the step-by-step portrayal of Moses as the ideal king.

Actually, the first hint of Philo's outline appears quite early in Book I, for he introduces the whole story of Israel's migration to Egypt and their oppression there to explain how it happened that Moses received a "royal upbringing" (τροφὴ βασιλική).[5] The story of Moses' exposure and his adoption by Pharaoh's daughter is expanded from the biblical account—either by Philo or, more likely, by the tradition before him—so that its main point is that Moses became heir apparent to the Egyptian throne.[6] His education and his miraculous progress as a child are typical of the θεῖος ἀνήρ;[7] he

---

[1] *Praem.* 53-55. If Goodenough is correct, this treatise forms the peroration to the Exposition of the Laws, as *Mos.* provided its introduction.

[2] *Mos.* i.1.

[3] *Mos.* i.334, cf. ii.1-7.

[4] Thus Bernard Botte, "La vie de Moïse par Philon," *Moïse, l'homme de l'alliance,* ed. H. Cazelles *et al.,* pp. 55-62. The significance of M. Botte's assertion, that Philo's attribution of kingship to Moses distorts "historical truth," escapes me.

[5] *Mos.* i.8, cf. 20.

[6] See especially *Mos.* i.13, 19.

[7] Bieler, I, 34-38.

soon displayed the extraordinary virtues which mark the semi-
divine king of Hellenistic royal ideology.[1] Recognized as the successor to Pharaoh, he was even called "the young king."[2] When he
was forced to leave Egypt, he nevertheless continued his practice
of philosophy and virtue[3] and received his final training for kingship
as Raguel's shepherd, "for the shepherd's business is a training-
ground and a preliminary exercise in kingship for one who is destined
to command the herd of mankind...."[4] Moses' appointment as
king is solemnly described and explained at the beginning of the
Exodus itself; the passage must be examined in more detail directly.[5] In the wilderness, the reader is told, God provided the
manna not only because of his own benevolence, but also "to honor
the leader he had appointed."[6] Moses' kingship thus emerges as the
organizing principle of Book I. Finally, while Philo inserts notes
which explain the attribution of other offices to Moses, his kingship
is unexplained. Evidently it is not only Moses' most important
"office" in Philo's presentation to Gentile inquirers, it is one which
is taken for granted in Philo's circle.

Aspects of Moses' kingship

At the turning point of the narrative, when Moses' preparation
for kingship is complete and he is inducted into the office, that is,
when the actual Exodus begins, Philo inserts an extraordinary
passage expounding the basis and characteristics of Moses' kingship.[7] He gives three explanations for Moses' election as king, which
may be called, for convenience, the haggadic, the philosophical, and
the mystic bases.

In simplest terms, God rewarded Moses with the kingship of
Israel because Moses had virtuously renounced the hegemony of
Egypt to which he was heir.[8] The reward was of course superior to
the forfeited honor, for Israel was "a nation more populous and
mightier, a nation destined to be consecrated above all others to

---

[1] *Mos.* i.18-31, cf. Goodenough, "Kingship," pp. 69-73, 86-89.
[2] *Mos.* i.32.
[3] *Ibid.*, 48.
[4] *Ibid.*, 60.
[5] *Ibid.*, 148-162.
[6] *Ibid.*, 198.
[7] *Ibid.*, 148-162.
[8] *Ibid.*, 148f.

offer prayers for ever on behalf of the human race . . .''[1] The same
motif is repeated in a subsequent paragraph, in different form, for
since Moses renounced the wealth which normally was a perquisite
of kingship, God rewarded him with ''the greatest and most perfect
wealth,'' the whole world.[2] This kind of divine *quid pro quo* is a
familiar feature in folklore; it can be plausibly conjectured, but not
demonstrated, that Philo here makes use of a bit of traditional
haggada which has not survived elsewhere. A very similar motif is
echoed in the New Testament, Hebrews 11.24-26.[3] Philo's own
typical interests come to the fore in the other two reasons.

Moses received kingship, in the second place, because the universal virtues he displayed marked him as the ideal ruler. He used
no force to acquire the throne, but was freely appointed.[4] He did
not establish a dynasty, but judged impartially the comparative
merits of his own sons and others.[5] His one aim was to benefit his
subjects.[6] He did not seek personal aggrandisement or levy tributes;
his only extravagance was in the accumulation of virtue.[7] Section
154 is a catalogue of virtues, and examples of Moses' practical exercise of kingly virtues are provided by Philo at every turn of his
narrative. For example, avoiding war with the Edomites displays
both Moses' prudence and his kindness;[8] he admonishes the tribes
of Reuben and Gad as a father.[9]

Philo's list of Moses' virtues reads like a ''mirror for kings.'' In
fact a strikingly close parallel is found in a fragment of the treatise
''On Kingship'' by Diotogenes, a Pythagorean:

> . . . He must excel the rest in virtue and on that account be
> judged worthy to rule, but not on account of his wealth, or
> power, or military strength. For the first of these qualities he
> has in common with all sorts of people, the second with ir-

---

[1] *Ibid.*, 149, trans. F. H. Colson (Loeb), VI, 355. This sentence is clearly
derived from Ex. 19.5f., where it is promised that Israel will be λαὸς περιούσιος
[θεῷ] ἀπὸ πάντων τῶν ἐθνῶν and βασίλειον ἱεράτευμα καὶ ἔθνος ἅγιον.

[2] *Ibid.*, 155.

[3] Πίστει Μωϋσῆς μέγας γενόμενος ἠρνήσατο λέγεσθαι υἱὸς θυγατρὸς Φαραώ,
μᾶλλον ἑλόμενος συγκακουχεῖσθαι τῷ λαῷ τοῦ θεοῦ ἢ πρόσκαιρον ἔχειν ἁμαρτίας
ἀπόλαυσιν, μείζονα πλοῦτον ἡγησάμενος τῶν Αἰγύπτου θησαυρῶν τὸν ὀνειδισμὸν
τοῦ Χριστοῦ.

[4] *Mos.* i.148.

[5] *Ibid.*, 150.

[6] *Ibid.*, 151.

[7] *Ibid.*, 152f.

[8] *Ibid.*, 249.

[9] *Ibid.*, 328.

rational animals, the third with tyrants, while virtue alone is
peculiar to good men. So that what king is self-controlled in
pleasure, given to sharing his possessions, and is prudent and
powerful in virtue, that man would be a king in very truth.[1]

It is also significant that Philo offers as an alternative explanation
of Moses' astonishing gifts of virtue the notion that "since he was
destined to be a legislator, long before that he became a living and
articulate law (νόμος ἔμψυχος καί λογικός) by divine providence,
which without his knowledge had appointed him to the office of
legislator."[2] Again Diotogenes provides the closest parallel:

> The most just man would be king, and the most lawful would
> be most just. For without justice no one would be king, and
> without law (there would be no) justice. For justice is in the
> law, and the law is the source (αἴτιος) of justice. But the king
> is Animate Law (νόμος ἔμψυχος), or is a legal ruler (νόμιμος
> ἄρχων). So for this reason he is most just and most lawful.[3]

There is no need to repeat in more detail Goodenough's well-
documented thesis that the predominant Hellenistic ideology of
kingship viewed the ideal king as a νόμος ἔμψυχος, a personal presence of the unwritten universal law, superior to all statutory law.[4]
Goodenough has also demonstrated how extensively this "living
law" conception has shaped Philo's portrait of all the Patriarchs,
but above all that of Moses.[5]

There is a third, more mystical interpretation of Moses' induction
into kingship which is extremely important:

> For he was named god and king (θεὸς καὶ βασιλεύς) of the whole
> nation. And he is said to have entered into the darkness where
> God was, that is, into the formless[6] and invisible and incor-

---

[1] Preserved in Stobaeus, IV, vii, 26, quoted and translated by Goodenough,
"Kingship," p. 70.

[2] *Mos.* i.162.

[3] Stobaeus, IV, vii, 61, cited by Goodenough, "Kingship," p. 65.

[4] Goodenough's findings are summarized in "Kingship," pp. 101f. The
small demur may be permitted that to speak of the king as an "incarnation"
of the Law = the Logos is an exaggeration and really misleading. The
adjective ἔμψυχος will not bear the translation "incarnate" or even "en-
souled," but can only mean "living," as in Mos. i.105, where Philo compares
dead frogs with those that are ἔμψυχα.

[5] *By Light, Light*, p. 89, and chaps. ii-vii *passim*.

[6] ἀειδῆ. It is difficult to see how the τῶν ὄντων παραδειγματικὴ οὐσία could
be "formless"; perhaps one should read "unseen" with Colson (Loeb), VII,
359, and Goodenough, *By Light, Light*, p. 186, n. 33.

poreal archetypal essence of existing things, perceiving (κατανοῶν) things invisible to mortal nature. And like a well-executed painting, openly presenting himself and his life, he set up an altogether beautiful and God-formed work as an example (παράδειγμα) for those who are willing to imitate it. Happy are those who have imprinted their souls or who have striven to imprint them with the image (τύπος). For let the mind bear if at all possible the perfect form (εἶδος) of virtue, but if not, then at least the unhesitating desire to possess the form.[1]

Here Moses' kingship assigns him an intermediary status between God and the rest of men; having perceived the invisible good, he so models his own life after it that he becomes a paradigm for his subjects. Again, Goodenough argues that this concept of double imitation is a common *topos* of Hellenistic kingship.[2] He illustrates his argument by impressive parallels from the second fragment on kingship attributed to Ecphantus by Stobaeus[3] and a fragment of Plutarch's "Discourse to an Unlearned Prince."[4] The argument is convincing, so far as Philo's interpretation is concerned. But perhaps it is more important for purposes of the present investigation to notice that in the Philonic passage Moses' paradigmatic office is founded upon a mystic vision, which in turn is identified allegorically with his ascent of Mt. Sinai.[5] This is not paralleled in the fragments cited by Goodenough. The implication is that Philo is uniting the Hellenistic ideology of kingship with an existing midrash which interpreted Moses' ascent of Sinai as a mystical "ascension." Puzzling is the double title "god and king." The first, θεός, Philo takes directly from Exodus 7.1,[6] but the scriptural context has no connection with the Sinai ascent, nor does it mention kingship. One is left then with the question how Philo came to connect Moses' installation as ideal king with (1) a mystic ascent, read into the Sinai episode, and (2) the scriptural report that Moses was called θεός. Evidence will appear below that Philo was not alone in making this peculiar connection.

---

[1] *Mos.* i.158f.

[2] *By Light, Light*, p. 186, n. 34; "Kingship," pp. 88-91; cf. p. 74.

[3] IV, vii, 65, cited by Goodenough, "Kingship," p. 89.

[4] *Moralia*, V, 11ff., cited by Goodenough, "Kingship," p. 96.

[5] Ex. 20.21 is the source of the statement εἴς τε τὸν γνόφον, ἔνθα ἦν ὁ θεός, εἰσελθεῖν λέγεται.

[6] Cf. *Sac.* 9; *Det.* 161f.; see above pp. 165f.

Kingship and the other offices

The transitional statements with which Philo punctuates his biography of Moses reveal that the whole is divided into four parts:

1. περὶ βασιλείας, Book I.
2. περὶ τῶν κατὰ τὴν νομοθετικὴν ἕξιν, II. 8-65.
3. περὶ ἱεροσύνης, II, 66-186.
4. περὶ προφητείας, II, 187-291.

Philo's summaries indicate plainly that the "offices" of legislator, priest, and prophet are really adjuncts to the primary office of king. At the close of Book I, he explains that, since Moses' royal activities have been recounted, it is now necessary to speak in turn of his accomplishments as legislator and as High Priest. "For these powers he also acquired," Philo continues, "as those especially befitting kingship."[1] Again, at the beginning of his treatment of prophecy, Philo recalls that "there are four adjuncts to the truly perfect ruler."[2] While Philo here inconsistently includes "kingship" among the "adjuncts," the following clause names only three, since obviously "king" and "ruler" are the same. Finally, in the summary of Moses' four offices in "On Rewards and Punishments," although the order differs from that in the *Vita*,[3] the relation of lawgiver, priest, and prophet to king is the same: "All these are one in kind; they should co-exist united with bonds of harmony and be found embodied in the same person, since he who falls short in any of the four is imperfectly equipped for government [ἡγεμονία], and the administration of public affairs which he has undertaken will limp and halt."[4]

The relation between kingship and legislation is particularly close and is found in the "living law" notion.

> It is a king's duty to command what is right and forbid what is wrong. But to command what should be done and to forbid what should not be done is the peculiar function of law; so that it follows at once that the king is a living law [νόμος ἔμψυχος], and the law a just king [βασιλέα δίκαιον].[5]

---

[1] *Mos.* i.334.
[2] *Ibid.*, ii.187, trans. Colson (Loeb), VI, 541.
[3] High priest and prophet are reversed.
[4] *Praem.* 56, trans. Colson (Loeb), VIII, 347.
[5] *Mos.* ii.4. Compare the νόμος ἔμψυχος and νόμιμος ἄρχων in the fragment of Diotogenes quoted above, p. 110.

Notice that the argument does not really explain why the king must be a legislator, but assumes it. Moreover, it will be recalled that the prooemium of Book I introduced Moses as "the Legislator," while the book turns out to be about his kingship. The two functions are almost interchangeable, just as they are in Hellenistic kingship theory in general. The king must legislate; the legislator is naturally the king.

However, the prooemium of the *Vita* also reveals that the title "Moses, the legislator of the Jews," is a common way of referring to him in Philo's environment. This observation is confirmed by the usage of the other extant Hellenistic Jewish sources[1] and by the fact that Philo himself, in ordinary discourse, calls Moses ὁ νομο-θέτης more frequently than any other title.[2] Philo's specific combi-nation of "king" and "legislator" thus represents the merging of the traditional Hellenistic Jewish title of Moses with the special content of pagan Hellenistic ideology of kingship. Whether Philo was the first to do this is difficult to say. Certainly the combination would be an obvious one, and the off-hand way in which Philo introduces it suggests that he is not the originator, though he has spelled out the implications of this view with special thoroughness.

That the king should be high priest is also regarded by Philo as a matter of necessity in the case of Moses, for the king must super-vise "divine matters" as well as "human matters," since τὰ θεῖα are necessary for the well-being of the kingdom. "Perfect rites" and "perfect knowledge of the service of God" ward off evil and secure good.[3] Again, Goodenough explains the combination from the ideo-logy of Hellenistic kingship, stressing especially the view of Dio-togenes that the priesthood is a necessary aspect of the kingly office.[4] It is true, as Goodenough says, that the Pentateuch itself did not provide the idea that Moses was high priest, but it should be noted that in some rabbinic traditions Moses was regarded as priest, because of Psalm 99.6, "Moses and Aaron [were] among his priests."[5]

---

[1] See below p. 132 and n. 2.

[2] Most of the occurrences have been collected by J. W. Earp in the Loeb edition, X, 386f., n. a, to which should be added *QG* ii.64; iii.48; iv.172, 244. In *QG* and *QE* προφήτης is the more frequent title.

[3] *Mos.* ii.5; cf. *Praem.* 56.

[4] *By Light, Light*, p. 190.

[5] Cf. Harry Austryn Wolfson, *Philo; Foundations of Religious Philosophy in Judaism, Christianity and Islam* (Cambridge: Harvard University Press,

There are several passages in Philo which indicate that he thought of priesthood as a kingly office, apart from Moses. Comparing the gifts prescribed for the priests by the Torah with the tribute ordinarily paid to kings, he remarks that "from all this it is evident that the Law ascribes royal dignity and honor (βασίλειον σεμνότητα καὶ τιμήν) to the priests."[1] Again he notes that a turban was part of the high priest's vestments, "for Oriental kings customarily use a turban instead of a diadem."[2] In his discussion of Deuteronomy 10.9, he apparently treats kingship as a standing honor accorded the Levites, "whom he calls the great kings":

> In face of this let those cease their proud boastings who have acquired royal and imperial sway, some by bringing under their authority a single city or country or nation, some by having over and above these made themselves masters of all earth's regions to the fullest bounds. . . . For even had they, besides controlling these, extended their empire . . . to the realms of the upper air . . . they would be reckoned ordinary citizens when compared with the great kings who received God as their portion; for the kingship of these as far surpasses theirs as he that has gained possession is better than the possession and he that has made than that which he has made.[3]

It is tempting to see here a reflection of the Hasmonean court ideology, or at least of the historical fact of the Hasmonean priest-kings. In his account of the making of the Septuagint, which mainly follows the *Letter of Aristeas*, Philo notes that at the time of Ptolemy Philadelphus the High Priest and King of Judaea "were the same person,"[4] and in the story of his mission to Gaius he has Agrippa I remark that his ancestors were both kings and priests, but that they considered their priesthood far superior to their kingship.[5] On the other hand, Philo suggests that one reason why Moses did not be-

---

1947), II, 337f., and below, pp. 287-289. Josephus is also a negative witness to this tradition, since he echoes a polemic against it (below, pp. 217f.). The polemic is also reflected in some extant rabbinic sources.

[1] *Spec. leg.*, i.142.

[2] *Mos.*, ii.116. A few paragraphs later, however, he interprets the turban as a sign of the priest's *superiority* to kings (par. 131).

[3] *Plant.*, 67f., trans. Colson (Loeb), III, 247f.; cf. *QE* ii.105. Wolfson (II, 344, n. 151), discussing the latter passage, rejects Goodenough's statement (*By Light, Light*, p. 113) that Aaron and his sons were regarded as kings. Oddly he makes no reference to the other passage I have just cited, which speaks much more directly of the βασιλεία of the Levites.

[4] *Mos.*, ii.31.

[5] *Leg.*, 278.

queath rule as well as priesthood to Aaron's sons may have been that he "reasonably enough considered that it was impossible for the same persons to do justice to both offices, the priesthood and sovereignty, one of which professes the service of God, the other the guardianship of men."[1] The implication is that Philo had a negative view of the Hasmonean experiment,[2] and would probably not have projected its ideals back to the ancient Levites, especially not to the Levite Moses.

The most likely probability remains that suggested by Goodenough, that Hellenistic kingship ideology was the source of the idea that a king must necessarily be a priest. For Philo, however, this was an ideal impracticable for ordinary mortals, so that its full exercise could be attributed only to Moses and, probably only in a figurative sense, to the ancient Levites. It seems that Moses' priesthood was itself traditional, while the uniting of priesthood with kingship was the result of the prevailing Hellenistic understanding of the ideal king.[3]

The situation is quite different in the case of Moses' prophetic office, for the Hellenistic kingship ideology offers no explanation for the peculiar combination of prophet with king.[4] A certain verbal analogy exists in Stoic aphorisms that refer to the ideal sage (σοφός) as "the only (true) king"[5] and could include, among the other functions that only the sage could truly fulfill, that of "diviner" (μάντις),[6] but Wetter and Fascher have made too much of the Stoic background of Philo.[7] The idea that "only the wise man is king" is

---

[1] *Virt.*, 54, trans. Colson (Loeb), VIII, 197.

[2] Cf. Wolfson, II, 339, who suggests, however, that the statement also might reflect polemic against pagan practice.

[3] Philo of course associates kingship with priesthood also in the case of Melchizedek (*Leg. all.*, iii.79-82), but the combination here is given in the biblical text. It has no influence on Moses' offices, although both Moses and Aaron, like Melchizedek, serve often to symbolize functions of the Logos.

[4] At least no parallel appears in Goodenough's essay on Hellenistic Kingship. Goodenough himself passes over in silence the question why prophecy should be an adjunct to kingship (*By Light, Light*, 192-198).

[5] The epigram, "Only the sage is king . . . ," usually attributed to Chrysippus, is often quoted by ancient authors. See Hans Friedrich August von Arnim (ed.), *Stoicorum veterum fragmenta* (Leipzig: B. G. Teubner, 1921-24), III, 81, 108, 158, 173; cf., on "kingship" of Cynics, Epictetus, *Diss.*, III, xxii, 63, 72.

[6] Chrysippus, *apud* Stobaeus: von Arnim, III, 164.

[7] Wetter, p. 35; Fascher, p. 160.

an axiom with Philo, applied especially to Abraham,[1] but he does not make any clear connection between σοφία and prophecy.[2] In fact, as Fascher cogently observes, Philo's fundamental view of prophecy as *ecstasy*, in which the prophet mystically perceives that which is *beyond* reason, stands in contradiction to the Stoic understanding of "wisdom."[3] The description of this ecstatic prophecy is, while not Stoic, still thoroughly Hellenistic,[4] but the attribution of prophecy to Moses as a distinctive office must derive primarily from the Bible itself[5] and the traditional Jewish view of Moses as "the prophet" and "first of the prophets."[6] While rabbinic haggada divides over the question whether Moses was king or priest, it is unanimous on the subject of his prophecy.

Of the three "adjuncts" to Moses' kingship, then, two turn out to receive their main content and their connection with kingship from the popular theories of royalty circulating in the Hellenistic world, although in each case there was a point of contact in Jewish tradition in which Moses was already known as priest and legislator. The content of the third "adjunct," prophecy, is likewise Hellenistic, but Hellenism offers no persuasive basis for connecting prophecy with kingship. Unless this connection originates with Philo, therefore, its source is to be sought in Jewish tradition, especially since the office of prophecy is universally ascribed to Moses in biblical and post-biblical Judaism.

Kingship and Moses' mystical function

In view of the stress which Philo places on Moses' kingship in the

---

[1] E.g., *Mut.*, 152; *Som.*, ii.244; *Abr.*, 261; *Agr.* 41; *Mig.*, 197; *Sobr.*, 57; *QG*, iv.76. Note that Philo has a scriptural basis for calling Abraham king, in Gen. 23.5f. (LXX). Abraham is called a prophet (*Quis her.*, 258f., 263-266; *Virt.* 218; *QG*, iii. 9,10) as well as king (besides the above-mentioned passages, *Abr.*, 261; *Virt.*, 216; *Mut.*, 151, 152, 153; *Som.*, ii.244), but so far as I can see the two "offices" are not connected in his case. Once Philo casually calls Samuel "the greatest of kings and prophets" (*Ebr.*, 143), a note which plays no part in Philo's own allegory of Samuel, but alludes to a tradition (see below, p. 150 and n. 1).

[2] *Contra* Wolfson, II, 32. See below, pp. 128f. and n. 8.

[3] Fascher, p. 160.

[4] *Ibid.*, see below, pp. 127-129.

[5] Moses' prophetic office is presupposed in the Pentateuch and becomes especially important in Dt., even though he is never directly called נביא. Cf. especially Dt. 18. 15-22 and 34.10 and, for a summary of the OT evidence, Fascher, pp. 110-114.

[6] Cf. Ginzberg, V. 404; VI, 125, and below, pp. 198-200.

Vita, it is remarkable that kingship does not play a significant role in any of his other writings. Apart from the summary in *Rewards and Punishments* and one instance in the treatise on the *Special Laws*,[1] both of which belong to the "introductory" exposition, Moses is never given the title βασιλεύς outside the *Vita*, and passages which speak of him as a ruler are rare.[2] Philo emphasizes Moses' kingship, and interprets it in terms of the ideal king of Hellenistic thought, only when he is telling the more or less literal story of Moses' leading Israel out of Egypt and constituting them as a nation. Elsewhere in Philo this journey out of Egypt is allegorized as the ascent of the soul or, by play on the etymology of "Israel," of "the man who sees God," out of slavery to the body and its passions toward the perhaps unattainable goal of the *visio dei*. Correspondingly, the predominant element in the portrait of Moses shifts from kingship to the role of hierophant or mystagogue.

It will be recalled that in a single passage of the *Vita Mosis* Philo based Moses' extraordinary appointment as "god and king of the whole nation" on Moses' mystical ascent and perception of the unseen archetype of existence.[3] In effect, that passage makes the king function as a hierophant. This is the nearest parallel to be found in Philo to the specifically revelatory function of kingship presented in John 18.37, and it is hardly comparable. Still it will be useful to explore briefly Moses' role as hierophant, which however can more logically be treated under the rubric of his priesthood.

Moses as High Priest and Mystagogue

Moses' high-priestly office

The third division of Philo's life of Moses concerns his priesthood.[4] In addition the summary of Moses' "rewards" in the treatise "On Rewards and Punishments" describes Moses' high priesthood,[5] and

---

[1] *Praem.*, 53-55; *Spec. leg.*, iv.176.

[2] *Praem.*, 77, ὁ τοῦ ἔθνους ἐπιμελητὴς καὶ προστάτης; *Virt.* 42, ὁ τοῦ ἔθνους ἡγεμών; with emphasis, only the interesting passage *QE*, ii.6, which applies Ex. 22.28b to Moses: ἐπεί, φησίν, οὐ περὶ παντὸς ἄρχοντος ἔοικε νομοθετεῖν ἀλλ' ὡσανεὶ τοῦ λαοῦ τοῦδε ἢ ἔθνους ἡγεμόνα σπουδαῖον ὑποτίθεται, διὰ πλειόνων, καταχρηστικῶς δὲ δυνατοὺς ἢ ἱερεῖς ἢ προφήτας ἢ ἁγίους ἄνδρας ὡς Μωυσέα. "'Ἰδοὺ γὰρ, ἔθηκά σε θεὸν Φαραώ," ἐλέχθη πρὸς Μωυσῆν. (Loeb, Supplement, II, 242).

[3] *Mos.*, i, 158f.; see above, pp. 110f.

[4] *Mos.*, ii.66-186.

[5] *Praem.*, 56.

it is briefly mentioned in two other passages.[1] Of these passages, one is an extravagant accumulation of titles which contributes nothing to the reader's understanding of Moses' priesthood,[2] while the others differ in their emphases. In "On Rewards and Punishments," Moses' office of high priesthood enables him "by prophesying to serve Being (τὸ ὄν) knowledgeably and to make thanksgivings for his subjects when they act aright and, if they should sin, prayers and supplications."[3] Moses' role as the intercessor for Israel appears once in the section of the *Vita* devoted to his priesthood. After the sin of the golden calf, when God has commanded him to return to the people, Moses did not leave Sinai until he had first placated God:

> He yet took the part of mediator and reconciler (μεσίτης καὶ διαλλακτής) and did not hurry away at once, but first made prayers and supplications, begging that their sins might be forgiven. Then, when this protector and intercessor (ὁ κηδεμὼν καὶ παραιτητής) had softened the wrath (ἐξευμενισάμενος) of the Ruler, he wended his way back in mingled joy and dejection.[4]

This theme recurs in *Quaestiones in Exodum* II.49, with the added notion that the forty days Moses spent on the mountain (Exodus 24.18b) corresponded to the forty years of the wilderness sojourn. Goodenough calls attention to the fact that, by reversing the order of Moses' two ascents of Sinai, Philo underlines the importance of Moses' intercession at the expense of Aaron's. In Philo's version, in contrast to the biblical account, Aaron and his sons have already been consecrated as priests *before* the golden calf episode and Moses' great act of appeasing God.[5] The idea that Moses was Israel's special mediator or "Paraclete" before God occurs already in Deuteronomy and was emphasized very frequently in post-biblical tradition.[6]

Moses' high-priesthood is allegorized by Philo in only one passage,[7] an explanation of Exodus 24.6. "The high priest Moses"[8] divides the blood of the covenant sacrifice, as a symbol that "ὁ ἱερὸς

---

[1] *Sac.*, 130; *Quis her.* 182.

[2] *Sac.* 130, ἡγεμόνα προστησάμενοι καὶ στρατηγὸν τὸν ἀρχιερέα καὶ προφήτην καὶ φίλον τοῦ θεοῦ Μωυσῆν πόλεμον . . . ἐπολέμουν (subject is the Levites, Ex. 32.28f.).

[3] *Praem.*, 56.

[4] *Mos.*, ii.166, trans. Colson (Loeb), VI, 531.

[5] *By Light, Light*, pp. 191f.

[6] See below, pp. 137, 159-161, 174, 200-204, 254f.

[7] *Quis her.* 182-185.

[8] Ἀρχιερεύς does not appear in the biblical text, but is added by Philo.

λόγος pours some of the blood on these bowls [representing the senses], thinking it fitting that our irrational part should be refreshed and in a sense become rational." While the high priest mentioned in the regulations of the Torah is frequently treated as a symbol of the Logos by Philo,[1] this is the only passage in which *Moses*, as high priest, is allegorized in this way. Moses, however, is treated elsewhere as a symbol of the Logos, and it seems that he represents a different Logos or the Logos in a different manifestation than does Aaron or the conventional high priest. In one place, the "meeting" of Moses and Aaron represents the ideal concomitance of thought (διάνοια) and speech (ὁ προφορικὸς λόγος), which is the "brother" of thought.[2] In another place Moses' "stability" and immutability is interpreted as his unique ability to cast off the bodily realm altogether and to have constant communion with the "divine spirit." This stability belongs to the act of "beholding Being (τὸ ὄν) by the soul alone, silently," in contrast to the instability of the articulated Logos (λόγος κατὰ προφοράν) represented by the high priest who can enter the holy of holies only once a year.[3] Thus the superiority of Moses' priesthood, that is, his mystical achievement, to that of Aaron is interpreted by Philo in terms of the familiar Stoic distinction between the λόγος ἐνδιάθετος and the λόγος προφορικός.[4] It should be noted that Melchizedek is also allegorized as the Logos which, in contrast to the Ammonites (= αἴσθησις) and Moabites (= νοῦς) provides not merely "bread and water," but wine, i.e., the "sober intoxication" of mystic transport, to the soul.[5] Melchizedek thus parallels Moses not only in his two offices, king and priest, but also in his symbolic function of leading the soul into a mystical experience.

The only extensive treatment of Moses' high-priesthood in explicit terms remains to be discussed: that of the third section of the *Vita* as a whole. Apart from the single passage already mentioned,[6] the biography does not describe Moses' priesthood in terms of leading worship or offering intercessions, but only in terms of establishing the cult. In other words, he is priest in the sense of ἱεροφάντης. In fact the verbal cognate of the latter title is used to

---

[1] *Cher.* 17; *Gig.*, 52; *Mig.*, 102; *Quis her.*, 303; *Fug.*, 106-116; *Som.* i.215.
[2] *Det.* 126-137.
[3] *Gig.* 45-54.
[4] Cf. Goodenough, *By Light, Light*, pp. 100-105.
[5] *Leg. all.* iii.82.
[6] *Mos.* ii.166.

describe Moses' "initiation" of Aaron and his sons into the rites of the sanctuary.[1] Yet Moses is never called "hierophant" in the *Vita*, while on the other hand he is called "high priest" only twice outside the *Vita*. "High Priest," like "king," is an office of Moses useful for presentation to the beginner, the Gentile inquirer. In the more allegorical writings, Philo drops both titles, replacing them to a large extent by "hierophant."

Moses as hierophant

Frequently the title ἱεροφάντης is used of Moses without emphasis, in formulae introducing quotations from the Pentateuch,[2] for "Some laws God delivered by his own agency alone (δι' ἑαυτοῦ μόνου), others through the prophet Moses (διὰ προφήτου Μωυσέως), whom he chose as a most serviceable hierophant (ἐπιτηδειότατος ἱεροφάντης) ranking above all.[3] But the contexts in which this title is applied instead of or in addition to the more common "the prophet" or "the legislator" are significant: in a quotation illustrating that the Exodus is a "leading out from the body";[4] introducing a regulation for purity (Deuteronomy 23.12) interpreted as an explanation how to control the body and "dig out" the passions;[5] in the account of Moses' destruction of the golden calf, symbolizing bodily pleasures;[6] introducing Moses' explanation of the manna, the food that gladdens the soul, namely the divine Logos.[7] The title thus calls attention to Philo's notion that Moses, in writing the Pentateuch, acted as God's agent to make known deeply symbolic secrets about the means by which the true mystic can learn to control the body and finally to escape its snares altogether. This usage implies that the Scripture itself is understood as the ἱερὸς λόγος, whether merely metaphorically or in some sense literally,[8] of the "Jewish mystery."

---

[1] ἱεροφαντῶν αὐτόν τε καὶ τοὺς ἀδελφιδοῦς ὠργίαζεν, (*ibid.*, 153).

[2] *Mig.* 14; *Som.* ii.3, 29, 109; *Virt.* 174; *Sac.* 94.

[3] *Dec.* 18. The connection of prophet with hierophant also occurs in *Mig.* 14 and *Leg. all.* iii.173; cf. *Virt.* 75.

[4] *Mig.* 14.

[5] *Leg. all.* iii.151.

[6] *Post.* 164.

[7] *Leg. all.* iii.173.

[8] It is unnecessary here to enter into the debate over Goodenough's controversial hypothesis of a "Jewish mystery." Cf. the review of his *By Light, Light* by Arthur Darby Nock in *Gnomon*, 13 (1937), 156-165, and Goodenough's reply, "Literal Mystery in Hellenistic Judaism," *Quantala-*

In other passages the specifically mystic sense is developed more fully. Commenting on Moses' request to see God (Exodus 33.18), Philo says, "Even before beginning this investigation, the hierophant seems to me to have considered its greatest element,[1] wherefore he beseeches Being itself to become the revealer of its own nature."[2] The actual *visio dei* was unattainable, but Moses achieved a position nearer to τὸ ὄν than that of any other man, even the patriarchs, "for he is the seventh from Abraham, no longer restricted to the outer circle of the holy precincts, like an initiate (μύστης), but spending his time in the inmost shrine as a hierophant."[3] This exceptional position, which was granted to Moses by the divine spirit because he was able to "disrobe" himself of all created things" and to "pitch his tent outside the camp" (Exodus 33.7), that is, outside "the whole array of bodily things." Entering into the "darkness" (Exodus 20.21),[4] he "abides there while he learns the secrets of the most holy mysteries. There he becomes not only an initiate (μύστης) but also the hierophant of rites and teacher of divine things, which he will impart to those whose ears are purified."[5] Thus Moses' mystic vision qualifies him to become the unique leader, the mystagogue, of his real disciples who pursue the same vision, for in Philo's view the genuine service (θεραπεία) of God, the highest meaning of Judaism, is the mystic ascent itself:

But the work proper to those who serve Being is not that of cupbearers or bakers or cooks, or any other earthly work, nor to shape or assemble bodily things like brick, but to ascend in mind (ἀναβαίνειν τοῖς λογισμοῖς) to the aethereal height, setting before them Moses, the God-loved type, as leader on the road (ἡγεμόνα τῆς ὁδοῦ). For then they will behold the "place," which is really the Logos,[6] where God, the immovable and immutable, stands, "and that which is under his feet, like brickwork of

---

cumque: *Studies Presented to Kirsopp Lake by Pupils, Colleagues, and Friends*, ed. R. P. Casey, Silva Lake, and Agnes K. Lake (London: Christophers, 1937), pp. 226-241.

[1] Τὸ μέγιστον αὐτῆς is peculiar, but Colson's emendation to "its futility" (τὸ ἄχρηστον αὐτῆς) seems unwarranted.

[2] *Post.* 16; cf. *Spec. leg.* i.41.

[3] *Post.* 173.

[4] Note that the same passage is explained in *Mos.* as the mystical foundation of Moses' *kingship* (above, p. 111 and n. 5).

[5] *Gig.* 53f.; translation based on that of Colson (Loeb), II, 471, 473, with slight alterations (cf. Whittaker's note, p. 503).

[6] Accepting Colson's emendation δὴ λόγος for the meaningless δῆλος of the MSS. The ensuing interpretation demands λόγος here.

sapphire and like a kind of firmament of heaven," the perceptible world, which he thus enigmatically portrays. For it
behooves those who have joined the association with knowledge
to long to see Being, but if they should not be able to, then to
see its image, the most holy Logos, and, next to that, the most
perfect work in the perceptible realm, the world. For to phi-
losophize is nothing other than to strive to see these things
accurately.[1]

One remaining occurrence of the title hierophant for Moses must be
mentioned, this in connection with his final ascension. The "Song
of Moses" (Deuteronomy 32) is set by Philo in a "divine assemblage
of the elements of all existence, . . . earth and heaven," which Moses
leads in chorus, all the while both convicting and admonishing
Israel.[2] What is depicted here resembles the mystic ascent on Sinai,
only raised to a higher key. Both "ascensions" of Moses now must
be examined briefly.

Moses' mystic ascents

Philo had learned from his own experience that a mystic cannot
exist always in an ecstatic state, but must "descend," "return to
himself."[3] Even the angels "descend" as well as "ascend" (Genesis
28.12), remarks Philo, and "the prophet" (Moses) has to come down
from Sinai.[4] Repeatedly Philo interprets Moses' ascent on Sinai as
a mystical translation; the incident becomes the persistent symbol
in his allegory of the experience which he sees as the goal of every
σοφός, every φιλόθεος. He makes much of Moses' entry into the
"thick darkness" (γνόφος, Exodus 20.21),[5] which he interprets as
"the unapproachable and formless (or, invisible: ἀειδεῖς) con-
ceptions about Being."[6] Moses not only enters this realm, but

---

[1] *Conf.* 95-97. The allegory is a "midrash" on Ex. 24.9f., καὶ ἀνέβη Μωυσῆς
καὶ Ααρων καὶ Ναδαβ καὶ Αβιουδ καὶ ἑβδομήκοντα τῆς γερουσίας Ἰσραὴλ καὶ
εἶδον τὸν τόπον, οὗ εἱστήκει ἐκεῖ ὁ θεὸς τοῦ Ἰσραήλ· καὶ τὰ ὑπὸ τοὺς πόδας
αὐτοῦ ὡσεὶ ἔργον πλίνθου σαπφείρου καὶ ὥσπερ εἶδος στερεώματος τοῦ οὐρανοῦ
τῇ καθαριότητι.

[2] *Virt.* 75. The prophetic "convicting and admonishing" is strikingly
similar to the function of the παράκλητος in Jn. 16.8. The Paraclete is also,
like the "hierophant" Moses, a "teacher of divine things" and a "guide" on
the way to truth (Jn. 14.26; 16.13). On Moses as Paraclete, see further Chaps.
IV and V below.

[3] *Spec. leg.* iii. 1-6.

[4] *QG.* iv.29.

[5] *Post.* 14; *Gig.* 54; *Mut.* 7; *Som.* i.186-188; *Mos.* i.158.

[6] *Post.* 14.

"abides" there, for he is able to "become bodiless."[1] His ascent was an initiation, the foundation of his office as king,[2] as high priest,[3] and as hierophant.[4] It was made possible by his asceticism, for "first he had to be clean, as in soul so also in body, to have no dealings with any passion, purifying himself from all the calls of mortal nature, food and drink and intercourse with women."[5] On the mountain, he needs no human food, for he has food sent from heaven, which Philo interprets as "the nourishment that comes through contemplation."[6]

The goal for which the mystic longed was the vision of God. The goal was unattainable, but the search itself, which led to a true understanding of "the things which lie below Being," was sufficient reward for the effort.[7] Philo hints that in the vision of the burning bush Moses already saw an "image of Being" (εἰκὼν τοῦ ὄντος), but lets it be called just "an angel" if the reader prefers.[8] Elsewhere the "Image of Being" is the Logos, and it is the Logos which Moses saw when he ascended the mountain.[9]

Nevertheless, Philo makes plain that Moses came nearer the goal than any other man has, so near that his ascent was virtually a deification. Philo interprets Deuteronomy 5.31, "Stand here by me," to mean that Being gives Moses a share in its own nature, that is, immutability,[10] and elsewhere he derives the same idea from Exodus 7.1, "I will give you as god to Pharaoh."[11] Exodus 24.2 says, "Moses alone shall come near to God," explains Philo, because

---

[1] *Som.* i.36: Μωυσῆν ἀσώματον γενόμενον. By this hyperbole Philo describes Moses' escape from all the body's desires, symbolized by his fast for forty days and nights (Ex. 24.18). Elsewhere he finds Moses' "bodilessness" symbolized in Moses' pitching the Tent of Meeting "outside the camp" (Ex. 33.7; *Gig.* 54; *Leg. all.* ii.54f.; iii.46-48; *Det.* 160; *Ebr.* 100, 124).

[2] *Mos.* i.158f.

[3] *Ibid.*, ii, 67-71.

[4] *Gig.* 53f.; see above, pp. 121f.

[5] *Mos.* ii.68, trans. Colson (Loeb), VI, 483. On Moses' asceticism, see below, p. 128.

[6] *Ibid.*, 69.

[7] *Mut.* 7-9; cf. *QE* ii.37. Contrast the view of Josephus, *Antt.* iii.88, which Philo would have regarded as naive.

[8] *Mos.* i.66.

[9] *Conf.* 95-97 (above, p. 121f.). Cf. Jacob Jervell, *Imago Dei; Gen.* 1, 26f. *im Spätjudentum, in der Gnosis, und in den paulinischen Briefen* (FRLANT, n.s. 58; 1960), pp. 52-70.

[10] *Post.* 28-31. Abraham is shown by Gen. 18.22f. also to have shared God's "standing," but not so perfectly as Moses (*ibid.*, 27).

[11] *Sac.* 9; see above, pp. 104f.

prophetic ecstasy changes the duality of the ordinary human mind
to resemble the "monad."

> But he who is resolved into the nature of unity, is said to come
> near God in a kind of family relation, for having given up and
> left behind all mortal kinds, he is changed into the divine, so
> that such men become kin to God and truly divine.[1]

The "calling up" of Moses to God on Sinai is explicitly called
"divinization":

> This [Exodus 24.12a] signifies that a holy soul is divinized by
> ascending not to the air or to the ether or to heaven (which is)
> higher than all but to (a region) above the heavens. And beyond
> the world there is no place but God.[2]

Again, it is called "a second birth better than the first," in a passage
that implicitly identifies the reborn Moses with the "heavenly man"
created in God's image.[3]

Philo takes for granted that Deuteronomy 34.6, "no man knows
his grave," means that Moses was translated. Doubtless this view
was traditional in Philo's circle, for he states matter-of-factly that
Enoch, "the protoprophet (Moses)," and Elijah all obtained this
reward.[4] The end of Moses' life was an "ascent,"[5] an "emigration to
heaven," "abandoning the mortal life to be made immortal"
(ἀπαθανατίζεσθαι).[6]

The striking thing about Philo's descriptions of Moses' translation is that they parallel exactly his descriptions of the ascent on
Sinai. In both cases, Moses leaves the mortal, bodily realm to enter
the "incorporeal and intelligible."[7] His ascension is at the "sum-
mons" of God.[8] Finally, his "immortalization" is defined as the
resolution of his twofold nature "into a single unity" (εἰς μονάδος

---

[1] *QE* ii.29, trans. Marcus (Loeb), Supplement, II, 70.

[2] *Ibid.*, 40.

[3] *Ibid.*, 46. On the "heavenly man," cf. *Leg. all.* i.31; ii.4f.; *Opif.* 134, and
see Jervell, pp. 56f., 64f. The description of Moses' δευτέρα γένεσις reminds
one at several points of the famous Tractate XIII of the *Corpus Hermeticum*.
Not only Moses, but also Noah was made the equal of the incorporeal first
man; Noah was therefore, like the first man, king of all the world (*QG* ii.56).

[4] *QG* i.86. In *Sac.* 8-10 he suggests that Abraham, Isaac, and Jacob also
received ἀφθαρσία, though Moses advanced even higher.

[5] *Ibid.*

[6] *Mos.* ii.288-292; cf. *Virt.* 53, 72-79.

[7] *Mos.* ii.288; *Virt.* 53, 76; *QG* i.86; cf. above, pp. 195f.

[8] *Mos.* ii.288.

φύσιν), "transforming his whole being into mind (νοῦς), pure as sunlight."[1] In the case of the final translation Philo adds that the "ascent is to heaven," but otherwise the imagery is essentially the same. To Philo's conception of Moses' Sinai ascent can be applied very precisely Bousset's observation about mystical ecstasy: "The ecstasy is nothing else but an anticipation of the heavenly ascent of the soul after the death of the man."[2] The mystic ascent is a kind of "realized eschatology"; the final ascension is a projection and fulfillment of the goal of the mystic ascent.[3]

Moses as Prophet

Usage

One of the most common titles by which Philo refers to Moses is "the prophet." Often this title is apparently chosen instead of another merely for variety, since it serves only to introduce a scripture quotation or an action by Moses in narrative.[4] There are of course other prophets—such as Abraham, Samuel, and Isaac—but Moses is *the* prophet, without further identification, the "chief

---

[1] *Ibid.*, trans. Colson (Loeb), VI, 593.

[2] Wilhelm Bousset, *Die Himmelsreise der Seele* (first published in *Archiv für Religionswissenschaft*, 4 [1901], 136-169, 229-273; rp. Darmstadt: Wissenschaftliche Buchgesellschaft, 1960), p. 5.

[3] The analogy raises the question whether, since Moses' ascent at Sinai institutes his mediatorial office in Israel, his final ascension is also thought to initiate some permanent function as intercessor for his "disciples." Goodenough answers this question affirmatively (*By Light, Light*, pp. 233f.), and he is probably correct, although the evidence he gives is ambiguous. Moses' "teaching" to his "disciples" is undoubtedly through the medium of the Pentateuch, since Philo defines Moses' γνώριμοι as those who can understand the Scripture's hidden meaning (*QG* iii.8). The "prayer" addressed to Moses as hierophant (*Som.* i.164f.) is quite possibly rhetorical, though admittedly the language is strong. The appeal to the "virtues of the founders of the race" (*Spec. leg.* iv. 180f.) does not imply continuing intercession, but comes very close to the familiar rabbinic idea of the *zekut abot*, on which see Solomon Schechter, *Aspects of Rabbinic Theology* (New York: Schocken Books, 1961), chapt. xii, especially pp. 171-175. On the other hand, *Praem.* 166, a passage that Goodenough, strangely enough, does not mention, clearly says that "the founders (ἀρχηγέται) of the nation," "whose souls are released from bodies," "never cease to make supplications on behalf of their sons and daughters." Moreover, Moses' perpetual intercession was known elsewhere, as shown by *Assump. Mos.* (below, pp. 159f.).

[4] *Quis her.* 4; *Fug.* 140; *Mut.* 11; *Som.* ii.277; *Mos.* i.156, ii.213, 229, 257, 275; *Virt.* 51; *Gig.* 49; *Vit. cont.* 64, 87; *Praem.* 1; *QG* iv.245; *QE* i.11; ii.44; *Leg. all.* ii.1 (vocative).

prophet" (ἀρχιπροφήτης),[1] the "primary prophet" (πρωτοπροφήτης).[2] He can be called "τὸ προφητικὸν γένος,"[3] by the same hyperbole that makes Homer τὸ ποιητικὸν γένος.[4] Significantly, he can also be called "the prophetic Logos"[5] or "the prophet, Logos, Moses by name,"[6] in each case introducing a scripture quotation.

Behind the frequency of the title are two factors: (1) the fact that, as Philo puts it, Moses is "everywhere hymned as prophet,"[7] and (2) the notion, also hardly original with Philo, that the Pentateuch itself, written by Moses, consists of prophetic oracles.[8]

It is not surprising that "the prophet" as a title for Moses readily interchanges or merges with others already considered. Especially is this the case with the two other titles which are similarly used to introduce scriptural quotations or allusions, νομοθέτης and ἱεροφάντης. Moses' giving of the laws is described as a prophetic action;[9] "interpretation and prophecy" are the great gifts which enable him to give the "divine laws."[10] Similarly, "prophet" is linked with "hierophant" as a hendiadys in two passages,[11] while in some places where "hierophant" would be expected, "prophet" stands instead. These are passages which speak of Moses' instituting rites,[12] of his leading the Exodus, understood as rescue from the body,[13] and of his final prayer for the tribes,[14] above all passages which speak of his ascent[15] and his intellectual vision.[16] In the last-mentioned passages, Philo identifies Moses' prophetic office with the ecstatic

---

[1] *Mut.* 103, 125; *Som.* ii.189; *QG* iv.8.

[2] *QG* i.86.

[3] *Fug.* 147.

[4] *Jos.* 2.

[5] *Leg. all.* iii.43; *Mig.* 151.

[6] *Congr.* 170.

[7] *Quis her.* 262. See above, p. 116.

[8] *Mos.* ii.188.

[9] *Congr.* 132; *Virt.* 51; *Spec. leg.* ii.104. Cf. Wolfson, II, 17f., who however goes too far in making Moses' legislative and priestly activities mere aspects of his prophecy. This is an example of Wolfson's tendency to force upon Philo constructive systems which, while logically derivable from Philo, were never expressed by Philo himself. It is only kingship to which Philo systematically connects the other offices, and that only in *Mos.*

[10] *Mut.* 126.

[11] *Leg. all.* iii. 173; *Dec.* 18.

[12] *QE* i.11.

[13] *Mig.* 15.

[14] *QG* iv.123.

[15] *QG* iv.29; *QE* ii.43, 46, 52.

[16] *Mos.* ii.209; *Spec. leg.* iii.125; *QE* ii.52, 67, 90. On Philo's connection of "seer" and "prophet," cf. Fascher, pp. 155f.

vision of the mystical "philosopher," which has already been mentioned in connection with the role of "hierophant."[1] The prophetic ecstasy, however, requires some additional words.

The three types of prophecy

In the *Life of Moses*, Philo classifies the oracles delivered through Moses under three categories: (1) those spoken by God "in person," with Moses an "interpreter," (2) those given as answers to Moses' questions, and (3) those spoken by Moses while in ecstasy.[2] The first type, in which Moses is the ἑρμηνεὺς θεοῦ, is called prophecy only by an improper use of the term, Philo says, so he does not discuss the cases of God's direct speaking in the *Vita*.[3] Elsewhere, however, he uses ἑρμηνεύς and προφήτης almost interchangeably.[4] The essential characteristic of prophecy conceived as ἑρμηνεία is that the word which is interpreted is not the prophet's own, but God's. The interpretation is prompted from within.[5] There is no need to discuss prophecy as question and answer, since instances of such prophecy "have a mixed character," that is, they are a combination of the other two types.[6]

For Philo the prophet in the strict sense (καθ'ὃ μάλιστα καὶ κυρίως νενόμισται προφήτης) is the ecstatic.[7] The prophet is οὐκέτ' ἐν ἑαυτῷ,[8] he is ἐπιθειάσας,[9] θεοφορηθείς,[10] or κατασχεθείς.[11] In this state he speaks

---

[1] Wolfson's schematization (II, chap. ix), which interprets Philo's view of prophecy as a harmonization of Plato with Scripture, so that the four different kinds of prophecy found in Scripture correspond to the four categories of "philosophic frenzy" in Plato and thus take the place of "recollection" in the threefold classification of knowledge in Plato, is an attractive simplification, but deceptive. To accept it, one would have to assume (a) that Philo was an academician who developed a theory of knowledge from Plato's writings directly, (b) that Philo systematized this theory into the same categories elucidated by Wolfson, (c) that Philo found the same fourfold classification of prophecy in scripture that Wolfson constructs from very diverse references, and (d) that Philo, like Wolfson, recognized a parallel between these and Plato's four kinds of "frenzy."

[2] *Mos.* ii.188.

[3] *Ibid.*, 191.

[4] *Praem.* 55; *Quis her.* 213 (ἑρμηνεὺς φύσεως), cf. *Mut.* 126; *Spec. leg.* iii.6; *Post.* 1; *Mos.* i.1.

[5] *Praem.* 55.

[6] *Mos.* ii.192; cf. Wolfson, II, 39f.

[7] *Mos.* ii.191, cf. 272.

[8] *Ibid.*, 251.

[9] *Ibid.*, 259, 263, 272.

[10] *Ibid.*, 251, 264, 273.

[11] *Ibid.*, 288.

κατὰ ἐνθουσιασμόν,[1] that is, he θεσπίζει.[2] He is changed both in appearance and in mind,[3] "transformed into a prophet."[4]

It accords with a widespread notion of ecstatic revelation when Philo mentions in passing that "for a long time, almost from the time he first began to prophesy and to be divinely possessed," Moses had disdained intercourse with his wife, "considering it fitting always to keep himself ready for the oracles."[5] This justification for Moses' asceticism is found in almost exactly the same words in the *Abot de Rabbi Nathan*;[6] the way Philo introduces the statement into his discussion of Moses' purification in preparation for his ascent of Sinai in the capacity of high priest shows that he is introducing a familiar tradition.

The prophet as mystic

Outside the *Vita*, Philo lays less emphasis on the nature of the ecstatic speech, interpreting the prophet's revelation more in the sense of the mystic vision. At times this is described more in philosophical terms, since "the name [prophet or interpreter] only befits the wise (σοφός), since he alone is the vocal instrument of God, smitten and played by his invisible hand."[7] It seems, as Fascher says, that "mystic-intuitive and rationalistic concepts" of prophecy, the latter related to the Stoic-Cynic idea of the σοφός as the true prophet, are joined together here.[8] To an extent this is true, but the essence of prophecy for Philo evidently consists in the power to penetrate beyond the reach of rational "wisdom." Prophecy is "the way of truth":

---

[1] *Ibid.*, 246, 258.

[2] *Ibid.*, 246, 251, 264, 270, 280, 288; i.175, 201.

[3] *Ibid.*, ii.272.

[4] *Ibid.*, 280, i.57.

[5] *Ibid.*, ii.68.

[6] Ed. Schechter, p. 10 (trans. Judah Goldin, *The Fathers according to Rabbi Nathan* ["Yale Judaica Series," ed. Julian Obermann, X; New Haven: Yale University Press, 1955], p. 19). Cf. *Debarim R.* XI, 10: "From the day when he received a revelation, he did not go in to his wife" (cited by Stein, p. 45). Two other traditions contained in *ARN* argue that Moses kept away from his wife –a very offensive course for the rabbis –only because of a specific commandment from God.

[7] *Quis her.* 259, trans. Colson (Loeb), IV, 417.

[8] Fascher, p. 160. Wolfson greatly exaggerates the latter notion as the controlling factor in Philo's view of prophecy (II, 32). Of the passages Wolfson cites connecting prophecy with σοφία, only one actually mentions προφήτης or προφητεία.

Now the way that leads to it [*sc.* truth, ἀλήθεια], *so far as it rests with us*, is knowledge and wisdom, for through these it is found. But *by an involuntary principle* (it is found) through prophecy. And since that which is proportioned and equal is a safe road, it leads to truth more evenly, briefly, and smoothly than the former.[1]

This passage could be used to support Fascher's thesis, that the connecting concept between rational and intuitive prophecy is the idea that true wisdom is the prerequisite for divine revelation.[2] The main point, however, seems to be that prophecy leads one *beyond* wisdom. The "connecting concept," then, is the more fundamental aspect, common to biblical as well as Hellenistic notions of prophecy, that the prophet does not speak on his own initiative. It is the way to truth "by an involuntary principle," which does not "rest with us." That the prophet does not speak his own words was already seen to be the primary characteristic of the kind of prophecy Philo calls "interpretation";[3] it is equally characteristic of ecstatic prophecy: "For a prophet utters nothing of his own, but everything he says is foreign to him, prompted by another."[4]

Summary of Findings

In general the atmosphere of Philo's writings is far removed from that of the Fourth Gospel. Specifically, great differences are apparent between Philo's description of Moses' prophetic and kingly functions and the symbolic depiction of Jesus as king and prophet in John. Nevertheless, there are elements in Philo's portrait of Moses that may serve to illuminate the background of John. Significantly, the closest parallels appear just in those elements which Philo probably inherited from Jewish tradition.

In Philo's introduction to Judaism for the gentile inquirer, Moses appears as the ideal king. Many elements in the royal portrait are

---

[1] *QG* iv.125, trans. Marcus (Loeb), Supplement, I, 409, emphasis mine. Cf. *ibid.*, iv.8.

[2] Fascher, p. 160.

[3] Above, p. 127.

[4] *Quis her.* 259; cf. *Spec. leg.* i.65, where Philo, closely following Dt. 18. 18-22, says of the prophet who "will suddenly appear" that "nothing of what he says will be his own, for he that is truly under the control of divine inspiration when he speaks but serves as the channel for the insistent words of Another's prompting" (trans. Colson [Loeb], VII, 137).

drawn directly from the ideal of kingship which was prevalent in the popular philosophy of late Hellenism, although not without some point of contact in the biblical text as commonly interpreted by wider circles of Judaism. For example, while the joining of kingship with priesthood is a commonplace of Hellenistic kingship literature, the tradition that Moses was a priest as well as a king is not unknown in "normative" Judaism and is in fact found even within the Bible itself. Again, the primary function of the king as legislator has deep roots in Hellenism, but at the same time coincides with the centrality of Moses' connection with the Torah in the biblical and in rabbinic traditions, as well as with the almost universal designation of Moses as "the legislator" in Hellenistic Jewish sources.

On the other hand, two prominent aspects of Philo's portrait of Moses are difficult to explain on the basis of pagan models. The first, and most immediately significant for the present inquiry, is the interrelation between kingship and prophecy. Philo's explanation for this connection is very weak, in contrast to his statements about the relationships between kingship and the other two "adjuncts," legislation and priesthood. The implication may be that the connection was not logical or philosophical, but traditional, drawn from the common stock of Jewish views and exegesis.

The second exceptional aspect of Philo's portrait is the suggestion that Moses was enthroned as king in the course of a mystic ascent to heaven from Sinai. While the pagan kingship models depict the ideal king as an intermediary between the gods and man, the notion of a heavenly enthronement has no place in the ordinary Hellenistic literature on the ideal king. Moreover, Philo connects the enthronement with Moses' designation as "god," based on Exodus 7.1. Why this designation should imply Moses' *kingship* and why Exodus 7.1 should be connected with Sinai are unexplained in Philo's statements. It will be seen in the next chapter, however, that precisely these connections can be found, in fuller and clearer form, in rabbinic tradition.

Moses' essential importance for Philo is as the prototypal mystic and the guide for those of his "disciples" who, like Philo himself, long to participate in the true "Exodus," an escape from the "Egypt" of the senses and passions. This aspect of the Moses portrait is so intimately associated with Philo's personal ideals, as they are disclosed in his occasional autobiographical asides, that the reader cannot determine from internal evidence alone the extent to which this mystical interpretation of Moses may have been already traditional rather than Philo's own creation.

MOSES IN THE WRITINGS OF JOSEPHUS

Josephus' Place within Judaism

Josephus' life and the character of his literary production demonstrate how fluid was the line between "Palestinian" and "Hellenistic" Judaism or, more accurately, that there was no line and that Palestine itself was only a special case within the manifold types of Hellenized lands and peoples. Josephus was a Palestinian Jew, a priest, a partisan in the Jewish war, by his own report a Pharisee. His first language was Aramaic, in which he wrote the first edition of his "Wars," and he required the help of editorial assistants to polish his writings for the Roman world. Yet Josephus' extant works are clearly Hellenistic from start to finish. His models were Hellenistic historians, and his major sources were all Greek.[1] Despite his passionate loyalty to the Jewish people as an *ethnos*—for all his works are clearly apologetic[2]—he was apparently little disturbed by the destruction of Jewish national hopes, and his values were predominantly the same as those of any educated citizen of the Greco-Roman empire. Josephus, like many of the other Hellenistic Jews whose works have survived, writes to show that Hellenism's best ideals were realized in Judaism.

Josephus' portrait of Moses is likewise composite. There is excellent reason for believing that many elements of the biography of Moses are drawn from haggadic traditions equally well-known in Palestine, some of which have survived in midrashim and in the Palestinian targums.[3] But at the same time Josephus portrays

[1] Cf. H. St. John Thackeray, "Josephus," *A Dictionary of the Bible*, ed. James Hastings, Extra Vol. (Edinburgh: T. & T. Clark, 1904), pp. 463f. Evidently Josephus used the Hebrew Bible along with the LXX, and Rappaport argues that he also used a Targum containing much haggadic material (pp. xvii-xxiv).

[2] Cf. Paul Krüger, *Philo und Josephus als Apologeten des Judentums* (Leipzig: Verlag der Dürr'schen Buchhandlung, 1906), 82pp.

[3] Rappaport, pp. xiii-xxxv, particularly pp. xxi-xxv. Rappaport's argument that Josephus must have depended upon a written source for the haggadah, as he did by his own statement in historical narrative, rather than upon oral traditions, is not completely convincing. Cf. Géza Vermès, "La figure de Moïse au tournant des deux Testaments," *Moïse l'homme de d'alliance*, ed. H. Cazelles *et al.* (Paris: Desclée & Cie., 1955), pp. 87f.

Moses with characteristic features of the Hellenistic θεῖος ἀνήρ.[1]

The Legislator

The most common title by which Josephus, like most Hellenistic
Jewish authors, refers to Moses is "legislator" (ὁ νομοθέτης).[2] Here
is an evident point of contact between the biblical-"normative"
view of Moses and that of Hellenism, for the mediation of the Torah
is one of the essential characteristics of Moses in the Rabbinic
haggadah.[3] Still, the Rabbis would not call Moses "the law giver" —
only God *gave* the Torah, while it came "by Moses' hand."[4] The
usual title in Rabbinic writings is rather "Moses our master"
(משה רבינו).[5] To call Moses νομοθέτης, then, is already to adapt for
Gentile understanding his primary role in Jewish sacred history.

The translation of Moses' legislative function into a Greek mode
is most apparent in Josephus' proemium to the Antiquities:

> I had indeed ere now, when writing the history of the war,
> already contemplated describing the origin of the Jews, the
> fortunes that befell them, the great lawgiver under whom they
> were trained in piety and the exercise of the other virtues

---

[1] Bieler, I, 18f.; II, 30-34. Vermès' statement, "En fin de compte, le
Moïse des *Antiquites judaïques* est identiquement celui de la tradition pales-
tinienne, mais habille parfois a la grecque" (p. 88), is misleading. In the first
place, the structure of the Moses' story, which is provided for Josephus by
the Hellenistic *Bios*, goes far beyond mere "clothing" of a fixed image.
Second, it becomes increasingly apparent that the "Palestinian tradition"
was far from untouched by Greek modes (cf. above, p. 100 and n. 2).

[2] *Antt.* ii.6, 18, 20, 23, 24; iii.180, iv.13, 150, 156; *C.Ap.* ii.75 (*noster
legislator*), 145 (ὁ νομοθέτης ἡμῶν Μωυσῆς), 154, 156, 161, 165, 169, 173, 209,
257, 286. In *Antt.* i.95 Μωυσῆς . . . ὁ Ἰουδαίων νομοθέτης appears in a quotation from Nicolas of Damascus; in i.240, from Alexander Polyhistor. Moses
also appears as subject of νομοθετέω *Antt.* iii.266, 268, 317; cf. iii.287, 320.
The statement by Isaac Heinemann, "Moses," Pauly-Wissowa, 1st Series,
vol. XVI, col. 374, that Josephus, unlike Philo, never calls Moses king,
priest, *or lawgiver* is a slip. On the use of the title by Philo and his circle, see
above, p. 113, n. 2. Cf. Letter of Aristeas, 131, 139, 148, 153; Aristobulus
apud Eusebius, *Praep. Ev.*, viii.10.4; Eupolemus, *ibid.*, ix.26; Clement Alex.,
Strom., i.153.4.

[3] Bloch, "Quelques aspects," p. 119.

[4] *Ibid.*, pp. 139f. The rabbinic view is known to Josephus, though he puts
it forth with some diffidence, lest his Gentile readers think that view too
"mythical" (*Antt.*, iii.320-322).

[5] Cf. *ibid.*, p. 92.

[ὑφ᾽ οἵῳ τε παιδευθέντες νομοθέτῃ τὰ πρὸς εὐσέβειαν καὶ τὴν ἄλλην ἄσκησιν ἀρετῆς] . . .[1]

The relationship between legislation and παιδεία is distinctively Greek. Moses is described after the model of the ideal founder of a Greek πόλις whose laws form the πολιτεία of the state.[2] Moses is more ancient than the Greek legislators,[3] as well as more capable, for the constitution he laid down is not monarchy, oligarchy, or rule by the masses, but "theocracy."[4] His success as a legislator stemmed, of course, from his superiority as a philosopher.[5] The model is ultimately Platonic; Hellenistic is the elevation of a single individual as the supreme, semi-divine source of society's pattern.

The Commander and Sovereign Leader

Moses the στρατηγός

According to Josephus, the voice from the burning bush announced to Moses that he was to be "commander and leader of the Hebrew hosts" (στρατηγὸν καὶ ἡγεμόνα τῆς 'Εβραίων πληθύος).[6] While not a frequent title of Moses in Josephus,[7] στρατηγός occurs in several summaries which make it appear that it represents one of Moses' most significant functions. In the summary at the end of Josephus' account of Moses' life, he describes him as a στρατηγός with few equals, a προφήτης equalled by none.[8] Moreover, the offices in which Joshua is installed as Moses' successor are the same, προφήτης and στρατηγός.[9]

---

[1] *Antt.*, i.6, trans. H. St. John Thackeray, *Josephus with an English Translation*, vol. IV ("The Loeb Classical Library," Cambridge: Harvard University Press, 1961), p. 5.

[2] *Antt.*, iii.322; *C. Ap.* ii.188.

[3] *C. Ap.*, ii.151-154.

[4] *C. Ap.*, ii.164-167.

[5] *Antt.*, i.18-26, cf. *C. Ap.*, ii.168-171. The former passage may be dependent on Philo, *Opif.*, as Thackeray suggests (*Dictionary of the Bible*, Extra Vol., p. 471), but the case is not clear. Similarity in content could be explained on the basis of common apologetic aim, the structure of the biblical material itself, and the general Hellenistic milieu. Rappaport (pp. xviiif.) also thinks Josephus used Philo, but Heinemann (Pauly-Wissowa, XVI, col. 375) finds no evidence for such dependence.

[6] *Antt.*, ii.268, trans. Thackery (Loeb), IV, 281.

[7] στρατηγός, *Antt.*, iii.2, 67, 102; iv. 165, 194, 329; *C. Ap.* ii.158. Cf. ἡγεμών, *Antt.*, iv.11.

[8] *Antt.*, iv.329.

[9] *Antt.*, iv.165.

One can only guess why Josephus chose this title to emphasize Moses' role as unique leader and governor of the Israelites during the period of national origins. On the one hand, the title carries a certain military connotation, which fits one aspect of the biblical picture of Moses, particularly of Deuteronomy, which idealizes him as the leader of Israel's holy war. The military aspect coincided also with one interest of Josephus, for one of his purposes in writing the *Antiquities* was to describe "all those wars waged by [the Jews] through long ages before this last in which they were involuntarily engaged against the Romans,"[1] and he always describes the scenes and stratagem of battle with a certain relish. On the other hand, the title in the Hellenistic world had taken on a much broader connotation than mere military leadership. In Diadochean times the στρατηγός was a provincial governor. It was to this office that the Hasmonean leaders were appointed when they had achieved a *modus vivendi* with the Syrian overlords.[2] Later, more secure in their positions, first Aristobulus I, then Alexander Jannaeus ventured to call themselves kings—a development viewed with distaste by Josephus.[3]

Moses not a king

For the purposes of this investigation it is particularly significant that Josephus never speaks of Moses as a king. This fact is remarkable not only because, as will be seen below, the idea that Moses was king is well attested in both Hebrew and Greek sources, but also because the functions which Josephus attributes to Moses were so naturally associated with kingship. Supreme command over the military forces, unique personal rule over the entire nation—these were certainly the ordinary perquisites of kingship. Above all, the task of legislation, in the sense of laying down the constitution of the state, was a fundamental element in the Hellenistic ideal of kingship, as Goodenough has shown, and as Philo makes plain in his own description of Moses.[4] Moreover, the opponents of Moses in

---

[1] *Antt.*, i.6, trans. Thackeray (Loeb), IV, 5.

[2] Jonathan, στρατηγὸς καὶ μεριδάρχης, by decree of King Alexander (1 Macc. 10.65); "Simon, στρατηγός from the Ladder of Tyre to the borders of Egypt" (*ibid.*, 11.59); ἀρχιερεὺς μέγας καὶ στρατηγὸς καὶ ἡγούμενος Ἰουδαίων (*ibid.*, 13.42); ἡγούμενος, ἀρχιερεύς, στρατηγός (*ibid.*, 14.42); ἀρχιερεύειν καὶ εἶναι στρατηγὸς καὶ ἐθνάρχης ... (*ibid.*, 14.47).

[3] Below, p. 135.

[4] Above, pp. 170-176.

Josephus' story call him a "tyrant,"[1] to which the favorable counterpart would surely be "king." Finally, the story of the boy Moses, who throws down Pharaoh's crown and tramples it with his feet,[2] certainly foreshadowed Moses' own kingship in some forms of the tradition,[3] though perhaps not clearly in the form in which the story reached Josephus.

If Josephus knew traditions in which Moses was described as a king, he had his own reasons for not repeating them. He was strongly opposed to monarchy, as he indicates on several occasions. As part of Israel's "constitution," he has Moses explain:

> Aristocracy, with the life that is lived thereunder, is indeed the best: let no craving possess you for another polity, but be content with this, having the laws for your masters (δεσπότας) and governing all your actions by them; for God sufficeth for your ruler (ἡγεμών). But should ye become enamoured of a king ... [there follows the "Law of the King" from Deuteronomy 17.14ff].[4]

Again, Moses' superiority as legislator was demonstrated just in the fact that he rejected monarchy, oligarchy, and democracy alike, but gave his constitution the form of a "theocracy."[5] In practical terms, this meant for Josephus that priests should control the government.[6] It was a fatal degradation of the "constitution" of Israel when Hyrcanus and Aristobulus sought to "change the nation to a different form of government" (εἰς ἄλλην μετάγειν ἀρχὴν τὸ ἔθνος).[7] and the result of the Roman intervention produced a still further degradation when kingship passed from the hands of "those of the high priestly family" to "commoners."[8] It was hardly to be expected that Josephus would have described the "legislator" of the Jews himself as a king, especially since, in Josephus' understanding, Moses was not a priest!

---

[1] τύραννος, *Antt.*, iv.16, 22, cf. 146f. Τύραννος here, as elsewhere in late Hellenism, is a distinctly pejorative term, no longer the neutral designation it had been in classical and early Hellenistic writing.

[2] *Antt.*, ii.233.

[3] Similar stories are told of the young Cyrus and of the founder of Constantinople (Rappaport, p. 116, nn. 136, 137).

[4] *Antt.*, iv.223, trans. Thackeray (Loeb), IV, 583.

[5] *C.Ap.*, ii.164-167.

[6] *C.Ap.*, ii.185. On Josephus' favoritism toward the priesthood, cf. Rappaport, p. xxxiv.

[7] *Antt.*, xiv.41-45.

[8] *Antt.*, xiv.78.

Thus it is impossible to be certain whether Josephus was acquainted with traditions that called Moses a king, despite some
hints of such traditions in his writings. His silence on the subject
is no proof that he was not, since his anti-monarchic tendency
affords sufficient reason for his having ignored the title.

Moses and the priesthood

It is equally interesting that Josephus denies to Moses the high-
priesthood. In this case the title is not merely absent, but Josephus
goes out of his way to insist that not Moses but Aaron received the
office. According to one passage, Aaron's appointment was contrary
to Moses' own reasonable expectations. In the convocation at Sinai,
when Aaron and his sons were to be consecrated, Moses says:

> "For my part, had the weighing of this matter been entrusted
> to me, I should have adjudged myself worthy of the dignity,
> alike from that self-love that is innate in all, as also because I
> am conscious of having laboured abundantly for your salvation.
> But now God himself has judged Aaron worthy of this honour
> and has chosen him to be priest, knowing him to be the most
> deserving among us. . . ." The Hebrews were pleased with this
> speech and acquiesced in the divine election; for Aaron, by
> reason of his birth, his prophetical gift, and his brother's
> virtues, was more highly qualified than all for the dignity.[1]

Furthermore, the divine election of Aaron to the priesthood had
been decreed long before, having been announced to Amram in the
dream that foretold Moses' birth.[2] Here Josephus has employed
traditions that deliberately exalted Aaron at the expense of Moses
for the sake of glorifying the priesthood;[3] very similar traditions
are found in Talmud and midrashim.[4] Elsewhere Josephus suggests
that it is because of Moses' humility that he deliberately declined
the honors which the people wished to confer on him.[5] These passages
reveal Josephus' own efforts to harmonize the priestly, Aaronic

---

[1] Antt., iii.188-192, trans. Thackeray (Loeb). IV, 409.

[2] Antt., ii.216.

[3] Cf. Rappaport, p. xxxiv.

[4] Especially Wayikra R., 11.6, cited by Rappaport, pp. 35, 122f., n. 164.
In addition to the other references mentioned by Rappaport, cf. ARN (ed.
Schechter, p. 10; trans. Goldin, p. 19), where Moses compares himself un-
favorably with Aaron, "who was anointed with the anointing oil and clothed
in many priestly garments."

[5] Antt., iii.212, cf. iv.28.

tendency of his sources with his own idealization of Moses. It should be noted that such humility is often a feature of the θεῖος ἀνήρ;[1] on the other hand, it is a frequent characterization of Moses in the Rabbinic traditions.[2]

Despite his rejection of the idea that Moses ever functioned as High Priest, Josephus emphasizes Moses' office as Israel's unequalled intercessor before God. Particularly important is the passage which describes the peoples' sorrow at Moses' death:

> But they were in tears and displaying deep regret for their general [στρατηγός], alike remembering the risks which he had run and all that ardent zeal of his for their salvation, and despondent concerning the future, in the belief that they would never more have such a ruler and that God would be less mindful of them, since it was Moses who had ever been the intercessor [παρακαλῶν].[3]

Here the tradition of Moses as defender and mediator for Israel before God's throne of judgment appears, a tradition also very important in Philo[4] and well known in Rabbinic Judaism.[5] It is important to see that this function of Moses can be described without any reference to his "office" of high priest.

The Prophet

Like Philo, though less frequently, Josephus can refer to Moses simply as "the prophet." Also like Philo, he regards "prophecy" as one of the distinct offices which Moses held. In the two summary passages already mentioned, he states that Moses had been στρατηγός and προφήτης as was his successor Joshua.[6] Moreover, while Moses may have had a few peers as a στρατηγός, as προφήτης there was no other like him.[7]

Moses' prophecy consists for Josephus precisely in the fact that in his words it was not he himself who spoke, but God. Thus the last-mentioned passage goes on, "so that whatever he uttered it

---

[1] Bieler, I, 59.
[2] From Num. 12.3. Cf. Ginzberg, III, 256f.; VI, 90f., n. 490.
[3] *Antt.*, iv.194, trans. Thackeray (Loeb), IV, 569.
[4] Above, p. 118.
[5] See below, pp. 200-204.
[6] *Antt.*, iv.165, 329; cf. ii.327; iv.320; *C.Ap.*, i.40.
[7] στρατηγὸς μὲν ἐν ὀλίγοις, προφήτης δὲ οἶος οὐκ ἄλλος (*Antt.*, iv.329). The second notion appears in Dt. 34.10.

seemed that one heard God himself speaking."[1] At Sinai Moses tells the assembled Israelites:

> In His name, then, and in the name of all that through Him has already been wrought for us, scorn not the words now to be spoken, through looking only on me the speaker, or by reason that it is a human tongue that addresses you. Nay, mark but their excellence and ye will discern the majesty of Him who conceived them and, for your profit, disdained not to speak them to me. For it is not Moses, son of Amaram and Jochabed, but He who constrained the Nile to flow for your sake a blood-red stream ... who favours you with these commandments, using me for interpreter [ἑρμηνεύς].[2]

From these passages it becomes apparent that prophecy is not identified with ecstatic experience and utterance for Josephus, as it was for Philo, but consists in the whole mission of Moses as God's representative, his ἀπόστολος on earth. Therefore Josephus' Moses does not hesitate to speak of himself and God in the same breath and in parallel: "'God,' said he, 'and I, though vilified by you, will never cease our efforts on your behalf.'"[3] It will be recalled that this is exactly the understanding of Jesus' prophetic mission found in the Fourth Gospel.[4]

The Divine Man

Bieler has emphasized the extent to which Josephus conforms the biography of Moses to the βίος of a typical Hellenistic θεῖος ἀνήρ.[5] The point is well taken, although, as Bieler himself recognizes, Josephus does not go so far in this direction as Philo and especially Artapanus. In a single passage Josephus actually applies the technical term θεῖος ἀνήρ to Moses.[6] It is important to notice, however, that the use here is occasioned by a specific apologetic context. The Jews are accused of despising τὸ θεῖον. On the contrary, retorts Josephus, a consideration of the institutions of worship which Moses founded will show that "the legislator" himself was a θεῖος ἀνήρ.

---

[1] ὥσθ' ὅ τι ἂν φθέγξαιτο δοκεῖν αὐτοῦ λέγοντος ἀκροᾶσθαι τοῦ θεοῦ (ibid.).

[2] Antt., iii.85-87, trans. Thackeray (Loeb), IV, 357, 359.

[3] ὁ θεός, εἶπε, κἀγὼ καίτοι κακῶς ἀκούοντες πρὸς ὑμῶν οὐκ ἂν ἀποσταίημεν κάμνοντες ὑπὲρ ὑμῶν ... (Antt., iii.298; trans. Thackeray [Loeb], IV, 463).

[4] Above, pp. 45f.

[5] Bieler, I, 18f., and esp. II, 30-34.

[6] Antt., iii.180.

Apart from the term itself, there are numerous elements in Josephus' life of Moses which remind the reader of the θεῖοι ἄνδρες. The story of Moses' birth, predicated by divine oracles and dreams,[1] and accomplished by Jochabed with miraculously painless labor,[2] has frequent parallels in the lives of the *theioi*.[3] The child's exceptional development, learning, and beauty,[4] less elaborately expounded than in Philo, belong to the typical motifs of the Hellenistic *Bios*.[5]

Typical of the Hellenistic divine men is the ability to foresee the future.[6] This ability is attributed to Moses by Josephus,[7] but it has little or nothing to do with Moses' office as prophet, which is depicted in the biblical mode. Josephus despises the γόεις of popular Hellenistic religiosity;[8] naturally he avoids every feature which would make Moses resemble these figures. Josephus' description of Moses' contest with the Egyptian magicians draws a very broad contrast between the two:

> Indeed, O king, I too disdain not the cunning (σοφία) of the Egyptians, but I assert that the deeds wrought by me so far surpass their magic and their art (ἡ τούτων μαγεία καὶ τέχνη) as things divine are remote from what is human. And I will show that it is from no witchcraft or deception of true judgment (οὐ κατὰ γοητείαν καὶ πλάνην τῆς ἀληθοῦς δόξης), but from God's providence and power that my miracles proceed.[9]

This passage illustrates also the reserve which Josephus displays toward Moses' miracles, which could have been expanded, as in Artapanus, to depict Moses as a virtual μάγος.[10] Towards miracles in general Josephus assumes an air of sophisticated rationalism,[11] although frequently this rationalism seems to go no deeper than a stylistic device to impress skeptical readers.

One might be tempted to include under the features resembling

---

[1] *Antt.*, ii.205: prediction by Egyptian ἱερογραμματεύς; ii.210-216; Amram's dream (or vision, ὄψις, 217).

[2] *Antt.*, ii.218.

[3] Cf. Bieler, I, 24-30.

[4] *Antt.*, ii.230f.

[5] Bieler, I, 34-38.

[6] *Ibid.*, 88-92; cf. Wetter, pp. 69f.

[7] *Antt.*, ii.237.

[8] Cf. Fascher, pp. 161-163.

[9] *Antt.*, ii.286, trans. Thackeray (Loeb), IV, 289.

[10] On the θεῖος as μάγος, cf. Bieler, I, 84-87.

[11] Thackeray, *Dictionary of the Bible*, Extra Vol., 470f.

a θεῖος ἀνήρ Josephus' heightened description of hostility towards Moses. The particular motif which Josephus emphasizes is the attempt to stone Moses. While the biblical account mentions an intent to stone Moses only at Rephaidm (Exodus 17.4), Josephus repeats this detail at the Red Sea,[1] at Enim,[2] and at the return of the scouts from Canaan.[3] Such opposition, as Bieler illustrates,[4] serves as a contrast motif to set the virtues of the *theios* in relief. However, resort to the ideology of the θεῖος ἀνήρ is unnecessary here, for the repetition is to be explained simply as the assimilation of details in accounts of similar incidents—an assimilation which could occur in any kind of narrative, but especially in oral tradition. The possibility that the multiplication of the Jews' attempt to stone Moses was taken by Josephus from older traditions is further supported by the fact that in the Rabbinic haggadah it is reported that Korah's mob also wanted to stone Moses.[5] It is worth recalling that in the Fourth Gospel repeated attempts to stone Jesus are reported.[6] Furthermore, Josephus reflects the notion that the rejection of Moses as God's messenger, implied by these uprisings, implied rejection of God: ... μὴ δι' ὧνπερ αὐτὸν βάλλουσι λίθων τοῦ θεοῦ κατακρίνειν νομισθῶσιν.[7] This note sets the hostility within the framework of the ἀπόστολος concept, so that it is closer to the world's hostility to the divine messenger than to the mere counterfoil of the divine man's own virtue.

At two points there are traces in Josephus' life of Moses of the ideas which dominate Philo's portrait: at the end of Moses' life and at his ascent of Sinai. The former is very vague in Josephus: when Moses has dismissed the elders and has bidden farewell to Eleazar and Joshua, but is "still conversing with them, a cloud suddenly stood over him and he disappeared down some ravine."[8] Here Josephus is almost certainly rationalizing, in his characteristic fashion, an account of Moses' ascension.[9] The next sentence contains,

---

[1] *Antt.*, ii.327.

[2] *Antt.*, iii.12-22.

[3] *Antt.*, iii.307; cf. the summary, iv.12.

[4] Bieler, I, 42-44.

[5] Rappaport, pp. 37, 124, n. 175, who cites *Bamidbar R.* 18.4 and *Tanhuma* קרח 3 (ed. Buber, par. 6).

[6] Jn. 8.59; 10.31-33; 11.8.

[7] *Antt.*, iii.21. A similar notion, based on Ex. 14.31b, is found in *Mekilta* (ed. Lauterbach, I, 252). Cf. Jn. 5.47.

[8] *Antt.*, iv.326.

[9] The translation of Moses is depicted in Philo (above, pp. 124f.) and

moreover, a polemic against a dangerous possibility inherent in the ascension tradition: "But he himself has written in the sacred books that he died, because he was afraid lest they would dare to say that on account of his superlative virtue he had departed to the divine."[1] That of course is precisely what Philo dared to say,[2] and he was certainly not alone. The polemic presupposes practice. Josephus here makes himself the mouthpiece, not of the tradition that Moses was translated, as Vermes says, but of a tradition that already fears that that notion leads to idolatry.[3]

Moses' ascent on Sinai was regarded by Philo and, as will be seen, in traditions preserved in Rabbinic haggadah, as a mystical ascent or translation to heaven. There are only traces of these traditions in Josephus, but these traces are clear enough. After his first ascent of the mountain, Moses returns to tell the Israelites that he has attained "a vision of God and become the auditor of an imperishable voice."[4] On the second ascent (by Josephus' reckoning, omitting the episode of the golden calf and combining the two forty-day sojourns on the mountain), the biblical account relates that Moses "ate no bread and drank no water" for forty days and nights. Josephus, however, says that he "had tasted no food of the kinds designated for men."[5] The implication is that Moses had been nourished by heavenly food, that is, the food of angels—a feature familiar in accounts of heavenly ascensions.[6] Presumably a fuller account of Moses' ascension was known to Josephus in one of his sources or oral traditions.

In summary, then, a definite tendency can be observed in Josephus to depict Moses, like the other great men in Jewish history, with the typical features of Hellenistic θεῖοι ἄνδρες. On the whole, however, the tendency is very moderate. Josephus' distaste for the

---

elsewhere (see below). Rappaport (pp. 39, 127, n. 185) and Vermès ("Moïse au tournant," p. 90) agree that an ascension is implied by Josephus' account.

[1] *Antt.*, iv.326.

[2] Above, pp. 124f.

[3] On the attempts in some circles to combat dangerous tendencies in the exaltation of Moses, see the note by Judah Goldin, "The First Chapter of the Abot de Rabbi Nathan," *Mordecai M. Kaplan: Jubilee Volume on the Occasion of His Seventieth Birthday; English Section* (New York: The Jewish Theological Seminary of America, 1953), pp. 279f.

[4] *Antt.*, iii.88: ... τῷ θεῷ γὰρ εἰς ὄψιν ἐλθὼν ἀκροατὴς ἀφθάρτου φωνῆς ἐγενόμην.

[5] *Antt.*, iii.99: οὐδενὸς σιτίου τῶν τοῖς ἀνθρώποις νενομισμένων γεγευμένος.

[6] Cf. Bieler, II, 33.

μάγοι or γόεις and his consciousness of writing for a sophisticated and skeptical audience led him to avoid the grosser features found in more popular versions of the lives of the divine men, even some of the features which were evidently found in or behind Josephus' own sources. Of particular importance is his handling of Moses' death, for it shows that legends of Moses' ascension to heaven were current and had awakened fears of idolatry.

The Prophet as Ruler

One other curious theme found in Josephus must be briefly examined because, while not directly related to Moses, it forms a distant parallel to the main phenomenon under investigation, the combination of kingship with prophecy. In his summary of the "constitution" of Israel, Josephus paraphrases Deuteronomy 17.8f.:

> But if the judges [of each city] see not how to pronounce upon the matters set before them—and with men such things oft befall—let them send up the case entire to the holy city and let the high priest and the prophet and the council of elders [ὅ τε ἀρχιερεὺς καὶ ὁ προφήτης καὶ ἡ γερουσία] meet and pronounce as they think fit.[1]

Comparison with the Hebrew and Septuagint texts shows that Josephus' version differs in three important respects: (1) for ἱερεῖς λευίτας he reads ὁ ἀρχιερεύς; (2) for ὁ κρίτης = שפט he reads ὁ προφήτης; (3) he adds ἡ γερουσία. The first and third alterations must bring the code into accord with the practice of his own time. The γερουσία with the High Priest, perhaps understood as presiding, corresponds to the Sanhedrin. Thackeray calls attention to the provincial council set up in Galilee by Josephus himself to try difficult cases.[2] But what is the meaning of his substitution of ὁ προφήτης for שפט? The implication is that "the prophet" is regarded as a regular administrative office, comparable to the High Priesthood on one hand and the Council of Elders on the other. Obviously this notion is not derived from contemporary practice. It must instead be connected with the idea of a prophetic succession, stemming from Moses' prophetic and ruling offices. It will be recalled that Joshua, as Moses' διάδοχος, acceded to the office of στρατηγός and to the προφητεία.[3]

---

[1] *Antt.*, iv.218, trans. Thackeray (Loeb), IV, 581.

[2] *BJ*, ii.57of., cf. Thackeray (Loeb), IV, 580f., n.a.

[3] *Antt.*, iv.165; above, p. 133.

The prophetic succession

There are other scattered hints of a "succession of prophets" in ancient Jewish and Christian literature. Justin Martyr, for example, has this very difficult passage in his *Dialogue with Trypho*:

> That therefore both prophet and ruler have ever[1] ceased in your race, from its beginning until the time when this Jesus Christ both came and suffered, you will not shamelessly assert, nor can you prove. For even though you say Herod, under whom he suffered [*sic*] was an Ashkalonite, at the same time in your race you say there was a high priest, so that even then there was someone who presented offerings for you. And since there have been prophets in succession until John, so that even when your people was carried away to Babylon, your land ruined by war and the holy vessels carried away, the prophet did not cease from you, who was 'Lord' and 'ruler' and 'prince' of your people [κύριος καὶ ἡγούμενος καὶ ἄρχων τοῦ λαοῦ ὑμων]. For the spirit in the prophets anointed and established kings for you.[2]

The passage is not altogether clear, but several conclusions can be drawn. Justin obviously wants to prove that the prophecy of Genesis 49.10 (Septuagint), that Judah's "ruler" and "prince" would not fail until the one came "for whom it is laid up," was not fulfilled before Jesus. Since there had clearly been no unbroken succession of kings, Justin is obliged to resort to the high priest in the time of Herod — a weak effort, since he does not attempt to make the priest a "ruler," but only remarks that he continued the Mosaic offerings — and the "succession of prophets until John." The latter presupposes two traditions: (1) the Christian tradition that John the Baptist was the last of the prophets (compare Luke 16.16) and (2) a tradition about a *succession* of prophets. But Justin goes on to call the prophet κύριος καὶ ἡγούμενος καὶ ἄρχων τοῦ λαοῦ. This is unparalleled, but must have some scriptural or traditional basis. Most likely he is thinking of the anointing of the prophets, which played an important role in the developing Christian view of Christ's "triple office."[3] At Qumran also the prophets were known as "the anointed ones."[4]

---

[1] The sense of the passage as a whole demands this translation, although the usual English versions read "never," which Justin's accumulated negatives admittedly suggest by strict rules of grammar.

[2] Justin, *Dial.*, 52.3.

[3] Cf. Eusebius, *HE*, I, iii.7, 19f.

[4] CD, ii.12; 1 QM, xi.7: "your [God's] anointed ones," CD, vi.1, "Moses

The succession of prophets must have been traced back to Moses. The notion is familiar from the mythical form attested in the Pseudo-Clementines, but it is also found in still other scattered references. The *Wisdom of Solomon* reports that Wisdom enters "holy souls" in each generation to prepare φίλους θεοῦ καὶ προφήτας.[1] "Friends of God" may be a reference either to Abraham[2] or to Moses;[3] hence the verse promises leaders in each generation who will perform the functions of (the Patriarch and) the Prophet. The same succession is implied in Josephus' own phrase, "the prophets after Moses,"[4] as well as in Philo's term for Moses, ὁ πρωτοπροφήτης.[5]

Cryptic as are the passages in Justin's *Dialogue* and Josephus' *Antiquities*, therefore, they can be taken as evidence for some tradition that a continuous succession of prophets, extending from Moses until the close of the age, would exercise for Israel both Moses' prophetic office and his rulership.

The "triple office" of John Hyrcanus

It is tempting to relate the "prophetic succession" to Josephus' singular description of John Hyrcanus:

> John lived the rest of his life in happiness and administered governmental affairs in a most excellent manner, thirty-one years altogether, and died, leaving five sons. He was truly happy; there was no occasion to blame fortune on his account. Indeed he alone held three magnificent offices: the rule of the nation, the high-priesthood, and prophecy. [τρία γοῦν τὰ κρατιστεύοντα μόνος εἶχεν, τήν τε ἀρχὴν τοῦ ἔθνους καὶ τὴν ἀρχιερωσύνην καὶ προφητείαν]. For the divine [τὸ δαιμόνιον] conversed with him, so that he was not ignorant of the future. Thus he foresaw and prophesied that two of his elder sons would not remain masters of their affairs.[6]

---

and the holy anointed ones." Cf. Karl Georg Kuhn, "The Two Messiahs of Aaron and Israel," *The Scrolls and the New Testament*, ed. Krister Stendahl (New York: Harper & Brothers, 1957), pp. 59f.

[1] *Wisd.* 7.27f.

[2] 2 Chron. 20.7; Isa. 41.8; Jas. 2.23; Philo, *Abr.* 50.89, cf. 273; *Sob.* 56; *Som.*, i.193f., calls Abraham θεοφιλής but not φίλος θεοῦ. For the frequent reference to Abraham as friend of God in rabbinic sources, cf. Bloch, "Quelques aspects," p. 119.

[3] Ex. 33.11; Philo frequently calls Moses φίλος θεοῦ (*Sac.* 130; *Ebr.* 94; *Mig.* 45; *Quis her.* 21; *Som.*, i.193f., 231f.; *Mos.*, i.156) as well as θεοφιλής.

[4] *C.Ap.* i.40.

[5] Above, p. 126. Cf. also Justin, *Apol.* I, 32.1: πρῶτος τῶν προφητῶν.

[6] *BJ*, i.68f.

However, Josephus does not see John's gifts as part of a regular succession, but unique: μόνος εἶχεν. The uniqueness obviously belongs to προφητεία, since this alone has to be explained by Josephus. The other two offices, ἀρχιερεύς and ἐθνάρχης, are common to the whole Hasmonean line. It seems, as Fascher argues,[1] and Franklin W. Young reiterates,[2] that in Josephus' view prophecy in the Old Testament sense had ceased with Malachi. It can therefore be argued, as Young does, that the three offices of Hyrcanus belong to a "firm tradition" that Josephus took over. But it does not follow that this passage shows that the exceptional gift of prophecy is "eschatological."[3] What Josephus took over from his source was evidently only the statement that John Hyrcanus had predicted his sons' "catastrophe" at the end of his own life. But death-bed prophecies are a very common element in ancient biography; nothing "messianic" or "eschatological" is implied. The summary statement, which treats this exceptional prophecy as if it were an "office," is probably Josephus' own; the objection that it contradicts his view that prophecy properly so-called had ceased demands too nice a consistency from an author like Josephus.

Of course this passage in Josephus is often connected by scholars with the puzzling reference in the *Testament of Levi* (8.14) to a king who will arise in Judah to establish a new priesthood, whose glory will be "like a prophet of the Most High."[4] There is, however, no real basis for interpreting the two passages by each other. The evidence that the Aramaic original form of the Testament of Levi originated in the Qumran sect makes the thesis that the passage in question belongs to Hasmonean court-ideology extremely dubious. But the *Testament of Levi* passage is very difficult and must be considered later.[5]

Summary of Findings

There is little in Josephus' portrait of Moses which directly suggests the "prophet-king" of the Fourth Gospel, although there

---

[1] Fascher, pp. 152-160, 161-164.

[2] "Jesus the Prophet; A Reappraisal," *JBL*, 68 (1949), 289f.

[3] *Ibid.*, pp. 291, 297.

[4] R. H. Charles (ed.), *The Apocrypha and Pseudepigrapha of the Old Testament* (Oxford: At the Clarendon Press, 1913, rp. 1964), II, 309; recently Riesenfeld, p. 141; Schnackenburg, p. 623.

[5] See below, pp. 151-153.

are a few intriguing parallels. Moses does have a double "office" in Josephus, for his mission as prophet is closely connected with his sovereign command of Israel. Furthermore, his position as "commander" or "governor" has many functional similarities to the Hellenistic ideal king, particualrly in the function of "legislator." Nevertheless, Josephus never calls Moses a king, and it is impossible to discover, since Josephus' own tendency is strongly anti-monarchic, whether his sources did or not. In addition, a hint was found that not only Moses, but a "succession of prophets" were thought to exercise the offices of prophet and ruler.

The nature of Moses' prophetic office is described in the biblical mode by Josephus and closely parallels Jesus' prophetic mission in the Fourth Gospel. The prophet is God's representative who speaks God's words, not his own. As apostle of God, he arouses opposition, illustrated by the repeated attempts to stone Moses. This element, perhaps drawn by Josephus from older traditions, is reminiscent of the hostility of "the Jews" toward Jesus in John.

In contrast to Philo, Josephus denies to Moses the high-priesthood. He has taken over polemical priestly traditions which exalted Aaron at the expense of Moses, but he has moderated these traditions by emphasizing Moses' humility. He also emphasizes Moses' role as Paraclete, Israel's "advocate" who ameliorates God's judgment. A few traces reveal that the sources from which Josephus drew were acquainted with more mystical views of Moses, including translation at the end of his life and an ascent to heaven from Sinai to obtain a vision of God. Evidently these ideas were of no importance to Josephus himself, perhaps even distasteful.

MOSES' KINGSHIP, PROPHECY, AND RELATED FUNCTIONS
IN APOCRYPHAL AND PSEUDEPIGRAPHICAL WRITINGS

The sources

No other Jewish writing of the first Christian century comparable in extent to the works of Philo and Josephus is extant. Most of those that have survived are fragmentary; only a few offer references to Moses that are germane to this investigation. In this section, then, it will be sufficient to record the results of a systematic survey of the remaining non-rabbinic sources, citing only particularly relevant passages and omitting detailed discussion of individual sources.

Included are the Old Testament apocryphal books and the writings usually collected under the category "pseudepigrapha," the fragments of larger works preserved by Eusebius and Clement of Alexandria (Artapanus, Demetrius, Aristobulus, Eupolemus, Ezekiel the Tragedian), and the anonymous "Book of Biblical Antiquities" attributed in the Middle Ages to Philo. The Qumran texts, because of their extent and special circumstances, will be treated separately in the following section.

Moses as prophet-king

There is one remarkable passage which depicts kingship and prophecy together as gifts to Moses from God, heralded on Sinai. The passage belongs to the drama "The Exodus" written in Greek iambic trimeter by one Ezekiel, otherwise unknown, fragments of which were quoted by both Eusebius and Clement of Alexandria from a catena by Alexander Polyhistor. The scene in question is a dialogue between Moses and his father-in-law, in which Moses describes a dream:

> Methought upon Mount Sinai's brow I saw
> A mighty throne that reached to heaven's high vault,
> Whereon there sat a man of noblest mien
> Wearing a royal crown; whose left hand held
> A mighty sceptre; and his right to me
> Made sign, and I stood forth before the throne.
> He gave me then the sceptre and the crown,
> And bade me sit upon the royal throne,
> From which himself removed. Thence I looked forth
> Upon the earth's wide circle, and beneath
> The earth itself, and high above the heaven.
> Then at my feet, behold! a thousand stars
> Began to fall, and I their number told,
> As they passed by me like an armed host:
> And I in terror started up from sleep.[1]

His father-in-law provides the interpretation:

> This sign from God bodes good to thee, my friend.
> Would I might live to see thy lot fulfilled!
> A mighty throne shalt thou set up, and be
> Thyself the leader and the judge of men!

---

[1] Eusebius, *Praep. Ev.*, ix.29, trans. E. H. Gifford, *Eusebii Pamphili, Evangelicae Praeparationis* (Oxford: The University Press, 1903), vol. III, part 1, pp. 469f.

And as o'er all the peopled earth thine eye
Looked forth, and underneath the earth, and high
Above God's heaven, so shall thy mind survey
All things in time, past, present, and to come.[1]

The introduction of a dream into the play follows the technique of
Greek drama,[2] but its content is a heavenly enthronement like
those of Daniel 7, 1 Enoch 37-71, Testament of Levi 8, 2 Enoch
24-36. The "man" (φώς) enthroned on Sinai can be no other than
God himself; he gives to Moses his own throne, diadem, and sceptre.
The meaning of this divine investiture is probably no different from
the more common apocalyptic imagery in which the ascended hero
is seated at God's left or right or shares God's throne, that is, Moses
becomes God's vicegerent. His exalted position is emphasized by
the obeisance of the stars, who also pass in review before him "like
a camp of mortal soldiers"; that is, the "heavenly hosts" of Yahweh
are at Moses' disposal.[3]

The ability of the enthroned man to see secrets ordinarily concealed from mortal eyes is a common feature of such heavenly
ascents, very elaborately developed in the Enochic literature and

---

[1] *Ibid.* The text is as follows:

<’Έδοξ’> ὄρους κατ’ <ἄκρα Σιναίου> θρόνον
μέγαν τιν’ εἶναι μέχρις οὐρανοῦ πτυχός,
ἐν τῷ καθῆσαι φῶτα γενναῖόν τινα
διάδημ’ ἔχοντα, καὶ μέγα σκῆπτρον χερὶ
εὐωνύμῳ μάλιστα. Δεξιᾷ δέ μοι
ἔνευσε, κἀγὼ πρόσθεν ἐστάθην θρόνου.
εἶπεν καθῆσθαι· βασιλικὸν <δ’ἔδωκέ μοι>
διάδημα, <κἀυτὸς> ἐκ θρόνων χωρίζεται.
Ἐγὼ δ’ἐσεῖδον γῆν ἅπασαν ἔγκυκλον,
κἄνερθε γαίας κἀξύπερθεν οὐρανοῦ,
καί μοί τι πλῆθος ἀστέρων πρὸς γούνατα
ἔπιπτ’ ἐγὼ δὲ πάντας ἠριθμησάμην,
κἀμοῦ παρῆγεν ὡς παρεμβολὴ βροτῶν.
Εἶτ’ ἐμφοβηθεὶς ἐξανίσταμ’ ἐξ ὕπνου.

Ὁ δὲ πενθερὸς αὐτοῦ τὸν ὄνειρον ἐπικρίνει οὕτως·
Ὦ ξένε, καλόν σοι τοῦτ’ ἐσήμηνεν θεός·
ζώην δ’ ὅταν σοί ταῦτα συμβαίη τοτέ.
Ἆρά γε μέγαν τιν’ ἐξαναστήσεις θρόνον,
κἀυτὸς βραβεύσεις, καὶ καθηγήσῃ βροτῶν.
Τὸ δ’ εἰσθεᾶσθαι γῆν ὅλην τ’οἰκουμένην,
καὶ τὰ ὑπένερθεν, καὶ ὑπὲρ οὐρανὸν θεοῦ,
ὄψει τά τ’ ὄντα, τά τε πρὸ τοῦ, τά θ’ ὕστερον.

[2] Heinemann, Pauly-Wissowa, XVI, 365.

[3] One is reminded of the emphasis on Moses as στρατηγός in Josephus, and
of the fact that ἀρχιστράτηγος, a title given an angel in Josh. 5.13-6.2, is
taken as a messianic title by Justin (*Dial.*, 34.2; 61.1; 62.5).

also, as will be seen, in some Moses traditions. Significant in the Ezekiel passage is the fact that this panoramic vision of heaven, earth, and underworld is interpreted by Reuel as a symbol of Moses' prophetic office: he will see "the things which are, those which were before, those afterward."

The presence of this extraordinary scene in Ezekiel's drama is the more remarkable because elsewhere in the extant fragments Ezekiel follows the narrative of the Septuagint very closely, with no evidence of influence from the Hellenistic "Moses novels."[1] The intended audience was probably Jewish; Schürer compares the drama with the medieval mystery plays, intended both to educate the audience in the biblical story and to provide "wholesome" entertainment in the place of pagan diversions.[2] It is apparent that Moses' kingship—one might even say "divine kingship"[3]—and the closely related office of prophecy were taken for granted by Ezekiel and his audience, as much a part of Moses' story as the elements found expressly in the biblical narrative. The lines of Ezekiel that have been preserved do not reveal how he may have portrayed the fulfillment of the Sinai vision—how Moses "set up a mighty throne" and practiced the gift of prophecy. For the prophetic endowment of Moses, the tragedian would have found sufficient basis in the scripture.[4] His general approach suggests that he must have also found support for Moses' kingship in biblical texts as they were interpreted in his circle. What such texts may have been is a question best deferred until the rabbinic midrashim are examined in the next chapter.

The date of Ezekiel is unknown, but the *terminus ad quem* is fixed approximately by the fact that Alexander Polyhistor quoted him. Since Alexander lived around 80-40 B.C.,[5] Ezekiel may safely be taken as a witness to traditions of the second century B.C. that God gave to Moses unique powers as king and prophet. The provenance of these traditions is scarcely illuminated by Ezekiel, although he himself must undoubtedly have belonged to the Greek-speaking Diaspora.

---

[1] Heinemann, Pauly-Wissowa, XVI, 365.

[2] Schürer, III, 502.

[3] Cf. Goodenough, *Jewish Symbols*, IX, 101, who connects the scene with Orphic notions.

[4] E.g., Deut. 18; 34.10; Num. 11. 24-30; 12.1-8.

[5] Schürer, III, 469.

Nowhere else in the literature here under discussion are the offices of kingship and prophecy so directly combined in the person of Moses as in Ezekiel, but there are several passages associating prophecy and rule which require some consideration. Only one of these applies directly to Moses.

In the treatise "Concerning the Kings in Judaea" by Eupolemus, also excerpted by Alexander Polyhistor, Moses appears as the founder of a succession of rulers of Israel, the first three of whom (Moses, Joshua, and Samuel) were "prophets"; the others, beginning with Saul, were "kings."[1] The idea that Samuel, as Moses' successor, was a king or prince as well as prophet is reflected in several places,[2] doubtless suggested by the biblical account itself, which regards Samuel as a נביא[3] but also places him among the "judges" of Israel.[4] In the *Biblical Antiquities* of pseudo-Philo, an oracle declares to the Israelites that the yet unborn Samuel "shall be prince over you and shall prophesy [*principabitur in vobis, et prophetabit*]; and from henceforth there shall not be wanting unto you a prince for many years."[5] Pseudo-Philo's description of Samuel's call has God in soliloquy explicitly compare Samuel with Moses (*tamen similis est Moysi famulo meo*),[6] and the call itself begins with God's description of the mission of Moses: "Verily I enlightened the house of Israel in Egypt and chose unto me at that time Moses my servant for a prophet, and by him I wrought wonders for my people. . . ."[7]

---

[1] "But Eupolemus says, in some comments on the prophecy of Elias, that Moses prophesied forty years; then Jesus the son of Nave thirty years, and he lived a hundred and ten years, and pitched the holy tabernacle in Silo.

"And afterwards Samuel rose up as a prophet: and then by God's will Saul was chosen king by Samuel, and died after a reign of twenty-one years.

"Then his son [*sic*] David reigned, who subdued the Syrians which live beside the river Euphrates . . . .

"When David had reigned forty years he gave over the government to Solomon his son . . ." (*apud* Eusebius, *Praep. Ev.*, ix.30; trans. Gifford, III/1, 475f.).

[2] Cf. Philo, *Ebr.* 143: ὁ καὶ βασιλέων καὶ προφητῶν μέγιστος Σαμουήλ.

[3] 1 Sam. 3.19-21; cf. 9.9.

[4] *Ibid.*, 7.15. The notion that Samuel continued a succession which began with Moses (and Aaron) is also implicit in the deuteronomistic summary 1 Sam. 12.6-15.

[5] *Bib. Antt.*, 49.7; trans. M. R. James, *The Biblical Antiquities of Philo* ("Translations of Early Documents, Series I, Palestinian Jewish Texts"; London: S.P.C.K., 1917), p. 214. Cf. 51.3.

[6] *Bib. Antt.*, 53.2.

[7] *Ibid.*, 53.8, trans. James, p. 221.

Clearly Samuel is regarded here as virtually a "new Moses," a successor to Moses' rulership and to Moses' prophetic mission.[1]

Much more problematical is the association of king, priest, and prophet in the *Testament of Levi*, chapter 8. In his vision at Bethel, Levi, after his investiture as priest by "seven men in white raiment," is told "Levi, thy seed shall be divided into three offices [τρεῖς ἀρχάς] for a sign of the glory of the Lord who is to come."[2] Then three "portions" (κλῆροι) are mentioned:

> And the first portion shall be great; yea, greater than it shall none be. The second shall be in the priesthood. And the third shall be called by a new name, because a king shall arise in Judah, and shall establish a new priesthood, after the fashion of the Gentiles [to all the Gentiles].[3] And his presence [παρουσία] is beloved, as a prophet of the Most High, of the seed of Abraham our Father.[4]

Charles' conviction that this passage stems from the court ideology of the Hasmonean priest-kings[5] has now become untenable because of the new evidence that the Aramaic original version of the Testament of Levi as well as the Book of Jubilees, to which the Testament is closely related, enjoyed great popularity with the strongly anti-Hasmonean sect of Qumran.[6] On the other hand, the passage as it stands would accord poorly with the eschatology of the Qumran texts, since it seems to combine all three eschatological figures into one person,[7] and because "King" is never used of the Messiah of Israel in the Qumran texts.[8] Moreover, the passage has some internal inconsistencies, since the "three offices" of verse 12 would

---

[1] For Pseudo-Philo, as for one strand of the biblical narrative, the change from rule by the prophet-princes to rule by kings is a degradation for Israel: "indigni sumus indicari propheta, tunc diximus: Constitue super nos regem qui indicet nos per omnia" (*Bib. Antt.*, 57.4, ed. Kisch).

[2] *T. Lev.*, 8.12, trans. Charles, *Apoc. and Pseud.*, II, 309.

[3] Charles brackets the words as a possible dittography, but without MS support. MS d omits the previous phrase κατὰ τὸν τύπον τῶν ἐθνῶν.

[4] *T. Lev.*, 8.12-15, trans. Charles, *Apoc and Pseud.*, II, 309.

[5] *Ibid.*, note on v.15.

[6] Cf. J. T. Milik, "Le Testament de Lévi en araméen. Fragment de la grotte 4 de Qumrân," *RB*, 62 (1955), 398-406, and *Ten Years of Discovery in the Wilderness of Judaea* (SBT, No. 26; 1959), pp. 34f.

[7] *Contra* Marc Philonenko, *Les interpolations chrétiennes des Testaments des Douze Patriarches et les manuscrits de Qoumrân* (Paris: Presses universitaires de France, 1960), *passim*. Philonenko tries to show that the entire *Test. XII* originated at Qumrân, in nearly its present form, but is able to do so only at the expense of an incredible number of unsupported suppositions.

[8] See below, p. 166 and n. 4.

seem to accord better with the "high priests, and judges, and scribes" of verse 17 than with the three κλήροι of verses 12-15. Marinus de Jonge has good reason, therefore, for regarding verses 13-15 as a later interpolation, in his opinion by the Christian compiler of the *Testaments of the Twelve Patriarchs*.[1] That the verses were written *de novo* by a Christian is difficult to believe, however. De Jonge's identification of the three "portions" as Abraham, "the father of all believers,"[2] the Aaronic priesthood, and Christ[3] is unconvincing; placing Christ and Abraham both within the lineage of Levi would be a blunder requiring an exceedingly obtuse editor.

Sense can be made of verses 12-15 only if it is recognized that the "king" of verse 14, who "will arise from Judah,"[4] is not the same as the "third portion" of Levi. The verse describes king and priest as separate figures. The most satisfactory explanation of these verses is therefore that offered by Van der Woude, who sees here not an eschatological reference, but a historical one. The king is David, the "new priesthood," the Zadokite line he established.[5] Less illuminating is Van der Woude's explanation of the clause "his *parousia* will be glorious as a prophet of the Most High" as an allusion to Melchizedek, applied to the Zadokite priesthood. Why should Melchizedek be called a "prophet"? If this puzzling clause stood in the original (Essene) Testament of Levi, it must have applied to the priesthood, the third κλήρος of Levi, not the king from Judah.[6] But perhaps the clause is best explained as a Christian gloss. In any event, the passage does not reflect a "triple office" ideology connected with the Hasmoneans, and it offers no evidence

---

[1] *The Testaments of the Twelve Patriarchs* (Assen: Van Gorcum & Comp., 1953), p. 46. De Jonge calls attention to the parallel in the blessing of Levi by Isaac in *Jub.* 31.15: "And they [*scil.* 'the seed of thy sons'] shall be judges and princes, and chiefs of the sons of Jacob." De Jonge's thesis that the present *Test XII* is a *Christian* compilation which made use of a variety of Jewish haggadic materials, including an older and much more extensive Testament of Levi (in Aramaic) and Testament of Naphtali (in Hebrew: fragments of both are known from the Cairo Geniza as well as from Qumrân, while fragments of a Greek recension of the former are also extant), remains the most satisfactory explanation of the origin of the complete work.

[2] Accepting, with some MSS, ὁ πιστεύσας, against Charles.

[3] De Jonge, p. 46.

[4] ἐκ τοῦ 'Ιούδα, thus all MSS. Charles, to fit his theory, emends to ἐν τῷ 'Ιουδα⟨ία⟩.

[5] Van der Woude, p. 213.

[6] In Lk. 1.76 the title προφήτης ὑψίστου is applied to John the Baptist Could it belong to the Elijah typology?

at all for an amalgamation of kingship and prophecy like that found in the Fourth Gospel.

Moses as king

Moses' dream in Ezekiel's drama of the Exodus shows that the idea of Moses' kingship was much older than Philo and that it was not just an apologetic notion intended for Gentiles, but belonged to traditions familiar enough to be incorporated in an account based mainly on the Old Testament and intended probably for a Jewish audience. Furthermore Ezekiel, like Philo, emphasizes that Moses' adoption by Pharaoh's daughter led to his receiving a "royal upbringing" (τροφαὶ βασιλικαί):

> The princess then through all my boyhood's years,
> As I had been a son of her own womb,
> In royal state and learning nurtured me.[1]

There are other hints that Moses was commonly known as a king. Both Demetrius and Eupolemus, Greek-speaking Jews included in Alexander Polyhistor's catena, wrote histories of Israel entitled, according to Clement of Alexandria, "Concerning the Kings in Judaea,"[2] which began with the story of Moses. Similarly Julius of Tiberius, a contemporary of Josephus and like him Palestinian by birth, wrote a "Chronicle of the Jewish Kings," which according to Photius "begins from Moses and relates events as far as the death of Agrippa the seventh."[3] Pseudo-Philo speaks of Moses' *ducatus* (= ἡγεμονία) which, he says, Moses "will exercise forever,"[4] and of his *principatus* (= ἀρχή), which was given to Joshua after Moses' death.[5] An anti-Jewish polemic by the Basilidean Gnostics, described by Irenaeus, may reflect Jewish practice of referring to Moses as "prince": "The prophecies were spoken by the world-making principalities [*principibus*], and the law by their chief [*principe ipsorum*], the one who led the people out of the land of Egypt."[6] It

---

[1] Eusebius, *Praep. Ev.*, ix.28 (trans. Gifford, III/1, 468) = Clement Alex., *Strom.*, i.157.7; cf. Philo, *Mos.*, i.8.

[2] *Strom.*, i.153.4 (Eupolemus) and i.21.141 (on Demetrius).

[3] Photius, *Biblioteca*, codex 33 (*PG*, Vol. CIII, col. 65.) Cf. Schürer, III, 472.

[4] *Bib. Antt.*, 9.10: *ipse ducatum aget semper.*

[5] *Ibid.*, 20.5: *post requietionem Moysi dabitur principatus Ihesu.*

[6] Irenaeus, *Adv. Haer.*, i. 24.5; trans. Robert M. Grant, *Gnosticism*; *A Source Book of Heretical Writings from the Early Christian Period* (New York: Harper & Brothers, 1961), p. 34. The mention of "the law" and "the prophe-

should be noted that here again, as in Philo, Moses' mediation of the law to Israel is connected with his princely office.

Moses as prophet

It is not surprising that "prophet" is one of the most frequent designations of Moses in the literature around the turn of the eras. Aristobulus, the Alexandrian Jewish apologete of the second century B.C.,[1] urges that, despite the offense of Moses' writings if taken literally, men of "good understanding" admire "his wisdom and the divine spirit because of which he has been proclaimed a prophet."[2] The Wisdom of Solomon, of approximately the same provenance and perhaps a century later than Aristobulus, calls Moses "a holy prophet"[3] and identifies the "divine spirit" with the hypostatized Wisdom:

> She (Wisdom) rescued a holy people and a blameless seed from a nation of oppressors
> She entered into the soul of a servant (θεράπων) of the Lord
> And withstood terrible kings by signs and wonders.[4]

In an earlier passage this extraordinary activity of Wisdom, regarded as an emanation (ἀπόρροια, ἀπαύγασμα) of God's glory, his Image (εἰκών),[5] is elaborated:

---

cies" and "the one who led the people out of Egypt" makes the identification of the "princeps principorum" with Moses practically certain. However, in i.24.4 the *princeps* of the angels who made the world is identified as "he that is thought by the Jews to be God" (*qui Iudaeorum putatur esse Deus*). The two passages taken together seem to imply identification of Moses with the God of the Jews in the eyes of the Basilideans. Is there behind this a confusion of Jewish traditions that exalted Moses as "god" on the basis of Ex. 4.16 and 7.1?

[1] The date depends on the assumption that the dedication of one of his works to Ptolemy Philometor is authentic and refers to Ptolemy VI (ca. 107-150 B.C.). The authenticity of the writings attributed to Aristobulus by Clement and Eusebius was questioned by many scholars at the end of the nineteenth century (cf. Gercke, "Aristobulus," Pauly-Wissowa, II [1895], 918-920, who dates the writings ca. 100 B.C.), but forcefully defended by Schürer (III, 516-522).

[2] Θαυμάζουσι τὴν περὶ αὐτὸν σοφίαν, καὶ τὸ θεῖον πνεῦμα, καθ'δ' καὶ προφήτης ἀνακεκήρυκται (Eusebius, *Praep. Ev.*, viii, 10.4).

[3] [scil. ἡ Σοφία] εὐόδωσεν τὰ ἔργα αὐτῶν [scil. τῶν Ἰσραηλίτων] ἐν χειρὶ προφήτου ἁγίου (11.1).

[4] *Ibid.*, 10.15f.

[5] *Ibid.*, 7.25-28; on this conception of σοφία as the εἰκὼν θεοῦ, cf. Jervell, pp. 46-50, 69.

But she being one can do all,
And abiding in herself makes all things new,
And generation by generation passing into holy souls,
Makes them friends of God and prophets.[1]

Reider refers to Philo's statement, "All wise men are friends of God,"[2] a stoic epigram quoted also by Philodemus.[3] But Philo applied the saying explicitly to Moses, on the basis of Exodus 33.11. That Moses as well as Abraham was known as "the friend of God" is a notion also well-attested by Pseudo-Philo[4] and by other sources,[5] and the combination "friends of God and prophets" is almost certainly an allusion to Moses. Thus the Wisdom passage implies a succession of leaders in Israel (including Solomon, as the context indicates) infused by σοφία to exercise the functions of Moses. The idea of a succession of prophetic leaders after the type of Moses is widely attested.[6] Pseudo-Philo calls Moses "the first of all the prophets" (*primus omnium prophetarum*), in a prayer of Gideon which takes Moses' request for a sign as a pattern for his own petition,[7] thus placing the "judge" Gideon in the Mosaic succession. Justin uses the same phrase for Moses,[8] and Eusebius describes him as "the most ancient of all prophets."[9]

Some sources especially magnify Moses' prophetic role and link it with other functions and dignities. The *Assumption of Moses* calls him "lord of the word, faithful in all things [an allusion to Numbers 12.7], God's divine prophet for the whole earth," as well as the "great messenger" (*magnus nuntius*) but relates his prophetic office particularly to his function as "advocate" (*defensor*) on Israel's behalf.[10] Elsewhere the same document speaks of Moses as *arbiter* for Israel and links Moses' prophecies with his sufferings in a manner

---

[1] 7.27, trans. Joseph Reider, *The Book of Wisdom* ("Dropsie College Edition, Jewish Apocryphal Literature"; New York: Harper & Brothers, 1957), p. 117.

[2] *Quis her.*, 21, cited by Reider, p. 117.

[3] Cited by Charles, *Apoc. and Pseud.*, I, 547.

[4] *Bib. Antt.*, xxiv.3; xxv.3, 5: *amicus domini*; *ibid.*, xxiii.9: *amicus meus*; xxxii.8: *dilectus suus*.

[5] Philo: see above, p. 103 and n. 7; cf. Sirach 45.1: ἠγαπημένον ὑπὸ θεοῦ καὶ ἀνθρώπου. Cf. Ginzberg, V, 207f., n. 4.

[6] In Eupolemus: cf. above, p. 150; in other sources: above, pp. 142-144; also in rabbinic sources (next chapter).

[7] *Bib. Antt.*, xxxv.6.

[8] *Apol.* I.32.1.

[9] προφητῶν ἀπάντων παλαιότατος (*HE*, I.ii.4).

[10] *Assump. Mos.*, xi.16f. On Moses' role as Paraclete, see below, pp. 159-161.

recalling the "servant songs" of Second Isaiah: "Is not this [the Exile] that which Moses did then declare unto us in prophecies, who suffered many things [*multa passus est*] in Egypt and in the Red Sea and in the wilderness during forty years: and assuredly called heaven and earth to witness against us . . .?"[1] The superiority of Moses to other prophets is emphasized by the tradition that God revealed all secrets to him, even that of the end of the ages.[2] A vulgarization of this tradition appears in an Egyptian magic papyrus, in which the conjurer says to the demon identified as Yeu-Osiris-Yabas-Yapos, "I am Moses your prophet, to whom you delivered your mysteries which were accomplished for (or celebrated by?) Israel. . . ."[3] The identification of Moses with Hermes, attested by Artapanus,[4] is probably also related to Moses' office as "messenger" and prophet, though Artapanus connects the name with Moses' "interpretation" (ἑρμηνεία) of the Hieroglyphics.[5]

It appears from these examples that "prophet" is a designation for Moses familiar in more diverse circles than any other. It is occasionally connected with his rulership and often with the notion that special mysteries were revealed to him. The latter notion must now be examined further in connection with traditions of Moses' heavenly ascents or journeys.

Moses' heavenly ascents and special revelations

It has already been noted that Philo found in Moses' vision of the burning bush, the ascent of Sinai, and the end of Moses' life occasions of extraordinary mystical revelations. A similar notion emerges in several of the sources here being considered.

As in Philo, little is made of the burning bush episode, beyond recital of the biblical account. The description by Ezekiel the Tragedian, however, is significant. God says to Moses:

---

[1] *Ibid.*, iii.11-13; trans. Charles, *Apoc. and Pseud.*, II, 417.

[2] *Jub.*, prologue; i.4, 26; 4 Ezra 14.5; *Syr. Bar.*, 59.8; *Bib. Antt.*, xix.14f.; on these passages see below and cf. Vermès, "Moïse au tournant," pp. 83f.

[3] Pap. Lond. 46; cited by Richard Reitzenstein, *Poimandres; Studien zur griechisch-ägyptischen und frühchristlichen Literatur* (Leipzig: B. G. Teubner, 1904), pp. 184f., who suggests that the formula may have originated in Samaria.

[4] Eusebius, *Praep. Ev.*, ix.27.

[5] Heinemann points out that Thoth was identified with Hermes by the same means, according to Diodorus, and that Artapanus gives to Moses Thoth's other, traditional functions, even including the foundation of Egypt's animal cults (Pauly-Wissowa, XVI, 368f.).

And from the bush the divine word shines forth for you;
Take courage, my child (or servant: ὦ παῖ), and hear my words,
For to see my face is impossible
For one born mortal, but you are permitted
To hear my words, for the sake of which I have come.[1]

It was suggested above that Philo's hint that Moses might have
seen "an image of the one that is," although a skeptical reader might
call it only "an angel," really meant that, in Philo's view, Moses
"saw" the Logos of God, as later on Sinai.[2] Ezekiel's mention of the
"divine word" (θεῖος λόγος) confirms the suggestion and shows that
a similar interpretation was at least a century older than Philo.

Moses' ascent of Sinai afforded more material for speculation.
The *Book of Jubilees* purports to be a secret revelation delivered to
Moses at Sinai, written down by the "angel of the presence."[3]
Similarly the apocalypse of Ezra models the special revelation to
Ezra on that of Moses, combining elements from the burning bush
episode with the revelation at Sinai.[4] Of the latter it says:

I told him many wondrous things,
    showed him the secrets of the times,
    declared to him the end of the seasons:
Then I commanded him saying:
These words shalt thou publish openly, but these keep secret.
    And now I do say to thee:
The signs which I have shewed thee,
    The dreams which thou hast seen,
    and the interpretations which thou has heard—lay them up
in thy heart! For thou shalt be taken up from (among) men,
and henceforth thou shalt remain with my Son,[5] and with such
as are like thee, until the times be ended.[6]

In Pseudo-Philo the secret is the covenant, "which no man hath
seen,"[7] but the author also knew traditions of Moses' actual entry
into Heaven at Sinai and his exploration of cosmological secrets.
Thus Moses came down from Sinai "covered with invisible light—

---

[1] In Eusebius, *Praep. Ev.*, ix.29.

[2] Above, p. 123 and n. 9; cf. p. 122.

[3] 1.26, cf. 1.4 and prologue.

[4] 4 Ezra 14.1-9. The chapter begins with a "voice out of a bush" that
cries "Ezra, Ezra!" and immediately proceeds to mention the revelation to
Moses "in the bush" (vv.1-3). Cf. Vermès, "Moïse au tournant," p. 77.

[5] Should this not be read "servant," as in 13.32? Does παῖς = עֶבֶד refer
to Moses, as so often?

[6] Vv. 5-9, trans. G. H. Box, in Charles, *Apoc. and Pseud.*, II, 621.

[7] ix.8, trans. James, p. 102.

for he had gone down into the place where is the light of the sun and moon. . ."[1] Again, God revealed to Moses not only the events of the past, which Moses was to record ("the years of the life of Noah") and the commandments about the festivals, but also "the ways of paradise," and "the place of birth and the color (?)."[2] Finally:

> And when he was dying (God) appointed unto him the firmament, and shewed him these witnesses whom now we have, saying: Let *the heaven where into thou hast entered* and the earth wherein thou hast walked until now be a witness between me and thee and my people. For the sun and the moon and the stars shall be ministers unto us.[3]

According to Syrian Baruch, God showed Moses the heavenly Jerusalem on Sinai,[4] and also:

> The measures of the fire, also the depths of the abyss, and the weight of the winds, and the number of the drops of rain: And the suppression of anger, and the multitude of long-suffering, and the truth of judgement: And the root of wisdom, and the riches of understanding, and the fount of knowledge: And the height of the air, and the greatness of Paradise, and the consummation of the ages, and the beginning of the day of judgement: And the number of the offerings, and the earths which have not yet come: And the mouth of Gehenna, and the station of vengeance, and the place of faith, and the region of hope: And the likeness of future torment, and the multitude of innumerable angels, and the flaming hosts, and the splendour of the lightnings, and the voice of the thunders, and the orders of the chiefs of the angels, and the treasuries of light, and the changes of the times, and the investigations of the law.[5]

This passage sounds like a summary of Enoch's "heavenly journeys";[6] Charles remarks, "Here one of Enoch's functions is for the first time transferred to Moses."[7]

---

[1] *Ibid.*, xii.1, trans. James, p. 110.

[2] *Ibid.*, xiii.7-9. Perhaps *colorem* is to be emended to *colubrum*, "the serpent," with James, p. 116.

[3] *Ibid.*, xxxii.9, trans. James, pp. 176f., emphasis mine. For the notion of the stars serving Moses, cf. the dream scene in Ezekiel, above, pp. 147f.

[4] Syr. Bar. 4.2-7.

[5] *Ibid.*, 59.5-11, trans. Charles, *Apoc. and Pseud.*, II, 514.

[6] Cf. 1 Enoch 17-36.

[7] *Apoc. and Pseud.*, II, 514 n. There are hints of secret revelations to the other patriarchs, as in Philo: to Jacob (an allusion to Gen. 28.10ff.), *Wisd. Sol.* 10.10; to Abraham, who alone saw God, Aristobulus *apud* Eusebius, *Praep. Ev.*, xii.12.12.

As the examination of Philo's writings showed, there was a tendency to assimilate traditions of Moses' (and other heroes') mystical ascent on Sinai with his translation at the end of his life.[1] Pseudo-Philo shows a similar development, for he expands the account of Moses' ascent of Mount Nebo to include not only the glimpse of the promised land, but also a vision of heavenly wonders, the latter reminiscent again of the cosmological and eschatological secrets showed to Enoch in his heavenly journeys or to Moses on Sinai:

> And he shewed him the place from whence the clouds draw up water to water all the earth, and the place whence the river receiveth his water, and the land of Egypt, and the place of the firmament, from whence the holy land only drinketh. He showed him also the place from whence it rained manna for the people, and even unto the paths of paradise. And he shewed him the measures of the sanctuary, and the number of the offerings, and the sign whereby (men) shall interpret (*lit.* begin to look upon) the heaven, and said: These are the things which were forbidden to the sons of men because they sinned.[2]

Despite this last heavenly ascent *before* death, Moses dies according to Pseudo-Philo; he is not translated. God himself takes Moses, "makes him sleep,"[3] and buries him "with his own hands on an high place of the earth, and in the light of the whole world."[4] In the *Assumption of Moses* death and translation are combined, for while Michael is commissioned to bury Moses, Joshua sees "the double Moses being taken up, the one with angels, the other on the mountain, accorded burial among the ravines."[5]

Moses as Israel's intercessor

In Philo and Josephus a strong tradition was found that Moses

---

[1] Above, pp. 124f.

[2] *Bib. Antt.*, 19.10, trans. James, p. 129. Note the similarity to the description of secrets revealed at Sinai, *ibid.*, xxxii.9.

[3] *dormificabo*, though two MSS read *glorificabo*.

[4] *Ibid.*, xix.12, 16, trans. James, pp. 130, 132.

[5] Thus the fragment preserved by Clement Alex., *Strom.*, vi.15: Εἰκότως ἄρα καὶ τὸν Μωυσέα ἀναλαμβανόμενον διττὸν εἶδεν Ἰησοῦς ὁ τοῦ Ναυῆ, καὶ τὸν μὲν μετ᾽ἀγγέλων, τὸν δὲ ἐπὶ τὰ ὄρη περὶ τὰς φάραγγας κηδείας ἀξιούμενον. (cited by R. H. Charles, *The Assumption of Moses* [London: Adam and Charles Black, 1897], p. 107). Origen records a slightly different version of the "double Moses": "Refertur enim quia duo Moses videbantur, unus vivus in spiritu, alius mortuus in corpore" (*In Iusuam hom.*, ii.1, cited by Charles, *Assump. Mos.*, p. 108).

acted as Israel's "advocate" before God, interceding on behalf of the people's sins and warding off God's judgment.[1] This role of Moses, already emphasized in the biblical narratives, particularly in the elohistic strand and in Deuteronomy,[2] was evidently expanded and elaborated in the intertestamental period. In the book of *Jubilees*, Moses is depicted as interceding for all the future generations of Israel, after he has been told by God of their destined sin.[3] It is significant that Moses' intercession in this passage stands over against the possibility that "the spirit of Beliar" may "accuse" the Israelites before God. In such a contest between accuser and defender before the seat of judgment Otto Betz finds the original *Sitz im Leben* of the concept of a "Paraclete."[4]

In *The Assumption of Moses* the hero's intercessory office is elevated beyond the limits of his earthly life. As Moses is preparing to depart, Joshua expresses his fear for the Israelites under his own leadership. Will not the Amorites now be able to conquer the Israelites, since when the latter sin they will not have Moses to atone for them?

> . . . They have no advocate [*defensor*] to offer prayers on their behalf to the Lord, as did Moses the great messenger [*magnus nuntius*], who every hour day and night had his knee fixed to the earth, praying and looking for help to Him that ruleth all the world with compassion and righteousness, calling to mind the covenant of the fathers and propitiating the Lord with the oath.[5]

But Moses reassures Joshua that his intercessions will not end with his departure from this life, for the Lord "hath on their behalf appointed me to pray for their sins and make intercession for them."[6] On the other hand, Moses' mediatorial office was established before creation: "Accordingly He designed and devised me [*excogitavit et invenit me*], and He prepared me before the foundation of the world,

---

[1] Above, pp. 118 and 137.

[2] Cf. Gerhard von Rad, *Theologie des Alten Testaments*, vol. I (München: Chr. Kaiser Verlag, 1961), pp. 288-294.

[3] *Jub.* 1.18-21.

[4] *Der Paraklet; Fürsprecher im häretischen Spätjudentum, im Johannes-Evangelium und in neu gefundenen gnostischen Schriften* ("Arbeiten zur Geschichte des Spätjudentums und Urchristentums," II; Leiden: E. J. Brill, 1963), pp. 36-55.

[5] *Assump. Mos.*, xi.17, trans. Charles, *Assump. Mos.*, pp. 47f.

[6] *Ibid.*, xii.6; trans. Charles, p. 49. Moses' continuing intercession is also attested in Philo: above, p. 125 and n. 3.

that I should be the mediator [*arbiter* = μεσίτης] of His covenant."[1]

Pseudo-Philo connects Moses' intercessory function with the titles "shepherd" and "judge." Moses predicts the future apostasy of Israel and warns:

> But then both ye and your sons and all your generations after you will arise and seek the day of my death and will say in their heart: Who will give us a shepherd like unto Moses,[2] or such another judge to the children of Israel, to pray for our sins at all times, and to be heard for our iniquities?[3]

"Judge" for the author is equivalent to "mediator," as comparison with another passage shows, in which God describes Moses' mission before his birth: "For in ancient days I thought of him, saying: My spirit shall not be a *mediator* among these men for ever, for they are flesh, and their days shall be 120 years."[4] The quotation is from Genesis 6.3, which Pseudo-Philo had quoted earlier in the Hebrew form, "My spirit shall not *judge* among these men for ever. . . ."[5] The curious application of this verse to Moses is suggested by the "120 years," which is the length of Moses' life. Here evidently Moses' office is limited to his earthly lifetime, a view consistent with the view of the author that Moses was "put to sleep" by God to arise at the last day. According to some traditions[6] Moses acts as intercessor also at the last Judgment. In the *Apocalypse of Ezra*, however, the possibility of such an intercession for the ungodly, raised by Ezra on the basis of the intercession of Abraham, Joshua, Samuel, David, Solomon, Elijah, Hezekiah, "and many for many," as well as of Moses,[7] is explicitly rejected. At the final Judgment, God himself will be the accuser, and "no man [shall] then be able to have mercy on him who is condemned in the Judgment, nor overwhelm him who is victorious."[8]

---

[1] *Ibid.*, i.14, trans. Charles, pp. 6f. The Greek fragment preserved by Gelasius of Cyzicum, *Comm. Act. Syn. Nic.*, ii.18, differs slightly from the Latin: καὶ προεθεάσατό με ὁ θεὸς πρὸ καταβολῆς κόσμου εἶναί με τῆς διαθήκης αὐτοῦ μεσίτην. (cited by Charles, *Assump. Mos.*, p. 6, n.).

[2] Cf. Num. 27.15-23.

[3] *Bib. Antt.*, xix.3, trans. James, p. 127.

[4] *Ibid.*, ix.8, trans. James, p. 102, emphasis mine.

[5] *Ibid.*, iii.2, trans. James, p. 79, emphasis mine.

[6] See below, chaps. IV and V.

[7] 4 Ezra 7.102-111.

[8] *Ibid.*, v.115, trans. Box in Charles, *Apoc. and Pseud.*, II, 590.

Moses' "signs and wonders"

The biblical narrative of the Exodus and wilderness wandering already emphasized the "signs and wonders" which Moses performed. In the summary of his life at the close of Deuteronomy, they are the epitome of his mission:

> And there has not arisen since a prophet in Israel like Moses, whom the Lord knew face to face, in all the signs and wonders (σημεῖα καὶ τέρατα) which the Lord sent him to do in the land of Egypt against Pharaoh and his servants and all his land, the great marvels (θαυμάσια) and the powerful hand which Moses did before all Israel.[1]

The literature surveyed in this chapter repeatedly magnifies this aspect of Moses' activity. In the passage already quoted from *Wisdom of Solomon*, Wisdom dwelling in Moses "withstood terrible kings by wonders and signs (τέρατα καὶ σημεῖα).[2] Before Moses' birth, according to Pseudo-Philo, God said, "By him will I do wonders [*mirabilia*] in the house of Jacob, and will do by him signs and wonders [*signa et prodigia*] for my people which I have done for none other, and will perform in them my glory and declare unto them my ways."[3] The promise is repeated in the vision of Miriam:

> Go and tell thy parents: behold that which shall be born of you shall be cast into the water, for by him water shall be dried up, and by him will I do signs [*signa*], and I will save my people, and he shall have the captaincy thereof alway.[4]

Numenius the Pythagorean knew the traditions of Moses' miraculous powers, as well as the apocryphal names of the Egyptian magicians who opposed him, Jannes and Jambres, and referred to Moses as "Musaeus."[5] The identicfiation of Moses with Musaeus, the legendary teacher of Orpheus, evidently belonged to an early stage of Hellenistic Jewish apologetic, for it is stated also by Artapanus, who painted Moses in the colors of a typical Greek hero.

---

[1] Dt. 34.10f., LXX.

[2] *Wisd. Sol.* 10.16.

[3] *Bib. Antt.*, ix.7, trans. James, p. 101.

[4] *Ibid.*, ix.10; James, p. 102. Cf. further liii.8: ". . . elegi mihi prophetam Moysen famulum meum et feci per eum prodigia populo meo. . . ."

[5] Eusebius, *Praep. Ev.*, ix.8. Numenius is also the author of the famous quip, "What is Plato but Moses speaking Attic?" (Clement Alex. *Strom.* i.150.4).

Furthermore Artapanus says that the Egyptian priests called Moses Hermes, and he attributes to Moses all the traditional functions of Hermes-Thoth.[1] It is noteworthy that Artapanus not only multiplies the miracles accomplished by or for Moses, but also stresses, even more than the E-account in Exodus, the part played by Moses' *rod* in the wonders. The same is true of Ezekiel the Tragedian, who has God say to Moses, "With this thy rod thou shalt work all these plagues,"[2] while an Egyptian messenger reports of the Red Sea crossing:

> And then their leader Moses, taking the *rod of God*, with which before he had contrived evil signs and wonders (σημεῖα κα τέρατα) against Egypt, struck the surface of the Red sea . . .[3]

In Pseudo-Philo, God places Moses' rod in the sky at his death, where, like the bow of Noah, it will remind God to spare the Israelites when they sin, thus in effect continuing Moses' own intercessory office.[4]

The emphasis on "signs and wonders" in Moses' mission led to a similar emphasis in the expectation of the "prophet like Moses" or of a *Moses redivivus*. This is especially clear in Josephus' description of Theudas and the other "magicians" (like Theudas, they doubtless called themselves "prophets"[5]) who promised or actually attempted to perform miracles in the wilderness.[6] It is commonly recognized that a Moses or Moses-Joshua typology is present here.[7] Moreover, the note on Jesus interpolated into Josephus' *Wars* in the Slavonic version relates that some Jews said, "This is our first legislator who has risen from the dead and who has shown *many cures and proofs* of his knowledge."[8] On the basis of these observations, Hahn is probably correct in seeing in the demand for and performance of signs in the synoptic traditions a reflection not of the Davidic

---

[1] Eusebius, *Praep. Ev.*, ix.27; cf. above, p. 156 and n. 5.

[2] Eusebius, *Praep. Ev.*, ix.29, trans. Gifford, III/1, 473.

[3] *Ibid.*, trans. mine.

[4] *Bib. Antt.*, xix.11.

[5] Fascher, pp. 162f., Teeple, p. 65.

[6] *Antt.*, xx.97; *BJ*, ii.259-262; vi.351; vii.438.

[7] Cf. J. Jeremias, *ThWbNT*, IV, 863; Teeple, pp. 65f.; Vermès, "Moïse au tournant," pp. 79, 84f.

[8] Cited by Vermès, "Moïse au tournant," p. 85, emphasis mine.

messianology—in which "there is no room for miracles"[1]—but of the expectation of a Mosaic eschatological prophet.[2] The performance of "signs and wonders" must have been a fundamental characteristic of the mission of the prophet like Moses. It will be recalled that the countertype of the Mosaic prophet, the "false prophet" of Deuteronomy 13 and 18, was also characterized by performance of "signs and wonders," but for the purpose of "leading astray" the people.[3]

KING, PROPHET, AND MOSES IN THE QUMRAN TEXTS

Significance of the Qumran Documents

The manuscripts discovered in the vicinity of the Dead Sea since 1947 have already led to a general revision of prevailing notions about Jewish eschatological hopes in the first century. The texts are of special importance because they are unaffected by the post-Jamnia consolidation of "normative" Judaism and uninfluenced by Christianity or by anti-Christian polemic. They are as important for their implications for understanding other sources of the same era as in their own content, for they reveal a manner of scriptural interpretation and haggadic expansion which is quite singular, yet at the same time bearing illuminating analogies to the use of the Old Testament in many New Testament passages on one hand and to the rabbinic midrashim on the other.[4] They also contain new clues which help fill in the imagery of traditions represented imperfectly by other sources. Hence, even though the work of editing and publishing the texts remains incomplete and although many important elements remain unsettled and confused in the process of scholarly evaluation, it is important to see whether these documents shed new light on the subject under investigation.

---

[1] Hahn, p. 219. He supports this statement by reference to Billerbeck, I, 593f., Bultmann, *Geschichte*, p. 275, and especially Joseph Klausner, *The Messianic Idea in Israel*, trans. W. F. Stinespring (New York: Macmillan, 1955), pp. 505-514.

[2] *Ibid.*

[3] Above, pp. 47-55.

[4] On the relation of the *pešarim* of Qumran to the *petirah* and other types of rabbinic midrashim, see Lou Silbermann, "Unriddling the Riddle; A Study in the Structure and Language of the Habakkuk Pesher," *RQ* 3 (1961), 323-364. On the significance of Qumran —and other recent discoveries —for the whole question of Scripture interpretation, see Vermès, *Scripture and Tradition*, *passim*.

The Qumran Eschatology

It is now generally agreed that the sect at Qumran awaited the coming "at the end of days" of two figures of fundamental importance: a High Priest, the Messiah of Aaron, and a Prince, the Messiah of Israel. In addition, at least at some stage of the sect's existence, a third eschatological figure, a prophet like Moses, was expected. The three figures were distinct individuals; there is no evidence that they were ever merged into the expectation of a single figure fulfilling two or all of these offices.[1] The relation of the dominating but anonymous historical figure in the sect's history, the Teacher of Righteousness, to the eschatological figures remains a subject of intense controversy, as it has been from the beginning.[2]

For the present investigation it is necessary only to examine the references to kingship, particularly in passages which speak of the royal Messiah; the limited references to an eschatological prophet; and the passages mentioning or alluding to Moses.

Eternal King and Eschatological Prince

Apart from references to kings of the Gentile enemies of Israel[3] and two passages that mention Israel's kings in OT times,[4] only God is regularly called "King" in the Qumran texts.[5] The "Messiah

---

[1] Unless perhaps the priestly Messiah-figure eventually absorbed the *functions* of the Prophet (below, p. 171). The view advanced by Dupont-Sommer and followed by others, including Brownlee and Philonenko, that the Teacher of Righteousness was expected to fulfill all three eschatological roles, can not be supported and is now generally rejected. It is true that CD uses the singular משיח where 1QS speaks of משיחי אהרון וישראל (the singular is not, as was thought formerly, an error of a medieval scribe, since unpublished fragments from Cave IV reveal the same reading in CD: G. Vermes, *The Dead Sea Scrolls in English* [Baltimore: Penguin Books, 1962], p. 49). Nevertheless the same document speaks of the two figures separately under their symbolic titles (cf. *ibid.*). For literature representing various positions, see Johan Maier, *Die Texte vom Toten Meer* (München: Ernst Reinhardt Verlag, 1960), II, 32f.

[2] The most painstaking and sober investigation of the figure of the מורה צדק is the recent monograph by Gert Jeremias, *Der Lehrer der Gerechtigkeit* (cited above). Jeremias rejects any eschatological role in the strict sense for the Teacher, but his argument will undoubtedly not lay the question to rest.

[3] 1QM i.4; xii.7, 14; xv.2; xix.6; 1QH fragment 7.10; 1Q16, 9.1; 1Q27, 9.3; 4QNah 2.3; CD i.6; viii.10-11 = xix.23-24; 1QpHab iv.2.

[4] 1QM xi.3; CD iii.9.

[5] 1QM xii.3, 7, 8, 16; xix.1,8 (though xii.16 and xix.8, וישראל למלכות עלמים may refer to the *community's* reign over the nations [so Vermes 'transla-

of Israel," the Davidic lay Messiah, is never called "king," but rather "the prince of (all) the congregation."[1] That the term מלך was deliberately avoided for the eschatological ruler, probably because of anti-Hasmonean sentiment,[2] is demonstrated by the exegesis of Amos 5.26-27 in the Damascus Document: "The King is the congregation" (המלך הוא הקהל).[3] The prophetic text, which referred to a specific king, has been allegorized to refer not to the Messiah, who is mentioned in line 20 as נשיא כל העידה, symbolized by שבט, but to the whole community of the covenanters.[4]

Nevertheless the "prince" is quite clearly the royal Messiah of the line of David, the figure known in the Talmud as the King-Messiah:[5]

---

tion, *Dead Sea Scrolls in English*, pp. 139, 148] but on the other hand cf. J. van der Ploeg, *Le Rouleau de la Guerre* ["Studies on the Texts of the Desert of Judah," I; Leiden: E. J. Brill, 1959], p. 47), 4QFlor i.3; 1QH x.8; 4QMa 12-13; 4QSl 39, I.i.17; cf. 1QSb iv.26, "royal temple" (היכל מלכות) in blessing of the priests.

[1] 1QM v.1; 1QSb v.20; CD vii.20; 4QpIs[a]2 (reconstructed). The title is probably drawn from Ezek., where kings, good and bad, are called נשיא; cf. especially 34.24; 37.25. Rabin (p. 30, n. 7.20) points out that Bar Koseba was called נשיא ישראל on his coins. He was also hailed as בר כוכבא the "star" of Num. 24.17. At Qumran the כוכב was interpreted as the *priestly* Messiah, the eschatological "Interpreter of the Law" (CD vii.18), never the נשיא העידה. (cf. Van der Woude, pp. 53-55). נשיא also becomes a title for "archangels" at Qumran (comparable to שר in later rabbinic angelology: cf. J. Strugnell, "The Angelic Liturgy at Qumran– 4Q Serek Sirot Olat Hassab-bat," *Congress Volume* ["Supplements to Vetus Testamentum," VII; Leiden: E. J. Brill, 1960], p. 324).

[2] Cf. Van der Woude, pp. 58, 116, 135.

[3] CD vii.17. The eschatological "reign" of the whole renewed Israel may have been indicated by the fragmentary lines 1QM xii.16 and xix.18 (cf. above, p. 165, n. 5).

[4] Rabin, p. 29, wants to "correct" this *non sequitur* by positing a "lacuna" to be filled with "[the king is] the prince . . ." But the Geniza MS has no lacuna at this point (see the facsimile edition by Solomon Zeitlin, *The Zadokite Fragments* ["JQR Monograph Series," No. 1; Philadelphia: The Dropsie College, 1952], plate VII), and none is likely to have existed in the *Vorlage*, for the logic of the midrashic interpretation is clear, if peculiar, as it stands: "Naar det da hedder 'KongensHytte' (ogHytte = Lovbøger), betyder 'Kongen' naturligvis '(den nye Pagts) Menighed'" (F. F. Hvidberg, *Menigheden af den Nye Pagt i Damascus* [Kobenhavn: G. E. C. Gads Forlag, 1928], pp. 118f.). Also in CD v.1, as Rabin himself points out (*ad loc.*), the sectarian interpreter substitutes נשיא for מלך in the Deuteronomic "Law of the King." It is evident that the avoidance of the title is deliberate. It may be the tendency to avoid מלך as a title for the Messiah had developed already in OT times (cf. Gerhard von Rad, "מלך und מלכות im AT," *ThWbNT*, I, 566).

[5] Cf. Millar Burrows, *More Light on the Dead Sea Scrolls* (New York: The Viking Press, 1958), p. 305; Van der Woude, pp. 58, 243f.

He is the Branch of David [צמח דויד] who shall arise with the Interpreter of the Law [to rule] in Zion [at the end] of time. As it is written, "I will raise up the tent of David that is fallen" (Amos ix, 11). That is to say, the fallen "tent of David" is he who shall arise to save Israel.[1]

In him the promise to David in 2 Samuel 7 will be fulfilled.[2] He is the "branch of David" (Jeremiah 23.5; 33.15; cf. Zechariah 3.8; 6.12),[3] the "Righteous Messiah,"[4] the "sceptre" of Numbers 24.17 and Genesis 49.10.[5] In distinction from the eschatological High Priest, the "Messiah of Aaron," the Prince of the Congregation is "Messiah of Israel."[6] Among the names written on his shield in the final holy war "Israel" will precede "Levi" and "Aaron,"[7] an exception to the usual order. Probably, as Van der Woude says,[8] this is because "the figure of the Prince is primarily connected with 'Israel.'" "Messiah of Israel," therefore, provides an analogy to the title "King of Israel" in the gospels, a title otherwise extremely rare.[9]

The functions of the Prince are royal, but limited by the community's hierocratic tendency. He receives the "Covenant of Kingship"[10] and will be "enthroned."[11] He has a certain role in the final War of the Sons of Light against the Sons of Darkness,[12] but the role is definitely secondary to the role of the High Priest and the other priests and Levites, for the war is a sacral undertaking.[13] The subordination of the Messiah of Israel to the Messiah of Aaron is further demonstrated by the fact that "Aaron" is always mentioned first when both are named[14] and especially by the description of the

---

[1] 4QFlor i.11, trans. Vermes, *Dead Sea Scrolls in English*, p. 244.
[2] *Ibid.*
[3] *Ibid.*, and 4QPB 3.
[4] 4QPB 3; again derived from Jer. 33.15 צמח צדק; the Targum on the passage reads משיחא צדקא (cited by Vermes, *Scripture and Tradition*, p. 159).
[5] 1QM xi.6f.; 1QSb v.27; CD vii.19.
[6] 1QS ix.11; 1QSa ii.12-20; cf. CD xii.23-xiii.1; xiv.19; xix.10; xx.1.
[7] 1QM v.1.
[8] P. 135.
[9] Cf. above, p. 80. Geo Widengren, *Sakrales Königtum im Alten Testament und im Judentum* (Stuttgart: Verlag W. Kohlhammer, 1955), pp. 41f., argues that "King of Israel" was a title applied properly only to the kings of the northern kingdom, used of David only once in irony.
[10] ברית המלכות 4QPB 4.
[11] 4QPB 2, and cf. Allegro, *JBL*, 75, p. 174, n. 4.
[12] 1QM v.
[13] Cf. Van der Woude, pp. 127f.
[14] See passages referred to above, n. 6.

sacral meal in the age to come, in which the Priest precedes the
Messiah of Israel and must bless the bread and wine before the
Messiah of Israel can "extend his hand over the bread."[1] A fragment
of a Testament of Levi found in Cave I says that ". . . the kingship
of the priesthood is greater than the kingship of . . .(?),"[2] and Van
der Woude thinks the reference to מלכות in a badly destroyed line
of the "blessings" appendix to the Rule of the Congregation is part
of a prayer for sovereignty to be given to the High Priest.[3] The
High Priest will dominate the eschatological kingdom, just as the
priests dominated the settlement at Qumran.

In the light of the relative positions and functions of the two
main eschatological figures, it is clear that no combination of kingship and priesthood in one figure, as was the case in Philo's Moses,
could be expected at Qumran. At the most one could say that the
eschatological High Priest usurps many of the functions and privileges of a king, but nevertheless the Prince remains a distinct figure.
By the same token the Prince bears no prophetic features, and the
prophet could be expected to exercise no kingly functions.

The Eschatological Prophet in Qumran Expectation

The expectation of an eschatological prophet is mentioned directly only in a single passage in the Qumran texts, at the conclusion to the regulations of the Rule of the Community:

> They shall depart from none of the counsels of the Law to walk
> in the stubbornness of their hearts, but shall be ruled by the
> primitive precepts in which the men of the Community were
> first instructed until there shall come the [or "a"[4]] prophet and
> the Messiahs of Aaron and Israel.[5]

Because of the absence of other references to the prophet by name,
some scholars have disputed the assumption that a specific figure
was meant.[6] However, the "Testimonia" document found in Cave
IV makes it all but certain that a definite eschatological prophet

---

[1] 1QSa ii.

[2] [. . .] בִּיךְ מלכות כהנותא רבא מן מלכות [. . .]

[3] 1QSb iii.5; Van der Woude, p. 110.

[4] נביא is anarthrous, but omission of the article with definite substantives
is common at Qumran, and almost all translators insert the article here.

[5] עד בוא נביא ומשיחי אהרן וישראל   1QS ix.11; trans. Vermes, *Dead Sea
Scrolls in English*, p. 87.

[6] Literature in Maier, II, 33.

was expected, and that the expectation was based on Deuteronomy 18.18. The "Testimonia" brings together Deuteronomy 5.28-29 and 18.18-19 with Deuteronomy 33.8-11, which certainly refers to the Messiah of Aaron, and Numbers 24.15-17, which here (passing over the "star," elsewhere identified with the priestly Messiah) refers to the Davidic Messiah.[1] Thus the "prophet" mentioned in Deuteronomy 18 is clearly interpreted as an eschatological figure of comparable importance to the Messiahs of Aaron and Israel. From the order of mention in the two passages, one might deduce that the Prophet was expected as a "forerunner" of the other two.

From these two brief passages little can be surmised about the functions of the expected prophet. The form of the Rule passage, however, is strikingly similar to the passages in 1 Maccabees in which the coming of a prophet is awaited to settle halakhic problems. The stones of the altar defiled by Antiochus are stored *"until there should come a prophet* to tell what to do with them" (4.46); and "the Jews and their priests decided that Simon should be their leader and high priest for ever, *until a trustworthy prophet* should arise" (14.41). So in the Qumran Rule, the original ordinances of the community are valid *"until there come a prophet* and the Messiahs of Aaron and Israel." The coming of the prophet will make possible the replacing of the provisional regulations with the eternally valid Torah.[2]

A problem is posed by the fact that in other passages which speak of the coming High Priest and Prince there is no further mention of the Prophet. In a richly suggestive article in 1953, N. Wieder sought to resolve this perplexity by proposing that the Teacher of Righteousnes was himself the eschatological prophet.[3] The Rule of the Community had been written at an early period, when the community still looked forward to the coming of a prophet, as yet unidentified. The Damascus Document was written at a later time when this hope had been fulfilled by the Teacher who organized the community, after it had "groped after the way for twenty years," and led it on "the way of God's heart."[4] Wieder supported his argument with an impressive array of evidence that four epithets

---

[1] 4Q Test, published by Allegro, *JBL*, 75, 182-186. Cf. Van der Woude, pp. 79f., Maier, II, 33.

[2] Cf. Schnackenburg, p. 636.

[3] N. Wieder, "The 'Law-Interpreter' of the Sect of the Dead Sea Scrolls: The Second Moses," *JJS*, 4 (1953), 170.

[4] CD i. 9-10.

applied to the Teacher (דורש התורה, מחקק, כלי, and כוכב, which Wieder interprets as "Mercury" — "Hermes") were commonly applied to Moses in Jewish traditions.[1] Furthermore, the whole organization of the Qumran sect indicated a copying of the wilderness and Exodus traditions, a typology in which a "new Moses" could scarcely fail.[2] Van der Woude accepted and elaborated Wieder's position,[3] and, with some variation, so did Geza Vermes.[4] Gert Jeremias, however, in his meticulous exegetical investigation of statements about the Teacher of Righteousness, rejects the thesis, arguing that (1) the Teacher himself was viewed as the founder and organizer of the community, so that the Rule could not have been written before his activity; (2) it would be difficult to construct a chronology for the documents such that between the Rule and the Damascus Document the whole activity of the Teacher, his death, and a considerable time after his death could intervene as the thesis of Wieder required; (3) there is no passage in the texts which actually suggests the identity of the Teacher and the Prophet.[5]

Even after Jeremias' labors the question remains, as Maier said earlier, "still debatable."[6] Jeremias himself shows that the Teacher is a prophet. "Every distinguishing characteristic of a prophet applies to him."[7] He receives his words "from the mouth of God"; he is chosen, sent, and commissioned by God; his hearers are put by his words into a situation requiring decision; those who reject his words are condemned, while those who accept his words are saved from final judgment.[8] The agreement of these characteristics with those of the promised prophet like Moses in Deuteronomy 18.18-22 is striking.[9] It can hardly be doubted that the Teacher of Righteousness functioned as *a* prophet like Moses; whether he was recognized as *the* eschatological prophet like Moses is another question. It should be noted that the Teacher was also a priest and that, like

---

[1] Wieder, pp. 161-170.

[2] *Ibid.*, pp. 171f.

[3] Van der Woude, pp. 84-87, 165.

[4] Vermes, *Scripture and Tradition*, pp. 59-66; "Moïse au tournant," pp. 79-84; *Dead Sea Scrolls in English*, p. 50 (see below, p. 172f.). Cf. also Teeple, pp. 51-55.

[5] G. Jeremias, pp. 297f.

[6] Maier, II, 138.

[7] G. Jeremias, p. 141.

[8] *Ibid.*: the characteristics are drawn from the statements of 1Q pHab.

[9] See above, pp. 45f.

him, the eschatological High Priest would "teach righteousness at the end of days"[1] and could be called "Searcher of the Torah."[2] Both, that is, combined prophetic functions with the priestly office. It is possible, therefore, that with the passage of time the eschatological High Priest may have absorbed *all* the functions of the eschatological Prophet —just as he took on many of the functions of the eschatological Prince.

Moses in the Qumran Texts

It is no surprise that Moses is most often mentioned in the Qumran texts in connection with the Torah. In this respect the sectarian documents are in accord with practically all Jewish sources. The Torah is "the Law of Moses,"[3] "commanded by the hand of Moses,"[4] or "by the hand of Moses and the prophets."[5] A quotation from the Pentateuch may be introduced by "As it is written in the Book of Moses . . .,"[6] or by "Moses said."[7] However, this aspect of Moses as mediator of the Torah was of peculiarly intense concern to the community of the Covenanters, for they saw Torah as in the process of renewal and their own obedience to it as an act of crucial significance in the final drama of judgment and redemption which was about to begin. Consequently the community's whole existence is determined by the relationship of its members to the Torah of Moses. To enter the sect meant to "take a binding oath to return to the Law of Moses,"[8] and "every man who enters the Council of Holiness . . . and who deliberately or through negligence transgresses one word of the Law of Moses, on any point whatever, shall be expelled from the Council of the Community and shall return no more. . . ."[9] At the same time the form of their obedience was determined by the special regulations—drawn to be sure from the written Torah—laid down by the new lawgiver, the

---

[1] CD vi.11, on which see Van der Woude, pp. 71-74, and G. Jeremias pp. 270-288.

[2] CD vii.18, on which see Van der Woude, pp. 54f.

[3] 1QS v.8; viii.22; CD xv.2, 12; xvi.2, 5.

[4] 1QS viii.15; 1Q M x.6; 1Q H xvii.12; 4Q Dib Ham, v.14.

[5] 1QS i.3; CD v.21.

[6] 4Q Flor i.2 (reconstructed).

[7] CD v.8; viii.14 = xix.26.

[8] 1QS v.8; cf. CD xv.9, 12; xvi.2, 5.

[9] *Ibid.*, viii.22, trans. Vermes, *Dead Sea Scrolls in English*, p. 86.

Mehoqeq, the Teacher of Righteousness.[1] The function of the new regulations is to restore the Covenant, which, while it could be called the "New Covenant,"[2] remains identical with "the covenant which Moses concluded with Israel, namely the covenant to return to the Law of Moses. . . ."[3] The apparent anomaly vanishes once it is understood that, in the view of the Qumran community, the commandments given through Moses and the other prophets *were intended in their fullness for the time of the end, the time of the community*. The words of Moses and the prophets were essentially eschatological revelations:

> Thou hast caused [the scourge] of Thy [plagues] to cleave to us of which Moses wrote, and thy servants the Prophets, that Thou wouldst send evil against us in the last days . . .[4]

The preparation of "the way of the Lord" commanded in Isaiah 40.3 was understood as "the study of the Law which He has commanded through Moses, so that all may be done according to all that which is revealed in each age and according to that which the prophets have revealed through His holy spirit,"[5] for in the Law of Moses "everything can be learnt."[6] The conviction that the mysteries of the end had been delivered to Moses is shown also by the expansion of the farewell discourse of Moses, based on Deuteronomy 31 and 32, in the document called "Sayings of Moses" of which small fragments were found in Cave I.[7]

The view of the Torah as a guide for the repentant Israel at the end of days has its place in the larger typological framework, often remarked by students of the scrolls, which connected the community's life and the events it anticipated with the time of the Exodus and the wilderness sojourn. The retreat to the wilderness to "prepare the way of the Lord" represents an attempt to recover the

---

[1] CD vi.2-11.

[2] CD vi.19; viii.21; xix.33; xx.12; 1Q pHab ii.3.

[3] CD xv.9, trans. Rabin, p. 72.

[4] 4Q Dib Ham, iii.12f., trans. Vermes, *Dead Sea Scrolls in English*, p. 203. The reference is presumably to passages like Dt. 8.11-20; 11.28; especially 28.15-68.

[5] 1QS viii.15, trans. Geza Vermes, *Discovery in the Judaean Desert* (New York: Desclee Company, 1956), p. 148.

[6] CD xvi.2, trans. Rabin, p. 74.

[7] 1Q "Dires du Moïse," in *Discoveries in the Judaean Desert: I, Qumran Cave I*, ed. D. Barthelemy and J. T. Milik (Oxford: at the Clarendon Press, 1955), pp. 91-97.

wilderness traditions of the generation under Moses.[1] The organization, the emphasis on the renewal of the covenant, the preparations for the final holy war between the Sons of Light and the Sons of Darkness[2] all demonstrate that the community saw the events of the Exodus, wilderness sojourn, and holy war being repeated in their own experience. The new redemption was to correspond with the first redemption.[3]

Moreover, the Qumran sect's view of the Torah shows that it conceived of Moses as a prophet, in fact, as the prophet *par excellence*. The repeated reference to revelations "by the hand of Moses and the prophets"[4] confirms this conception. Moses is regarded, as Schnackenburg points out, as the "Urprophet,"[5] the first in the series,[6] and superior to those who follow. It is significant that the mysteries delivered to the other prophets were not understood by the prophets themselves, but first divulged "from the mouth of God" to the Teacher of Righteousness.[7] There is no hint of such a limitation in the case of Moses, nor was there likely to be, since Numbers 12 made plain that God spoke to Moses, not as with ordinary prophets, but "mouth to mouth, plainly and not in riddles."[8]

Of other possible offices of Moses there are only hints in the Qumran scrolls. Related to the prophetic function, but also to the priestly, is the title "Teacher" in the third column of the Damascus Document,[9] which may refer to Moses.[10] There is no mention of any

---

[1] Cf. Wieder, pp. 171f.; Van der Woude, pp. 48f., 58, 103, 116; G. Jeremias, pp. 107-109, 118, 154f., 270. The unpublished Göttingen dissertation by W. Wiebe, *Die Wüstenzeit als Typus der messianischen Heilszeit*, mentioned by Jeremias, was not available to me.

[2] 1QM x especially makes clear that the war is a holy war, following the prescriptions of Moses. Cf. also 1QM iii.13f., where the organization of the 12 tribes corresponds to that in Num. 2 (cf. Van der Woude, p. 103).

[3] Cf. Vermès, "Moïse au tournant," pp. 76-79.

[4] 1QS i.3; viii.15; CD v.21.

[5] Schnackenburg, p. 632.

[6] Cf. similar references to Moses at the head of a succession of prophets, above, pp. 133 and 143f.

[7] 1Q pHab ii.2-10; vii.1-8. The resultant similarity between the Teacher and Ezra as a new Moses in 4 Ezra 14 is pointed out by Vermès, "Moïse au tournant," pp. 83f.

[8] Num. 12.8, trans. *The Torah*, p. 269.

[9] יוריהם CD iii.8.

[10] "... nur als Bezeichnung des *Mose* zu verstehen ...," Van der Woude, p. 72, but most scholars understand the participle as parallel to עשיהם and referred to God (Rabin, p. 11; cf. Maier, II, 46).

royal function of Moses, although the term "faithful shepherd," an epithet applied to Moses in rabbinic sources[1] and reminiscent of Philo's description of the ideal king,[2] appears in one fragment.[3] It probably refers to the Teacher of Righteousness,[4] but in his role as a new Moses. Likewise there is no reference to Moses as priest; Aaron is the High Priest *par excellence* in this priestly community.[5] However, Moses' role as intercessor and mediator between Israel and God comes to clear expression in one passage:

> We pray Thee, O Lord, act in accordance with Thyself, in accordance with the greatness of Thy might, Thou who didst pardon our fathers when they rebelled against Thy word. Thou wert angry with them so as to wish to destroy them, but because of Thy love for them and for the sake of Thy Covenant —for Moses had atoned for their sin [כיא כפר מושה בעד חטאתם]— and in order that Thy great might and the abundance of Thy mercy might be known to everlasting generations, Thou didst take pity on them. So let Thine anger and wrath against all [their] sin turn away from Thy people Israel.[6]

Here Moses' great act of propitiation stands as the model for intercession and the basis for hope for forgiveness.

Conclusions

The Qumran texts are important for the present investigation mainly because they attest clearly the expectation of an eschatological prophet like Moses and show that the expectation was based on Deuteronomy 18. However, the texts give little insight into the expected functions of the prophet, and provide no basis for understanding the peculiar combination of kingship and prophecy in the Fourth Gospel. Kingship belongs first of all to God, in the view of the sect, and human royalty is the perquisite of the Messiah of the line of David, even though he does not receive the title "King" and

---

[1] Cf. Aaron Rosmarin, *Moses im Lichte der Agada* (New York: Goldblatt Publishing Co., 1932), p. 82, n. 293; J. Jeremias, *ThWbNT*, IV, 877; Bloch, "Quelques aspects," p. 138f.

[2] See above, p. 108.

[3] 1Q 34bis ii.8.

[4] Cf. CD xix.7b-9, where Zech. 13.7 is evidently applied to the Teacher. Cf. Rabin, p. 30; Van der Woude, p. 64.

[5] Cf. the exaltation of Aaron in Josephus, above, pp. 136f.

[6] 4Q Dib Ham, trans. Vermes, *Dead Sea Scrolls in English*, p. 202.

is subordinated to the priestly Messiah of the line of Aaron.

Moses was seen by the sect of the Dead Sea as the mediator of the Torah and founder of the Covenant, as the first and greatest of the prophets, and as the mediator between Israel and God, propitiating God's wrath. There is no hint of Moses' kingship, and, despite his propitiatory role, he is not called priest.

The importance of the typology of the wilderness sojourn under Moses' leadership for the images of eschatological preparation and redemption emerges with exceptional clarity in the scrolls. Within this typological framework, the sect's principal midrashic teacher and lawgiver functioned as a new Moses, although he is never *called* by that name. The relation of this mysterious figure to the three explicitly eschatological figures, particularly to the eschatological prophet, remains a puzzle whose satisfactory solution has yet to be achieved.

CHAPTER FOUR

MOSES AS PROPHET AND KING
IN THE RABBINIC HAGGADA

INTRODUCTION

The difficulties encountered by historical research in the rabbinic sources are notorious. The dating of the sources themselves is frequently determinable only within a very wide range, and the task of dating any given tradition even more complex, since the midrashim characteristically combine traditions of quite divergent date and origin. So far the techniques of the history of traditions developed in folkloric and Old Testament studies have been applied only in rare instances to rabbinic haggada. Nevertheless, the rich material in these sources cannot be overlooked for an investigation like the present one.

The method employed here has followed the principles of investigation laid out by Renée Bloch, a pioneer in this field whose early death cut short her labors, and elaborated by Geza Vermes.[1] Earlier sources are preferred, but not to the exclusion of the possibility that later sources may retain earlier traditions. The biblical starting point is sought for each midrashic statement, and where evidence warrants, the attempt is made to see how the tradition may have evolved. Wherever possible, stages of the traditions are dated by comparison with parallels in datable sources, particularly Philo, Josephus, and Alexander Polyhistor.

The midrashim are more extravagant in their portrayal of Moses than of any other of Israel's heroes. To survey the whole variety of traditions about the various aspects of his life would lead far beyond the scope of this monograph.[2] Instead the attempt has been made

---

[1] Renée Bloch, "Note méthodologique pour l'étude de la littérature rabbinique," *Recherches de Science Religieuse*, 43 (1955), 194-227; cf. her art. "Midrash," *Dictionnaire de la Bible, Supplement*, vol. V (Paris: Libraire Letouzey et Ane, 1957), cols. 1263-1281, and "Quelques aspects," pp. 95-97 Geza Vermes, *Scripture and Tradition*, pp. 1-10.

[2] Such surveys, without an attempt to distinguish stages or separate strands of development, are found in Ginzberg, II, 243-375, III, 1-481, and Rosmarin, *passim* (older compilations are listed in Rosmarin's bibliography).

to examine the passages which attributed kingship to Moses, and those which emphasized his superiority or singularity as a prophet. Even within these limits no claim can be made for complete coverage.[1] Both because of connections found in the rabbinic materials and because of associations discovered in non-rabbinic material in the previous chapter, certain related elements in the Moses haggada have been included: his designation "shepherd of Israel," his heavenly ascents, his role as defender or "Paraclete" of Israel, his eschatological role.

KING AND PROPHET

Confession by the Sons of Koraḥ

The midrashim on the Ḳoraḥ chapter (Numbers 16) all amplify the story of the Ḳoraḥites' destruction by supplying the words of their "cry" as they were swallowed by the earth. One version of the legend, found in the Tanḥuma compilation, is significant for purposes of this investigation:

> As they were being swallowed they were crying out saying: "Moses is King and Prophet, and Aaron is High Priest, and the Torah was given from Heaven." Their cry went through all the camp of Israel, as it is said, "And all Israel that was round about them fled at the cry" (Num. 16.34).[2]

It is impossible to date the tradition. Jacob Z. Lauterbach argues that the Tanḥuma Midrash was compiled in the fifth century,[3] but the collection was extremely fluid,[4] and the tradition just quoted occurs in none of the Hebrew manuscripts but only in a medieval

---

Cf. also J. Jeremias, ThWbNT, IV, 852-878. An analytical treatment of certain aspects of the Moses haggadah, especially the birth narratives, is found in Bloch, "Quelques aspects."

[1] The voluminous notes in Ginzberg, supplemented by Rosmarin and occasionally by Billerbeck, have served me as a "concordance" of the haggadic literature, since an independent survey of all the sources would have been impossible.

[2] Solomon Buber (ed.), מדרש תנחומא על חמשה חומשי תורה (Wilna: Verlag v. Wittwe & Gebrüder Romm, 1885), IV, 97 (hereafter referred to as Tanḥuma, ed. Buber).

[3] "Tanḥuma, Midrash," JE, XII, 45.

[4] Cf. Hermann L. Strack, Introduction to the Talmud and Midrash (Philadelphia: The Jewish Publication Society of America, 1959), p. 212.

Latin manuscript used by the editor, Solomon Buber.[1] In Buber's opinion "it is certain that this whole addition was added by the translator of the Latin manuscript from the lost *Yelammedenu.*"[2]

The midrashic starting point of the tradition is clear: What was the "cry" of the descending Ḳoraḥites mentioned in Numbers 16. 34? The haggada provides at least four different answers to the question beside the one already quoted. (1) "Righteous is the Lord, and His judgment is truth, and the words of his servant Mosheh are truth; but we are wicked who have rebelled against him. . . ."[3] (2) "Moses is truth and his Torah is truth."[4] (3) "Moses, Moses, have mercy on us!"[5] (4) "Moses our Teacher, save us!"[6] In the last two traditions the cry is an appeal for mercy. It recalls the frequent notion of Moses' intercession for Israel,[7] appropriate here because the rabbis agreed that the Ḳoraḥites, having "descended alive to Sheol," would be raised and restored to Israel in the world to come. The form of the other three versions is that of a *Gerichtsdoxologie,*[8] a *confession* which acknowledges the justice of God's judgment.

That a *Gerichtsdoxologie* on the lips of the Ḳoraḥites should have been felt by the rabbis to be appropriate is not surprising. The tantalizing question is why one version of the doxology should take precisely the form of a confession that Moses was King and Prophet, Aaron High Priest, and the Torah from Heaven. In one sense this form is closer to the scriptural account than are the others, for the point of contention of the Korahite group was that Moses "made himself a prince" and that Aaron usurps the priestly privileges that rightly belong to the whole congregation (Numbers 16.3, 10, 13).

---

[1] See Buber's note at ויקח קרח IV, 94.

[2] *Ibid.*, IV, 95, note. On the relation of *Tanḥuma* and *Yelammedenu*, see Lauterbach, *JE*, XII, 45f.

[3] Targ. Pseudo-Jonathan on Num. 16.34, trans. J. W. Ethridge, *The Targums of Onkelos and Jonathan ben Uzziel on the Pentateuch; with the Fragments of the Jerusalem Targum* (London: Longman, Green, Longman, and Roberts, 1865), II, 395.

[4] מדרש לקה טוב המכונה פסיקתא זוטרתא, ed. Solomon Buber (Wilna: Verlag v. Wittwe & Gebrüder Romm, 1884), II, 230 (hereafter referred to as *Lekah-Ṭob*).

[5] L. Grünhut, *Sefer-ha-Likkutim; Sammlung älterer Midraschim und wissenschaftliche Abhandlung* ([Jerusalem and] Frankfurt a/M.: J. Kaufmann [1898-1903]), I, 23b.

[6] *Tanḥuma*, ed. Buber, IV, 93.

[7] See above, pp. 118; 125, n. 3; 137; 159-161; 174 and below, pp. 200–204, 254f.

[8] For description of the genre, see Von Rad, *Theologie*, I, 355f.

Hence it is not impossible that this version of the "confession" was constructed solely from a rational analysis of the scriptural story. However, there is a striking resemblance to the Samaritan confession, which finds its place in actual liturgical usage:

> Lord, we will not worship any but thee forever, and we will not put our trust in any but thee and in Moses thy prophet and in thy true Scripture and in thy place of worship, Mt. Gerazim, House of God, etc.[1]

The question therefore has at least to be raised whether there was ever a situation in Jewish liturgical life in which such a confession could have been formulated.[2] There is at present no basis for answering the question, so the *Tanḥuma* passage proves definitely only that some circle of rabbinic Judaism, at indeterminate date, took for granted that Moses' two basic offices were "king and prophet."

Joshua's Succession as Prophet-King

A similar conclusion is to be derived from a passage in the late midrash *Peṭirat Mosheh* ("The Departure of Moses") compiled for use in synagogue services for Tabernacles.[3] The midrash brings together a number of traditions on similar themes within a framework of the last days and hours of Moses' life, which is provided by editorial insertions of a *bat kol*, announcing the time remaining to Moses, between successive pericopes. At the beginning of the last day a tradition in the name of Rabbi Josia[4] is inserted:

---

[1] A. E. Cowley (ed.), *The Samaritan Liturgy* (Oxford: At the Clarendon Press, 1909), I, 3 and often. Cf. John Bowman, *BJRL*, 40, 309f.

[2] There is some resemblance to the seventh of the "Thirteen Principles" composed by Maimonides (in his commentary on Mishnah *Sanh.* 10.1, 1168 A.D.), now embodied in the order of daily synagogue prayer: "I believe with perfect faith that the prophecy of Moses our teacher, peace be unto him, was true, and that he was the chief of the prophets (אב לנביאים) both of those that preceded and of those that followed him" (*Authorized Daily Prayer Book* [9th ed.], p. 90).

[3] Adolph Jellinek (ed.), *Bet ha-Midrasch; Sammlung kleiner Midraschim und vermischter Abhandlungen aus der älteren jüdischen Literatur* (2d. ed.; Jerusalem: Bamberger & Wahrmann, 1938), I, xxi.

[4] I do not know whether this R. Josia is to be identified with the third generation Tanna (130-160 A.D.) or with one of the two Babylonian Amoraim by the same name, of the second and third generations respectively. (Cf. Strack, *Introduction*, pp. 114 and 126). In any case the tradition would be not later than ca. 300 A.D.

At that time Moses gave great honor to Joshua and great distinction before Israel. A herald went forth before him throughout Israel's camp, proclaiming: "Come and hear the words of the new prophet [הנביא חדש] who has arisen over us [שיקו‹ם› עלינו] today." All Israel went up to honor Joshua. Then Moses commanded (them) to bring a golden throne, a crown of pearls, a turban of kingship, and a purple robe. Moses stood up and ordered and arranged the seats of the Sanhedrin, of the captains of the troops, and of the priests. Then Moses went to Joshua, robed him and put the crown on him, installed him on the throne of gold, and stationed an interpreter [תורגמן] beside him to interpret before all Israel. And who was the interpreter? Caleb the son of Japhoneh. And Joshua interpreted before all Israel, and before Moses his teacher.[1]

The scene corresponds to the tradition that the king was enthroned before the people at the festival of Tabernacles, on every seventh year, to read the Torah to the people.[2] Joshua, as Moses' successor, is thus portrayed as the ideal king of Israel. The following pages of the midrash depict Moses serving Joshua as his disciple—a motif connected in various forms with stories of Moses' last days—in which Joshua's kingship is repeatedly emphasized.[3] But it must not be overlooked that Joshua is introduced in Rabbi Josiah's story as "the new prophet who has arisen over us." The allusion to Deuteronomy 18.15 and 18 is manifest, including the words of the herald, "Come and hear!"[4] Joshua is portrayed here as the Prophet like Moses, but the prophet is the one who is enthroned as Israel's king. The dominant motif in this as in the similar traditions associated with it in the midrash is the exchange of roles by Moses and Joshua. Therefore the tradition takes for granted that Moses was prophet and king of Israel.

The tradition of Joshua's succession to Moses' offices of prophecy

---

[1] Text in Jellinek, I, 122. Cf. the German translation in Aug. Wünsche, *Aus Israels Lehrhallen; kleine Midraschim zur späteren legendarischen Literatur des Alten Testaments* (Leipzig: Verlag von Eduard Pfeiffer, 1907), I, 148f.

[2] Mishnah, *Soṭa* 7.8; cf. Dt. 17.18-20; 31.10. On the enthronement of the king at *Sukot* and his role as "possessor of Torah," cf. Widengren, *Sakrales Königtum*, chaps. ii, iii.

[3] E.G., p. 123. The Israelites lament: "'Woe to you, for your king is a youth (נער),' but a *Bat Kol* said, 'For Israel was a youth, and I loved him,' and the earth opened its mouth and said, 'I have been a youth, but now am old.'"

[4] Dt. 18.15:

נביא · · · · יקים לך
· · · · אליו תשמעון.

Petirat Mosheh:

בואו ושמעו דברי הנביא
חדש שיקו' עלינו · · ·

and rule calls to mind the various hints of a concept of a succession of ruler-prophets which were discovered in non-rabbinic sources. What is especially significant about the present passage is its clear connection of this succession with the promise of "a new prophet" in Deuteronomy 18.

MOSES AS KING OF ISRAEL

King and Priest

There is a tradition, occurring frequently in slightly varying forms, that Moses surmised from the moment when God first called him that he was to be both king and priest. To this tradition was later attached a polemic interpretation that Moses' surmise was after all wrong. In a midrash on Exodus 3.1 preserved in the *Tanḥuma* collection both offices are associated with the wilderness. Moses "longed for the wilderness," because "he saw that he was to receive greatness from the wilderness." Among the gifts to come "from the wilderness" are listed the Torah, the commandments, the Tabernacle, the *Shekinah*, kingship and priesthood, the well, the manna, the clouds of glory.[1] According to another tradition, both offices are implicit in Moses' reply to God's call at the burning bush, since "Here am I" for Moses as for Abraham (Genesis 22.11) meant "Here am I for priesthood, Here am I for kingship."[2] Only the positive interpretation is given in *Tanḥuma*; the other sources add that "Do not approach" meant that Moses' hopes were dashed by God. However the Talmud still preserves differing opinions on the subject.

> 'Ulla said: Moses desired kingship, but He did not grant it to him, for it is written, *Draw not nigh halom (hither)*; 'halom' can only mean kingship, . . . Raba raised an objection: R. Ismael said: Her [Elisheba's] brother-in-law [Moses] was a king? —said Rabbah b. 'Ulla: He ['Ulla] meant, for himself and for his descendants.[3]

---

[1] *Tanḥuma*, ed. Buber, II, 7, emending מלכיות to מלכות, cf. *Shemot R.* on Ex. 2.4 and *Shir R.* on 3.6.

[2] *Tanḥuma*, ed. Buber, II, 9; *Mekilta de R. Šim'on*, ed. Hoffmann, p. 167; Talm. B., *Zeb.* 102a; *Bereshit R.* 55.6; *Shemot R.* 2.6; *Debarim R.* 2.7; *Midrash ha-Gadol*, ed. Hoffmann, p. 26, ll.12-16.

[3] *Zeb.* 102a, trans. H. Freedman, *Soncino Talmud*, Seder Kodashim, I, 492. *Shemot R.* 2.6 also records a positive interpretation, based on Dt. 33.5.

That is, 'Ulla's son accepts Ismael's objection and explains that kingship was denied only to Moses' descendants. Earlier in the same discussion it is suggested by some that Moses was king, but not high priest, by others that he was both, but that his high priesthood was taken away after seven days (the tradition given in the name of "the Sages"). Still others say that Moses was king and high priest throughout his life, though his descendants were forbidden to receive the offices.

The earliest form of the tradition is that preserved in *Tanḥuma*, in which Moses, like Abraham, was both king and priest.[1] The various traditions which contest or try to interpret this statement all presuppose it. They are probably the result of later schematizations which make Aaron *the* type of priesthood, David *the* type of kingship.[2]

Kingship Taken for Granted

The Levitic blessings

There are numerous statements in the midrashim which take Moses' kingship for granted. Among these are several occurring in different contexts but having a common form, listing Moses' kingship as one of a series of honors which have accrued to the family of Amram. The form occurs in two contexts in the homilectic midrashim in the chapter "After the death of Aaron's sons" (Leviticus 16.1). The homilies begin with Ecclesiastes 2.2, "I said to laughter, you are 'mixed,'" and apply this to Aaron's wife Elisabeth, who saw "four joys on one day," which were however quickly turned to mourning. "She saw her brother-in-law king, her husband high priest, her brother a prince, and two of her sons priests-coadjutor. . . ."[3] Further on in the same chapter is the tra-

---

[1] The parallel between Moses and Abraham, both seen as kings and prophets, has turned up before, in Philo. The assimilation of the Moses and Abraham legends to each other is very frequent. E.g., the birth narratives: cf. Ginzberg, V, 209, n.8; 213, n. 34, Bloch, "Quelques aspects," pp. 102-118.

[2] This concern emerges clearly in *Shemot R.* 2.6, ". . . the priesthood has already been alloted to your brother Aaron. . . . Kingship is already assigned to David." (Trans. S. M. Lehrmann, *Midrash Rabbah*, ed. H. Freedmann and Maurice Simon [London: Soncino Press, 1939]) (henceforth: "Soncino Midrash"), III, 57.

[3] *Tanḥuma*, ed. Buber, III, 56f. *Yalkuṭ Šimʿoni*, *ad loc.*, is identical. *Pesikta de R. Kahana* (Salomon Buber, ed., *Pesikta, die älteste Hagada, redigiert in Palästina von Rab Kahana* [Lyck: Selbstverlag des Vereins Mikize

dition of Rabbi Levi, who adds an explanation to Abba Ḥanin's statement that the sons of Aaron died because they had no wives:

> R. Levi said, They were very arrogant, and they used to say, 'What woman is fit for us?' Many women remained single, waiting for them, but they would say, 'Our father's brother is king, our father is high priest, our mother's brother is a prince, and we are priests-coadjutor. What woman is fit for us?'[1]

Again a similar statement is put in the mouth of Koraḥ to explain his jealousy.[2] Disregarding the contexts, which may all be secondary, the statement, "Moses is king, Aaron is High Priest, Naḥshon is a prince, Nadab and Abihu are priests-coadjutor," with its variations, has the sole function of exalting the family of Amram or, perhaps, the Levitic tribe. One is reminded of the "three portions of Levi" in the Testament of Levi, although the parallel is not exact.[3] The antiquity of the tradition is indicated by the fact that it is accepted in the Talmud as proof that Moses was a king, with the further information that it was told in the name of Rabbi Ishmael, the famous contemporary of Akiba (early second century).[4] Even though its original intent is not entirely clear, the formula stands as a witness to a relatively early tradition that Moses was certainly king of Israel during the wilderness sojourn. This time the tradition stems from circles which do not attribute the high priest-

---

Nirdamim, 1868], Piska 27, p. 107a, has the same tradition, with different order: husband, brother-in-law, brother, sons. *Midrash Tehillim* on Ps. 75 names the personages in the same order as *Tanḥuma*. *Kohelet R.* on 2.2 presents the tradition in a corrupt form: "Sie sah nämlich Mose als ihren Schwager, ihren Bruder Nachschon als König und Haupt aller Fürsten [*sic*!], ihren Mann Aaron als Priester mit dem Ephod bekleidet, und ihre beiden Söhne als Stellvertretende Priester" (trans. Aug. Wünsche, *Bibliotheca Rabbinica*, vol. III, 1. Lieferung, *Der Midrasch Kohelet* [Leipzig: Otto Schulze, 1880], pp. 26f.). *Wayikra R.* 20.2 and Talm. B. *Zeb.* 102a add Phineas, "the priest anointed for war," as does *Shir R.* on 3.6, "Who is this that arises from the wilderness?"

[1] *Tanḥuma*, ed. Buber, III, 63; *Pesikta de R. Kahana*, Piska 27, p. 107a. So also *Midrash Tehillim* on Ps. 78.63, which however mistakenly attributes the whole tradition to Abba Hanin.

[2] *Tanḥuma*, ed. Buber, IV, 85, "Amram was first-born; Aaron his son received the privilege of the high priesthood; Moses his brother, kingship . . .";
cf. Grühut, *Sefer ha-Likkutim*, IV, 39b; *Bamidbar R.* 18.2, cf. 10. A variant of the same tradition occurs in *Tanḥuma*, ed. Buber, IV, 87 and *Bamidbar R.* 18.4.

[3] *Test. Lev.* 8.12-15, above, pp. 151-153.

[4] *Zeb.* 102a; see above, p. 181.

hood to Moses. The prophetic office, moreover, is not mentioned.

Miscellaneous traditions

There are a number of other traditional statements in which Moses' kingship is the starting point rather than the result of argument. Of all the names by which Jethro was called, for example, "the most excellent for him" was "the father-in-law of Moses" (Numbers 10.29), for this meant "that he was called the father-in-law of the King."[1] Similarly Jethro's staying with Moses is interpreted as his becoming the model proselyte. If he had not done so, the other proselytes would have said, "If Jethro, the father-in-law of the king did not take it [the 'yoke of the kingdom'] on himself —how much more the rest of mankind!"[2] On the other hand a mild polemic against the notion of Moses' kingship is implicit in both versions of *Mekilta* on Exodus 18.14:

> *And when Moses' Father-in-law Saw*, etc. What did he see? He saw him behaving like a king who sits on his throne while all the people around him stand. He, therefore, said to him: 'What is this thing that thou doest to the people? . . .'[3]

Here "sitting alone" (יושב לבדך) is interpreted as "sitting on his throne" (יושב על כסאו).

The Midrash on Psalms applies Psalm 24.3, "Who shall ascend into the mountain of the Lord" and "Who shall stand in his holy place" to Moses. It follows that the subsequent clauses also refer to Moses, including "He shall receive the blessing from the Lord" (verse 5), which means "Moses was made king and master of all Israel." The second gift, "righteousness," is interpreted as the Torah, "given to Israel by his hand."[4] It should be noted that the

---

[1] *Sifre Num.*, par. 78; cf. the German translation by Karl Georg Kuhn, *Der tannaitische Midrasch Sifre zu Numeri* ("Rabbinische Texte," ed. G. Kittel and K. H. Rengstorf, 2d series, vol. III; Stuttgart: W. Kohlhammer Verlag, 1959), p. 207.

[2] *Sifre Num.*, par. 80; cf. Kuhn, p. 211.

[3] *Mekilta*, Yitro 2, trans. Jacob Z. Lauterbach, *Mekilta de-Rabbi Ishmael* ("The Schiff Library of Jewish Classics"; Philadelphia: The Jewish Publication Society of America, 1949), II, 179. Similarly *Mekilta de-Rabbi Simon b. Jochai*, ed. D. Hoffman (Frankfurt a/M.: J. Kaufmann, 1905), p. 89 (critical ed.: J. N. Epstein and E. Z. Melamed, eds., *Mekhilta d' Rabbi Sim'on b. Jochai* [Jerusalem: Mekize Nirdamim, 1955], p. 132).

[4] *Midrash Tehillim* on 24.5; trans. William G. Braude, *The Midrash on Psalms* ("Yale Judaica Series," ed. Leon Nemoy, Saul Liebermann, and

context associates Moses' appointment as "king and master" with his ascent of Sinai and his receiving the Torah. While the sometimes "atomistic" nature of midrash makes argument from context precarious, these same associations will be seen to recur with more and more importance. In *Midrash Rabbah* on Exodus 34.27, God is made to say to Moses, "as soon as you received My Torah, I made a covenant with you and I promoted you, and not only Israel alone (have I promoted) but also thee, their king."[1] On the other hand, *Mekilta* in one passage finds the basis for Moses' elevation as king to his song of praise at the Sea of Reeds. Since the hymn concludes "The Lord will reign for ever and ever" (Exodus 15.18), "The Holy One, blessed be He, therefore, said: 'He who was the cause of My being proclaimed King at the sea, him will I make king over Israel.'"[2]

The silver trumpets Moses was commanded to make in Numbers 10.1-2 were taken in the midrashim to indicate Moses' kingly rank. Furthermore, the words, "Make *for yourself* . . ." indicated that "*you* are to use them, for you are king, but no other is to use them — except David the king."[3] According to another interpretation, not even David could use them, and they were withdrawn and hidden by God even before Moses' death.[4] Finally, Moses' kingship is presupposed by the traditions of his death in the older midrashim, which describe his pleading with God to be permitted to enter the promised land:

> He said before Him: Lord of the world: Was there at all any decree made against my entering the land? 'Therefore ye shall not bring this assembly,' etc. (Num. 20.12), only means that in my position as a king [במלכות] I may not enter. Let me then enter as a private man [הדיוט = ἰδιώτης]. God said to him: A king cannot enter as a private man.[5]

Harry A. Wolfson, vol. XIII; New Haven: Yale University Press, 1959), I, 341. Other interpretations apply the same verses to Abraham and Jacob respectively.

[1] *Shemot R.* 47.3, trans. Lehrmann, *Soncino Midrash*, III, 538. The same tradition is found in *Tanḥuma*, ed. Buber, II, 118, but mentioning only Moses' "greatness" (גדולה) without further specification.

[2] *Mekilta*, Beshallaḥ, 6; ed. and trans. Lauterbach, I, 235.

[3] *Tanḥuma*, ed. Buber, IV, 53; *Kohelet R.* 8.8 (end) (trans. Wünsche, p. 115); *Bamidbar R.* 15.13, 15. Less clear is *Sifre Num.*, par. 75.

[4] See the same sources cited in previous note.

[5] *Mekilta*, Amalek 2, trans. Lauterbach, II, 151f. The same tradition is in *Midrasch Tannaim zum Deuteronomium*, ed. D. Hoffmann (Berlin: H. Itzkowski, 1908-09), I, 17; in abbreviated form in *Sifre Num.*, par. 135.

The Scriptural Basis: Deuteronomy 33.5

The traditions cited so far have all assumed Moses' kingship and have therefore offered no explicit scriptural authority for the notion. Yet it is fundamental to the nature of midrash that some scriptural starting point or at least point of contact must exist for every tradition.[1] There are apparently two texts which serve as midrashic proof that Moses was king, and of these the primary one is Deuteronomy 33.5. Evidence for this conclusion is found in the traditions which cite this text directly.

The third recension of the "Tanḥuma" group of homilies[2] preserves a comment by Rabbi Nathan, a fourth generation *Tanna* (late second century), which compares the two great kings, Joseph and Moses:

> 'And Moses took the bones of Joseph' (Exodus 13.19). . . . This goes to show you that by what measure a man measures it shall be measured to him. Joseph buried his father, as it is said, 'And Joseph went up to bury his father' (Genesis 50.7), and there was none among his brothers greater than he, for he was a king, as it is written, 'And there went up with him both chariots and cavalry' (Genesis 50.9). So he merited to go forth from the tomb by the hand of Moses. Moses took the bones of Joseph from Egypt, and no one in the world is greater than Moses, for he was a king, as it is said, 'And he became king in Jeshurun' (Deuteronomy 33.5). Therefore Moses merited that the *Shekinah* should occupy itself with him, as it is said, 'And he buried him in a valley' (Deuteronomy 34.6).[3]

A simpler and probably earlier form of the tradition found in the Mishnah merely says that Joseph's greatness is proved by the fact that Moses took trouble to bury him, while Moses' superior greatness is shown by the fact that God himself took trouble to bury him.[4] To this have been added at some stage of development two additional elements, (1) performing burial for an Israelite wins merit[5] and (2) Joseph and Moses were alike because both were kings. The proof-text of the latter point in Moses' case is Deuteronomy 33.5.

In the midrash on Song of Songs two comments apply "The king

---

[1] Cf. the works by Bloch cited above, p. 175, n. 1.

[2] Cf. Lauterbach, *JE*, XII, 46.

[3] מדרש תנחמא והוא מדרש ילמדנו וגו׳, (reprinted New York and Berlin: Horeb, 1924), p. 218.

[4] *Soṭah* 1.9.

[5] Cf. the story of Tobit.

is held captive in the tresses" (Canticles 7.6) to Moses, while another interpretation understands "king" as God, bound by his covenant. Rabbi Berekia, a Palestinian Amora of the fifth generation, takes "king" as Moses, on the basis of Deuteronomy 33.5, and "tresses" (רהטים) as "streams" of Meribah, because of which Moses and Aaron were forbidden to enter the promised land.[1] Rabbi Nehemiah, a third generation Tanna, also takes "king" as a reference to Moses, citing Deuteronomy 33.5, and adds the additional proof that Moses, like a king, was told by God to "command the children of Israel" (Leviticus 24.2).[2]

The Masoretic text of Deuteronomy 33.5 is ambiguous, since either Moses or Yahweh can be understood as the subject of ויהי בישרון מלך. All but one of the medieval Jewish commentators found in common editions of the Rabbinic Bible took God to be the subject, and modern Christian interpreters agree with them. However, Ibn Ezra (a twelfth century Spanish scholar) says: "'King': this is Moses. When the heads of the people heard the Torah interpreted from his mouth and his sound reasoning, that he was like a king, the heads of the tribes gathered to him."[3] The Targumim divide in their interpretation of the passage. Onkelos follows the Hebrew closely and is similarly ambiguous. Pseudo-Jonathan, however, makes it clear that Moses is meant:

> The sons of Israel said, Mosheh commanded us the law, and gave it for an heritage to the tribes of Jakob. And he was king in Israel: when the chiefs of the people were gathered together, the tribes of Israel were obedient to him.[4]

On the other hand, a fragment of the ancient Jerusalem Targum gives the verse an eschatological interpretation:

> The sons of Israel said, Mosheh commanded us the law: he gave it for an inheritance and possession to the congregation of the house of Jakob. And a king shall arise from the house of Jakob, when the heads of the people are gathered together: unto Him shall the tribes of Israel be obedient.[5]

---

[1] Cf. Num. 20.10-13.

[2] *Shir R.* 7.6 (*Soncino Midrash*, IX, 289).

[3] Note that Moses is pictured as interpreting the law before the national assembly. Again, as in the case of Joshua (above p. 180), the imagery is from the king's enthronement and formal reading of Torah at Tabernacles.

[4] Trans. Ethridge, II, 673.

[5] *Ibid.*, p. 674.

The interpretation offered by Pseudo-Jonathan is probably the basis for Ibn Ezra's comment.

All three interpretations suggested by the three Targumim are to be found in the midrashim. For example, in the collection of tannaitic material on Deuteronomy which Hoffmann extracted from Midrash ha-Gadol, there is one paragraph which offers all three. One interpretation states matter-of-factly: "'And he became king in Jeshurun': this is Moses our teacher," another, "this is the King Messiah." In the latter יחד שבטי ישראל is understood as *"He will gather* the fugitives of Israel." The third interpretation, that God is meant, takes a novel form:

> 'And he became king in Jeshurun': the Scripture declares that when the prince (הנשיא) installed the council of elders below, the kingdom of heaven was established among those on high.[1]

Here Moses is not king, but he is "prince," and the assembly on earth is matched by the heavenly counterpart, the "kingdom of heaven" (i.e., of God). Moses is therefore understood as the earthly vice-regent of the heavenly King.

One final instance of the use of Deuteronomy 33.5 to support Moses' kingship must be discussed at some length because in its context several related themes which have been emerging in the foregoing discussion come to clarity. The Midrash on Psalms, in the process of interpreting Psalm 1.1, "Blessed is the man that . . . *sits* not in the seat of scoffers," introduces 2 Samuel 7.18, "Then David the king went in and *sat* before the Lord." After a discussion of the problem provoked by the idea of sitting in the presence of God, the midrash proceeds to discuss the remainder of the new passage, 2 Samuel 7.18-19. The last clause, "For this is the Torah of Man" evokes the statement that האדם here means "he who is foremost [משובח] among Prophets; he who is foremost among kings."[2] There follows the general heading "You find that whatever Moses did, David did," under which eight points of similarity are listed: Both led Israel out of servitude, both fought the "battles of the Lord"; both became King in Israel and in Judah; both divided a sea; both built an altar; both brought offerings; both gave five books to Israel; both blessed

---

[1] *Midrasch Tannaïm*, II, 213.

[2] Trans. Braude, I, 4. This statement raises anew the question of "Man" as an eschatological title in Judaism (see above, p. 7off. and 72 n. 4), a question which needs independent investigation.

Israel.[1] The third point of comparison uses Deuteronomy 33.5 as a proof-text:

> As Moses became king in Israel and in Judah, for it is said *And he became king in Jeshurun, when the heads of the people . . . were gathered together . . .* , so David became king in Israel and in Judah.[2]

Attached to the comment on verse 3 is a very similar comparison of Moses and Samuel.[3] Here again it is said, "The one became king, and the other became king."[4] At the end of the paragraph is a significant addition:

> Indeed Scripture alludes to this likeness in the verse: *A prophet will the Lord thy God raise up unto thee, from the midst of thee, of thy brethren, like unto me* (Deut. 18:15). So, too, you find of [Moses and] Jeremiah, that what is said of the one is also said of the other.[5]

The idea that Samuel was "greatest of kings and prophets" has appeared in the non-rabbinic sources, in isolated instances,[6] but here is striking evidence that Samuel could be understood as prophet-king *like Moses*, in fulfillment of the promise in Deuteronomy 18.15, 18. The laconic note on Jeremiah does not indicate whether he, like David and Samuel, was thought in some fashion to have received kingship as well as the prophetic office in the succession of Moses, but it will be seen below that Deuteronomy 18.15 was sometimes applied to Jeremiah.[7] It is now quite clear that in some circles of Judaism there was a persistent notion of a *succession of prophetic rulers* of Israel, beginning with Moses, passed on to Joshua, continuing in Samuel and, presumably, also found in the remaining great prophets of Israel, especially Jeremiah. Perhaps it was also projected into the future. To this succession, according

----

[1] Cf. Braude, I, 5.

[2] *Ibid.*

[3] This paragraph seems misplaced, for it has nothing to do with the comparison of David's attributes with God's that immediately precedes it. It begins כוצא בדבר אתה אומר אם יעמוד וגו', i.e., "another example is provided by the verse 'If Moses and Samuel stood before me.'" Braude is probably correct in connecting this paragraph with the one comparing Moses and David.

[4] Braude, I, 6.

[5] *Ibid.*

[6] See above, pp. 116, n. 1; 150f.

[7] P. 200, and n. 2.

to some traditions, belonged Ezra[1] and the "Teacher of Righteousness" of the Qumran community.[2]

What is the meaning of the fact that David is brought into the Mosaic succession? There is certain anomaly in the paragraph comparing David and Moses, because while the heading distinguishes them as *respectively* foremost of prophets and foremost of kings, yet one point of comparison is that both are kings. Perhaps behind the extant midrash was a tradition that "'The Man' means the one who is foremost among prophets *and* kings," namely Moses and "the man" in each generation who succeeds to Moses' office.[3] In this case the present form of the midrash *might* represent an attempt to unify two divergent eschatological traditions, one of a prophet-king like Moses, the other the more familiar expectation of the King Messiah of the Davidic line. These suggestions, however, cannot go beyond conjecture. Nevertheless some such combination of traditions seems also to lie behind the text of the Fragmentary Targum on Deuteronomy 35.5,[4] since the interpretation that makes "the King Messiah" the subject of "And he will become king in Jeshurun" (understood as future by ignoring the waw-consecutive) must have proceeded from a tradition that Yahweh was *not* the subject. The only alternative, represented by Pseudo-Jonathan, was Moses. That is, the Palestinian Targum substituted "the King Messiah" for "Moses."[5]

Kingship from the wilderness

The tradition has already been quoted from *Tanḥuma* which spoke of Moses' yearning for the wilderness because "from the wilderness" he was to receive great gifts, including kingship.[6] Now it is possible to determine on what occasion and in what circum-

---

[1] Above, p. 157.

[2] Above, pp. 196f., 174.

[3] David also could be called a prophet by the rabbis: cf. Ginzberg, VI, 249f., n. 24. Note that the statement that Moses was foremost among prophets is supported by a proof-text, while the statement "the foremost among kings –he is David" is unsupported. Thus the balanced structure of the passage breaks down at this point. "The Man" (but איש, not אדם) as a title for Moses (derived from Dt. 33.1) is important in Samaritan tradition below, p. 255f.)

[4] Quoted above, p. 187.

[5] The analogy, "As was the first redeemer, so will be the last redeemer," is a familiar one in rabbinic sources (see below).

[6] Above, p. 181.

stances Moses was made king in the wilderness, according to the rabbinic haggada. According to the fundamental proof-text, Deuteronomy 33.5, he became king "when the heads of the people were assembled." The rabbinic sources which have been examined so far all agree that "the heads of the people" were the "seventy elders" who gathered on Mt. Sinai (Exodus 24) when the Torah was given. The association between the giving of the Torah and Moses' elevation to kingship has been noted frequently in these pages and was already familiar from the non-rabbinic sources discussed in the previous chapter. Furthermore, the enthronement of Joshua as Moses' successor—as prophet-king—was characterized above all by his being given the Torah to read before all the people.[1]

What was the connection between becoming king and the giving of the Law? As was seen above, Philo made the connection through the prevailing understanding of the ideal king in Hellenism as "living law." As "legislator," therefore, Moses was king. In rabbinic traditions, however, Moses was not the *giver* of the Law, but only the mediator of it. What has to be explained is the way in which his *receiving* and/or *transmitting* the law could be understood as constituting his enthronement as king of Israel. A valuable clue is provided by this passage from Targum Pseudo-Jonathan on Deuteronomy 34.5:

> A voice fell from heaven, and thus spake: Come, all ye who have entered into the world, and behold the grief of Mosheh, the Rabban of Israel, who hath laboured, but not to please himself, and who is ennobled with four goodly crowns:—the crown of the Law is his, because he brought it from the heavens above, when there was revealed to him the Glory of the Lord's Shekinah, with two thousand myriads of angels, and forty and two thousand chariots of fire. The crown of the Priesthood hath been his in the seven days of the peace offerings. The crown of the kingdom they gave him in possession from heaven: he drew not the sword, nor prepared the war horse, nor gathered he the host.[2] The crown of a good name he possesseth by good works, and by his humility. Therefore is Mosheh, the servant of the Lord, gathered in the land of Moab, by the kiss of the Word of the Lord.[3]

---

[1] Above, pp. 179f.

[2] On Moses' peaceful acquisition of kingship, cf. Philo, *Mos.* i.148.

[3] Trans. Ethridge, II, 683. The four crowns are mentioned in a saying of R. Simeon, *Abot* 4.13; according to *ARN*, version "B," chap. 48, p. 130, Moses received only the crown of Torah, the crowns of priesthood and kingship belonging to Aaron and David, respectively. For different interpre-

Two of the crowns, that of Torah and that of Kingship, were given
to Moses "from heaven." The description of the things Moses saw
shows that "heaven" here is not just a circumlocution for God.
What is involved is an ascent to heaven, where Moses, despite the
terrifying sights of "the glory of the Lord's *Shekinah*, two thousand
myriads of angels, and forty-two thousand chariots of fire," obtained the Torah for Israel and was himself crowned as king. A
similar view lies behind a comment on Exodus 31.2 in *Shemot Rabbah*:

> You find that when Moses ascended on high, God showed him
> all the vessels of the Tabernacle and told him: 'Thus and thus
> shalt thou do. . . .' When Moses was about to descend (from
> heaven), he was under the impression that he was to make
> them, but God called unto him: 'Moses, I have made thee a
> king; it does not befit a king to do anything (himself), but he
> gives orders and others do the thing for him. Thou, likewise,
> must not do anything thyself, but just command others and
> let them do it.'[1]

Thus Moses became king in heaven, where he ascended to obtain the
Torah. Allusions to Moses' "heavenly journeys" and to his enthronement "on high" have been seen already in nonrabbinic
sources.[2] Still more evidence for such traditions of Moses' mystical
ascension and heavenly enthronement will be seen in the ensuing
pages.

Moses as Divine King

Among the homilies in the *Tanḥuma* compilation edited by Buber,
there is one which provides an important clue to the traditions here
under investigation. The homily interprets Numbers 10.1-2, "The
Lord said to Moses, 'Make for yourself two trumpets of silver,'" by
introducing Psalm 24.7, "Lift up your heads, O Gates . . .," which,
according to the midrash, was spoken by Solomon when he brought
the Ark into the Temple. The connection of the two passages is not
at once apparent, for the cardinal point, that the trumpets are a
sign of royalty, does not emerge until the end of the midrash. Once
introduced, however, the Psalm text is now interpreted:

---

tations of the four crowns, see *ARN*, version "A," chap. 41, p. 130; Talm.
B., *Yoma* 72b; *Sifre Num.*, par. 119; *Shemot R.* 34.2; *Midrash Kohelet* 7.1.

[1] *Shemot R.* 40.2; trans. Lehrmann, *Soncino Midrash*, III, 461.

[2] Above, pp. 110f. 120-125, 140f., 147-149, 156-159.

Another interpretation: What (does this mean): "The Lord of Hosts, he is the King of Glory"? (This means that) he apportions some of his glory to those who fear him according to his glory. How so? He is called "God," and he called Moses "god", as it is said, "See, I have made you a god to Pharaoh" [Exodus 7.1]. He vivifies the dead, and he apportioned some of his glory to Elijah, for the latter vivified a dead person, as it is said, "Elijah said, See your son lives" [1 Kings 17.23]. Thus the Holy One, blessed be He, apportions some of his glory to those that fear him. To the King Messiah he grants to be clothed in his robes, as it is said, "Splendor and majesty thou dost put on him" [Psalm 21.6(5)]. Our rabbis teach us that no king of flesh and blood rides on God's steed or puts on his robes or uses his crown or sits on his throne, but the Holy One, blessed be He, apportions all these to those who fear him, and gives them to them. How do we know this? It is said, "In storm and whirlwind are his ways" [Nahum 1.3], and he gave this to Elijah, as it is said, "And he went up in a whirlwind of heaven" [2 Kings 2.11]. And none puts on his robes. What is written? "Thou art clothed in splendor and majesty" [Psalm 104.1]. And of the King Messiah it is written, "Splendor and majesty thou dost put on him" [Psalm 21.6(5)]. And none makes use of his crown. What is written of 'Moses? "And Moses did not know that his face beamed with light" [Exodus 34.29]. And none sits on his throne. It is written, "Solomon sat on the throne of the Lord as king" [1 Chronicles 29.23]. And none makes use of his sceptre, for it was given to Moses, as scripture says, "Take this rod in your hand," etc. [Exodus 4.16]. What is written of the Holy One, blessed be He? "God has gone up with a shout, the Lord, with the sound of the horn (שופר)" [the next verses of the Psalm are required for the midrash, though assumed without being quoted: "Sing to God, sing; sing to the King, sing; for God is King of all the earth; sing a Maskil. God reigns over the nations; God sits on his holy throne" (Psalm 47.6-9 [5-8])]. The Holy One, blessed be He, said to Moses, "I have made you a king," as Scripture says, "He became king in Yeshurun" [Deuteronomy 33.5]. Just as they blow trumpets before the King when he goes forth, so in your case, when you go forth they will sound trumpets. "Make for yourself two trumpets of silver."[1]

The context makes plain that the last sentence quoted from the midrash compares Moses not with earthly kings, but with God who is preceded by the sound of the Shofar when he "goes up" as King. The silver trumpets, which, as has already been seen, were not to be used by any other earthly king save perhaps David,[2] are there-

---

[1] *Tanḥuma*, ed. Buber, IV, 51f., cf. 53. Also in *Bamidbar R.* 15.13.
[2] Above, p. 185.

fore understood as a sign that Moses shared *God's* kingship. This accords with the theme of the whole homily, that God "shares his glory with his worshippers." As God the supreme King made Moses "god," so also he made him "king."

It will be recalled that Philo also derived Moses' kingship from the passage, "See, I have made you a god to Pharaoh."[1] In discussing the Philonic passage in the previous chapter, it was remarked that the link between the scriptural text and Philo's conclusion, "He made him god *and king* over the whole nation," was puzzling and must presuppose some traditional exegesis not made explicit by Philo. That surmise is now confirmed and the tradition behind Philo's statement can be seen to be substantially the same as that just quoted from *Tanḥuma*. (1) The main theme of both is that "God shares his glory with those who fear him" (*Tanḥuma*), in Philo's language, "The good man (ὁ σπουδαῖος ἄνθρωπος) . . . partakes of the precious things of God (τῶν . . . τοῦ θεοῦ κειμηλίων) so far as he is able."[2] (2) Both hinge on the verse, "I have made you a god to Pharaoh." (3) This verse is interpreted to mean that God made Moses "king" as well, since "king" is one of the attributes of "God." This point is only implicit—though absolutely necessary for the argument—in Philo; in the midrash it is explicitly grounded by proof-texts: Psalm 47 for God's kingship, Deuteronomy 33.5 for Moses'. The passage in Philo becomes much clearer when read alongside the midrash. Philo in fact skipped one step in the argument, namely, that "God" implies "king," though he clearly implies this when he speaks of "the Father and Maker of all."[3] The central element of the midrash, therefore, turns out to be older than Philo: that is, it was current prior to 40 A.D.

Another peculiarity of the passage in Philo is that while the biblical context of the statement, "I have made you a god to Pharaoh," was a conversation between God and Moses in Egypt, Philo connects it, understood as Moses' installation as king, with Moses' entry "into the thick darkness" (Exodus 20.21), that is,

---

[1] Philo, *Mos.* i.155-158; above, pp. 110f.

[2] *Mos.* i.157. Cf. 155: κοινωνὸν γὰρ ἀξιώσας ἀναφανῆναι τῆς ἑαυτοῦ λήξεως ἀνῆκε πάντα τὸν κόσμον..., especially 158, οὐχὶ καὶ μείζονος τῆς πρὸς τὸν πατέρα τῶν ὅλων καὶ ποιητὴν κοινωνίας ἀπέλαυσε προσρήσεως τῆς αὐτῆς ἀξιωθείς; ὠνομάσθη γὰρ ὅλου τοῦ ἔθνους θεὸς καὶ βασιλεύς.

[3] *Ibid.*, 158. Furthermore, it was a commonplace for Philo that God was known as King.

with Moses' mystic ascent from Mt. Sinai.[1] This connection is not quite clear in the *Tanḥuma* homily, although it is implied in the proof-text Deuteronomy 33.5, as seen above, and also in the identi-fication of the corona of light which surrounded Moses' face when he descended with the "crown of God."

That rabbinic circles did commonly connect Exodus 7.1 with Moses' ascent to heaven on Sinai is demonstrated by the midrashim on the phrase "Moses, the man of God" in Deuteronomy 33.1. One of several interpretations of the phrase is this:

> "A man, god": "A man" when he ascended on high; "god" when he descended below. "And Aaron and all the sons of Israel saw Moses and behold! his face emitted beams of light." (Exodus 34.30)[2]

Thus it was in heaven that Moses was made "god" (and, therefore, king), which meant that Moses became imbued in some sense with God's fiery substance[3] or, in the pictorial language of the *Midrash Tanḥuma*, was crowned with God's own corona as the heavenly King's earthly vice-regent.

Summary

The tradition that Moses was the king of Israel during the wilderness sojourn has been found to be very widespread in rabbinic haggada. It was found sometimes linked with the office of high priest, but could still be affirmed by circles that denied that Moses was priest. Again, it is found frequently associated with his office as prophet, particularly in connection with the notion that the double function, prophecy and sovereignty, was passed on to Moses' successors, beginning with Joshua. But Moses' kingship is found

---

[1] Above, pp. 110f.

[2] *Pesikta de Rab Kahana*, Piska 32, p. 198b. Cf. *Debarim R.* 11.4; *Midrash Tehillim* 90.1 (Braude, II, 88f.). Other interpretations of Dt. 33.1 found in the same sources are summarized by Ginzberg, III, 481.

[3] This is the clear implication of *Midrash Tehillim* 90.1, "When a mortal goes up to the Holy One, blessed be He, who is pure fire, and whose ministers are fire –and Moses did go up to Him –he is a man. But after he comes down, he is called 'God'" (trans. Braude, II, 88f.); cf. *Debarim R.* 11.4 (*Soncino Midrash*, VII, 175f.). It will be recalled that for Philo Moses could symbolize the manifestation among men of the divine Logos, conceived of as an emanating "light stream" (cf. Goodenough, *By Light, Light*, pp. 201-203, 211, 220, 231).

very often in passages which do not speak of any other "office" and is frequently taken for granted rather than argued. The fundamental text on which the idea of Moses' kingship was grounded was Deuteronomy 33.5. In various ways the idea is expressed that Moses was made king directly by God and that he served as God's earthly vice-regent. A particularly close connection appeared between Moses' installation as king and his mediation of the Torah. In some circles at least the connection lay specifically in the notion that when Moses went up Mt. Sinai he was enthroned in heaven as king and descended from there with the Torah to exercise his reign.

The Shepherd of Israel

Both because of the general connection between "king" and "shepherd" in the symbolic language of antiquity and because of the special connection in Philo between Moses' tending sheep and his preparation for kingship and, moreover, because of the relation between the discourse on the "good shepherd" in John 10 and the ironic exaltation of Jesus by Pilate as "King of the Jews," the designation of Moses as "shepherd" by the Rabbis deserves a brief discussion at this point.

For Philo herding sheep was the best possible preparation for the royal office,[1] and that was why the Scripture said "Now Moses was keeping the flock" (Exodus 3.1). Similar opinions were expressed by the rabbis when they came to comment on the same verse. For example the homily in *Tanḥuma* on this verse says, "'And he led the flock' indicated to him that he would lead Israel forty years. . ."[2] *Shemot Rabbah* suggests that Moses, like David, was tested for rule by having to tend a flock, for "before God confers greatness on a man He first tests him by a little thing and then promotes him to greatness."[3]

More often the rabbis refer to Moses as "faithful shepherd" (רועה נאמן), a title which seems to be connected not with Moses'

---

[1] *Mos.* i.60-62; cf. *Jos.* 2-3.

[2] *Tanḥuma*, ed. Buber, II, 7.

[3] *Shemot R.* 2.3, trans. Lehrmann, *Soncino Midrash*, III, 49; cf. 2.2. The quoted sentence is almost indentical with the last clause in Philo, *Mos.* i.62 (cf. Stein, p. 45, where further similarities of form as well as content are noted. Stein concludes that a common haggadah lies behind Philo and the midrash. It is possible, however, that in isolated cases Philo could have influenced the midrashim).

kingship but with his prophetic office and especially with his role as Israel's defender or "Paraclete" before God. For example, one of the Proems to *Ruth Rabbah* begins thus:

> R. Nehemiah introduced his exposition with the verse, *O Israel, thy prophets have been like foxes in ruins* (Ezek. xiii,4). Just as the fox looks about it in the ruins to see where it can escape if it sees men coming, so were thy prophets in the ruins. *Ye have not gone up in the breaches (ib.)* like Moses. To whom can Moses be compared? To a faithful shepherd whose fence fell down in the twilight. He arose and repaired it from three sides, but a breach remained on the fourth side, and having no time to erect the fence, he stood in the breach himself. A lion came, he boldly withstood it; a wolf came and still he stood against it. But ye! Ye did not stand in the breach as Moses did. Had ye stood in the breach like Moses, ye would have been able to stand in the battle in the day of God's anger.[1]

The simile which compares Moses with a faithful shepherd describes the model for succeeding prophets. The image "standing in the breach" derives from Psalm 106.23, "And he said he would have destroyed them had not Moses his chosen one stood in the breach before him," a verse frequently quoted in descriptions of Moses' intercessory role. Thus according to *Esther Rabbah*, Elijah went to Moses after the decree of Ahasuerus had been issued for Israel's destruction and said "O thou faithful shepherd, how many times hast thou stood in the breach for Israel and quashed their doom so that they should not be destroyed, as it says, 'Had not Moses his chosen one stood in the breach. . . .'"[2]

From these instances it seems that Moses' herding sheep could be understood as a symbol of or introduction to his kingship, but that the common term "faithful shepherd" implied instead Moses' peculiar function as Israel's defender before God. The latter function is connected with the office of prophet.[3]

---

[1] Proem V, trans. L. Rabbinowitz, *Soncino Midrash*, VIII, 8.

[2] vii, 13, trans. Maurice Simon, *Soncino Midrash*, VII, 99. Additional instances of the title applied to Moses in similar situations are given by Ginzberg, V, 414, n. 109, cf. II, 300-303; IV, 308.

[3] Ginzberg notes that "this designation is a favorite with Zohar, a part of which work is called רעיא מהימנא ('The Faithful Shepherd'), after Moses, who is introduced as revealing certain mystic doctrines" (V, 414, n. 109).

MOSES AS THE SUPREME PROPHET

The Father of the Prophets and Similar Titles

An often repeated tradition warns that "if even Moses, the father of the prophets, once forgot his words because he lost his temper — how much more the rest of mankind!"[1] Variants of the tradition call him "the great wise man, father of the wise men, father of the prophets,"[2] "the wisest of the wise, the greatest of the great, the father of the prophets,"[3] the father of wisdom and of prophecy."[4]

In *Midrash Rabbah* on Leviticus it is said that Moses was called "Father of Soko" (1 Chronicles 4.18) because "he was the father of the prophets who see [סוכין] by means of the Holy Spirit" or, according to another interpretation by Rabbi Levi, from the Arabic word for prophet, *sakya*.[5] *Bereshit Rabbah* calls Moses "the chosen one of the prophets," comparing him with Jacob, "the chosen one of the patriarchs."[6] Here the epithet "chosen" (בחיר), which is the point of comparison, is drawn from Psalm 106.23. The Psalm text does not call Moses a prophet; that is taken for granted.

The originator of prophecy

The traditions quoted so far might mean only that Moses was the first of the prophets in temporal sequence. Other passages, however, show that more is involved. *Midrash Rabbah* on Deuteronomy calls Moses "the teacher (רבן) of all the prophets,"[7] while the midrash on Psalms calls him "the greatest of the prophets."[8] The meaning of these statements is revealed by a statement in *Midrash Rabbah* on Exodus:

> Another explanation of 'They have turned aside quickly' [Exodus 32.8] was given by R. Jonah in the name of R. Samuel

---

[1] *ARN*, version "B," chap. 1, p. 3.

[2] *Sifre Num.*, par. 134, ed. Friedmann, p. 50b; cf. *Sifre Dt.*, par. 306, ed. Friedmann, p. 132b: משה שהוא חכם חכמים גדול שבגדולים.

[3] *Seder Eliahu Rabbah* 5, 6, 13; *Eliahu Zuta* 12 (*Seder Eliahu rabba und Seder Eliahu zuta*, ed. Meyer Friedmann [Vienna: Verlag "Achiasaf," 1902], pp. 21, 33, 68, 194.

[4] *Midrash Mishle* 25.97 (Wünsche, *Bibliotheca Rabbinica*, III, Lieferung 33, p. 63).

[5] *Wayikra R.* 1.3; trans. J. Israelstam, *Soncino Midrash*, IV, 5.

[6] *Bereshit R.* 76.1, cf. ET by H. Freedmann, *Soncino Midrash*, II, 701.

[7] *Debarim R.* 1.10; cf. ET by J. Rabbinowitz, *Soncino Midrash*, VII, 10.

[8] *Midrash Tehillim* on Ps. 5.11, trans. Braude, I, 90.

b. Naḥman: Every prophet who arose repeated the prophecy of his predecessor in order to clarify his prophecy. R. Joshua b. Levi said: Each one was fully occupied with his own prophecy, save Moses, who delivered the prophecies of all the prophets as well as his own, so that every one who has prophesied has drawn his prophecy from one source, the prophecy of Moses.[1]

Rabbi Joshua belonged to the first generation of Palestinian Amoraim (third century A.D.), but the tradition that Moses received all prophetic secrets on Sinai is much older, as the books of Jubilees and 4 Ezra show.[2] Corresponding to this is the notion, very widespread, that all halakic traditions, written and oral, were delivered to Moses at Sinai.[3] This explains also why the passage from the Midrash on Psalms 1.3 already discussed[4] supports the statement that Moses was "foremost among prophets" by the text "And Moses went up to God."[5]

The scriptural basis

One does not need to seek far to discover the scriptural basis for traditions like those which have just been cited. Two texts are of primary importance. Deuteronomy 34.10 states, "There has not arisen since in Israel a prophet like Moses." The haggadot often cite this verse, but the rabbis generally add that among the Gentiles Moses had one equal: Balaam. The two are often compared and contrasted.[6]

The second text of importance is of course Deuteronomy 18.15, 18, which speaks of a prophet like Moses who will arise from Israel. The text receives surprisingly little attention from the rabbis.

---

[1] *Shemot R.* 42.8, trans. Lehrmann, *Soncino Midrash*, III, 490. I have departed from Lehrmann's translation in R. Joshua's statement to bring out more fully the force of the original.

[2] See above, pp. 156-159.

[3] Talm. Y., *Peah* 2.4; Talm. B., *Meg.* 19b; *Kohelet R.* 1.9; cf. *Abot* 1.1.

[4] Above, pp. 188f.

[5] It is interesting that while the homily says, "Whatever Moses did, David did," there is no claim that David "went up to God." In another homily in the same collection precisely this point becomes the main distinction between Moses and David: Moses, who had gone up to heaven, knew heaven and earth, as a king's house steward knows the affairs of both palace and field (Num. 12.7 is presupposed), while David, "who had not gone up to heaven," knew only the earth, like the field steward who knows nothing of palace affairs (*Midrash Tehillim* on Ps. 24.1, trans. Braude, I, 339f.).

[6] *Seder Eliahu R.* 18 (ed. Friedmann, p. 142); *Seder Eliahu z.* 10 (ed. Friedmann, p. 191); *Sifre Dt.*, end (ed. Friedmann, pp. 227f.); *Wayikra R.* 1.13; *Midrasch Tannaïm*, p. 227; *Bamidbar R.* 14.20.

Where it is cited, it is applied in most cases to the succession of prophets beginning with Moses. For example, the *Mekilta* interprets the verse to mean that God had intended to raise up a prophet in the future, but the merits obtained by the Israelites in sending Moses as their intermediary to accept the Torah (Exodus 20.19) resulted in God's advancing the promise, so that Moses himself became the first.[1] In particular Jeremiah is singled out, as the climax and virtual end of the series of prophets.[2]

Summary

The haggada universally takes for granted that Moses was a prophet and moreover the *first* and *greatest* in Israel. The basis for these assumptions is primarily Deuteronomy 34.10. Moses' supremacy in prophecy is connected (1) with his ascension of Sinai, which was widely regarded as an ascent to heaven, and (2) with his receiving there mysteries which were not revealed to any other single prophet. Thus Moses became the inaugurator of a succession of prophets, each of whom used as the source of his prophecies the secrets revealed through Moses. Traditions cited in the previous section showed that this succession could also take the form of a series of prophetic *rulers* of Israel. The idea of a prophetic succession was derived from Deuteronomy 18.15 and 18.

Israel's Defense Attorney

In the extra-rabbinic literature on Moses the idea that Moses acted as Israel's supreme mediator and intercessor to assuage God's anger toward Israel appeared again and again.[3] It was seen that Josephus rejected the tradition of Moses' priesthood, but retained the idea of his intercession for Israel.[4] In Philo the two functions were also separable, although at times the priesthood was interpreted in the sense of Moses' intercession.[5] The situation is similar in

---

[1] *Mekilta*, Baḥodesh 9, ed. Lauterbach, II, 271. So also *Mekilta de R. Simon* (ed. Hoffmann, p. 114), *Agadath Bereshith*, par. 80, p. 153.

[2] *Pesikta dè Rab Kahana*, ed. Buber, p. 112a; cf. *Midrasch Tannaïm*, p. 111, and *Midrash Tehillim* 1.3, where Samuel and Jeremiah are both mentioned (above p. 189).

[3] Above, pp. 118, 137f., 159-161, 174.

[4] Above, p. 137.

[5] Above, p. 118.

rabbinic sources. They offer divergent traditions on the question whether Moses was high priest,[1] but the tradition of Moses' intercessory and advocative office is very strong and never contradicted.[2]

Excerpts from a few typical passages will illustrate how the rabbis conceived of Moses' defense of Israel. The model example of Moses' intervention to turn away God's wrath was the episode of the golden calf, particularly in the extensive description found in Deuteronomy 9.[3] Part of a midrash on this passage found in *Yalkut Shim'oni* follows:

> 'And he said to him, Arise, go down quickly from here, for your people have acted corruptly (Deuteronomy 9.12). Moses said to him: Do '*my* people' sin and *your* people do not sin? The Holy One, blessed be He, said to him: *Your* people sin. He said to him: Who will convince me that my people have sinned? He replied, He by whom creation was made is convincing you. Moses said to him: And does he (Israel) know? [i.e., does he sin knowingly?] The Holy One, blessed be He, said, 'The ox knows his owner' (Isaiah 1.3): he knows the Torah. . . . (Moses) said to him: 'Israel does not know; my people do not understand' (*ibid.*)—for this reason I leap to the defense (סניגוריא = συνηγορία) of my people. They have not sinned and your people have not sinned; do not destroy my people. When Moses spoke in their defense, immediately 'The Lord repented of the evil which he had said he would do to his people' (Exodus 32.14). When Moses, the defender (סניגורין)[4] of Israel, died, the Holy One, blessed be He, remembered him, for there was found no defender like him, as Scripture says, 'And he remembered the days of old, of Moses his servant' (Isaiah 63.11). The Holy One, blessed be He, said: In this world a mortal was made their defender, and he saved them. But in the time to come I in my glory will be their defender before the princes of the nations of the world and will save them from them, as scripture says, 'It is I, announcing vindication, mighty to save' (Isaiah 63.1).[5]

---

[1] Above, pp. 181f.

[2] Cf. Bloch, "Quelques aspects," pp. 123-127, and Nils Johansson, *Parakletoi: Vorstellungen von Fürsprechern für die Menschen vor Gott in der alttestamentlichen Religion, im Spätjudentum und Urchristentum* (Lund: Gleerupska Universitetsbokhandeln, 1940), pp. 161-166.

[3] On this passage, see Von Rad, *Theologie*, I, 293.

[4] סניגורין, if correct, is to be taken as a singular nominal formation in ין-, not as a plural. Elsewhere in the passage סניגור is the spelling. The text of the whole passage seems to be in some disarray, but the lines quoted here are clear.

[5] *Yalkut Šim'oni*, par. 852 on Dt. ‏(ילקוט שמעוני לדרש על תורה על נביאים‎ ‏וכתובים‎ [Warsaw: Br. Levin-Epstein, 1925], I, 588).

The second motif mentioned here, that after Moses' death no other defender like him was found for Israel, is elaborated in a passage found in several midrashim:

> [When Moses died] The Holy One, blessed be He, said: "Who will rise up for me against the wicked? (Psalm 94.16) And who will stand up for Israel in the time of my anger? And who will stand up in the wars of my sons? And who will stand up and seek mercy for them when they sin before me?"[1] At that moment Meṭaṭron came and fell on his face and said before him, "Lord of the world, while Moses lived he was yours, and in his death he is yours." The Holy One, blessed be He, replied: "I'll tell you a parable. What is the matter like? A king who had a son, and day after day the father was provoked with him and wanted to kill him, for he did not respect his father. But his mother would save the son from his hand. In time the mother died, and the king was crying. His servants said to him, "O King, why are you crying?" He said to them, "Not for my wife alone am I crying, but for my son, for many times I have been provoked with him and wanted to kill him, but she saved him from my hand.' "In the same way the Holy One, blessed be He, said to Meṭaṭron, "Not for Moses alone am I weeping, but for him and for Israel. For how many times have they provoked me and I have been provoked with them, and he stood in the breach before me" [Psalm 106.23].[2]

The biblical account of Moses' intercession after the golden calf was made is treated expansively in a passage of the Talmud, in *Berakot* 32a. There the statement of Rabbi Abbahu[3] is found which, as he says, would be impossible if not explicitly supported by Scripture (Deuteronomy 9.14). He says, "Moses took hold of the Holy One, blessed be He, like a man who seizes his fellow by his garment and said before Him: Sovereign of the Universe, I will not let Thee go until Thou forgivest and pardonest them."[4]

Midrash Rabbah on Exodus 32.11 contains the statement by Rabbi Ḥama ben Ḥanina that "Moses was one of the two advocates [סניגורין] that arose to defend Israel and set themselves, as it were,

---

[1] Compare the almost identical complaint in the mouth of Joshua, *Assump. Mos.* xi.17, quoted above, p. 160.

[2] *Tanḥuma*, ed. Buber, V, 13; cf. *ARN*, version "B," p. 156; *Debarim R.* at the end; Talm. B., *Soṭa* 13b and 14a; *Peṭirat Mosheh* in Jellinek, I, 129, 2d. recension, VI, 383.

[3] Third generation Palestinian Amora.

[4] Trans. Maurice Simon, *Soncino Talmud*, Seder Zera'im, I, 196f.

against the Holy One, blessed be He." The familiar proof-text, Psalm 106.23, is introduced and explained as follows:

> When Israel made the Golden Calf, Satan stood within (before God) accusing them, while Moses remained without. What then did Moses do? He arose and thrust Satan away and placed himself in his stead. . . .[1]

The scene here is the heavenly court, where accuser and defender stand before God's throne.[2] That means that the "forty days and nights" on Sinai, when Moses "lay prostrate before the Lord" (Deuteronomy 9.25) were understood to have been spent in heaven, arguing Israel's case in the heavenly Council.

The *Assumption of Moses* and, probably, Philo bear witness to traditions that Moses' intercession did not cease at death, but continues on high.[3] Was such a tradition known in rabbinic circles? The passages quoted so far in this section exclude the notion of continuing intercession, for death deprives Israel of Moses' advocacy. There are other traditions, however, that "Moses stands and serves" after his departure from this world, just as he "stood and served" on Sinai. These traditions, which will be discussed shortly in connection with Moses' ascension, probably imply a notion similar to that found in the *Assumption of Moses*. A rather different conception lies behind the traditions already mentioned that speak of Moses' being recalled to life together with the Patriarchs to plead for Israel at significant crises,[4] for these presuppose Moses' burial.

The biblical accounts of Moses' intercession already suggested that Moses "laid down his life" for Israel, in the sense of offering to die in their stead.[5] In late sources, notably in tractate *Soṭa* (14a) of the Talmud, this theme is elaborated and connected with the description of the "suffering servant" in Isaiah 53. A parallel passage in the *Sifre*, however, uses Isaiah 53.12 only to show that in the age to come Moses will enter at the head of the whole nation into the promised land, without any allusion to Moses' suffering.[6] The consistent exegesis of the "servant" passage to explicate his suffering

---

[1] *Shemot R.*, par. 43; trans. Lehrmann, *Soncino Midrash*, III, 494.
[2] Cf. Betz, pp. 36-55 and above, p. 160.
[3] Above, p. 125, n. 3.
[4] Above, p. 197.
[5] Ex. 32.32; Dt. 9.18; cf. Von Rad, *Theologie*, I, 292f.; Bloch, "Quelques aspects," p. 129.
[6] *Sifre Dt.*, par. 355, ed. Friedmann, p. 147b.

on Israel's behalf may therefore be a later development. The notion of Moses' vicarious suffering has sometimes been exaggerated,[1] but it was at least a minor theme in the Pentateuch itself and in the midrashim. The most important element seems to be Moses' identification in his death with the wilderness generation. Moses is forbidden to enter the promised land because he cannot be separated from the generation he led in the wilderness—otherwise people would say that they had no part in the world to come. Instead, Moses himself must remain in the wilderness with them until the time comes to arise and lead them into the land in the age to come.[2] The controlling idea here is not *vicarious* suffering or death, however, but Moses' *identification* with the wilderness generation, a point developed very illuminatingly by Renée Bloch.[3]

Summary

Diverse circles of Judaism, including the rabbis, were virtually unanimous in seeing Moses as Israel's great intercessor and "counsel for the defense" before God's throne of judgment. For some circles, this function ceased, lamentably, with Moses' death, although God would still "remember" Moses' intercessions of the past, as he remembered the "merits" of the Patriarchs. For other circles, however, who believed that Moses did not die but ascended to heaven at the end of his life, apparently Moses' intercession continued. Connected with Moses' defense of Israel was his willingness to give his life for Israel, which at least in Talmudic times was connected with the figure of the suffering servant in Isaiah 53. More common is the notion that Moses had to die in the wilderness together with the generation that he led out of Egypt, so that in the age to come he could arise with them and lead them into the promised land.

---

[1] Notably by J. Jeremias, *ThWbNT*, IV, 867f., 877f. The four elements listed by Jeremias on p. 867 can be understood as examples of Moses' suffering only by a very strained interpretation. That Rev. 11 is evidence for an early tradition of a dying Messiah (p. 868) is questionable. The basic point in Acts 7 is hardly Moses' vicarious suffering (877f.), but only his rejection.

[2] *Shemot R.* 2.4 (ET: *Soncino Midrash*, III, 51); *Bamidbar R.* 19.13 (ET: *ibid.*, VI, 762); *Tanḥuma*, ed. Buber, IV, 121f.; *Sifre Dt.*, par. 355, ed. Friedmann, p. 147b. Other traditions in these sources, however, say Moses was punished for his *own* sin, on the basis of Num. 20.12.

[3] "Quelques aspects," pp. 129f.; see especially p. 130, n. 104.

MOSES' HEAVENLY ASCENTS

The Ascent on Sinai

It is almost a commonplace in rabbinic traditions that when Moses "went up to God" on Mt. Sinai, he ascended "on high," that is, to heaven. For example, the midrash on Psalm 24.1 already quoted in another connection found in Moses' ascent to heaven and his intimate knowledge of heavenly affairs the principal mark of his great superiority to David.[1] Even in passages where a mild polemic can be detected against too great an exaltation of Moses— and perhaps against dangerous mystical preoccupation with heaven-ly mysteries—Moses' ascent is taken for granted, as in the midrash on Psalm 106.2: "Not even Moses who went up into heaven to receive the Torah from God's hand into his own could fathom heaven's depth."[2] The reaction was sometimes so strong that Moses' ascent was denied—and Elijah's along with it!—as in *Mekilta* on Exodus 19.20.[3] That such a strong protest could be registered in a Tannaitic source shows the strength of interest in such ascensions and their connection with the figures of Moses and Elijah in the early centuries of the Christian era. The sources discussed in the previous chapter have already shown how early and how important the tradition was in certain non-rabbinic circles; sufficient evidence has emerged in this chapter that not all those who belonged within "normative" Judaism denied Moses' ascent with the vigor of *Mekilta*!

Very often Moses' Sinai ascent takes the form of an almost Promethean conquest. The most overt expression of this theme occurs in the midrash *Peṭirat Mosheh*. When Sammael, the death-angel, comes to claim Moses' soul, Moses defies him. He is superior to Sammael and to all the angels, he claims, for "I ascended to heaven . . ., spoke face to face with the Lord of the world, conquered the heavenly household (נצחתי פמליא של מעלה) received the Torah, wrote down at the command of the Holy One, blessed be He, the 613 commandments, taught them to the children of Israel, . . ."[4] Stated less radically, the tradition occurs elsewhere. The animosity

---

[1] Trans. Braude, I, 339f. Cf. above, pp. 188f. and p. 199, n. 5.
[2] Trans. Braude, II, 188.
[3] *Mekilta*, Baḥodesh 4, ed. Lauterbach, II, 224.
[4] Jellinek, I, 128.

of the angels to Moses' presence in heaven is often mentioned. "What is man," they complain, "that thou art mindful of Him?" (Psalm 8.2) "What is this offspring of woman who has come up on high?"[1]

The object of Moses' ascent on Sinai was of course to acquire the Torah for Israel. The Torah is generally understood by the rabbis as pre-existent, having been created on the eve of the first Sabbath. Hence Psalm 68.19 (18), "You ascended on high, you led captivity captive; you took gifts . . ." is applied to Moses.[2] Perhaps it is not accidental that the motif of the angels' opposition makes the mediation of the Torah by Moses in effect a Jewish counterpart to the Prometheus myth.

It was not only the Torah that Moses obtained on high, but other heavenly secrets as well. Passages have already been quoted to the effect that Moses received all the canonical books, the Mishnah, Talmud, and haggada, even the answers to all questions that a clever disciple might ask his teacher in future times.[3] There are later sources which describe Moses' heavenly journeys and the secrets he saw there in more detail, often strongly reminiscent of passages in the Enoch literature. In two manuscripts of the Hebrew book of Enoch Moses' ascension, after fasting "121 fasts," is described. The angels seek to burn up Moses, but when Moses prays for mercy, God sent "eighteen hundred advocates" and the "Prince of the Presence, Meṭaṭron" to protect him.[4] A similar, even more elaborate, description of the heavenly journeys is found in the *Gedulat Mosheh*.[5] This document describes Moses' visit to heaven and his encounter with the various angels. He ascends through seven heavens, visits Hell and Paradise. Certain similarities to 3 *Enoch* are very striking: God sends Meṭaṭron to Moses to "change his flesh into fire." Meṭaṭron tells Moses, "I am Enoch the son of Jared, thy father's father." Then "Meṭaṭron changed Moses' tongue into a tongue of

---

[1] *ARN*, version "A," chap. 2, p. 10; trans. Goldin, p. 20; cf. *Midrash Tehillim* on Ps. 8.2 (ET: Braude, I, 122); Talm. B., *Shab.* 88b; *Shir R.* 8.11.

[2] *ARN*, version "A," p. 10; Talm. B., *Shab.* 88b; *Shir. R.* 8.11.

[3] Talm. Y., *Peah* 2.4; Talm. B., *Meg.* 19b; *Kohelet R.* on 1.9; cf. above, pp. 198f.

[4] Hugo Odeberg, ed. and trans., 3 *Enoch: or the Hebrew Book of Enoch* (Cambridge: at the University Press, 1928), chap. xvB, pp. 40-43.

[5] Trans. Moses Gaster, "Hebrew Visions of Hell and Paradise," rp. in *Studies and Texts in Folklore, Magic, Medieval Romance, Hebrew Apocrypha, and Samaritan Archaeology*, vol. I (London: Maggs, Brothers, 1925-28), 125-141. A shorter recension of Moses' heavenly visions is found in Jellinek, I, 58-61, trans. Gaster, *Studies and Texts*, I, 141-143.

fire, and his eyes he made like the wheels of the heavenly chariot, and his power like unto that of the angels, and his tongue like a flame, and brought him up to heaven."[1] The description exactly parallels that of Enoch-Meṭaṭron's own transformation in 3 *Enoch* 15.1.[2] The enthronement of Enoch-Meṭaṭron in 3 *Enoch* also betrays interesting similarities to Moses' traditions. Meṭaṭron says:

> And he made me a royal crown in which were fixed forty-nine costly stones *like unto the light of the globe of the sun. For its splendour went forth* in the four quarters of the *Araboth Raqia* [the highest of the seven heavens] and in (through) the seven heavens, and in the four quarters of the world. And he put it on my head.[3]

To this may be compared the notion, preserved in *Midrash Tanḥuma*, that Moses received God's crown, identified with the "horns of light" that streamed from Moses' face.[4]

There are still other connections between rabbinic traditions of Moses' ascension at Sinai and the more outspokenly mystical speculations. One of these is Moses' ascetic preparation for the ascent:

> R. Nathan said: "Why was Moses made to wait all these six days before the word came to rest upon him? So that he might be purged of all food and drink in his bowels, before he was sanctified and became like the ministering angels."[5]

Moses needed no food nor drink in heaven because, like the heavenly creatures around the throne, he subsisted on the radiance of the *Shekina*.[6] From the time when God first spoke to Moses, according to the unanimous view of the haggada,[7] Moses withdrew from cohabitation with his wife. The purpose of his continence, according to one view found both in Philo and in rabbinic sources, was to

---

[1] Trans. Gaster, *Studies and Texts*, I, 126.

[2] Odeberg, 3 *Enoch*, p. 39.

[3] 3 *Enoch*, xii.3f., trans. Odeberg, pp. 32f. (emphasis mine).

[4] Above, pp. 193-195.

[5] *ARN*, version "A," chap. 1, p. 1; trans. Goldin, p. 3. Goldin points out that the other traditions contained in the same paragraph are examples of the polemic, visible in many rabbinic sources, against according superhuman dignities to Moses (*Kaplan Jubilee Volume*, pp. 278-280).

[6] *Shemot R.* 47.5, cf. 3.1; but according to another tradition found here and in *Tanḥuma*, ed. Buber, II, 120, he "ate the bread of the Torah . . . and drank the water of the Torah."

[7] So Bloch, "Quelques aspects," p. 127, n. 84.

make sure that he was always ready to receive divine revelations.[1]
According to Scholem, the "mystical ascent is always preceded by
ascetic practices."[2]

The secrets which Moses saw on high could be summed up in the
expression "what is above and what is below; what is before and
what is behind; what was and what will be."[3] This expression is
important because, while it is found in a late source, the antiquity
of the formulation is shown by the fact that it is almost identical
with the last line of the interpretation of Moses' dream of enthronement on Sinai in Ezekiel the Tragedian.[4] Moreover, the Mishnah, in
a halakah forbidding the discussion of mystical lore, including the
Maaseh Bereshit and the *Merkabah* chapter, says:

> Whosoever gives his mind to four things it were better for him
> if he had not come into the world—what is above? what is
> beneath? what was beforetime? and what will be hereafter?[5]

With good reason Scholem suggests that the Mishnah prohibition
refers to the mystical, quasi-gnostic speculations about heavenly
mysteries. Scholem compares the well-known formula of the gnostic
Theodotus, "the knowledge of who we were, what we have become,
where we were or where we are placed, whither we hasten, and from
what we are redeemed."[6]

It would be foolhardy to assume with Gaster that the elaborate
descriptions of Moses' heavenly journeys in the *Gedulat Mosheh*
belong to "the oldest extant Revelations."[7] Nevertheless, Scholem's
explorations have shown that skepticism about the early origins of
Merkabah and *Hekalot* mysticism is unwarranted. Furthermore
there are hints in a number of early sources, mentioned in this and

---

[1] *ARN*, version "A," chap. 2, p. 10; *Tanḥuma*, ed. Buber, III, 46; cf.
Philo, *Mos.* i.68f. According to Zohar ii, 198a (as quoted by Ginzberg, II,
316), Moses' continence made possible his union with the Shekinah, "that
she may descend upon earth for his sake." Cf. Philo's complicated notion of
Moses' (and the Patriarchs') union with Sophia, as interpreted by Goodenough, *By Light, Light*, pp. 22f., 157-160, 164, 201.

[2] *Major Trends*, p. 49. Compare the "121 fasts" which were necessary
before Moses ascended according to 3 Enoch, xvB.

[3] *Sifre Zuta*, 84, quoted by Ginzberg, III, 258; cf. Yalḳut Sim'oni, I, 483:
כל מה שבמעלה ושבמטה גליתי לו כל מה שבים וכל מה
שבחרבה, אף על מלאכי השרת ועל בת המקדש הוא נאמן.

[4] Above, p. 148.

[5] *Ḥag.* 2.1, trans. Danby, *The Mishnah*, p. 213.

[6] Scholem, *Major Trends*, p. 74.

[7] Gaster, *Studies and Texts*, I, 124.

the previous chapter, of heavenly journeys and revelations of Moses. There is no way of knowing how the early traditions may have pictured these journeys, but there is inherent probability that the descriptions would have had many points in common with those found in the medieval documents like *Gedulat Mosheh* and *3 Enoch*.

The medieval "revelations" show that Moses, like Enoch, Ezra, Baruch, Rabbi Akiba, Rabbi Joshua ben Levi, and others, was in some circles regarded as the pathfinder to the heavenly mysteries so ardently desired by mystical circles of Judaism. These documents present only the end-product of a development many centuries long. At the other end of the development are the tantalizing hints of Moses' ascent in early portions of the midrashim, in Josephus, in Pseudo-Philo, in Ezekiel the Tragedian, and above all the mystical function of Moses as hierophant in Philo. To these must be added the extraordinary paintings of Moses in the Dura synagogue, which undoubtedly implied some analogous function.[1] In between lies an unknown world, but enough has been seen to guess many of its contours.

The Ascent at the End of Moses' Life

There are many varied legends surrounding Moses' death, beginning with the biblical statement, "No man knows his grave."[2] The dominant traditions, following the biblical text, say that Moses died by the kiss of God and was mysteriously buried by God himself in an unknown grave. But even these sober traditions contain extraordinary elements. In particular Moses' contention with God to be permitted to live and his contest with Sammael are elaborately developed.[3] According to one view, Moses' request to see God's glory was finally granted him, for God revealed himself to Moses at the time of his death.[4]

On the other hand there is a persistent tradition that Moses did not die, but ascended to heaven. Thus *Yalkuṭ Šim'oni* preserves a statement from the older *Yelammedenu* midrash that God said to Moses "All creatures descend to Sheol, as it is said, 'All who descend

---

[1] Goodenough, *Jewish Symbols*, IX-XI.

[2] Cf. Schürer, III, 301f.; J. Jeremias, *ThWbNT*, IV, 858-860.

[3] See especially *Peṭirat Mosheh*, ed. Jellinek, I, 115-129, *passim*.

[4] *Debarim Zuṭa* (Salomon Buber, ed., [זוטא] לקוטים ממדרש אלה הדברים [Vienna: Druck von Löwy & Alkalay, 1885], p. 10, *Peṭirat Mosheh*, Jellinek, I, 128 (German trans. Wünsche, *Lehrhallen*, I, 161).

to silence' (Psalm 115.17), but you are to ascend, as it is said, 'Go up into this mountain of Abarim' (Numbers 27.12)."[1] Even the verse "And Moses died there" (Deuteronomy 34.5) is interpreted to mean that Moses ascended, for "in another place it is written 'he was *there* with the Lord' (Exodus 34.28). As in the one case he was standing and ministering on high, so in the other case he stands and ministers on high."[2] With good reason Ginzberg compares Moses' "ministering" (שמש) on high with the function of the "ministering angels."[3] Version "B" of *Abot de Rabbi Nathan* contains the statement "Moses our teacher was like a man, but thenceforth he is not, but is like the ministering angels. God has hidden him for the life of the age to come."[4] It is significant that the midrashic connection in the midrash on Deuteronomy 34.5 is with Moses' ascent on Sinai. To be sure the connection is very strained; one can only conclude that Moses' final ascension was already connected with his ascent on Sinai and that the exegetical connection by the coincidence of the word שם "there," was secondary. This accords with the general tendency already observed in non-rabbinic sources to regard the mystical ascent on Sinai as a foretaste of the final ascent to heaven.

There is also a tradition that Moses was "taken up by the wings of the *Shekina*" at the end of his life.[5] In its present form, the tradition says that the wings of the *Shekina* carried Moses only "four miles" from the "portion of Reuben" where he died to the "portion of Gad" where he was buried. But perhaps two traditions have merged here, for mention of the "wings of the *Shekina*" would more naturally fit an account of an ascent to heaven, as in the very similar passage in 3 *Enoch*:

> When the Holy One, blessed be He, took me away from the generation of the flood, he lifted me on the wings of the wind [or spirit?] of *Shekina* to the highest heaven and brought me into the great palaces of the *Araboth Raqia* on high, where are the glorious Throne of *Shekina*, the *Merkaba*, the troops of anger [etc.] ... And he placed me (there) to attend [שמש] the Throne of Glory day after day.[6]

---

[1] *Yalkuṭ Šim'oni*, III, 958.

[2] *Midrasch Tannaïm*, p. 224; so also *Sifre Dt.*, par. 357; Talm. B., *Sota* 13b; *Yalkuṭ Sim'oni*, I, 686 and 687.

[3] Ginzberg, V, 157.

[4] Ed. Schechter, p. 157.

[5] *Midrasch Tannaïm*, p. 219; Tosefta, *Soṭa* 4.8; Talm. B., *Sota* 13b.

[6] Odeberg, 3 *Enoch*, p. 22.

What has apparently happened in the Moses' haggada is that by combining the legend of Moses' ascent to heaven on the wings of the Shekina with the interpretation that Moses died in the portion of Reuben and was buried in the portion of Gad, the rabbis sought to render harmless a dangerous form of speculation. A similar intent might very well lie behind the story of God's vigorous rejection of Moses' plea to be allowed to live, which fills most of the *Peṭirat Mosheh*. There Deuteronomy 3.26 is interpreted thus: "The Holy One, blessed be He, said to him, 'Let it suffice you! If you remained alive then (others) would go astray because of you; they would make you a god and serve you.'"[1] This protest recalls the similar danger cited by Josephus.[2] Were there actually synagogues or groups of Jews for whom the ascended Moses became such a danger? Even Philo, for all the divine attributes he gave to Moses, was careful to maintain the distinction between him and God. Yet some of Philo's statements could have led a "normative" rabbi to issue a warning like that in Josephus or *Peṭirat Mosheh*, and ample evidence has been reviewed in this chapter for views preserved within rabbinic sources themselves that differed but little from Philo in the exaltation of Moses.

MOSES' ESCHATOLOGICAL ACTIVITY

Since the eschatological significance of the figure of Moses is the aspect of the Moses haggada most frequently discussed by scholars interested in New Testament problems, this aspect can be treated very briefly here.[3] In discussions of this subject the analogy drawn between Moses and the King-Messiah in later midrashim is particularly often emphasized. The most useful treatment is that by Bloch, who cites numerous passages in which it is said that the future deliverer(s) will repeat characteristic features of Moses' life and work.[4] A typical example is from the Midrash on Ecclesiastes 1.28:

---

[1] Jellinek, I, 118.

[2] *Antt.* iv.326; above, p. 141f.

[3] See especially Teeple, *Mosaic Prophet, passim,* and Bloch, "Quelques aspects," pp. 149-167. Also cf. J. Jeremias, *ThWbNT,* IV, 86off. Hahn makes no use of rabbinic sources in his appendix on the eschatological prophet, but gives a valuable survey of other material.

[4] "Quelques aspects," pp. 156-161.

R. Berekiah said in the name of R. Isaac: As the first redeemer was, so shall the latter Redeemer be. What is stated of the former redeemer? *And Moses took his wife and his sons, and set them upon an ass* (Ex. iv.20). Similarly will it be with the latter Redeemer, as it is stated, *Lowly and riding upon an ass* (Zech. ix.9). As the former redeemer caused manna to descend, as it is stated, *Behold, I will cause to rain bread from heaven for you* (Ex. xvi, 4), so will the latter Redeemer cause manna to descend, as it is stated, *May he be as a rich cornfield* [פסת read as פתם 'pieces of bread'] *in the land* (Ps. lxxii, 16). As the former redeemer made a well to rise, so will the latter Redeemer bring up water, as it is stated, *And a fountain shall come forth from the house of the Lord, and shall water the valley of Shittim* (Joel ix, 18).[1]

As Bloch points out, the passages which use Mosaic typology to describe the awaited King Messiah are never connected with Deuteronomy 18,[2] but with Exodus and Song of Songs. This is no longer so surprising, since it is now known on the basis of the Qumran texts that the eschatological *prophet* whose expectation was derived from Deuteronomy 18.18 was a figure quite distinct from the King Messiah.

More important in the rabbinic traditions themselves is the view that Moses will appear in the wilderness to lead the wilderness generation into the promised land. Thus the Palestinian Targumim on Deuteronomy 33.21 describe the marvelous cave prepared for Moses' burial, where he is to be hidden for his future task, for "as he went in and out at the head of the people in this world, so will he go in and out in the world to come."[3] In another place the verse "every valley will be raised up" (Isaiah 40.4) is interpreted eschatologically and applied to Moses, "for he was buried in a valley." "A voice crying in the wilderness" refers to God. As a man who lost a pearl searches for it where he lost it, so God, who lost Israel in the wilderness, goes and searches for it there.[4] Moses, who for the sake of the wilderness generation was himself buried in the wilderness, will arise and lead them.[5]

---

[1] Trans. L. Rabbinowitz, *Soncino Midrash*, VIII, 33.

[2] "Quelques aspects," p. 161; cf. J. Jeremias, *ThWbNT*, IV, 861, 864.

[3] Fragmentary targum, trans. Ethridge, II, 679; cf. Targ. Pseudo-Jonathan, *ibid*. The same tradition is found in *Sifre Dt.*, par. 355, p. 147a, and in *Midrasch Tannaïm*, p. 219.

[4] *Agadath Bereschith; Midraschische Auslegungen zum ersten Buche Mosis*, ed. Salomon Buber (Krakau: Verlag von Josef Fischer, 1902), par. 67, p. 133.

[5] *Tanḥuma*, ed. Buber, II, 7; IV, 121f.; *Bamidbar R.* 19.13; *Shemot R.* 2.4. See above, p. 203f. Cf. also *Midrash Tehillim* on Ps. 78 (ET, Braude, II, 28).

In the traditions just quoted, Moses' eschatological task is associated with the notion that he shared the death of the wilderness generation. Hence this view is not to be sought in the same circles which believed that Moses ascended to heaven at the end of his life. On the other hand, a late tradition recorded in Midrash Rabbah on Deuteronomy does apparently presuppose the ascension. Here God says, "Moses, I swear to you, as you devoted your life to their service in this world, so too in the time to come when I bring Elijah, the prophet, unto them, the two of you shall come together."[1] Here the eschatological role of Moses is assimilated to that of Elijah, to which, in this form, it is obviously secondary. This does not exclude the possibility that Moses' own ascension and eschatological return could have been originally independent of the Elijah expectation and as old.[2] In one tradition Moses will initiate the „new song" of praise in the world to come, as he conducted the song by the Sea of Reeds.[3] The antiquity of this tradition is attested by Revelation 15.3, which clearly presupposes a similar eschatological interpretation of "the Song of Moses." Still another tradition says that Moses will be Israel's teacher *par excellence* in the age to come, since he "learned the Torah from God himself."[4]

One final passage will help to clarify the possible relation between Moses' eschatological role and that of the King Messiah. The Fragmentary Targum of Palestine on Exodus 12.42 says:

> Four nights are there written in the Book of Memorial. Night first; when the Word of the Lord was revealed upon the world as it was created . . . Night second; when the Word of the Lord was revealed unto Abraham between the divided parts. . . . The third night; when the Word of the Lord was revealed upon the Mizraee, at the dividing of the night. . . . Night the fourth; when the end of the age will be accomplished, that it might be dissolved, the bands of wickedness destroyed, and the iron yoke broken. Mosheh [comes][5] forth from the midst of the desert; but the King Meshiha (comes) from the midst of Roma. The

---

[1] *Debarim R.* 3.17, trans. J. Rabbinowitz, *Soncino Midrash*, VII, 88. On the possible date of the tradition, cf. Teeple, *Mosaic Prophet*, p. 45.

[2] Cf. Hahn, p. 354.

[3] *Kohelet R.* 1.9 (ET: *Soncino Midrash*, VII, 31); cf. *Mekilta* on Ex. 15.1 (ed. Lauterbach, II, 1), where אז ישר משה is understood as a *future*, "then Moses will sing," and is used as a proof-text for the resurrection.

[4] *Shemot R.* 2.6 (ET: *Soncino Midrash*, III, 56f.).

[5] Ethridge translates "came," but the next sentence shows that a contemporaneous appearance of Moses and the King Messiah is meant.

Cloud [precedes][1] that one and the cloud will go before this one;
and the Word of the Lord will lead between both, and they
shall proceed together.[2]

The basic imagery is all Mosaic; the cloud preceding each figure
belongs to the Exodus tradition. But what is meant by the extraordinary emphasis on Moses and the King Messiah appearing and
proceeding *together*? With his usual acute insight Ginzberg paraphrases the last sentence, "The Word of God will *mediate* between
them, *causing them to walk with one accord in the same direction.*"[3]
This brings out what was very likely the intent of the passage: to
avoid any suggestion of a difference of rank or purpose between the
King Messiah and the awaited return of Moses himself "from the
wilderness." Probably then the Targum represents the blending and
harmonizing of two divergent eschatological traditions, one of which
fixes its hope on Moses, the other on a Messiah of David's line.

Conclusions

It has now become quite clear from rabbinic as well as non-
rabbinic sources, that in some circles of Judaism over an extended
period of time, from at least the second century B.C. until the
middle ages, Moses was regarded as Israel's ideal king as well as
prophet. In isolated traditions the two titles were found closely
connected, as the basic offices of Moses, and evidence was found
for a notion of a succession of prophetic kings continuing the
functions of Moses.

More frequently the traditions speak of Moses as either king or
prophet without any necessary connection with the other title.
Almost everywhere Moses was regarded as the supreme prophet of
Israel, the originator of all prophecy and the model for all subsequent prophets. Somewhat less extensive are the traditions that
Moses was the prototypal king of Israel; more often in the rabbinic
sources it is David who is the king *par excellence*. However there are
passages which clearly emphasize Moses' superiority to David,
which set David within the succession of rulers like Moses, and
which make Moses the ideal king of Israel. Moreover evidence has
been found in several places which suggests attempts to harmonize

---

[1] Ethridge, "preceded," cf. previous note.
[2] Trans. Ethridge, I, 48of.
[3] Ginzberg, II, 373, emphasis mine.

the Mosaic traditions with those exalting David as King or Aaron as High Priest, or an eschatological figure, the King Messiah or Elijah.

Both Moses' kingship and his prophetic office were found to be grounded in the idea that "Moses went up to God," that is, to heaven, where he received the Torah, was crowned king of Israel and thus God's vice-regent, and learned the secrets which made him teacher of all prophets. The traditions that Moses was king and prophet were connected with scriptural texts.

Deuteronomy 18.15 and 18 are not interpreted eschatologically in extant rabbinic sources. However, in some instances these verses are definitely connected with the notion of successors of Moses who like him act as Israel's prophets and kings.

Very extensive is the tradition that Moses was Israel's "defense attorney" without equal. Mostly this function was connected with his prophetic office, and occasionally with his designation "faithful shepherd" as well.

Some striking similarities were found between descriptions of Moses' ascent to heaven and the descriptions of "heavenly journeys" or mystic visions in apocalyptic and mystical literature. The elaborate accounts appear only in late sources, but there are numerous evidences in early traditions that some such view of Moses was prevalent in the early Christian centuries. In view of the similar findings in the non-rabbinic sources it can hardly be doubted that in New Testament times Moses was regarded by some Jews as one of the great prototypes of the mystic ascent to heaven. As such he seems to have been viewed as the mediator of heavenly secrets of all kinds, which were delivered to him when he went up from Sinai.

CHAPTER FIVE

MOSES AS KING AND PROPHET
IN SAMARITAN SOURCES

INTRODUCTION

Importance of the Samaritan sources

The figure of Moses dominates Samaritan religious literature to an extent scarcely equalled in any circle of Jewish tradition, with the possible exception of Philo. For this reason alone the Samaritan sources demand attention in the present investigation, but their significance is heightened by the fact that the Samaritan traditions, while springing from scriptural roots in large part common also to Judaism and shaped by many of the same environmental influences in Greco-Roman Palestine, yet developed in a distinct line little influenced, if at all, by the consolidation of "normative" Judaism. Furthermore, the eschatology of the Samaritans was certainly not Davidic,[1] a point of considerable importance in view of the absence of the Davidic traditions from the christology of the Fourth Gospel.

John Macdonald, who has attempted a systematic theology of Samaritanism, declares, "Any claim for Samaritan borrowing from Judaism is nonsense."[2] James A. Montgomery, nearly sixty years earlier, assumed the opposite position: "No intellectual independence is to be found in our sect; it was content to draw its teachings and stimulus from the Jews, even long after the rupture was final."[3] Against the latter view, Macdonald's reaction is perhaps justified, but the Samaritans and Jews were hardly so isolated from each other as he assumes. Both Montgomery and, recently, John Bowman have shown from the references in the Talmud that in the

---

[1] This point is illustrated by Hegisippus' list of the "sects" among "the circumcision" who opposed *"the tribe of Judah and the Messiah,* as follows: Essenes, Galileans, Hemerobaptists, Masbothei, *Samaritans,* Sadducees, and Pharisees" (*apud* Eusebius, *HE,* IV, xxii, 6, trans. Kirsopp Lake [Loeb], I, 377, emphasis mine).

[2] John Macdonald, *The Theology of the Samaritans* ("The New Testament Library"; London: SCM Press Ltd., 1964) [hereafter cited as *Theology*], p. 29, cf. p. 452.

[3] *The Samaritans: The Earliest Jewish Sect; Their History, Theology, and Literature* (Philadelphia: The John C. Winston Co., 1907), p. 205.

age of the Tannaim "in those places where both sects were found there existed very intimate intercourse between them in many most important matters of life."[1] Adalbert Merx,[2] Moses Gaster,[3] and John Bowman[4] have all collected parallels, some of them quite striking, between Rabbinic and Samaritan *haggadot*. Evidently the developing lines of Samaritan and Jewish traditions had more points of contact than the "common matrix" of Torah and pre-exilic traditions emphasized by Macdonald.[5] For present purposes interest lies only in certain specific features of the Samaritan tradition about Moses and about the eschatological redeemer. Where these coincide with certain Jewish traditions, often in such a way that Jewish and Samaritan versions help to explain one another, there is no reason a priori to exclude historical interaction.

The situation in Samaritan studies

Samaritan studies are still in their infancy, even on the basic levels of textual criticism and philology. A lexicon of Samaritan Aramaic is still wanting, and no comprehensive study of the dialect's grammar has been attempted since Petermann's brief and not very satisfactory work of 1873.[6] For many years after European scholars first made contact with modern Samaritans research depended upon letters from the Samaritans and impressions gathered by visits to Samaritan villages.[7] The collection and critical evaluation of manuscripts have proceeded slowly, and even today very much remains to be done. Macdonald's critical edition of the *Memar Marqah*,

---

[1] *Ibid.*, p. 174, cf. John Bowman, *BJRL*, 40, 298.

[2] *Der Messias oder Ta'eb der Samaritaner* (BZAW, XVII; 1909) [hereafter cited as *Ta'eb*], 92 pp.

[3] *The Samaritan Oral Law and Ancient Traditions*, Vol. I: *The Samaritan Eschatology* ([London:] The Search Publishing Company, 1932), 277 pp. [hereafter referred to as *Eschatology*]; *The Asatir; The Samaritan Book of the "Secrets of Moses"; Together with the Pitron or Samaritan Commentary and the Samaritan Story of the Death of Moses* ("Oriental Translation Fund," n.s., XXVI; London: The Royal Asiatic Society, 1957), 352+59 pp. (henceforth: *Asatir*).

[4] "The Exegesis of the Pentateuch among the Samaritans and among the Rabbis," *Oudtestamentische Studien*, ed. P. A. H. DeBoer, vol. VIII (Leiden: E. J. Brill, 1950), pp. 230-262.

[5] Macdonald, *Theology*, p. 29.

[6] Cf. Franz Rosenthal, *Die aramäische Forschung seit Th. Nöldeke's Veröffentlichungen* (Leiden: E. J. Brill, 1939), pp. 133-143, especially p. 137: "Grammatik und Lexikon bleiben aber hier dringlichste Desiderate . . ."

[7] Cf. Montgomery, pp. 1-12.

published only last year, marks a new phase in this area. A series of doctoral dissertations completed at Leeds University, so far unfortunately unpublished, have undertaken comparative studies and English translations of parts of the Samaritan Liturgy,[1] a critical text of which was published by Cowley fifty-five years ago.[2] A new critical text of the Samaritan targum is being prepared by José Ramon Díaz.[3] The interpretation of these sources, it is fair to say, has hardly begun.

The place of Samaritanism within the history of religions remains very much unsettled. Because of Simon Magus' origin in Samaria, and especially because of Justin's statement that "almost all" his countrymen had become adherents of Simon,[4] it has long been assumed that the Samaritans were intimately involved in the early development of Palestinian Gnosticism. Most recently Geo Widengren has pointed out the extensive overlapping of technical terminology in the Samaritan liturgies and in the patristic reports about Simon and Dositheos.[5] Yet Macdonald insists repeatedly that the Samaritan circles which produced the extant literature were influenced only by the terminology, not by the substance, of gnostic thought.[6] Similarly the relation between Samaritan traditions and those of Christianity and Islam remains largely unclarified. For example, Hugo Odeberg proposed with some cogency that Samaritan concepts had influenced the formulation of parts of the Fourth Gospel,[7] a hypothesis renewed by John Bowman.[8] Yet Macdonald argues that the earliest extant Samaritan sources show direct borrowings from Christianity, particularly from the Fourth Gospel, so that the Samaritan description of Moses is shaped in part by Christology.[9] These opposing claims will have to be evaluated in specific instances below.

---

[1] See the bibliography in Macdonald, *Theology*, pp. 460f., and *Publications and Titles of Theses* (Leeds: Leeds University) since 1954.

[2] Arthur E. Cowley, *The Samaritan Liturgy* (cited above).

[3] Cf. Paul Kahle, *The Cairo Geniza* (2d ed.; Oxford: B. H. Blackwell, 1959), p. 53.

[4] *Apol.* I, 26.3.

[5] *The Ascension of the Apostle and the Heavenly Book*, Vol. III of *King and Saviour* ("Uppsala Universitets Arsskrift," VII; Uppsala: A. B. Lundequistska Bokhandeln, 1950), pp. 48-51. Cf. also Rudolf, *Mandäer*, I, 121, 217.

[6] Macdonald, *Theology*, p. 72, cf. pp. 118, 123, 164, 166, 477, *et passim*.

[7] Odeberg, *Fourth Gospel*, pp. 171-190.

[8] *BJRL*, 40, pp. 299, 310f.

[9] *Theology*, chap. xxii *et passim*.

From this brief survey it is evident that Samaritanism before the fourth century A.D. remains largely in the dark. Only long and painstaking labor in the history of traditions and in comparative studies can illuminate the period. Given the present state of critical tools, an investigator who is not a Samaritan specialist must be content with very tentative results. Nevertheless an attempt to trace the internal connections of a few specific points and to compare these points with the Jewish traditions of Moses which have emerged so far may not be unfruitful.

The sources

So far as possible this investigation has been founded on the earliest sources. Unfortunately even the earliest sources do not lead directly to a point much earlier than the fourth century A.D., when a major literary revival and re-constitution of Samaritan life and thought took place.[1] At that time the *Memar Marqah*[2] and a large part of the *Defter*, the oldest portion of the Liturgy,[3] were composed. The Targum[4] may have been composed at that time as well, although possibly it stems from a much earlier period. In any case the Targum is a quite literal translation, so that it offers few of the clues to midrashic starting points often discernible in the Jewish Palestinian Targum. More important are the passages in which the text of the Samaritan Pentateuch itself, and of course the Targum with it, differs significantly from the Masoretic text. Several of these passages, which presumably go back to a very early date, have dogmatic significance. In addition, one of the Hellenistic "Jewish" authors quoted by Eusebius, a certain Theodotus, was evidently a Samaritan, for the passages preserved by Eusebius glorify the "holy

---

[1] Cowley, II, xx; Macdonald, *Theology*, pp. 36f., 447; T. H. Gaster, "Samaritans," *The Interpreter's Dictionary of the Bible* (New York: Abington Press, 1962), IV, 196.

[2] John Macdonald, ed. and trans., *Memar Marqah*; *The Teaching of Marqah* (BZAW, LXXXIV; 1963), 2 vols.

[3] Cowley, I, 3-92.

[4] The only edition of the Targum based on more than one MS is that published under the (misleading) title *Pentateuchus Samaritanus*, ed. H. Petermann [Gen. and Ex.] and K. Vollers [Lev.-Dt] (Berlin: W. Moeser, 1872-93), 5 fascicles. The text is very unreliable (cf. Rosenthal, pp. 137f.). Since only the first fascicle (Gen.) was accessible to me, I have used the reprint of the old Polyglot text, transcribed into square characters by Adolf Brüll, ed., *Das samaritanische Targum* (Frankfurt a/M: Verlag von Wilhelm Erras, 1875), 248+18pp.

city" Shechem.[1] Unfortunately Theodotus offers nothing relevant to the present study.

Some use has been made of medieval sources, particularly (1) the *Asatir*, whose date is uncertain but doubtless nearer the twelfth or thirteenth century A.D. suggested by T. H. Gaster[2] than to the third century B.C. proposed by Gaster's father;[3] (2) the "Book of Joshua," fourteenth century chronicle published in an Arabic version in 1848, later discovered and published in Samaritan Hebrew (the English translation of the Arabic has been used here);[4] (3) the eschatological hymns in the Atonement Day service which were explored by Adalbert Merx.[5] While these sources were all composed between the twelfth and fourteenth centuries, they undoubtedly contain older traditions, and in some cases they provide clues which help in outlining the development of a particular strand of tradition.

MOSES THE GREAT PROPHET

Common Titles

Most frequently the Samaritan sources refer to Moses as "the great prophet Moses" (נביא רבה משה). Very often he is called "the faithful prophet" (נביא מהימן or נאמן),[6] or "the prophet who was entrusted" (with the Torah, with secrets, with "the unseen," but often used absolutely).[7] Of virtually the same signification are the

---

[1] Schürer, III, 499f.; apparently it is Theodotus whom T. H. Gaster has in mind when he speaks of "a Greek poem on Gerizim" without further identification (*IDB*, IV, 196). Gaster, like B. W. Bacon (*Gospel of the Hellenists*, p. 83), thinks Eupolemus was a Samaritan, but this is improbable, for Eupolemus includes David and Solomon in his account and speaks positively of the Jerusalem temple. Gaster's identification of Ezekiel the Tragedian as a Samaritan is possible, but has no positive support.

[2] *IDB*, IV, 196.

[3] *Asatir*, p. 65. Cf. also the criticism of the elder Gaster's method by Rappaport, *Agada und Exegese*, xi-xii, n. 3.

[4] Oliver Turnbul Crane, trans., *The Samaritan Chronicle or the Book of Joshua the Son of Nun* (New York: John B. Alden, 1890), 178pp. [cited henceforth as *Sam. Josh.*].

[5] *Ta'eb, passim.*

[6] E.g., *Memar Marqah*, ii.10 (ET, p. 77); iv.9 (ET: p. 170); *ibid.* (p. 171); iv.10 (ET: p. 175); Cowley, I, 36, 'מ; 53, 'א, 'ח; 81, 1.4; 84, 11.23, 25.

[7] E.g., Cowley, I, 50, 'ד, 'ה; 60, 'מ; cf. I, 38 (the *Durran*, 'א).

titles "true prophet" (נביא קשיט, נביא אמת)[1] and "righteous prophet" (נביא צדיק).[2]

Other titles emphasize Moses' uniqueness as mediator between God and men;

> This is the prophet whose prophethood is a treasure [סימי] which will not be removed from him as long as the world lasts—the father of wonders, the store [כרי] of miracles, the companion of the covenants, the light of the two worlds, the sun of prophethood, like whom there is no prophet from the whole human race.[3]

He is the "treasure of prophethood" (כרי נבייתה),[4] "master of the prophets" (רבון דנבייה),[5] "seal of the prophets" (מחתם נבייה),[6] the "sea of prophethood" (ים דנבייתה).[7] The last metaphor is explained in another passage: "His prophethood was like the surrounding sea, for from it seventy prophets prophesied without any diminishing of it."[8] In various ways all these terms express Moses' unique status among all prophets. In comparison to Moses, to whom all secrets were revealed, other prophets have only derivative and partial messages. The same view of Moses' relation to other prophets was found in the Jewish midrashim, where Moses was described as "the first of the prophets," "the teacher of the prophets," and similar titles.[9]

In the Jewish haggada, Moses' preeminence among the prophets involved his status at the beginning of a succession of prophets who, in a diminished and secondary measure, carried on his prophetic function. In the Samaritan sources, on the other hand, some passages seem to exclude the possibility of such a succession. Again and again in *Memar Marqah* and in the liturgy Deuteronomy 34.10 is paraphrased in an exclusive sense: "Who can compare with

---

[1] E.g., Cowley, I, 38, last line; 56, 'ד; 59, 'ג; *Memar Marqah*, iv.8 (ET: p. 162). Widengren, *Ascension*, pp. 55f., calls attention to the importance of this term in the Pseudo-Clementine writings and its equivalent, "true Apostle," in Mandaean literature.

[2] *Memar Marqah*, ii.10 (ET: p. 77); iv.8 (ET: p. 166); 9 (ET: p. 170); Cowley, I, 4.

[3] *Memar Marqah*, vi.9, trans. Macdonald, p. 240.

[4] *Ibid.*, v.3 (text, p. 123).

[5] *Ibid.*, and Cowley, I, 13, 'ט and 15.

[6] *Memar Marqah*, v.3 (text, p. 123).

[7] *Ibid.*, ii.3 (ET: p. 51).

[8] *Ibid.*, ii.12, trans. Macdonald, p. 82.

[9] Above, pp. 198-200.

Moses the prophet, the like of whom has not arisen and *never will arise?*" Markah urges, "Let us therefore not listen to anyone but him, for it is death to disobey him and judgement too to bring it to nought," and asks, "Who can succeed him?"[1] The death of Moses brought an end to the unique gifts which had enriched Israel's life:

> The pillar of cloud which went before him has been removed and will not be seen ever again. The pillar of fire which shone by night and day will not appear ever again.
> The Manna which descended from heaven through him at God's command has been cut off and will no more descend after his passing.
> The shining light which abode on his face is with him in his tomb. It will not abide ever again on another's face.
> The prophethood [נביותה] with which he was vested, of which he was worthy, has been hidden away and no man will ever again be vested with it.[2]

There are hints here and there in the sources of a tradition in which Moses may have been the *end* rather than the beginning of a succession of prophets, which would have begun with Adam. In *Memar Marqah*, for example, is found a list of seven "first fruits" or "choice things":[3] "the light, the Sabbath, Mount Gerizim, Adam, the two stone tablets, the great prophet Moses, and Israel."[4] Not only are Moses and Adam conspicuous as the only *persons* in the list, Adam is described as "the most special [דמע] of all creatures, for from him prophets and righteous men arise in the world," while Moses is called "a special one [דמע] who magnifies every special thing [דמע]."[5] Again Markah can vary the usual formula of Moses' greatness to read, "Great is this prophet the like of whom has not arisen *since* [or, from] *Adam* and never will arise."[6] The comparison between Adam and Moses is very frequent in the sources. Moses' leadership of the Exodus and delivery of the Torah are regarded by Markah as a renewal of creation[7] and a re-opening of the Garden of Eden.[8]

---

[1] *Memar Marqah*, iv.10, trans. Macdonald, p. 175.

[2] *Ibid.*, v.4, trans. Macdonald, p. 207.

[3] "First fruit" seems the best translation of דמע in this context, as in Talmudic Aramaic. Macdonald renders the word "special," "best thing."

[4] *Memar Marqah*, ii.10, trans. Macdonald, p. 73.

[5] *Ibid.*, p. 74.

[6] *Ibid.*, iv.2, trans. Macdonald, p. 139, emphasis mine.

[7] *Ibid.*; cf. Bowman's discussion in *Oudtestamentische Studiën*, VIII, 231, 248.

[8] *Memar Marqah*, ii.2 (ET: p. 47).

The *Asatir* relates that "the rod of Adam and his clothes were given to Moses" when he was commissioned,[1] a tradition which may be ancient, since it coincides with Jewish traditions attested in the Palestinian Targum and elsewhere.[2] Very likely related to this tradition is the notion, appearing in some late sources, that "a drop of light" was transmitted through a succession of righteous descendants of Adam, culminating in the purest manifestation of this light in Moses.[3] In passages like these Moses is depicted apparently as the new Adam, the ultimate prophet, after whom there could never be another prophet for the Samaritans.[4]

The view that Moses was the last prophet accords poorly with the fact that Deuteronomy 18.18, the promise of a future prophet like Moses, apparently lies at the foundation of Samaritan eschatology from early times.[5] Three solutions to the anomaly are possible: (1) the statements which make Moses the final prophet may represent a non-eschatological or even anti-eschatological circle of Samaritanism;[6] (2) the statements that no prophet like Moses "will ever arise" are not to be taken literally since the eschatological era would be excepted from such a statement; or (3) no prophet *like* Moses but Moses himself was expected at the end of days. There is evidence to support the third possibility, but there is also evidence that some traditions did in fact speak of successors to Moses. The question must be deferred until the matter of kingship and the position of Joshua in Samaritan tradition are discussed below.

Characteristics of Moses' Prophetic Function

For the Samaritans Moses' prophetic office consisted in the revelation of heavenly secrets through him. Markah has God say to Moses, "Were it not for your prophethood, I would not have

---

[1] *Asatir*, ix.22, trans. M. Gaster, p. 280; cf. iii.25; ix.32; xii.24.

[2] Cf. Diaz, *Novum Testamentum*, 6, p. 78. Also the sources cited by M. Gaster, *Asatir*, p. 280, and Bowman, *BJRL*, 40, pp. 303f.

[3] Montgomery, p. 228; cf. Macdonald, *Theology*, pp. 165-172. The similarity between this notion and that of the "true prophet" in the Pseudo-Clementines is striking.

[4] Montgomery took this to be the general view of Samaritanism (p. 229).

[5] Below, pp. 250-254.

[6] Bowman has advanced the hypothesis that conservative, priestly circles resisted the "sectarian" doctrine of the Taheb until possibly as late as the 14th century ("The Importance of Samaritan Researches," *ALUOS*, I [1959], 49f., cf. 46).

revealed myself, and my voice would not have been heard as long as the world lasts."[1] Moses owed his unique status above other mortals to the fact that "mysteries were unravelled for him into revelations; the creations exulted at him."[2] He is compared with "water from the Euphrates containing mysteries,"[3] to him "his Lord revealed what He had never before revealed to any man."[4] The fourteenth century *Book of Joshua*, describing the investiture of Joshua as Moses' successor, tells that God commanded Moses to deliver to Joshua "information of the profound secret, and reveal to him the vision of his dream and the science of knowledge, as much as he was capable of bearing . . . and that he should also inform him of the Name, by which he should put to flight hostile armies. . ."[5]

The things which were revealed to Moses are described as "wonders and miracles," "mysteries new and old."[6] Included in the first instance was the Torah itself, "tablets containing life for the generations."[7] The Torah is frequently called "life" or by terms symbolic of life, as in this poem from the *Defter*:

Glorious is the prophet who was clothed with your divine name;
He honored your greatness with exalted glories.
Your glorious handwriting he received in greatness, the great scripture which was from the days of creation [or, of the Covenant: בריתה]
To the world you revealed life by the hand of Moses; to his right hand you handed over life from your right hand.
Apart from Moses there is no man descended from [or, since] Adam
who received from his Lord choice water and choice fire.[8]

---

[1] *Memar Marqah*, i.9, trans. Macdonald, p. 32.

[2] *Ibid.*, ii.9, trans. Macdonald, p. 71.

[3] *Ibid.*, ii.12, trans. Macdonald, p. 82. Cf. vi.3 (ET: pp. 223f.), where Moses is compared with "Euphrates," "Tree of life," "Eden", metaphors which are usually reserved for the Torah itself. Cf. the hymn of Marḳah in *Defter*, Cowley, I, 23f. (German trans.: Paul Kahle, "Die zwölf Marka-Hymnen aus dem 'Defter' der Samaritanischen Liturgie," *Opera Minora*; *Festgabe zum* 21. *Januar* 1956 [Leiden: E. J. Brill, 1956], pp. 203-205).

[4] *Memar Marqah*, iv.1, trans. Macdonald, p. 135.

[5] Chap. ii, trans. Crane, p. 16.

[6] *Memar Marqah*, ii.9; cf. i.1; echoed in the 12th (?) century poem by Ab-Gelugah in the *Defter*, Cowley, I, 77, ll.17-19.

[7] *Memar Marqah*, iv.3, trans. Macdonald, p. 144.

[8] Cowley, I, 33, strophes מ׳-ר׳. John Macdonald, "The Theological Hymns of Amram Darah," *ALUOS*, II (1961), 70-72, gives a translation which differs in several details from mine. One instance, "to his left" for לימינה is evidently just a slip; cf. also Widengren, *Ascension*, p. 43. Macdonald thinks

But the "mysteries old and new" included also secret lore, for Moses saw "the unseen world," including all the angels which were "assembled before him" when he ascended on Sinai,[1] and the secrets which he received and made known included cosmological and eschatological mysteries:

> The great glory honoured him; the light before him lit up the darkness and it was dispelled before it and the wind bore it away. His place was opened up for him. The deep darkness confronted him. He stood at the very foundations of the Creation and he knew its mystery. He disclosed it to all the generations.[2]

His knowledge embraces all time:

> None has arisen or ever will arise like Moses!
> His span includes the knowledge of the Beginning [בראשית] and it goes on to the Day of Vengeance.[3]

The passage just quoted summarizes Markah's midrash on the Song of Moses, Deuteronomy 32, which occupies his fourth book. There he demonstrated that the Song speaks of both Creation and the Day of Vengeance. The secrets made known through Moses, then, include the knowledge of creation's mysteries and the secrets of the end of days, all concealed in the Torah but discernible through midrashic interpretation. A very similar view was found in diverse circles of Judaism.

Principally the secrets are communicated and the "life" made available to the Samaritans, but there is also a universalistic strain in the traditions about Moses' prophetic office. Markah can call him "the illuminer of the whole house of Adam,"[4] and Ab-gelugah (twelfth century) names him "the prophet of the world."[5] Potentially therefore the truth possessed by the Samaritans because of Moses' revelations was intended for the restoration of all mankind.[6]

---

the prayer, attributed in the Arabic rubric to Markah, is by Amram Darah of the fourth century, but Cowley (II, lxxvii) thinks it is probably by Eleazar (b. Pinhas, 14th century).

[1] See below.

[2] *Memar Marqah*, iv.3, trans. Macdonald, p. 143.

[3] *Ibid.*, v.1, trans. Macdonald, p. 193; cf. Macdonald, *Theology*, pp. 180, 184.

[4] *Memar Marqah*, i.2.

[5] Cowley, I, 77, 1:17.

[6] Macdonald tries to connect this understanding of Moses' prophecy with a view that Moses was the Logos: ". . . The Samaritans emphasize an aspect

At one point the extant Samaritan traditions are unanimous: the moment at which the revelations to Moses occurred was at Sinai, when Moses ascended into heaven and joined the angelic assembly:

> When He said, *Moses, Moses*, it was as though He were saying to him, "You are the harbinger in the world of glorious life." "It is your greatness, Moses, above all men, that you are entrusted with secret things ancient and new," preserved by the Proclaimer of Good, and laid out before him on the top of Mount Sinai.[1]

It was the experience on Sinai that established Moses as the prophet-revealer who could never be equaled. Other aspects of the Sinai ascension must be considered below.

MOSES THE APOSTLE OF GOD

In the *Memar Marqah* and in late portions of the *Defter* Moses is occasionally referred to as the "Apostle" (שליח) of God.[2] The basis

of the *nabi* (prophet) which receives less emphasis in the other religions. The prophet is the *spokesman* of God, who knows at first hand the divine will. It is obvious that this definition of prophecy is based on the nature of Moses, and therefore it could not be applied to persons like Zephaniah, Isaiah, etc. It is Moses' Logos role *in the world* that makes him prophet of the world" (*Theology*, pp. 205f., italics original). This is a curiously confused argument. In the first place the statement that the Samaritans are virtually alone in emphasizing that the prophet is "the spokesman of God" is clearly incorrect. Not only is this the fundamental OT view of the prophets, but Fascher's monograph demonstrated that it was central to the Greek understanding of prophecy from Homer to Hellenistic times. Second, Macdonald admits (p. 174) that it was not until the 14th century that the notion of Moses as "the Word" was explicitly stated "although from the evidence supplied by Markah the notion was at least implicit in the thought of his day." It is hard to come to grips with ideas that are only supposed to be "implicit in the thought" of authors who never expressed these notions in words– particularly in documents 1600 years old. Moreover, "the word" by which God is said to have created the world in most of the passages Macdonald refers to, seems to me from the context to be simply the יהי, "let there be . . .," of Gen. 1. Unfortunately, Macdonald has paid all too little attention to the midrashic character of the *Memar Marqah*; without careful analysis of the scriptural basis or point of connection of each homily, many statements of the *Memar*– as of any midrash– remain unintelligible.

[1] *Memar Marqah*, i.1, trans. Macdonald, p. 4.

[2] *Ibid.*, i.9 (ET: p. 32); v.3 (ET: p. 201); vi.3 (ET: p. 223); vi. 7 ("chosen for apostleship" [שליחותה] ET: p. 233); Cowley, I, 82, 1.28 (probably Pinḥas b. Joseph, 14th century); 81, 1.15 (Muslim b. Murjan, 18th century). Macdonald's translation of the *Memar Marqah* also uses "apostle" of Moses in ii.5, p. 54, possibly on the basis of the Arabic version. The Aramaic reads מתבחר, "chosen one."

for this title was already present in the Torah, in passages like Exodus 3.13 and 4.28, as Widengren points out.[1] Markah connects Moses' apostleship with his ascension: "O great prophet Moses, whom God specially chose for apostleship, he opened before you the gateway to the unseen."[2] Furthermore, "apostleship" and "prophecy" are closely connected. *Memar Marqah* v.3 calls Moses "apostle of God" in a poem in which three parallel verses call him "seal of the prophets" and "the great prophet Moses." In another passage Markah says:

> This is a true prophet sent from God [אה נביא קשט משגר מדילה דאלה] Blessed are they who believe in him.[3] Let us love him[3] and keep his[3] commandments, that our Lord may love us and send us deliverance.[4]

The last passage uses שגר (pa'el) instead of שלח, but the meaning is the same: the "true prophet" is God's representative; response to the prophet is response to God.

Widengren thinks that this concept of God's representative, the שליח, belongs originally to the Babylonian "pattern" of divine kingship.[5] Whether or not this is the case, the specific words for "sending" and "the sent one" are used in the Samaritan sources in connection with Moses' prophetic function. Apart from the notion of "sending," there are some more clearly royal elements in the Samaritan description of Moses as God's vice-regent, which will be discussed in the next section. The parallel to the Fourth Gospel's characterization of Jesus as "the one sent from God" (ὁ ἀπεσταλμένος) and "truly the prophet coming into the world" (John 6.14) will be explored further in Chapter VII.

MOSES AS KING

Rarity of Title

Moses is almost never called "king" in the Samaritan sources consulted for this investigation. For the Samaritans, as for virtually

---

[1] *Ascension*, p. 31.

[2] *Memar Marqah*, vi.7, trans. Macdonald, p. 233.

[3] Macdonald capitalizes these pronouns, but the passage is more coherent if they are understood as referring to Moses rather than God. The underlying notion is that by "believing in" Moses, "the true prophet," the Samaritans are being faithful to God. To believe in Moses is to believe in God (see below).

[4] *Memar Marqah*, iv.8, trans. Macdonald, p. 162.

[5] *Ascension*, pp. 31, 47, *et passim*.

every circle and age of Judaism, God is the king *par excellence*. In the *Defter* God is regularly called "the great King" and Moses, "the great prophet." For example an anonymous poem in praise of the Sabbath begins and ends with an ascription to God, and the last line adds Moses:

> Peace to the Great King and peace to the Scripture and peace to the Seventh Day, greatest of the festivals
> Peace to the Great King and to the Prophet who prophesied it [the Sabbath commandment], and to this great day which he called by the name 'Sabbath.'[1]

However, the theocratic notion certainly does not exclude human kingship, and Samaritan traditions do speak of Joseph and of Joshua as kings.

Joseph and Joshua as Kings

In fourth century sources, references to Joseph's kingship are frequent. In Marḳah's paraphrase of Exodus 3.7 God says to Moses, "Surely I know about the anguish. The crown of Joseph is cast away and there is none to inherit it."[2] The kingdom of Joseph is the kingdom to which the Samaritans belong:

> We are the descendants of Joseph following trial. Shall we leave his kingdom? That would not be right![3]

Among the tribes which were blessed on Mount Gerizim (Deuteronomy 27) were "Joseph and Benjamin who were made great with the crown of kingship."[4] Jacob was glorified because he was buried by "Joseph the king," just as Aaron was glorified by being buried by Eleazar and by "the great prophet Moses" and Moses because he was buried by God himself.[5] In lists of the righteous forebears,

---

[1] Cowley, I, 74, ll.7 and 30. Macdonald (*Theology*, p. 427) states that in one instance the title "the great king" is given to Moses, but I am unable to discover the passage. It is *not*, as he says, in the Dream of Abisha printed by Cowley, I, 366f.

[2] *Memar Marqah*, i.2, trans. Macdonald. p. 6.

[3] *Ibid*., iv.6, trans. Macdonald, p. 157.

[4] *Ibid*., iii.3, trans. Macdonald, p. 94.

[5] *Ibid*., v.4, trans. Macdonald, p. 208. The tradition is very similar to that found in *Tanḥuma* [3d recension], Beshallaḥ 2, in which significantly both Joseph and Moses are called kings. Cf. Mishnah, *Soṭah* 1.9 and above, pp. 156f.

Joseph is characterized as "the king,"[1] or "the king, the freed one."[2] Again he is eulogized in the words, "O Joseph the king who was vested with freedom,"[3] and Markah says, in a passage that compares Joseph with both Moses and the Taheb, "Joseph came; so he was recompensed with a kingdom after servitude and those who had oppressed him sought his favour."[4]

From the last three passages, which connect Joseph's kingship with his having been "set free," the scriptural basis of the tradition becomes clear. The reference is to Joseph's liberation from prison in Egypt and his appointment as Pharaoh's vice-regent (Genesis 41), which is interpreted as kingship. But why should this modification of the Joseph story have taken on such significance for the Samaritans?

Adalbert Merx held that the kingdom of Joseph was emphasized because it was from Joseph's tribe that the Taheb was to come, who, in Merx's view, would be a *Joshua redivivus*.[5] Now it is true that the fourteenth century chronicle "The Book of Joshua" regularly calls Joshua "the king," never "prophet," while it calls Moses only "the prophet," never "king."[6] Joshua is the first of a succession of kings constituting the "First Kingdom."[7] To this "First Kingdom," presumably, corresponds the "Second Kingdom" which is to be initiated by the Taheb. Furthermore Merx quotes some passages in late sources which speak of the Taheb as "Joshua." An evaluation of Merx's argument must await the section below on the Taheb. In the meantime, it can be shown that the emphasis on Joseph's kingship in the early sources can be more readily explained on another basis than eschatological typology.

The fact that Joseph's kingship is linked with his liberation suggests that in these traditions "Joseph" is an eponym or type for the Israelite nation, that is, the Samaritans, who could speak of themselves, in distinction from the Jews, as the descendants of Joseph or Ephraim. The liberation of Joseph was a prototype of the

---

[1] *Memar Marqah*, iv.10 (ET: p. 174).

[2] יוסף מלכה חורה in the *Durran* of Amram Darah (4th century), strophe ט' Cowley, I, 42, l.12.

[3] *Memar Marqah*, i.10, trans. Macdonald, p. 41.

[4] *Ibid.*, iv.12, trans. Macdonald, p. 185.

[5] *Ta'eb*, pp. 41, 43, 49.

[6] In Crane, pp. 16, 35, 38, 45, 46, 50, 53, 54, 55, 57, 58, 59, *et passim*.

[7] *Sam. Josh.*, chaps. ii, xxxix; Crane, pp. 15-18, 99-101. Cf. Macdonald, *Theology*, pp. 14, 16f., who draws a similar description from the earlier, as yet unpublished, "Chronicle II."

liberation from Egypt. This line of interpretation is supported by several passages, based on Exodus 19.6,[1] which speak of all the Samaritans as kings, whose kingdom began with the Exodus.[2] Thus when the firstborn of the Egyptians, including their gods,[3] were destroyed, "the kingdom of Ham came then to an end, while the kingdom of Shem then began."[4] And Exodus 15.14, "The peoples have heard, they tremble," is interpreted by Marḳah:

> This is a true prophecy from the mind of God by which He was magnified. True is the great prophet Moses in what he said. The kingdom of Israel has now been created.[5]

From these passages it is apparent that in Marḳah's view it was Moses who restored the kingdom of Joseph through the Exodus,[6] not Joshua. Moses and Joseph are associated in two significant passages in the *Memar Marqah*. The first states that "two were coupled together" because each "inhabited a place," Joseph the place of his father and Moses the place of his Lord.[7] Oddly this statement is one of the two midrashim comparing *two* figures in a chapter constructed as a series of lists of *three*. Perhaps there is some relation to the tradition quoted by Moses Gaster from his manuscript of the *Book of Joshua* which compares "three pious [righteous]: Abraham, Isaac and Jacob"—the same three who precede Moses and Joseph in the Memar—with "three kings," Joseph, Joshua, and the Taheb.[8] At any rate, another midrash in *Memar Marqah* connects Moses, Joseph, *and* the Taheb, each of whom is said to "reign":

> The Taheb will come in peace to repossess [rather, "to reign over": וימלך] the place which God chose for these good people. Joseph came; so he was recompensed with a kingdom after servitude and those who had oppressed him sought his favour. . . Where is there the like of Joseph, illumined, wise, possessing the spirit of God. He possessed ["was king in": מלך] the place. Therefore his bones were borne by a prophet who was the faithful one of his Lord's house. There is none like Joseph the king and there is none like Moses the prophet. Each of them

---

[1] As shown by *Memar Marqah*, v.2 (ET: p. 198).
[2] *Ibid.*, ii.2 (ET: p. 47); ii.3 (ET: p. 52).
[3] Cf. Targ. Pseudo-Jonathan on Ex. 12.12.
[4] *Memar Marqah*, i.9, trans. Macdonald, p. 37.
[5] *Ibid.*, ii.9, trans. Macdonald, p. 70.
[6] This is also evident in the call of Moses, *ibid.*, i.2, quoted above.
[7] *Ibid.*, iv.9, trans. Macdonald, p. 169.
[8] *Studies and Texts*, I, 647.

possessed high status [דרג; תריין מלכו דרגין רמין] can also mean "throne"]; Moses possessed [מלך] prophethood, Joseph possessed [מלך] the Goodly Mount. There is none greater than either of them.[1]

Furthermore, in the *Memar Marqah* Joshua is only Moses' disciple and successor (חליף),[2] and even in the "Book of Joshua" itself when Joshua's investiture with "kingly authority" is described it is made clear that Joshua receives this office not by virtue of his connection to Joseph, but because he is Moses' *ḥalîph*.[3] In the fourth century, therefore, so far as extant sources can show, mention of Joseph's kingship did not connote a kingship initiated by Joshua, but a kingship which belonged to all Israel (Samaritans), lost in Egypt but restored by Moses.

Deuteronomy 33.5

In Chapter IV above evidence was produced to show that in certain circles of Judaism Deuteronomy 33.5 was interpreted as referring to Moses, who was made king when "the heads of the people assembled" on Sinai. In his wide-ranging study of Samaritan eschatology, Moses Gaster indicated that the same was true of Samaritan tradition: "The first king, according to Samaritan tradition, was Moses, for he is the one who is mentioned in Deut. xxxiii.5, 'and he was king in Jeshurun.'"[4] Unfortunately Gaster did not reveal his evidence for this conclusion, and the early sources offer no direct support for it. The Samaritan Targum on the verse is a literal translation of the Hebrew and is equally ambiguous;

---

[1] *Memar Marqah*, iv.12, trans. Macdonald, pp. 185f. Cf. Bowman's translation of the last sentence, "There is no king like Joseph and no prophet like Moses, Moses is king of the prophets and Joseph king of the blessed mountain" (*Oudtestamentische Studiën*, VIII, 247).

[2] *Ibid.*, iii.10 (ET: pp. 126, 127); v. 2 (ET: p. 195).

[3] *Sam. Josh.*, chap. ii, Crane, pp. 15-18; Crane says of the term חליף, "successor," "This is strictly a Mohammedan term ..." (p. 135, n. 2). But *Memar Marqah*, in pre-Islamic times, already says of Joshua, "He [*sc.* Moses] appointed him his successor" (אקימה חליפתה, iii.10). The similarity between the account in *Sam. Josh.* of Joshua's enthronement and that in *Peṭirat Mosheh* (quoted above, pp. 179-181 is noteworthy, although the Samaritan account is less elaborate and, surprisingly, lacks the central motif of the delivery of the written Torah to Joshua and his public reading of it. It is interesting, however, that this element appears prominently in the investiture of the king of the 2-1/2 trans-Jordanian tribes by Joshua (chap. xxiii, Crane, p. 64).

[4] *Eschatology*, p. 223.

either God or Moses could be understood as the subject of the clause. Markah presents an extensive midrash on parts of Deuteronomy 33 in Book V, section 2 of his *Memar*, but he omits all reference to verse 5. Nowhere in the *Memar* is there an explicit interpretation of this verse. The *Defter*, as already mentioned, does not call Moses king.

Nevertheless it may be that Gaster was correct, for when Markah lists the "twenty names"[1] of Moses, he includes "King" (מלך).[2] Unfortunately he gives no hint where he derives this title. However there are numerous clues which point to Moses' installation as king, which must now be examined.

Moses' Enthronement and Coronation

In Chapter IV traditions were found in the Jewish haggada which described Moses' ascent of Sinai as a heavenly enthronement. In Samaritan literature such traditions are common and are more extensively elaborated. Repeatedly it is said that Moses was "crowned with light":

> Exalted is the great prophet Moses whom his Lord vested with His name. He dwelt in the mysteries and was crowned with the light. The True One was revealed to him and gave him His handwriting; He made him drink from ten glorious fountains, seven on high and three below.[3]

In one passage, a midrash which compares Moses with Adam in six points, one common element is that "the two of them were clad in two crowns of great light."[4] Alternatively, it is said that Moses was

---

[1] שמהתה עסרין, not, as Macdonald translates (p. 207), "his names are ten"! (Cf. Bowman, *Oudtestamentische Studien*, VIII, 250). To multiply confusion, Macdonald's translation lists *seventeen* names. To obtain the correct count, *each word*, including "Man," "God" (not "Man of God"), and even "Portion," *Meḥokek*, and "Reserved One" from Dt. 33.21 (not, "A commander's portion was reserved") must be reckoned as a separate title.

[2] *Memar Marqah*, v.4.

[3] *Ibid.*, ii.12, trans. Macdonald, pp. 80f.; similarly *ibid.*, iv. 7 (ET: p. 158) and Cowley, I, 56 ג (an anonymous alphabetical hymn of uncertain date).

[4] *Memar Marqah*, vi.3, trans. Macdonald, p. 221. The basic structure of the passage, obscured somewhat by Macdonald's translation and punctuation, consists simply of alternate statements about creation and the giving of the Torah: (1) The "Divine appeared and established the Covenant"; "The Glory appeared and magnified what was good," ("and it was very good," Gen. 1.31). (2) Angels came to "magnify what was glorious" (the Torah), as "they were all assembled for Adam" (when he was created). (3) Adam received the breath of life; Moses was made "complete with a great spirit." (4) The one was glorified with speech, the other with "perfect knowledge." For the comparison between Moses and Adam, see above, pp. 222f.

"clothed with light,"[1] a formulation recalling the "garment of light" which Adam had worn until he was expelled from Eden.[2] Both the "crown of light" and the "garment of light" refer of course to the light which beamed from Moses' face when he descended from Sinai (Exodus 34.29f.). As in the *Midrash Tanhuma* passage discussed in the previous chapter,[3] the "horn of light" is interpreted as a nimbus or corona, the equivalent of God's own crown, or, differently from the Jewish midrash, as a "robe."[4] The "robe of light" is also a royal garment, even though it is as a prophet that Moses is adorned with it:

> They assembled on Mount Sinai on the day when the Scripture came down.
> The *Shofar* began to proclaim,
> and the voice of the prophet was raised.
> And the Good said: "A prophet shall be exalted; the prophet shall be magnified; his prophecy shall be exalted."
> And he adorned and glorified and brought (him) to *Arafel*,[5]
> When he was clothed with a garment in which no king is able to be clothed;
> when he was hidden in the cloud
> and his face clothed with a beam of light,
> that all peoples should know that Moses is the servant of God and faithful.[6]

The last passage can only be understood as the description of a heavenly enthronement. So also this passage from the *Memar Marqah*, which also stands in the context of the giving of the Torah on Sinai:

> Glory came to strengthen him, as when [more likely, simply "when"] the good came and vested him with the crown of holiness [or, "his holy crown"]. It appeared and anointed his body with faith; it came and set out laws for him.[7]

Here three elements which are fundamental to Israelite enthronement ritual are mentioned: coronation, anointing, and the giving of the Torah. Still other passages speak directly of Moses' instal-

---

[1] In the *Durran* of Amram Darah (4th century), Cowley, I, 41, 1.3; in a hymn by Markah, *ibid.*, I, 61, 1.21 and 62, 1.6; cf. *Memar Marqah*, iv.6, "He wore the brightness of light" (trans. Macdonald, p. 155).

[2] See above, p. 223.

[3] Above, pp. 192-195.

[4] It is worth noting, however, that the *Tanhuma* passage does speak of God's "robe of slendor," which however is reserved for the King Messiah!

[5] In Jewish mystical literature, Arafel is one of the seven heavens.

[6] From the 6th hymn of the *Durran* cycle by Amram Darah, Cowley, I, 40f.

[7] *Memar Marqah*, vi.2, trans. Macdonald, p. 219.

lation on a throne in heaven: "God seated him upon a throne[1] upon which no king is able to sit, and God appointed him below and he entrusted him with the unseen world."[2] Like Enoch in other traditions, Moses "sat on a great throne and wrote what his Lord had taught him."[3] Similarly, the rod he received from God ("from the fire") is a sceptre of sovereignty: "This will be a wonder to you—in it is great and powerful rulership [שלטנו]."[4]

The crown, the robe, the throne, the sceptre received from God — all these are varying aspects of the imagery of Moses' enthronement in heaven at the time of the Sinai revelation. Central to all the images is the concept that when Moses received the Torah he was made God's vice-regent. In two passages in the *Memar Marqah* this concept comes to direct expression. In the midrash on Exodus 4, Markah has God say to Moses, after describing the miracles Moses is to perform, "No one will be able to do them except you, for you are my second [תניני] in the lower world."[5] Further on in the same midrash Moses' relationship to Aaron is elaborated: "You will be my vice-regent [תניני literally, my 'second'] and he will be your prophet."[6] The second statement is the midrash on Exodus 4.16, "He shall be a mouth for you and you shall be a god (אלהים) to him," but the midrash more closely paraphrases the parallel verse, "See, I have made you a god (אלהים) to Pharaoh, and Aaron your brother shall be your prophet" (Exodus 7.1).[7] Significantly both biblical texts call Moses אלהים, while the midrash substitutes "my (God's) second." That is, Moses is understood as a "second God," the "God of the lower world," or as Macdonald quite reasonably translates, God's "vice-regent" in the world.[8]

---

[1] דרג is unusual in this sense, but context requires this translation.

[2] From hymn 'א of the *Durran*, Cowley, I, 38, ll.24-26.

[3] *Memar Marqah*, iv.6, trans. Macdonald, p. 156; cf. 1 Enoch 12.3, 4; 15.1; Jub. 4.23; Targ. Ps.-Jon. on Gen. 5.23; cf. Scholem, *Jewish Gnosticism*, p. 51, n. 24.

[4] *Memar Marqah*, 1.2, trans. Macdonald, p. 7. On the staff as a symbol of kingship, cf. Widengren, *Ascension*, p. 9 and n. 1. The rod of Moses, which had been Adam's and —in one tradition at least —cut from the tree of life (*ARN*, Version "B," ed. Schechter, p. 157; cf. Widengren, *Ascension*, p. 9, n. 1, who sees this as a Babylonian motif), plays an important part in diverse Jewish as well as Samaritan traditions. (Cf. above, pp. 259f., 352.)

[5] *Memar Marqah*, i.2, trans. Macdonald, p. 12.

[6] *Ibid.*

[7] Macdonald, *ibid.*, fails to notice this and refers only to Ex. 4.16.

[8] One is tempted to see a parallel to the "lesser Yahweh" (יהוה קטן), a title of Enoch-Metatron in the earlier texts of Jewish Merkabah and Hekalot

It is not surprising therefore that several passages are found in which Moses' coronation or investiture is said to be "with God's name" rather than "with a crown" or "with light."[1] Twice the phrase "vested with [God's] name" occurs in the same passage with and parallel to the phrase "crowned with the light."[2] The "name" which is meant in all these passages is אלהים,[3] and Exodus 7.1 is the scriptural basis, as this passage at once makes plain:

> The first name, with which Genesis opens, was that which he was vested with and by which he was made strong. *See, I make you as God to Pharaoh.*[4]

The "name with which God vested him" is distinguished from "the name which God revealed to him," which is always יהוה.[5] Moses' "twenty names" includes אלהים,[6] and the congregation lamenting Moses' final departure salutes him "O you who were called אלהים."[7] When the decree that he was to die was made known, "the name with which he was vested on the top of Mount Horeb asked its Lord that death should not come near him."[8] The following acrostic on אלהים shows clearly that this is the name with which Moses was "vested."

From the passages just quoted it is evident that Exodus 7.1, the naming of Moses with God's name, is transferred to Sinai in Samaritan tradition and incorporated in the description of the enthronement of Moses in heaven and his commissioning as God's earthly regent, his "second." Receiving the name *Elohim* from God is

---

mysticism (cf. Scholem, *Jewish Gnosticism*, chap. vii; *Major Trends*, pp. 68-70). One oft-repeated etymology of the name Meṭaṭron derives from μετὰ θρόνου, i.e., "vice-regent," but Scholem disputes this on philological grounds (*Major Trends*, pp. 69f.). In two passages of *Memar Marqah* an angel is apparently called God's שלטן which Macdonald translates "vice-regent" and "regent" respectively (i.2, p. 5 and i.9, p. 35).

[1] "Crowned" with the name: *Memar Marqah*, i.9 (ET: p. 31); Cowley, I, 54, l.26 (poem by Marḳah); "vested" or "clothed" with the name: *Memar Marqah*, ii.12 (ET: p. 81); v.1 (ET: p. 194); Cowley, I, 33, ᵔ.

[2] *Memar Marqah*, ii.12 (ET: p. 80); iv.7 (ET: p. 158).

[3] Macdonald apparently missed this fact, for he tries to explain all these allusions on the basis of a supposed *gematria*, in which שמה ("the name," the Samaritan substitute for יהוה) = משה (*Memar Marqah*, II, 31, n. 94, and elsewhere).

[4] *Memar Marqah*, ii.12, trans. Macdonald, p. 81.

[5] *Ibid.*

[6] *Ibid.*, v.4; cf. above, p. 232 and n. 1.

[7] *Ibid.*, v.3, trans. Macdonald, p. 203.

[8] *Ibid.*, v.1, trans. Macdonald, p. 194.

equivalent to becoming the divine king on earth. Additional support is found in a line from a Markah hymn in the *Defter*, addressed to God:

> The wealth of your deity (אלהותך)
>   was set forth on Mount Sinai;
> The wealth of your kingship (מלכותך):
>   who can estimate it?[1]

The parallelism shows that God's "Elohim-ness" is equivalent to his kingship.

Now it is evident that the basic outline of Moses' enthronement as God's vice-regent is exactly the same in the fourth-century Samaritan traditions as it was discovered to be in one passage in Philo and in a midrash preserved by the collection *Tanhuma*.[2] In both the Jewish and the Samaritan traditions Exodus 7.1 is the central text, in both traditions the naming of Moses as "God" is transferred to Sinai and connected with his "crowning" with the nimbus of light, and in both traditions naming Moses "God" is equivalent to his appointment as God's vice-regent, the divine king of the earthly sphere or of Israel.

King or Prophet?

The puzzling fact remains that, with all the trappings of kingship which are applied to Moses' Sinai ascension and his earthly office, nevertheless he is almost never called "king" in the extant Samaritan sources. Instead the title "prophet" appears precisely in the places where one would expect "king." For example, the "crown" with which Moses was vested can be identified with his prophetic office: "Prophecy was for him a crown from the days of the Covenant,[3] the glory of Moses, who was worthy to be clothed with it."[4] Most significantly, Exodus 7.1 and Moses' title "God" are connected directly with his office as prophet:

---

[1] Cowley, I, 24, 'ע ; cf. the German trans. by Kahle, *Opera Minora*, p. 206.

[2] See above, pp. 192-195.

[3] יומי בריתה could be translated "Days of creation," since the Samaritans write בריאתה defectively as בריתה (so Macdonald, *ALUOS*, II, 69; cf. Cowley, II, lii, s.v. ברי). But the context requires "covenant" as in the very next line and in line 'ל, "tablets of the covenant," לוחי בריתה.

[4] A prayer by Amram Darah (4th century), Cowley, I, 32, 'נ. Cf. *Memar Marqah*, vi.5, where it is said that all *priests* wear "the crown of prophethood" (כליל נביותה).

Then He said, I am the God of your fathers (Ex. iii.6). Take from me divinity [אלהו] and with it make your prophethood strong.[1]

The idea that the name אלהים made Moses "strong" has been encountered before.[2] Furthermore, the repetition of Moses' name in God's call at the bush meant that "he would be vested with prophethood and the divine name."[3]

> ... Divinity and prophethood were combined to honour him. Divinity willed deliverance with wonders, and prophethood was established to elevate his status. Divinity was glorified and prophethood magnified.[4]

One can only speculate about the reasons for this curious identification of the prophetic office and title with royal imagery and mission. Since there is some evidence that Moses was at least occasionally called "king," and since he was regarded as the restorer of the "kingdom of Joseph," it may be that in some instances the title "prophet" has secondarily replaced "king" in the tradition. Possibly the fourth-century sources, which apparently belonged to an extensive realignment and systematization of Samaritan worship and belief, present a harmony of previously distinct lines. On the other hand, it is possible that even in the centuries prior to Marḳah and Amram Moses was always regarded as the prophet who, *qua* prophet, performed all the tasks and held all the prerogatives which in the surrounding world were attributes of kingship.[5] Only one conclusion can safely be drawn—and it is one that is rather significant for the present investigation—: the title and functions of the

---

[1] *Memar Marqah*, i.2, trans. Macdonald, p. 5.

[2] *Ibid.*, ii.12, quoted above, p. 235.

[3] *Ibid.*, i.1, trans. Macdonald, p. 4. Cf. the Jewish midrashim on the same passage, in which the two offices promised there were kingship and priesthood (above, p. 181, and the references given there). For both Jews and Samaritans the double address suggested comparison with Abraham and Jacob.

[4] *Memar Marqah*, ii.9, trans. Macdonald, pp. 67f.

[5] Certain parallels are to be found in descriptions of prophets' missions in OT and in Judaism from which Widengren concludes, "We can clearly perceive that it is from royal ideology that the prophet has adopted both the idea of 'sending out' and the ritual scene of the heavenly investiture where he receives his commission, sometimes the heavenly tablets" (*Ascension*, p. 33). Yet he admits "that in some passages it might be difficult to ascertain whether the royal pattern, as applied to the prophet, really has been taken over from the Israelitic king or possibly existed only as a pattern for such a prophetic leader" (*ibid.*, n. 3). This exactly describes our situation here.

prophet are more closely connected with the functions and prerogatives, but not the title, of the divine *king* in the Samaritan traditions
of Moses than in any other material which has so far been explored.

BELIEF IN GOD AND IN MOSES

Perhaps the most striking difference between the Samaritan traditions and those of Rabbinic Judaism is the existence of a "Samaritan creed" of which one essential element is "belief in Moses."[1]
In the liturgy and in the *Memar Marqah* a two-member credal
formula, with slight variations, forms the stereotyped conclusion to
many homilies or prayers:

> Praised be the Merciful One . . . Let us believe in Him and in
> Moses His prophet, and let us bow down before Him and
> testify, saying, "There is only one God."[2]

The formula can be stated negatively, in an evidently polemical
variation:

> We will not listen to any scripture but this; there is no God
> great as its Giver; and we will not listen to the word from any
> prophet but from the prophet who received it.[3]

In addition to the "credal" form, employing the verb אמן or its
equivalent in these contexts, שמע "to heed," the same two elements
can be stated in simple affirmative statements:

> YHWH is the God of the generations, and Moses the prophet
> of all generations.[4]

In one passage belief in Moses has soteriological significance:

> Believe in him —you will be safe from all wrath, in the Day of
> Vengeance you will find rest; in the fire you will not be. It will
> have no power over you.

---

[1] The term "Samaritan creed" was first used by Montgomery, p. 207. For
a survey of the probable development of the "creed," see Macdonald,
Theology, pp. 49-55, and cf. Bowman, *BJRL* 40, 302-310.

[2] *Memar Marqah*, iv.8, trans. Macdonald, p. 167; cf. *ibid.*, ii.9 (ET: pp. 72,
73); ii.10 (ET: pp. 75, 76); iv.7 (ET: p. 160), 11 (ET: p. 181), 12 (ET: p.
189); vi.6 (ET: p. 233); Cowley, I, 50, ll.18f.; 84, ll.3-5.

[3] Liturgical poem by Marḳah, Cowley, I, 60, ll.3f.; cf. the more elaborate
(and evidently much later) formulation, *ibid.*, p. 3, a prayer for the eve of
Sabbath often quoted (e.g., Macdonald, *Theology*, p. 55).

[4] From a prayer by Amram Darah, Cowley, I, 32, ש; cf. *Memar Marqah*,
ii.9 (ET: p. 69); ii.12 (ET: p. 83); iv.4 (ET: p. 147); iv.12 (ET: p. 187).

He who believes in him believes in his Lord. Woe to us if we do not remember that. Let us believe in the Lord and in Moses His servant.[1]

It is in statements like that just quoted that Macdonald finds the strongest evidence for Christian influence on the Samaritan doctrine of Moses. He says, "That Christian influence helps towards the formulation of the Samaritan concept of belief in Moses seems beyond doubt."[2] This is an attractive assumption at first glance, but it rests on faulty reasoning. Macdonald finds a "close parallel" to the sentence quoted above, "He who believes in Moses believes in his Lord," in John 14.1, "You believe in God, believe also in me," and apparently this "parallel" is in his opinion sufficient to prove dependence.[3] Against this hasty conclusion several things can be said: (1) The statement by Marḳah is not really parallel in form to John 14.1; a closer parallel would be John 5.46, "If you believed in Moses, you would believe in me." (2) The *Memar* statement is a close paraphrase of Exodus 14.31, a fact of which Macdonald must have been aware, since earlier in his *Theology* (but nowhere in his edition of the *Memar* itself) he calls attention to the fact that this Old Testament verse is probably at the root of the "two-member creed" of the Samaritans.[4] (3) As for Christian influence being the only possible source for formulation of "belief in" a person (if indeed the Samaritan formulas mean the same as "belief in Jesus," rather than "fidelity to" Moses and his Torah), reference ought at least to have been made to two significant parallels in Jewish sources. (a) *Mekilta* on Exodus 14.31 develops an extended statement on the Jewish "faith," including these remarkable statements:

> If you say they believed in Moses, is it not implied by *Kal vahomer* that they believed in God? But this is to teach you that having faith in the shepherd of Israel is the same as having faith in Him who spoke and the world came into being. In like manner you must interpret: "And the people spoke against God, and against Moses" (Num. 21.5). If you say they spoke

---

[1] *Memar Marqah*, iv.7, trans. Macdonald, p. 160.

[2] *Theology*, p. 150.

[3] *Ibid.*, cf. p. 180.

[4] *Ibid.*, p. 51, n. 1 and p. 53. Yet, later on, discussing the same formula, he says, "Ex. 4.5 may implicitly suggest the germ of such belief . . .," but that it was only developed under NT influence. Had Macdonald forgotten his own earlier statements? More than a "germ" of Marḳah's statement is resent in Ex. 14.31.

against God, is it not implied *Kal vaḥomer* that they spoke against Moses? But this comes to teach you that speaking against the shepherd of Israel is like speaking against Him who spoke and the world came into being.[1]

(b) Even the soteriological aspect of belief is present in the much-discussed statement from the Habbakuk Commentary of Qumran:

> God will deliver them from the house of judgment because of their work (or, "merit", עמל) and their fidelity to (or, "faith in") the Teacher of Righteousness.[2]

In connection with this passage it should be remembered that the Teacher of Righteousness bears many traits from the Moses traditions.[3] When these other factors are considered, the contention that the fourth-century Samaritan description of Moses is based to a large extent on Christian doctrine, far from being "beyond doubt," appears very flimsy indeed.[4]

Actually the Samaritan "belief in" or "fidelity to" Moses, which is always united with the "belief in" or "fidelity to" Yahweh, is a logical concomitant to the notion that Moses is God's representative, his "Apostle" or "vice-regent." The connection is explicit in this passage:

> When Moses recounted the records of the ancestors before the children who succeeded them, they believed in the True One [קשטה] and knew that the apostleship [שליחותה] of Moses was true.[5]

Moses, the prophetic ruler of Israel, is God's representative on earth. His mission, founded in his heavenly enthronement on Sinai,

---

[1] *Mekilta*, Beshallah 7, trans. Lauterbach, I, 252.

[2] 1QpHab viii.2f. For the translation, cf. Maier, I, 153, and contrast Dupont-Sommer, p. 263. The latter's tendentious exegesis has found little acceptance.

[3] Above, pp. 169f.

[4] On the whole, although Macdonald repeatedly asserts that Christian doctrine had a strong formative influence on Samaritan theology, he never demonstrates more than the *possibility* of such influence. It may be granted that the possibility existed, since as he says Samaritans and Christians must have been in early contact in Palestine, and the medieval chronicles have references to Christian events and writings. But Macdonald's lists of purported "parallels" (cf. especially *Theology*, pp. 189-194) are the only evidence he presents for *actual* influence —and none of these parallels is more convincing than the one just analyzed.

[5] *Memar Marqah*, ii.9, trans. Macdonald, p. 72.

consists in mediating God's teaching to the world, as the prophetic *šaliaḥ*, and in ruling on God's behalf, as the royal vice-regent or "second God."

MOSES' ASCENSIONS

The Ascension on Sinai

In common with certain circles of Judaism which were examined in the previous two chapters, the Samaritans understood Moses' ascent of Mount Sinai as an ascent to heaven, where he was enthroned in glory, commissioned for his earthly assignment, and entrusted with secrets from God which would mean life for men. Since several aspects of the Sinai ascension have already been discussed in connection with Moses' prophetic office as revealer of secrets and his enthronement, it will be sufficient at this point merely to add some elements of the tradition not yet mentioned and to summarize the whole.

The Sinai ascension was the central, all-important event in Moses' life, so far as the Samaritan traditions are concerned. Upon this single event, to an even greater extent than on the Exodus itself and the crossing of the Sea, Moses' unique position is founded. Every ascription of honor addressed to Moses, every panegyric describing him, focuses attention on the ascension, like this hymn with which Marḳah has the congregation of Israel address Moses just before his death:

> Peace be to you, O treasure of prophethood.
> Peace be to you, O piercer of veils.
> Peace be to you, you who trod the fire.
> Peace be to you, you who approached the deep darkness.
> Peace be to you, you who wear the brightness of light.
> Peace be to you, O receiver of the two tablets.
> Peace be to you, whom the Lord addressed face to face openly, not secretly.
> Peace be to you, the like of whom has not arisen and will never arise.[1]

In the descriptions of and allusions to Moses' ascension there is a rather consistent pattern of images, which has several points of striking coincidence with the typical description of a mystical ascent

---

[1] *Memar Marqah*, v.3, trans. Macdonald, p. 201.

in traditions like the Enoch literature and the *Merkabah* and *Hekalot* texts. Fundamental to the whole is Moses' "entry" into "the unseen," the "hidden world" (כסיאתה), a term which is frequently paired with its opposite, "the revealed things," "the visible world" (גליאתה). The term is the equivalent to "heaven," but it includes all the "angels," "powers," "mysteries," and "secrets" which are not seen by ordinary mortals, so that its meaning approaches that of the gnostic *pleroma*. When God said to Moses "Come up to me" (Deuteronomy 10.1), he brought him "into the Sanctuary of the Unseen."[1] Moses "pierced the veil" and "is above the unseen and dwells among the angels. His head reached into the deep darkness."[2]

Very frequently it is said that Moses "trod the fire." Of the "ten wonders" that crowned Moses,

> *The first* [was] in his feet, for he walked with them on the fire and he was not harmed by it. When did he tread in the fire except on the Day of Horeb? The fire was at the front—as He said, *"Because the Lord descended upon it in fire"* (Ex. xix.18; Targ.), and there was darkness behind it and cloud in the midst of it.[3]

The "fire" is associated with God's presence; Moses received the tablets of the Covenant "from the fire," and they were written "by a finger of devouring fire."[4] This image, which was suggested by such biblical texts as Exodus 19.18 and Deuteronomy 18.16, also calls to mind the threat often encountered by a mystic upon entering heaven, that he might be consumed by the heavenly or angelic fire. That Moses "trod the fire" demonstrates his immunity.

Another element found in the mystical literature is that the ascendant mortal becomes like the angels, sometimes having his flesh transformed into flame, their substance, or subsisting on their food. One of the main elements in the Sinai theophany, according

---

[1] *Ibid.*, iv.7, trans. Macdonald, p. 158.

[2] *Ibid.*, iv.3, trans. Macdonald, p. 142f. Nothing can be made of the present tense of the first two verbs, for they could equally well have been translated by the past tense.

[3] *Ibid.*, ii.12, trans. Macdonald, p. 82. Cf. v.3 (quoted above); vi.3 (ET: p. 224); Cowley, I, 41 (the *Durran*); *Sam. Josh.*, chap. vii, Crane, p. 32; and often elsewhere.

[4] Cowley, I, 23, 'מ (a poem by Marḳah, cf. Kahle's trans., *Opera Minora*, p. 204); cf. Cowley, I, 50, l.14 (also by Marḳah).

to the Samaritans, was the assembly there of the angels.[1] "Powers
and creatures gathered there; . . . All the powers of the invisible
world came forth into the visible world. . . ."[2] Moreover, Moses
"ascended from human status to that of the angels."[3] The angels'
food was given him, and he even received angelic ablutions:

> From their store he had been supplied. At their table he had
> sat and with their bread he had been satisfied. He had washed
> in their trough and he had been established in their dwelling
> place.[4]

As in the Jewish midrash *Gedulat Mosheh*, his flesh was made angelic,
for "His body mingled with the angels above, and he dwelt with
them, being worthy to do so."[5]

The climax of Moses' ascension, his enthronement and his receiving of heavenly secrets including the Torah itself, has already been
discussed above.[6] The two aspects are closely related, for "he sat on
a great throne and wrote what his Lord had taught him. He had
learned at a schoolhouse[7] among the angels.[8] Furthermore, in at
least one tradition of late attestation, the passing on of the secrets
Moses received on high formed an essential part of the enthronement
ceremony of Joshua the King and, presumably, of his successors
during the "First Kingdom."[9]

Finally, Moses' priesthood, occasionally mentioned in the Samaritan sources, is connected with his Sinai ascension, for before he
served in the earthly ("visible") sanctuary (the Tabernacle), he
was first inducted into the priesthood of the heavenly Sanctuary
("the Sanctuary of the Unseen"): "He was a holy priest in two
sanctuaries,"[10] the "priest of the mysteries" (or, of the unseen world:
כסיאתה).[11] In one passage Marḳah even suggests that Moses might

---

[1] For the notion that a heavenly assembly formed the counterpart to the
assembly of Israel, below, cf. *Midrasch Tannaïm*, II, 213, quoted above, p.
188.

[2] Cowley, I, 23, 'ח and 'כ ; cf. Kahle's trans., *Opera Minora*, p. 204.

[3] *Memar Marqah*, v.3, trans. Macdonald, p. 206.

[4] *Ibid.*, iv.6, trans. Macdonald, p. 156; cf. *Sam. Josh.*, chap. vii, Crane,
p. 32.

[5] *Ibid.*, vi.3, trans. Macdonald, p. 224.

[6] Pp. 223-225, 232-236.

[7] בית ספרא=ביספר, "synagogue"; cf. the Jewish term בית המדרש.

[8] *Memar Marqah*, iv.6, trans. Macdonald, p. 156.

[9] Above, p. 224.

[10] *Memar Marqah*, iv.6, trans. Macdonald, p. 155.

[11] *Ibid.*, v.3, trans. Macdonald, p. 202.

serve as a hierophant, having prepared the way which others may
follow:

> Thanks be to the Merciful One . . . He who follows in the foot-
> steps of Moses the faithful prophet will not go astray, nor be
> guilty of sin, but will serve in both worlds.[1]

This passage suggests that Moses' ascension may have been so
extraordinarily important for the Samaritans not only because of
the secrets Moses obtained and passed on, but also because the
ascension itself served as a prototype, as in Philo, of the ascent to
heaven which every disciple of Moses hoped to be granted, whether
after death or during life as a mystical translation. So far, however,
the sources present no other evidence which could corroborate this
suggestion.

Moses' Final Ascension

The accounts of Moses' departure from earthly life are as ambiguous and contradictory in the Samaritan sources as in the Jewish.
The *Memar Marqah* describes Moses' entry into the cave on Mount
Nebo and his obedient death there,[2] and Montgomery, basing his
opinion at this point on Markah, could say flatly that "there is no
doctrine of the assumption of Moses."[3]

Nevertheless, there is a certain ambiguity even in Markah's de-
scription.[4] For example, the biblical command of God to Moses,
"Die on the mountain . . . and be gathered to your people . . ."
(Deuteronomy 32.50) receives a peculiar twist:

> No prophet like Moses has arisen or ever will arise. He was
> exalted above the whole human race and he progressed until
> he was gathered with the angels—as was said to him, *"Be
> gathered."*[5]

The "progress" of Moses to status equal to angels recalls an element

---

[1] *Ibid.*, iv.9, trans. Macdonald, pp. 169f. The words read literally,
"will serve here and there," אנה ושם. Macdonald observes that both words
are unusual in Samaritan Aramaic (p. 170, n. 191) and suggests that they
are "maybe a mystical idiom reflecting a divine name." It may not be mere
coincidence that שם in Ex. 34.28 and Dt. 34.5 is interpreted in *Sifre Dt.*, par.
357, *Yalkut Šim'oni* on Dt., par. 962, 965 (pp. 686f.), and Talm. B. *Soṭa* 13b
to mean "standing and serving" on high (above, p. 210).

[2] Bk. v, *passim*.

[3] Montgomery, p. 229.

[4] Cf. Macdonald, *Theology*, p. 216.

[5] *Memar Marqah*, iv.12, trans. Macdonald, p. 186.

in the description of the Sinai ascent,[1] and in fact Marḳah draws a plain parallel between the Sinai and Nebo ascents:

> The great prophet Moses said, "O congregation, happy are you if you hearken to all this address that I make before you! Three times my Lord said to me, *"Go up to it,"*[2] and I went up with the mind of prophethood[3] on the (first) two occasions. I delivered the first and second tablets and on this (third) occasion I receive the portion that He presented me through Adam.[4] Twice I ascended and descended as God commanded me; on this occasion I go up and will not come down. Behold, before I die, I bless you with a beneficial blessing in the name of God.[5]

As Macdonald cogently points out, Marḳah describes the ascent of Nebo with imagery drawn from the Sinai tradition.[6] The crown of light, the assembly of the angelic hosts, the descent of the "powers," the enveloping cloud[7] are all part of the final ascent, as of the first.[8] This assimilation between a final ascension to heaven and the mystical transport, conceived of as a prolepsis of the final ascent, has appeared often before. In this context Marḳah's description of Moses' "going up" Mount Nebo certainly implies an assumption,[9] a notion which logically contradicts Marḳah's description of the burial. Such contradictions are commonplace in descriptions of the deaths of heroes, however, and the *Memar Marqah* is no more am-

---

[1] Above, pp. 242f.

[2] אסק לידה; cf. Sam. Targ. (ed. Brüll) on Ex. 24.1, סק ליד יהוה; 34.2, ... סק לטור ... לטור סיני; Dt. 32.49, ... ותסק.

[3] במדע נביותה.

[4] The חלקה presented through Adam *may* refer to the notion developed earlier in this section (ET: pp. 195, 198), that Adam's sin brought death to all, including Moses (so Macdonald, *Theology*, pp. 217f.). This would be a curious way to express that idea, however, and the reference may be to the חלקת מחקק of Dt. 33.21, applied in Samaritan as in Jewish tradition to the place of Moses' grave (cf. *Memar Marqah*, v.4, where Dt. 33.21 provides 3 of Moses' "20 names").

[5] *Memar Marqah*, v.2, trans. Macdonald, p. 198.

[6] *Theology*, p. 220.

[7] The cloud that hides Moses at the end was found also in Josephus, *Antt.* iv.326. In view of this fact and the Sinai parallelism Macdonald's suggestion that the cloud "indicates the New Testament influence on the Samaritans" from Acts 1.9 (*Theology*, p. 442) is strange. His additional proposal that Moses gives a final blessing in *Memar Marqah* because Jesus does in Acts 1.9 is absurd; see Dt. 33.1!

[8] *Memar Marqah*, v.3.

[9] So also Macdonald, *Theology*, p. 216.

biguous in this respect than, for example, the *Assumption of Moses* quoted by Christian Fathers.[1]

The situation is quite reversed in the medieval chronicle "The Book of Joshua." As in Markah and Josephus, the actual departure of Moses is shrouded in mystery, for "a pillar of divine fire"—replacing the cloud of the older accounts—"descended and separated between them and their master . . . and no one knows what happened to him after this, even unto this time."[2] The grave and burial, however, are not mentioned, and the following passages make clear that Moses ascended and serves in heaven:

> His allotted period of life had reached its limit, and the term of his existence among men—peace be unto him—and now his dealings were with his Lord and His angels. And of God do we beg that he would unite us to him through His mercy. Behold He [or, "he"] is over all things powerful [i.e., "all the powers"], and He [or, "he"] is my sufficiency and illustrious Protector.[3]

To sum up the results of this section, the notion that Moses ascended to heaven was a fundamental element in his symbolic and religious value to the Samaritans. Sources of all ages agree on the centrality of the Sinai ascension(s), but in the older sources the relation between a final ascension at the end of his life and his biblically attested death and burial is fluid and not rationalized.

THE ESCHATOLOGICAL FUNCTIONS OF MOSES

The Coming of Moses

Several passages in the Samaritan sources reveal an expectation that Moses himself would return at the end of days. In the medieval *Book of Joshua* this expectation is clearly stated in a passage which summarizes the content of Moses' last address before his ascent of Nebo:

> He expounded intelligence of the days of Divine favor which were to come, and the cause of Wrath and Error. And he informed the children of Isrâil concerning the deluge of fire, and the day of vengeance and reward, *and defined the time of his return unto them*. Then he announced unto them what should

---

[1] See above, p. 159.
[2] *Sam. Josh.*, chap. vi, trans. Crane, p. 31.
[3] *Ibid.*

happen unto every tribe, and that he would marshal them complete in the days of final perfection and completion.[1]

The reference is to the "song of Moses," Deuteronomy 32, and the "blessing of Moses," Deuteronomy 33, which were interpreted eschatologically from an early time. The *Memar Marqah*, a millennium earlier than the *Book of Joshua*, contains in its fourth book an extensive midrash on Deuteronomy 32 which describes the "fire" (Deuteronomy 32.22), the "day of vengeance" (Deuteronomy 32.35 in the Samaritan recension), and the coming of the *Taheb*.[2] The questions arise then whether at the time of Markah a tradition about Moses' coming at the end of days was already known and, if so, what the relation was between Moses and the "Taheb."

The first question has to be answered affirmatively, for Markah assigns a prominent role to Moses on the "Day of Vengeance." When the obedient Samaritans rise from the grave, "the light will shine on them and the great prophet Moses will glorify them."[3] His intercession on behalf of them will be a primary factor in their salvation, as of old at the time of the Golden Calf. The evildoers, however, will have no part in the bliss of the righteous, for "the great prophet Moses was too righteous for them."[4] A prayer in the *Defter*, attributed by the rubric to Markah but evidently much later,[5] also connects Moses with the Day of Vengeance as well as with creation:

> Remember for good forever the prophet, righteous, perfect, pure, faithful, Moses the son of Amram, the Man of God, the prophet of the whole world, whom YHWH appointed over the Beginning and over the Day of Vengeance, like whom no prophet has arisen in the world. The peace of YHWH be upon him.[6]

The story preserved by Josephus of a Samaritan "tumult" under Pilate shows that the name of Moses was connected with eschatological hopes in the early first century, but the nature of the con-

---

[1] *Sam. Josh.*, chap. vi, trans. Crane, p. 30, emphasis mine.
[2] *Memar Marqah*, iv.10, on Dt. 32.15, 11, on Dt. 32.30, 12, on Dt. 32.36 (ET: pp. 176, 180, 188). Cf. iii.4 (ET: pp. 101f). For a different translation and interpretation, see Bowman, *Oudtestamentische Studien*, VIII, 222, n. 4.
[3] *Memar Marqah*, iv.12, trans. Macdonald, p. 182.
[4] *Ibid.*, p. 183.
[5] The language is more Hebrew than Aramaic.
[6] Cowley, I, 84, ll.25-28.

nection is not at all clear. According to Josephus, an unnamed man gathered a large following by promising that on Mount Gerizim he would "show them the sacred implements buried there, which Moses had deposited."[1] It is difficult to see how the tradition could have arisen that Moses *hid* the vessels on *Gerizim*, and Merx thinks that "the name Μωυσέως here . . . is certainly wrong . . ."[2] The chronicles relate the hiding of the vessels by Uzzi the High Priest, after the death of Samson and the onset of the *Fanuta* (time of God's disfavor).[3] Josephus may have received a garbled report, although it is risky to argue from the medieval sources or from ordinary logic that the Samaritans *could not* have had a tradition that Moses himself hid the vessels, especially since their midrash sometimes identifies the various mountains in Moses' life. All that can be said with certainty from the story as it now stands is that the figure who promised to restore true worship to the Samaritans was associated in some way with the Moses traditions.

Much clearer is this poem inserted by Marḳah into his midrash on the victory over Pharaoh's army at the Sea of Reeds:

> May the great prophet Moses come in peace,
>   who was trustworthy in what he said (when) the
>   creatures were beseeching.[4]
> May the great prophet Moses come in peace,
>   who revealed truth and abolished falsehood.
> May the great prophet Moses come in peace,
>   who glorified righteousness and destroyed the
>   wicked ones.
> May the great prophet Moses come in peace;
>   may he magnify the good and enfeeble the guilty.
> May the great prophet Moses come in peace;
>   may he reveal a good reward for men (who[5]) do good.[6]

---

[1] *Antt.* xviii.85.

[2] *Ta'eb*, p. 40; cf. Crane, p. 169, p. 81.

[3] *Sam. Josh.*, chap. xlii, Crane, p. 105.

[4] This clause is difficult to construe. Analogy with the other strophes (except the last, which also is problematical in syntax) demands that the *waw* introduce a second ptcp. or finite verb with Moses as subject. The text may be corrupt. Reading the text as it stands, ובוראיה שאלין could be parenthetical, "the creatures are beseeching (that Moses come)" or even, with Macdonald, "the creatures say 'Greeting!'" But the context suggests rather a reference to the pleas of the Israelites at the Sea of Reeds.

[5] In place of אטיבו one would expect a ptcp.; I have supplied the relative particle.

[6] *Memar Marqah*, ii.8 (text, I, 40).

Compare this poem, also from the *Memar Marqah*, this time about the Taheb:

> May the Taheb come in peace
>   and expose the darkness that has become powerful in the world.
> May the Taheb come in peace
>   and destroy the opponents who provoke God.
> May the Taheb come in peace
>   and offer a correct sacrifice before the House of God.[1]
> May the Taheb come in peace
>   that Yahweh may have pity, and reveal his favor,
>   and that Israel may sacrifice at evening.[2]
> May the Taheb come in peace
>   and separate the chosen from the rejected,
>   that this oppression may be turned to relief.
> The fourteenth day which he made is the crown of creation and
>   the beginning of a creation. . . .[3]

It is evident at once that the coming of the Taheb exactly parallels the coming of Moses, and that the functions of Moses at the time of the Exodus are analogous to the functions which both he and the Taheb are hoped to perform in the future: Moses "revealed truth and abolished falsehood"; the Taheb "reveals" or "exposes" darkness. Moses destroyed the enemies; so will the Taheb. Moses instituted the first Tabernacle; the Taheb will restore true worship.[4] Moreover, the Taheb poem stands in Markah's interpretation of Exodus 12.14, "This day (fourteenth Nisan) shall be for you a memorial day." This verse evokes an eschatological interpretation, for "the fourteenth day" identified with the Exodus is also identified with the final redemption. But in this context the redemption cannot be separated from the work of Moses, and it will be recalled that the Palestinian Targum on the parallel verse, Exodus 12.42, says that "Moses will come from the desert."[5]

---

[1] Or "Bethel." Bethel and Gerizim are identified.

[2] Literally, "between the evenings."

[3] *Memar Marqah*, i.9 (text, I, 22). I have abandoned Macdonald's translation for both poems (II, 33 and 63) mainly because it obscures the fact that the first line of each strophe has exactly the same form in both poems. In the Moses poem the second lines of the first 3 strophes show a participial construction, referring to Moses' past actions, while the last 2 strophes, like all strophes of the Taheb poem, show the imperfect (jussive) construction, expressing the petition for future activity.

[4] At this point the tradition agrees with the implication of Josephus' narrative.

[5] Above, p. 213; cf. M. Gaster, *Eschatology*, pp. 232f., and Bowman, *Oudtestamentische Studien*, VIII, 231f.

From these passages a few conclusions can now be drawn about early Samaritan eschatology. First, the events reported by Josephus indicate a popular Samaritan hope that someone associated with Moses, in a way no longer clear, would recover the hidden cult implements of the Gerizim temple, making possible the restoration of true worship. Second, the *Memar Marqah* shows that a similar hope was alive in at least one circle of Samaritanism in the fourth century A.D., and that the expected eschatological figure was called, then as later, "the Taheb."[1] Third, the Taheb for Markah was none other than Moses.

The Taheb

It would be impossible here to attempt a systematic discussion of the Taheb, and it is very doubtful whether sufficient information is yet available to make such a discussion possible.[2] A few statements about the Taheb, however, may throw additional light on the Moses traditions.

The most important biblical proof-text for the expectation of the Taheb is Deuteronomy 18.18, which promises a prophet like Moses. Surprisingly Markah offers no midrash on this verse in the *Memar*, and the Samaritan Targum of the verse adds nothing to the Hebrew. Nevertheless, the verse must have been extremely important to the Samaritans from a very early date, for it is one of the elements in the composite tenth commandment in the Samaritan Pentateuch, added after Exodus 20.19.[3]

In later sources Deuteronomy 18.18 is clearly applied to the coming of the Taheb. Particularly important are the fourteenth century hymns by Abisha ben Phinhas, to which Adalbert Merx devoted his attention, and which in Bowman's judgment represent a compendium of fully developed Samaritan eschatology.[4] The sixth

---

[1] תהבה or תאבה active ptcp. of the verb תוב = Hebrew שוב. Scholars have not yet agreed whether the title ought to be understood transitively, "the Restorer," or intransitively, "the Returning One."

[2] Cf. Macdonald's survey, *Theology*, pp. 362-371.

[3] M. Gaster points out that in the Hexapla the Samaritan 10th commandment, marked with an asterisk by Origen, was found in one text of the Greek OT. From this he concludes that the addition is as old as the LXX (*Eschatology*, pp. 128f.) and that the foundation of the eschatological belief in a Taheb or eschatological prophet like Moses is equally old. Unfortunately the first step in the argument is faulty.

[4] John Bowman, "Early Samaritan Eschatology," *JJS* 6 (1955), 63. Bowman's criticism of Merx in this article is based only on the latter's paper

hymn quotes, "I will raise up a prophet for them from the midst of their brothers, like you," and adds: "and he will be king and will be clothed in fearfulness. . . ."[1] Significantly, the Taheb here is both prophet and king. The poem also mentions Moses in parallel with the Taheb, but the relation between them is not clear. A reference to Deuteronomy 18.18 probably lies also in the cryptic statement at the end of the fifth hymn, "He who says, 'The Prophet like Moses' will see what his greatness is."[2] Most likely this means: He who recites the passage 'The prophet like Moses,' i.e., Deuteronomy 18.15-22, will understand the prophecy of the Taheb as set forth here. The same phrase occurs in the fourth century *Durran*:

> God seated him [Moses] upon a throne [דרג] upon which no king is able to sit, and God appointed him below, and he entrusted him with the unseen world. He who says "A Prophet like Moses" will see what his greatness is.[3]

The fifth Abisha hymn also applies Numbers 24.5-7 and 17 to the Taheb's advent, and again suggests that he is to rule as a king.[4] Eschatological interpretation of these verses among the Jews is attested by the interpretative translations in the Septuagint and the Targums, by Philo's interpretation, and by the Qumran texts. It is also significant that they were applied by the Samaritans to Moses.[5] Numbers 24.17 is probably also the source of the peculiar title קדקד applied occasionally to the Taheb, as in the "Midrash on the Deluge and the Advent of the Taheb" published by Merx:

> He has chosen Isaac, and the name of the Taheb is from him, for Isaac, Phinḥas, Qodqod have the same number.[6]

The Samaritan Pentateuch has קדקד for the Masoretic Text's קרקר, so that the last stich has to be translated, "And (he will be) the

---

of 1893 and makes no mention of Merx's monograph of 1909 in which the latter corrected several of his own former errors (see Bowman's n. 1, p. 63).

[1] Following the text printed by Merx, pp. 8f. and his translation, p. 9.

[2] Merx, p. 29, 1.56; cf. his translation, p. 32.

[3] Cowley, I, 38, ll.24-28. Cf. above, p. 233.

[4] Cf. Merx, pp. 31, 35-37. The text is printed on pp. 28f.

[5] *Asatir* x.45 refers the "star" to Phinhas and the "sceptre" to Joshua, thus agreeing with the Qumran texts in making the star a priest, the sceptre a royal figure.

[6] Merx, p. 80. This translation seems preferable to Merx's.

crown of all the sons of Seth."[1] The "oracle" contained in *Asatir*,
chapter XII, consists of twenty-four strophes, each beginning with
the words "Qodqod will arise" (קעם קדקד or קדקד יקום). Gaster
understood this as the prediction of twenty-four consecutive
princes, twenty during the age of evil, four in the time of favor, but
this is by no means clear. Gaster himself notes that strophe 24 describes the Qodqod in terms of the Moses traditions:

> A prince will arise who will write the Law in truth, the rod of
> miracles in his hand.
> There will be no light and no darkness.[2]

But this is equally true of strophe 22, "A prince will arise from the
section (portion) of the Lawgiver [מחקק] ...," referring to the
"portion of Gad" in Deuteronomy 33.21, where Moses was buried,
according to both Samaritan and Jewish legend, and of strophe 23
which paraphrases Numbers 24.17.

The sources which mention the Taheb generally agree in making
him the "prophet like Moses" promised in Deuteronomy 18, and on
the basis of Numbers 24.5-7 and 17 he was also expected to reign as
king.[3] In the *Memar Marqah* the Taheb is Moses himself;[4] in the
medieval sources the relation between Taheb and Moses is less
clear,[5] but the description of the Taheb is always drawn largely
from the Moses traditions.

Merx argued that the Taheb was to be a "Joshua redivivus," a

---

[1] Seth is always regarded positively in Samaritan tradition, so קדקד is
not to be taken, as normal syntax would dictate, as the object of מחק. Similarly, the targ., רום כל בני שת, has to be translated "And (he will be) the
highest of all the sons of Seth," as Moses' title in the liturgy רום נבייה is
"highest of the prophets" (Cowley, II, lxix).

[2] M. Gaster, *Asatir*, p. 55: "probably no one else than Moses Redivivus."
Cf. p. 98.

[3] Macdonald denies that the Taheb was either "primarily a prophet" or
a king (*Theology*, pp. 362f., 367), but his case is poorly supported. He ignores
the fact that Amram Darah (Cowley, I, 45) could call the Taheb "the
prophet" even though he himself quotes the passage (p. 364). Also, when he
says "Markah has quite a lot to say about the kingdom, though there is no
king as such, only the Taheb" (p. 367), he fails to mention that in the passage
he is referring to (*Memar Marqah*, iv.12) the word he translates "repossesses"
is מלך, "reign, be king." (Cf. above, p. 364.)

[4] Cf. Bowman, *Oudtestamentische Studiën*, VIII, 226f., n. 7; Macdonald,
Theology, p. 363.

[5] Bowman notes that modern Samaritans regard the Taheb as a prophet
like Moses (*JJS* 6, 69).

figure inferior to Moses. His suggestion that this was the reason for the prominence of Joseph's kingship in the early sources has already been discussed and rejected.[1] At this point other aspects of his hypothesis must be briefly mentioned. The inferiority of the Taheb to Moses, Merx thought, was reflected in the notion that he would live only 110 years, ten less than Moses. But this tradition is attested only by Petermann's report of conversations with *modern* Samaritans; it says nothing for the earlier periods.[2] More important, Merx prints an Arabic polemic composition from the sixteenth century, which contains, in Aramaic, a quotation attributed to Markah: "The Ta'eb will arise at the end and will rule over Edom seven times seven, and he is not like Moses, but the Tabernacle will be established." The Arabic tract proceeds, "that is, that he will not be like Moses and not like his prophecy, but that he will be like Joshua the son of Nun. . . ."[3]

Even in this late document the situation is confused, however, for the author, a certain Ibrahim al-Kabasi,[4] states further on that he thinks the Taheb is Enoch.[5] What the relationship is between this assertion and "the right teaching" that the Taheb is Joshua, Ibrahim does not explain. From the polemical character of the tract one can infer that Ibrahim's opponents *did* regard the Taheb as a new Moses, and the anomaly in the tract itself is that the Taheb who is supposed to be only a new Joshua (or perhaps Enoch returned) is described throughout with the imagery belonging to Moses.[6] Thus it looks as if the notion that the Taheb was *Joshua redivivus*, far from representing the general opinion of Samaritans even in the sixteenth century, was rather only one line of tradition

---

[1] Above, pp. 228-231.

[2] Merx, p. 41.

[3] *Ibid.*, p. 43.

[4] On the identification, see Moses Gaster's review of Merx in *Studies and Texts*, I, 644. Gaster criticizes Merx for drawing conclusions about the overall doctrine of the Taheb from only a few late sources.

[5] Merx, p. 74.

[6] (1) "By his hand" the pillars of cloud and fire will reappear (p. 72); (2) his reign will be preceded by the reign of a "great king" compared explicitly with the "disbelieving Pharaoh" (*ibid.*); (3) he will set up the Tabernacle (pp. 74, 76); (4) the trumpets will be returned (p. 78; cf. Num. 12.1 and the Jewish midrashim thereon); (5) he will choose 70 leaders, corresponding to the 70 elders who assembled with Moses (p. 78; cf. Ex. 24 and Dt. 33.5); (6) he will be the most humble of men, "gleich dem Herrn Moses . . ." (p. 76); (7) he will be a servant in the house of God (p. 78; cf. Num. 12.7); (8) his life will be —not 110 years, but 120 years! (p. 78).

which had to contend with various others.[1] All in all, it was the imagery of the Moses traditions that dominated Samaritan eschatology.

OTHER SIGNIFICANT ASPECTS OF THE SAMARITAN MOSES

Moses as Intercessor

In the Samaritan traditions, just as in the Jewish, Moses is regarded as Israel's intercessor *par excellence,* their "defense attorney" before God. For this reason the news of Moses' impending death brought great sorrow. Moses himself wept "not for himself, but for the congregation," for he said:

> You will go astray after my death (cf. Deut. xxxi.29).
> Who will make supplication for you? Who will make entreaty on your behalf? Who will seek forgiveness for you? Who will have compassion for you after me?[2]

This recalls the Jewish tradition that *God* wept, "not for Moses . . . but for him and for Israel," for the same reason.[3] Israel laments as Moses slowly ascends Mount Nebo:

> Who will pray for us after you? Who will make atonement for our sins after you? Who will have compassion for us after you? Who will extinguish the fire of wrath from upon us after you?[4]

In the later *Book of Joshua* this lament is greatly expanded and put

---

[1] The tradition of a returning Joshua might be quite early however. Bishop Eulogius of Alexandria reported a division between two sects of the Samaritans in the sixth century, one group claiming that Joshua was meant by the prophet like Moses in Dt. 18.18, the others applying the text to Dositheos (*apud* Photius, *Bibliotheca,* codex 230, PG CIII, 1084f.; mentioned by Macdonald, *Theology,* p. 35). However, the text does not state that the former group meant Joshua *redivivus.* It may have been a conservative group which denied the whole Taheb doctrine and regarded the Scripture passage as having been fulfilled by the historical Joshua. (The application of Dt. 18.18 to Dositheos is attested also by Origen, *Contra Celsum,* i.57.) M. Gaster, *Studies and Texts,* I, 647f., also suggested that there were at least two different strands of tradition in the Taheb expectation, one "Ephraimite," awaiting a new Joshua, the other "Levite," awaiting a new Moses. Cf. also Bowman, *ALUOS,* I, 48-50.

[2] *Memar Marqah,* v.2, trans. Macdonald.

[3] *Tanḥuma,* ed. Buber, V, 13; cf. above, p. 202. and the other sources referred to there. Note also Jub. 1.18-21 and Ps. Philo, *Bibl. Antt.* 19.3.

[4] *Memar Marqah,* v.3, trans. Macdonald, p. 203.

in the mouth of Joshua, in a passage closely resembling *Assumption of Moses*, xi, 17.[1]

The notion that Moses continues to intercede for Israel in heaven is not to be found in the early Samaritan sources, although the *Book of Joshua* in one passage indicates that he serves in heaven,[2] and according to Macdonald prayers began in medieval times to be addressed to Moses, probably because of Christian influence.[3]

On the other hand, Marḳah already attests a strong belief that Moses will make a decisive intercession on the Day of Vengeance.[4] This is a notion scarcely mentioned in extant Jewish sources, although there are a few hints of a polemic against such a notion.[5]

Related to Moses' own intercession are the many prayers for forgiveness which are made "by the merit (עמל) of Moses," often in conjunction with the other "righteous ones," the Patriarchs.[6] The idea is the same as the Jewish זכות אבות.[7]

Moses as "the Man"

At several points during this investigation it has been remarked that "the Man" appears in the Jewish sources occasionally as a title, sometimes evidently of an eschatological figure. Moreover, in the trial narrative of the Fourth Gospel ὁ ἄνθρωπος was treated as a throne name parallel to "the King of the Jews." Therefore it is worth-while to notice that "the Man," is one of the titles frequently given to Moses in the *Memar Marqah*.[8] The title is derived from Deuteronomy 33.1, where Moses is called איש האלהים. Since אלהים was a title already given to Moses (Exodus 7.1), a fact frequently

---

[1] Above, p. 160.

[2] Above, p. 246.

[3] *Theology*, p. 213.

[4] Above, pp. 247f.

[5] Thus according to *Yalḳuṭ Simʿoni* on Dt., par. 852 (ed. 1925, I, 588) God himself would take Moses' place as defender in the future world (above, p. 201), while in 4 Ezra 7.102-115, the question whether intercession for the wicked like that by Moses and his successors will be permitted on the last day is emphatically denied (above, p. 161). But in the Samaritan view also Moses' intercession at the end would only be valid for Samaritans who observed the Torah (cf. *Memar Marqah*, iii.9).

[6] E.g., Cowley, I, 4, 10, 11, 12, 15, 48, 66, 75, 76, 77, 86, *et passim*.

[7] The Samaritan doctrine is discussed at length by Macdonald, *Theology*, pp. 320-327, where he compares the Jewish counterpart.

[8] *Memar Marqah*, iv.3 (text I, 89); 4 (p. 91); v.2 (p. 119), 3 (p. 124, again, p. 126); vi.6 (p. 141).

referred to by the Samaritans, איש is taken, not as a construct, but as absolute, and treated as a distinct title.[1] It may be that the title is connected with the tradition which describes Moses as a new Adam, the genuine Adam who renews creation,[2] but this is an area which needs more detailed exploration than is possible here.

Conclusions

This inquiry into Samaritan sources has shown that Moses was for the Samaritans the supreme prophet, indeed virtually the only prophet. His prophecy was understood as the mediation to Israel of heavenly secrets, imparted by God when Moses ascended Mount Sinai into "the unseen world." These secrets, including the Torah, brought "life" to the world, and both the Torah and Moses himself are symbolized by such terms as "water" and "light." Closely related to Moses' prophetic office is the notion that he was God's "apostle," belief in whom was equivalent to belief in Yahweh himself.   *see p. 258*

More ambiguous is Moses' kingship in Samaritan sources, since he is only very rarely called king in the extant texts, although he functions as God's vice-regent. However, there is some evidence that older traditions may have used the title. It was Moses' enthronement in heaven which established his position as God's vice-regent, at which time he was "crowned" or "vested" with God's name, that is, he was called "Elohim." Thus the tradition of Moses' heavenly enthronement was found to be the same as that attested by Philo and the *Tanḥuma* collection of Jewish midrashim. Moreover, Moses was evidently regarded in the early sources as the founder of "the First Kingdom," even though in the chronicles it is Joshua who is first called its king. Whatever else Joshua may have become in Samaritan legend, he was always essentially Moses' successor, and his features were modeled on Moses.'

The Sinai ascension took on great importance in Samaritan lore, and served as the basis for both Moses' prophetic and his more obscure royal functions. The sources are ambiguous about a final

---

[1] This is shown by Markah's list of "20 names" of Moses (*Memar Marqah*, v.4), where the words must be counted separately to achieve the correct total (above, p. 232, n. 1, cf. pp. 234f.). Jewish midrashim on Dt. 33.1 also deal with איש as if it were in the absolute state (cf. above, p. 195 and n. 3.

[2] Above, pp. 222f.; cf. Macdonald, *Theology*, p. 221, and Bowman, *BJRL* 40, 304.

ascension, but suggestions of such an ascent are found already in the *Memar Marqah*. One passage hints that Moses' followers hoped to follow the same path and, like him, "serve in both worlds," but there is nothing to indicate how widespread such a hope may have been.

No evidence was found to substantiate Macdonald's contention that the Samaritan description of Moses had been influenced by Christology even before Markah, and Macdonald's arguments to this effect were found unconvincing. On the other hand the points common to Samaritan and Jewish haggada about Moses are so numerous and so striking that they can only stem from a common origin. One need not speak of Samaritans and Jews "borrowing" from each other, but rather the evidence points to an area of overlapping traditions and mutual influence in the fluid situation in Palestine, perhaps as early as the first century. To be sure it is only in Greek writings among the extant Jewish sources that the prophetic-royal and "hierophantic" roles of Moses are so central as they are in Samaritanism, while in extant rabbinic literature these traditions are found only at the periphery. Yet the survival of the traditions at all in the rabbinic material shows that at an early period the mystical interpretation of Moses was important even in circles close to the Tannaim.

In what region could such mutual cultivation of tradition by Jew and Samaritan have taken place? Only conjectures are possible, but Galilee is easily the most plausible place. Its geographical contiguity to Samaria, its susceptibility to Hellenistic influence, the ambiguities of its relationship to Jerusalem and Judea would all help to explain the actual incidence of the traditions in question. If Galilee and Samaria were once the center of the growth of these traditions, it would be quite natural that they would persist at the center of Samaritan and certain Hellenistic Jewish literature, while only occasionally and peripherally in "normative" Jewish documents. There will be occasion in the final chapter to return to this quite tentative working hypothesis.

CHAPTER SIX

KING AND PROPHET IN MANDAEAN SOURCES

THE SITUATION IN MANDAEAN RESEARCH

The discovery of the Mandaeans by modern western scholarship parallels in many respects the rediscovery of the Samaritans. In both cases a remnant of the ancient sect survived in isolation, preserving very old cultic practices and traditions as well as a literature of great importance. Both groups became known to the West through the reports of travelers, and the investigation of their documents has proceeded alongside eye-witness descriptions of present rites and oral traditions.

The quality and extent of the research devoted to the Mandaeans, however, have produced a much more fortunate situation for the student of their history than for the student of Samaritan lore. In 1875 the great Semitist and Orientalist Theodor Nöldeke published his monumental grammar of the Mandaean dialect of Aramaic,[1] a work so thorough and precise that it remains the fundamental philological tool despite many subsequent discoveries and publications of texts. Building on this foundation, another renowned semitic scholar, Mark Lidzbarski, devoted much of his life to the collection, editing, and translation of the major Mandaean documents.[2] More recently the remarkable Lady Ethel Stefana Drower, who has lived most of her life in the Near East, not only has won an intimacy with the living Mandaeans which permitted detailed description of their continuing rituals[3] and the acquisition of valuable manuscripts, but has acquired the philological skills necessary for the publication of a large number of texts with translations.[4] Finally, the publication of *A Mandaic Dictionary*, based on Nöldeke's notes and on the independent studies by Lady Drower

---

[1] *Mandäische Grammatik* (Halle: Verlag der Buchhandlung des Waisenhauses, 1875 [reprinted, with an appendix containing Nöldeke's later notes, Darmstadt: Wissenschaftliche Buchgesellschaft, 1964]), 486 pp.

[2] See below, p. 262, nn. 4,6; p. 263, n. 1.

[3] E. S. Drower, *The Mandaeans of Iraq and Iran: Their Cults, Customs, Legends, and Folklore* (Oxford: At the Clarendon Press, 1937), 436 pp.

[4] See below.

and R. Macuch,[1] makes the published texts accessible even to a non-specialist.

Despite the solid progress of basic research into Mandaeanism, major problems of interpretation remain. Foremost among them is the problem of understanding the Mandaean myths. These myths are of central interest to the historian of religions and to the New Testament scholar, for they have been widely regarded as a key to the puzzle of pre-Christian gnosticism and, in some circles, as the key to the interpretation of the Fourth Gospel.[2] Certainly the Mandaean religion, as revealed by the literary compilations of the seventh century and later, is aptly termed "gnostic." Therefore the Mandaean texts are extraordinarily valuable because they portray a gnostic group as seen from within rather than through reports of opponents. Until the recent discoveries of Coptic gnostic papyri at Chenoboskion, the Mandaean texts were the only extensive primary documents of a gnostic sect. Consequently two generations of scholars have labored to analyze the Mandaean texts and to construct a synthetic outline of "the gnostic redeemer myth" portrayed by them[3] without bringing the problem to rest.

Each of the attempts at a systematic description of the Mandaean religion has assumed that there is a unitary, organic myth at its heart. Yet careful reading of the published Mandaean texts leaves the impression rather of a multiplicity of myths, an extremely diverse vocabulary of names and images, and great fluidity in the description of mythical actions. To be sure, there are certain patterns

---

[1] E. S. Drower and R. Macuch, *A Mandaic Dictionary* (Oxford: At the Clarendon Press, 1963), 491 pp.

[2] See above, pp. 7-11.

[3] The first attempt at a description of the sect's ideology on the basis of the texts was Wilhelm Brandt, *Die mandäische Religion; ihre Entwicklung und geschichtliche Bedeutung* (Leipzig: J. C. Hinrichs, 1889), 236 pp. Then followed the bold proposals by Richard Reitzenstein, *Das mandäische Buch des Herrn der Grösse und die Evangelienüberlieferung*, elaborated in *Das iranische Erlösungsmysterium* (Bonn: A. Marcus & E. Weber, 1921), pp. 43-92. Bultmann's brilliant synthesis built upon Reitzenstein's proposals (above, pp. 6-12). Hans Jonas set the Mandaean myth within his fourfold schema of gnostic "types" (*Gnosis und Spätantiker Geist*, I, 255-283). More recently, Lady Drower made an attempt at a synthetic description of the Mandaean religion in *The Secret Adam; A Study of Naṣoraean Gnosis* (Oxford: At the Clarendon Press, 1960), 123 pp. Rudolph, in his double monograph which is now fundamental for all further work on Mandaeanism, concerned himself with historical questions and with the phenomenonology of the cult. He attempts no unitary synthesis of the myth, but approves the synthesis of Jonas (*Die Mandäer*, I, 141-176).

which occur repeatedly, with differences only in the *dramatis personae* and in the descriptive details. For example, there are numerous accounts of the "fall" or rebellion of various divine figures, followed by their respective punishments and restorations. There are several accounts of the emanation or procreation of the successive lower stages of the Light World and several stories of bumbling attempts at creating the earthly world and its inhabitants, finally made possible in each case by intervention from the Light World. Apart from these and other cosmogonic and theogonic myths, there are many descriptions of the soul's ascent past the hostile "watchers" who capture the non-Naṣoraean and the apostate. Now the question which has to be faced is whether it is legitimate to abstract from the manifold myths the similar points which can comprise one logically coherent pattern. Rudolph recognizes the tendency to construct such patterns as a special problem of gnostic research, and he offers cogent criticism of "patternism" in the work of Widengren and others who have sought to connect Mandaeanism with general Mesopotamian religion.[1] Cannot an analogous criticism be turned against the construction of patterns out of even *internal* parallels among the varying Mandaean myths? Until further research elucidates the interrelationship among the various personages and images of the various myths, it will be well to heed the *caveat* of Carsten Colpe, "The Mandaean mythology cannot be represented systematically. . . ."[2]

A special aspect of the problem of Mandaean mythology is the question how the myths themselves are related to salvation. Most of the extant myths are theogonic and cosmogonic, describing events in the superterrestrial worlds, mostly before the creation of the earth and man. On the other hand, the center of interest in the liturgical texts is undoubtedly the ascent of the individual soul after death. Both kinds of material are of course typical of gnostic documents. What is lacking in the Mandaean texts is a clear connection between the two. One can guess that the theogonic myths were

---

[1] Rudolph, I, 195-222, especially 199f., 215.

[2] "Die m.[andäisch]e *Mythologie* kann nicht systematisch dargestellt werden, weil sie in eine uneinheitliche Sammel-literatur eingebettet ist. Inwieweit dem umfangreichen m.en Pantheon wirkliche Götter- und Funktionszusammenhänge, -spaltungen und -vereinigungen zugrunde liegen und inwieweit bestimmte Figuren und Themen einander nur literarisch zugeordnet sind, ist im einzeln noch nicht untersucht" ("Mandäer," *RGG*, 3. Aufl., IV, cols. 709f.).

intended to explain the origins of the obstacles—the "sentry posts" or purgatories in the intermediary spheres—which the ascending soul must pass. But the texts themselves do not make this connection explicit.

Similarly the relation of the myth to the cult is not always self-evident, even though it is certainly in the cult that "the heart of the Mandaean thought-world beats,"[1] and "to a large extent the Mandaean mythology is an explanation of the cultic phenomena."[2] Some few myths serve an aetiological function, grounding the cultic act in an act performed in the primeval time in the World of Light,[3] but others seem as little connected with the cultic acts as with the final ascent toward which the cult points. Moreover, even the connection between the soul's ascent itself and the cultic acts may be secondary.[4]

The pre-literary history of the Mandaeans remains largely in the dark, although consensus has been achieved by scholars on a few salient points.[5] It is generally agreed now that Lidzbarski was correct in fixing the origins of the sect or of its direct precursor in the West, in Syria-Palestine, and probably among the Transjordanian baptizing sects.[6] Furthermore, it seems assured that Jewish elements belong to the fundamental stratum of the Mandaean traditions,[7] and that later influences included that of Byzantine Christianity, although perhaps there were also earlier contacts and conflicts between proto-Mandaeans and Syrian Christians.[8]

PROCEDURE AND SOURCES

This chapter will be limited to the very modest task of describing the various passages within which the terms "king" and "prophet" and the related imagery occur. As in previous stages of this investi-

---

[1] Rudolph, II, 13.

[2] Colpe, *RGG*, IV, col. 709.

[3] Rudolph, II, 17.

[4] So Colpe argues: "Die gnostische Seelen-, Urmensch- und Erlösermythologie hängst keinesfalls von Anfang an mit ihrem Kult zusammen, sondern ist später übernommen und umgebildet worden" (*RGG*, IV, col. 711).

[5] The historical development of the sect and particularly the probable influence of various other religious groups form the subject of Rudolph's first volume.

[6] Rudolph, I, 59-252.

[7] *Ibid.*, pp. 51-54, 80-101.

[8] *Ibid.*, pp. 101-118, especially p. 112.

gation, the primary aim will be to explain the function of these notions within their existing contexts. Because of the complex problems surrounding the Mandaean myths and liturgy, no attempt will be made to explain the functions of kingship and prophecy within a presumed over-all pattern of myth, although specific parallels, both within the Mandaean material and between Mandaean material and other traditions already studied, will of course be pointed out.

The three largest Mandaean sources furnish almost all the information which is of direct relevance to the present work. The first of these is the *Qulasta*[1] or book of liturgies, of foremost importance because of the centrality of the cult in the life of the sect. The hymns in the liturgies and in parts of the *Ginza* may belong to the earliest parts of the extant sources.[2] Drower's edition of the complete prayerbook[3] supersedes Lidzbarski's,[4] which contained only about one-third of the material Lady Drower was able to discover, although Lidzbarski's notes are frequently still helpful. The text reproduced in Drower's edition is not a critical collation, but the photographic facsimile of a single manuscript, supplemented from others only to fill lacunae.[5]

The second and longest of the basic texts is the *Ginza* ("treasure"), also called "the Book of Adam." While it was first assembled around the time the Mandaeans came under Muslim supremacy, most of its contents existed in writing before that time.[6]

---

[1] For the transliteration of Mandaean words, I have adopted the simplified system of Drower-Macuch (*Dictionary*, p. xii, cf. p. vi), which abandons the attempt to represent pronunciation. In quotations from other authors, I have left their transliterations as they stood.

[2] So Rudolph, I, 26f.

[3] E. S. Drower (ed. and trans.), *The Canonical Prayerbook of the Mandaeans* (Leiden: E. J. Brill, 1959); text 257 pp., translation and notes, 325 pp. Cited hereafter as *CP*.

[4] Mark Lidzbarski, *Mandäische Liturgien* ("Abhandlungen der Königlichen Gesellschaft der Wissenschaften zu Göttingen, Philologisch-historische Klasse," n.s. XVII, 1; Berlin: Weidmannsche Buchhandlung, 1920), 295 pp. Cited as *ML*.

[5] Drower, *CP*, p. vii.

[6] Lidzbarski, *Ginza*, pp. xii–xiii; cf. Rudolph, I, 27. Citations from the *Ginza* in the following pages are all from Lidzbarski's translation and use the customary abbreviations, *GR* for "Right Ginza" (*ginza yamin*) and *GL* for "Left Ginza" (*ginza smala*). References are to page and line and usually to book and section as well; e.g., *GR*, II, 1, p. 33:20 means "Zweites Buch, erstes Stück, p. 33, line 20." I have not had access to the text edited by J. H. Petermann.

The third major Mandaean compilation is the "Book of John,"[1] so called from the tractate on John the Baptist (iahia as in Arabic; in earlier passages iuhana) which it contains. The title, like much of the tractate on John itself, is late. Like "the Book of Adam," it was probably adopted under Muslim pressure, since both Adam and John were personages of importance in Islamic tradition.[2] An older title was "Discourses of the Kings" (dršia d-malkia), but this title also fits only one of the tractates, that concerned with Iušamin.[3] The relation of the "Book of John" to the Ginza is somewhat like that of the Jewish Tosefta to the Mishnah, for its kernel consists of old traditions which circulated independently, some of which are similar to elements incorporated into the Ginza, but the accumulation of new material continued over a longer period of time. The final compilation of the "Book of John" was considerably later than that of the Ginza, so that most of its contents originated, at least in written form, in Islamic times.[4]

Some of the smaller published documents have been examined, but these prove to contain very little that is directly pertinent to the limited subject at hand: the Haran Gawaita, the Baptism of Hibil-Ziwa,[5] the Diwan Abatur,[6] and the older magic texts and inscriptions.[7]

---

[1] Mark Lidzbarski (ed. and trans.), Das Johannesbuch der Mandäer (Giessen: Verlag von Alfred Töpelmann, 1905/1915), Part I: Text; Part II, Introduction, Translation, Commentary. Cited hereafter as Johannesbuch, by section, page, and line of Lidzbarski's translation.

[2] Ibid., p. v-vi.

[3] Ibid.

[4] Ibid., p. vii; Rudolph, I, 27.

[5] E. S. Drower (ed. and trans.), The Haran Gawaita and the Baptism of Hibil-Ziwa ("Studi e Testi," 176; Città del Vaticano; Biblioteca Apostolica Vaticana, 1953), 96 pp. + inserted facsimile of the Haran Gawaita text.

[6] E. S. Drower (ed. and trans.), Diwan Abatur; or Progress Through the Purgatories ("Studi e Testi," 151; Città del Vaticano: Biblioteca Apostolica Vaticana, 1950), 45 pp. + text facsimile.

[7] H. Pognon, Inscriptions mandaites des coupes de Khouabir (Paris: Imprimerie Nationale, 1898), 328 pp.; Mark Lidzbarski, "Mandäische Zaubertexte," Ephemeris für semitische Epigraphik (Giessen: Alfred Töpelmann, 1900-1902), I, 89-105; James A. Montgomery, Aramaic Incantation Texts from Nippur ("Publications of the Babylonian Section, the Museum, University of Pennsylvania," III; Philadelphia: The University Museum, 1913), pp. 244-255.

Deities and Demons as Kings

An astonishing array of figures are called "king" in the Mandaean sources. Royal imagery is ubiquitous in the liturgy and throughout the mythology, to such an extent that it sometimes seems no longer to carry any particular significance. The pleroma is peopled with "kings"; the description will begin with the highest of the deities.

The Light-King

At the pinnacle of the Mandaean pantheon in some segments of the literature is a figure called the "King of Light" (*malka d-nhura*), "the exalted King of Light" (*malka rama d-nhura*).

> He is the exalted King of Light, the Lord of all worlds of light, the exalted one above all uthras, the God above all [gods],[1] the King of the kings, the great Lord above all kings. A radiance that does not change, a light that does not cease, beauty, radiance, and glory that are not contemptible. Life: a super-life; radiance: a super-radiance; light: a super-light; in him is neither fault nor flaw.[2]

In the tract that stands in two different recensions at the beginning of the *Right Ginza*[3] the King of Light is the hidden Creator: without him nothing would exist.[4] When he spoke "with great power and powerful speech," "kings (angels) of light" came into existence.[5] The first recension contains an additional discourse from a different source,[6] which describes in greater detail the creative activity of the King of Light and the world of Light which emanated from or was created by him.[7] The Light King is "guarded, hidden, not revealed";[8]

---

[1] Inserting *alahia* with Lidzbarski, *Ginza*, p. 6, n. 9.

[2] *GR* I, p. 6: 20-25.

[3] Book I and Book II, section I, are different adaptations of the same underlying document: this much remains certain from Reitzenstein's analysis of the two sections (*Das mandäische Buch, passim*). Cf. Lidzbarski, *Ginza*, pp. 3f.

[4] *GR* I, p. 6: 1 = II, 1, p. 31:32.

[5] *GR* I, p. 10: 25-28 = II, 1, p. 31: 24-27.

[6] Lidzbarski, *Ginza*, p. 4.

[7] *GR* I, p. 6:6 - p. 10:24, p. 11:20 - p. 14:21. Lidzbarski (p. 4) points out that *GR* XII, 6, which begins, "First, I taught you about the King of Light . . ., I spoke to you of the world of Light . . .," and which then describes the world of Darkness, must originally have belonged to the same source, while XII, 7 was evidently by the same author.

[8] *GR* I, 6:19.

his name "the uthras have not revealed."[1] Yet the "sparks of his crown" penetrate every place,[2] and from him come emanations of light, fragrance, his voice, his speech, and the beauty of his form, which create and nurture the "uthras and kings" of the world of Light.[3] Several passages emphasize the necessity of "belief in the King of Light."[4]

The "King of Light" appears regularly as the highest being in the portions of the *Ginza* already mentioned—the doublets in the first book and the first section of the second book, the remainder of the first book and the closely related sixth and seventh sections of the twelfth book—in certain other parts of the *Right Ginza*,[5] very frequently in the "Book of John,"[6] and occasionally in the liturgy.[7] He is known by other titles as well as "King of Light" in these portions of the literature, especially "Lord of Greatness."[8] He is the "Lord of all worlds,"[9] "the King of all *'utria* and *škinata*,[10] probably he is also meant by "the King of Glory."[11]

The terminology is evidently derived from certain limited strands of the early Mandaean traditions, for in the great bulk of the Mandaean texts the supreme deity is called simply "Life" (*hiia*),[12]

---

[1] *GR* XV, 16, p. 360:36f.

[2] *GR* I, p. 7:25-27.

[3] *GR* I, p. 7:30-p. 8:5.

[4] *GR* II, 4, p. 62:9, 12; VII, p. 214:3f.; XVI, 6, p. 392:33f.

[5] Throughout Bk. II, Bk. IV, but occasionally elsewhere: III, p. 73:9-17; IX, 2, p. 237:33 (perhaps an interpolation, cf. Lidzbarski's n. 7); XV, 16, p. 360:36; p. 361:17; p. 363:15; p. 365:9; p. 391:17; XVI, 6, p. 392:33. The single occurrence in *GL* (I, 2, p. 436:29) is bracketed by Lidzbarski as a gloss.

[6] Sect. 3, p. 21:19, 22, 24; p. 23:1; p. 24:4; p. 25:1; sect. 5, p. 29:9; sect. 8, p. 34:11-15; p. 36:8, 21. Also called "the Great King" (sec. 3, p. 24:15) or simply "the King" (sect. 3, p. 20:4; p. 24:15; sect. 4, p. 28:6; sect. 7, pp. 32f. *passim*).

[7] *CP* no. 176 (p. 159).

[8] *GR* I, p. 6:8; p. 7:13; p. 14:25; p. 30:10; II, 1, p. 31:13, 14; p. 32:36; p. 45:1; p. 54:20; II, 4, p. 61:17; p. 62:27; IV, p. 142:19; p. 143:26, 33; p. 144 (often); p. 145 (often), p. 146:17. The title occurs also in contexts where the King of Light is not mentioned: V, 1, p. 173:5; V, 5, p. 197:11; IX, 2, p. 235:30 (bracketed by Lidzbarski as an interpolation); XIV, p. 290: 17 (questioned by Lidzbarski); XV, 2, p. 302:26; p. 303:20; p. 304:25 (context speaks of "the Great [Life]"); XV, 8, p. 326:22; XV, 16, p. 370:11; XVII, 1, p. 401:33, 34, 37; *GL* I, 1, p. 423:16 (superscription).

[9] *GR* I, p. 5:14f.

[10] *GR* I, p. 10:14; cf. *CP*, no. 185 (p. 164), no. 171 (? p. 156).

[11] *Johannesbuch*, sect. 57, p. 203:8, 11; cf. sect. 58, p. 205:15ff.; cf. *GR* II, p. 73:10f.

[12] "Life, the primordial deity of Mand. religion" (Drower-Macuch, s.v. *hiia*).

"the Great Life" (*hiia rbia, hiia rurbia*) or "the First Great Life"
(*hiia rurbia qadmaiia*).[1] "The Great Life" can also be called" king,"
although this usage is rare.[2] There are clear signs in a few passages
of the merging of separate strands, both in places where one of the
titles "king of Light" or "Lord of Greatness" has, in Lidzbarski's
view, been interpolated into a passage that otherwise speaks solely
of "Life,"[3] and also occasionally in the pre-literary stage of tradition. An important example of the latter is the poem in which
"Life" explains to Manda ḏ-Hiia, his son and messenger, the successive emanations which have produced the worlds and deities of
Light.[4] Here "Life" and "the King of Light" appear not as alternative designations of the highest being, but as inferior and superior
emanations. Somewhat more surprising is the fact that Manda ḏ-
Hiia can also be called "King of Light."[5] In this case, however, the
term should probably be regarded as an appellative rather than as
a fixed title which has passed from one figure to another.[6]

---

[1] *Ibid.* Less frequently the supreme god is called "the Great Mana"
(*mana* = "spirit," "soul": *mana rba, mana rba qadmaia*, etc.; *ibid.*, s.v. *mana*).

[2] *GR* II, 12, p. 472:34; "King of the great ones" refers to "the Great Life,"
as does "the King," Adam's ruler and father, *GL* I, 2, p. 435:21.

[3] E.g., *GR* IX, 2, p. 237:33; *GL* 1, 2, p. 436:29; *GR* V, 1, p. 173:5; V, 5,
p. 197:11; IX, 2, p. 235:30; XIV, p. 290:17.

[4] Bevor alle Welten entstanden/war diese grosse Frucht da.
Als die grosse Frucht in der grossen Frucht war, entstand der grosse
    Lichtkönig der Herrlichkeit.
Aus dem grossen Lichtkönig der Herrlicheit entstand der grosse
    Glanzäther.
Aus dem grossen Glanzäther/entstand das lebende Feuer.
Aus dem lebenden Feuer/entstand das Licht.
Durch die Macht des Lichtkönigs
    entstand ‹das Leben und› die grosse Frucht.
Die grosse Frucht entstand,/und in ihr entstand der Jordan.
Der grosse Jordan entstand,/es entstand das lebende Wasser.
Es entstand das glänzende, prangende Wasser,
    und aus dem lebenden Wasser bin ich, das Leben, entstanden.
Ich, das Leben, entstand,/und alsdann entstanden alle Uthras.
(*GR* III, p. 73:7-26)

[5] *CP* no. 71 (p. 60); no. 106 (? p. 107); cf. no. 123 (p. 117); *GR* II, 3,
p. 61:1-4. Yauar-rba, "King of the worlds of light" in *CP* no. 171 (p. 156)
may be not Manda d-Hiia but the Exalted King of Light, but cf. *GR* XV, 2,
p. 302:38 and *Alma Rišaia Rba* (Bodleian MS. *DC* 41), quoted by Drower,
Secret Adam, p. 24.

[6] It is also well to keep in mind that a certain deliberate mixing or un-
conscious fluidity of titles and images is evident throughout the Mandaean
literature, as in much other gnostic material. Cf. Waldemar Sundberg,
Kushṭa; A Monograph on a Principal Word in Mandaean Texts (Lund:
C. W. K. Gleerup, 1953), whose major conclusion is that "there is no sharp

The kings of darkness

The dualism which is basic to Mandaean myth, as to all gnostic systems, comes to expression in the frequent opposition between the world of light and the world of darkness. In the largest continuous description of the two worlds, the account now broken into fragments in the first book and the sixth section of the twelfth book of the *Right Ginza*, the dualism is complete. The two worlds stand over against one another, one the reverse image of the other. As the King of Light stands at the pinnacle of the world of light, so there is a King of Darkness as his counterpart:

> Out of the black water the King of Darkness came to be, formed by his own evil nature, and came forth.[1]

As the King of Light produced the 'utria and other beings of the world of light, so the King of Darkness calls forth a horde of all kinds of demons and monsters.[2] When he sees the light world and its King, he wants to make war on the latter: "I will take away his crown, set it upon my head, and become king of the height and of the depth."[3] His plans naturally come to nothing, although the outcome of the strife is not developed in this passage.[4] In a passage in the "Book of John," catechetical in form, the dualism is carried back still another step by making the two kings coeval:[5]

> The Good [the faithful Mandaeans] speak, take counsel, and say: "Who will come, who will tell me, who will inform me, who will teach me, who will come, who will tell me, whether (in the beginning) there was one king or two?" The Good speak and let themselves be taught: "Two kings existed; two natures

---

dividing line between person and thing," between one person and another, between one thing and another, between means and end, between darkness and light (pp. 111-118).

[1] *GR* XII, 6, p. 277:31f.

[2] *Ibid.*, pp. 277f. A similar myth must be presupposed by the Mandaean magic incantation published by Lidzbarski, *Ephemeris*, p. 103: "Zum Fesseln des Abugdana, des Königs der Dämonen und des grossen Beherrschers aller Nachtgeister. . . ." Nearly identical phrases are found in two inscriptions published by Montgomery, *Aramaic Inscriptions*, no. 11, l.5 (p. 168) and no. 18, l.4 (p. 192). These two inscriptions are not Mandaean, but are in square Aramaic script and are called by Montgomery, "'Rabbinic' Texts," although he suggests Mandaic and Syriac influence.

[3] *GR* XII, 6, p. 279: 25-27.

[4] *Ibid.*, p. 280.

[5] Cf. Lidzbarski's introduction to the passage, *Johannesbuch*, p. 54.

were made; a king of this world and a king from beyond the worlds. The king of this age put on a sword and a crown of darkness. . . . The king from beyond the worlds put on a crown of light. A crown of light he put on and took the Kušṭa in his right hand . . .[1]

More often the dualism is limited and the king(s) of darkness are not full countertypes to the deities of the light world. In the third book of the *Right Ginza*, for example, the "king of darkness" is 'Ur, the son of Ruha; he is described as a giant or dragon who brings chaos into the kosmos and seeks to swallow up the whole world.[2] In the first part of the fifth book, an elaborate account of Hibil-Ziua's descent to restore order in the lower world, 'Ur appaears again as the King of Darkness who creates a disturbance, at the instigation of his mother.[3] But the same section mentions other kings of the lower world, including "the great Šdum, the grandson of darkness," "warlike Šdum, the king of the dark world," as well as the other two of the "three kings" mentioned in the passage, Giu (Lidzbarski, *Gēw*) and Krun,[4] and, in another place, Gap the father of 'Ur.[5] There are hints in the same book of an identification of "Krun, the great mountain of flesh," with the supreme King of Darkness, for 'Ur appears to be an inferior demon ultimately descended from Krun.[6] Within the framework of the more limited dualism, several other kings of darkness appear, including the king of the planets, Šamiš (the sun),[7] who is also identified with the god of the Jews, Adunai-Iurba;[8] Zan-Hazazban, "the swift, valiant king of powerful wrath and destruction," one of the "sentries" in one version of the

---

[1] *Ibid.*, sect. 13, p. 55:7-19; cf. sect. 4, p. 27:6f. and n. 3.

[2] 'Ur is called King of Darkness *GR* III, p. 72:3; pp. 81f.; p. 85:23; p. 87: 33, also apparently 'Ur is meant in XV, 17, p. 375:1 and *GL* III, 1, p. 507:25. He is "the Lord of the world," *GR* III, p. 86:21 and "King of the world," *ibid.*, p. 100:12; cf. *GR* IV, p. 147:20-23.

[3] *GR* V, 1, p. 169:6-15; cf. p. 170:13.

[4] *GR* V, 1, pp. 156f. The original must have described the successive opening of three doors, one for each king, but only the release of Šdum is preserved.

[5] *GR* V, 1, p. 160:4.

[6] *GR* V, 1, p. 157:1-8 and cf. IV, pp. 142f.

[7] *CP* no. 147 (p. 129); *GR* V, 1, p. 176:21-23.

[8] Adunai: *GR* I, p. 25:7 = II, 1, p. 43:1f.; III, p. 135: 9f. Iurba (Yuh or Yah, i.e., Yahweh, the Great): *GR* III, p. 132:12-14; cf. *GL* II, 22, p. 494: 5-15; n.b. *GR* XVIII, p. 410:9, "Jorābbā, den die Juden Adōnai nennen."

ascent of the soul but otherwise not identifiable.[1] Once the twelve Zodiak figures are called kings.[2]

Rebellious kings

Even more prominent than the theme of opposition between darkness and light in the Mandaean traditions is the theme of error or rebellion by deities on the lower echelons of the light world itself.[3] These deities are frequently described as kings. The punishment for their rebellion involves displacement from their thrones and stripping away their insignia of office, while the restoration which follows their repentance and recognition of the higher powers of light invariably is depicted as a coronation in which the former rebel is again called king and is invested with wreath and robes of light.[4] Less clear is the altercation between Nbaṭ, "the King of the Ether" (malka d-ayar), and 'Tinṣib-Nhura, mentioned in the Iušamin section of the "Book of John."[5] Adam can also take the role of "king of the world," as a vice-regent of the powers of light. Thus in the third book of the Right Ginza a "beloved son" "who was formed out of the bosom of radiance" comes and forms "a world,"[6] for which he then "creates a king and casts a soul into his body."[7] Again in the same book Ptahil declares, against Ruha and the Planets who plot against his new creation, "Before I go to the Father's house,/I shall set over this world a Lord," who is Adam.[8] These passages refer to the earthly Adam; others call "First Adam"

---

[1] GR V, 3, p. 185:10f.; VI, p. 208:19f.

[2] GR XVIII, p. 419:20.

[3] This is the "Urfall" motif which, in Jonas' schema characterizes "Syrian-Egyptian" gnosis (Gnosis und spätantiker Geist, I, 280-283; cf. 328-362; cf. The Gnostic Religion; The Message of the Alien God and the Beginnings of Christianity (2d ed., rev.; Boston: Beacon Press, 1963), pp. 236f. As Rudolph points out (I, 145f.), Mandaean myth stands in "einer Mittelstellung" between this and the "Iranian" dualism, but with the "Schuldmotiv" dominating its cosmogony. The limits to Mandaean dualism, Rudolph plausibly suggests, derive from the Jewish influence in its earliest stage.

[4] E.g., Ptahil, GR XV, 3, p. 312:5-8; GL II, 14, p. 478-33:36; Iušamin, Johannesbuch, sects. 9-10, n.b., p. 40:1-8, p. 41:8, 13; p. 42:11; even Iurba, Johannesbuch, sect. 52, especially p. 184:16-18; p. 185:13-19.

[5] Johannesbuch, sect. 3, pp. 19-21; cf. pp. 19f., n. 6, and, on the usua characterization of Nbaṭ, GR XIV, p. 288 and Lidzbarski, ML, p. xx.

[6] GR III, p. 91:29. The beloved son is evidently Manda dHiia, although this is not certain, since the passage fits poorly into its present context.

[7] Ibid., lines 33f.

[8] Ibid., p. 106:5-9; cf. p. 107:21f.: "Wir wollen Adam schaffen, dass er König über die Welt sei . . ."

(*adam qadmaia*) or "Hidden Adam" (*adam kasia*, abbreviated as *adakas*) a king. He is "Adam, the king of *'utria*,/whom all worlds honor";[1] like the rebels, he is tempted to regard himself as "a king without a peer! . . . lord of the whole world!" until awakened by the light of Water of Life and enlightened by a message from the light world.[2]

Kings and 'utria

Apart from the demiurges and other significant kings over certain spheres in the light world, there is a tendency in the Mandaean texts, apparently heightened in later strata, to designate all the gods and demigods as kings. In the "Salutation of the Kings" (*asut malkia*), a litany which now forms part of the daily prayers (*rahmia*) and is also "recited before all baptisms and ritual meals, and rites,"[3] the following personages are specifically addressed as "king": King Mara ḏ-Rabuta- laita, King Iušamin the Pure, son of Nišibtun, King Manda ḏ-hiia, son of Nišibtun, King Hibil-Ziua, King Anuš-'Utra, King Šišlam-Rba, King Shaq Ziua Rba Qadmaia ("the-Great-First-Radiance-was-Bright"), King Sam Ziua, pure, eldest, beloved, great, first Radiance, King Barbag 'Utra, King Šingilan 'Utra, King Abatur Rama, King Uṣṭuna Rba, King Abatur Muzania, King Ptahil, son of Zahriel, King Iahia-Iuhana (John the Baptist), King Adam, the first man, King Šitil, son of Adam the first man.[4] The litany concludes:

> O (ye) kings and 'uthras [sic],
> And Indwellings and jordans,
> And running streams and *škintas*
> Of the worlds of light,
> All of you, healing and victory (be yours!)[5]

Even in the *Asut Malkia*, expansive as is the list of royal personages, "king" is not yet the simple equivalent of *'utra* or angel, as it becomes in some texts. Originally the figures who were called "kings"

---

[1] *GR* III, p. 118:22, a puzzling passage in which Adam is named "ganz unmotiviert" at the end of a list of the three *'utria*, Hibil, Anuš, and Šitil, which is itself unconnected with the preceding verses (Lidzbarski, *Ginza*, p. 118, n. 6).

[2] In the singular myth described in *Alma Riṣaia Rba*, Bodleian Library MS *DC* 41, quoted by Drower, *Secret Adam*, pp. 25f.

[3] Drower, *Mandaeans*, p. 245.

[4] *CP*, no. 105, pp. 104-106.

[5] *Ibid.*, p. 106.

occupied some special position above the rank and file of *'utria*. When Hibil-Ziua says, "An armed *'utra* am I, the king over all worlds,"[1] he is expressing his special rank above the ordinary *'utria*. Moreover, Iušamin complains about his deposition in these terms:

> While I myself was a king, they made me an *'utra*, who must stand before a king. When I was gentle and humble, the *'utria* who belonged to me hated me.[2]

Hibil-Ziua, sent by his father Iauar (Manda ḏ-Hiia) to "pure Taruan" to "teach the Uthras," establishes there "seven worlds of light" and installs over them "seven perfect kings," which are called "kings of light."[3] Anuš calls himself "the son of the mighty kings of glory" as well as "the son of the great Šitil son of the great Adam."[4]

The most prominent of the heavenly kings are the messengers who are sent from the world of light, either to restore order in some lower region of the pleroma or to instruct men. Foremost among these is Manda ḏ-Hiia, who is very frequently called "King of *'utria*"[5] as well as "king in the ether"[6] and "King of Light."[7] "Envoy" or "Apostle" (*Šliha*, compare Hebrew שליח) and "king" (*malka*) are parallel self-designations of Manda ḏ-Hiia in one passage:

> I, the envoy of Light,
> the king, who have come from the Light.[8]

Any messenger from the light world can be called a king, like the "king from the firmament" who is sent to confound the (Persian) "King of Kings"[9] or a messenger sent to fetch the soul of a dying Naṣoraean, who is told:

---

[1] *Johannesbuch*, sect. 40, p. 165:3f.

[2] *Ibid.*, sect. 10, p. 42:11-13.

[3] *GR* XV, 2, pp. 303f.

[4] *GR* XII, 1, p. 269:10, p. 270:9.

[5] *CP*, no. 130 (p. 122), cf. no. 150 (p. 131); no. 132 (p. 122); no. 134 (p. 123); *GR* III, p. 68:3-6; *Johannesbuch*, sect. 6, p. 30:11; sect. 69, p. 231:17. Of Iauar, generally an epithet for Manda ḏ-Hiia (Rudolph, II, 37, n. 6): *CP*, no. 180 (pp. 162f.); no. 188 (p. 166); no. 200 (? p. 172); no. 210 (p. 178); no. 374 (p. 267).

[6] *GR* XV, 16, p. 361:17f.

[7] See above, p. 266, n. 5.

[8] *GR*, II, 3, p. 57:33f.

[9] *GR* XVIII, p. 417.

Stand up, go with him,
with the King of the Great (Life), who has come to you.[1]

Coronation of the messengers and investiture with the various
insignia of the kings of light have a significant place in the descriptions of their missions to lower worlds. Before they descend the
envoys regularly receive a "robe of light" and a "crown" or "turban"
of light or of fire or a "wreath of victory," to which may be added
"a staff of living waters."[2] These royal vestments are the counter-
parts of the Mandaean priest's garb, so these heavenly enthrone-
ments may have a certain aetiological function.[3] Within the myths
themselves, however, the vestments of light clearly have as their
main function protection against the powers of darkness. This
apotropaic function is evident in the report by Manda ḏ-Hiia of his
encounter with rebellious 'Ur:

As I appeared to him in expanded radiance,
    expanded and surpassing all the world,
I showed him the olive staff of living waters,
    which my father gave to me.
I showed him the olive staff of living waters,
    with which rebels are conquered.
I showed him the wreath of living fire,
    at the sight of which the demons are terrified.[4]

In some passages "kings" becomes a general term for all heavenly
beings, that is, the equivalent of 'utria or "angels." Thus prayer
246 in the Canonical Prayerbook speaks of the enthronement of all
'utria,[5] while prayer 249 calls them "kings."[6] In an old portion of
the Ginza "angels of radiance" are said to receive robes, coverings,
girdles, and wreathes of light, that is, all the paraphernalia of
Mandaean kingship.[7] Several times "utria and kings" appears as a

---

[1] GL III, 28, p. 554:22 = p. 555:8.
[2] E.g., GR III, p. 79:11f., cf. pp. 82f.; IX, 2, p. 236:15-20; cf. XV, 15,
p. 356:13f.; Johannesbuch, sect. 47, pp. 173f.; sect. 66, p. 223:15f.; cf. sect.
69, p. 231:8f. Before his attempt at creation, in one account, Ptahil is
similarly invested: GR XV, 13, p. 348:30-33.
[3] On the priests as kings, see below, pp. 274f.
[4] GR III, p. 82:39- p. 83:6.
[5] CP, no. 246 (p. 203).
[6] CP, no. 249 (p. 206); cf. no. 376 (p. 279).
[7] GR I, p. 11:4-18 = II, 1, p. 32:18-30. The Leiden MS has malkia, 'kings,'
instead of malakia, 'angels,' in the former passage (p. 11, n. 1).

hendiadys,[1] as does "gods and kings" in a single instance.[2] "All the beings (or, 'worlds') and kings" that stand before the King of Light are the equivalent of *'utria*,[3] as are the offspring of Simat Hiia, "Mother of all kings."[4] In one passage which is preserved in a double recension in the *Ginza*, one version speaks of "angels" (*malakia*) where the other speaks of "kings" (*malkia*).[5] Since the two words differ by only a single letter, the variant is readily explained as a scribal error, but behind it lies also an actual change of vocabulary. The general Semitic word for "angel," *mal'ak*, does not belong to the basic Mandaean vocabulary,[6] but is probably a later intrusion under the influence of Arabic. Perhaps Arabic influence also caused the extension of the usage of *malka*, "king," as a term equivalent to "angel" or *'utra*, as Lidzbarski has suggested.[7]

Kings in the Human Sphere

Leaving out of account the chronicles and other passages which speak of political kings, there are three significant uses of the title king and of the imagery of kingship for human beings in the Mandaean texts: for priests, for bridegrooms, and for the ascending soul of the faithful Mandaean after death. Of these only the last is of importance for present purposes; the first two need be mentioned only briefly.

Lady Drower has not only described carefully the modern ordination ritual for priests and modern weddings,[8] but has also

---

[1] *CP*, no. 174 (p. 158); *GR* I, p. 7:16,27; p. 12:18; p. 13:10; p. 22:7; II, 1, p. 31:32; p. 32:6 (as emended by Lidzbarski), 35; V, 5, p. 199:7; XI, p. 257:8; XII, 7, p. 280:32; XV, 2, p. 304:22; *GL* I, 1, p. 429:21; cf. *GR* I, p. 8:21; p. 10:40.

[2] *GR* XVIII, p. 412:16. *Alaha* is rare in Mandaean, and here probably alien gods are meant.

[3] *GR* I, p. 6:4: *almia umalkia*; cf. Lidzbarski's n. 3.

[4] *CP*, no. 171 (p. 155).

[5] *GR* I, p. 10:26f. = II, 1, p. 31:25f. Cf. also the places mentioned above, p. 272, n. 7.

[6] "Nicht eigentlich mand. [ist] מלאכא, seltner מאלאכא 'Engel' (מַלְאָךְ) ..." (Nöldeke, *Mandäische Grammatik*, p. 129, n. 1); cf. Drower-Macuch, s.v. *malaka*: "a loan-W. ... used of both good and evil spirits, but preferably of the evil. ... Good angels are preferably indicated as *malka*. ..."

[7] Mark Lidzbarski, "Uthra und Malakha," *Orientalische Studien Theodor Nöldeke zum siebzigten Geburtstag gewidmet*, ed. Carl Bezold (Giessen: A. Töpelmann, 1906), pp. 544f.

[8] *Mandaeans*, pp. 59-72 (marriages), 146-177 (consecration of priests).

published the Mandaean ritual text with translation.[1] These descriptions are important, but the primary sources for understanding the "coronation" of priest and bridegroom are the hymns and prayers for these occasions found in the *Qulasta*.[2] The first cycle of coronation hymns, which are used for both marriage and ordination,[3] describe the investiture of Manda *d*-Hiia or Iauar Ziua, "King of *'utria*."[4] The coronation is depicted as if it were taking place in the light world. The priests represent the *'utria*, and the postulant (or bridegroom) represents Manda *d*-Hiia (Iauar). Having received the vestments and the wreath (*klila*), the new priest (or bridegroom) is saluted:

> Who hath sent thee, new king,
> Cause of all these rites?
> Thou hast illumined the world of Ether
> And brightened the whole earth from end to end.
> Who sent thee, new king
> That sitteth in the *saka* of his teacher?
> Thou hast watered it with a great watering (?)
> And thou hast illumined and ordered
> The uthras in their dwellings (*škinata*)
> From end to end.[5]

Here is perhaps the strongest clue to the relation between the cult and the myth. The priest is the manifestation of the light world in the earth. Perhaps the coronation becomes even the *Vergegenwärtigung* of Manda *d*-Hiia's descent to instruct the Naṣoraeans and to bring light into the darkness. The vestments themselves, all white, are light symbols, as the hymns repeatedly emphasize. References to the radiance of vestments, especially of the crown or wreath, abound, and in the later Šišlam-Rba cycle the king is called a mirror of the light world.[6] Furthermore both wedding and ordination

---

[1] *The Coronation of the Great Šišlam* (Leiden: E. J. Brill, 1962), 39 pp.

[2] *CP*, nos. 179-329 (pp. 160-233).

[3] *CP*, nos. 179-199 (pp. 161-169) = nos. 293-304. (p. 220).

[4] Perhaps Iauar Ziua is only an appellative for Manda *d*-Hiia (see above, p. 427, n. 87). Whether the passages speaking of Iauar are later than the Manda *d*-Hiia passages, as Rudolph urges (II, 239-244), is uncertain, but undoubtedly "das Durcheinander der Verschiedenen Engelwesen zeigt teilweise die sekundäre Ausgestaltung dieser Stücke" (*ibid.*, p. 315, n. 2).

[5] *CP*, nos. 192, 193 (pp. 167f.) = nos. 297, 298; cf. the additional hymn to the bridegroom, no. 210, p. 179.

[6] *CP*, no. 313 (p. 223), cf. the similar address to Manda *d*-Hiia, *Johannesbuch*, sect. 69, p. 231:17. See also *CP*, no. 306 (p. 221). no. 308 (pp. 221f.), no. 310 (p. 222).

liturgies contain purely mythical material in the hymn-cycle *Kt azil bhira dakia* ("When the Proven One, the Pure One Went"),[1] which according to Drower is a selection from "a volume of gnostic poems with this title."[2]

A second group of hymns, used only for weddings, not for the ordination of priests, also mentions Manda *d*-Hiia and Iauar and adds Anuš 'Utra, Šitil, and especially Hibil Ziua as significant personages.[3] But in the last series of hymns, used for ordination alone, a new figure, Šišlam Rba, is the prototype of the postulant.[4] In these hymns Manda *d*-Hiia and Iauar are not mentioned, and there is good reason for believing that the Šišlam Rba passages belong to a later stratum of Mandaean tradition than the others,[5] for Šišlam plays no role in the mythological passages and is never mentioned in either *Ginza* or "Book of John." Perhaps this figure is merely a personification of the priesthood.[6] In these hymns just as much as in the Manda *d*-Hiia hymns the priest is a king and a representative of the light world.[7]

For the faithful Naṣoraean the goal of his ascent after death is both "seeing the light world" and enthronement as a king like the *'utria* on high:

> Hail to him who gives heed to himself. A man who gives heed to himself has not an equal in the world. He will be a king in the Light and will be like the great ones, a great one in the place of Light.[8]
> He who keeps himself unblemished in it (this world), his *škina* will be at the head of the world of Light. Uthras gather around him and extend *kušta* to him. *Kušta* they extend to him and

---

[1] *CP*, nos. 233-256 (pp. 186-213) = nos. 261-284 (see pp. 217f.).

[2] *CP*, p. 213. Three others of the poems are found in *GR*, two in Lidzbarski's and Petermann's editions, another in a MS possessed by Drower. Drower gives a summary on p. 214.

[3] *CP*, nos. 200-214 (pp. 171-184).

[4] *CP*, nos. 305-329 (pp. 220-231).

[5] Rudolph, II, 315.

[6] *Ibid.*, cf. Drower, *CP*, p. 220. According to Drower-Macuch (s.v), the title refers to "Adam kasia as perfect Man, anointed and crowned Priest and Bridegroom." For a radically different, but weakly supported, view of Šišlam's significance, see Cyrus H. Gordon's review of Drower's *The Coronation of the Great Sislam*, *JBL* 82 (1962), 464.

[7] Cf. Rudolph, II, 29 and n. 5, 305, 314-322.

[8] *GR* XV, 1, p. 300:30-33. Somewhat different is the conception in VII, p. 213:17, where a "man of proven righteousness" is said to be "like a king, with the crown set upon his head, who wages war in the world of the evil ones and liars and conquers the darkness and its helpers."

take from him . . . [a lacuna] and on their [sic: read "his"] head they place a great crown, that illumines the world. They place upon him a wreath, a wreath of victory, and name him "Illuminer of the Škinas."[1]

The soul returns to its "original home" and dwells among "the uthras, his brothers"; its throne is established again "as it was before."[2] The ascending soul is met by 'utria, who present it with a "turban of light," a "robe of radiance," a "wreath of ether," and "whatever else the Great (Life) has conveyed to the uthras."[3]

In a poem of the *Left Ginza*, often called "the Mandaean Book of the Dead," the soul addresses the body, declaring the impossibility of the body's accompanying the soul on its upward flight. If the body were "a girdle of radiance and light," "a wreath of radiance and light," "a staff of radiance and light," "sandals of radiance and light," then it could ascend.[4] Thus it is clear that the garments and appurtenances of light *replace* the earthly body with a "body of light."[5]

As the hymns and prayers of the *Masiqta* (death ritual; the name means "raising up" or "ascent"), the dying Mandaean is washed, robed, and crowned.[6] The ritual investiture corresponds to the heavenly investiture which is described in the hymns; undoubtedly it is intended both to symbolize and sacramentally to help bring about the heavenly enthronement.[7]

At the same time the white garments, turban, and wreath which are put on the dying person have an apotropaic function during his

---

[1] *Johannesbuch*, sect. 56, p. 200:5-11.

[2] *GL* II, 1, p. 456; cf. II, 12, p. 473:29-31; III, 5, p. 513:9-16; III, 14, p. 532:3-20.

[3] *GL* III, 7, p. 517:14-19; cf. III, 2, p. 509:15f. A primary motif in the *Masiqta* (funeral) prayers: *CP*, no. 67 (p. 54, top), no. 69 (p. 56, middle), no. 70 (p. 57, top), no. 73 (p. 63), no. 75 (p. 78), no. 76 (p. 81), no. 94 (p. 97), no. 98 (p. 100), no. 114 (p. 111). The enthronement of Iuhana (*GR* II, 1, p. 51:18-25) is also a model of the enthronement of a good Naṣoraean.

[4] *GL* III, 17, p. 537:1-20; another version: III, 58, pp. 589f.

[5] Cf. *GL* III, 50, p. 577:21-28: "Er zog mich aus dem körperlichen Gewande,/aus dem nichtigen Gewande./Er bekleidete mich mit Glanz von sich,/ bedeckte mich mit teurem Licht von sich . . ." See Rudolph, II, 181-188, who compares Mandaean and Christian "Gewandsymbolik."

[6] For a description of the *Masiqta* as conducted in modern times, see Drower, *Mandaeans*, pp. 178-203. Rudolph gives a detailed analysis of the *Masiqta* and other funeral ceremonies (II, 259-296).

[7] As Rudolph says, the basis of the robing lies in the conception "dass eine unbekleidete Seele nicht in die Lichtwelt aufgenommen wird . . ." (II, 57).

ascent, facilitating the passage of his soul through the hostile spheres. The aetiology of the white Turban, found at the beginning the *Qulasta*, makes it clear that the "crown of light" has this function.[1] It symbolizes "the great mystery of radiance, light and glory" which "every Naṣoraean man who is righteous and believing" must take "on arising from sleep."[2] The first man, "Adam-Yuhana son of Mahnuš," describes the time when "Evil was formed and emerged" from the "black waters":

> The Seven were wroth with me, were outraged and said, "The man who set out and came toward us hath not bound a circlet [*klila*] about his head!"

But when Adam complained,

> Then that Lord of Lofty Greatness took a circlet of radiance [*klila dziua*] and set it on my head.[3]

The crown of light, together with the other vestments which are somewhat less frequently mentioned, thus both facilitates the passage of the soul on high by warding off the planetary evil powers and also serves as a symbol and ἀπαρχή of the goal of the ascent, the soul's installation as a king of light.

The descriptions of the heavenly investiture, particularly the crown which is essentially beams of light, immediately recall the descriptions of Moses' enthronement in Jewish sources. The simplest explanation for this similarity is doubtless that both Moses' crown (and occasionally robe) of light and the Mandaean symbols are merely specialized developments of the extremely widespread representation of royal crowns as light emblems or aureoles throughout the ancient Near East. However there is at least one passage which suggests that specifically Mosaic traditions may have had some role in the formation of the Mandaean description of the soul's

---

[1] The *Masiqta* hymns speak most often of a wreath (*klila*) but also of turban (*burzinqa*) or crown (*taga*: a rounded fillet of white silk), as well as a *ṭarṭbuna*, usually translated "turban" also, but of uncertain etymology and meaning. (Drower-Macuch, s.v., and Drower, *CP*, p. 81, n. 1.) All these are equivalent to a crown of light, like that worn by the King of Light and imparted to the kings, ʿutria, and messengers of the light world. The wreath alone may be original: Rudolph, II, 175-181, especially 177; cf. II, 80, n. 1.

[2] *CP*, no. 1 (p. 2). Note that "arising from sleep" could be a double-entendre, since this is a familiar metaphor for the recovery of the soul from its oblivion to its heavenly origins. Cf. *CP*, no. 114 (p. 111).

[3] *Ibid.*, pp. 1f.

ascent. The passage, at least in its present form, describes the ascent of "a man of proven righteousness"[1] and his encounter at the first "sentry post," that of the "voracious, rabid dogs." The soul speaks to them of death, of life, to no avail, and is stricken with terror. Then a cry comes from the light world:

> O man, who call to Life and whom Life answers: believe firmly in Life. You are like a man 120 years of age, a man who holds staff and rattle in his hand and follows behind the flock. But suddenly they grasp him, clothe him in honor, robe him with honor, bind a diadem upon him, set him upon a horse, and make him king in the cities. Moreover you are like a man who stands in a space of 160 miles in a dry plain, thirsts after water, and then smells the fragrance of life. His soul is then like the good Anuš in his glory.[2]

The parallels to Moses' exaltation from "following the flock" to being "King of Israel" are immediately apparent. Furthermore, in Jewish tradition the age of 120 years invariably calls to mind the extent of Moses' life and that of the later righteous men who were compared with him (such as Akiba and Yoḥanan b. Zakkai). The second comparison also would not be inappropriate to the Moses haggada: desert wandering and the satisfaction of thirst. Of course there is no hint of a conscious reference to Moses in the passage in its present form in the *Ginza*. Yet, considering the evidence for a Jewish origin of the proto-Mandaeans, it is altogether possible that this passage is a Mandaean adaptation of a specifically Jewish tradition.[3] The Jewish form would have described the ascent and enthronement of Moses, the Shepherd of Israel, as the prototype of the ascent for which every righteous "disciple of Moses" hoped.

The similarities to the Moses tradition in the single *Ginza* passage

---

[1] Reitzenstein, *Das Mandäische Buch*, pp. 80-85, thinks this originally spoke of Manda d-Hiia, in his view identical with the *Urmensch*. Whether this reconstruction, which requires a number of conjectural assumptions, can be accepted is perhaps not crucial for understanding the text. But Reitzenstein's claim that the Mandaean redactor misunderstood the original, so that p. 183:29-33 describes the *descent* of the "god" and his preaching on earth, rather than the *ascent* of the soul past the first sentry post (*ibid.*, p. 80) is completely unconvincing.

[2] *GR* V, 3, p. 184:3-13.

[3] Lidzbarski's notes on the passage are not very enlightening. The shepherd is not necessarily merely "ein alter verächtlicher Hirt" (p. 184, n. 2), and the suggestion that the author had in mind "vielleicht das Märchenmotiv von dem plötzlich zum König erhobenen armen Manne" (*ibid.*, n. 3) does not explain the graphic details of the simile.

could readily be dismissed as accidental if it were not for the fact that motifs from the Exodus are prominent in several other passages which are connected with the ascent of the soul. In particular the Sea of Reeds (*yama d̲-sup*, Hebrew יֽם סוף) is depicted as a major barrier into which apostates as well as Ruha, the planets, and Christ will fall. "Crossing over" the Sea of Reeds means for the true Naṣoraean ascent into the world of light.[1] The Mandaean world-chronicle in the fourteenth book of the *Right Ginza* mentions major events in Israel's history, including the Exodus, the crossing of the Sea, the wandering in the wilderness, settling in "Jerusalem," and (out of its normal order), the destruction of Pharaoh in the sea.[2] Remarkably enough, Moses is not mentioned in this context, perhaps for polemical reasons.[3] Lidzbarski suggested that the use of Psalm 114.3-6 in one Mandaean hymn[4] "is probably connected with eschatological interpretations of the Exodus."[5] He calls attention also to the similarity between Mandaean allegorical interpretation of the *Yam Suf*, which is sometimes understood as *yama d̲-sop* ("Sea of the End") or *yuma d̲-sop* ("Day of the End"), and the Alexandrian Jewish allegories.[6] For Philo the crossing of the Sea meant escape from the body (Egypt) and the drowning of the passions.[7] Now a Jewish iconographic parallel is probably to be seen in the remarkable mural at Dura-Europas,[8] significantly near the eastern home of the Mandaeans. Thus the group which was to become the Mandaeans must have known, at an early stage of its development, an interpretation of the Exodus as a symbol for the ascent of the soul, an interpretation shared with some widely diffused circles of Judaism. Whether the proto-Mandaeans also shared with these Jewish circles the central conception of Moses as the hierophant of that ascent is no longer possible to determine, but it

---

[1] *GR* I, p. 20:12-18; IX, 1, p. 229:26f; XV, 7, p. 323:21-27; XVI, 6, p. 391: 28 - p. 292:2; *GL* II, 14, p. 477:34; *Johannesbuch*, sect. 14, p. 60:6-9; sect. 23, p. 90:13-15; sect. 30, p. 105:5; especially sect. 57, p. 203:19-26, where the negative image "Sea of Reeds" flows into the positive one of "Jordan"; also *ibid*, p. 205:1-3; cf. *GR* XVI, 10, p. 395:3-8 and XVII, 2, p. 405:18f.

[2] *GR* XVIII, p. 410:14-30.

[3] Cf. Rudolph, I, 83, n. 3.

[4] The hymn occurs both in *GR* V, 2, pp. 177-183, and *CP*, no. 75, pp. 72-78.

[5] *GR*, p. 177, introduction to V, 2.

[6] *Johannesbuch*, p. xxi. On the permeation of the early strata of Mandaean traditions and vocabulary by Jewish elements, see pp. xvi-xxviii. Cf. also Rudolph, I, 16of. and n. 4.

[7] Cf. Goodenough, *By Light, Light*, pp. 204-207.

[8] Goodenough, *Jewish Symbols*, X, 105-139.

remains a possibility at least suggested by the "shepherd-king" passage. The anti-Jewish polemic which abounds in the basic strata of the Mandaean sources, alongside strong elements of Jewish tradition, could explain how the figure of Moses might have been expunged from Mandaean ideology—especially if the Jewish groups which opposed the Mandaeans saw in Moses their primary savior. The question then arises whether at one stage of its development the Mandaean ideology may have found its saviors in docetically interpreted figures of Jewish history, to whom the heavenly figures Hibil (Abel), Šitil (Seth), and Anuš (Enosh) must have once belonged, while the now dominant emanation-saviors with abstract and artificially contrived names might have entered the picture around the time the Mandaeans separated from Judaism. But these conjectures leave far behind the facts which can so far be gleaned from the sources.

Conclusions

From this survey of kingship in Mandaean sources, the aspect which has most bearing on the attempt to clarify the prophet-king christology of John is the designation of the Mandaean "apostles" or "messengers" of the light world as kings. These figures are "sent by the father" and come bringing light into darkness. Their main mission is certainly "to testify to the truth," that is, these "kings" are essentially revealers. Yet no passage makes an explicit connection between kingship as such and the revelatory-juridical function, as John 18.37 does. The imagery of kingship serves only to symbolize the identity of the messengers with the light world and their power over the powers of darkness that resist them. Furthermore, none of these apostle-kings is ever called "prophet."

Both in the case of the apostles of light and in the case of the individual soul, kingship is connected in the Mandaean sources with the descent into the world of darkness and the ascent into the world of light—just the aspect of gnostic myth which has attracted most attention in New Testament scholarship. The center of the Mandaean cult, however, seems to be just the *ascent* of the soul, with enthronement as its reward and culmination. And the connection of enthronement with the ascent of the soul is a notion that pervades Mediterranean syncretism in the Greco-Roman age, even in circles which cannot strictly be called gnostic. It is in the descriptions of this ascent and enthronement that Jewish motifs—perhaps even an echo of Moses traditions—are to be found in the Mandaean literature.

PROPHETS IN MANDAEAN LITERATURE

False Prophets

In the Mandaean texts the word "prophet" is used almost exclusively in a negative sense, to characterize representatives of religions opposing the Mandaeans. In the declaration of innocence which the soul must make as it passes the seven planets, it affirms:

> I did not do your works
>   and I was not counted yours.
> (I did not name) your names
>   and did not speak your speech.
> I was no Chaldaean,
>   no soothsayer and no prophet.[1]

Prophecy is thus identified with the work of Ruha and the seven planets.[2] Similarly, when Abraham and Moses are called "prophets of Ruha," the polemic associates Judaism with the powers of darkness[3]—even though these passages contain a contradictory positive evaluation of the work of Abraham and Moses which can only be a relic of the Jewish traditions which were used here.[4]

In two long polemic sections of the *Ginza*, the tract found in two forms in the first and second books and the tract in the ninth book called "The Downfall of the Seven Stars,"[5] the advent of "false prophets" (*nbihia ḏ-kadba* or *nbihia ḏšiqra*) "who walk in falsehood and deception" is described.[6] To these belong the Jews,[7] Mohammed,

---

[1] *GL* III, 56, p. 587:1-8.

[2] Cf. *GR* II, 4, p. 61:13-15, where Mandaeans are admonished, "Gleichet nicht den Propheten des Truges, noch den Richtern der Lüge; nicht steigen sie empor aus dem Jordan, noch wurden sie gefestigt durch diesen Herrn, der in der oberen Höhe sitzt." The context does not reveal who are meant, but suggests that a rival group, outwardly resembling the Mandaeans, is intended.

[3] *GR* II, 1, pp. 43, 46:10. The other recension of this material does not mention Abraham and Moses (I, p. 25:10ff., p. 28:14f.).

[4] See above, pp. 53-55.

[5] See Lidzbarski's introduction to *GR*, IX, 1, p. 223.

[6] *GR* I, p. 25:22; cf. II, 1, p. 44:1. On the possible influence of Jewish apocalyptic notions of a false prophet at the end of days, see above, pp. 54f.

[7] See the references in n. 3 above.

who is the last, the "most degraded," and "the seal" of the false prophets,[1] and above all the Christians.

In one passage Christ himself is called "the prophet of the Jews," who joins forces with the planets against the true faith.[2] Elsewhere it is Christian priests or monks who are the false prophets. In one passage the emphasis is on the schismatic character of the Christians (treated here as a direct outgrowth, really a sect, of Judaism), as opposed to the unity of Nasoraean faith:

> One king reviles the other king, one prophet punishes the lies of the other prophet. They summon the children of men, make them greedy for gold and silver, money and property, fill them with lust, and seduce them.[3]

Reitzenstein thought the reference was specifically to the sons of Constantine and the struggle between Arians and Catholics,[4] but more likely the "kings" represent the various powers to whom the Mandaeans have been subject in their history, while the "prophets" indicate the various religions—Judaism, Christianity, and Islam—which have attacked their religion.[5] The reference to Christian monks becomes clear in other passages where their outward resemblance to the Mandaeans is suggested[6] and their asceticism condemned,[7] and is detailed in the ninth book of the *Right Ginza*. Kiuan (Saturn) is said to be the author of ascetic Christianity:

---

[1] *GR* II, 1, p. 54:13-17; cf. I, p. 30:15-17, where however the word "prophet" is not used; *Haran Gawaita*, p. 12.

[2] *GR* I, p. 28:22. The parallel , II, 1, p. 46:29-39, calls Christ (also Nbu or Nbu-Christ) a "seducer" and "falsifier" and a "messenger" sent into the world by Šamiš, but not "prophet."

[3] *GR* I, p. 26:1-8. The parallel, II, 1, p. 44:3-8, does not mention kings and prophets, but only "die Engel des Fehls," who are however identical with the "Gesandte des Fehls" who were incarnated as prophets (p. 43:28-33 = p. 25:22-31).

[4] *Das mandäische Buch*, p. 14.

[5] As Reitzenstein says (*ibid.*, pp. 14f.), the following passage about idolatry and star worship evidently refers to paganism.

[6] *GR* I, p. 26 = II, 1, pp. 44f.

[7] *GR* III, p. 136:6-19. The "Adam, son of Adam" in the same book (pp. 129f.) who is called a false prophet after he is seduced by Ruha may be a symbol for Mandaeans who have become Christians. N.b. the false cultus which Ruha and the planets found to mislead Adam. Her insistence that the male/female division is a distortion of the originally androgynous human *mana* may also reflect the views of Syrian Encratism or of Christian gnosticism (cf. *Gospel of Thomas*, logia 22, 114).

He created a covering[1] and perverted the sign. He sent out
false prophets; he laid the cross of darkness on their left
shoulder and took them captive from their houses. . . .[2]

There follows a description of the monks' asceticism and the assertion that demons (*diuia*) and liliths sleep with the celibates to
reproduce their kind. The cult (eucharist) is described in perverse
terms, and it is especially objected that "like my[3] disciples they
establish for themselves a *masiqta* and a memorial feast."[4] It is
specifically said that the monks "call themselves prophets of falsehood."[5] Is there a recollection here of Christian monks who really
called themselves "prophets"? This may very well have been the
case in early Syrian Christianity, which seems to have resembled
in other respects the Mandaean description of these "false prophets."[6]

Exceptions: Naṣoraean Prophets

There are a few passages in which prophets are referred to positively in the Mandaean texts. The *Ginza* passage which describes
the advent of Anuš-'Utra "in the years of Palṭus (Pilate) the king
of the world" tells of "three hundred and sixty prophets" who went
forth from Jerusalem and "testified to the name of the Lord of
Greatness," after which Anuš ascended to the world of light.[7] The
parallel version does not mention these 360 prophets,[8] but in another
passage, describing Ruha's foundation of Jerusalem, it is said that
finally "365 disciples came forth from the place Jerusalem."[9]

The only major exception to the negative usage of "prophet" is
in the titulature of John the Baptist, who is regularly called a

---

[1] The monks' robes.

[2] *GR* IX, 1, p. 223:23 - p. 224:2.

[3] The speaker is either Manda ḏ-Hiia or Hibil-Šitil-Anuš (Lidzbarski,
p. 223, n. 2).

[4] *GR* IX, 1, p. 224.

[5] *Ibid.*, line 18.

[6] Cf. Rudolph, I, 112, Reitzenstein also points out elements in the polemic
of *GR* I that are parallel to Celsus' descriptions of the Syrian and Palestinian
mendicant prophets (*Das mandäische Buch*, pp. 22f.).

[7] *GR* I, p. 30:1-14. As Anuš' activity is described in terms similar to the
synoptic accounts of Jesus' healings, so this passage reminds one of the
early chapters of Acts. The Mandaean passage is late (Lidzbarski, *Ginza*, p.
xii), and dependence on Christian traditions is not impossible.

[8] *GR* II, 1, p. 48:15-18.

[9] *GR* XV, 11, p. 341:28-33; cf. Reitzenstein, *Das mandäische Buch*, pp. 33f.

prophet.[1] But this title, which is applied to no other important figure in the sources, must have been firmly attached to John in the traditions before they came to the Mandaeans. Moreover, the "Book of John" itself makes clear that the importance of this designation for John arose from the encounter with Islam, for the persecutors would characteristically inquire:

> Who is your prophet? Tell us who your prophet is; tell us what your scripture is; tell us whom you worship.[2]

The same apologetic necessity that produced the compilations of Mandaean writings, that they, like Jews and Christians, could be recognized by the Arabs as "a people of a book," thus also made necessary that "their prophet" be discovered or elevated to new prominence.[3] It is interesting that in one passage John is addressed as "a false prophet" because he is unmarried, a fault which has to be corrected for him to fit Mandaean ideology.[4] Evidently not all elements of the old traditions about the Baptist were acceptable to the Mandaeans.

Surprisingly enough, there is only one passage that suggests that the heavenly messengers could be called prophets. A priest's prayer, a late piece[5] found in the *Ginza*, mentions "the blessing which was pronounced over the earth with its condensation, over the heaven with its canopy, over the shining sun, the moon . . ., the stars . . ., the air, the living water, the fruit of the earth, over Adam the first man, his wife Eve, his children and descendants, over the apostles and prophets (*šlihia unb'iia*), over the elect and perfect, over the faithful and perfect of Light. . . ."[6] But there is no hint of the identity of the "apostles and prophets."

Conclusions

There is no evidence that at any point the Mandaeans expected a prophet as a savior figure or that they called any of their revealers

---

[1] *Johannesbuch*, sects. 18-33, *passim* (pp. 75-123). N.b. p. 78:1-3; p. 80:11, 26; p. 82:3-6; p. 85:10f.; p. 117:7f. = p. 118:1; *Haran Gawaita*, pp. 5-7 ("prophet of *kušṭa* and apostle").

[2] *Johannesbuch*, sect. 22, p. 89.

[3] Cf. Lidzbarski, *Johannesbuch*, pp. v-vi; Rudolph, I, 66.

[4] *Johannesbuch*, sect. 31, pp. 109f.

[5] Lidzbarski, *Ginza*, p. 283.

[6] *GR* XIII, pp. 284f.

"prophet." The emphasis on John the Baptist as "our prophet" is a secondary development in the face of Islamic pressure; "Iaia" or "Iuhana" is never a significant revealer and not one of the apostles sent from the light world in the earlier texts. Of course the possibility cannot be entirely foreclosed that the "messengers" or "apostles" may have been called prophets at one time and that polemic against a Christian group of "prophets" might have led to suppression of the title. But there is no evidence for any such alteration of the traditions.

Furthermore, while the revealers could be called "king," and royal imagery has an important function in the cosmogonic myths and in the description of the soul's ascent, yet kingship as such is not associated with revelation, and the title "prophet" is never associated with the title "king."[1]

---

[1] The one polemical passage quoted above, p. 282, forms an exception to this statement, but not a significant one.

CHAPTER SEVEN

MOSAIC TRADITIONS IN THE FOURTH GOSPEL

In Chapter II analysis of the thematic functions of "prophet" and "king" in John led to the hypothesis that this peculiar combination of the two figures was connected with traditions about Moses. Exploration of Moses' legends and midrash of very diverse provenance has now shown clearly that Moses was frequently described by just such a combination of royal and prophetic images. In some circles of both Judaism and Samaritanism Moses was regarded as the prototypal king and prophet of Israel. The foundation of his prophetic-royal mission, in this view, was his enthronement in heaven (the Sinai theophany), where he received the Torah and, with or within it, all truth. From that moment he became God's emissary or agent (his *šaliaḥ*) and his vice-regent on earth. It is reasonable to assume that such traditions were cultivated by groups that exalted Moses as the center of their religious concerns, as the intermediary, in some sense, between them and God. There is considerable evidence to support this assumption: the secrets revealed to Moses were the source of apocalyptic knowledge and legal regulation; his enthronement was sometimes the model for mystical "ascent" and for the elevation of the righteous at death; his leadership in the Exodus and the wilderness was the model for expectations of final redemption; his intercession was the basis for hope at the last judgment.[1]

On the other hand, the prophet-king combination is completely

---

[1] E. R. Goodenough has for years been arguing for the existence of such a Moses-centered mystical piety in Judaism (*By Light, Light, passim*, and now with great persuasiveness in his analysis of the synagogue paintings at Dura-Europas, *Jewish Symbols*, IX-XI, especially IX, 197-226, cf. 110-123, and X, 105-139). Goodenough's theory has been vigorously controverted, the debate turning especially on the question whether such a Jewish religion might have taken the form of an organized "mystery" (above, p. 120, n. 7). The evidence I have presented above, while it sheds little new light on the question of a possible cultic organization in mystical Judaism, certainly harmonizes with Goodenough's general theory, and even adds a measure of corroboration beyond the sources he had used. In particular, it shows that the kind of piety Goodenough postulates was not limited to certain "Hellenized" Diaspora Jews, but was known in Palestine, by Samaritans as well as Jews, even in circles whose traditions have been preserved in the literature of "normative" Judaism.

absent from the Mandaean sources, even though "king" is a frequent title for the divers revealers, who also have in common with the Johannine Christ their missions as "apostles" or envoys of the highest God.

Thus the Moses traditions do offer an adequate background for the prophetic-royal christology of John. The question to be answered now is what the Fourth Gospel says about Moses.

DIRECT MENTION OF MOSES IN THE FOURTH GOSPEL

Moses is mentioned by name eleven times in John. Most of the occurrences speak of the "gifts" of God through Moses, pre-eminently "the Law," i.e., the Torah. A few passages suggest a Moses-centered Jewish piety. Beginning from these direct references, one can discover in the gospel a large number of fairly clear allusions to the Moses traditions. Only those allusions closely related to the "prophet-king" themes can be discussed here.[1]

Gifts through Moses and through Jesus

The gift of the Torah

"The Law was given through Moses . . .," declares the evangelist (1.17), in a clause formulated exactly as the rabbis would put it.[2] Moses did not give the Law, but it was given *through* him. The distinction was not always preserved by Greek-speaking Jews, who customarily referred to Moses as "our legislator."[3] John 7.19a thus sounds more like the Hellenistic formulation: "Did not Moses give you the Law?" However, perhaps this clause should be translated as a statement rather than a question, like the precisely parallel clause, "Moses did not give you the bread from heaven . . ." (6.32a). The result in 7.19 would be awkward, requiring the reader to supply

---

[1] There is a temptation, once one is familiar with the Moses stories, to find hidden parallels to them throughout the gospel. But every such suggested parallel would have to be subjected to a rigorous historical criticism, to discover whether the Johannine motif in question could be better explained in another way. For an example of the extraordinary number of allusions to Moses that an imaginative reader can discover in John, cf. the monograph by T. F. Glasson already referred to several times.

[2] The Torah was given "by the hand of Moses" (על ידי משה or ביד משה): Bloch, "Quelques aspects," pp. 139-141; Odeberg, *Fourth Gospel*, pp. 149f.; Barrett, p. 141; cf. above, pp. 171, 205f., 224.

[3] Above, pp. 107, 112f., 132f. and n. 2.

a clause like 6.32b, ". . . but my Father gives you [the real Law]."
But the resulting construction would be similar to that of 7.22-23,
where the direct statement, "Moses gave you circumcision," is
immediately corrected by the parenthetic remark, "Not that it is
from Moses, but from the Fathers." By "circumcision" the commandment is meant, as verse 23, "the Law of Moses," shows. For
John, then, as for the New Testament in general and also for
Judaism, the Law is the "Law of Moses" in the sense that it is
delivered by God through him. Similarly "Scripture" can be called
γράμματα Μωϋσέως (5.47), or it can be said that "Moses wrote in
the Law . . .," with "and the Prophets" added as an afterthought
(1.46).[1]

In each passage which mentions the Law or Scripture of Moses,
the Fourth Gospel indicates a direct relationship between that Law
and Jesus. The relationship is emphatically ambivalent. On the one
hand, Jesus and his revelation stand over against or at least superior to the Torah. While "the Law was given through Moses,
grace and truth came through Jesus Christ" (1.17).[2] Like Pilate
(18.31) Jesus can speak of "your Law" (8.17; 10.34; cf. 7.51 and
15.25). Use of Scripture proof-texts can lead to false conclusions
(7.40-52; cf. 5.39, δοκεῖτε). On the basis of "our Law" Jesus is
condemned to death (19.7).

On the other hand, Jesus is the one of whom "Moses wrote in the
Law" (1.45; 5.46), so that a faithful comprehension of "the Scriptures" would discover testimony to Jesus (5.39, 46-47). Hence the
fourth evangelist uses Scripture proofs, in the form of direct quotations introduced by a formula, more extensively than any other

---

[1] νόμος = תורה can be used loosely for "Scripture," as in the formula οὐκ
ἔστιν γεγραμμένον ἐν τῷ νόμῳ ὑμῶν . . .; (10.34; 15.25), which in these passages
introduces quotations from Psalms.

[2] This verse itself expresses the ambivalence, for while it implies a contrast
between the gift through Moses and the gift through Jesus Christ, its form
also suggests that the gifts are parallel. There is nothing in the formal
structure of the two clauses which requires them to be understood anti-
thetically (cf. J. Jeremias, ThWbNT, IV, 877), though the δε inserted in P66
and W attests such an understanding in antiquity. Modern commentators
generally interpret the parallelism as antithetic simply because they see in
the words νόμος and χάρις the Pauline antinomy, which however finds no
distinct echo elsewhere in the gospel (cf. Bultmann, Ev. Joh., p. 53). ἡ χάρις
καὶ ἡ ἀλήθεια, however, is to be understood as a unified expression, as in v. 14,
equivalent to the OT חסד ואמת (Ex. 34.6 and elsewhere; cf. Barrett, p. 139,
and Dahl, "The Johannine Church and History," p. 132). There is no real
connection with the Pauline antithesis.

New Testament writer except Matthew.[1] The Torah is not rejected, for if "the Jews" really kept the Torah they would not seek to kill Jesus (7.19), and the Johannine Jesus can defend his violation of the Sabbath by a *ḳal weḥomer* argument from "the Law of Moses" itself (7.22-24).[3]

Most significant of all is the way in which the "words" of Jesus are made functionally parallel to the Scripture. The same Scripture-fulfillment formula which introduces Old Testament quotations seven times in John is applied twice to Jesus' words.[3] To his version of the traditional saying about destruction and rebuilding of the Temple the evangelist appends the note, "So when he was raised from the dead, his disciples remembered that he had said this, and *they believed the Scripture and the word which Jesus had said*" (2.22).[4] The taunt is addressed to "the Jews," "If you do not believe his [*sc.* Moses'] Scriptures, how can you believe my words (ῥήματα)?" (5.47).

In the light of this relationship between the Torah and the words of Jesus, his statement in the final prayer to the Father takes on new significance: "The words (ῥήματα) which you gave to me I have given to them, and they received them . . ." (17.8). Almost identical

---

[1] γεγραμμένον ἐστιν (ἐν τῷ νόμῳ, ἐν τοῖς προφήταις): 2.17 (quoting Ps. 69. 10); 6.31 (Ps. 78[77].24, the basis for the discourse on "bread from heaven"); 6.45 (Isa. 54.13; n.b. the deduction: "Everyone who hears from the Father and learns comes to me," which could be taken as a charter for Christian missionary interpretation of OT texts); 10.34 (Ps. 82[81].6); 11.15 (a catena of Isa. 40.9 and Zech. 9.9); 15.25 (Ps. 35 [34].19 = 69[68].5). ἵνα (ἡ γραφή, ὁ λόγος . . . , κτλ.) πληρωθῇ: 12.38 (Isa. 53.1); 13.18 (Ps. 41[40].10); 15.25 (see above); 19.24 (Ps. 22[21].19); 19.36 (source not certain: cf. Ex. 12.46, Num. 9.12, Ps. 34.21); 19.37 (Zech. 12.10). ἵνα τελειωθῇ ἡ γραφή: 19.28 (Ps. 22[21]. 16). Introduced more freely: πάλιν εἶπεν Ἠσαιας 12.40 (Isa. 6.9f.), following closely upon a formula-quotation, v.38. The quotation from Ps. 118.25f. in the cry of festival crowds (11.13) is taken over by the evangelist from his source; in any case a formula would be inappropriate to the context. N.b. also 20.9, where however no specific OT text is cited to support the resurrection.

[2] The same view is implicit in the argument of Nicodemus (7.51), which suggests that ὁ νόμος ἡμῶν itself, if one judges τὴν δικαίαν κρίσιν (7.24), would lead to *hearing* from Jesus and *knowing* what he does (v. 51; cf. 6.45), and thus to recognition that he is the true messenger of God.

[3] ἵνα πληρωθῇ ὁ λόγος ὃν εἶπεν . . . (18.9, 32). The two λόγοι referred to are found at 17.12 (cf. 6.39; 10.28) and 12.32f. (cf. 3.14; 8.28).

[4] Possibly the γραφή which is referred to here is the quotation from Psalm 69.10 introduced in v. 17 (ἐμνήσθησαν οἱ μαθηταὶ αὐτοῦ ὅτι γεγραμμένον ἐστίν . . .), but more likely v. 22 refers only to the vague conviction that ἡ γραφή, without further specification, attests the Resurrection (cf. 20.9).

language is used repeatedly, already in the Pentateuch as well as in the later tradition of both Jews and Samaritans, to describe the fundamental element of Moses' mission: the transmission of the Torah on Sinai. As a single example, the Septuagint translation of Deuteronomy 10.4, describing the delivery of the second set of tablets, may be quoted:

καὶ ἔγραψεν [*sc.* κύριος] ἐπὶ τὰς πλάκας κατὰ τὴν γραφὴν τὴν πρώτην τοὺς δέκα λόγους, οὓς ἐλάλησεν κύριος πρὸς ὑμᾶς ἐν τῷ ὄρει ἐκ μέσου τοῦ πυρός, καὶ ἔδωκεν αὐτὰς κύριος ἐμοί.[1]

The point which is emphasized, especially in the Deuteronomic account, is that Moses had to *mediate* between God and the people:

κἀγὼ εἱστήκειν ἀνὰ μέσον κυρίου καὶ ὑμῶν ἐν τῷ καιρῷ ἐκείνῳ ἀναγγεῖλαι ὑμῖν τὰ ῥήματα κυρίου, ὅτι ἐφοβήθητε ἀπὸ προσώπου τοῦ πυρὸς καὶ οὐκ ἀνέβητε εἰς τὸ ὄρος.

(Deuteronomy 5.5)[2]

Moreover, the prophet like Moses promised in Deuteronomy 18 was to have the same mediatorial function, again described in similar language: δώσω τὸ ῥῆμά μου ἐν τῷ στόματι αὐτοῦ, καὶ λαλήσει αὐτοῖς καθότι ἂν ἐντείλωμαι (Deuteronomy 18.18). Reason has already been found for connecting Jesus' repeated insistence that his words were "not his own" with the authentication of the true Prophet.[3] Now it can be seen that these prophetic words actually take on the same function in John as the Mosaic Torah, and thus effectively supplant it. It is also in this context that Jesus' "new commandment" (13.34) belongs. It is by keeping Jesus' commandments, which means to "remain in his love" by "loving one another," that one becomes and remains Jesus' true disciple,[4] just as study and obedience of Moses' commandments makes the Jew a true disciple of Moses (תלמידו של משה, γνώριμος Μωϋσέως).[5]

Not only did Jesus deliver to his disciples the "words" and "commandment" which God gave to him, he also revealed the *name* of God, which was likewise *given* to him (17.6, 11-12). It can scarcely be doubted that this reference to a special revelation of

---

[1] Cf. Ex. 19.6bf.; 23.22b; 24.3; 34.28; Dt. 4 *passim*; 5.5; 9.10.
[2] On this mediatorial function, see Bloch, "Quelques aspects," pp. 139-141.
[3] Above, pp. 45f.
[4] 14.15, 21; 15.10; cf. 8.31.
[5] See above, p. 103; Talm. B., *Yoma* 4a.

God's name is derived from the tradition of the revelation of the ineffable name YHWH to Moses, described in Exodus 3.13-14 and 6.2-3, and vastly elaborated in post-biblical tradition.[1] Thus John 17, which stands as a formal summary of Jesus' total mission, connects that mission in two important respects with the Sinai theophany, that is, with precisely the event that established Moses as Prophet and King of Israel in the traditions explored above.

The gift of "bread from heaven"

The theme of Jesus' discourse on "the bread of life" in John 6 is stated in these words: "It is not Moses who gave you the bread from heaven, but my father is giving you the real bread from heaven" (6.32). Thus the second "gift" associated with Moses is brought into a christological perspective. The polemic intent is evident: Moses is reduced to a mere mediator of the gift, and the gift itself is derogated in comparison with its Christian countertype.

Since the bread discourse has been discussed in detail,[2] it will suffice here to recall a few of the salient points of the previous analysis. The gift which is given through Jesus is depicted as parallel to that which came through Moses. Like the manna of the wilderness, the gift is "bread from heaven." But the discourse emphasizes that Jesus' gift is superior to that which came by Moses' hand: as the "real bread" it gives "eternal life," while the fathers who ate the manna died. The new gift is symbolized by the multiplication of the loaves and the gathering of the fragments, for the "living bread" is the means of "gathering into one the children of God who are scattered." But this means that the gift is nothing less than Jesus himself, ὁ καταβὰς ἐκ τοῦ οὐρανοῦ, "given" in death.

The lifting up of the serpent

There remains the familiar passage in which the "lifting up" of the Son of Man, that is, his crucifixion and paradoxical "exaltation," is compared with the "lifting up" of the serpent by Moses (3.14). Here is one clear case of "typology" properly so called, as the form

---

[1] Cf. Ginzberg, *Legends*, II, 319f., who quotes *Shemot R.*, 3.6; *Tanhuma, Shemot* 20; Tal. B., *Ber.* 9b, and *Pirke de R. Eliezer*, 40. On Samaritan traditions, see above, pp. 224, 235. Gilles Quispel has suggested that esoteric forms of this speculation about the "hidden name" underlie certain notions in Valentinian gnosticism ("Christliche Gnosis und jüdische Heterodoxie," *Evangelische Theologie* 14 (1954), 479-484).

[2] Above, pp. 91-98.

καθώς . . . οὕτως . . . indicates. As is often pointed out,[1] this is not an example of "Moses-typology," for it is the serpent or, more precisely, the act of "lifting up" that is the *tertium comparationis*. Hence the passage compares an action which takes place through Moses with an action associated with Jesus. For this reason it is properly considered among the "gifts" through Moses. Again the main thrust of the passage is that what takes place through Jesus is parallel to, but far superior to that which was enacted by Moses. The bronze serpent was erected to save the Israelites who were dying from snake-bite (Numbers 21.8-9), but "everyone who believes in him [*sc.* the Son of Man] will have *eternal* life."

Summary

A common pattern has emerged from the analysis of each of the "gifts" connected by John with the name of Moses, the Torah, the manna, and the lifting up of the serpent. (1) Each of these gifts has its parallel in a gift made by God through Jesus. (2) In each case Jesus' gift presents "life"—real life, eternal life—which was only supposed to be available or was only superficially or temporally available through the corresponding gift of Moses. "In them [*sc.* the Scriptures] you *think* you have life": 6.49; ". . . that everyone who believes in him may have *eternal life*": 3.15). (3) In each case the new gift is symbolically identical with Jesus himself.

Moses as the Center of Jewish Piety

The remaining occurrences of the name "Moses" in John are in 9.28-29, in the context of an interrogation by "the Jews" of the man born blind who has been healed by Jesus. When the man taunts his inquisitors with "Do you want to become his disciples?" they retort:

> You are his disciple, but *we* are Moses' disciples. We know that God spoke to Moses, but as for this man, we do not know where he is from.

The interrogation is in effect a formal trial, which culminates with the expulsion from the synagogue of the man who was blind but

---

[1] E.g., Teeple, p. 96.

now sees (verse 34). But the chapter concludes with the revelation that, by judging him, "the Jews" or "the Pharisees" have in fact condemned themselves (verses 40-41). Thus the trial becomes a parallel to the trial of Jesus himself before Pilate,[1] and a paradigm of the notion, emphasized in the farewell discourses,[2] that followers of Jesus must endure from "the world" the same hostility that Jesus met. In particular the healed man in chapter 9 illustrates the prediction of 15.27 - 16.1: "You will testify, because you have been with me from the beginning. . . . They will put you out of the synagogue." The man in chapter 9 is a witness on Jesus' behalf; for this reason he is expelled from the synagogue. But he must be compared with the healed man in chapter 5, who, when similarly interrogated, becomes a witness *against* Jesus (5.15-16).

Bultmann has cogently pointed out that chapters 5 and 9 not only share a common formal pattern, but "are evidently to be understood from the same historical situation,"[3] namely, the relationship between an early Christian group and a hostile Jewish community. What is significant for present purposes is that in both chapters Moses is mentioned as of central importance in the religion of the Jewish opponents. From the details of the two stories it is possible to reconstruct some important aspects of the *Sitz im Leben*.

The "witnesses"

In neither story does the healed person represent the Christian community as such, but rather persons still standing within Judaism who have come under the influence of the Christian proclamation.[4] The first man does not even know who Jesus is when first interrogated (5.13) and never enters into a positive relationship with him. The second is "found" by Jesus and makes his confession only *after* his testimony at the trial and his expulsion (9.36-38). The situation of persons who remain in the synagogues, but who are attracted to Christianity, is presupposed also by the note in 12.42: "Even many of the rulers believed in him, but because of the Pharisees they did not confess, lest they be expelled from the synagogue." Perhaps like the former blind man they recognized in Jesus "a prophet," a true

---

[1] This parallelism, which can be extended in part even to the formal structure, was pointed out to me by Prof. Paul W. Meyer.

[2] 15.18-25; 17.14.

[3] *Ev. Joh.*, p. 178.

[4] *Ibid.*

prophet who had come "from God" (19.18, 31-33).[1] Thus at least substantial portions of the Johannine tradition were shaped by a fluid situation of missionary and polemical interaction with a strong Jewish community.

The opponents

The stories also reveal important features of the Jewish community. In each case, the controversy begins with the question of Sabbath observance. As in the case of the synoptic controversies, this must indicate that while the opponents were Torah-practicing Jews, the Johannine Christians were not—hardly a surprising deduction. However, the question of Sabbath observance is merely the starting point of the argument in John 5 and 9, which is on the whole an expressly *christological* controversy. As the Christians see the situation, the Jewish opposition is directed especially against the claim that Jesus is "equal to God" (5.18). Moreover, the Jews claim that anyone who violates the Sabbath commandment even vitiates the claim to "come from God" (9.16).

Not only do the opponents of the Johannine community faithfully observe the Torah, they also practice midrash, since in the Scripture, they are convinced, "life" is to be found (5.38). Most important, they "put their hope in Moses" (5.45) and "believe" in him (5.46) and declare themselves, over against the disciples of Jesus, to be "disciples of Moses" (9.28). The nature of their "hope in Moses" is further illuminated by the taunt, "The one who accuses (ὁ κατηγορῶν) you [before the Father] is Moses, in whom you put your hope." The full irony of this taunt becomes clear only when it is recalled that in almost every circle of Judaism and in Samaritanism Moses was regarded as the primary *defender* (συνήγορος, παράκλητος) of Israel before God.[2] In a number of places the act of intercession for Israel was particularly linked with Moses' prophetic office.[3] And it is just on the question of the prophetic functions of Moses and of Jesus that the controversy in chapters 5 and 9 finally turns: "We know that God spoke to Moses, but as for this man, we do not know where he is from" (9.29). The point at issue, both in the "trial" in

---

[1] See above, p. 34.

[2] Thus Philo, Josephus, *Assump. Mos.*, Pseudo-Philo, Qumran, and the rabbinic midrashim, as well as Samaritan sources: above, pp. 118, 125, n. 2, 137, 159-161, 174, 200-204 254f.

[3] Philo, *Praem.* 56; elsewhere: above, p. 155, cf. p. 197; Samaritan sources, *passim*: see p. 254.

chapter 9 and in 5.19-47, is whether Jesus is the true or the false prophet predicted in Deuteronomy 18.[1]

Even the notion of "believing in Moses," suggested by 5.46 (together with the parallel idea, "believing his Scriptures"), is probably not merely a Christian formulation by analogy, for the importance of belief in Moses is attested in several places in Jewish and throughout Samaritan sources. The Mekilta on Exodus 14.31 remarks, "Having faith in the shepherd of Israel is the same as having faith in Him who spoke and the world came into being."[2] The confession of belief in "God and in Moses the Great Prophet" is basic to the "Samaritan creed,"[3] and occurs in an isolated rabbinic midrash on Numbers 16.[4]

The two controversy stories in John 5 and 9 therefore provide valuable glimpses of at least *one* segment of the environment in which the Johannine traditions were formed. The Johannine circle was engaged in polemics with a Jewish community of the type of which rare glimpses have been seen in the variegated literature surveyed in Chapters III and IV above. This community put its trust in Moses as the supreme prophet, God's emissary and revealer, and the defender in the heavenly court of the true Israelites who trusted him.

THE ASCENT OF MOSES AND THE EXALTATION OF JESUS

The Ascensions of Moses

One of the most widespread of the legendary motifs connected with Moses' mission is that which interprets his meeting with God on Mount Sinai as an enthronement in heaven.[5] Moses' ascent "on high" is understood as his inauguration as King and Prophet of Israel. From this point he was God's agent on earth: as prophet, his unique messenger, conveying divine secrets; as king, his vice-regent.

---

[1] See above, pp. 44-61.

[2] Mekilta, *Bešallaḥ*, 7; ed. Lauterbach, I, 252; the passage is quoted *in extenso* above, p. 239. The importance of this passage as a parallel to John 12.44 and 14.1 (curiously without mention of 5.46!) was pointed out long ago by Paul Fiebig ("Die Mekilta und das Johannes-Evangelium," ΑΓΓΕΛΟΣ, I [1925], 58).

[3] Above, pp. 238-241.

[4] Above, pp. 177-179.

[5] Above, pp. 110f., 117, 122-125, 141, 147-149, 156-159, 205-209, 232-236, 241-244.

This agential relationship to God was expressed in several of the traditions—traditions as diverse as Philo, the Samaritan Book of Markah, and a midrash preserved in a medieval rabbinic collection—by transferring to the Sinai event the commission of Exodus 7.1, "See, I have appointed you *god!*"[1] The bearing of God's name (here אלהים, θεός) signifies that Moses is God's emissary, that he acts as king and prophet for God, not in his own right.

Very much less frequent are the legends that Moses ascended at the end of his life as well, for these legends after all contradict the flat statement of Deuteronomy 34.5, "So Moses . . . died there . . ." Nevertheless Philo elaborates a tradition that Moses "was translated" instead of dying,[2] Josephus betrays knowledge of such a tradition by his polemic against it,[3] and in the Rabbinic sources there is a persistent strand that ingeniously finds in the very verse that speaks of Moses' death a cryptic indication that he really ascended and "serves on high."[4] The Samaritan sources, like the Jewish ones, present a mixed picture. The Book of Markah speaks of Moses' death, but describes it with all the imagery of an ascension, while medieval sources speak directly of Moses' assumption.[5] Similarly ambiguous is the description in the *Assumption of Moses*.[6]

The Return of Jesus to Heaven

In the Fourth Gospel one of the central themes in Jesus' discourses, a theme which leads to a climax in the crucifixion and resurrection narratives, is the notion that he is "ascending (ἀναβαίνων) to the Father."[7] More often the notion is expressed by the less specific verbs ἔρχεσθαι,[8] πορεύεσθαι,[9] ὑπάγειν,[10] but again the paradoxical ὑψωθῆναι[11] and δοξασθῆναι[12] emphasize the idea of an ascension.

---

[1] Above, pp. 110f., 192-195, 235f., cf. 147f.

[2] Above, pp. 124f.

[3] Above, pp. 140f.

[4] Above, pp. 209-211.

[5] Above, pp. 244-246.

[6] Above, p. 159.

[7] ἀναβαίνειν: 6.62; 20.17; cf. 3.13 and also 10.1, in the light of the exegesis by Paul W. Meyer, *JBL* 75, p. 434.

[8] 7.34; 13.33; 17.11, 13.

[9] 14.2f., 12, 28; 16.7, 28.

[10] 7.33; 8.21f.; 13.33-36; 14.14f., 28; 16.5, 10, 17; cf. 8.14; 13.3.

[11] 3.14; 8.28; 12.32.

[12] 7.39; 8.54; 11.4; 12.16, 23, 28; 13.31f.; 16.14; 17.1, 5, 10.

Now just as in the Moses traditions, an essential aspect of the ascension of Jesus in the Fourth Gospel is his enthronement as King of Israel, as the trial and crucifixion narratives demonstrate.[1] However, the enthronement of the returning messenger in the upper world is very important feature in the Mandaean myths as well,[2] and these provide in this respect a closer analogy to the Johannine theme than do the Moses legends. As in the gnostic myths, the *ascent* of Jesus in the Fourth Gospel cannot be separated from his prior *descent*: "No one has ascended into heaven except he who descended . . ." (3.13); "What if you should see the Son of Man ascending *where he was before?*" (6.62). This pattern of descent/ ascent of a heavenly messenger has no direct parallel in the Moses traditions (except for an isolated statement by Philo);[3] it has been and remains the strongest support for the hypothesis that the Johannine christology is connected with gnostic mythology.

The most striking aspect of the Johannine description of Jesus' ascension, however, is paralleled neither in the gnostic myths nor in the Moses legends. This is the central paradox that Jesus' "being lifted up," his "glorification," takes place in and through his death on the cross. There is to be sure a distant analogy in the ambiguity of some traditions of Moses' death,[4] but this analogy is hardly more. Since the Johannine ambiguity turns on the double use of ὑψοῦν, it could only arise on the presupposition that the person in question died by crucifixion or hanging. The Johannine paradox is the exclusive product of Christian interpretation of the passion tradition.

Comparison of the legends of Moses' ascenion with the Johannine theme of the exaltation of the Son of Man thus leads to negative results. The notion of Jesus' paradoxical enthronement is not dependent on the Moses traditions for its fundamental structure.

The Polemic

If the legends of Moses' ascensions did not directly help form the Johannine theme of Jesus' return to the Father, nevertheless there are polemical notes in the gospel which indicate that these legends

---

[1] Above, pp. 61-81.

[2] Above, pp. 271f.

[3] *Sac.* 8-10, discussed above, pp. 104f.

[4] E.g., in *Assump. Mos.*, where some observers see Moses' burial while a few perceive his assumption; or in the *Memar Marqah*, where the narrative of his death is dominated by the language of ascension.

may have played a part in the religion of the opponents of the Johannine community.

The most direct of these polemical notes is the one already quoted, "No one has ascended into heaven except he who descended from heaven, the Son of Man" (3.13). This statement comes near the end of a dialogue between Jesus and Nicodemus, who significantly is identified as "a ruler of the Jews" (verse 1) and "the teacher of Israel" (verse 10). Jesus' discourse sets forth the prerequisite for anyone who wants to "see" or "enter the kingdom of God." Commentators regularly point out that the synoptic and, presumably, primitive Christian phrase "Kingdom of God" occurs only here (verses 3, 5) in John. This apocalyptic notion seems distinctly an alien intrusion in the Johannine context. Yet, if one puts aside the connotations which the phrase has in the synoptic gospels,[1] the context in John 3 suggests an independent but coherent range of meaning.

Jesus' description of the man who, born "again" or "from above" (ἄνωθεν), is able to enter/see the Kingdom of God is at the same time and even primarily a description of himself—in Johannine terms. The life of such a man is the life of the Spirit (οὕτως, verse 8), but of the Spirit if is said that one "hears his voice," men do not know "where he comes from and where he goes"—precisely the language which John uses for Jesus himself.[2] In short, the life of the Christian, through the mediation of the Spirit, participates in the movement of Jesus' own life. But applied to Jesus the ambiguous term ἄνωθεν clearly means "from above." Moreover, Jesus has "seen" the things of God, the "heavenly things" (ἐπουράνια: that is the content of his μαρτυρία (verses 11f., compare verse 32). Verse 13, then, claims that no one else has seen these things. Indeed "the teacher of Israel" does not even understand "earthly things"—how could he perceive "heavenly things"? (verse 12).

In this context "seeing the Kingdom of God" would naturally mean seeing God reigning in heaven, while "entering the Kingdom of God" would mean to ascend to heaven. Now Gershom Scholem has shown that the earliest Jewish mysticism was a "throne mysticism," closely related to an exaggerated emphasis on God's king-

---

[1] On which see Karl Ludwig Schmidt, "Die βασιλεία Gottes [im N.T.]," *ThWbNT*, I, 582-591.

[2] Above, pp. 37f.

ship.[1] The same emphasis has been apparent in the traditions of Moses' heavenly ascents. Alongside the apocalyptic concept of God's reign, which has dominated gospel research in this century, it is therefore necessary to postulate the existence in some circles of Judaism of a mystical notion of God's kingship, in which the individual's relationship to the βασιλεία was expressed pre-eminently in terms of "ascending" and "seeing." This notion is the one connected with the notions of Moses' kingship, and it is the one which best fits John 3.3 and 5. Verses 3, 5, and 13 thus in effect say the same thing: only the Son of Man has ascended to heaven, "entered," and "seen" the Kingdom of God. No one else has ascended or can ascend, enter, and see, except through him. But the polemic expressed in these three statements clearly implies that the circle represented by "the teacher of Israel" did think such an ascent and the vision of "heavenly things" was possible. That a "throne-mysticism" was practised in Palestine in the first century, even by Pharisaic leaders, is shown by the traditions about Yohanan ben Zakkai and his associates and disciples.[2] Was such a mysticism practised by the Johannine opponents? Was their mystical ideology connected with Moses?

Other elements of the Johannine polemic suggest affirmative answers to these questions. Parallel to 3.13, "No one has ascended . . .," stands 1.18, "No one has ever seen God . . ." Moreover, 1.17 explicitly contrasts the gift of the Torah through Moses with the event of grace and truth through Jesus. The same statement, "No one has seen God," in slightly varying language, is made again in 5.37, 6.46, and 1 John 4.12. Of these 5.37 is particularly important, for here the statement belongs to a series of allusions to the Sinai theophany.[3] The immediate context is an exposition of the way in which God himself attests (μαρτυρεῖν) the mission of Jesus, a testimony which the opponents do not accept. They are told:

His voice (φωνή) you have never heard;
his form (εἶδος) you have never seen,
and his word (λόγος) you do not have staying in you,
because you do not believe the one whom he sent.

---

[1] *Major Trends*, pp. 54-57.

[2] Jacob Neusner, *A Life of Rabban Yohanan ben Zakkai, ca. 1-80 C.E.* ("Studia Post-Biblica," ed. P. A. H. DeBoer *et al.*, VII; Leiden: E. J. Brill, 1962), pp. 97-103.

[3] Cf. Dahl, "The Johannine Church and History," p. 133.

The resemblance to the Deuteronomic description of the theophany at Horeb is striking:

καὶ ἐλάλησεν κύριος πρὸς ὑμᾶς ἐκ μέσου τοῦ πυρός· φωνήν
ῥημάτων ὑμεῖς ἠκούσατε καὶ ὁμοίωμα οὐκ εἴδατε, ἀλλ'ἢ φωνήν.

(Deuteronomy 4.12)

The Deuteronomic homily develops the theme that, while the Horeb (Sinai) assembly did not see God's "form," yet they heard the "voice," and the words of the Covenant, which Moses himself delivered to them, provided the continuing, sufficient basis for their responsible relationship to God. The Johannine verse denies that the opponents have either seen God's form or heard his voice. Moreover, τὸν λόγον αὐτοῦ οὐκ ἔχετε ἐν ὑμῖν μένοντα may well be an allusion to Deuteronomy 30.11-14, particularly verse 14: ἔστιν σου ἐγγὺς τὸ ῥῆμα σφόδρα ἐν τῷ στόματί σου καὶ ἐν τῇ καρδίᾳ σου καὶ ἐν ταῖς χερσίν σου αὐτὸ ποιεῖν.[1]

All three aspects of the Sinai event—voice, vision, and abiding word—are denied to the opponents in John "because you do not believe the one whom he sent." Who is this envoy of God who is not believed? In the context ὃν ἀπέστειλεν ἐκεῖνος could refer not only to Jesus but equally well to Moses, for it is Moses in whom the opponents "hope" (5.45), and belief in Moses is tantamount to belief in Jesus (verse 46).[2] Perhaps the reference in verse 38 is deliberately ambiguous, that is, inclusive. Furthermore, Deuteronomy 18.16 says that the prophet like Moses will be sent because the people beg, "Let us not again hear the voice of the Lord our God and see this great fire . . ." The prophet was understood in Jewish and Samaritan midrash to refer to Moses himself or to a succession of prophets or to an eschatological redeemer; in the Fourth Gospel the prophet is Jesus.

In sum the polemic of John 5.36-45 says: the Sinai theophany and the word delivered there, namely, the Torah, τὰ γράμματα Μωϋσέως, is nothing other than the "testimony" by which the Father attests his ultimate prophetic agent, the Son. By rejecting this final agent, the opponents reveal that in fact they have rejected the first prophet, Moses, and the whole revelation of which he was mediator. But this polemic would be pointless unless the opponents

---

[1] Cf. Dt. 6.6.
[2] Above, pp. 289, 294f.

actually did practice a Moses-centered piety. Therefore this analysis corroborates the hypothesis suggested above on different grounds.

To return to John 3.13, the statement "No one has ascended to heaven" would in this context carry the pointed implication, "not even Moses."[1]

JESUS AND MOSES AS GOD'S "APOSTLES"

The One Sent from God

The descent of Jesus from heaven in John was found to have no genuine parallel in the Moses traditions, but the Fourth Gospel describes his mission also in another way which turns out to bear significant similarities to the descriptions of Moses' mission. The designation of Jesus as "he whom God sent" (ὃν ἀπέστειλεν ὁ θεός) is far more significant (and frequent) than ὁ καταβὰς ἐκ τοῦ οὐρανοῦ and its equivalents.[2] Even more often God is referred to by the corresponding phrase ὁ πέμψας με (πατήρ).[3] As the one sent from God, Jesus does not come ἀφ' ἑαυτοῦ (7.28; 8.42). He does not come in his own name, but in the name of the Father (5.43). He does not do his own works or will, but the works and will of the Sender (4.34; 5.30; 6.38f.; 9.4). Likewise he does not speak his own words, but the words of the Sender (7.16, 18; 8.26; 12.49; 14.24). He does not seek his own glory, but the glory of the Sender (7.18), so whoever honors or dishonors the Son actually is honoring or dishonoring the Sender (5.23). In all these aspects the Johannine Christ exemplifies

---

[1] Thus the proposal made many years ago by Odeberg (*Fourth Gospel*, pp. 75-89, 98) is in large measure vindicated. Had Odeberg devoted his unusual perception as much to careful analysis of the gospel itself as he did to the discovery and analysis of invaluable parallels, his intuitive suggestion that behind the Fourth Gospel stood a polemic against "the traditions of ascensions into heaven by great saints, patriarchs, and prophets of old . . . , such as Enoch, Abraham, Moses, Elijah, Isaiah . . ." might have commanded more attention from subsequent scholarship.

[2] Some form of the phrase ἀπέστειλεν ὁ θεὸς τὸν υἱόν occurs 16 times in the gospel: 3.17, 34; 5.36, 38 (perhaps referring to Moses: see above); 6.29, 57; 7.29; 8.42; 10.36; 11.42; 17.3, 8, 18, 21, 23, 25; 20.21. Cf. also 9.7, where the name of the pool *šiloah* is, I believe, used to symbolize Jesus as ὁ ἀπεσταλμένος (n.b. the masc. form).

[3] Twenty-four times: 4.34; 5.23, 24, 30, 37; 6.38, 39, 44; 7.16, 18, 28, 33; 8.16, 18, 26, 29; 9.4; 12.44, 45, 49; 13.20; 14.24; 15.21; 16.5. Karl H. Rengstorf, "ἀποστέλλω, (πέμπω), ἐξαποστέλλω, ἀπόστολος, ψευδαπόστολος, ἀποστολή," *ThWbNT*, IV, 404, counts 26, apparently through error. His analysis of the relation between πέμπειν and ἀποστέλλειν in Jn. is suggestive.

the common rule of agency (שליחות) in Judaism: שליחו של אדם כמותו, "the agent of a man is as himself."[1] But the elements of his "sending" or "commissioning" overlap with the characteristics of the true prophet.[2] Jesus is God's agent specifically as his prophet. Furthermore, his prophetic agency is closely connected with the functions of "testifying" and "judgment." The κρίσις of the world is the demand to "believe" that God sent Jesus (11.42; 17.8, 21) or to "know" this (17.23, 25), which is identical with the act of believing in him whom God sent (6.29) or knowing him (17.3). Furthermore belief in the one sent or belief that he was sent is the same as belief in the Sender (12.44f.; 17.3; 5.24; cf. 5.23, 38, also 8.19).

Moses as God's Commissioned Agent

In the Samaritan traditions Moses' שליחותא, his "apostolate" or "commission," is particularly emphasized.[3] Moreover, it is closely connected to his prophetic office and his enthronement at Sinai. There is no comparable theme in the Rabbinic haggada, although occasionally Moses is called the שליח of God in the context of a specific task he had to do.[4] However, the scriptural account of Moses' commissioning already suggests the formal appointment of an agent: note particularly the use of the verb (ἐξ)ἀποστέλλειν (שלח) in Exodus 3-4. Moreover, the same account relates that God gave to Moses both the ineffable name YHWH and the "signs" (σημεῖα) that the Israelites might believe (πιστεύειν) that God had sent him (3.12, 13f., 4.1, 8) and "hearken" to his "voice" (4.1).[5] This suggests the means of authentication of the prophet, who is at the same time God's agent.[6] The same connections are present in the summary of Moses' whole mission at the end of Deuteronomy:

---

[1] Mishnah, Ber. 5.5; Tal. B., Kidd. 41b; Hag. 10b. Naz. 12b; B.M. 96a; Men. 93b; Mekilta, Pisḥa 3.5 (ed. Lauterbach, I, 25, 40), cited Billerbeck, III, 2; cf. Rengstorf, ThWbNT, I, 415. The importance of this concept for Johannine christology was recognized by Théo Preiss, p. 16.

[2] Above, pp. 45f.

[3] Above, pp. 226f.

[4] Talm., B.M. 86b; Shemot R. 5.14, cited by Billerbeck, III, 3; Tanḥuma, wa'era, par. 5, f. 95a (trans. G. G. Montefiore and H. Loewe, A Rabbinic Anthology [Philadelphia: The Jewish Publication Society of America, 1960], pp. 8f.); cf. Assump. Mos., xi, 17, where Moses is called magnus nuntius (but Johansson, p. 67, thinks the original was μέγας ἄγγελος).

[5] A similar notion lies behind the passage in Mekilta on belief in God and Moses (above, pp. 239f., 295).

[6] The mediation of the Torah was commonly regarded as a prophetic

καὶ οὐκ ἀνέστη ἔτι προφήτης ἐν Ἰσραὴλ ὡς Μωϋσῆς, ὃν ἔγνω κύριος
αὐτὸν πρόσωπον κατὰ πρόσωπον, ἐν πᾶσι τοῖς σημείοις καὶ τέρασιν,
ὃν ἀπέστειλεν αὐτὸν κύριος ποιῆσαι αὐτά . . . ἃ ἐποίησεν Μωϋσῆς
ἔναντι παντὸς Ἰσραήλ.

(Deuteronomy 34.10-12)

Correlation

The prophetic aspect of the commission, the "signs" which are
to evoke "belief" in the messenger and thus belief in the Sender, all
argue strongly for a connection between John's view of Jesus'
mission and Moses' traditional function. Notice that "the crowd"
in John 6.30 asks Jesus, who has just spoken of belief "in him whom
he [sc. God] sent," "What sign do you do, then, that we may see and
believe you?" Then they immediately refer to a sign of *Moses*
(verses 31f.). Previously, it was the men who "saw *the sign* which
he did" that said, "Is not this truly *the prophet* who is coming into
the world?" (6.14). Since the "works" and "words" of Jesus are
"not his own" but God's, the works (= "signs") and words "bear
witness" that he is the Sent One (5.36; 17.8), and the word (λόγος)
which Jesus has spoken will be the judge "on the last day" (12.48).
Moreover, the sending Father himself "bears witness" to Jesus
(5.37; 8.16, 18).

The correlation is especially clear in two passages, 5.19-47 and
chapter 17, each of which has been analyzed above in part. The
theme of 5.19-47 is stated in verse 19 and again in verse 30: οὐ
δύναται ὁ υἱὸς ποιεῖν ἀφ' ἑαυτοῦ οὐδέν. This theme already shows that
the whole passage is an exposition of Jesus' function and authority
as God's agent. The first section, verses 19-29, explain that the
agent does only the Sender's works. He only does what he sees the
Father doing (verse 19). The Father designates certain of his own

---

function (or, as in Philo and elsewhere, prophetic and royal at once): above,
pp. 110f., 112f., 126f., 154, 171-173, 184f., 187, 198f., cf. 224f., 233f.
That the essence of Moses' prophecy was speaking *another's* words, not his
own, is emphasized, especially by Josephus (above, p. 137f.). The signs of
Moses play a large part in the legends; for their connection with prophecy,
see above, pp. 50 and 162-164. The notion that the prophet was God's agent
is certainly implicit in all the OT prophetic books, not least in the fact that
the "messenger-formula" is the fundamental genre in the prophetic pro-
nouncements. According to Rengstorf, the Rabbis did not use the noun
שָׁלִיחַ to refer to prophets, but did use the verb שָׁלַח as a *terminus technicus*
for the authorization of a prophet (*ThWbNT*, I, 420).

works to the Son (verse 20), (a) raising the dead (verses 21, 24-26),[1] (b) judgment (verses 22, 27-29). The second section, verses 30-40, shows that the agent does not *witness* to himself, but is attested by the Sender. The four "witnesses" claimed by Jesus are (a) John the Baptist (verses 33-35), (b) the works given the agent by the Sender (verse 36), (c) the Sender himself (verse 37), and (d) the Scripture (verse 39b). The allusions to the Sinai theophany in this section have already been discussed. The final section (41-44) shows that the agent does not seek his own *glory* but the glory of the Sender. Those who seek their own glory or glory from men (the meaning is the same) are not open to the agent who seeks only the Sender's glory.

The prayer of John 17 serves as a kind of quittance by the agent, a summary of his mission and an affadavit that he has faithfully discharged his assigment. Briefly, the following points are important: (a) accomplishment: "I have glorified you upon the earth; I have completed the work which you gave me to do" (verse 4).[3] (b) authority: ". . . You gave him [*sc.* the Son] authority over all flesh" (verse 2). (c) revelation of the name: "I have revealed your name to the men whom you gave me" (verse 6, compare 11b). (d) revelation of the words: "The words which you gave me I have given to them, and they accepted them . . ." (verse 8, compare 14). The allusions to the delivery of the ineffable Name and the Torah through Moses have already been pointed out above.[3]

---

[1] An interesting passage in the Midrash on Psalm 78.5 (trans. Braude, II, 25) states that God never gives the key to three things to a שליח –except in the rare instances recorded in Scripture when he appointed a just man as agent. The three are: the keys to the womb, *to the graves for the resurrection*, and to the rain. The three exceptions, in the case of the resurrection, are Elijah, Elisha, and Ezekiel. (Cited by Billerbeck, III, 3.)

[2] The "accomplishment of the work" is a theme that recurs throughout the gospel (4.34; 5.36; 9.3f.; 10.25, 32-38: 14.10, 12; 15.24), culminating in the cry from the cross, τετέλεσται! (19.30). The crucifixion is the completion of the work; the summary in chapter 17 of course presupposes the crucifixion as accomplished.

[3] It is tempting to compare the whole notion of the "farewell discourses" in Jn. with the closing chapters of Dt., which are presented as Moses' farewell sermons and blessing to Israel. The similarities are even stronger when Jn. is compared with the later midrashim on Moses' "departure." E.g., cf. Jn. 13.1 with *Debarim R.*, xi. 8, "When Moses was about to depart this world, God said to him, 'Behold thy days approach' . . ." (trans. Rabbinowitz, *Soncino Midrash*, VII, 179). To the request of Philip, "Show us the Father" (Jn. 14.8), cf. Moses' request: "Master of the Universe, I ask of Thee one favour before I die, that I may enter, and that all the gates of heaven and the

It seems quite likely, on the basis of the strong similarities, that the frequent description of Jesus as the prophetic agent or envoy of God in John was actually modeled in part on the traditions of Moses' mission. The hypothesis is the more probable since one of the passages in which this notion is developed most fully (5.19-47) is one that evidently grew out of a controversy with a Jewish circle especially devoted to Moses.

THE JURIDICAL SETTING OF THE PROPHET-KING'S MISSION

The Forensic Character of Jesus' Revelation

A number of scholars in recent years have emphasized the significance of forensic terminology in John. They have suggested that the action in the gospel adds up to a cosmic legal process, in which witnesses produce their testimony, accusations and counter-accusations are delivered, and judgment is rendered. The trial bears a highly ironic character, for the principal witness, the "Son of Man," though he is "attested" by the Baptist, by his own "works," by the Scripture of Moses, and by God himself, becomes the accused because "the world" refuses to accept his "testimony" or his attestation. It is this very refusal, leading to the condemnation and execution of the witness, which exposes "the world" as condemned in the judgment of God. Thus the "trial" of Jesus becomes his enthronement as King and judge and at the same time the "judgment of this world." There is no need to repeat in more detail what has been said so frequently by others.[1] The exegetical analysis in Chapter II above showed how the motifs represented by μαρτυρία

---

deep be opened and people shall see that there is none beside Thee." (*Debarim R.*, xi, 8, trans. Rabbinowitz, *ibid.*). To the reluctance of Moses to die, often elaborated extensively in the midrashim, contrast the Johannine abbreviation and alteration of the "agony" tradition (Jn. 12.27). Both Moses and Jesus choose successors who will continue their functions, but in a lesser way. Each *serves* his successor(s) in menial tasks (Jn. 13; cf. *Peṭirat Moseh* on Moses' serving Joshua, above, p. 180). The spirit is distributed to their successors (Num. 11.25; Dt. 34.9); the Spirit is specifically *prophetic* (Num. 11.25, 29; cf. Jn. 16.13). Both Moses and Jesus predict what is to come (Jn. 14.29; cf. 16.4; Dt. 32-34 and Dt. *passim*). Now that Jesus is leaving, the disciples are grieved, but "another Paraclete" will come to them. Cf. the many traditions of Israel's (and God's) grief that after Moses' departure they will be left without a paraclete or συνήγορος.

[1] See above, pp. 65f., n. 1 and Betz, pp. 120-126.

and κρίσις are closely intertwined in the Fourth Gospel and reach their climax in the trial before Pilate.[1]

The forensic elements in the Fourth Gospel have important implications for the way in which Jesus' function as a revealer is to be understood. Jesus' "words" are a revelation from on high; he speaks "what he has seen and heard." Thus his revelation is formally analogous both to the secrets brought by the redeemer in the gnostic myths and to the secrets procured in heaven by Moses (or, in other traditions, by such figures as Enoch and Baruch). But in the Johannine pattern the secrets constitute a μαρτυρία, a testimony which becomes God's complaint against "the world" (3.11-21, 31-36; compare 7.7). The "testimony" of Jesus is closely connected with his mission as God's agent, the "sent one." The judgment is ultimate because rejection of the one whom God sent means the rejection of the Sender himself.[2] Thus the "word" Jesus spoke will "judge on the last day" (12.48).

The gnostic myths provide no real analogy to this forensic function of Jesus' revelation. There is nothing in the Mandaean texts, for example, that could be compared with the Johannine modification of the trial before Pilate or with the specifically juridical themes that coalesce in that narrative. In the traditions about Moses, however, the connection between the revelation from on high and God's judgment of Israel is at least as old as the book of Deuteronomy.

The Juridical Aspect of Moses' Mission

A forensic setting for the revelation to Moses was always implicit in the fact that the revelation consisted primarily in the transmission of *Torah*. The Torah, which Moses brought down from heaven and delivered to Israel, was naturally the standard by which Israel was to be judged. The book of Deuteronomy makes this juridical function of the Torah quite explicit. Of special importance is the "Song of Moses" (Deuteronomy 32), which is written down "for a testimony (לעד, εἰς μαρτύριον) against the sons of Israel" (31.19, 21). In the same passage, moreover, Moses commands the Levites to place the whole "book of this Law" (originally, the book of Deuteronomy, "the words of Moses," 1.1) into the ark

---

[1] Above, pp. 65f.
[2] See especially 15.22, and the passages discussed above, pp. 302f.

of the Covenant, to be "a testimony against you" (31.26). Frequently the rabbis identify the "song" with the entire written Torah, so that verses 19, 21, and 26 are made to say the same thing.[1]

The forensic character of the revelation was recognized and emphasized by the translators of the Septuagint.[2] Philo, who often refers to Moses as a witness (μάρτυς or subject of the verb μαρτυρεῖν) weakens the legal terminology to a mere figure of speech to introduce a Scripture text to prove a point.[3]

Judaism and Samaritanism regarded Moses as the "defense attorney" for their respective groups in the heavenly court.[4] Sometimes, especially in the Samaritan traditions, this defense had an eschatological setting.[5] Deuteronomy 31-32, however, already suggested that Moses would become the *accuser* of a disobedient Israel, through his words which were solemnly inscribed and preserved to serve as a "witness." It is this negative possibility of Moses' testimony that is explicitly claimed in the Fourth Gospel (5.46f.), so that Moses is made one in the chain of witnesses that condemn "the world" = "the Jews" and testify in behalf of Jesus. But this forensic function of Moses in the gospel is then parallel to Jesus' own function as God's witness, for Jesus' word, like Moses', will be an accusing witness "on the last day."[6]

THE GOOD SHEPHERD

The Shepherd in the Themes of the Fourth Gospel

Exegetical analysis in Chapter II led to the conclusion that the

---

[1] Mekilta, *Nezikin* 1.6 (ed. Lauterbach, III, 1); Talm. B. *Sanh.*, 21b (where "write for yourselves this song" is connected with the law of the king in Dt. 17.19, "And he shall write for himself a book of Torah"), *Ḥul.* 133a. Cf. Jacob Schachter in *Soncino Talmud, Seder Nezikin, Sanhedrin*, I, p. 118, n. 6

[2] Hermann S. Strathmann, "μάρτυς, [κτλ.]," *ThWbNT*, IV, 488f.

[3] *Det.* 138; *Post.* 57; *Mig.* 3; *Congr.* 160; *Som.* ii,222; *Abr.* 262; *Mut.* 258; cf. *Som.* i, 231.

[4] Above, p. 294, n. 2; on the function of prophetic intercessors in Israel as "witnesses" in what was always conceived as a "purely juridical action" see Johansson, pp. 41-48, cf. 222-227 and Betz, p. 45.

[5] Above, pp. 254f.

[6] The form of the Deuteronomic homily, in part a *vaticinium ex eventu*, sets the apostasy of Israel and the accusation by Moses' words in "later times" (באחרית הימים). But the temporal phrase could be understood as "at the end of days," as in LXX, ἔσχατον τῶν ἡμερῶν, leading to eschatological interpretation of the Song of Moses in the midrashim. Cf. Jn. 12.48, ἐν τῇ ἐσχάτῃ ἡμέρᾳ.

"Good Shepherd" symbol of John 10 could not be explained apart from its thematic connections with the trial narrative. (1) The call of the shepherd, equivalent to the "testimony" of the King, pro- vokes the κρίσις of the world: those who "hear" recognize their King and shepherd, those who refuse to hear choose a "robber" and, left without "the truth," have finally "no king but Caesar." (2) The *Good* Shepherd is the one who "lays down his life" for the sheep, just as the true King of the Jews is enthroned in death. (3) The Shepherd, like the "King of the Jews" in John 18-19, is both a royal and a prophetic figure. His shepherding function focuses in his "call" which must be "heard"; his kingship consists in testimony to the truth.[1]

Attempts to derive the Johannine symbol of the Good Shepherd directly from the Old Testament usage of the term shepherd for rulers, prophets, and God fail to illuminate the most striking features of John 10.[2] Description of the imagery as "messianic"[3] also goes astray, even though David could be called a "good shepherd,"[4] and the *Psalms of Solomon* use the shepherd imagery, but not the title, for the Davidic Messiah.[5] The designation of rulers and deities as "shepherd" is very widely attested in Greek literature—from Homer on, with special application in Plato and in the Stoic-Cynic writings on kingship[6]—and in Near Eastern sources of various provenance,[7] but these occurrences also offer only a very general analogy to the Johannine discourse. Hence Bultmann turned to the Mandaean sources for an illustration of the kind of symbolic usage most nearly comparable to the Johannine.[8] His solution must now be examined in some detail.

---

[1] Above, pp. 66-68.

[2] Most recently, Dodd, pp. 358-361; more cautiously Barrett, pp. 310f., who thinks that "John is primarily dependent upon the biblical and messi- anic meaning of the shepherd imagery, but he is doubtless aware also of other ideas of divine kingship . . ." For a penetrating criticism of similar views, cf. Odeberg, *Fourth Gospel*, pp. 317f., and n. 2, and Bultmann, *Ev. Joh.*, p. 279.

[3] E.g., Barrett, p. 310.

[4] *Shemot R.*, 2.2: רועה יפה

[5] *Ps. Sol.* 17.45.

[6] Cf. Goodenough, "Hellenistic Kingship," pp. 60-62, 84, and n. 93.

[7] Numerous references are collected by Bauer, pp. 143f.; cf. iconographic material in Goodenough, *Jewish Symbols*, III, 77-79.

[8] *Ev. Joh.*, pp. 279-281.

The Mandaean Parallels

Eduard Schweizer, in a dissertation carried out under Bultmann's direction, has worked out in greatest detail the argument for a proto-Mandaean origin of the Johannine Good Shepherd discourse.[1] There are three main passages in the extant Mandaean texts which refer to Manda ḏ-Hiia as a shepherd. The oldest of these, in its literary form, is a simple metaphor in the *Right Ginza*:

> Trust in Manda ḏ-Hiia. Like a good shepherd who protects (his sheep), he keeps you far from every spirit of apostasy. Like a good shepherd who leads his sheep to their fold, he establishes you and plants you before him.[2]

Schweizer devotes his primary attention to the two more expansive allegories found in the *Book of John*,[3] in which the redeemer figure speaks in the first person. The two passages are evidently of independent origin and betray signs that they have undergone several stages of development.[4] By excluding a central section of the first allegory, in which the danger of a flood suggests a Babylonian background,[5] Schweizer thinks he can arrive at the earliest stage of the discourse which could go back to the west-Palestinian origins of the Mandaean sect. He argues that the reconstructed kernel is a close parallel to John 10.1-18, but that it must be earlier because it is more mythical.[6]

Schweizer's argument for common origin of the Johannine and Mandaean passages is based on similarities of terminology: (a) "I am a shepherd";[7] (b) "sheep"; (c) "fold"; (d) "wolves"; (e) "thief"; (f) the "iron knife"[8] of the thief, which Schweizer compares with John 10.10, ἵνα ... θύσῃ ...; (g) the "typically Johannine *Wiederaufnahme*," in which the key word at the end of one clause is repeated at the beginning of the next.[9] He seeks to establish the priority

---

[1] *Ego Eimi; Die religionsgeschichtliche Herkunft und theologische Bedeutung der joh. Bildreden* (Göttingen: Vandenhoeck & Ruprecht, 1939), pp. 64-66.
[2] *GR* V, 2; p. 181:18-21, following Lidzbarski's German translation.
[3] *Johannesbuch*, sects. 11, 12; pp. 42-54.
[4] Cf. Lidzbarski, *Johannesbuch*, p. 43.
[5] Cf. *ibid.*
[6] Schweizer, pp. 65f., 81f.
[7] *Johannesbuch*, sect. 11, p. 44:27.
[8] *Ibid.*, p. 45:11f.
[9] Schweizer, pp. 64f., cf. p. 45, nn. 243, 244.

of the Mandaean version as follows: (a) The adjective καλός, appearing in John 10.11, 14 but absent from the Mandaean discourse, indicates a polemic in which the *good*, that is, the *real* shepherd, is distinguished from any figure which might be designated merely *a* shepherd, as in the Mandaean passage. (b) Similarly, the absence of the significant Johannine element of the *death* of the shepherd argues for the priority of the more mythical version. (c) The use of the "wolf" and the "thief" in John to show the uniqueness of the shepherd is secondary to the more commonplace use in the Mandaean allegory, where these figures are simply part of the general picture of the task of a shepherd.[1]

Schweizer's arguments for dependence will hardly bear the weight he places on them. Of the terminological parallels he cites, only the first is actually significant. Once a shepherd is mentioned, references to "sheep" and "sheepfold" are only to be expected. Moreover, while the "fold" has special significance in the Mandaean passage, since it is the fold that protects the flock against dangers, it is entirely incidental to the Johannine imagery. Similarly, mention of "wolves" and "thieves" is commonplace in the most diverse folkloric stories of shepherds. In the Mandaean source the wolf and the thief are only two in a series of typical dangers, the others of which have no parallel in John. To connect the "iron knife" with John 10.10 is forced. Finally, the *Wiederaufnahme* in this passage and generally in Mandaean texts is not at all "typically Johannine." In Johannine parallelism clauses are connected in a chain-like sequence; when a key-word is repeated, it is with the addition of new predicates (synthetic parallelism) or in negative form (antithetic parallelism). The Mandaean form, which is monotonously frequent, consists of a couplet in which the second clause is identical to the first except for the mere reversal of word-order.[2] Of the terminological parallels, then, there remains only the similarity between the Mandaean "I am a shepherd" and the Johannine "I am the Good Shepherd."

The arguments for priority would be valid only if dependence were proved. But the three arguments Schweizer advances could just as well be evidence for independence of the two traditions as

---

[1] *Ibid.*, p. 66.

[2] A glance at the examples Schweizer himself cites (p. 45, nn. 243, 244) is sufficient to show the difference.

for priority of one. Formal analysis of the Mandaean and Johannine passages thus leads to quite inconclusive results.[1]

Both Bultmann and Schweizer admit that two of the most important elements in the Johannine discourse, the contrast between Jesus and the "hirelings" and the necessity for the Good Shepherd to "lay down his life," are completely absent from the Mandaean traditions. Over against this difference, Bultmann stresses the fact that Mandaean sources offer a significant parallel to the equally important notion that the shepherd "calls" his own and they "hear his voice," and that they know one another.[2] In content as well as form, therefore, comparison leaves the question of dependence open.

Moses the Faithful Shepherd

The traditions about Moses frequently call him "the shepherd of Israel" or "the faithful shepherd."[3] This metaphor, moreover, is connected with characteristics which have several points of similarity with the Johannine discourse. Moses' designation as shepherd is closely connected with both his prophetic and his royal functions. It is chiefly the character of fidelity that marks him as shepherd,[4] and to this corresponds the notion of belief or trust in "the shepherd of Israel."[5]

The notion of judgment implicit in "hearing the voice" of the shepherd is not to be found in any of the Old Testament passages in which the shepherd metaphor appears, as Bultmann has properly noted, nor in the post-biblical passages that call Moses "shepherd." However, this motif is not connected exclusively with the shepherd in John, but is an important theme throughout the gospel. Furthermore, it has been shown above that this motif is related to the Sinai

---

[1] In view of this uncertainty, it should be pointed out that the *GR* passage which compares Manda *d*-Hiia with "a good shepherd" stands in close proximity to a passage which compares Christ with a *bad* shepherd (*GR* V, 3; p. 189:5-9). Since the latter passage may be the result of secondary redaction (so Reitzenstein, *Das mandäische Buch*, pp. 82f., and Lidzbarski, *ad loc.*, in an argument which, however, I find unconvincing), one cannot argue from this fact for dependence of the Mandaean upon Christian tradition. Nevertheless, it calls for greater caution in asserting dependence in the opposite direction.

[2] *Ev. Joh.*, p. 280. The mutual recognition theme is not found in the Mandaean shepherd discourses, but appears elsewhere (Schweizer, p. 66).

[3] Above, pp. 108, 161, 196f.

[4] Cf. Bloch, "Quelques aspects," p. 138.

[5] Above, p. 295 and nn. 2-4; cf. Fiebig, p. 58.

theophany and the emphasis on hearing God's voice *via* Moses' words,[1] and also to the special mission of the Prophet like Moses.[2] Hence this theme is at least as readily explicable on the basis of Moses traditions as of gnostic mythology.

Especially significant for the interpretation of John 10 is the fact that Moses' designation as Israel's shepherd is frequently associated with his function as intercessor or advocate, his "standing in the breach before God" for Israel.[3] Moreover, his intercession went to such lengths that the haggada could speak of his "offering his life" for the sake of Israel, a notion suggested already by Exodus 32.32. Mekilta on Exodus 12.1 is particularly important:

> And so you find that the patriarchs and the prophets offered their lives (נתנו נפשם) in behalf of Israel. As to Moses, what did he say: "Yet now, if thou wilt forgive their sin; and if not blot me, I pray Thee, out of the book which Thou hast written" (Ex. 32.32); "And if Thou deal thus with me, kill me, I pray Thee, out of hand, if I have found favour in Thy sight. . . ."[4]

The phrase נתן נפש is the precise equivalent to τὴν ψυχὴν τιθέναι.[5]

Conclusions

The Moses traditions provide analogies to some essential features of the "Good Shepherd" discourse in John which were absent from the Mandaean traditions, while offering an alternative explanation for the notion of "hearing the voice" of the shepherd.[6] These analogies are not adequate to suggest that the whole discourse, John 10.1-18, was derived exclusively from Moses traditions. On the contrary, the central themes of the discourse are most likely the product of specifically Christian reflection on the passion tradition. Moreover,

---

[1] Above, pp. 299f.

[2] Above, pp. 67f.

[3] Above, pp. 161, 197.

[4] *Pisḥa*, I, trans. Lauterbach, I, 10. Cf. Fiebig, pp. 58f.

[5] Cf. Fiebig, *ibid.*, who also cites as a parallel Mekilta, *Shirata*, I (ed. Lauterbach, II, 3f.), where however the phrase . . . נתן משה נפשו על means merely, "Moses devoted himself to . . .," without any sense of risking death.

[6] The derivation of the Good Shepherd symbol from Moses traditions has been suggested previously by Adolf Schlatter, *Sprache und Heimat des Vierten Evangeliums*, p. 124 (cited by J. Jeremias, *ThWbNT*, IV, 877, n. 252), and Odeberg, *Fourth Gospel*, pp. 138f., 314f., as well as by Fiebig. Jeremias expresses himself more cautiously, but holds open the possibility of such derivation (*ibid.*).

the figure of the shepherd is too widespread in the Old Testament and in older and younger literature throughout the Mediterranean religious and political world for one to insist on an exclusive derivation of the Johannine figure from any single tradition.[1] Nevertheless, the analogies suggest that Moses traditions did provide some of the material for the Good Shepherd symbolism, adding another element to the cumulative evidence for the Mosaic background for the prophet-king christological images in the gospel.

GEOGRAPHICAL SYMBOLISM IN THE FOURTH GOSPEL

Galilee and Samaria

It has become an axiom for modern New Testament scholarship that the Fourth Gospel, in contrast to the Synoptics, reduces "Galilee to a completely subordinate province of Jesus' activity,"[2] which is centered instead in Jerusalem. If the analysis of Galilee's symbolic significance in Chapter II above is valid, however, the axiom has to be modified, with important results for future discussion of the gospel's provenance. It is true that Jerusalem is central theologically in the sense that the decisive confrontations take place there. Judaea is Jesus' πατρίς, his ἴδια. There Jesus is manifested openly and rejected by "his own"; there he is enthroned and finally rejected by "the Jews"; there "the judgment of this world" and of its ruler takes place. Yet it is in Galilee that he is "accepted," there that he performs his first two "signs." It is because he himself comes from Galilee, in earthly terms, that he offends the Scripture-based expectations of "the Jews," while in some passages "Galileans" is the symbolic equivalent to "disciples of Jesus." The basic geographical scheme in John is therefore not Jerusalem-centered or Galilee-centered, but a movement back and forth between the two.[3]

---

[1] The similarities between the imagery of John 10.1-18 and the allegory of the Exodus in 1 Enoch 89.10-40, where *God* is the shepherd, Israel the flock, and Egypt the wolves, are at least as striking as similarities to the Mandaean discourses. Here, as in Jn., the sheep hear and follow "the Lord of the sheep," and he leads them out and gives them pasture.

[2] Bacon, *The Gospel of the Hellenists*, p. 72. Bacon adds the corollary that, to a greater extent even than Luke-Acts, "John relies on traditions of Judaean origin."

[3] Above, pp. 35-41.

A similar judgment must be made about Samaria, although Samaria has a much smaller role than Galilee in the Gospel. The story of Jesus' encounter with the Samaritan woman receives its literary setting from the note "He left Judaea and went away again into Galilee" (4.3), which is repeated five times in the following episode (4.43, 45, 46, 47, 54). The Samaritan story must therefore have a similar significance to that of the story of the official's faith (4.46-53): a non-Judaean group "receives" Jesus as a true prophet and savior after he has been rejected in "his own fatherland."[1]

Moreover, as "Galilean" could be a taunt directed by "the Jews" against a sympathizer with Jesus (7.52), "Samaritan" is a taunt hurled at Jesus himself (8.48). Furthermore, while the accompanying taunt, ". . . And you have a demon," is denied, the accusation that Jesus is a Samaritan is passed over in silence (8.49).[2] Could the Johannine community, or the community in which part of the Johannine traditions were nurtured, have been of such character that Jewish polemics would have included this kind of taunts? If so, was there a historical reason why the community would be willing tacitly to accept an identification as "Samaritans" or "Galileans"? Could these elements be harmonized with the evangelist's recognition that Jesus was a Jew (4.9, compare verse 22) and "King of the Jews," or is it necessary to postulate either a combination of "Galilean-Samaritan" traditions with "Judaean-Jerusalem" traditions or a conflict between tradition and redaction? Any attempt to answer all these questions is bound to remain conjectural, but such conjectures may help indicate a further implication of the viewpoint developed here.

Local Traditions

In 1925 Karl Kundsin put forth the thesis that the topographical notes in the Fourth Gospel were the product of specific local traditions cultivated by Palestinian Christian communities.[3] To

---

[1] Cf. above, pp. 39f. and 41, n. 2. Odeberg's comparison of Jn. 4 with the dialogue with Nicodemus in chap. 3 is also suggestive. Odeberg shows that the outcome of the latter is inconclusive, but with "the teacher of Israel" cast in an unfavorable light compared with the Samaritan woman, while the Samaritan episode ends with an extraordinary confession of faith (*Fourth Gospel*, pp. 169f.).

[2] Cf. *ibid.*, p. 304.

[3] *Topologische Überlieferungsstoffe im Johannes-Evangelium* (FRLANT, n.s., XXII; 1925), 80 pp. This seminal work has not had the recognition it

support this hypothesis he adduced the following evidence: (1) Archaeological and literary evidence shows the topographical details in John to be predominantly realistic in character, not the product of literary fancy.[1] (2) Many of the place names are attested by the Church Fathers as pilgrimage sites; others seem, from Jewish sources, to have been centers of Christian influence.[2] (3) Some of the stories seem to contain elements of cult-aetiology, analogous to the Patriarch-sagas of Genesis (as interpreted by

deserves. While Bacon used Kundsin's hypothesis to reinforce his own highly conjectural reconstruction of the early history of "Galilean" and "Judaean" Christianities (Gospel of the Hellenists, pp. 71f.), and Bultmann occasionally refers to Kundsin's work in his commentary, Barrett and Dodd in their commentaries make no reference to Kundsin. Even in his large monograph on traditional material in Jn. (Historical Traditions in the Fourth Gospel [Cambridge: The University Press, 1964], 453 pp.), Dodd never mentions Kundsin's study.

[1] Kundsin, pp. 14-20; details in analysis of particular stories, pp. 20-50. Kundsin's polemic against the allegorical interpretation, while justified over against such extreme viewpoints as those of Hönig and Grill which he cites (pp. 14f.), goes too far in its tendency to eliminate all symbolical elements (but n.b. the concession on p. 69). The demonstration that places with the names and physical character mentioned in the gospel actually existed excludes the view that the names were *invented* for a symbolic purpose, but not the possibility that the evangelist or the tradition before him anchored a given story in a particular place because of its symbolic potential. Alternatively, the evangelist may in some cases have incorporated a "local tradition" because this tradition could serve a useful function within his larger symbolism. For example, the indubitable fact that a pool called Šiloaḥ had existed in Jerusalem from pre-exilic times is no proof that a healing miracle was not connected with this particular pool because of the etymological significance of the name, rather than because the pool was a cultic center for Christian baptism. Even if there was such a local, cultic tradition, the evangelist's addition of the note ὃ ἑρμηνεύεται ἀπεσταλμένος strongly suggests his symbolic use of the tradition, since ἀπεσταλμένος in Jn. designates Jesus. Kundsin's own analysis, which suggests that the story of Jn. 9 springs from the fact of Christian baptism at Šiloaḥ, while Jn. 5 reflects the possession of the Bethzatha pool by Jews (pp. 36-38) is unconvincing. His interpretation of the etymological note as a *Nebenmotiv* of aetiology—the Christians asserted that the pool was called Šiloaḥ because Jesus had *sent* the blind man to be washed there (p. 52)—cannot be maintained. There is no characteristic of the aetiology proper in the story. If the motif were aetiological, one would expect the name to be mentioned in a note such as: "The pool is therefore called Šiloaḥ to this day." Instead, the name is mentioned in Jesus' command, which shows that the familiar name was taken for granted and that there is no intention to connect its *origin* with Jesus' action or statement. The note is rather a symbolic interpretation by the evangelist, suggesting that the only healing for this "blindness" is provided by the "sent one." That "washing in the Sent One" might still refer to Christian baptism is naturally not excluded by this interpretation.

[2] Ibid., pp. 17-19, 34, 60, 70.

Gunkel) and to aetiologies of the expansion of the Dionysus cult in Greece.[1]

Kundsin's development of his hypothesis is somewhat extravagant in face of the available data. He goes too far in discounting the symbolic character of the topology of the gospel, and his argument from the analogy of the Genesis sagas and the Dionysus myths and legends often leads to a *petitio principii*. Few formal characteristics of the aetiology are to be observed in the Johannine stories. Hence Kundsin's reconstruction of the intention of the individual units of Johannine tradition is dubious.[2]

Nevertheless Kundsin succeeds in showing the importance of the actual topographical background of Johannine narratives and in making extremely plausible his explanation that the geographical and physical details were preserved because they were significant to Christian communities and missionary endeavors in the places described.

Of particular importance is Kundsin's analysis of the references to Galilean and Samaritan topography. It is especially in the Samaritan pericope (John 4) and the feeding narrative (John 6.1-14), along with the Judaea-situated stories of Lazarus, the passion, and the burial, that he discovers an extraordinary wealth of accurate topographical detail,[3] but the special prominence given to Cana, he thinks, must also be the result of firm traditions localized there.[4] Therefore, although Kundsin accepts the prevailing view that Jerusalem dominates the Fourth Gospel,[5] he concludes that many of the Johannine traditions were shaped in Christian communities situated in Samaria and in Galilee and engaged there in intensive missionary propaganda.[6] With this general conclusion the results of the analysis of the Johannine symbolism are in complete harmony.

---

[1] *Ibid.*, pp. 1-6, 30,36-38, 51f., 54-58, 76f.

[2] This is particularly clear in his interpretation of the wine at Cana and the feeding episode as aetiologies of the victory of a "hellenistisch-mystischen (sakramentalen)" Christianity over a "jüdisch-nüchternen" Christianity (pp. 33, 57f.). The argument depends too much upon supposed analogies in extra-biblical myths, with too little attention to the exegetical analysis which alone could demonstrate that the analogies are actual.

[3] *Ibid.*, p. 50.

[4] *Ibid.*, pp. 22-25, 50, 70f.

[5] *Ibid.*, pp. 76f.

[6] *Ibid.*, pp. 28f., 35, 39f., 24f., 52f., 69-71, 76f.

Clues from the Moses Legends

No direct connection between Moses and Galilee has turned up in the traditions investigated in the course of this study.[1] Furthermore, the traditions of Moses' heavenly enthronement as king and prophet are found in such diverse sources that the Moses-centered mystical piety postulated above must have thrived in many places throughout the Mediterranean area in the Greco-Roman period.[2] Still, a distinct variant of the traditions was certainly localized in Samaria. The coincidence between the specifically Samaritan ideology and some elements in Jewish tradition, both rabbinic and especially extra-rabbinic, leads to the probability of mutual interaction between Jews and Samaritans in the formation of the traditions. As suggested above, Galilee would for several reasons be the most reasonable place to expect such interaction.[3]

The clear connection between the relevant Moses legends and Samaria and their hypothetical connection with Galilee would accord very well with the symbolic function of Samaria and Galilee in the Fourth Gospel, and particularly with the hypothesis that the symbolism developed out of actual local traditions.

At the same time it should be emphasized that Johannine Christianity could not have been exclusively Galilean-Samaritan. The geographical symbolism itself demonstrates the importance of Jerusalem and Judaea. Moreover, the very controversy stories which evidently reflect a historical confrontation between the Johannine community and a Moses-centered Jewish piety are set not in Galilee or Samaria, but in Jerusalem.[4] Now this connection with Jerusalem might be secondary, for since Jerusalem is understood in this gospel as the center of *judgment* and *decision* —precisely the main themes of John 5 and 9—one must reckon with the possi-

---

[1] Further research on the place of Galilee in Jewish history and tradition might prove fruitful, although the sources are exceedingly limited. The evidence from the N.T. and Josephus for a strong expectation of an eschatological *prophet* in Galilee (cf. Teeple, *Mosaic Prophet*, pp. 65f., Hahn, p. 361), together with characterization of Galileans in rabbinic traditions as people looking "for daily miracles, signs and wonders" (Neusner, *Yohanan*, p. 32), suggest that Moses traditions were cultivated there.

[2] It was at home, it seems, at least from Alexandria to Dura-Europas.

[3] Above, p. 257.

[4] Jn. 5; 9; cf. above, pp. 292-295. In both stories Kundsin would find evidence for locally fixed cult-aetiologies, but his arguments seem particularly weak at this point: see above, p. 315, n. 1.

bility that the evangelist may have transferred to Jerusalem traditions that were formed in Galilee. Nevertheless, it is clear that the
gospel as it stands is the product of the consolidation of traditions
of differing provenance. While Jesus fulfills the expectations of a
"prophet-king" like Moses, he is also the "Messiah" awaited by the
Judaeans—thought not the Bethlehemite son of David they expect.[1]

In this connection it is significant that the oft-mentioned "uni-
versalism" of the Fourth Gospel is expressed on a very concrete
level by the universal geography of its scenes, which includes all
Palestine.[2] Hence it could be that the peculiarities of the Johannine
material result from a period of consolidation of Palestinian Christianity, with an accompanying juxtaposition and partial assimilation to one another of several strands of tradition.

A CONCLUDING NOTE

This exegetical and historical investigation of two Johannine
christological motifs has led to two general conclusions about the
content of the gospel traditions and their provenance. First, the
Johannine traditions were shaped, at least in part, by interaction
between a Christian community and a hostile Jewish community
whose piety accorded very great importance to Moses and the Sinai
theophany, probably understood as Moses' ascent to heaven and
his enthronement there. Second, it is clear that the Johannine
church had drawn members from that Jewish group as well as from
the Samaritan circles which held very similar beliefs, and it has been
demonstrated to a high degree of probability that the depiction of

---

[1] N.b. that the title Μεσσίας has even been put in the mouth of the
Samaritan woman (4.25), a clear sign of the leveling of different termi-
nologies.

[2] It may be that this fact ought to be connected with the reference in
10.16 about "other sheep" which must be "gathered," and the "prophecy"
11.52, that Jesus' death would result in the gathering into one of "the
scattered children of God." The following note, that Jesus ended his "open"
appearance among the Jews by concealing himself in "Ephraim, near the
wilderness" may be related. Who if not a prophet-king of the character of
Moses (or God himself) would be expected to gather the scattered tribes
again, Ephraim and Judah together, as in the assembly at Sinai? (See above,
pp. 188, 190). Bowman's suggestion that the evangelist intended to show
"that Jesus is the fulfillment of all Israel's hope, the hope of Judah and also
of the Samaritans who claimed to be the descendants of Northern Israel"
(*BJRL*, 40, p. 302) thus points in the right direction, though his connection
of Jn. 10.16 with Ezek. 34.22-24 goes astray.

Jesus as prophet and king in the Fourth Gospel owes much to traditions which the church inherited from the Moses piety.

Now the thesis advocated here is not that the fourth evangelist wished to depict Jesus as a "new Moses." If that were the case, the typology would have to have been much more explicit. Rather it is to be assumed that he regarded Jesus as greater than Moses, just as he was "greater than our [the Samaritans'] father Jacob" (4.12) and "greater than our [the Jews'] father Abraham" (8.53). In describing Jesus in this way the evangelist—or the congregations that formed his traditions (the two points of view are not mutually exclusive)—used materials ready at hand, among which were evidently traditions about Moses very similar to those described in Chapters III-V above. The Fourth Gospel is not so constructed that the reader, in order to understand it, would have to perceive that Jesus, the "Son of Man," is like Moses—that is the error of the numerous typological treatments of John that have proliferated in recent years. On the other hand, its form and content are such that, if the reader *were* acquainted with those Moses-traditions described above, he would recognize (1) that Jesus fulfills for the believer those functions elsewhere attributed to Moses and (2) that the Christian claims he does this in a superior and exclusive way, so that Moses is now stripped of those functions and made merely a "witness" to Jesus (like John the Baptist). Therefore one who had formerly accounted himself a "disciple of Moses" would now have to decide whether he would become instead a "disciple of Jesus." If he did not, then from the viewpoint of this gospel he had in fact deserted the real Moses, for Moses only wrote of Jesus and true belief in Moses led to belief in Jesus.

BIBLIOGRAPHY

Primary Sources
Including Translations

Biblical and Early Christian Literature

Clement of Alexandria. *Clemens Alexandrinus.* Edited by Otto Stählin. (Die griechischen christlichen Schriftsteller der ersten drei Jahrhunderte.) Vol. II: *Stromateis Buch I-VI.* Leipzig: J. C. Hinrichs, 1906. 519 pp.

Eusebii Pamphili. *Evangelicae Praeparationis.* Ed. and trans. E. H. Gifford. Oxford: The University Press, 1903. 4 vols. in 5.

Eusebius. The Ecclesiastical History; With an English Translation. Edited by Kirsopp Lake. (The Loeb Classical Library.) London: Wm. Heinemann, 1926-32. 2 vols.

Die älteste Apologeten; Texte mit kurzen Einleitungen. Edited by Edgar J. Goodspeed. Göttingen: Vandenhoeck & Ruprecht, 1914. 380 pp.

Bruchstücke des Evangeliums und der Apokalypse des Petrus. Edited by Adolf von Harnack. Leipzig: J. C. Hinrichs, 1893. 98 pp.

Biblia Hebraica. Ed. Rud. Kittel, textum masoreticum curavit P. Kahle. 7th ed. Stuttgart: Privileg. Württ. Bibelanstalt, 1951. 1434 pp.

The Apostolic Fathers; With an English Translation. Edited by Kirsopp Lake. (Loeb Classical Library.) Cambridge: Harvard University Press, 1952. 2 vols.

Novum Testamentum Graece; cum apparatu critico curavit. Eberhard Nestle. 24th ed. rev. Erwin Nestle and Kurt Aland. Stuttgart: Privileg. Württ. Bibelanstalt, 1960. 671 pp.

Photius. *Myriobiblon sive Bibliotheca.* Edited by J. P. Migne. Vol. CIII of *Patrologiae cursus completus, series Graeca.* Paris: Garnier Fratres Editores, 1900.

Septuaginta; id est vetus testamentum graece iuxta LXX interpretes. Ed. Alfred Rahlfs. 6th ed. Stuttgart: Privileg. Württ. Bibelanstalt, 1959. 2 vols.

The Torah: The Five Books of Moses; A New Translation of the Holy Scriptures According to the Masoretic Text. Philadelphia: The Jewish Publishing Society of America, 1962. 393 pp.

Extra-Rabbinic Jewish Literature

Allegro, J. M. "Further Messianic References in Qumran Literature," JBL 75 (1956), 174-187.

——. "Further Light on the History of the Qumran Sect," *ibid.*, pp. 89-95 (pNah and pPs xxxvii fragments).

——. "Fragments of a Qumran Scroll of Eschatological *Midrasim*," JBL 77 (1958), 350-354 (4Q Florilegium so far as known).

Altjüdisches Schrifttum ausserhalb der Bibel. Ed. and trans. Paul Riessler. Augsburg: Dr. Benno Filser Verlag, 1928. 1342 pp.

The Apocrypha and Pseudepigrapha of the Old Testament. Oxford: at the Clarendon Press, 1913 (rp. 1964). 2 vols.

Artapanus: see Eusebius, *Praep. Ev.* and Clement of Alexandria, *Stromateis.*

The Assumption of Moses. Edited by R. H. Charles. London: Adam & Charles Black, 1897. 117 pp.

Baillet, Maurice. "Un recueil liturgique de Qumran, Grotte 4: 'Les paroles des luminaires," *Revue Biblique* 68 (1961), 195-250.

The Biblical Antiquities of Philo. Trans. M. R. James. (Translations of Early Documents, Series I, Palestinian Jewish Texts.) London: SPCK, 1917. 280 pp.

The Book of Wisdom. Edited by Joseph Reider. (Dropsie College Edition, Jewish Apocryphal Literature, ed. Solomon Zeitlin *et al.*) New York: Harper & Brothers, 1957. 233 pp.

The Dead Sea Scrolls in English. Trans. G[eza] Vermes. Baltimore: Penguin Books, 1962. 255 pp.

The Dead Sea Scrolls of St. Mark's Monastery. Vol. 1. Edited by Millar Burrows. New Haven: American Schools of Oriental Research, 1950-51.

Die Oracula Sibyllina. Edited by Joh. Geffcken. (Griechische christliche Schriftsteller der ersten drei Jahrhunderte, Vol. VIII.) Leipzig: J. C. Hinrichs, 1902. 240 pp.

Discoveries in the Judaean Desert. Vol. I: Qumran Cave I. Edited by D. Barthélemy and J. T. Milik. Oxford: at the Clarendon Press, 1955. 165 pp.; xxxvii plates.

Documents of Jewish Sectaries. Vol. I: Fragments of a Zadokite Work. Edited by Solomon Schechter. Cambridge: The University Press, 1910. lxiv and 20 pp., 2 plates.

3 *Enoch or The Hebrew Book of Enoch.* Ed. and trans. Hugo Odeberg. Cambridge: University Press, 1928. 192 + 179 + 74 + 36 pp.

Eupolemus: see Clement of Alexandria, *Stromateis*, and Eusebius, *Praep. Ev.*

Ezekiel the Tragedian: see Clement of Alexandria, *Stromateis*, and Eusebius, *Praep. Ev.*

The Greek Versions of the Testaments of the Twelve Patriarchs. Edited by R. H. Charles. Oxford: at the Clarendon Press, 1908. 324 pp.

Hunzinger, Claus-Hunno. "Fragmente einer älteren Fassung des Buches Milḥamā aus Höhle 4 von Qumrān," *Zeitschrift für die alttestamentliche Wissenschaft*, n.s. 28 (1957), 131-151.

Josephus, Flavius. *Opera Recognovit.* Edited by Benedict Niese. Berlin: Weidmann, 1888-95. 6 vols.

Josephus; With an English Translation. Edited by H. St. J. Thackeray and Ralph Marcus. (Loeb Classical Library.) London: Wm. Heinemann, 1926-65. 9 vols.

Philo; With an English Translation. Edited by F. H. Colson and G. H. Whitaker [*et al.*]. (Loeb Classical Library.) London: Wm. Heinemann, 1929-64. 10 vols.; 2 supplements.

Philo Judaeus. *Opera quae supersunt.* Edited by Leopold Cohn and Paul Wendland. Berlin: G. Reimer, 1896-1930. 7 vols.

Pseudo-Philo's Liber Antiquitatum Biblicarum. Edited by Guido Kisch. (Publications in Mediaeval Studies, ed. Philip S. Moore and Joseph N. Garvin, Vol. X.) Notre Dame: The University of Notre Dame, 1949. 277 pp.

Strugnell, J. "The Angelic Liturgy at Qumran, 4Q Serek Sirot Olat Hassabat": Congress Volume (Supplements to Vetus Testamentum, VII). Leiden: E. J. Brill, 1960, pp. 318-345.

The Zadokite Documents. Edited by Chaim Rabin. 2d rev. ed. Oxford: at the Clarendon Press, 1958. 103 pp.

The Zadokite Fragments; Facsimile of the Manuscripts in the Cairo Genizah . . .

Edited by Solomon Zeitlin. (The Jewish Quarterly Review Monograph Series, No. 1.) Philadelphia: The Dropsie College for Hebrew and Cognate Learning, 1952. 32 pp. and 20 plates.

Rabbinic Literature

Aboth de Rabbi Nathan. Edited by Solomon Schechter. Vienna: 1887; rp. New York: Philipp Feldheim, 1945. 176 pp.

Agadath Bereschith; Midraschische Auslegungen zum ersten Buche Mosis. Edited by Salomon Buber. Krakau: Verlag von Josef Fischer, 1902. 166 pp.

Aus Israels Lehrhallen; Kleine Midraschim zur späteren legendarischen Literatur des alten Testaments. Ed. and trans. Aug. Wünsche. Leipzig: Verlag von Eduard Pfeiffer, 1907-10. 5 vols. in 6.

The Authorized Daily Prayer Book of the United Hebrew Congregations of the British Empire, with a new translation by S. Singer. 9th American ed. New York: Hebrew Publishing Company [n.d.]. 338 pp.

The Babylonian Talmud . . . translated into English with notes, glossary and indices. Edited by Isidore Epstein. London: Soncino Press, 1935-52. 35 vols.

Bibliotheca Rabbinica; Eine Sammlung alter Midraschim. Ed. and trans. Aug. Wünsche. Leipzig: Otto Schulze, 1880-85. 3 vols., containing separately paginated fascicles.

Debarim Zuta: לקוטים ממדרש אלה הדברים רבה הנמצאים מפוזרים בילקוט Edited by Salomon Buber. Vienna: [Druck von Löwy & Alkalay], 1885. 35 pp.

Der tannaitische Midrasch Sifre zu Numeri. Ed. and trans. Karl Georg Kuhn. (Rabbinische Texte, ed. G. Kittel and K. H. Rengstorf, 2d series, Vol. III.) Stuttgart: W. Kohlhammer Verlag, 1959. 831 pp.

Die Tosefta; Text, Übersetzung, Erklärung. Edited by Gerhard Kittel, *et al.* Stuttgart: W. Kohlhammer, 1933-63.

The Fathers According to Rabbi Nathan. Trans. Judah Goldin. (Yale Judaica Series, Vol. X.) New Haven: Yale University Press, 1955. 277 pp.

Gaster, Moses. "Hebrew Visions of Hell and Paradise," in *Studies and Texts in Folklore, Magic, Medieval Romance, Hebrew Apocrypha, and Samaritan Archaeology.* Vol. I. London: Maggs Bros., 1925-28. Pp. 124-164.

Jellinek, Adolph (ed.). *Bet ha-Midrasch; Sammlung kleiner Midraschim und vermischter Abhandlungen aus der älteren jüdischen Literatur.* 2d. ed.; Jerusalem: Bamberger & Wahrmann, 1938. 6 vols.

Mekilta de-Rabbi Ishmael. Ed. and trans. Jacob Z. Lauterbach. (The Schiff Library of Jewish Classics.) Philadelphia: The Jewish Publication Society of America, 1949. 3 vols.

Mekhilta d'Rabbi Sim'on b. Jochai; Fragmenta in Geniza Cairensi reperta digessit apparatu critico, notis, praefatione instruxit. Edited by J. N. Epstein and E. Z. Melamed. Jerusalem: Mikize Nirdamim, 1955. 303 pp.

Mechilta de-Rabbi Simon b. Jochai; ein halachischer und haggadischer Midrasch zu Exodus. Edited by D. Hoffmann. Frankfurt a.M.: J. Kaufmann, 1905. 180 pp.

Midrasch ha-gadol zum Buche Exodus. Edited by D. Hoffmann. Berlin: H. Itzkowski, 1913-21. 242 pp.

Midrash Lekah Tob: מדרש לקה טוב המכונה פסיקתא זוטרתא על ·חמשה חומשי תורה Edited by Salomon Buber. Wilna: Verlag Wittwe & Gebrüder Romm, 1884. 2 vols.

The Midrash on Psalms. Trans. William G. Braude. (Yale Judaica Series, ed.

Leon Nemoy, Saul Lieberman, and Harry A. Wolfson; Vol. XIII.)
New Haven: Yale University Press, 1959. 2 vols.

Midrash Tanḥuma: מדרש תנחומא על חמשה חומשי תורה Edited by Salomon
Buber. Wilna: Verlag Wittwe & Gebrüder Romm, 1885. 5 vols. in 1.

Midrash Tanḥuma ("B"): מדרש תנחומא והוא מדרש ילמדנו על חמשה חומשי תורה
Reprinted New York and Berlin: Horeb Press, 1924. 692 pp.

Midrash Tannaïm zum Deuteronomium. Edited by D. Hoffmann. Berlin: H.
Itzkowski, 1908-09. 2 vols.

Midrash Tehillim: מדרש שוחר טוב על תהלים. Jerusalem:"Midraš", 1960. 203 pp.

Midrash Rabbah: מדרש רבה מפורש פירש וגו'. Edited by Moshe Aryeh Mirkin.
Tel-Aviv: 1956-62. 8 vols. (incomplete).

Midrash Rabbah. Trans. under the editorship of H. Freedmann and Maurice
Simon. London: Soncino Press, 1939. 10 vols.

Midrash Rabbah: מדרש רבה על חמשה חומשי תורה וחמש מגלות New York and
Berlin: Horeb, 1924. 132 (264) pp.

Mishnah: ששה סדרי משנה Edited by Enoch Albeck. Jerusalem + Tel Aviv:
Bialik Institute and Divir Co., 1957-58. 6 vols.

The Mishnah. Trans. Herbert Danby. Oxford: at the Clarendon Press, 1933.
844 pp.

Pesikta, die älteste Hagada, redigiert in Pälastina von Rab Kahana. Edited by
Salomon Buber. Lyck: Selbstverlag des Vereins Mekize Nirdamim, 1868.
207 (413) pp.

Seder Eliahu rabba und Seder Eliahu zuta. Edited by Meyer Friedmann.
Vienna: Verlag "Achiasaf," 1902. 200 pp.

*Sefer-ha-Likkutim; Sammlung älterer Midraschim und wissenschaftlicher Ab-
handlung.* Edited by L. Grünhut. [Jerusalem &] Frankfurt a.M.: J.
Kaufmann [1898-1903]. 6 vols.

Sifre: ספרי דבי רב עם תוספות מיר עין. Edited by Meyer Friedmann. Vienna:
1864. Reprinted New York: Om Publishing Co., 1948. 150 (300) pp.

Talmud Babli: תלמוד בבלי עם כל המפרשים כאשר נדפס מקדם ועם. הספות חדשות
[New York: S. Goldman-Otzar Hasefarim, Inc., 1958]. 20 vols.

Le Talmud de Jerusalem traduit pour la première fois. Trans. Moise Schwab.
Paris: Libraire Maisonneuve et Cie., 1878-90. 11 vols.

Talmud Yerushalmi: תלמוד ירושלמי או תלמוד המערב ויש קורין לו תלמוד ארץ
ישראל Jerusalem: Israel-American Offset, 1960. 4 vols.

*The Targums of Onkelos and Jonathan ben Uzziel on the Pentateuch; with the
Fragments of the Jerusalem Targum.* Trans. J. W. Ethridge. London:
Longman, Green, Longman, and Roberts, 1862. 2 vols.

Targum (Pseudo-) Jonathan ben Uzziel. [Printed copy without title page.
Sterling Memorial Library, Judaica/mlb/ + 900t.]

Tractate Sanhedrin; Mishnah and Tosefta. Trans. Herbert Danby. (Translations of Early Documents, Series III, Rabbinic Texts.) London:
Society for Promoting Christian Knowledge. 1919. 148 pp.

Yalkut Šim'oni: ילקוט שמעוני מדרש על תורה נביאים וכתובים [n.n.] Warsaw:
Br. Levin-Epstein, 1925. 3 vols. in 2.

Samaritan Literature

*The Asatir; The Samaritan Book of the 'Secrets of Moses'; Together with the
Pitron or Commentary and the Samaritan Story of the Death of Moses.* Ed.
and trans. Moses Gaster. (Oriental Translation Fund.) London: The
Royal Asiatic Society, 1927. 352 + 59 pp.

The Samaritan Chronicle or the Book of Joshua the Son of Nun. Trans. Oliver
Turnbul Crane. New York: John B. Alden, Publisher, 1890. 178 pp.

The Samaritan Liturgy. Edited by Arthur E. Cowley. Oxford: at the Clarendon Press, 1909. 2 vols.

Das samaritanische Targum. Edited by Adolf Brüll. Frankfurt a.M.: Verlag von Wilhelm Erras, 1875. 248 + 18 pp.

Der hebräische Pentateuch der Samaritaner. Edited by August Freiherr von Gall. Giessen: A. Töpelmann, 1914-18, 5 vols.

Kahle, Paul. "Die zwölf Marka-Hymnen aus dem 'Defter' der samaritanischen Liturgie," *Opera Minora; Festgabe zum 21. Januar 1956.* Leiden: E. J. Brill, 1956. Pp. 186-212.

Macdonald, John. "The Theological Hymns of Amram Darah," *Annual of Leeds University Oriental Society,* Vol. II. Leiden: E. J. Brill, 1961. Pp. 54-73.

Memar Marqah; The Teaching of Marqah. Ed. and trans. John Macdonald. (Beihefte zur Zeitschrift für die alttestamentliche Wissenschaft, No. 84.) Berlin: A. Töpelmann, 1963. 2 vols.

Mandaean Literature

The Canonical Prayerbook of the Mandaeans. Edited and trans. by E. S. Drower. Leiden: E. J. Brill, 1959. 324 + 495 pp.

Diwan Abatur; or Progress Through the Purgatories. Edited by E. S. Drower. (Studi e Testi, 151.) Città del Vaticano: Biblioteca Apostolica Vaticana, 1950. 45 pp. + text facsimile.

Ginza; Der Schatz oder Das Grosse Buch der Mandäer. Ed. and trans. Mark Lidzbarski. (Quellen der Religionsgeschichte, Vol. XIII.) Göttingen: Vandenhoeck & Ruprecht; Leipzig: J. C. Hinrichs, 1925. 619 pp.

The Haran Gawaita and the Baptism of Hibil-Ziwa [maṣbuta ḏ-hibil ziua]. Edited by E. S. Drower.)Studi e Testi, 176.) Città del Vaticano: Biblioteca Apostolica Vaticana, 1953. 96 pp. + inserted facsimile of Haran Gawaita text.

Inscriptions mandaïtes des coupes de Khouabir. Edited by H. Pognon. Paris: Imprimerie Nationale, 1898. 328 pp.

Das Johannesbuch der Mandaer. Edited by Mark Lidzbarski. Giessen: Verlag von Alfred Töpelmann, 1905-15. 2 vols. in 1.

Lidzbarski, Mark. "Mandäische Zaubertexte," *Ephemeris für semitische Epigraphik.* Giessen: Alfred Töpelmann, 1900-02. I, 89-105.

Mandäische Liturgien. Trans. Mark Lidzbarski. (Abhandlungen der königlichen Gesellschaft der Wissenschaften zu Göttingen, Philologisch-historische Klasse, n.s. XVII/1.) Berlin: Weidmann, 1920. 295 pp.

Montgomery, James A. *Aramaic Incantation Texts from Nippur.* (Publications of the Babylonian Section, the Museum, University of Pennsylvania, Vol. III.) Philadelphia: The University Museum, 1913. 326 pp.; 41 plates.

Other Sources

Epictetus. *Epicteti Dissertationes ab Arriano digestae.* Edited by H. Schenkl. Leipzig: B. G. Teubner, 1916. 713 pp.

Epictetus. *The Discourses as Reported by Arrian, the Manual, and Fragments.* Ed. and trans. W. A. Oldfather. (Loeb Classical Library.) London: W. Heinemann, 1926-28. 2 vols.

Gnosticism: A Source Book of Heretical Writings from the Early Christian Period. Edited by Robert M. Grant. New York: Harper & Brothers, 1961. 254 pp.

Quellen zur Geschichte der christlichen Gnosis. Edited by Walther Völker. Tübingen: J. C. B. Mohr [Paul Siebeck], 1932. 147 pp.

Stoicorum veterum fragmenta. Edited by Hans Friedrich August von Arnim. Leipzig: B. G. Teubner, 1921-24. 4 vols.

Works of Reference

Bacher, Wilhelm. *Die exegetische Terminologie der jüdischen Traditionsliteratur.* Leipzig: J. C. Hinrichs, 1899-1905. 2 vols.

Blass, F., and Debrunner, A. *A Greek Grammar of the New Testament and Other Early Christian Literature.* Translated and revised by Robert W. Funk. Chicago: The University of Chicago Press, 1961. 325 pp.

Clavis Patrum Apostolicorum; catalogum vocum in libris patrum qui dicuntur apostolici non raro occurrentium. Edited by Henricus Kraft. Darmstadt: Wissenschaftliche Buchgesellschaft, 1963. 501 pp.

A Concordance to the Greek Testament according to the Texts of Westcott and Hort, Tischendorf, and the English Revisers. Edited by W. F. Moulton and A. S. Geden. Edinburgh: T. & T. Clark, 1957. 1033 pp.

A Concordance to the Septuagint and the Other Greek Versions of the Old Testament (Including the Apocryphal Books). Compiled by Edwin Hatch and Henry A. Redpath. Graz-Austria: Akademische Druck- u. Verlagsanstalt, 1954. 2 vols.

A Dictionary of the Targumim, the Talmud Babli and Yerushalmi, and the Midrashic Literature. Compiled by Marcus Jastrow. New York: Pardes Publishing House, Inc., 1950. 2 vols.

Goodwin, William Watson. *Greek Grammar.* Rev. by Charles Burton Gulick. [Boston:] Ginn and Company, 1958. 472 pp.

A Greek-English Lexicon. Compiled by Henry George Liddell and Robert Scott. New ed. rev. by Henry Stuart Jones. Oxford: at the Clarendon Press, 1961. 2111 pp.

A Greek-English Lexicon of the New Testament and Other Early Christian Literature. A translation and adaptation of Walter Bauer's Griechisch-Deutsches Wörterbuch zu den Schriften des Neuen Testaments, etc., by William F. Arndt and F. Wilbur Gingrich. Chicago: The University of Chicago Press, 1957. 909 pp.

Hyman, Aharon M. תורה הכתובה והמסורה. Tel-Aviv: Dvir Company, 1939. 3 vols.

Index apologeticus sive clave Iustini martyris operum aliorumque apologetarum pristinorum. Edited by E. J. Goodspeed. Leipzig: J. C. Hinrichs, 1912. 300 pp.

Indices ad Philonis Alexandrini Opera. Edited by Johannes Leisegang. Vol. VII of *Philo Judaeus, Opera quae supersunt,* ed. Leopold Cohn and Paul Wendland. Berlin: Walter de Gruyter & Co., 1930. 878 pp.

Konkordanz zu den Qumrantexten. Edited by Karl Georg Kuhn. Göttingen: Vandenhoeck & Ruprecht, 1960. 237 pp.

Kühner, Raphael. *Ausführliche Grammatik des griechischen Sprache.* 2. Teil: *Satzlehre.* 3d ed. rev. by Bernhard Gerth. München: Max Hueber Verlag, 1904. Reprinted: Darmstadt: Wissenschaftliche Buchgesellschaft, 1963. 2 vols.

A Lexicon to Josephus. Edited by Henry St. John Thackeray. Part II, ἀργύρεος to διαστέλλειν. Paris: Libraire Orientaliste Paul Geuthner, 1934.

A Mandaic Dictionary. Compiled by E. S. Drower and R. Macuch. Oxford: at the Clarendon Press, 1963. 491 pp.

Mielziner, M. *Introduction to the Talmud.* 3d ed.; New York: Bloch Publishing Company, Inc., 1925. 395 pp.

Nöldeke, Theodor. *Mandäische Grammatik*. Halle: Verlag der Buchhandlung des Waisenhauses, 1875. Rp.: Darmstadt: Wissenschaftliche Buchgesellschaft, 1964. 486 pp.

Rabbinovicz, Raphael. *Variae Lectiones in Mischnam et in Talmud Babylonicum*. Reprinted: Brooklyn *et al.*: Jerusalem Publishing Company, 1940. 13 vols.

Real-Encyklopädie der christlichen Altertumer. Edited by F. X. Kraus. Freiburg i.B.: Herder Verlag, 1886. 2 vols.

Strack, Herman L. *Introduction to the Talmud and Midrash*. Philadelphia: The Jewish Publication Society; and New York: Meridian Books, 1959. 372 pp.

Synopsis of the First Three Gospels. Edited by Albert Huck. 9th ed. revised by Hans Lietzmann. English ed. by F. L. Cross. New York: American Bible Society, 1954. 213 pp.

General Works

Albright, W. F. "Recent Discoveries in Palestine and the Gospel of St. John," *The Background of the New Testament and Its Eschatology*. Ed. W. D. Davies and David Daube. Cambridge: The University Press, 1956. Pp. 153-171.

Audet, Jean-Paul. *La Didachè; Instructions des Apôtres*. Paris: Librairie Lecoffe, 1958. 498 pp.

Bacon, Benjamin W. *The Gospel of the Hellenists*. Ed. Carl H. Kraeling. New York: Henry Holt & Company, 1933. 432 pp.

Bailey, John Amedee. *The Traditions Common to the Gospels of Luke and John*. (Supplements to Novum Testamentum. Ed. W. C. van Unnik, *et al.*, Vol. VII.) Leiden: E. J. Brill, 1963. 121 pp.

Barrett, C. K. *The Gospel According to St. John; An Introduction with Commentary and Notes on the Greek Text*. London: S.P.C.K., 1955. 531 pp.

Bauer, Walter. *Das Johannesevangelium*. 2d rev. ed. (Handbuch zum Neuen Testament. Ed. Hans Lietzmann, *et al.*, Vol. VI.) Tübingen: J. C. B. Mohr [Paul Siebeck], 1925. 244 pp.

Bernard, J. H. *A Critical and Exegetical Commentary on the Gospel according to St. John*. (The International Critical Commentary.) New York: Charles Scribner's Sons, 1929. 2 vols.

Betz, Otto. *Der Paraklet; Fürsprecher im haretischen Spätjudentum, im Johannes-Evangelium und in neu gefundenen gnostischen Schriften*. (Arbeiten zur Geschichte des Spätjudentums und Urchristentums. Ed. Otto Michel, Institutum Iudaicum; Vol. II.) Leiden/Köln: E. J. Brill, 1963. 242 pp.

Bickermann, Elias. *From Ezra to the Last of the Maccabees; Foundations of Post-Biblical Judaism*. New York: Schocken Books, 1962. 186 pp.

Bieler, Ludwig. ΘΕΙΟΣ ΑΝΗΡ; *Das Bild des "göttlichen Menschen" in Spätantike und Frühchristentum*. Vienna: Buchhandlung Oskar Höfels, 1935-36. 2 vols.

Blank, Josef. "Die Verhandlung vor Pilatus Jo 18, 28-19, 16 im Lichte johanneischer Theologie," *Biblische Zeitschrift*, n.s. (1959), 60-81.

Blinzler, Joseph. *The Trial of Jesus; The Jewish and Roman Proceedings against Jesus Christ Described and Assessed from the Oldest Accounts*. Trans. Isabel and Florence McHugh. Cork: Mercier Press, 1959. 312 pp.

Bloch, Renée. "Midrash," *Dictionnaire de la Bible, Supplément*. Ed. L. Pirot, *et al.* Vol. V. Paris: Librairie Letouzey et Ane, 1957. Cols. 1263-1281.

——. "Note méthodologique pour l'étude de la littérature rabbinque," *Recherches de Science Religieuse*, 43 (1955), 194-227.

——. "Quelques aspects de la Figure de Moïse dans la Tradition Rabbinque," *Moïse, l'homme de l'Alliance*. Ed. H. Cazelles, *et al.* (Special issue of *Cahiers Sioniens*.) Paris: Desclée & Cie., 1955. Pp. 93-167.

Borgen, Peder. "Observations on the Midrashic Character of John 6," *Zeitschrift für die neutestamentliche Wissenschaft*, 54 (1963), 232-240.

——. "Philo and a Haggadic Tradition." Unpublished paper read before 99th meeting of the Society of Biblical Literature, New York, January 2, 1964.

——. "The Unity of the Discourse in John 6," *Zeitschrift für die neutestamentliche Wissenschaft*, 50 (1959), 277-279.

Bornkamm, Günther. "End-Expectation and Church in Matthew," *Tradition and Interpretation in Matthew*, by Günther Bornkamm, Gerhard Barth, and Heinz Joachim Held. Trans. Percy Scott. (New Testament Library.) Philadelphia: Westminster Press, 1963. Pp. 15-51.

——. *Jesus of Nazareth*. Trans. Irene and Fraser McLuskey with James M. Robinson. New York: Harper & Brothers, 1960. 239 pp.

Botte, Bernard. "La vie de Moïse par Philon," in *Moïse, l'homme de l'alliance*. Ed. H. Cazelles, *et al.* (Special issue of *Cahiers Sioniens*.) Paris: Desclée & Cie., 1955. Pp. 55-62.

Bousset, Wilhelm. *Der Antichrist in der Überlieferung des Judentums, des Neuen Testaments, und der alten Kirche*. Göttingen: Vandenhoeck & Ruprecht, 1895. 186 pp.

——. *The Antichrist Legend: A Chapter in Christian and Jewish Folklore*. Trans. A. H. Keane. London: Hutchinson and Co., 1896. 307 pp.

——. *Die Himmelsreise der Seele*. (Originally published in *Archiv für Religionswissenschaft*, 4 [1901], 136-169, 229-273.) Reprinted: Darmstadt: Wissenschaftliche Buchgesellschaft, 1960. 83 pp.

Bowman, John. "Early Samaritan Eschatology," *The Journal of Jewish Studies*, 6 (1955), 63-72.

——. "The Exegesis of the Pentateuch among the Samaritans and among the Rabbis," *Oudtestamentische Studiën*. Ed. P. A. H. DeBoer, Deel VIII. Leiden: E. J. Brill, 1950. Pp. 220-262.

——. "The Importance of Samaritan Researches," *The Annual of Leeds University Oriental Society*. Ed. John Macdonald. Vol. I. Leiden: E. J. Brill, 1959. Pp. 43-54.

——. "Samaritan Studies," reprinted from the *Bulletin of the John Rylarch Library*, 40 (1958), 298-327.

Brandt, Wilhelm. *Die mandäische Religion; ihre Entwicklung und geschichtliche Bedeutung*. Leipzig: J. C. Hinrichs, 1889. 236 pp.

Braun, F. M. "L'arrière-fond judaïque du quatrième évangile et la communauté de l'alliance," *Revue Biblique*, 62 (1955), 5-44.

Bultmann, Rudolf. "Die Bedeutung der neuerschlossenen mandäischen und manichäischen Quellen für das Verständnis des Johannesevangeliums," *Zeitschrift für die Neutestamentlichen Wissenschaft*, 24 (1925), 100-146.

——. *Das Evangelium des Johannes*. (Kritisch-Exegetischer Kommentar über das Neue Testament, begründet von H. A. W. Meyer.) 16th ed. Göttingen: Vandenhoeck & Ruprecht, 1959. 563 pp. + Ergänzungsheft.

——. *Die Geschichte der synoptischen Tradition*. (Forschungen zur Religion und Literatur des Alten und Neuen Testaments, n.s., vol. XII.) 5th ed. Göttingen: Vandenhoeck & Ruprecht, 1961. 408 pp. + Ergänzungsheft.

——. "The Interpretation of the Fourth Gospel," *New Testament Studies*, 1 (1954-55), 77-91.
——. "Johannesevangelium," *Die Religion in Geschichte und Gegenwart*. 3d ed.; ed. Kurt Galling, *et al.* Tübingen: J. C. B. Mohr [Paul Siebeck], 1959. Vol. III, cols. 840-850.
——. "Der religionsgeschichtliche Hintergrund des Prologs zum Johannes-Evangelium," EYXAPIΣTHPION; *Hermann Gunkel zum 60. Geburtstage . . .* Ed. Hans Schmidt. Part 2. (Forschungen zur Religion und Literatur des Alten und Neuen Testaments, n.s. XIX.) Göttingen: Vandenhoeck & Ruprecht, 1923. Pp. 1-26.
——. *Theology of the New Testament*. Trans. Kendrick Grobel. New York: Chas. Scribner's Sons, 1951-55. 2 vols.
Burrows, Millar. *More Light on the Dead Sea Scrolls*. New York: The Viking Press, 1958. 434 pp.
Cerfaux, Lucien. "La multiplication des pains dans la liturgie de la Didachè (IX, 4)," *Biblica*, 40 (1959), 943-958.
Colpe, Carsten. "Mandäer," *Die Religion in Geschichte und Gegenwart*. 3d ed. Kurt Galling, *et al.* Vol. IV. Tübingen: J. C. B. Mohr [Paul Siebeck], 1960. Cols. 709-712.
——. *Die religionsgeschichtliche Schule; Darstellung und Kritik ihres Bildes vom gnostischen Erlösermythus*. (Forschungen zur Religion und Literatur des Alten und Neuen Testaments, n.s. LX.) Göttingen: Vandenhoeck & Ruprecht, 1961. 265 pp.
Conzelmann, Hans. *The Theology of St. Luke*. Trans. Geoffrey Buswell. New York: Harper & Bros., 1960. 255 pp.
Corssen, Paul. "'Εκάθισεν ἐπί βήματος," *Zeitschrift für die neutestamentliche Wissenschaft*, 15 (1914), 338-340.
Cullmann, Oscar. *The Christology of the New Testament*. Trans. Shirley C. Guthrie and Charles A. M. Hall. Philadelphia: The Westminster Press, 1959. 342 pp.
——. *Königsherrschaft Christi und Kirche im Neuen Testament*. 2d. ed. (Theologische Studien. Ed. Karl Barth, XI.) Zollikon-Zürich: Evangelischer Verlag, 1946. 48 pp.
Dahl, Nils Alstrup. "Der erstgeborene Satans und der Vater des Teufels (Polyk. 7.1 und Joh 8.44)," *Apophoreta; Festschrift für Ernst Haenchen*. Ed. Walther Eltester. Berlin: Alfred Töpelmann, 1964. Pp. 70-84.
——. "Der gekreuzigte Messias," *Der historische Jesus und der kerygmatische Christus*. Ed. Helmut Ristow and Karl Matthiae. Berlin: Evangelische Verlagsanstalt, 1960. Pp. 149-169.
——. "The Johannine Church and History," *Current Issues in New Testament Interpretation*. Ed. William Klassen and Graydon F. Snyder. New York: Harper & Brothers, 1962. Pp. 124-142.
——. "Manndraperen og hans far (Joh 8:44)," *Norsk Theologisk Tidskrift*, 64 (1963), 129-162.
——. *Das VolkGottes; Eine Untersuchung zum Kirchenbewusstsein des Urchristentums*. 2d ed. Darmstadt: Wissenschaftliche Buchgesellschaft, 1962. 351 pp.
Daube, David. *The New Testament and Rabbinic Judaism*. London: The Athlone Press, 1956. 460 pp.
Descamps, Albert. "Le Messianisme royal dans le Nouveau Testament," *l'Attente du Messie*. Ed. Lucien Cerfaux, *et al.* Paris: Desclée de Brouwer & Cie., 1954. Pp. 57-84.
Díaz, José Ramón. "Palestinian Targum and New Testament," *Novum Testamentum*, 6 (1963), 75-80.

Dibelius, Martin. *An die Thessalonicher I, II; An die Philipper*. (Handbuch zum Neuen Testament. Ed. Hans Lietzmann.) Tübingen: J. C. B. Mohr [Paul Siebeck], 1925.

Dodd, C. H. *The Interpretation of the Fourth Gospel*. Cambridge: The University Press, 1953. 477 pp.

Drower, E. S. *The Mandaeans of Iraq and Iran; Their Cults, Customs, Legends, and Folklore*. Oxford: at the Clarendon Press, 1937. 436 pp.

The Secret Adam: A Study of Naṣorean Gnosis. Oxford: At the Clarendon Press, 1960. 123 pp.

Elliger, Karl. *Das Buch der zwölf kleinen Propheten*. Edited by Volkmar Herntrich and Artur Weiser. (Das Alte Testament Deutsch. Vol. XXV.) Göttingen: Vandenhoeck & Ruprecht, 1950. 217 pp.

Fascher, Erich. Προφήτης; *Eine sprach- und religionsgeschichtliche Untersuchung*. Giessen: Alfred Töpelmann, 1927. 228 pp.

Fiebig, Paul. "Die Mekilta und das Johannes-Evangelium," ΑΓΓΕΛΟΣ, *Archiv für neutestamentliche Zeitgeschichte und Kulturkunde*. Ed. Johannes Leipoldt. I (1925), 57-59.

Gärtner, Bertil. *John 6 and the Jewish Passover*. (Coniectanea Neotestamentica, XVII.) Lund: G. W. K. Gleerup, 1959. 52 pp.

Gaster, Moses. "Merx (Adalbert): Der Messias oder Ta'eb der Samaritaner" [a review], *Zeitschrift der Deutsch-Morgenländischen Gesellschaft* (1911), 445-455. Reprinted: in *Studies and Texts* . . . (London: Maggs Bros., 1925-28), I, 638-648.

——. *The Samaritans: Their History, Doctrines and Literature*. (The Schweich Lectures, 1923). London: Oxford University Press, 1925. 208 pp.

——. *The Samaritan Oral Law and Ancient Traditions*. Vol. I: *The Samaritan Eschatology*. [London:] The Search Publishing Company, 1932. 277 pp.

——. *Studies and Texts in Folklore, Magic, Medieval Romance, Hebrew Apocrypha and Samaritan Eschatology*. London: Maggs Bros., 1925-28. 3 vols.

Gaster, T. H. "Samaritans," *The Interpreter's Dictionary of the Bible*. Vol. IV. New York: Abington Press, 1962. Pp. 190-197.

Gercke, A. "Aristobulus, 15," *Paulys Real-Encyclopädie der classischen Altertumswissenschaft*. Ed. Georg Wissowa. Vol. II. Stuttgart: J. B. Metzler, 1896. Cols. 918-920.

Giblet, J. "Prophétisme et attente d'un Messie prophète dans l'ancien Judaïsme," *L'Attente du Messie*. Ed. L. Cerfaux, *et al.* (Recherches Bibliques.) Paris: Desclée de Brouwer, 1954. Pp. 85-130.

Ginzberg, Louis. *The Legends of the Jews*. Philadelphia: The Jewish Publication Society of America, 1909-61. 7 vols.

Glasson, T. F. *Moses in the Fourth Gospel*. (Studies in Biblical Theology, No. 40.) London: SCM Press Ltd., 1963, 115 pp.

Goldin, Judah. "The First Chapter of the Abot de Rabbi Nathan." *Mordecai M. Kaplan: Jubilee Volume on the Occasion of His Seventieth Birthday. English Section*. New York: Jewish Theological Seminary of America, 1953. Pp. 263-280.

Goodenough, Erwin R. *By Light, Light: The Mystic Gospel of Hellenistic Judaism*. New Haven: Yale University Press, 1935. 436 pp.

——. *Jewish Symbols in the Greco-Roman Period*. (Bollingen Series, XXXVII.) New York: Pantheon Books, 1952-64. 11 vols. (Vol. 12 in preparation.)

——. "John a Primitive Gospel," *Journal of Biblical Literature* 64 (1945), 145-182.

——. "The Political Philosophy of Hellenistic Kingship," in *Yale Classical*

Studies, Vol. I. Ed. Austin M. Harmon. New Haven: Yale University Press, 1928. Pp. 55-102.

——. "Literal Mystery in Hellenistic Judaism," *Quantulacumque*; *Studies Presented to Kirsopp Lake by Pupils, Colleagues and Friends*. Ed. Robert P. Casey, Silva Lake, and Agnes K. Lake. London: Christophers, 1937. Pp. 227-241.

Grant, Frederick C. "Was the Author of John Dependent upon the Gospel of Luke?" *Journal of Biblical Literature*, 56 (1937), 285-307.

Guilding, Aileen. *The Fourth Gospel and Jewish Worship*; *A Study of the Relation of St. John's Gospel to the Ancient Jewish Lectionary System*. Oxford: at the Clarendon Press, 1960. 247 pp.

Haenchen, Ernst. "Jesus vor Pilatus," *Theologische Literaturzeitung*, 85 (1960), cols. 93-102.

——. "Johanneische Probleme," *Zeitschrift für Theologie und Kirche*, 56 (1959), 19-54.

——. "Probleme des johanneischen 'Prologs,'" *Zeitschrift für Theologie und Kirche*, 60 (1963), 305-334.

Hahn, Ferdinand. *Christologische Hoheitstitel; Ihre Geschichte im frühen Christentum*. (Forschungen zur Religion und Literatur des Alten und Neuen Testaments, LXXXIII.) Göttingen: Vandenhoeck & Ruprecht, 1963, 442 pp.

Heinemann, Isaac. "Moses," *Paulys Real-Encyclopädie der classischen Altertumswissenschaft*. Ed. Georg Wissowa. 1st Series, Vol. XVI. Stuttgart: J. B. Metzler, 1933.

——. *Philons Griechische und Jüdische Bildung: Kulturvergleichende Untersuchungen zu Philons Darstellung der jüdischen Gesetze*. Breslau: M & H. Marcus, 1929-1932. Reprinted: Darmstadt: Wissenschaftliche Buchgesellschaft, 1962. 606 pp.

Hirsch, Emanuel. *Studien zum vierten Evangelium*. (Beiträge zur historischen Theologie, XI.) Tübingen: J. C. B. Mohr [Paul Siebeck], 1936. 190 pp.

Hoskyns, Edwyn Clement. *The Fourth Gospel*. Edited by Francis Noel Davey. London: Faber and Faber, 1947. 604 pp.

Howard, W. F. *The Fourth Gospel in Recent Criticism and Interpretation*. 4th ed. rev. by C. K. Barrett. London: The Epworth Press, 1955. 327 pp.

Hvidberg, Flemming F. *Menigheden af den Nye Pagt i Damascus*. København: G. E. C. Gads Forlag, 1928. 303 pp.

Jeremias, Gert. *Der Lehrer der Gerechtigkeit*. (Studien zur Umwelt des Neuen Testaments. Ed. Karl Georg Kuhn. II.) Göttingen: Vandenhoeck & Ruprecht, 1963. 376 pp.

Jeremias, Joachim. *Golgotha*. (ΑΓΓΕΛΟΣ Beihefte. Ed. Gottfried Polster. I.) Leipzig: Verlag von Eduard Pfeiffer, 1926. 96 pp.

——. "Μωϋσῆς," *Theologisches Wörterbuch zum Neuen Testament*. Ed. Gerhard Kittel. Vol. IV. Stuttgart: W. Kohlhammer, 1942. Pp. 852-878.

Jervell, Jacob. *Imago Dei; Gen. 1, 26f. im Spätjudentum, in der Gnosis, und in den paulinischen Briefen*. (Forschungen zur Religion und Literatur des Alten und Neuen Testaments, n.s., LVIII.) Göttingen: Vandenhoeck & Ruprecht, 1960. 379 pp.

Johansson, Nils. *Parakletoi: Vorstellungen von Fürsprechern für die Menschen vor Gott in der alttestamentlichen Religion, im Spätjudentum und Urchristentum*. Lund: Gleerupska Universitetsbokhandeln, 1940. 323 pp.

Jonas, Hans. *Gnosis und Spätantiker Geist. Teil I: Die mythologische Gnosis*. (FRLANT, n.s. 33.) Göttingen: Vandenhoeck & Ruprecht, 1934. 375 pp.

3d ed. rev. and enlarged, 1964. 456 pp. Teil II: *Von der Mythologie zur mystischen Philosophie.* (FRLANT, n.s. 45.) 1954. 223 pp.

——. *The Gnostic Religion; The Message of the Alien God and the Beginnings of Christianity.* 2d ed. rev. Boston: Beacon Press, 1963. 355 pp.

Jonge, Marinus de. *The Testaments of the Twelve Patriarchs.* Assen: Van Gorcum & Comp., 1953. 171 pp.

Käsemann, Ernst. "Aufbau und Anliegen des Johanneischen Prologs," *Libertas Christiana; Friedrich Delekat zum 65. Geburtstag.* Ed. W. Matthias u. E. Wolf. Muenchen: Chr. Kaiser Verlag, 1957. Pp. 75-99.

Kahle, Paul. *The Cairo Geniza.* 2d ed. Oxford: B. H. Blackwell, 1959. 370 pp.

Klausner, Joseph. *The Messianic Idea in Israel.* Trans. W. F. Stinespring. New York: Macmillan, 1955. 543 pp.

Klostermann, Erich. *Das Markus Evangelium.* (4th ed., Handbuch zum Neuen Testament. Ed. Hans Lietzmann. III.) Tübingen: J. C. B. Mohr, 1950. 180 pp.

Knopf, Rudolf. *Die Lehre der zwölf Apostel; Die zwei Clemensbriefe.* (Handbuch zum Neuen Testament. II. Ed. Hans Lietzmann. Ergänzungsband. I.) Tübingen: J. C. B. Mohr [Paul Siebeck]. 1920. 184 pp.

Kraus, H. J. *Psalmen.* (Biblischer Kommentar zum A.T. XV.) Neukirchen: Verlag des Erziehungsvereins, 1961. 2 vols.

Krüger, Paul. *Philo und Josephus als Apologeten des Judentums.* Leipzig: Verlag der Dürr'schen Buchhandlung, 1906. 82 pp.

Kuhn, Karl Georg. "The Two Messiahs of Aaron and Israel," *The Scrolls and the New Testament.* Ed. Krister Stendahl. New York: Harper & Brothers, 1957. Pp. 54-64.

Kundsin, Karl. *Topologische Überlieferungsstoffe im Johannes-Evangelium.* (Forschungen zur Religion und Literatur des Alten und Neuen Testaments, n.s., 22.) Göttingen: Vandenhoeck & Ruprecht, 1925. 80 pp.

Labriole, Pierre. *La Réaction païenne; Étude sur la polemique antichrétienne du Ier au Vie Siècle.* Paris: l'Artisan du Livre, 1942. 519 pp.

Lauterbach, Jacob. "Tanḥuma, Midrash," *The Jewish Encyclopedia.* New York: Funk and Wagnalls Company, 1907. Vol. XII, pp. 45-46.

Lidzbarski, Mark. "Uthra und Malakha," *Orientalische Studien Theodor Nöldeke zum siebzigsten Geburtstag gewidmet.* Ed. Carl Bezold. Giessen: A. Töpelmann, 1906. Pp. 537-545.

Liberman, Saul. *Hellenism in Jewish Palestine.* (Texts and Studies of the Jewish Theological Seminary of America. Vol. XVII.) New York: The Jewish Theology Seminary, 1950. 231 pp.

Lightfoot, R. H. *Locality and Doctrine in the Gospels.* New York: Harper & Brothers, 1938. 166 pp.

Lohmeyer, Ernst. *Das Evangelium Markus.* (Kritisch-Exegetischer Kommentar über das Neue Testament, begründet von H. A. W. Meyer, vol. II.) 4th ed. Göttingen: Vandenhoeck & Ruprecht, 1954. 368 pp. — Ergänzungsheft (ed. Gerhard Sass).

——. *Die Offenbarung des Johannes.* (Handbuch zum Neuen Testament. Ed. Hans Lietzmann, et al., Vol. XVI.) Tübingen: J. C. B. Mohr [Paul Siebeck], 1926. 203 pp.

Loisy, Alfred. *Le Quatrième Évangile.* 2d ed. Paris: Emile Nourry, 1921. 602 pp.

Macdonald, John. *The Theology of the Samaritans.* (The New Testament Library.) London: SCM Press, 1964. 480 pp.

Maier, Johan. *Die Texte vom Toten Meer.* München: Ernst Reinhardt Verlag, 1960. 2 vols.

Marti, Karl. *Das Dodekapropheton.* (Karl Marti, *et al.* [eds.]. Kurzer Hand-Kommentar zum Alten Testament. Vol. XIII.) Tübingen: J. C. B. Mohr [Paul Siebeck], 1904. 492 pp.

Merx, Adalbert. *Der Messias oder Ta'eb der Samaritaner.* (Beihefte zur Zeitschrift für die alttestamentliche Wissenschaft, XVII.) Giessen: Alfred Töpelmann, 1909. 92 pp.

Meyer, H. A. W. *Kritisch Exegetisches Handbuch über das Evangelium des Johannes.* (Kritisch exegetischer Kommentar über das Neue Testament. Ed. H. A. W. Meyer.) 5th rev. ed. Göttingen: Vandenhoeck und Ruprecht, 1869. 684 pp.

Meyer, Paul W. "A Note on John 10.1-18," *Journal of Biblical Literature,* 75 (1956), 232-235.

Milik, J. T. *Ten Years of Discovery in the Wilderness of Judaea.* Trans. J. Strugnell. (Studies in Biblical Theology, No. 26.) London: SCM Press, 1959, 124 pp., 25 plates.

——. "Le Testament de Lévi en Araméen. Fragment de la grotte 4 de Qumran," *Revue Biblique,* 62 (1955), 398-406.

Moffatt, James. *An Introduction to the Literature of the New Testament.* New York: Charles Scribner's Sons, 1911. 630 pp.

Montefiore, C. G., and Loewe, H. *A Rabbinic Anthology.* Philadelphia: The Jewish Publication Society of America, 1960. 853 pp.

Montgomery, James A. *The Samaritans: the Earliest Jewish Sect; Their History, Theology, and Literature.* Philadelphia: The John C. Winston Co., 1907. 358 pp.

Moore, George Foot. *Judaism in the First Centuries of the Christian Era: The Age of the Tannaim.* Cambridge: Harvard University Press, 1927-1930. 3 vols.

Moule, C. F. D. "A Note on Didache IX.4," *The Journal of Theological Studies,* n.s. 6 (1955), 240-243.

Mowinckel, Sigmund. *He That Cometh.* Trans. G. W. Anderson. Nashville: Abingdon Press, 1954. 528 pp.

Mowry, Lucetta. "The Dead Sea Scrolls and the Background for the Gospel of John." *Biblical Archaeologist,* 17 (1954), 78-97.

Neusner, Jacob. "Jewish Use of Pagan Symbols after 70 C.E.," *The Journal of Religion,* 43 (1963), 285-294.

——. *A Life of Rabban Yohanan ben Zakkai, ca.* 1-80C.E. (Studia Post-Biblica. Ed. P. A. H. DeBoer, *et al.* Vol. VI.) Leiden: E. J. Brill, 1962. 200 pp.

Noack, Bent. *Zur johanneischen Tradition; Beiträge zur Kritik an der literarkritischen Analyse des vierten Evangeliums.* København: Rosenkilde og Bagger, 1954. 172 pp.

Nock, Arthur Darby. "Review of Erwin R. Goodenough's *By Light, Light,*" *Gnomon,* 13 (1937), 156-165.

Odeberg, Hugo. *The Fourth Gospel; Interpreted in its Relation to Contemporaneous Religious Currents in Palestine and the Hellenistic-Oriental World.* Uppsala, Stockholm: Almquist & Wiksells Boktryckeri, 1929. 336 pp.

Oesterley, W. O. E. *The Jewish Background of the Christian Liturgy.* Oxford: at the Clarendon Press, 1925. 243 pp.

Philonenko, Marc. *Les interpolations chrétiennes des Testaments des Douze Patriarches et les manuscripts de Qoumrân.* Paris: Presses universitaires de France, 1960. 66 pp.

Ploeg, J. van der. *Le Rouleau de la Guerre.* (Studies on the Texts of the Desert of Judah. Ed. J. van der Ploeg. II.) Leiden: E. J. Brill, 1959. 198 pp.

Preiss, Théo. "Justification in Johannine Thought," *Life in Christ.* Trans. Harold Knight. (Studies in Biblical Theology, No. 13.) Chicago: Alex R. Allenson, Inc., 1954. Pp. 9-31.

Potterie, I. de la. "Jesus King and Judge According to John 19.13," *Scripture,* 13 (1961), 97-111.

——. "Jesus Roi et Juge d'après Jn 19.13; 'Εκάθισεν ἐπὶ βήματος," *Biblica,* 41 (1960), 217-247.

Quispel, Gilles. "Christliche Gnosis und jüdische Heterodoxie," *Evangelische Theologie,* 14 (1954), 474-484.

Rad, Gerhard von. "מֶלֶךְ und מַלְכוּת im AT," *Theologisches Wörterbuch zum Neuen Testament.* Ed. Gerhard Kittel. Vol. I. Stuttgart: W. Kohlhammer, 1933. Pp. 563-569.

——. *Theologie des Alten Testaments.* München: Chr. Kaiser Verlag, 1961. 2 vols.

Rappaport, Salomo. *Agada und Exegese bei Flavius Josephus.* (Veröffentlichungen der Oberrabbiner Dr. H. P. Chajes Preisstiftung an der Israelitisch-theologischen Lehranstalt in Wien, III.) Frankfurt a/M: J. Kauffmann Verlag, 1930. 140 pp.

Reitzenstein, Richard. *Die hellenistische Mysterienreligionen, nach ihren Grundgedanken und Wirkungen.* 3d ed. rev. Leipzig: B. G. Teubner, 1927. 438 pp.

——. *Das iranische Erlösungsmysterium.* Bonn: A. Marcus & E. Weber, 1921. 272 pp.

——. *Das mandäische Buch des Herrn der Grösse und die Evangelienüberlieferung.* (Sitzungsberichte der Heidelberger Akademie der Wissenschaften; Philosophisch-historische Klasse, Jahrgang 1919.) Heibelderg: Carl Winter, 1919. 98 pp.

——. *Die Vorgeschichte der christlichen Taufe.* Mit Beiträgen von L. Troje. Leipzig und Berlin: B. G. Teubner, 1929. 399 pp.

Rengstorf, Karl H. "ἀποστέλλω (πέμπω), ἐξαποστέλλω, ἀπόστλος, ψευδαπόστολος, ἀποστολή," *Theologisches Wörterbuch zum Neuen Testament.* Ed. Gerhard Kittel. Vol. I. Pp. 397-448.

Risenfeld, Harald. "Das Brot von den Bergen, Zu Did. 9,4," *Eranos,* 54 (1956), 142-150.

——. "Jesus als Prophet," *Spiritus et Veritas; Festschrift for Karl Kundsin.* Edit Auseklis. Societas Theologorum Universitatis Latviensis, "In Exile." (San Francisco: Rev. A. Ernstons, 1953). Pp. 135-148.

Robinson, J. Armitage. "The Problem of the Didache," *The Journal of Theological Studies,* 13 (1911/12), 339-356.

Robinson, T. H., and Horst, Friedrich. *Die Zwölf Kleinen Propheten.* (Handbuch zum Alten Testament. Ed. O. Eissfeldt. Vol. XIV.) Tübingen: J. C. B. Mohr [Paul Siebeck], 1954. 275 pp.

Rosenthal, Franz. *Die aramäische Forschung seit Th. Nöldeke's Veröffentlichungen.* Leiden: E. J. Brill, 1939. 307 pp.

Rosmarin, Aaron. *Moses im Lichte der Agada.* New York: The Goldblatt Publishing Co., 1932. 157 pp.

Rudolph, Kurt. *Die Mandäer.* Vol. I: Prolegomena: Das *Mandäerproblem.* Vol. II: *Der Kult.* (Forschungen zur Religion und Literatur des Alten und Neuen Testaments, n.s., 56, 57.) Göttingen: Vandenhoeck & Ruprecht, 1960-21.

Schechter, Solomon. *Aspects of Rabbinic Theology.* New York: Schocken Books, 1961 (1st published 1909). 384 pp.

Schlier, Heinrich. "Jesus und Pilatus nach dem Johannesevangelium," *Die*

Zeit der Kirche; Exegetische Aufsätze und Vorträge. Freiburg: Herder Verlag, 1956. Pp. 56-74.

Schmidt, Karl Ludwig. "Die βασιλεία Gottes im NT," *Theologisches Wörterbuch zum Neuen Testament.* Ed. Gerhard Kittel. Vol. I. Stuttgart: W. Kohlhammer Verlag, 1933. Pp. 582-591.

Schnackenburg, R. "Die Erwartung des 'Propheten" nach dem Neuen Testament und den Qumran-Texten," *Studia Evangelica.* (Texte und Untersuchungen zur Geschichte der altchristlichen Literatur, Series V, Vol. 18.) Berlin: Akademie-Verlag, 1959. Pp. 622-639.

Scholem, Gershom G. *Jewish Gnosticism, Merkabah Mysticism, and Talmudic Tradition.* New York: The Jewish Theological Seminary of America, 1960. 126 pp.

——. *Major Trends in Jewish Mysticism.* New York: Schocken Books, 1946. 460 pp.

Schubert, Paul. "The Structure and Significance of Luke 24," *Neutestamentliche Studien für Rudolf Bultmann.* Ed. W. Eltester. 2d ed. (Beihefte zur Zeitschrift für die neutestamentliche Wissenschaft, XXI.) Berlin: A. Töpelmann, 1957. Pp. 165-186.

Schürer, Emil. *Geschichte des jüdischen Volkes im Zeitalter Jesu Christi.* 4th ed. rev. Leipzig: J. C. Hinrichs'sche Buchhandlung, 1901-1909. 4 vols.

Schweizer, Eduard. *Ego Eimi; Die religionsgeschichtliche Herkunft und theologische Bedeutung der joh. Bildreden.* Göttingen: Vandenhoeck & Ruprecht, 1939. 180 pp.

Silbermann, Lou H. "Unriddling the Riddle; A Study in the Structure and Language of the Habakkuk Pesher," *Revue de Qumran,* 3 (1961), 323-364.

Smith, Dwight Moody, Jr. *The Composition and Order of the Fourth Gospel; Bultmann's Literary Theory.* (Yale Publications in Religion, 10.) New Haven and London: Yale University Press, 1965. 272 pp.

——. "John 12.12ff. and the Question of John's Use of the Synoptics," *Journal of Biblical Literature,* 82 (1963), 58-64.

Smith, Morton. "A Comparison of Early Christian and Early Rabbinic Tradition," *Journal of Biblical Literature,* 82 (1963), 169-176.

——. "Palestinian Judaism in the First Century." *Israel: Its Role in Civilization.* Ed. Moshe Davis. New York: The Seminary Israel Institute of the Jewish Theological Seminary, 1956. Pp. 67-81.

Staerk, Willy. *Soter; Die biblische Erlöserewartung als religionsgeschichtliches Problem.* 1. Teil: *Der biblische Christus.* Gütersloh: C. Bertelsmann, 1933. 170 pp.

Stein, Edmund. *Philo und der Midrasch: Philos Schilderung der Gestalten des Pentateuch verglichen mit der des Midrasch.* (Beihefte zur Zeitschrift für die alttestamentliche Wissenschaft, 57.) Giessen: Alfred Töpelmann, 1931. 52 pp.

Strack, Herman L., and Billerbeck, Paul. *Kommentar zum Neuen Testament aus Talmud und Midrasch.* München: C. H. Beck, 1924-61. 6 vols. in 7.

Strathmann, Hermann. "μάρτυς, μαρτυρέω, [κτλ.]," *Theologisches Wörterbuch zum Neuen Testament.* Ed. Gerhard Kittel. Vol. IV. Stuttgart: Verlag von W. Kohlhammer, 1942. Pp. 477-520.

Sundberg, Waldemar. *Kushṭa; A Monograph on a Principal Word in Mandaean Texts.* Lund: CWK Gleerup, 1953. 144 pp.

Taylor, Vincent. *The Names of Jesus.* London: Macmillan and Co., Limited. 1953. 179 pp.

Tcherikover, Victor. *Hellenistic Civilization and the Jews.* Trans. S. Applebaum. Philadelphia: The Jewish Publication Society of America, 1961. 563 pp.

Teeple, Howard M. *The Mosaic Eschatological Prophet.* (Journal of Biblical Literature Monograph Series, Vol. X.) Philadelphia: Society of Biblical Literature, 1957. 122 pp.

———. "Qumran and the Origin of the Fourth Gospel," *Novum Testamentum*, 4 (1960), 6-25.

Thackeray, H. St. John. "Josephus," *A Dictionary of the Bible.* Ed. James Hastings. Extra Volume. Edinburgh: T. and T. Clark, 1904. Pp. 461-473.

Vermes, Geza. *Discovery in the Judaean Desert.* New York: Desclee Company, 1956. 237 pp.

———. "La Figure de Moïse au Tournant des Deux Testaments," *Moise, l'homme de l'alliance.* Ed. H. Cazelles *et al.* (Special issue of *Cahiers Sioniens.*) Paris: Desclée & Cie., 1955. Pp. 63-92.

———. *Scripture and Tradition in Judaism: Haggadic Studies.* (Studia Post-Biblica. Ed. P. A. H. DeBoer, *et al.*, Vol. IV.) Leiden: E. J. Brill, 1961. 243 pp.

Volz, Paul. *Die Eschatologie der jüdischen Gemeinde im neutestamentlichen Zeitalter.* Tübingen: J. C. B. Mohr [Paul Siebeck], 1934. 458 pp.

Wellhausen, Julius. *Das Evangelium Johannis.* Berlin: Georg Reimer, 1908. 146 pp.

Wetter, Gillis P. *Der Sohn Gottes; Eine Untersuchung über den Charakter und die Tendenz des Johannes-Evangeliums.* Göttingen: Vandenhoeck & Ruprecht, 1916. 201 pp.

Widengren, Geo. *The Ascension of the Apostle and the Heavenly Book.* (King and Saviour III; Uppsala Universitets Arsskrift, VII.) Uppsala: A. B. Lundequistska Bokhandeln, 1950. 117 pp.

———. *Sakrales Königtum im Alten Testament und im Judentum.* Stuttgart: Verlag W. Kohlhammer, 1955. 127 pp.

Wieder, N. "The 'Law-Interpreter' of the Sect of the Dead Sea Scrolls: the Second Moses," *The Journal of Jewish Studies*, 4 (1953), 158-175.

Wikenhauser, Alfred. *Das Evangelium nach Johannes.* (Regensburger Neues Testament. Ed. Alfred Wikenhauser and Otto Kuss, Vol. IV.) 2d rev. ed. Regensburg: Verlag Friedrich Pustet, 1957. 360 pp.

Winter, Paul. *On the Trial of Jesus.* (Studia Judaica Series, Bd. I.) Berlin: W. de Gruyter, 1961. 216 pp.

Wolfson, Harry Austryn. *Philo; Foundations of Religious Philosophy in Judaism, Christianity, and Islam.* Cambridge: Harvard University Press, 1947. 2 vols.

Woude, A. S. van der. *Die messianische Vorstellungen der Gemeinde von Qumran.* (Studia Semitica Neerlandica. Ed. M. A. Beek, J. H. Hospers, Th. C. Vriezen.) Assen: Van Gorcum & Co., 1957. 276 pp.

Young, Franklin W. "Jesus the Prophet: A Re-Examination," *Journal of Biblical Literature*, 68 (1949), 285-299.

Zahn, Theodor. *Das Evangelium des Johannes.* (Kommentar zum Neuen Testament. Ed. Theodor Zahn, *et al.*, Vol. IV.) 4th ed. rev. Leipzig: A. Deichert'sche Verlag, 1912. 729 pp.

INDEX OF REFERENCES

1. OLD TESTAMENT

2. THE NEW TESTAMENT AND

OTHER EARLY CHRISTIAN LITERATURE

3. EXTRA-RABBINIC JEWISH LITERATURE

4. RABBINIC LITERATURE

5. SAMARITAN LITERATURE

6. MANDAEAN LITERATURE

SUBJECT INDEX

INDEX OF AUTHORS

PROPHET-KING ERRATA

Page	Line	Text	Should be
11	2	bases	basis
26	4 f.b.	Micah	Malachi
40	17	πατσίς	πατρίς
44	7 f.b.	after "and" a line has been omitted: "the four verses preceding it—directly with the end"	
47	n.4	erstgeborene	Erstgeborene
77	n.3	הדוס	הדוף
85	n.1	Harper E. Brothers	Harper & Brothers
88	top	a line of Greek at the end of the quotation is omitted: φεύγει πάλιν εἰς τὸ ὄρος αὐτὸς μόνος	
89	5	wordy	worldly
91	15	It ist his	It is this
162	4 f.b.	identicfiation	identification
163	11	κα	καὶ
163	12	sea . . .3	Sea . . .3
191	header	PORPHET	PROPHET
201	n.5	שרדל	שרדם
239	last	resent	present
289	5	3	2
298	1of.b.	(ἐπουράνια	(ἐπουράνια)

312	n.6	title of the Schlatter book is: *Die Sprache und Heimat des vierten Evangeliums*	

312   n.6   title of the Schlatter book is: *Die Sprache und Heimat des vierten Evangeliums*

318   6   thought   though

327   16 f.b.   *Rylarch*   *Rylands*

328   20 f.b.   *erstgeborene*   *Erstgeborene*

337   under "Numbers" insert "11:24–30 149f." and delete "24–30 149f."

339   left col. 3:13 296n.–299, 301   3:13 296n., 299, 301

341   left col., *1 Corinthians*, 10:18 83n.   10:18 82n.

341   mid. col.   Clment Alex.   Clement Alex.

342   after Aristeas, insert:

Aristobulus 154

Artapanus 162f.

After *Eupolemus,* insert:

Ezekiel Trag. 147–50, 156f.

346   7 f.b.   Beshallaḥ   Beshallaḥ 7

354   under "Bloch, Renée," delete "144n."

355   under "Ginzberg, Louis," 210n.   210

72789022R00219

Made in the USA
Middletown, DE
08 May 2018